State of the Apes 2013

Extractive Industries and Ape Conservation

Current dominant thinking and practice in the private and public sectors continually assert that peoples' development needs are in conflict with, or mutually exclusive to, the need to conserve the biosphere on which we depend. Consequently, we are asked to either diminish development in the name of conservation or diminish conservation in the name of development. Efforts to identify complementary objectives, or mutually acceptable trade-offs and compromises indicate, however, that this does not always have to be the case. *Extractive Industries and Ape Conservation*, the first volume in the new *State of the Apes* series draws attention to the evolving context within which great ape and gibbon habitats are increasingly interfacing with extractive industries.

Aimed at a broad range of policy makers, industry experts and decision makers, academics, researchers, and NGOs these publications aim to influence debate, practice and policy, seeking to reconcile ape conservation and welfare, and economic and social development, through objective and rigorous analysis.

D1597433

State of the Apes

Series editors
Helga Rainer   Arcus Foundation
Alison White
Annette Lanjouw Arcus Foundation

The world's primates are among the most endangered of all tropical species. All great ape species – gorilla, chimpanzee, bonobo and orangutan – are classified as either Endangered or Critically Endangered. Furthermore, nearly all gibbon species are threatened with extinction. Whilst linkages between ape conservation and economic development, ethics and wider environmental processes have been acknowledged, more needs to be done to integrate biodiversity conservation within broader economic, social and environmental communities if those connections are to be fully realized and addressed.

Intended for a broad range of policy makers, industry experts and decision makers, academics, researchers, and NGOs, the *State of the Apes* series will look at the threats to these animals and their habitats within the broader context of economic and community development. Each publication presents a different theme, providing an overview of how these factors interrelate and affect the current and future status of apes, with robust statistics, welfare indicators, official and various other reports providing an objective and rigorous analysis of relevant issues.

State of the Apes 2013

Extractive Industries and Ape Conservation

CAMBRIDGE
UNIVERSITY PRESS

CAMBRIDGE
UNIVERSITY PRESS

University Printing House, Cambridge CB2 8BS, United Kingdom

Published in the United States of America by Cambridge University Press, New York

Cambridge University Press is part of the University of Cambridge.

It furthers the University's mission by disseminating knowledge in the pursuit of education, learning and research at the highest international levels of excellence.

www.cambridge.org
Information on this title:
www.cambridge.org/9781107067493

First published 2014

Printed in Spain by Grafos SA, Arte sobre papel

A catalogue record for this publication is available from the British Library

ISBN 978-1-107-06749-3 Hardback
ISBN 978-1-107-69621-1 Paperback

Credits

Editors
Helga Rainer, Alison White and Annette Lanjouw

Coordinator
Alison White

Designer
Rick Jones, StudioExile

Cartographer
Jillian Luff, MAPgrafix

Copy Editor
Judith Shaw

Proofreader
Sarah Binns

Indexer
Caroline Jones, Osprey Indexing

Referencing
Eva Fairnell

Cover photographs

Log pile: © Global Witness

Bonobo: © Takeshi Furuichi

Gibbon: © Andybignellphoto/Dreamstime.com

Gorilla: © Annette Lanjouw

Orangutan: © Jurek Wajdowicz, EWS

Chimpanzee: © Nilanjan Bhattacharya/Dreamstime.com

Foreword

Apes, including gorillas, chimpanzees, bonobos, orangutans and gibbons, inhabit tropical forests across Africa and Asia. The alarming rate at which these forests are disappearing, due to deforestation and land degradation, is cause for global concern. Forest loss is one of the factors linked to climate change, which is resulting in a range of impacts on our planet. Forests also secure a host of important ecosystem services, as well as providing a habitat for a rich biodiversity of species. Charismatic species such as apes can act as ambassadors for these important forests. Apes also serve to illustrate our link to all other species on this planet. The shared evolutionary linkages between humans and non-human apes, and the similar genetic make-up and physiology are evident in our shared behaviors and intelligence. The conservation and protection of apes is of paramount importance as we look to secure the futures of humans, biodiversity and the planet.

The 2013 *State of the Apes* report is the first in a series, and unprecedented not only in its presentation of the current status of great apes and gibbons globally but also in demonstrating our understanding of how the survival of apes is impacted by extractive industry practice. The report discusses the relationship between global, national and local processes that interact with extractive industry activity and ape conservation. It presents an overview of our current understanding of the impacts of extractive industries on ape communities, acknowledging that a fundamental shift in approach is required, one that recognizes the importance of both extractive industries and the environment. Although there is little doubt that any form of extractive industry negatively impacts the wellbeing of great apes and gibbons, the report notes that there is scope for industry practice to mitigate its impacts on their wellbeing, and that these practices have yet to be broadly implemented.

A key message contained in this report is that the indirect impacts of extractive industry action are often more destructive and extensive, for both apes and their habitats, than the direct impacts. Policies and investments that focus on improved practice and recognition of the rights of indigenous peoples can reduce the environmental impacts of the industry, thus contributing to the protection of these important species. Although there are still gaps in our understanding of the interaction between ape conservation and extractive industry, examples show how nation states and individual projects strive to reconcile these disparate entities through partnership, research and dialogue.

Ultimately it is only through engagement across sectors, and acknowledgment of the importance of the different goals that meaningful conservation of apes and other species can be achieved. To this end, the *State of the Apes* is a resource that provides a benchmark against which progress in overcoming the challenges and opportunities for ape conservation will be measured.

Zhang Xinsheng
President IUCN
(International Union for
Conservation of Nature)

Contents

Section 1

1. From global to local: the megatrends at the interface of apes and industry and the case of trade, law, and finance

2. Land tenure: industry, ape conservation, and communities

3. Ecological impacts of extractive industries on ape populations

4. Avoiding the chainsaws: industrial timber extraction and apes

5. Mining/oil extraction and ape populations and habitats

The Arcus Foundation

The Arcus Foundation is a private grant-making foundation that advances social justice and conservation goals. The Arcus Foundation works globally and has offices in New York City, USA, and Cambridge, UK. For more information on the Foundation visit arcusfoundation.org or connect with Arcus at: twitter.com/ArcusGreatApes, and facebook.com/ArcusGreatApes.

Great Apes Program

The long-term survival of humans and the great apes is dependent on how we respect and care for other animals and our shared natural resources. The Arcus Foundation seeks to increase respect for and recognition of the rights and value of great apes and gibbons, and to strengthen protection from threats to their habitats. The Great Apes program supports conservation and policy advocacy efforts that promote the survival of apes in the wild and in sanctuaries that offer high-quality care, safety and freedom from invasive research and exploitation.

Contact details

New York office:

44 West 28th Street, 17th Floor
New York, New York 10001
United States

Phone: 212.488.3000
Fax: 212.488.3010

Cambridge office (Great Apes program):

Wellington House, East Road
Cambridge CB1 1BH
United Kingdom

Phone: +44.1223.451050
Fax: +44.1223.451100

Notes to readers

Acronyms and abbreviations

A list of acronyms and abbreviations can be found at the back of the book on page 319.

Annexes

All annexes can be found at the back of the book, starting on page 306 except for Annex IV, which is available from the State of the Apes website www.stateoftheapes.org

Glossary

There is a glossary of scientific terms and key words at the back of the book, starting on page 324.

Chapter cross-referencing

Chapter cross-references appear throughout the book, either as direct references in the body text or in brackets. For example, in Chapter 1: 'The resulting increases in forest degradation and fragmentation, hunting, and poaching of animal species are explored in Chapter 7.' And: 'As great apes and gibbons primarily inhabit tropical forest in Asia and Africa, the impact on their survival is likely to be significant (see Chapter 3).'

Acknowledgments

The first edition of *State of the Apes* has been an extensive undertaking, and one that we hope will not only encourage the critical engagement of current conservation, industry and government practice but also expand support for great apes and gibbons. To all who contributed, from those who attended our stakeholder meeting, to our contributors and reviewers and all those involved in the actual production and design of the book, thank you for your input, advice, expertise, support, flexibility and patience!

The support of Jon Stryker and the Arcus Foundation Board of Directors was essential to realise the production of such a publication and we thank them for supporting our vision to bring an overview of critical ape conservation issues to important audiences.

Without a comprehensive global view of the status of apes, this publication would not have been possible and we would also like to thank all the great ape and gibbon scientists who contributed, and continue to contribute, their valuable data to improving the robustness of the Ape Populations, Environments and Surveys (A.P.E.S.) database, which led to the creation of the A.P.E.S. Portal. It is through such collaborative efforts that effective and efficient conservation action can be achieved.

Authors, contributors, and those who provided essential data are named at the end of each chapter, and we thank them again here. We could not have produced this book without them. Detailed chapter and whole book reviews were provided by: Marc Ancrenaz, Elizabeth Bennett, Susan M. Cheyne, Wendy Elliot, Kay Farmer, Barbara Filas, Chris Hallam, Tatyana Humle, Nigel Kieser, Cyril Kormos, Rebecca Kormos, Sally Lahm, Sam Lawson, Jerome Lewis, Andrew Marshall, Rob Muggah, Sten Nilsson, Tim Rayden, Jamison Suter, Serge Wich, and David Wilkie. Most of the photographs included were generously contributed by their creators, who are credited alongside each one. We are also grateful to those organisations that allowed us to include extracts from previously published books and reports and from internal documents; they are acknowledged alongside these entries.

Particular thanks also go to the following: ArcelorMittal, Artisanal Small-scale Mining in and around Protected Areas and Critical Ecosystems, Cambridge University Press, Tom Clements, Lori Ann Conzo, Doug Cress, Bruce Davidson, Fauna and Flora International, Ruth Fletcher, Forest Peoples Programme, Forest Stewardship Council, Neba Funwi-Gabga, Elisa Gerontianos, Jo Gilbert, Global Witness, Great Apes Survival Partnership, Liz Greengrass, David Greer, Martin Griffiths, Groupe Rougier, Paul Hatanga, Matthew Hatchwell, John Howell, Paul-Emmanuel Huet, Kirsten Hund, International Finance Corporation, International Union for Conservation of Nature, Nigel Kieser, Justin Kenrick, Estelle Levin, Julia Marton-Lefèvre, Linda May, Max Planck Institute, Yekoyada Mukasa, Fiona Napier, Pallisco-CIFM, Guy Parker, Bardolf Paul, People and Nature Consulting International, Adam Phillipson, Signe Preuschoft, Chris Ransom, Ben Rawson, Jamartin Sihite, Société des Mines de Fer de Guinée, Marie Stevenson, Indrawan Suryadi, Reiner Tetgmeyer, Melissa Tolley, Cristina Villegas, Wildlife Conservation Society, Glenys White, Lee J.T. White, Serge A. Wich, Elizabeth A. Williamson, World Conservation Monitoring Centre, World Wide Fund for Nature, Yayasan Tambuhak Sinta, and the Zoological Society of London. Thanks also to Phoenix Design Aid for the translation and re-design of the French and Indonesian editions.

Many others contributed in various ways that cannot be attributed to the content of specific chapters, by providing introductions, anonymous input, strategic advice, and helping with essential, if sometimes tedious, administrative tasks. We also thank all those who provided invaluable moral support.

**Helga Rainer, Alison White
and Annette Lanjouw**
Editors

X

Photo: King, orphan gorilla in Gabon. © Alison White

INTRODUCTION

Current dominant thinking and practice in both the private and public sectors continually assert that people's development needs are in conflict with, or mutually exclusive to, the need to conserve the biosphere on which we depend. As a consequence, we are asked to either diminish development in the name of conservation or diminish conservation in the name of development. The efforts to identify complementary objectives, or mutually acceptable trade-offs and compromises, described in this publication indicate, however, that this does not always need to be the case. *State of the Apes: Extractive Industries and Ape Conservation*, the first in a series, draws attention to the evolving context within which great ape and gibbon habitats are increasingly interfacing with extractive industries.

Commissioned by the Arcus Foundation, the *State of the Apes* objective is to raise awareness about the status of apes around the world and the impacts of human activities on apes and ape habitat. Apes are closely related to humans and vulnerable to many threats posed to their habitat

Bonobo (formerly known as the "pygmy chimpanzee")

Male adult bonobos reach a height of 73–83 cm and weigh about 40 kg, while females are slightly smaller and tend to weigh around 30 kg. Bonobos live in communities of up to 100 individuals. The lifespan of bonobos in the wild is unknown but in captivity they can live for 40 years.

Unlike chimpanzees, in bonobo society the females are dominant over the males and establish a social hierarchy, and the status of a male appears to be derived from his mother's hierarchical position.

Bonobos are frugivorous, but they appear to consume more herbaceous plants than chimpanzees. They also consume small vertebrates and invertebrates, and hunting of monkeys and duikers has also been reported.

Bonobos occur only in the Democratic Republic of Congo (DRC).

There are estimated to be fewer than 50 000 bonobos remaining in the wild, but accurate population estimates are difficult to obtain.

Classified as endangered (EN), also listed on Appendix I of CITES (for more information see text box: IUCN Red List categories and criteria, and CITES Appendices, at the end of the Introduction).

Chimpanzee

Adult males are less than 170 cm in height when standing and weigh up to 70 kg, but females are somewhat smaller. Chimpanzees live in multi-male, multi-female communities of up to 150 individuals. Chimpanzees live for up to 50 years.

There is a strong dominance hierarchy within chimpanzee groups and males are dominant over females.

Chimpanzees are ripe-fruit specialists, but they also consume nuts and leaves, in addition to insects and small mammals, including monkeys and duikers. Chimpanzees are well known for their use of tools in obtaining food: they use stones to crack open nuts, and modify sticks to extract termites from underground or to get honey from beehives.

Chimpanzees are split into four subspecies, which occur in different regions of tropical Africa. Chimpanzees inhabit not only lowland rainforests, but also dry savanna and montane forest regions up to 3000 m elevation.

There are estimated to be between 170 000 and 300 000 chimpanzees remaining in the wild, but accurate population estimates are difficult to obtain.

All subspecies are classified as endangered (EN) and listed on Appendix I of CITES.

Together with the bonobos, chimpanzees are the closest living relatives to humans, sharing 98.7% of our DNA.

Gibbon

Gibbons form the family of *Hylobatidae,* which can be divided into four genera: *Hoolock, Hylobates, Symphalangus,* and *Nomascus,* which in total comprise 19 species in some taxonomic schemes. They inhabit a wide range of habitats across Southeast Asia, occurring in ten countries. Gibbons have been confirmed to live for upwards of 40 years in captivity, in some instances, but in the wild they likely live for 25–30 years.

Depending on the species, adult size ranges from 45–90 cm and weight from 5–12 kg, and there is little difference in body size between males and females.

Gibbons are largely monogamous, with family groups consisting of an adult male and female and their offspring; however, considerable variation and flexibility have been noted. They are also territorial, defending an area against neighboring groups, advertised through the production of loud vocalizations.

Gibbons are generally characterized as frugivorous, with a significant part of their diet composed of fruits, with additional elements of leaves, flowers, and, in some instances, insects and small vertebrates.

All gibbons are classified as critically endangered (CR) or endangered (EN) with the exception of the eastern hoolock (*Hoolock leuconedys*), which is classified as vulnerable (VU) and the northern yellow-cheeked gibbon (*Nomascus annamensis*), which was recently described and has not yet been assessed. They are all listed on Appendix I of CITES.

Gorilla

Gorillas are the largest of the great apes, with adult males reaching a height of 140–200 cm and a weight of 120–210 kg. Gorillas are very social animals that typically live in groups of between 2 and 40 individuals. Normally a group consists of one or more mature adult males (silverbacks) who lead the group, and several females and their offspring. Gorillas live for up to 40 years.

Gorillas inhabit a variety of environments across equatorial Africa, from lowland swamp to montane forest.

Gorillas are largely herbivorous and/or frugivorous, with their diets consisting mainly of leaves and herbs or a large amount of fruit.

There are estimated to be approximately 150 000 gorillas left in the wild, but accurate population estimates are difficult to obtain.

All subspecies of gorilla are classified as critically endangered (CR), except for Grauer's gorilla (*Gorilla beringeigraueri*), which is classified as endangered (EN). They are all listed on Appendix I of CITES.

Gorilla DNA is about 97.7% identical to human DNA.

Orangutan

Adult male orangutans can reach a height of 150 cm and a weight of 100 kg, while females are smaller and typically do not exceed 125 cm and 45 kg. Orangutans are largely solitary, and strong social bonds exist only between adult females and their offspring. Adults of both sexes live either as resident individuals in a defined home range or as transient individuals. In defined ranges, the dominant flanged adult male is the primary breeder. Orangutans live for up to 50 years.

Orangutans are divided into two species that are each endemic to the islands of Borneo and Sumatra in Southeast Asia.

The orangutan diet consists mainly of fruits, but also of leaves, shoots, and bark.

There are estimated to be around 60 000 orangutans left in the wild, but accurate population estimates are difficult to obtain.

The three subspecies of Bornean orangutan are classified as endangered (EN), whereas the Sumatran orangutan is classified as critically endangered (CR). They are all listed on Appendix I of CITES.

Their DNA is about 97% identical to human DNA.

All information from the A.P.E.S. Portal: http://apesportal.eva.mpg.de/

Additional information from Elizabeth A. Williamson and Ben Rawson.

Photo credits:

Bonobo – Takeshi Furuichi;

Chimpanzee – Ian Nichols;

Gibbon – Pakhnyushchyy/Dreamstime.com;

Gorilla – Annette Lanjouw;

Orangutan - Perry van Duijnhoven 2013.

and their survival, by humans. To understand both the severity and extent of those threats, as well as the possibilities and potential for avoiding and mitigating the threats, the publication brings together leading scholars and practitioners from various sectors, including conservation, industry, and academia.

The aim of this Arcus Foundation initiative is to create a biennial series of publications that influence debate, practice and policy by seeking to reconcile ape conservation and welfare, and economic and social development through objective and rigorous analysis of relevant issues. Robust statistics on the status and welfare of apes will be derived from the Ape Populations, Environments and Surveys (A.P.E.S.) Portal (apesportal.eva.mpg.de).

This first publication presents a narrative of research, analysis, case studies, and best practice from a range of key stakeholders relating to the interface between ape/biodiversity conservation and extractive industries. The publication incorporates related factors such as governance, corporate social responsibility (CSR), land tenure, social development, and international trade and trends. Through objective presentation, the contents of this publication can contribute to further improvements in current conservation practice and inform and influence communities that include commerce (logging, mining, oil and gas), law (legislative protections, industry regulation) and development (human) by showing how they interrelate and affect the current and future status and welfare of apes, and of people who are dependent on their habitats. As a policy document, the aim is to introduce ape conservation into local, national, regional,

---

BOX I.1

Definition of extractive industry

The State of the Apes uses the term "extractive industry" to cover the extraction of specific resources from the land for commercial exploitation. The term is used to encompass mineral (industrial and artisanal), oil, gas, and round wood or industrial timber extraction. The term does not cover the clearing of land for agriculture or plantations, nor does it cover non-timber forest products (NTFPs) or the hunting of wildlife living in the forest.

Oil and gas: refers to the extraction of petroleum oil hydrocarbons and/or natural gas through drilling and pumping of drilling fluids (a mix of chemicals and fluids) into a borehole and extracting the oil or gas.

Mining: there are two general types of mining techniques, surface mining and underground mining. Surface mining removes the surface vegetation and soil or rock that covers the mineral deposits. Open pit/open cast mining consists of removing minerals from a pit, and strip mining consists of removing strips of surface layers to expose the minerals underneath. Mountaintop removal refers to the removal of mountaintops to get at deep mineral deposits below. Underground mining consists of digging tunnels or shafts to reach the minerals.

Industrial, large-scale mining (LSM): typically involves capital intensive and high technological input to extract minerals.

Artisanal and small-scale mining (ASM): refers to the use of low-level technology and manual labor to extract minerals.

Round wood or industrial timber extraction: refers to the extraction of wood from natural forest or timber plantations and includes saw logs, veneer logs, and pulpwood. There are two types of industrial logging: clear felling and selective logging. Clear felling normally results in the conversion of forests to plantation or some other land use. Selective logging incorporates reduced-impact logging (RIL), which is a limited form of extraction that maintains minimal removal rates and stem diameter, undertaken in conjunction with minimizing the impact on the environment of the removal of timber. Other forms of selective logging remove specific valuable species from a forest with no regard to the environmental effects of extraction.

and international policy dialogs, as well as into development and economic planning.

The focus of the publication is on all non-human ape species, including chimpanzees, gorillas, bonobos, orangutans, and gibbons, and the specific analysis is for countries where apes are found. This encompasses much of the tropical belt of Africa and Southeast Asia. To achieve this, contributions commissioned from a range of expertise that includes conservation organizations and individuals, industry, academics, and social and environmental justice organizations are collated to present a holistic overview of current thinking and practice in this arena.

Chapter highlights

Eight of the ten chapters examine various aspects of the interface of extractive industries with ape conservation from impacts on the individual species of ape through to global processes that drive the demand for commodities. The first thematic chapter (Chapter 1) discusses the various global drivers that impact extractive industry action and how this in turn impacts ape habitats and ape populations. The chapter highlights a number of cases that consider trade, finance, and law. The subsequent chapter (Chapter 2) considers the implications for land tenure, in particular protected areas and community lands that overlap with ape habitat and extractive industries. Chapter 3 presents detail on current understanding of ape socioecology in relation to impacts from mining, oil and gas extraction, and industrial-scale logging. Although a relatively new area of focus with few long-term studies (particularly on mining and oil and gas), the data are reviewed in light of extractive industry trends in ape range states. The following chapters (Chapters 4 and 5) describe the various phases of logging and mining industries, respectively, and how they impact apes. The chapters present some

of the mitigation strategies that can potentially protect conservation goals in areas where there is an overlap of ape distribution with logging or mining activities. Chapter 6 is also concerned with mining but focuses on the interface of ASM, and the implications for ape conservation. Chapters 7 and 8 consider the broader impacts of extractive industries, including the indirect impacts of all the extractive industries (Chapter 7), and how national responses in three ape range countries (Guinea, Gabon, and Indonesia) are reframing their extractive industry practice to more explicitly consider the environment (Chapter 8).

Section 2 presents two chapters that focus on the status of apes *in situ* (Chapter 9) and in captivity (Chapter 10). Chapter 10 concludes by highlighting some of the linkages between captive apes and extractive industry.

Photo: Great ape and gibbon habitats are increasingly interfacing with extractive industries . . . a lone orangutan. © Serge Wich

Section 1: the interface of extractive industries and ape conservation

Chapter 1 (Global drivers)

Rapidly growing global demand for natural resources is at the center of the encroachment of extractive industries into ape habitats. With human populations expected to increase to 10.1 billion by 2100 (UN, 2011) and the global economy expected to grow 2–4 times by 2050 (OECD, 2012; Randers, 2012; Ward, 2012), this trajectory is not expected to simply continue to grow, but to become increasingly complex. This chapter presents an overview of some of the megatrends that influence extractive industry action within ape ranges and how their impacts, such as infrastructure development and biodiversity loss and deforestation, are particularly relevant. It also presents detail on the role that trade agreements can play in influencing industrial logging, although the extent of the impact of this is still unknown. The complexity of ensuring the conservation of apes in projects financed by the International Finance Corporation (IFC) is considered. There are pragmatic approaches that civil society can engage with through contract law, but poor understanding of how megatrends interact limits the extent to which global processes can be influenced to the benefit of ape conservation.

Chapter 2 (Land tenure)

Land tenure is a critical issue for conservation and in clarifying its relevance in relation to extractive industries, this chapter presents detail across two themes – extraction within protected areas and extraction from community lands. By illustrating the contested nature of tenure within these two contexts, it presents detail on how weak some of the current tenure legislation relating to rights and access really is. It shows how the economic pressures to exploit resources regardless of the negative impacts result in direct conflict with conservation and contribute to the issue of "land grabbing." Further detail on the role that civil society plays in increasing transparency and an analysis of mitigation strategies that promote stakeholder engagement are also included. Unless mitigation occurs across all levels, supplemented with clear land-use planning, little in terms of redressing encroachment onto protected areas or community lands will change. In general, policy and regulatory frameworks do not provide adequate protection for conservation and it is through multi-stakeholder engagement that opportunities for reconciliation potentially exist.

Chapter 3 (Ecological impacts)

Our analysis suggests that there are no simple conclusions to be drawn about the impact of the extractive industry on apes. The severity and extent of impact vary significantly depending on the type of industry, quality of management, type of forest in which a company operates, and a range of other factors. This chapter reviews the socioecology of great apes and gibbons, and the ways in which this can be influenced by different extractive industries. There is significant variation between ape species in their social organization and ecology, yet all apes reproduce slowly and infants remain dependent on the care of their mother for many years. This leads any population of apes to recover slowly when mortality rates are increased, due to killing, increased morbidity from disease or stress, or loss of habitat and food. The impacts of the extractive industry, such as habitat disturbance, building of roads and infrastructure, and the introduction of noise and pollution, as well as influx of people, resulting in a range of impacts (hunting, introduction of disease, agriculture and habitat disturbance, etc.) are examined in relation to how they affect

different ape species. The different impacts of oil and gas extraction at a local scale are presented and compared with the more extensive, but sometimes less severe, impact of forestry practices. Some forms of forestry, such as RIL, can be compatible with ape conservation in some areas, but this depends on the ape species (with some apes being more sensitive to habitat disturbance than others) and the type of management practices adhered to.

Chapter 4
(Industrial timber extraction)

The recent trend towards more ecologically informed logging practices is changing the nature of how decisions are made and offers a chance to remedy policy failures and lack of accountability that has typified most timber operations in the past. However, there has been a slow uptake of some of these logging practices within tropical forests and there is also a lack of clarity regarding the impacts on biodiversity and ape conservation. This chapter examines the various facets

of Sustainable Forestry Management (SFM) and showcases examples of where conservation practitioners are engaging with logging companies to mitigate their impacts on apes and other species. While some changes in current practice result in relatively positive impacts to forest biodiversity, there is consensus that any form of logging results in changes in ape behavior. The lack of long-term research makes it difficult to evaluate the true sustainability of large-scale logging. Economic pressures complicate the challenges of influencing logging practice more broadly and working with logging companies in general is about mitigating the impact of logging rather than achieving conservation.

Chapter 5
(Industrial mining, oil and gas)

Extraction of minerals and oil/gas overlaps with ape habitat in both Asia and Africa, but the impact of these industries has been little studied, compared with forestry. Although the scale of overlap tends to be small, the growth in mineral and hydrocarbon development

Photo: Apes are closely related to humans . . . a bonobo relaxes in the forest. © Takeshi Furuichi, Wamba Committee for Bonobo Research

has led to significant loss of forest, through both the direct and the indirect impacts of the industry. This chapter describes the phases of mining and hydrocarbon project development, and the impacts of each phase on habitat and wildlife. Where specific data on the impacts on apes exist, these are presented. Examples are provided of projects that have developed strategies based on the conservation "mitigation hierarchy" of prevention, avoidance, minimization, and reduction, prior to reparation and restoration. Reviewing the overall impact of industrial mining and oil and gas extraction on ape populations and habitats, the chapter presents the extent of overlap (only 5 of 27 ape taxa have no mining projects in their range) and emphasizes the importance of gathering evidence on the effect on ape distribution, ecology, and behavior.

Chapter 6
(Artisanal and small-scale mining (ASM))

Photo: Cooked and smoked bushmeat for sale, including ape meat, at a market in the Central African Republic. © David Greer/WWF

ASM is known to occur in or around 96 of 147 protected areas in 32 countries of a 36 country study (Villegas *et al.*, 2012). It represents a serious and growing threat to biodiversity due to extraction methods and as a result of large numbers of miners in areas of high biodiversity. Artisanal miners have also been described as being amongst the poorest and most marginalized members of society. This chapter integrates the extent of artisanal mining activity within previously identified ape habitats and presents detail on mitigation strategies currently in existence. In the context of conservation, economic activity, and human rights, it illustrates the negative environmental impacts of uncontrolled ASM, which encompass direct impacts such as habitat destruction, and indirect impacts such as water pollution and increased hunting pressure. As ASM further encroaches into critical ape habitats, approaches that include policy and legislative development, coupled with poverty alleviation measures, are likely to have the greatest impacts. However, little has been achieved in this direction as ASM continues to remain poorly understood and regulated, further exacerbated by inadequate and corrupt governance structures.

Chapter 7 (Indirect impacts)

The preceding chapters describing the direct impacts of extractive industries on apes all highlight the relative significance of the indirect impacts. These are similar for industrial timber extraction, industrial mining, oil and gas extraction, as well as for ASM. The influx of people, linked to the opportunities for employment and economic benefit, brings with it a range of impacts on habitat and ape populations. The chapter looks at the impacts of road and rail construction, pipeline and industry transects, in-migration and development of population centers, individually driven logging and fuel-wood collection, clearing of land for agriculture, and the introduction of exotic species and livestock, while focusing on three of the most pressing threats: (1) increased levels of hunting and poaching, (2) habitat fragmentation and degradation, and (3) the spread of disease. Whereas the direct impacts of extractive industries come to an end after a project is closed, the indirect impacts generally continue, and continue to grow. The chapter also illustrates areas of best practice and describes some of the efforts of industry to contain and limit these indirect impacts, and ensure that conservation objectives can be maintained.

Chapter 8 (Range state responses)

Industry and national governments face a number of challenges to ensure that natural habitats and wildlife populations are not destroyed in the process of natural resources exploitation and economic development. With the ever-increasing demands for raw materials in an advancing global society, commercially viable areas for exploitation will continue to be identified and developed. Mining and logging operations can be significant economic engines and can contribute to broad development goals. This chapter examines three specific cases where efforts have been made to ensure that exploitation of natural resources is undertaken in a manner compatible with biodiversity conservation. In the Republic of Guinea, West Africa, efforts to develop a national strategy to offset the impacts of mining on biodiversity are described and evaluated. In Gabon, Central Africa, the efforts of the government to ensure environment and protected area legislation are considered in the development of extractive industries are described, and the history of this process examined. Finally, in Indonesia, the experience of the government in establishing and implementing a logging moratorium is evaluated, in light of the history of logging and its contribution to Indonesia's high greenhouse gas emissions.

Section 2: The status and welfare of great apes and gibbons

Chapter 9 (Global distribution and environmental conditions)

This chapter presents detail on the spatial distribution of apes across Africa and Asia derived from the A.P.E.S. Portal. Declines in "suitable environmental conditions" for African apes between the 1990s and 2000s have resulted in varying impacts on different species and ape range states. Further analysis of the interaction of ape densities with levels of protection, socioeconomic contexts, and human population density presents some insights into the interrelation between great apes and gibbons and human presence and action.

Finally, a global overview of current knowledge of ape population hotspots is presented, drawing attention to areas of critical importance for the survival of great apes and gibbons.

Photo: Artisanal mining in Liberia. © Cristina Villegas

Chapter 10
(Apes in captivity and extractive industry)

Across most ape range states, the fact that there are apes in captivity is a result of both ineffective enforcement of legislation protecting apes, as well as the destruction of their habitat. In all ape range states, apes benefit from legal protection from hunting or live trade. The destruction of their habitats, and the direct and indirect impacts associated with this destruction, as well as the intentional hunting and capture of apes, have resulted in the creation of a number of sanctuaries to care for confiscated apes. The existence of industries that exploit captive apes, as performers in exhibits and entertainment, or as pets and displays in zoos, also contributes to the threats to apes in the wild.

The issue of apes in captivity is closely tied to the conservation of apes in the wild. This chapter presents the background context to ape welfare and captivity in both non-range states and ape range states, and then focuses specifically on the impact of extractive industries on ape sanctuaries and rescue centers.

Conclusion

This edition of *State of the Apes* seeks to extend our understanding of the various direct and indirect linkages between the conservation of apes and economic development tied to extractive industry. The publication reviews and provides details from the local context to the global dynamics and explores best options for responding to and reconciling these different trajectories. Positive measures

TABLE I.1

Great apes and gibbons

Common name	Scientific name	Countries where present
Western chimpanzee[1]	*Pan troglodytes verus*	▪ Ghana ▪ Guinea ▪ Guinea Bissau ▪ Ivory Coast ▪ Liberia ▪ Mali ▪ Senegal ▪ Sierra Leone
Nigeria–Cameroon chimpanzee[1]	*Pan troglodytes ellioti*	▪ Cameroon ▪ Nigeria
Central chimpanzee[1]	*Pan troglodytes troglodytes*	▪ Angola ▪ Cameroon ▪ Central African Republic ▪ Equatorial Guinea ▪ Gabon ▪ Republic of Congo ▪ Democratic Republic of Congo
Eastern chimpanzee[1]	*Pan troglodytes schweinfurthii*	▪ Burundi ▪ Central African Republic ▪ Rwanda ▪ Democratic Republic of Congo ▪ Tanzania ▪ Uganda
Bonobo	*Pan paniscus*	▪ Democratic Republic of Congo
Grauer's gorilla[2]	*Gorilla beringei graueri*	▪ Democratic Republic of Congo
Mountain gorilla[2]	*Gorilla beringei beringei*	▪ Uganda ▪ Rwanda ▪ Democratic Republic of Congo
Cross River gorilla[3]	*Gorilla gorilla diehli*	▪ Cameroon ▪ Nigeria
Western lowland gorilla[3]	*Gorilla gorilla gorilla*	▪ Angola ▪ Cameroon ▪ Central African Republic ▪ Equatorial Guinea ▪ Republic of Congo
Sumatran orangutan	*Pongo abelii*	▪ Indonesia
Northeast Bornean orangutan[4]	*Pongo pygmaeus morio*	▪ Indonesia ▪ Malaysia
Southwest Bornean orangutan[4]	*Pongo pygmaeus wurmbii*	▪ Indonesia
Northwest Bornean orangutan[4]	*Pongo pygmaeus pygmaeus*	▪ Indonesia ▪ Malaysia
Bornean white-bearded gibbon	*Hylobates albibarbis*	▪ Indonesia
Müller's gibbon/Bornean gray gibbon	*Hylobates muelleri*	▪ Indonesia
Abbott's Gibbon/West Bornean gray gibbon	*Hylobates abbotti*	▪ Malaysia ▪ Brunei Darussalam ▪ Indonesia
East Bornean gray gibbon	*Hylobates funerus*	▪ Malaysia ▪ Indonesia
Agile gibbon	*Hylobates agilis*	▪ Thailand ▪ Malaysia ▪ Indonesia
Pileated gibbon	*Hylobates pileatus*	▪ Cambodia ▪ Lao People's Democratic Republic ▪ Thailand
White-handed gibbon	*Hylobates lar*	▪ Indonesia ▪ Lao People's Democratic Republic ▪ Malaysia ▪ Myanmar ▪ Thailand ▪ China
Javan gibbon	*Hylobates moloch*	▪ Indonesia
Kloss' gibbon	*Hylobates klossii*	▪ Indonesia
Southern yellow-cheeked gibbon	*Nomascus gabriellae*	▪ Cambodia ▪ Viet Nam
Northern yellow-cheeked gibbon	*Nomascus annamensis*	▪ Cambodia ▪ Lao People's Democratic Republic ▪ Viet Nam
Southern white-cheeked gibbon	*Nomascus siki*	▪ Lao People's Democratic Republic ▪ Viet Nam
Northern white-cheeked gibbon	*Nomascus leucogenys*	▪ Lao People's Democratic Republic ▪ Viet Nam ▪ China
Western black-crested gibbon	*Nomascus concolor*	▪ China ▪ Lao People's Democratic Republic ▪ Viet Nam
Eastern black-crested gibbon/Cao Vit gibbon	*Nomascus nasutus*	▪ China ▪ Viet Nam
Hainan gibbon	*Nomascus hainanus*	▪ China
Western hoolock	*Hoolock hoolock*	▪ Bangladesh ▪ India ▪ Myanmar
Eastern hoolock	*Hoolock leuconedys*	▪ China ▪ Myanmar ▪ India
Siamang	*Symphlangus syndactylus*	▪ Thailand ▪ Malaysia ▪ Indonesia

Notes:

1. Subspecies of chimpanzee (*Pan troglodytes*); 2. Subspecies of eastern gorilla (*Gorilla beringei*); 3. Subspecies of western gorilla (*Gorilla gorilla*); 4. Subspecies of Bornean orangutan (*Pongo pygmaeus*)

IUCN Red List Categories and Criteria, and CITES Appendices

The IUCN Species Survival Commission has defined various categories for each species and subspecies (IUCN, 2012). The criteria can be applied to any taxonomic unit at or below the species level. In order to be ascribed a specific definition, a taxon must fulfill a number of criteria. As all great apes and gibbons are placed within the categories of critically endangered, endangered or vulnerable, this text box presents detail on a selection of the criteria for these three categories.

Full details of the IUCN Red List Categories and Criteria (in English, French, or Spanish) can be viewed and downloaded at:

http://www.iucnredlist.org/technical-documents/categories-and-criteria/2001-categories-criteria.

Detailed guidelines on their use can also be seen at:

http://www.iucnredlist.org/documents/RedListGuidelines.pdf.

A **vulnerable** taxon is considered to be facing a high risk of extinction in the wild. It will number fewer than 10 000 mature individuals, there will be evidence of continuing decline, and a significant reduction (upwards of 50%) in the size of the population over the last 10 years or three generations.

An **endangered** taxon is considered to be facing a very high risk of extinction in the wild. It will number fewer than 2500 mature individuals, there will be evidence of continuing decline and a significant reduction (upwards of 50%) in the size of the population over the last 10 years or three generations.

A **critically endangered** taxon is considered to be facing an extremely high risk of extinction in the wild. It will number fewer than 250 mature individuals, there will be evidence of continuing decline and a significant reduction (upwards of 80%) in the size of the population over the last 10 years or three generations.

CITES Appendices I, II, and III to the Convention are lists of species afforded different levels or types of protection from overexploitation.

All non-human apes are listed on **Appendix I**, which includes species that are the most endangered among CITES-listed animals and plants. They are threatened with extinction and CITES prohibits international trade in specimens of these species except when the purpose of the import is not commercial, for instance for scientific research. In these exceptional cases, trade may take place provided it is authorized by the granting of both an import permit and an export permit (or re-export certificate). Article VII of the Convention provides for a number of exemptions to this general prohibition. For more information go to: http://www.cites.org/eng/app/.

All information from http://www.iucnredlist.org/technical-documents/categories-and-criteria and http://www.cites.org/eng/app/.

are possible but future work requires verification of the impact of existing approaches as well as the formulation of bold recommendations that further secure reconciliation and ensure implementation becomes standard government and industry practice.

The wellbeing of humans, as well as non-human beings, depends on a healthy environment. The most critical habitats for great apes occur in some of the most isolated and impoverished regions of the world. In these areas, people depend on forest products, including land and food, for both subsistence and economic growth, with few alternatives. Until there are realistic alternatives and people are able to select those alternatives as well as understand the ecological ramifications of continuing with destructive practices, they will continue to hunt and clear the forest. People need to be supported by national and international legislation and governance that enables them to make decisions about their lives that can ensure a sustainable and life-giving environment for themselves and their children. Partnerships between government, development/conservation non-governmental organizations (NGOs) and extractive industries can provide people with such choices.

Understanding the impacts, on the ecosystems and biodiversity that sustain life, of natural resource exploitation to meet global needs, is essential. This will enable decision-makers, at the national and family level, to make informed choices about how to meet immediate needs and preserve resources for future generations. This deeper examination of the impact of natural resource extraction on one particular taxonomic group of animals, and the experience of trying to reconcile their survival with human economic development, contributes to building this understanding.

Principal authors: Helga Rainer, Annette Lanjouw, and Alison White

14

Photo: It is the rapidly growing global demand for natural resources that lies at the heart of encroachment into ape habitats. © Global Witness

CHAPTER 1

From global to local: the mega-trends at the interface of apes and industry and the case of trade, law, and finance

Introduction

The greatest threats to the conservation of great apes and gibbons are forest loss and poaching. These impacts are manifested in a number of ways that include habitat loss, fragmentation and degradation by logging, expanding agriculture and food production for commercial and subsistence purposes, expanding infrastructures, forest fires, expanding mining, and changed land use. Other factors such as expanding human settlements in, or in the vicinity of, ape habitats, growing tourism, increased hunting for bushmeat, the live pet trade, and increased spread of human diseases also contribute to the loss of great ape and gibbon populations. It is the rapidly growing global demand for natural resources including land, water, minerals, energy, food, and forest products that lies at the heart of encroachment into ape habitats and there are a number of different drivers underlying these trends. This chapter focuses on the drivers that influence the expansion of extractive industries into ape habitats, highlighting various megatrends.

By focusing on megatrends, which are major societal and transformative forces, this chapter initially presents detail on the following global drivers: economic development, demographics, globalization, and infrastructure. The impacts of these drivers on minerals and mining, biodiversity, and industrial logging are further explored as these three factors are considered most relevant to presenting the linkages between global processes, extractive industries, and the status and welfare of apes.

The final section of this chapter interrogates three elements of the megatrends – trade, law, and finance – and presents examples of how these factors are being utilized to influence ape conservation. In particular, this section examines the role of EU Forest Law Enforcement Governance and Trade (FLEGT), contract law, and the International Finance Corporations (IFC) Performance Standard 6 (PS6) that prescribes biodiversity conservation to its clients.

Key findings from this chapter include:

- Substantial economic growth within ape range countries and beyond over the next several decades will exert intense pressure on natural resources and ape habitats.
- Substantial increases in the size of the middle classes in emerging economies will have a dramatic impact on ape habitats due to their consumption patterns.
- Impacts of globalization are likely to be a factor in armed conflicts, especially in sub-Saharan Africa, with subsequent direct and indirect impacts to great apes and their habitats.

- The impacts of global trends in production, consumption, and demography are interconnected. New approaches to risk strategies and management, that move beyond focusing on individual issues but rather concentrate on systems and patterns, promote alternatives to managing the myriad of interconnected trends and impacts.
- Industry behavior can be influenced through civil society action, particularly when targeting international financial institutions.
- Recent trade agreements seek to incorporate conditionalities that mitigate habitat destruction and degradation but coverage is still limited.

Global drivers of megatrends

This section presents detail on a selection of global drivers of the megatrends. By highlighting the role of economy, demographics, and infrastructure on natural resources and the environment especially in the tropical forest belt, it demonstrates the linkages between global processes, extractive industries, and ape conservation and welfare. An illustration of some of these drivers and their impacts is presented in Figure 1.1. A detailed treatment of all the drivers (highlighted in Figure 1.1) is beyond the scope of this publication but the three drivers elaborated on in this section are considered most relevant for their impact on extractive industries and ape habitats.

Economy

While there is uncertainty on how the global economy will develop, its importance as a key driver of most of the megatrends and their impacts is less disputed. The financial crisis at the onset of the twenty-first century developed into a recession, which in turn developed into political economic crisis and on to a global crisis of confidence. The Bank for International Settlements (often referred to as the Bank of Central Banks) concluded that the greatest risks for the economies are the developed economies, but also those emerging economies whose rapid growth was through exports. The Bank also concluded that a sustainable growth path can only be achieved by restructuring the banking and financial industry. These conditions create huge uncertainties in making any assessment about the long-term development of the global economy.

However, a number of predictions indicate that the global economy will grow by 2–4 times between 2010 and 2050 (Ward, 2011; OECD, 2012; Randers, 2012; Rubin, 2012; Ward, 2012). The variation in growth is shown to depend on the direction of policy development and implementation by both the international and national communities. Various scenarios that include business-as-usual models and other scenarios that consider using investments to solve problems related to resource depletion and environmental destruction have been articulated. Furthermore, rapid growth in the middle class will have dramatic impacts on ape habitats due to their consumption patterns. The growth of the middle class (defined as house-

FIGURE 1.1

Examples of drivers and impacts of megatrends

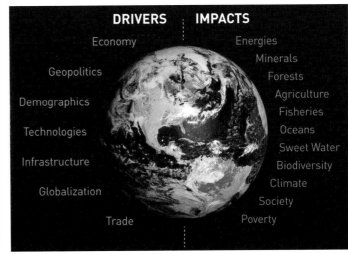

Courtesy of S. Nilsson

holds with daily expenditures of US $10–100 per person in purchasing parity terms (PPP) is expected to change from 1.8 billion in 2009 to 4.9 billion in 2030. This represents an increase in purchasing power from US$21 trillion in 2009 to US$56 trillion in 2030. If current consumption patterns are maintained, it is highly likely that global resources will be unable to accommodate such levels in 20–30 years (Wilson and Dragusanu, 2008). The shifts of the middle classes during the next 40 years will be dominated by the emerging economies (Kharas, 2010).

TABLE 1.1

Total GDP (gross domestic product) growth per year in the developed world, Asia and sub-Saharan Africa per decade from 2010–50

Time period	Developed world	Asia	Sub-Saharan Africa
2010–20	1.8	5.8	4.6
2020–30	1.8	5.1	5.1
2030–40	1.9	4.7	5.2
2040–50	2.1	4.3	5.3

Ward, 2012

BOX 1.1

Forever Sabah

Forever Sabah (http://www.forever-sabah.com/) is a new initiative that aims to transition the Malaysian state of Sabah toward a diversified, equitable and ecologically sustainable "green" economy. Sabah's 74 000 km^2 (7.4 million hectares) on the island of Borneo harbor some of the world's most biologically diverse and ecologically significant habitats, including critical lowland forest habitat for the endangered Bornean orangutan and gibbon (Wikramanayake et al., 2002). Over the last 40 years, intense natural resource extraction (logging and subsequent conversion of land to large-scale agriculture) has helped fuel exponential growth in Malaysia's GDP at the cost of lowland forests. This growth is expected to continue, with the federal government proposing a new economic program intended to achieve a high-income economy by 2020 (Prime Minister's Department of Malaysia, 2010).

Amidst relentless pressure, the state remains committed to protection of forests and biodiversity, setting aside vast protected areas and implementing sustainable forest management strategies. However, these initiatives lack support amongst an increasingly urban society and the business community, and have contributed to marginalization of indigenous communities – placing additional pressure on remaining forests.

Forever Sabah offers an integrated approach to reverse current trends by engaging a diverse group of stakeholders – government, communities, industry, civil society, scientists, and conservation groups – to jointly develop a concept for a common sustainable future. With a national policy framework geared to stimulate business development and economic wealth, a business "model" approach was chosen as the most viable mechanism to attract investment, gain political traction, and ensure the establishment of legal and policy frameworks to incentivize, sustain, and enforce a transition to sustainability.

The aim is to catalyze fundamental changes in the way natural resource conservation and economic development interface. For businesses, this means instilling a focus on a "triple bottom line" – measuring benefits to economy, equality, and ecology. For natural resource managers, this entails engaging in sustainable enterprise approaches to fund management and restoration of ecosystems. Research and technology transfer, as well as impact accounting, will be emphasized to ensure verifiable net ecological gains.

To accomplish this, Forever Sabah will identify and facilitate implementation of a suite of "model" projects designed to transform and diversify standard practices in areas including habitat conservation, renewable energy, waste management, and agriculture, with significant focus on rural areas to create "green jobs" and alleviate pressure on dwindling forest resources. Model projects will be underpinned by business financial models and designed to move beyond "best practice" to demonstrate a positive and accountable ecological footprint on all fronts – from energy, resource utilization, and waste management to equitable social benefits.

Once implemented, projects will be scaled-up to achieve wider impacts. For example, community-based micro hydro enterprises will provide electricity and sustainable water supply as well as incentives for watershed protection locally – with significant potential to generate additional power to feed into the state grid, decreasing overall dependence on fossil fuels.

Together, the suite of model projects are intended to provide innovative and practical solutions to meet policy goals of creating a greener economy, alleviating dependence on traditional economic drivers, achieving long-term protection of lowland forests and biodiversity, and decreasing CO$_2$ and methane emissions.

Consensus that there will be substantial economic growth in the emerging economies is rarely disputed (see Table 1.1) and the resultant accelerating shift of global economic power alongside the newly emerged economic balance will be the driving force for global and international policy setting. With great apes and gibbons found in many of the countries that will have substantial economic growth over the next few decades, the resulting pressure on natural resources and their habitats will therefore increase substantially. Extractive industries will increasingly expand their operations into pristine habitats that include ape ranges in order to meet the demands of the growing economy.

Strongly linked to innovations and technological development is the creation of a ubiquitous Green Economy. A Green Economy is based on principles of sustainable development of natural resources. In comparison to a conventional economy, a Green Economy is based on resource efficiency and renewable raw materials, generating little waste and pollution. This in turn means that there would be a substantial increase in the use of renewable energy, green buildings, clean transportation, sustainable waste management, and sustainable management of water and land, to mention but a few characteristics. With predictions that the global population is using 50% more natural resources than the Earth can sustainably provide, an alternative to current economic models is being increasingly considered and debated. The potential positive impact on the habitats of great apes is enhanced in Green Economy models with more value ascribed to protecting critical ecosystems and biodiversity in comparison to business-as-usual models.

Demographics

The global human population is likely to increase from 7 billion (2010) to 9.3 billion by

2050 and to 10.1 billion by 2100. The population in sub-Saharan Africa is estimated to increase by nearly 1.2 billion between 2010 and 2050 (an increase of 130%) and in Southeast Asia by nearly 200 million people (Population Reference Bureau, 2011). With population growth expected to be much more dramatic in Africa than Asia, it is likely that there will be an accelerated rate of impact on the natural environment in Africa while the rate of impact on the natural environment in Asia will be slower.

Impacts on the natural environment are further compounded when predictions are disaggregated to show the increases in rural populations. In the least developed countries the rural population will increase by 268 million, or 45%, between 2010 and 2050. The total rural population in sub-Saharan Africa is expected to increase by 300 million people, or 57%, over the same period. In comparison, in Southeast Asia the rural population is expected to decrease by 73 million people, or 22%. Rural population increases in sub-Saharan Africa and especially in Western Africa will probably cause an increased pressure on the natural resources, especially as poverty is an overriding issue, and significant impacts on ape habitats in these countries are therefore likely to occur.

Finally, an additional component of future demographic patterns is the increase in life expectancies, which are expected to converge substantially across all the world's regions by 2050. Currently approximately 0.5 billion people are 65 or older and this number is predicted to increase to 1.5 billion in 2050 and 2.2 billion in 2100. Impacts on the economies of governments will manifest themselves in the pensions, health, and care that are currently in the range of 10–20% of GDP but will rise to 30–40% in 2050 (Franklin and Andrews, 2012).

Globalization

One definition of globalization is "the widening, deepening, and speeding up of worldwide interconnectedness." However, no clear definition has emerged (see Box 1.2) and while globalization impacts the global society in many dimensions (such as demographics, politics, social and cultural changes, education, etc.), this section will explore the impact of globalization on severe conflicts in

Photo: A remote village in Gabon. Rural population increases in sub-Saharan Africa will probably increase pressure on natural resources and significant impacts on ape habitats are likely to occur. © Alison White

The many faces of globalization

In 2007, the United Nations Environment Programme (UNEP) themed its February issue of *Our Planet* magazine on globalization and the environment. For some of the eminent contributors, globalization provides opportunities for growth and more efficient allocation of resources. For the remainder, globalization is the main vector of environmental degradation chiefly by virtue of encouraging increased consumption. The journal issue is worthy of mention because the dissonance among its authors reflects the diversity of meanings inherent in globalization. Consequently, it is exceedingly difficult to define: no single author in the issue attempted it explicitly. Yet for those seeking a greater understanding of the connections between globalization and environmental change – and a decline in biodiversity in particular – the absence of a definition is frustrating and compounded by the traditional separation of the two discourses. This section explores what is generally meant by globalization.

Space and its politics

Globalization has obvious spatial connotations but economic connotations are dominant. Advocates of economic globalization – globalists – presuppose and champion a geographical spread of free markets that those skeptical of globalization – globoskeptics – dismiss as limited to the developed world. Implicitly then, globalists see globalization as more inclusive than globoskeptics. Conservationists have tended to be cognizant of global trends but more keenly aware of their differentiated impact across local spaces.

Decline of the state

For such reasons, many prefer the term 'internationalization' as this highlights the role of nation states in the processes linked to globalization. Globalization is an engineered process for globoskeptics while being a "natural" process for globalists that is best left unfettered by government regulation. The two camps differ in their assessment of the benefit of deregulation. Historically, the conservation movement has advocated for greater regulation, which is most notable in the expansion of international treaties since the 1970s.

Political agendas

Globalists are often associated with the neoliberal economic thinking of the political right, whereas globoskeptics tend to belong to the left of the political spectrum. However, there are exceptions to this rough guide. Some members of the left accept that globalization has changed the role of the nation state but have judged this to be a cause for lament rather than celebration. They see the responsibility for negative externalities that markets generate left to governments to solve with costs that burden citizens more than business. From this perspective, global markets frequently fail rather than flourish with calamitous effects on the environment.

Movement

Globalization is frequently taken to mean movement of goods, people, capital and ideas that is more intensive or more extensive than any seen historically. Many perceive levels of immigration, the influx of transnational companies into local markets, the penetration of foreign cultural products, and so on, as more marked than before (Smith, 1990). Of course, much movement is subject to control in the form of state regulation or deregulation. Clearly other forms – such as the movement of greenhouse gases or the spread of introduced species – prove difficult, if not impossible, to control.

Beyond interdependence

The recent global financial crisis has underlined the financial and economic connections between different parts of the globe, but more importantly the degree to which collective action is required by governments to solve problems that spill over state boundaries. However, the various strands of globalization theory look beyond governmental interdependence to other dimensions of globalization, such as the growth of civil society (Martell, 2007).

Interconnectivity

New types of interconnection among and between populations rather than governments and markets are closely and powerfully associated with globalization. These understandings are not merely the result of movements of people but of technological advances in the field of telecommunications. The increased speed and volume of information transfer since the onset of the Internet appears to negate the importance of physical distance. It has become possible to envision social relations as stretched across vast expanses of space.

Global consciousness

Developments in television broadcasting allow for news and events to be viewed virtually simultaneously through satellite links in disparate places across the world, thus amplifying the perceptions of global interconnection. Not only do advances in telecommunications help to broaden audience horizons, they help to engender a global consciousness. Transnational movements, including environmentalist and anti-globalization variants, can *also* arouse precisely this type of consciousness.

Inequality and culture

Increases in movement and interconnection across space impact cultures to varying degrees. With magnified exposure to foreign ideas, products, and people, cultural convergence is perceived by many but cultural hybridity by others. Anxieties arise over both the loss of cultural uniqueness and the domination of Western and especially American cultures over others. Remarkably similar worries plague conservationists keen to protect ecosystems from invading species. Ironically for local populations, the inundation of international environmental organizations tasked with environmental protection may itself be seen as an invasion.

Neo-imperialist understandings of globalization gain potency in certain quarters, among them anti-globalization movements. Such groups point to the unevenness in the distribution of the costs and benefits of globalization. Elsewhere, concerns mount for the overall socioeconomic consequences of globalization. Globalists interpret the trends as an aggregate improvement in population wealth but detractors point to growing relative poverty in the same figures (Hirst and Thompson, 2000).

Global governance

Worries over rising inequality help evoke desires to shape globalization for the better. While the goal of global democracy is currently merely an aspiration, the diffusion of global governance forges ahead. The proliferation of norms, decision-making procedures, and international law over an array of issues continues. One could reasonably suggest that environmental governance is paradigmatic of global governance (Biermann and Siebenhuner, 2009); itself a form of globalization it is, paradoxically, the key means by which globalization's negative impact on the environment is addressed (Zimmerer, 2006).

Asia and Africa and the subsequent impact on apes and their habitats. An additional treatment of globalization and the environment is explored in Box 1.2.

Globalization has the potential to increase both armed and non-armed conflict over natural resources. Over the last 20 years there have been severe armed conflicts in Africa and Asia that have impacted the habitats and conditions of great apes and gibbons living in these regions. Since 1946 all great ape range states, except for Tanzania, have experienced some form of civil conflict. Post the cold war, civil wars occurred in 40% of the great ape states (Benz and Benz-Schwarzburg, 2010). In the last 50 years there has been an increase in the proportion of global internal armed conflicts in sub-Saharan Africa and this upward trend is likely to continue. With warring parties utilizing tropical forests for protection, and also to harvest and trade forest resources that in turn finance conflict, the impact on great ape populations in these regions is a reality. Examples include dramatic declines in eastern lowland gorilla populations in Kahuzi Biega National Park in Eastern DRC (Democratic Republic of Congo) and massacring of mountain gorillas in the same region (Yamagiwa, 2003; Jenkins, 2008). Linkages to the extraction of valuable minerals from areas that include ape habitats have been cited as a driver of the conflict in the region.

Factors that exacerbate and potentially initiate conflict are linked to both the scarcity and abundance of certain natural resources (Cater, 2003). Other factors such as poverty, poor education, ethnicity, inequality, corruption, and external aggression also contribute to the onset and perpetuation of armed conflicts. Additionally, weak government effectiveness, a lack of rule of law, and low control of corruption increase the likelihood of a country descending into civil war by 30–45% (World Bank, 2011a). The use of increased wealth and growth to implement necessary reforms that reduce poverty and improve education and security has been cited as a critical factor to prevent future conflict. A significant proportion of the 1.5 billion people currently living in countries affected by or recovering from organized crime and political violence depend on access to and use of natural resources for their survival. This in turn has further impacts on natural resources as compromised communities unsustainably utilize resources to ensure their survival during periods of conflict and post conflict (McNeely, 2007). This section highlights the necessity of monitoring future conflicts especially in great ape range states in sub-Saharan Africa in order to better protect the habitats and populations of great apes in the region.

Infrastructure

Physical infrastructure is considered critical to enable economic growth and development. Infrastructure is not only an issue of economy and physical assets through the opening and connecting of markets, connecting jobs and improving competitiveness, it also improves the overall quality of life in the form of increased mobility, better housing, safer lives, and reductions in poverty. Infrastructure development is thus perceived as contributing to better economies and society; however, some investments have negative impacts on land use and the environment. For example, investments in transport infrastructure increase emissions and pollution, and lead to increased and often times uncontrolled exploitation of natural resources (Wright, 2010).

There is concern that today's infrastructure planning is insufficient as it builds upon existing structures or even worse on infrastructure established 30–40 years ago. Future generations and the type of societies that would be desirable should be the focus of planning, as well as the needs for the next 50–100 years rather than just working to meet current demands.

Countries in tropical Africa and Southeast Asia are expected to capitalize on the global demand for their commodities driven by economic growth and demographic developments. However, current transportation networks constitute a constraint on these ambitions; for example, Indonesia has the lowest road density in all of Southeast Asia, and the government is not surprisingly prioritizing the development of infrastructure to unlock the economic potential of its natural resource base (Moser, 2011). With future investments by the World Bank and African Development Bank aimed at providing assistance that will target connecting rural African populations (some 75% of the total population) with markets, similar to the planning in Southeast Asia, the impact on great apes and gibbons is likely to be significant. Their habitats will become more fragmented as a result of increased road networks, which will in turn increase the exploitation of natural resources as previously inaccessible areas open up. The resulting increases in forest degradation and fragmentation, hunting, and poaching of animal species are explored in Chapter 7.

Impacts of megatrends

Although this section focuses on exploring some of the impacts of the drivers and their subsequent role in the status of great apes and gibbons, there is no absolute division between the two. When impacts reach a tipping point they in turn become drivers of developments, predominantly in unfavorable directions, and often no clear boundaries exist to distinguish between cause and effect. Maintaining the focus on the interface of extractive industries and ape conservation means that this section only explores the following impacts of mega-

trends: minerals and mining, biodiversity, and industrial logging.

Minerals and mining

Minerals and metals underpin the global economy with sectors such as transport, energy, housing, health, and agriculture heavily dependent on the raw materials that are extracted around the world. Due to growth in economies and the human population, there has been a tremendous increase in the consumption of minerals over the last 100 years. Over the period 1900–2005, the extraction of construction materials grew by a factor of 34 and ores and industrial mining extraction by a factor of 27 (UNEP, 2011a). A number of scenarios for future demand for minerals for 2050 have been analyzed. If business-as-usual models prevail, total resource use by 2050 will be some 140 billion tons per year. This means that from an extraction rate of 8–9 tons/capita/year in 2005 it will increase to 16 tons/capita/year in 2050. Extraction at such levels is considered to be unsustainable, and if investments in sustainable-oriented innovations are made then predicted substantial structural changes in industry consumption and production could generate far more per unit of resources than the current rates (UNEP, 2011a).

The impact of increased competition over land, changed land use and significantly extended infrastructure as a result of expansion in extraction of the magnitude along the business-as-usual model will influence and disturb ecosystems and wildlife habitats. The implications for Africa and Asia are that it is likely that countries on these two continents will utilize mining and mineral resources as a key strategy to ensure economic growth and development. The African Union developed a mining vision in 2009, identifying resources from this sector as key to Africa's development. This highlights not only the economic incentives for expansion but

also the strong political support of developments in this direction (African Union, 2009).

An additional dimension of minerals and mining to the environment is the increase in the use of lower grades of minerals and its impact on waste and energy. This is illustrated by the decline in average global lead grade from about 0.75% in 1998 to 0.5% in 2009 (ICMM, 2012). The extraction of lower grade ores and minerals requires more energy and results in increased waste production. In the 1940s, the production of 1 ton of copper generated 25–50 tons of waste, whereas current production results in 250 tons of waste per ton of copper. Increasing energy requirements to extract relevant ores are likely to be prohibitive, especially for elements such as aluminum, iron, silicon, magnesium, and titanium. Furthermore, many of the new environmental technologies such as wind turbines, energy efficient light bulbs, and electric car batteries are dependent on the use of a range of rare earth metals (REM),

which constitute a limited resource, predominantly extracted from China. This will have repercussions on international tensions for resources and there will continue to be a scramble for resources, especially in Africa (Bloodworth and Gunn, 2012).

A number of ape range states are key producers of minerals, such as Guinea for bauxite and the DRC for cobalt. The establishment of mining concessions in ape habitats has known impacts on habitat fragmentation and loss. Furthermore, mineral wealth in poorer countries is often linked to poverty and instability, which is considered to be a driver for informal artisanal and small-scale mining (ASM) on which millions of people are economically dependent. The direct and indirect environmental impacts in ape habitats of both industrial-scale mining and ASM are explored in greater depth in Chapters 5 and 6, and the increasing extent of exploration and exploitation will further expand into ape ranges.

Photo: The impact of increased competition over land as a result of expansion in extraction of the magnitude along the business-as-usual model will significantly influence and disturb ecosystems and wildlife habitats. © Jabruson, 2013. All Rights Reserved. www.jabruson. photoshelter.com

Biodiversity loss and deforestation

Understanding and knowledge of biodiversity is incomplete; current estimates put the total number of species on earth at between 2 and 100 million, of which some 45 000 have been assessed. Of the assessed species, 2% are already extinct, 7% are critically endangered, and 11% are classified as endangered (Convention on Biological Diversity (CBD) Secretariat, 2010). The importance of biodiversity for human welfare is not fully understood and species such as cockroaches could, for example, provide the key to controlling bacterial infections and outbreaks. Cockroaches have nine molecules that are toxic to bacteria and, with increasing levels of resistance to antibiotics (Bouamama *et al.*, 2010), the opportunities to exploit solutions from nature (and in this case from cockroaches!) are likely to be increasingly critical.

However, significant declines in biodiversity are expected over the next decades. Terrestrial biodiversity, measured as mean species abundance, is projected to decrease by an additional 10% by 2050 with mature forests in particular decreasing by 13% over that period (OECD, 2012). The driving forces for this decline will be as a result of expansion of agriculture and commercial forestry, infrastructure development, human encroachment, fragmentation of habitats, climate change, and pollution. The greatest losses in biodiversity will be in Africa, Latin America, the Caribbean, and Asia. International trade has been associated with declines in biodiversity stocks as consumers in developed countries increase demand for commodities produced in developing countries which have high levels of biodiversity.

Deforestation is expected to have a particularly significant impact on tropical biodiversity. Under business-as-usual scenarios, severe impacts on extinction of species by deforestation were detected for Latin America, sub-Saharan Africa, and Southeast Asia. Depending on the methodology employed, out of 4500 forest-dependent species, deforestation will cause the extinction of mammal and amphibian species to the range of 9–27% by 2100 (Strassburg *et al.*, 2012). In fact, gross yearly deforestation in Africa is 32 000 km²/year (3.2 million ha/year) and in Asia it is assessed to be 24 000 km²/year (2.4 million ha/year), although there is no net loss for the region due to the large plantations being developed in China. Gross forest loss is occurring primarily in the tropical regions with forest gains in other climatic domains (FAO and JRC, 2011).

As great apes and gibbons primarily inhabit tropical forest in Asia and Africa, the impact on their survival is likely to be significant (see Chapter 3). There is, however, no clear consensus on the causes of deforestation, although these include subsistence farming (Sanz, 2007; Kissinger *et al.*, 2012), commercial large-scale farming including increased demand for biomass for biofuels and edible oils, and shifting cultivation (FAO, 2010a, 2010b). Extractive industries often require substantial infrastructure not only to access viable deposits of minerals and metals or remove valuable timber but also to transport the commodity to markets. In this way, extractive industries contribute to increasing fragmentation of tropical forests and loss of biodiversity. This was highlighted in the development of the Chad–Cameroon oil pipeline that not only cut through ape habitat but also impacted the indigenous Bagyéli community whose sacred sites were threatened and many of whom had to move their camps (Nelson, 2007).

However, it is likely that there has been a shift over time of drivers of deforestation with the demands of growing urban populations and agricultural trade currently having the greatest impact. With consensus that deforestation will continue, it is unlikely that zero deforestation will be achievable in the foreseeable future, especially considering increased demand for food and biofuels, and the subsequent increase in conversion to croplands to meet these demands.

Industrial round wood

Globally, over 2 million people are estimated to be employed by the forestry industry in the tropical timber sector, over half of these in Southeast Asia (FAO, 2011a). In this region forestry contributes almost US$20 billion to the region's economy annually, whereas for the Congo basin, the figure is US$1.8 billion which, although smaller than that for Southeast Asia, represents a similar proportion of GDP (FAO, 2011b).

Demand for industrial round wood, which includes industrial wood in the rough (i.e. saw logs and veneer logs, pulpwood, and other industrial round wood) is likely to increase from 1.5 billion cubic meters to 2.3 billion cubic meters by 2020 (FIM, 2012) and 3.9 billion cubic meters by 2030 (Indufor, 2012). Key drivers in the increased demand for industrial round wood include population growth, with much of the expansion expected to occur in emerging markets such as India, China, Latin America, and the Caribbean, as well as Africa. Demand from emerging economies will constitute the larger share of increased demand for round wood despite a lower per capita consumption of wood products compared to mature markets. Other drivers include economic growth, where round wood consumption follows the increasing growth in GDP as a result of higher standards of living. However, when GDP reaches a certain level, consumption of forest products and wood starts to decrease as people switch from traditional paper-based products to electronic products.

In 2012, wood from plantations was supplying approximately 33% of the total

Photo: As increased supply for demand of industrial round wood is predicted to come from natural sources, the overlap with ape habitats is already a reality and will increase. © Alison White

global industrial round wood demand. This is expected to be in the region of 24–35% by 2050. With the remainder of the wood obtained from tropical and boreal natural and semi-natural forests, an increase in pressure on these resources is expected and, with access to boreal forests limited, pressure will mount in areas that are easier to access (Indufor, 2012). As of 2010, approximately 116 million hectares of the equatorial forests in Africa were allocated for the production of wood and non-wood products. Forest coverage has continued to decline since 1990 in Central, West and East Africa where *Gorilla* and *Pan* spp. are found (FAO, 2011b). In Indonesia, a similar scenario emerges with over half of the remaining forests earmarked for production (FAO, 2010a, 2010b) of which half again are primary forest, the majority in Papua and Kalimantan, the latter a stronghold for the endangered Bornean orangutan (*Pongo pygmaeus*). As increased supply for the demand for industrial round wood is predicted to come from natural sources, the overlap with ape habitats is already a reality and will increase. This interface is further explored in Chapter 4.

Interconnections, complexity, and a new paradigm?

Current scientific knowledge of the impacts of megatrends and options for substantial mitigation are known and understood (FAO, 2009; Lambin and Meyfroidt, 2011; WWF, 2011; Franklin and Andrews, 2012), however little in the way of meaningful implementation that can lead to the fundamental changes required is occurring. This is further compounded when one acknowledges that the impacts of one factor create a chain reaction on to other factors. The drivers and impacts of megatrends explored in the previous section are explicitly linked to impacting apes and their habitats, but these also further influence, to mention just a few, climate change, poverty, and food consumption. These interconnections are complex and a simple illustration of the change in demographics is used as an example to demonstrate these interactions (Figure 1.2).

Figure 1.2 presents, through the connections illustrated by the red line, how the demographic megatrend contributes to economic growth as a result of increasing demand and size of workforce. The growing economy will in turn generate more consumption and increased emissions contributing to climate change. The increased human population will also result in increased food demand, which together will influence the upward trajectory of energy demand. This will also contribute to changes in the global climate as increased energy consumption increases emissions of greenhouse gases. Further impacts of increased food consumption will be manifested in increased consumption of fresh water and the knock-on effects of increased energy consumption will lead to increases in the use of minerals and biomass energy, further impacting terrestrial ecosystems and biodiversity.

FIGURE 1.2

Example of megatrend interconnections

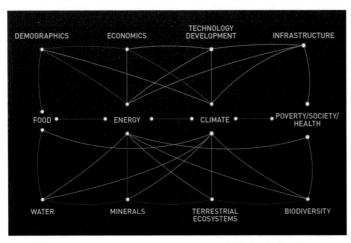

Courtesy of S. Nilsson

While the simple interconnections can be identified, there is limited knowledge of the extent of these impacts and exactly where the tipping points into drivers occur is poorly understood. Furthermore, defining interconnections in situations with several megatrends occurring in parallel is more complex and current knowledge is limited.

A systems and paradigm shift is considered necessary with new approaches to risk strategies and management moving beyond focusing on individual trends but instead concentrating on systems and patterns. Information is predominantly dealt with in silos but the paradigm shift would require knowledge to be nested and networked thereby promoting alternative premises to managing the myriad of interconnected trends and impacts.

Trade agreements, finance, and contract law reconciling extractives and conservation

The previous discussion highlighted the impact of global drivers of increasing globalization, human populations, economies, and infrastructure on mining and minerals, biodiversity and industrial round wood. Considering the necessity for governments to exploit opportunities for economic development, creating opportunities to influence policy- and decision-makers to consider conservation of apes and their habitats is challenging. This is further compounded when impacts are the result of interactions among a number of factors and contexts are continually evolving.

With global demand and extraction of minerals, mining, and logging expected to increase significantly, this section presents a number of existing and theoretical frameworks that encompass trade, finance, and contract law. It showcases examples of how

sustainably sourced timber from tropical forests is increasingly considered in trade, highlights opportunities for conserving apes through contract law that interfaces with extractive industries, and concludes by presenting the challenge for multilateral finance institutions to reconcile environmental conservation and economic development.

European Union Forest Law Enforcement Governance and Trade (FLEGT) Action Plan

Considering the impact of consumers on tropical forests, there has only recently been the recognition that policies within tropical timber consumer countries could be a potent tool for driving change in environmental and social standards within the tropical timber sector, in particular with regard to addressing the myriad of issues associated with illegal logging. It is estimated that, between 1990 and 2005, Africa lost over 570 000 km² (57 million hectares) of forests, representing 1.5% of the world's total forests. Deforestation and forest fires are recognized as significant factors, but the inability of forest agencies to manage these resources in a sustainable manner due to financial limitations is also considered to be part of the problem (Powers and Wong, 2011).

Policies that seek to ensure that timber is produced in accordance with producer country laws, including wildlife, forestry, and indigenous people's rights, are being promoted as avenues that could make a significant contribution to addressing one of the major threats to wildlife in tropical forests.

Bilateral agreements between timber producing countries and consumer countries to ensure legal and sustainable supplies of timber are emerging. A major example is the EU FLEGT action plan linked to the EU's "due diligence" regulation designed to stop illegal timber entering the region's markets. This initiative combines a licensing system with capacity-building measures for verification and enforcement in producer countries. Other global initiatives by the World Bank are Africa Forest Law Enforcement and Governance (AFLEG) and Europe and North Asia Forest Law Enforcement and Governance (ENAFLEG). One fundamental difference between these initiatives and FLEGT is the incorporation of the trade component. The World Bank supported initiatives do not provide binding power to require countries to take action or face sanction. Despite showing initial promise there has been little progress on these initiatives since their inception, just over and just under 10 years ago respectively (Powers and Wong, 2011).

Within developed nations the state is a major purchaser of goods and services, accounting for an estimated 10% of GDP (Brack, 2008). Many states have sought to use this purchasing power to ensure that the public sector purchases only legal and sustainable timber. These include Belgium, Denmark, France, Germany, Japan, the Netherlands, New Zealand, Norway, and the UK. Within the UK, certified timber now accounts for 80% of the timber product market (Moore, 2012), a substantial portion of which is thought to be driven by public procurement policies which can act as major drivers for suppliers (Simula, 2006). Procurement policies have the advantage of being more easily legislated for and implemented than the other methods described above.

The FLEGT process is realized through Voluntary Partnership Agreements (VPAs) negotiated on a country-by-country basis with Ghana one of the earliest to sign up, in 2009. Since then Cameroon, Liberia, Republic of Congo, and Indonesia are amongst those who have signed VPAs. Each agreement is country specific, defines concepts of legality and standards of production and verification with producer countries com-

mitting to legislation changes as required, and are sovereign, legally binding trade agreements. Once VPAs have been signed, exporter countries receive financing from the EU to develop appropriate systems to regulate the forestry sector including tracing products and licensing their export to the EU. These systems have to be in place after an allocated period, from which point only licensed timber is permitted to enter the EU. Benefits to the exporting countries are improved access to EU markets, EU political and financial reinforcement of forest governance, increased revenue from taxes and duties, increased development assistance from the EU, additional enforcement tools to combat illegal activities, and improved reputation by demonstrating a commitment to good governance (Powers and Wong, 2011).

The VPA lists criteria, indicators, and verifiers that will form the basis for enforcement and uses an approach that resembles the voluntary forest certification process. Although the VPA does not have to include all of the country's timber production, including domestic trade, thus far all countries that have signed agreements have opted to do so (S. Lawson, email communication, July 2013). A licensing process, under a designated licensing authority and overseen by independent verifiers, is designed to ensure compliance. The process places strong emphasis on legality, governance, transparency, and local stakeholder involvement and differs from other mechanisms in its countrywide coverage and strong capacity-building aspects. Several other bilateral trade agreements exist, between, for example, Australia and Papua New Guinea, and Indonesia and China, although it has been noted that none of these is yet to be associated with any change in exporters' behavior and, if purely free-trade based, the lifting of trade barriers may actually exacerbate existing situations (Brack and Buckrell, 2011).

Currently a small portion of timber traded internationally is licensed and/or verified as being legally harvested – approximately 8% of forests globally (FAO, 2010a, 2010b); a fact recognized in measures taken by the EU and United States to try to ensure only legal timber enters their markets. In the United States this takes the form of the Lacey Act, which extends the concept of illegality of goods imported or exported in the United States to include definitions of illegality in their country of origin, making it unlawful to: "import, export, transport, sell, receive, acquire or purchase in interstate or foreign commerce . . . any plant taken, possessed, transported or sold . . . in violation of any foreign law" with the onus on importers to verify that their goods are

Photo: Currently a small portion of timber traded internationally is licensed and/or verified as being legally harvested – approximately 8% of forests globally. © Serge Wich

legitimately sourced. Within the EU this comes under the Timber Regulation. It requires due diligence, which places the responsibility for verifying legality on to the supplier that initially places the product on the EU market. Timber produced under a VPA is automatically approved. This system only came online in 2013, so how it functions remains to be seen. However, areas of concern relate to possible corruption and the ability of companies to have timber verified as legal despite not meeting the relevant criteria and standards (BBC, 2013).

Ultimately, all measures driven by consumer countries (in common with certification schemes) are dependent on the quality and implementation of the standards and criteria they use. They are also vulnerable to weak enforcement, fraud, and leakage to other consumer nations that are not part of FLEGT. Properly implemented, however, they have the potential to be a potent driver promoting legal and sustainable production of tropical timber as well as improving forest governance in producer countries. The use of such initiatives can also be extended to mining; however, consumer-orientated initiatives are less likely to be effective where the supply chain between consumer and mine is longer and more convoluted, and determining the chain of custody becomes impossible.

Conserving apes through contract law

A number of major international laws govern the lives and treatment of apes, of which the most important is the Convention on International Trade in Endangered Species of Wild Fauna and Flora (CITES). In relation to regulating the timber industry, it is increasingly being used by states to ensure that trade in listed timber species is legal,

sustainable, and traceable. Around 350 tree species are listed under CITES Appendices, and trade in their products is therefore subject to regulation to avoid utilization that is incompatible with their survival. CITES also partners with the International Tropical Timber Organization (ITTO) to promote sustainable forest management and to build the capacity of developing states to effectively implement the Convention as it relates to listed tree species. However, enforcement is uneven; even within certain states of the United States differences exist. In the United States, implementation demands federal, state, and local coordination and monitoring US practice is itself complex. The reality is that much of ape conservation is governed by contracts and informal agreements and this is most developed in the extractive industry sector.

There is acknowledgment that extractive industries are moving away from traditional strategies and toward partnership working through engagement with public and private institutions. Examples are highlighted throughout this publication, demonstrating various successes that have shifted industry behavior as a result of the concerted effort of visionary individuals and networks of nongovernmental organizations (NGOs). This section focuses on how NGOs establish effective "laws" by leveraging the contract approach. Although lessons must be learned from engaging in legal proceedings, the reality is that a majority of issues arising, tied to great apes and gibbons, occur outside of a courtroom through contracts, legislative, or executive action. However, laws that govern the conservation of apes and practice of extractive projects emerge from a combination of public and private law, as well as domestic, foreign, and international law. They therefore share a common group of legal documents and sources including private and public contracts, loan agreements, regulations, executive documents such as

> 66 There is acknowledgment that extractive industries are moving away from traditional strategies and toward partnership working through engagement with public and private institutions. 99

Presidential Directives and white papers. It is at the interface of the laws that govern apes and the extractive sector where the conservation and welfare of many apes is determined and typically the details of apes in the extractive sector are woven into contract clauses.

Even though contracts play a central role, in how the tendering of projects is shaped by government regulations, often procurement laws are also relevant. With mediation occurring in the rules governing tendering to construction and operation of projects, the question of rights and their realization is included in this process and interacts with extractives' sites in many ways. The process of procurement is not the realm of private law and private players only, with governments and international organizations both involved throughout. Furthermore, the laws of international organizations also play a key role. For instance, the World Bank's Multilateral Investment Guarantee Agency (MIGA) might be more important than governments and certain private players. MIGA issues insurance for private parties to a contract (MIGA, 2013b). The Agency is part of the World Bank Group and presents a promising area for promoting the conservation of apes because they insure private corporate behavior (MIGA, 2013a). However, the political risk insurance (PRI) provided by MIGA excludes regulations enacted by governments that are non-discriminatory and may result in regulations that are considered expropriation from the investor's perspective (Comeaux and Kinsella, 1994). This likely affects the number of mining companies that use the MIGA PRI. This, however, does not diminish the potential that a condition tied to conservation could readily cohere and it may be effective to target the Agency to secure ape conservation and welfare.

The current law of contracts is part of a wider effort to assert anti-neoimperialism and NGOs are often the site of attack and defense. They provide a communication function by letting others know what is going on. Box 1.3 showcases the ability to bring NGOs to a single but broad issue resulting in an increased focus on contract and financial expertise. Having said that, as a great deal is known of the legal facets of the extractive sector, it can serve as a model from which a number of lessons can be drawn for the protection of apes. These include:

> NGOs establish effective "laws" by leveraging the contract approach.

1. **Leverage:** By mapping all of the domestic and foreign as well as public and private players involved in a project, one can determine who and how to target participating institutions so as to advance public values.

2. **Responsibility**: Despite the large numbers of players in a project, one can target the specific one(s) with primary responsibility over a project. For instance, although 50 international banks finance the bulk of projects, realistically only 10 or so take the lead.

3. **Repeat player**: Related, a movement away from targeting states has happened over time. For globally oriented NGOs, it is more efficient to target private actors and international organizations. Both are often involved in projects in far reaching parts of the globe.

4. **Choose your issue**: Because different organizations of a major project have distinct roles and responsibilities, it is important to choose a Bank Group, which is a more likely ally when it comes to apes than are governments.

5. **Litigate sparingly**: Litigation takes enormous time and other resources. Oftentimes the payout in a successful case is not worth much. The most effective international legal forum is the International Centre for the Settlement of Invest Disputes (ICSID), which is part

Extractive Industries Transparency Initiative (EITI): a model for great ape conservation?

The Extractive Industries Transparency Initiative (EITI) offers a model for the reporting of public-interest information, with the active participation of civil society groups in many developing countries. This initiative has been put into practice by more than 30 governments, shortly to be joined by the United States. Although the long-term effects of the EITI have yet to be determined, the initiative has been successful in attracting the endorsement not only of governments but also of civil society groups and multinational extractive companies (EITI Secretariat, 2012b). Could this initiative have relevance for the conservation of apes and ape habitat?

The theory behind the EITI, which has inspired legislation in the United States (Securities and Exchange Commission, 2012) and regulatory proposals in the European Union (European Commission, 2011), is that accurate and timely information will enable citizens to better hold their governments and extractive companies to account. The core activity of the EITI is the production and distribution of reports in each country, under the auspices of a "multi-stakeholder group" (MSG), which provides detailed information on revenue payments by companies and receipts by the relevant states (EITI Secretariat, 2012a).

The EITI is now in the middle of a debate about its future. The issues at the center of the debate include questions about other kinds of information that should be included in EITI reports, how countries should be incentivized to broaden and deepen the initiative beyond the minimum requirements of the rules, and how to better connect its work in each country to broader discussions about governance and public policy.

Is EITI relevant to conservation issues?

EITI is designed to address the specific problem of managing natural resource revenues: it does not include conservation issues within its ambit and is unlikely to in the near future, at least at the international level. It does not currently cover logging or other industries apart from oil and mining, which involve the conversion of natural forest. One country (Liberia) has chosen to report on logging revenues (LEITI Secretariat, 2010), but it is not assessed by the EITI Board on its reporting in this area because it lies outside the international requirements of the initiative.

That said, countries can choose to report on any area under the EITI and there is nothing to stop a country extending EITI reporting to conservation issues if it chooses. Due, in part, to the initiatives of some countries to move beyond the minimum rules, the focus of EITI is starting to broaden. The EITI Board is considering new systems of evaluation, which would give governments a reputational incentive to extend the scope of EITI reporting within their countries. It cannot be ruled out that at some point in the future, some countries could opt to include the impact of extractive activities on the conservation of natural resources in their EITI reports and have this form of reporting evaluated by the Board. The form this reporting should take will likely be hotly debated by EITI's supporters: a conservation NGO in a central African country, for example, might take a wholly different view of what such reporting should involve, and what the consequences of failing to meet established standards should be, from that of a mining company hoping to explore for minerals in a forested area of that country.

The centrality of civil society participation to EITI

There are safeguards to ensure the participation of local civil society groups in the country concerned, although their effectiveness depends on the attitude of the government and the ability of civil society activists to make their voices heard. Almost all civil society groups value the ability to engage within the umbrella of protection created by EITI, in which they can engage with government and company officials, but many are frustrated by its limited effect, so far, on underlying problems of poor governance. The rules on data quality in EITI are quite loose, reports from some countries in West and Central Africa have often been late, and there have been particular problems with the quality of some government data (Ravat and Ufer, 2010).

Is EITI relevant to great ape conservation?

A weakness of the EITI in some countries is that it has little connection with the communities in areas of natural resource extraction. A conservation initiative that involved local communities in forest areas, not just in monitoring activities but also in the decision-making structures of the initiative, might gain some useful legitimacy from being part of an international reporting system like the EITI. Weighed against this advantage, however, are the very long and complex negotiations that would be necessary to create such an international system: the EITI was first mooted in 2002 and can only be said to have reached a critical mass of country reporting around 2011–12.

Conclusion: what does the EITI offer for ape conservation?

EITI occupies a terrain which is some distance away from the issue of ape conservation, but may nonetheless offer some general value. The strengths and limitations of its multi-stakeholder model provide useful rhetorical arguments for strengthening existing conservation initiatives so as to ensure deeper participation by local communities in forested areas. EITI is widely seen as a successful collaboration between stakeholders from government, the private sector, and civil society, and thus could be cited as a model to replicate.

The governments of countries whose extractive industries have a significant impact on ape conservation might be persuaded to include reporting on this issue in their EITI reports, as a way of showing that they are attempting to address a range of problems associated with resource extraction, not just the financial. EITI cannot compel this form of reporting and, at the moment, has no means of evaluating the reliability of reporting, which does not relate directly to financial flows from extractive companies to governments, but this may change in the future. Some governments and companies would oppose the extension of the international EITI rules to conservation issues and it is possible that a country would not be able to tap the funding and technical support provided to EITI by development agencies for conservation issues, but there is nothing to stop a government from including conservation issues in EITI if it chooses.

of the World Bank Group and hears disputes mainly over projects. NGOs have no standing to sue; oftentimes they have not even been able to participate in a hearing.

6. **International public organizations**: Groups such as the World Bank or export credit agencies like the Export–Import Bank have been a fertile area for rule-making and implementation.

The approach employed in the extractives sector is generally to make little mention of international agreements. Instead, the target for change is usually a repeat player with sway over how a project happens. Therefore the integration of extractive industry and ape conservation NGO networks presents a case that is potentially beneficial to both groups.

NGOs in the extractive industry sector focus on the myriad of public international law institutions to achieve change; these include the International Finance Corporation (IFC), the African Development Bank (AfDB), the Asian Development Bank (ADB), the European Bank for Reconstruction and Development (EBRD), the European Investment Bank (EIB), and the Inter-American Development Bank (IDB). Their strategies focus on either internal or external reforms to the international institution. Internal reforms target governance-incorporating issues that include transparency, accountability, and democracy/participation; while external ones address the impact of the international institution on a broader political and environmental landscape. These may target a policy or project of which three common areas are the specific projects (e.g. extractive industries, power, dams, and transportation), debt relief, and structural adjustment. The mechanism for implementing meaningful change often happens in partnership with government institutions. Important NGO success stories include the establishment of the World Commission on Dams (WCD) (WCD, 2000) and the World Bank Inspection Panel (World Bank Group, 2011).

NGOs utilize a number of tools to effect change and these include networking between local, national and international civil society actors, protest, lobbying, use of media, public–political mobilization, building local capacity, and engaging in legal action. Other tools incorporate "naming and shaming" strategies, independent research, and also diplomacy to educate the general public and government representatives on the impacts of international financial institutions and ultimately influence contract detail. Going forward, the fields of apes and extractives might find themselves allies. Each brings with it capital, moral or strategic advantage, and extractives can utilize the experiences from NGO networks that are making the law bottom-up to resolve frustrations over the implementation of basic agreements or having to use the courts. From a resource perspective it is best to approach NGOs, integrate strands, and create enforceable contracts.

International Finance Corporation and Performance Standard 6

Financial institutions are a major source of capital for extractive industry projects with no more than 50 international banks providing the bulk of monetary resources. With civil society having been more successful in placing democratic conditions on projects through these lending institutions than through governments or legal systems, improving the environmental safeguards of lending institutions presents an opportunity to influence private sector behavior to mitigate against environmental and social risks. However, the reality of extractive industry action and conserving biodiversity continues to present conflicting realities. Alternative responses that still enable extraction to occur in areas of environmental value are emerging and being integrated into lending structures. This section focuses on the experience of the IFC, a member of the World Bank Group and the largest source of multilateral private sector funding. The IFC "further[s] economic development by encouraging the growth of productive private enterprise in member countries, particularly in the less developed areas, thus supplementing the activities of the International Bank for Reconstruction and Development" (IFC, 2012a).

Through eight performance standards (PSs), the IFC manages its reduction in lending exposure to environmental and social risk. In 2009, the Board of Executive Directors of IFC requested a review of all the PSs. At the time of the review PS6 – Biodiversity Conser-

vation and Sustainable Natural Resources Management – it was stated that "in areas of critical habitat, the client will not implement any project activities unless the following requirements are met: there are no measureable adverse impacts on the ability of the critical habitat to support the established population of species . . . or the functions of the habitat [and] there is no reduction in the population of any recognized critically endangered or endangered species" (IFC, 2006).

Given the nature of large-scale mining, which involves the removal of all vegetation and top soil, the construction of wide roads and almost continual use of heavy machinery, it would be virtually impossible to guarantee the protection of chimpanzees and other apes, or almost any critically endangered (CR) or endangered (EN) species, without placing large areas of a number of mining concessions off limits.

Photo: With civil society having been more successful in placing democratic conditions on projects through lending institutions, improving the environmental safeguards of lending institutions presents an opportunity to influence private sector behavior. Oil extraction plant, Gamba, Gabon. © Jabruson, 2013. All Rights Reserved. www. jabruson.photoshelter.com

The IFC approved revised PSs in January 2012 and two standards in particular affect biodiversity and great apes – PS1[1] and PS6.[2] PS1 generally requires the IFC clients to conduct social and environmental impact assessments and to develop management systems and action plans to respond to environmental impacts. PS1 also requires that clients follow a "mitigation hierarchy" in addressing environmental impacts. The mitigation hierarchy states that the first objective is to "avoid" risks and impacts, but that "where avoidance is not possible" the client must "reduce, restore, or compensate/offset for risks and impacts." Thus, PS1 establishes offsetting as a key environmental response measure for IFC projects. PS6 provides the framework for responding to the risks and impacts to biodiversity identified by the assessments required under PS1. As with the 2006 version, the 2012 version of PS6 is organized around a classification system of three habitat types: Modified Habitat (MH), Natural Habitat (NH), and Critical Habitat (CH), where the latter can be a subset of either modified or natural habitat. Annex I summarizes how each of these habitat types is defined by the IFC. Biodiversity and endangered species concerns are addressed in the context of these habitat types, which are redefined in the 2012 version.

In addition to laying out the habitats framework, PS6 also restates the mitigation hierarchy described in PS1. With respect to biodiversity offsets, PS6 notes that offsets should achieve conservation outcomes that can "reasonably be expected" to achieve no net loss (NNL) of biodiversity, though in the case of CH, offsets must not only achieve NNL, but must achieve a net gain. The revised PS1 and PS6 therefore resolve the problem for projects that will impact EN and CR species by creating an offset option.

A report (Kormos and Kormos, 2011a) submitted to the IFC noted that the revised performance standards limited the definition of CH via the concept of discrete management units, which would have the effect of excluding wide-ranging species such as great apes. The IFC attempted to address this issue by including a footnote to the Guidance Note for PS6, which states:

> In terms of the definition of Tier 1[3] habitat, special consideration might be given to some wide-ranging, large EN and CR mammals that would rarely trigger Tier 1 thresholds given the application of the discrete management unit concept. For example, special consideration should be given to great apes (i.e., family Hominidae) given their anthropological and evolutionary significance in addition to ethical considerations. Where populations of CR and EN great apes exist, a Tier 1 habitat designation is probable, regardless of the discrete management unit concept. (IFC, 2012b, p. 24)

The IFC notes that Tier 1 projects are highly unlikely to be funded; however, they do not categorically exclude projects in Tier 1 because CH impacts can be addressed via the IFC's mitigation hierarchy. There are still unresolved concerns about the lack of clarity regarding the footnote, particularly in relation to the extent it includes species other than great apes whose ranges are also wide. The footnote also raises important ethical aspects of offsetting but stops short of providing clear criteria – even for chimpanzees, where a finding of CH is only "probable."

In addition to this, the new CH definition is applied on a project-by-project basis and the cumulative impacts of the IFC's development activities are not taken into account (Kormos and Kormos, 2011a; C. Kormos, unpublished data). A recent process to develop a national biodiversity-offsetting plan for Guinea, West Africa, seeks to address some of these issues, although biodiversity offsets are a relatively new and unproven concept with few clear successes to date (see Chapter 8). The Business and Biodiversity

Offsets Program (BBOP) has developed guidelines about biodiversity offsets, published several case studies, and continues to implement additional research (see Chapter 5).

Furthermore, the performance standards, in most cases, apply to relatively advanced projects – towards the end of feasibility studies – when significant environmental damage may have already been caused. The inclusion of legal requirements for companies to comply with IFC PS6 from the onset, regardless of when they apply for funding from IFC, could impact industry action at the pre-feasibility stage. Currently any enforcement of reducing social and environmental impacts at the pre-feasibility stage is dependent on individual company policies or if there is IFC investment at the exploration stage, which is not common.

The importance of major lending institutions attaching conditions that seek to mitigate environmental and social impacts is proving to be a key avenue to ensure that extractive industries integrate these considerations. The recent review of PS6 and subsequent changes highlights the complexity of resolving species conservation of CR and EN species with extractive industries, which is further compounded if funding is not sought from IFC early in the project cycle. Consultation with civil society and the private sector continue to inform this process. Furthermore, banks that fall outside of multilateral oversight have less incentive to implement standards that may affect their profit margins and do not oblige environmental and social considerations to be part of the lending conditions.

Conclusion

Global drivers of deforestation and hunting that impact ape populations and their habitats, particularly the impacts of demography, economies, and globalization, require a substantial response if the gloomy trends are to be reduced, halted, or reversed. While there is a good understanding of the linkages between individual megatrends, less is known about the extent to which the various impacts interact.

Although policy responses to the impact of changes in rates of extraction of minerals and timber on ape populations and their habitats are emerging, including processes that address consumer behavior and demand, these are still unproven and require stringent oversight by consumer nations to ensure their effectiveness.

This chapter acknowledges the pragmatic approach of action at the interface of contract law and in so doing highlights the current weak enforcement of existing laws and conventions that are explicitly linked to ape conservation. It presents detail on how contract law can be shaped to influence ape conservation through action of civil society and potentially in partnership with industry partners.

Further reform of conditionality around lending works to modify industry behavior within critical ape habitats, and influences national policy development, showcasing some of the complexity of reconciling aspects of ape conservation with industry practice and, in so doing, options that have not been proven in ape ranges are gaining traction. Further reform of lending conditionality is required if lack of clarity and risks associated with unproven approaches are to be resolved.

However, responses are still siloed and considering the interrelated and poorly understood nature of the drivers, a call for shifts in approaches that acknowledge the interconnected nature of global processes and their ultimate impact on ape conservation appears necessary but requires a paradigm shift away from current modes of practice. Future research at this interface is critical if meaningful responses are to be developed.

> Lending institutions attaching conditions that seek to mitigate environmental and social impacts is a key avenue to ensure that extractive industries integrate these considerations.

Acknowledgments

Principal author: Helga Rainer

Contributors: Eric Arnhem, Laure Cugnière, Oliver Fankem, Global Witness, Cyril Kormos, Rebecca Kormos, LEAP, Michael Likosky, Lorraine MacMillan, Sten Nilsson, Paul De Ornellas, Chris Ransom, and ZSL

Endnotes

1   PS1 Assessment and Management of Environmental and Social Risks and Impacts: http://www1.ifc.org/wps/wcm/connect/3be1a68049a78dc8b7e4f7a8c6a8312a/PS1_English_2012.pdf?MOD=AJPERES

2   PS6 Biodiversity Conservation and Sustainable Management of Living Natural Resources: http://www1.ifc.org/wps/wcm/connect/bff0a28049a790d6b835faa8c6a8312a/PS6_English_2012.pdf?MOD=AJPERES

3   "Habitat required to sustain ≥ 10 percent of an IUCN Red-listed CR or EN species where there are known regular occurrences of the species and where that habitat could be considered a discrete management unit for that species"; or

"Habitat with known regular occurrences of IUCN Red-listed CR or EN where that habitat is one of 10 or fewer discrete management sites globally for that species."

Guidance Note 6 defines a discrete management unit as:

"an area with a definable boundary within which the character of biological communities and/or management issues have more in common with each other than they do with adjacent areas. A discrete, management unit may or may not have an actual management boundary (e.g., legally protected areas, World Heritage sites, KBAs, IBAs, community reserves) but could also be defined by some other sensible ecologically definable boundary (e.g., watershed, interfluvial zone, intact forest patch within patchy modified habitat, seagrass habitat, a coral reef, a concentrated upwelling area, etc.)."

CHAPTER 2

Land tenure: industry, ape conservation, and communities

Introduction

The issue of tenure, the ownership or access to an area of land, has long been recognized as a critical factor for conservation, since it determines the linkages between responsibility and authority over land and natural resources, and also the incentive structures for sustainable use (Murphree, 1996). The impact of extractive industries (and thus the effect on great ape conservation) is, however, less clear at this interface. Whether or not conservation gains will outweigh other forms of land use is dependent on a number of both subsistence-based benefits (food, fuel, cultural) and those that are increasingly market-based (ecotourism, non-consumptive and consumptive use, sale of primary and secondary products, carbon, etc.), but is also linked strongly to issues of tenure and access. Ignoring ownership linked to the right to benefit, and thus to the potential for sustainable use, may lead to alternative land uses (e.g. conservation) being viewed as an unimportant economic and/or cultural component of land use. Likewise, the presence of natural resources on state-controlled land that has been demarcated for either communal use or biodiversity protection can often lead to encroachment by actors interested in more profitable uses such as logging, mining, and exploration for oil and gas.

This chapter attempts to clarify two themes related to land tenure issues around extractive industries, specifically:

1. their exploitation within protected areas, and

2. their impact on local communities.

It examines how efforts to attract foreign investment related to the extraction of natural resources in Asia and Africa limits access to land and resources by local communities and indigenous peoples, alongside the claim that as proprietors and stakeholders in any extraction they are more likely to better manage these lands for both conservation and social outcomes.

The first two case studies presented in this chapter illustrate issues of contested tenure in the context of protected areas and national parks. The chapter then looks at the interface between extractive industries, local communities, and rights of access to natural resources. It gives an overview of some of the concepts/principles that have been promoted by civil society actors to help facilitate alliances between communities and industry, including notions of self-determination and Free Prior and Informed Consent (FPIC). A further case study from Indonesia highlights the importance of governance in building these kinds of relationships, and looks at the growing issue of "land

grabbing," and the role of civil society in promoting transparency in the sector. The chapter closes with an analysis of a number of mitigation strategies that promote stakeholder engagement, and the challenges that can arise in trying to instigate them.

Key findings include:

- The need to recognize the importance of extractive resource use for socio-economic development and of partnerships for sustainable development, while also addressing the environmental, economic, health, and social impacts that accompany it.

- More integrated and incorporative strategies for land-use management are less likely to marginalize one aspect of environmental services to the benefit of some stakeholders over others.

- Capacity building within the political and institutional environment of those countries involved may also be needed. This includes raising awareness on the linkages in question, improved enforcement of the relevant laws, and the clarification of contradictory policies under different ministries.

- Both large- and fine-scale mitigation strategies need to be supplemented with meticulous land-use planning, with both voluntary and regulatory mechanisms at national and international levels underpinned by more robust policy.

- There is a growing need for business entities to incorporate strong corporate social responsibility (CSR) policies, as well as for government legislation to develop in a way that preserves world heritage, both in terms of charismatic fauna and habitat, but also at the intersection with indigenous rights.

- More effective holistic management strategies would be developed by clearly determining the fiscal, social, and environmental obligations of companies according to international good practice, making consultation with local communities compulsory, and by initiating a participatory, land-use planning approach for local development.

Extractive industries in protected areas

In 1962, there were some 1000 official protected areas worldwide; today there are 108 000, with more being added every day. The total area of land now under conservation protection worldwide has doubled since 1990, when the World Parks Commission set a goal of protecting 10% of the planet's surface. That goal has been exceeded, with over 12% of all land, a total area of 30 432 360 km² now protected (Dowie, 2009). At the same time, global demand for oil, gas, minerals, and metals has been increasing rapidly, and is expected to continue to do so in the coming decades (Chapter 1). To supply the growing global demand, extractive companies will intensify their prospecting and production efforts by moving into remote and hitherto unexplored areas, many of which are currently protected or are candidates for protection (McNeely, 2005). For example, the World Resources Institute (WRI) reported that almost a quarter of active mines and exploration sites overlapped with or were within a 10 km radius of protected areas categorized under the International Union for Conservation of Nature (IUCN) system (Miranda *et al.*, 2003).

Photo: A settlement established along a logging road. Natural landscapes are targets for unprecedented levels of exploitation and settlement.
© Noelle Kumpel, ZSL

Governments thus have to make tough decisions about how best to balance economic development and environmental protection. States may be understandably reluctant to forgo potential revenue from developing their natural resources and may resist calls to expand their protected areas system into areas that might hold mineral or hydrocarbon reserves, or choose to delineate boundaries to exclude mineralized zones. As these protected areas become increasingly ecologically isolated and encroached upon by agricultural and industrial development, deforestation, human settlement, and the active elimination of wildlife on adjacent lands, the task now is to design strategies that not only ensure the long-term viability of species and ecosystems, but that will also be politically and economically acceptable to local communities and governments, as well as being enforceable on the ground.

Protected areas in ape range states are usually surrounded by a mosaic of forest types, habitats, and human land-use zones, many of which can contain ape populations and also be radically altered by the extraction of those resources found within them. In Indonesia, for example, and certainly if current logging trends continue, most national parks are likely to be severely damaged within the next decade, because they are amongst the last areas to hold valuable timber in commercially viable amounts. Furthermore, illegal logging occurs in 37 of Indonesia's 41 national parks, but is most severe in Gunung Palung, Danau Sentarum, Gunung Leuser, Tanjung Puting and Kutai (Ministry of Forestry, 2006). Recent research on the overlap between orangutan distribution and a variety of land-use categories in Kalimantan suggests that, while 22% of this distribution lies in protected areas, 29% lies in natural forest concessions (Wich *et al.*, 2012b). The first case study on Kutai National Park shows how important these zones are thus likely to be for the continued survival of the species in the future, and how necessary it is to try and find solutions to competing claims to the land in question.

In Africa, the Democratic Republic of Congo (DRC) contains more than half of the continent's remaining rainforest within its borders, including lowland and mountain rainforest, bamboo forest, savannahs, and marshes. As it begins to emerge from nearly a decade of civil conflict, the DRC's natural landscapes are targets for unprecedented levels of exploitation and settlement. Its protected areas and national parks face threats from immigration by people seeking access to forest resources, arable land, bushmeat, gold, diamonds, coltan (a key component in the manufacture of cell phones), and other minerals. Illegal mining, poaching of ivory and other resources, and extensive cattle herding threaten wildlife and their habitats; problems that are often exacerbated by the presence of armed militias (see Chapter 6). These challenges can also

FIGURE 2.1

Map of Kutai National Park and KPC mine, Kalimantan, Indonesia

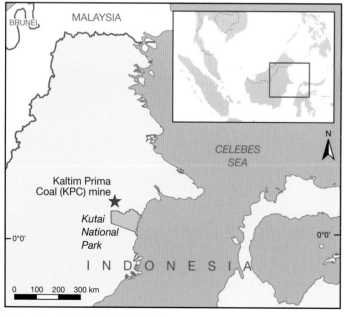

Developed from IUCN and UNEP-WCMC, 2013

Kutai National Park, Kalimantan

Kutai National Park is a 1986 km² IUCN category II protected area in East Kalimantan Province, Indonesia (IUCN and UNEP-WCMC, 2010) (see Figure 2.1). The park is one of seven terrestrial National Parks in Indonesian Borneo and hosts a range of globally threatened lowland Bornean species including important orangutan (*Pongo pygmaeus*) and Bornean gibbon (*Hylobates muelleri*) populations (MacKinnon et al., 1996; Singleton et al., 2004). The protected area has had a long and complicated history and provides a clear example of how legally protected status does not necessarily confer long-term protection to an area.

While the Kutai area has had some form of protected status since the mid-1930s, the area has still been exposed to decades of legal and illegal resource exploitation. Historical instances of certain areas being excised from the reserve and allocated to logging companies meant that by the early 1980s the eastern third of the remaining reserve had been significantly degraded as a result of ongoing logging, oil exploration, and agricultural expansion. The national park in its current form was declared in 1982 (but was not officially gazetted until 1996). Exploitation of high quality thermal coal in the region began in 1989 under the management of PT Kaltim Prima Coal (KPC), originally an Indonesian-registered joint venture between Rio Tinto and British Petroleum (BP), but now a fully owned Indonesian company. A large open-pit mine, together with support infrastructure, was established on the northern boundaries of the park, and a new township for mine workers and their families was built, with access roads constructed that cut through the park (MacKinnon et al., 1996). KPC has supported the management of the park for many years, sponsoring the production of a park management plan in 1991, and since 1995 has been a central partner in an initiative known as Friends of Kutai, in which nine private-sector developers from the mining and forestry industries cooperate with the park's management authority, providing advice and annual budgetary support (KPC, 2012).

In spite of government and private-sector initiatives, threats to the park remain severe. Intense wild fires linked to an El Niño Southern Oscillation (ENSO) weather event, and exacerbated by logging damage, devastated about 1000 km² of the eastern part of the park in 1982–83. The park authorities' lack of capacity to manage such a large area of land, coupled with increasing pressure due to growing human populations around the park, and demand for timber, continued to degrade the forest (Jepson, Momberg, and van Noord, 2002). In 2009 the Ministry of Forestry proposed the excision of a further 240 km² as an enclave on land occupied by over 24 000 people. In addition, a 2009 research team including experts from the Indonesian Institute of Sciences (LIPI), Gajah Mada University in Yogyakarta, the Ministry of Energy, Minerals and Human Resources, and the Forestry Ministry found that the Pertamina oil concession in the east of the park had cleared a reported 80 km² of forest for 800 oil wells and support infrastructure (Jakarta Globe, 2009). Pressure from the mining industry also continues. In 2006 and 2008, 350 km² of coal exploration licenses overlapping with Kutai were awarded to the Indonesian company Ridlatama Group, which is now owned by the British Company Churchill Mining (Churchill Mining, 2012). In 2010, however, these licenses were revoked by the East Kutai district government. Churchill Mining is now suing the district government to repeal this decision and allow continued exploration (Wall Street Journal, 2011). In resource-rich ape range states, pressures such as these are often the rule rather than the exception.

Given Kutai's tragic history, it is perhaps surprising that the park still appears to support a large population of orangutan, Bornean gibbon, and other globally threatened species. The orangutan population was estimated at 600 in 2004 (Singleton et al., 2004), but more recent surveys suggest that the population could be as high as 2000 (OCSP, 2010). KPC continues to support the park and orangutan conservation, collaborating with the USAID funded Orangutan Conservation Services Program (OCSP) in 2009 as a pilot site for the development of orangutan conservation management plans and best practice guidelines (OCSP, 2010). Parts of the KPC mining concession still retain remnant patches of lowland forest that are used by orangutan passing through the area. The company agreed to set aside 45 km² of forest for orangutan conservation (equivalent to 5% of the concession) (OCSP, 2010), and developed a program for relocating orangutan that were found in areas due to be mined. They are also establishing a monitoring program, and are continuing to support research and conservation efforts in the national park (KPC, 2010). Several of the industries working in the area have committed to supporting the park, and KPC in particular is taking extra measures to protect orangutans in their license area and the park. The current Indonesian President has made many public statements in support of forest conservation, and its importance is now widely recognized in this rapidly developing emerging economy. Under these circumstances, there might be hope that Kutai's story of planned and unplanned degradation could soon be halted.

Virunga National Park, DRC

Virunga National Park (Virunga NP) in the eastern Democratic Republic of Congo (DRC) is the oldest national park in Africa, as well as the richest in terms of its biodiversity. Established in 1925 and located at the heart of the Albertine Rift, it covers an area of 7900 km² and embraces a wide diversity of habitats ranging from savannah ecosystems to a chain of mountains and active volcanoes. Besides its spectacular scenery, the park is best known for its population of mountain gorillas (*Gorilla beringei beringei*) which, although still listed by IUCN as critically endangered, represents a true conservation success story, having expanded from about 130 individuals in 1978 to 201 in 2010 (out of a total global population of 880 animals).

Congolese legislation governing national parks, passed in 1969, prohibits "excavations, earthworks, surveys, sampling of materials and all other work liable to alter the appearance of the terrain or vegetation," except in the context of scientific research. Unusually for such legislation, there is no language in the 1969 law relating to commercial activities in integrally protected areas. Although the park is part of the national network of protected areas whose management is the responsibility of the ICCN (*Institut Congolais pour la Conservation de la Nature* – The Congolese Wildlife Authority), it is currently the subject of a private–public partnership agreement between the government of DRC and the UK-based African Conservation Foundation (ACF), which has secured significant funding from the European Union to support park management. In recognition of its great natural wealth, Virunga NP was declared a World Heritage Site in 1979. As such, under the terms of the World Heritage Convention (which was ratified by the DRC in 1974), the government agrees "to do all it can do . . . to ensure that effective and active measures are taken for the protection, conservation and presentation of the cultural and natural heritage situated on its territory." Further weight was given to this treaty commitment by the new Constitution, approved by referendum in 2006, which assigns precedence over national legislation to the country's obligations under international conventions.

However, Virunga NP is located in an exceptionally fragile zone, due in no small part to its proximity to international borders and its wealth of natural resources. Civil conflict that began even before the Rwandan genocide in 1994 has resulted in profound governance difficulties throughout eastern DRC over the past two decades. Virunga NP management has suffered in particular from the activities of rebel groups, from the general breakdown in law and order, and from the settlement of displaced people in the low-lying savannah area of the park to the southwest of Lake Edward. The gorillas themselves are continually threatened by poachers and habitat loss, mainly through the burning of charcoal. Over 150 national park rangers have been killed in the line of duty since 1990, along with over 20 mountain gorillas. As a direct consequence of this loss

of management control, Virunga NP was declared a World Heritage Site in Danger by the World Heritage Committee in 1994 and has remained on that list ever since.

On the Ugandan side of Virunga NP, expectations of greater economic prosperity have increased as a result of exploration in the early 2000s that led to oil discoveries inside Murchison Falls National Park and further south around Lake Albert, just a few miles across the Albertine Rift from the national boundary with DRC. Not surprisingly, since 2006, the government of DRC has issued exploration licenses to several companies, two of which overlap with Virunga NP – Bloc III to the French company Total and Bloc V to the UK-based company Soco International (see Figure 2.2). In the case of Bloc V, 52% of the concession lies within the national park, divided between terrestrial ecosystems and Lake Edward.

While Total has pledged not to work in the section of Bloc III inside the national park, "in compliance with Congolese legislation and international conventions," in 2011 Soco International sought and was granted permission by the DRC Ministry of Hydrocarbons to proceed with oil exploration inside Bloc V, including inside Virunga NP. Also in 2011, the Ministry of the Environment gave permission for Soco to go ahead with aeromagnetic and aerogravimetric surveys that would not require ground incursions into the national park. Soco was instructed to work with ICCN to monitor and manage any negative socio-economic impacts resulting from the surveys. Soco and ICCN signed an agreement granting the former access to the park in return for a fee payable to ICCN to cover the costs of access and monitoring of Soco's activities while inside the park and, in April 2012, Soco received clearance from ICCN for a range of specific activities including boat access to Lake Edward and limited vehicular access to Virunga NP.

The response from the conservation community has been swift. Since 2011, UNESCO, the World Heritage Committee, the British and Belgian governments, IUCN, and a range of national and international conservation organizations have roundly condemned oil exploration inside Virunga NP as being incompatible with its status as a World Heritage Site. Soco, for its part, protests that the part of the park where it will be conducting its surveys is many miles from the Mikeno sector where mountain gorillas live, that its activities will bring socio-economic benefits to local people, that it has not done anything illegal, and that it has acted at all times in compliance with DRC legislation and government directives. What has become clear, in that respect, is that the government is seeking to strike a balance between the sustainable management of natural resources on the one hand and, on the other, the pressure to exploit those resources as the basis for local and national economic growth. Realizing the fears of many conservationists, the partial or even total degazettement of the national park has been openly discussed by the government as a possible way forward. The illegality of such a move under the country's own national constitution in respect to its treaty obligations as a signatory to the World Heritage Convention is seemingly being ignored.

While this highlights how fragile tenure arrangements can be when there exist strong financial incentives to circumnavigate them, further difficulties arise at the interface with local land ownership. Congolese legislation does not include any obligation for the government to provide information to local populations and obligations for oil companies regarding local development fall far short of international best practice (ICG, 2012). In the troubled North Kivu region of the park, civil society opposition is fierce. Although about 40 deputies signed a petition in favor of oil exploration in Bloc V and some deputies tried to persuade the public to support oil exploration, some local associations have opposed oil production and criticized Soco for, allegedly, not consulting the population as part of the environmental impact assessment (EIA), not providing local jobs, and threatening Pygmy communities' fishing interests and habitat (ICG, 2012).

The managers of Virunga NP itself – notably the ACF working under contract with ICCN – are in a difficult position. The ICCN operates at the national level under the Ministry of the Environment, and is therefore bound to align itself with the official government position. Meanwhile, its managers on the ground are committed to a daily life-and-death struggle to protect the national park and its rich biodiversity against the multiple pressures that beset them, and are reluctant to agree to anything other than a total prohibition on oil exploration inside the park. A strong coalition has emerged in support of this position, based largely on the World Heritage status of Virunga NP as a "line in the sand" upon which the global conservation community and parties to the World Heritage Convention cannot and should not compromise. The Virunga case has served to unite conservation nongovernmental organizations (NGOs) against the erosion of World Heritage values that many believe is now under way.

At the same time, there is a strong sense in some quarters that degazettement – even partial – of Virunga NP would constitute the worst of all possible outcomes and that unwillingness on either side to enter into discussions over limiting, managing, and offsetting the negative impacts of oil exploration and extraction may actually hasten such a move. Furthermore, international NGOs feel that they simply cannot engage in such a process due to the illegality of the actions being undertaken. While presenting the government's position as promoting local and national economic growth is a commonly stated rhetorical position, evidence on the ground points to these extractive industry expansions largely benefiting national elites and international investors, with local people rarely seeing more than marginal benefits such as temporary low-paid employment opportunities which are unlikely to compensate them for the loss of land and resource access they may suffer. With positions so polarized, there has been little talk so far of trade-offs and compromise between parties, despite the fact that neither side is likely to see its entire agenda fulfilled.

Encroachment on protected areas in this way highlights how weak some of the current tenure legislation relating to rights and access really is. Legislation differs from country to country, and proposals to locate such industries in or adjacent to protected areas do not always require rigorous application of the kinds of planning and decision-making tools that might help capture the cumulative impacts that can occur across a landscape.

Both the Virunga and Kutai examples demonstrate that, despite the fact that the operations of extractive industries are rarely compatible with the mission and objectives of protected areas, the governments of both DRC and Indonesia may feel forced by economic pressures to make decisions to exploit resources regardless of their negative impacts. Additionally, large financial incentives (in the form of interest-free loans for access to mineral resources, for example) can be a more common route of access for the extractive industries than depersonalized economic pressures alone. So while protected areas may well be a key strategy for conserving biodiversity, they do not necessarily secure this biodiversity when lucrative extraction is possible.

FIGURE 2.2

The Virungas and oil block concessions

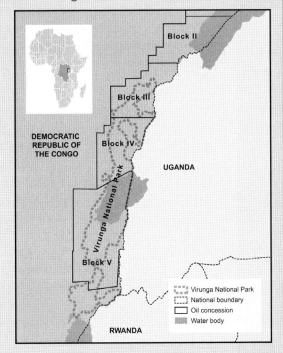

Courtesy of © WWF

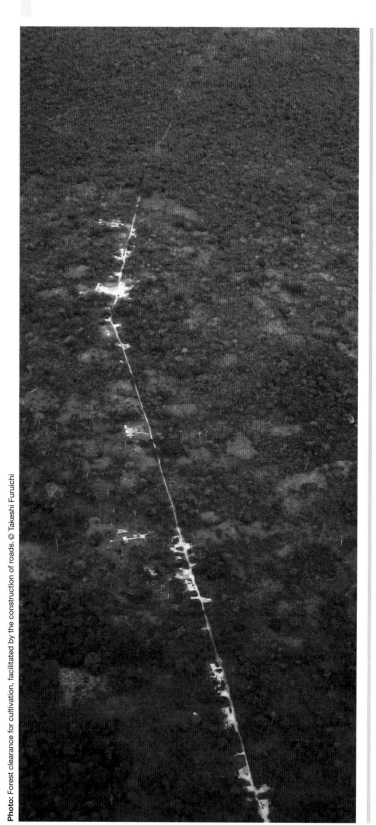

Photo: Forest clearance for cultivation, facilitated by the construction of roads. © Takeshi Furuichi

be compounded by continuing interest in industrial-scale resource extraction within these landscapes, unmarked boundaries and, in some cases, lack of public respect for the parks (WCS, 2012). The second of the case studies, on oil exploration in Virunga National Park, highlights the need for the conservation community and the extractive industry to engage each other in a constructive dialog over issues of contested tenure, and where possible, to find solutions that benefit both biodiversity preservation as well as economic development.

Extractive industries and local communities

It has long been recognized that biodiversity will not be conserved without understanding how humans interact with the natural world. Many of the world's protected areas have historically been occupied by indigenous peoples, and creating protected areas has frequently entailed at least some degree of restriction on access to natural resources upon which local communities have long depended. Many indigenous peoples argue that they are effective custodians of the land, and indeed are largely responsible for the rich biodiversity that often characterizes indigenous territories. Others point out that indigenous peoples are as likely to over-exploit as anyone else, given the pressures of increasing populations and the demands of expanding economies (McNeely, 2005). However, these kinds of stereotyping should not be accepted uncritically, as the penetration of market economics and infrastructural developments that may facilitate abusive resource extraction are less likely to be undertaken by indigenous people and more by those with economic traditions more compatible to these kinds of activities.

Based on the principle that a balanced compromise between the needs of people and those of biodiversity is indeed possible, popular community-based conservation programs place the sustainable management of natural resources as their principal objective (Barrow and Murphree, 2001). As a result, for more than a decade now, policy reforms aimed at decentralizing and devolving natural resource management to local stakeholders have been underway throughout the developing world (Agrawal, 2001; Edmunds *et al.*, 2003). But while significant areas of biodiversity and ape habitats are under the custody of local communities, a variety of challenges to the ownership, management, and access to their natural resources commonly arise. These challenges come from a range of actors, including national governments, multinational corporations, multilateral institutions, such as the World Bank, large landowners, and paramilitary groups. In their pursuit of economic development, profit, or power, legislation may be introduced that enables governments and/or corporations to exploit resources without the consent or approval of local communities, to actively repress local communities, or even bypass the relevant laws altogether (Gupta *et al.*, 2011).

As seen in the Virungas case study, conflict that arises through contested tenureship and the management of natural resources can have negative impacts on all the actors in a given environment. At this level of interaction, some of the following processes and questions may be of relevance to these stakeholders, be they local communities, extraction companies, or conservationists protecting biodiversity:

- how to effectively (and where possible equitably) participate in the management and use of natural resources,
- which mechanisms are, or should be, at their disposal for doing so, and
- how should potential conflict between these interests be mitigated?

There is a growing acceptance that if forest-dwelling communities are supported by national and international legislation and governance to make their own decisions about how best to manage their resources, then it might be possible to ensure a sustainable existence for them as well as for the environment in which they live. Indeed, indigenous peoples have long emphasized the role of their customary institutions (such as common property regimes), practices (e.g. conflict resolution), and representative organizations in some of the above processes. However, both large-scale extractive industries and also top-down conservation can alienate local people from their environments in a way that might hinder the sustainable use of resources.

With increasing international attention now being placed on how both governments and industries manage these kinds of competing claims, building an alliance with indigenous groups could not only help achieve conservation goals much more sustainably, but might also provide corporations with a means of mitigating some of the tension that can exist between themselves and local communities, something that certain parts of the extractive industries have recognized and are now acting on.

Several concepts/principles have been promoted by civil society actors to help facilitate such alliances. These include the concepts of FPIC, self-determination, and the development of an Extractive Industries Review (EIR). The following sections present some detail on these concepts.

Free prior and informed consent (FPIC)

FPIC is the principle that a community has the right to give or withhold its consent to proposed projects that may affect the lands they customarily own, occupy, or otherwise use. FPIC is now a key principle in international law and jurisprudence related to indigenous peoples.

FPIC implies informed, non-coercive negotiations between investors, companies and/or governments and indigenous peoples prior to the development and establishment of mining concessions, logging concessions, timber plantations, oil palm estates, or other enterprises on their customary lands. This principle means that those who wish to use the customary lands belonging to indigenous communities must enter into negotiations with them. It is the communities who have the right to decide whether they will agree to the project or not once they have a full and accurate understanding of the implications of the project for them and their customary land. As most commonly interpreted, the right to FPIC is meant to recognize customary systems as legitimate ways of making decisions, and that such decisions should be considered binding by large powerful interests such as multinationals and central government proposing activities that will affect peoples' access to their land and resources. It is thus crucial for addressing power imbalances between local people and the industrial sector.

One challenge for indigenous peoples in their efforts to exercise their right to FPIC is to ensure that their systems of decision-making are genuinely representative and made in ways that are inclusive of, and accountable to, members of their communities. Colchester and Ferrari (2007), through their experience with third-party audits for the Forest Stewardship Council (FSC) in Indonesia, suggest that verifiers are sometimes unduly lenient about what constitutes adequate compliance, thereby weakening any leverage that communities may gain from companies' obligations to respect their rights and priorities in accordance with FSC voluntary standards.

Another key issue here is that national governments often deny the status of indigenous peoples within their borders and so companies may argue that they cannot – or do not need to – undertake FPIC. In Liberia, for example, the government has claimed that it alone speaks on behalf of the people and can make agreements with companies on their behalf, thus avoiding the need for FPIC. However, as a case study later in this chapter illustrates, the agreement signed between the government of Liberia and the palm oil producer Sime Darby is explicit about Sime Darby abiding by a given list of principles and thus the government has – through this process – accepted the community's right to FPIC (Lomax, Kenrick, and Brownell, forthcoming).

Self-determination

The United Nations Declaration on the Rights of Indigenous Peoples (UNDRIP) affirms many rights already contained in international human rights treaties, and applies these to the collective rights of indigenous peoples, for whom many aspects of life are shared, such as ownership of lands and resources. UNDRIP states:

Article 3
"Indigenous peoples have the right to self-determination. By virtue of that right they freely determine their political status and freely pursue their economic, social and cultural development."

Article 4
"Indigenous peoples, in exercising their right to self-determination, have the right to autonomy or self-government in matters relating to their internal and local affairs, as well as ways and means for financing their autonomous functions."

Here and elsewhere, international law recognizes custom as a source of rights, that these rights exist independently of whether the state has recognized them or not, because

> The importance of the quality of governance with respect to biodiversity conservation within the context of extractive industry operations should not be underestimated.

their rights derive from indigenous peoples' own laws and practices. In line with international human rights law and jurisprudence, forest peoples can thus claim the right to own their lands and forests in accordance with their customary norms and with their right, as peoples, to self-determination (Colchester, 2008).

The Extractive Industries Review (EIR)

While several international expert mechanisms, including the World Bank's World Commission on Dams and the UN Permanent Forum on Indigenous Issues, have provided guidance on how to implement FPIC, the key question is how to make FPIC work in practice. The lack of enforcement of these rules and regulations means that there are still cases where companies completely ignore the presence of indigenous peoples, or pretend that they do not exist. Despite collaboration between the Forest People's Program (FPP) and the World Bank (WB) on their EIR, the International Council on Metals and Mining (ICMM) is only now beginning to accept the standards proposed (ICMM, 2013). This historical refusal to accept a "best practice" standard – and the fact that the WB routinely failed to adhere to its own lower standards that it had incorporated into its safeguarding policies – meant that the extractive industries operated in ways that had a destructive impact on both indigenous peoples and their environment (Caruso *et al.*, 2003; World Bank, 2011b). However, there are also some examples of successful engagement, as the below case study shows.

The importance of governance

The importance of the quality of governance with respect to biodiversity conservation (including that of great apes) within the context of extractive industry operations should not be underestimated. In 2002, the mining industry first began to engage collectively with sustainable development issues through the Mining, Minerals and Sustainable Development (MMSD) initiative (MMSD, 2002), an industry-funded independent review on how the industry had performed in relation to sustainable development objectives. Over the last 10 years, the attitudes of both conservation and developmental organizations have begun to change, with a growing recognition that collaborative partnerships with the extractive industries can ensure that unique and fragile habitats are properly managed and protected for the benefit of both human and non-human communities.

Yayasan Tambuhak Sinta (YTS), an Indonesian-based foundation, was formed in 1998 by the junior exploration company Kalimantan Gold Corporation Limited (KLG), in order to have a vehicle that would address social development concerns in the communities close to where the company was conducting exploration activities, and to create conditions that would be supportive for future development of a large-scale mine in a wilderness area. One of the prime concerns was to establish good relationships within these communities and within the region, especially with local government: thinking that was far ahead of normal practice in the sector, and anticipated what is described above as FPIC.

An important influence on the company's thinking and the focus of YTS was the EIR. As a result of recommendations coming out of the EIR, YTS started to build a program approach that would address the need to strengthen local governance. The foundation spent several years testing and refining its approach and methodology. Since then, it has spread its program approach to 21 villages in the region around KLG's mineral concession, as well as to other locations in Kalimantan and eastern Indonesia, where mineral exploration is taking place. Specific steps in this process that are of relevance included:

- **Participatory planning.** A group of locals selected by the community were trained to facilitate an intensive process of analysis and planning that generated a preliminary community development plan, with all members of the community identifying opportunities and constraints, and deciding on the needs and priorities to be included. This established a platform for all other activities, creating an agenda for action, and addressing needs in three broad areas – local infrastructure, economic livelihoods, and social and cultural aspects.

- **Institution building.** Of equal importance to participatory planning was the mobilization of more active community participation in the formation and running of these institutions. An informal village management group was established to implement actions arising out of the community development plan.

- **Bridging the gap with local government.** There was a gap both in knowledge of community needs, as well as in the provision of services, so information flows were improved and meetings set up between the government and villagers to facilitate this.

- **Strengthening government capacity.** Technical support was provided to the district government as a means of improving its capacity to engage more effectively with communities.

Photo: YTS learned that a good three-way partnership between itself, local government, and communities close to its operations could help facilitate a smooth and successful development process. Community group meeting facilitated by YTS.
© Bardolf Paul

Governance encompasses all the elements that enable and determine how society functions – the formal institutions, policies, laws, and regulations, as well as informal mechanisms that influence how things run. Contested tenure (either official or customary) and rights of access can impact negatively on many of these elements. At the present time in Central Kalimantan, the regulatory framework is very weak, and there is very poor enforcement of existing laws and regulations. Not only is the overall capacity of government to govern low, but the ability to provide programs and services that match local needs is limited. This is partly due to the fact that many administrative jurisdictions are relatively new, barely 10 years old, so many government staff lack experience. Thus any company that intends to develop a mineral prospect into an operating mine needs a clear and well-functioning policy, and legal and regulatory environment in which to operate. It also needs the relationship between government and communities to be functioning well, otherwise there is a tendency for both government and communities to expect the company to provide services that are the responsibility of government. YTS learned that a good three-way partnership between itself, local government, and communities close to its operations could help facilitate a smooth and successful development process for any resource prospecting that then took place. All of these factors and conditions might also apply to other kinds of local development initiative, including investment in long-term management of local natural resources or biodiversity and species conservation.

Land grabbing

In the past decade considerable concern has emerged amongst policy analysts, conservationists, and local populations about the effect of large-scale acquisitions of land in Africa, Asia, and elsewhere. These acquisitions, now known as acts of "land grabbing," were initially triggered by sharp rises in food prices in 2007, and have also been influenced by increases in the price of oil and growing European demand for biofuels. For local populations, the benefits of such large-scale land acquisitions are hard to separate from the costs that so often accompany them, and foreign investment has resulted in the eviction of many thousands of smallholder farmers from their land, sometimes by force, and typically with minimal compensation. Underlying this is the notion that land should be worked in ways that benefit international markets in order to have value, indeed, the World Bank calls the 4 million square kilometers of savannah grasslands in Africa, between the rainforest and the deserts, "the world's last large reserve of underused land" (Pearce, 2012). While this suggests, incorrectly, that millions of peasant farmers, fishers, and hunter-gatherers are not working their land, the inverse is true, and that while they may not be contributing directly to international markets, they are certainly contributing to local and national economies.

It is important to note, however, that the term "land grabbing" has been deliberately chosen in order to draw attention to these processes of dispossession by outside actors. Such interventions have a long and checkered history, with colonialism's laws and policies paving the way for foreign intervention and local dispossession in sectors such as mining, agriculture, and environmental conservation. Some of the key concerns for both local communities and wildlife that arise from such broad-scale changes to the environment might also be of relevance to the extractive industry. These center on the ways in which land deals are negotiated and the resultant structures of

CASE STUDY 3

Liberia: forests, communities' livelihoods, and certification schemes

Awareness of these kinds of social and ecological impacts of land change in places such as Malaysia and Indonesia is slowly leading to new standards and certification schemes for acceptable development of the industries in question. The Roundtable on Sustainable Palm Oil (RSPO), for example, is a third-party voluntary certification process, which adopted a set of principles and criteria that is substantially consistent with a rights-based approach, and which seeks to divert palm oil expansion away from primary forests and areas of critical high conservation value (HCV) while prohibiting the takeover of customary lands without communities' FPIC. Increasingly, adherence to the RSPO standard is becoming a requirement for access to the European market and major palm oil producing conglomerates seeking to maintain market share are now members of the RSPO.

With industrial-scale resource extraction rapidly expanding in many ape range states, certification procedures such as this mean that conflict can be caught and addressed earlier in the cycle. In 2011, in Grand Cape Mount, Liberia, local communities denounced the takeover and destruction of their lands for palm oil development by the Malaysian conglomerate Sime Darby. In response to a formal complaint, Sime Darby froze its operations in the contested area and, via the RSPO secretariat, agreed to bilateral negotiations with the communities to resolve their differences.

Negative impacts such as these have encouraged affected communities to mobilize opposition to extractive resource use, many times impeding access to the areas and to these resources (Orellana, 2002). Important lessons that have come out of this process include the willingness of the company managers in Malaysia to become centrally involved, the willingness of the community's lawyer to speak out strongly, and the provision of facilitation services by an international civil society group which sought to support people to regain their rights while finding a way for the company to act.

Navigating these complex trade-offs without drastically scaling back the speed and extent of business operations requires engagement with all stakeholders in an environment. If the major buyers of a particular resource are susceptible to civil society pressure, their major international suppliers are more likely to seek to ensure that they are seen to be abiding by the relevant social and environmental safeguards so that they do not lose their market share. Although the RSPO is a voluntary certification process, established through civil society pressure from outside and inside the industry, it is based on the key principles of mitigating the impacts on biodiversity and ensuring that palm oil developments recognize communities' rights both to their lands and to give or withhold their FPIC to what happens on this land. This provides a key basis for ensuring that stakeholders can enter into dialog with companies. Regardless of the resource in question, such schemes can also help inform the current debate over the appropriate tools in advancing these kinds of standards and roles.

However, whether the dialog is meaningful or not often depends on the level of engagement. This can include community awareness and mobilization, national and international civil society support, and a willingness by corporations to recognize their obligation to both protect the environment and respect human rights. Such issues are all the more pertinent with regards to the encroachment onto both community land and protected areas by the extractive industries. No one would deny the need for increased foreign investment to often-poor ape range states, but mechanisms need to be put into place to ensure that this does not result in the eviction of smallholder farmers, nor come at the expense of threatened ape populations.

any new land tenure dispensation. A number of important questions then result:

- What is the capacity of the local populations with a claim to the affected lands to secure their preferred outcomes?
- Can they block the deals if they do not want them?
- What are the consequences of these land acquisitions for local populations and the country's biodiversity in general?

While proponents say the deals are beneficial to the states and local communities, critics argue that they are likely to have negative impacts on food security, essential ecosystem services, and access to land by the poor (Pearce, 2012). While the need for foreign investment remains a necessity, policies that transfer land to investors motivated primarily by profit, to feed populations in other countries or to supply biofuel markets across the globe are likely to end up exacerbating poverty. In Cambodia, nearly three-quarters of the country's arable land has been transferred in so-called "economic land concessions" to private companies, usually without consultation or compensation (Neef and Touch, 2012).

Although both the direct and indirect impacts of these massive deals on great apes have yet to be quantified, increasing competition for land may well have an effect on other extractive industries, too. The lowland forests of Central and West Africa, prime great ape habitat, are even now being parceled up for industrial-scale conversion to agricultural land. Understanding how to navigate land investment deals, both in terms of their effects on wildlife conservation and local tenure rights, is thus likely to be an important part of future land-use management strategies for both governments and the extractive resource industry itself. The Liberia case study opposite illustrates how this might be done.

Mitigation strategies

Extractive resource development in both Africa and Asia has traditionally operated on the assumption that there are always winners and losers, with the broad needs of biodiversity conservation generally being on the losing end of the equation. High levels of poverty, severe infrastructure deficits, and the continuing weak voice of stakeholders in negotiating development contracts have exacerbated this condition (ECA, 2011). Within the context of weak tenure arrangements and the extractives sector, conservation practitioners now have to work with a wide range of tools and measures intended both to minimize impacts on great apes and their habitat, and to improve biodiversity conservation in general.

The human interface: strengthening tenure and local community rights

As highlighted in both the Indonesian case studies and in Global Witness' work on transparency and civil society engagement detailed below, one of the more recent developments in regards to tenure is the consideration of a rights-based approach to ensure local community involvement in land management and development. This is illustrated by an increase in discussion, action, and movement to preserve cultural heritage, health, life, and civil and political rights at a variety of local and multilateral levels. But while these ideals are grounded in several UN treaties, rarely do state policies broadly embrace them, nor is local and regional implementation effective when they do.

In order to advance these goals, infrastructure needs to be put into place to facilitate them. In many local communities living in landscapes threatened by megaprojects, the lack of community voice in the decision-making process can be a major weakness and thus source of conflict. Though international agreements protect communities' rights to decide what development projects are implemented on their lands, indigenous and tribal peoples often face difficulties simply accessing information about projects that will affect them. Even with calls for participatory development from institutions such as the UN and the WB, governments and private companies often fail to meet with communities to discuss local priorities, determine the impact of potential projects or agree upon viable alternatives.

Mechanisms for strengthening governance

Supporting the rights of local communities to manage their natural resources and protect their communities and livelihoods from the negative impacts of certain development projects requires a multifaceted approach. In Kalimantan, YTS began working with communities on a mechanism that would strengthen their ability to run their own affairs, and thus improve the overall quality of governance in the area of the Kalimantan Gold Corporation Limited (KLG) mineral concession. This was not an easy task, as these communities did not have a cultural history of making collective decisions. Moreover, there was a culture of passivity and dependency regarding their relationship and interaction with local government and other outside agencies. The objective therefore was to put in place a process that would encourage and reward collective decision-making and promote more proactive engagement with outside entities, such as government, companies, or civil society organizations. At the same time, YTS was mindful to involve local government at the district and sub-district levels as much as possible, to keep them well-informed about the work in the villages, and to obtain their formal approval as well as to get letters of endorsement.

As improving the quality of governance is a lengthy and complex process, it not only requires dedication and persistence from all parties, but also a commitment of resources for funding and to provide the necessary expertise. It is particularly difficult to find funding for strengthening government capacity and, without this, it is extremely difficult to bring about any significant systemic change. Ultimately, the long-term protection and conservation of biodiversity and natural habitat for great ape species requires an environment in which the quality of governance will support efforts to achieve this objective. This requires a concerted effort to improve the capacity of communities and government to engage effectively, and as equal partners, with one another. An extractive company such as Kalimantan Gold, that has an independent, well-functioning development partner like YTS, can have a catalytic impact by providing financial and other resources to parties interested in improving the quality of governance. And with more capable partners, it is much easier to discuss and tackle complex issues such as protection and conservation of biodiversity and species habitats.

The Making the Forest Sector Transparent program

As a means of engaging citizens and activists in tropical forest-rich countries in the fight against deforestation, Global Witness has, since 2008, been implementing the *Making the Forest Sector Transparent* program (Global Witness, 2008–12). The aim of this program is to improve governance of these countries' forests by helping local activists and citizens living in forest areas to demand more information from their governments on how these forests are managed. *Making the Forest Sector Transparent* works with civil society groups in forest-rich countries to engage with policy-makers and advocate for capable, responsive, and accountable forest-sector governance. It supports local environmental and human rights campaigners in seven countries to monitor transparency and to advocate on issues of importance to local communities, including issues of tenure. To achieve this, Global Witness has formed partnerships with local NGOs in Peru, Ecuador, Ghana, Cameroon, DRC, Guatemala, and Liberia. The main element of the program consists of the following:

Forest Transparency Report Card

The program has developed an innovative Forest Transparency Report Card and an Annual Transparency Report to assess the level of information in the public domain (Global Witness, 2008–12). The methodology compares disclosure and dissemination of information such as forest management plans, concession allocation, and revenues and infractions in forest-rich, low-governance countries. Its development involved a literature review of a number of similar report card approaches in other sectors (Global Witness, 2009).

The 2011 report card (Table 2.1) consists of 20 indicators on key aspects of forest-sector governance. A simple traffic-light system of "yes," "partial," or "no" shows whether the criterion is met or not. The full, Internet-based database and assessment (Global Witness, 2008–12) shows clearly how people need information about rights to access forests and benefit from their use; and about government policies, to have a say in the management of forest resources. In Peru, for example, the report card was the basis for dialog with a number of government agencies, and for more information to be made available to citizens.

The report card has been a useful tool to help civil society groups to analyze gaps

TABLE 2.1

Forest-sector transparency assessments in seven countries, 2011

Key:

- ◐ Yes: the information exists and is available
- ○ Partial: the information is incomplete or only partially available
- ● No: the information does not exist or is not available
- ● Not applicable to the country-specific context

	Cameroon	Ghana	Liberia	Peru	Ecuador	Guatemala	DRC
Freedom of information legislation	○	○	○	○	○	○	○
National forest policy	○	○	○	○	○	○	●
Codified forest law and supporting norms	○	○	○	○	○	○	○
Signed international agreements related to forest products	○	○	○	○	○	○	○
Provisions for transparency in forest laws and norms	○	○	○	○	○	●	○
Legal recognition of customary rights in forest laws and norms	○	○	○	○	○	●	○
Legally recognized procedure for consultation on new forest norms	●	○	●	○	○	○	○
Legal recognition of the right to free prior and informed consent	●	○	○	○	●	○	○
National land tenure policy	●	●	●	●	○	○	○
Forest ownership and resource-use maps	○	●	○	○	○	○	●
Regulated System of Permits for Commercial Logging Operations	○	○	○	○	●	○	○
Legal requirement for consultation before commercial logging allocation	●	○	○	●	○	○	○
Verification process (due diligence) on eligibility of commercial operators	●	○	○	●	○	○	○
Forest management plans	○	●	●	●	○	○	○
Regulation of environmental services	●	●	●	○	●	○	●
Strategic environmental assessment	●	●	●	○	○	○	●
Independent forest monitoring	○	●	●	●	●	○	○
Fiscal systems to distribute forestry royalties or incentives	○	○	○	○	○	○	○
Information on forest law infractions	○	●	●	●	○	○	●
Annual forest authority report	●	○	○	●	○	○	●

Global Witness, 2012b, p.2, courtesy of Global Witness

in what information their government is providing to citizens. In some cases it has also promoted real policy change, by strengthening civil society capacity to effectively use information on forest use and management in their country to demand changes to forest management. People need to have the motivation and skills to convince governments to listen to and respond to their needs. In Ghana, the program has enabled nearly 7000 people to engage directly with local officials, through a large number of community-level grants (Cowling, Wiafe, and Brogan, 2011). Civil Society activists consider such interactions, happening as they do at the level at which forest-dependent people operate, key to a long-term change in power relations. These kinds of capacity-building activities are vital if civil society is to effectively advocate to their governments for measures that will more effectively protect apes.

Stakeholder collaboration: engaging both communities and the extractives sector

Over the last decade, conservation organizations have been making great strides towards recognizing that protected areas should respect the rights of indigenous peoples, as enshrined in international law, including the right to give or withhold their FPIC to the establishment of new protected areas in their customary territories. And yet, despite setting aside a "protected" land mass the size of Africa, global biodiversity continues to decline (Dowie, 2009).

Successfully conserving forests and species requires a remedy that should include all stakeholders, and that balances often-competing claims for resources. Rather than imposing protected areas and seeking to buy local people into the process, the right to own and manage the resources upon which communities depend needs to be rec-

ognized and supported. Support could be given to small-scale landowners; in contrast to industrial logging, for example, many community-level timber and non-timber forest management options, often in combination with other small-scale economic alternatives, have proven to lead to the protection of reasonably intact tropical forest ecosystems while promoting sustainable livelihoods (Bray et al., 2008). The common thread of these models of successful common-pool resource management in the tropical forestry sector is governance – if only at the local or community level – but only when it is fostered by national legislation, especially the ratification of community land tenure (Zimmerman and Kormos, 2012).

In order to manage the conflict that can arise over competing claims for resources, it is also necessary to identify the interests of the extractive sector in protected areas and help design measures that might be undertaken in order to make them partners of protected area managers rather than opponents. Beyond the financial contributions that extractive industries may provide, the sector can also contribute to environmental planning and management, carry out important research that is relevant to the environments where they work, and contribute to building stronger public support for protected areas (McNeely, 2005).

On the ground, companies may be able to leverage additional conservation funding through their partnerships, and also provide effective "in-kind" support to ease the financial burden of protected area management (e.g. covering the salaries of park staff, donating equipment, and providing office space). However, one critical element is a commitment by the extractive companies to be explicit about their impact on biodiversity and protected areas, and to design and implement management measures to minimize any negative impacts and – in the best case – to provide net benefits to the protected area system of a country. While the larger multinationals may have stricter codes regarding both environmental and social responsibility, smaller companies may take higher risks in pursuit of profits. In the mining industry, for example, their business might be to explore and discover new resources and negotiate an interest in operating a mine with a larger company. In the oil industry, these "independents" specialize in finding and developing fields that are of little interest to the larger companies that are searching for a larger "prize." The competitive nature of this kind of exploration may see some of those same environmental and social responsibility codes being overlooked in the pursuit of profits.

Spatial planning

However, providing much needed, long-term financial support to protected areas is not compensation or a substitute for avoiding harming protected ecosystems, habitats, and species. This fundamental issue – promoting economic development while formally recognizing systems of customary land tenure and traditional usage rights and still conserving resources and thus biodiversity – remains a significant hurdle to protecting ape populations. Given the complex nature of tenure systems in areas containing both wildlife and other natural resources, the need for comprehensive land-use management plans, designed in such a way that will benefit all stakeholders, is clear.

Spatial planning uses existing and original data to provide a broad-scale perspective on the conditions, threats, and opportunities for improved resource management across a specific geographic area. The use of spatial-planning tools typically includes measures to coordinate the spatial impacts of sectoral policies in order to achieve a more even distribution of economic development across a region or between regions than would

otherwise be created by market forces, and to regulate the conversion of land and property uses (Economic Commission for Europe, 2008). Some of the decisions and actions that spatial planning typically seeks to support, in the context of tenure issues, include:

- More socially and economically balanced development within regions, and improved competitiveness;
- Enhanced communication networks;
- Greater access to information and knowledge by affected stakeholders;
- Reduced environmental damage from all infrastructure and extractive development;
- Enhanced protection for natural resources and natural heritage; and
- Enhancement of cultural heritage as a factor for development.

Since most of these issues are cross-sectoral in nature, effective spatial planning should help to avoid the duplication of efforts by all actors engaged in development across a region or landscape, including governments, industry, civil society, communities, and individuals (Economic Commission for Europe, 2008). In the context of ape conservation, comprehensive, landscape-wide planning could enable stakeholders to view competing claims for resources in the context of change to viable habitat. In the Virungas, for example, the oil exploration process has been marked by a disregard for the established legal frameworks, by a lack of transparency or consultation of important stakeholders, and by an absence of any strategic or participatory land-use planning process regarding how best to use the DRC's natural resources in the long term. The DRC government's decision-making on this issue has also taken place in the absence of a national land-use or zoning plan. Such a plan might help the government to decide between potentially overlapping or conflicting land uses such

> " Effective spatial planning should help to avoid the duplication of efforts by all actors engaged in development across a region or landscape. "

as mining, oil extraction, forestry, conservation, and other activities. Furthermore, zoning and gazetting can establish secure user rights in a way that makes it possible to introduce some degree of regulation and clarity into a system which often suffers from a lack of transparency.

Technologies and management techniques for mitigating many of the impacts of mining and oil and gas development are well known and documented in the industry literature (McNeely, 2005). However, no "technical fix" can manage all risks to biodiversity from exploration and production, and so if the biodiversity values of an area are to persist, projects have to be planned in a way that will minimize these risks (Chapters 5, 6, and 7). A comprehensive landscape assessment could contain:

- a description of the area's natural and social environment;
- cartographic data;
- a forest management inventory;
- a definition of zones and user rights, the marking of boundaries; and
- a calculation of the area's resource production potential.

Traditional rights could also be surveyed by the concession holder, and socioeconomic and ecological surveys and consultation used to define and secure customary user rights within a given area. In the Karoo region of South Africa, for example, the outcome of such an assessment led to the production of a multi-use landscape plan that allocated areas for conservation, traditional grazing

Photo: No "technical fix" can manage all risks to biodiversity . . . projects have to be planned in a way that will minimize these risks. Abandoned mine workings inside the East Nimba Nature Reserve, Liberia. © Chloe Hodgkinson, FFI

rights, and more intensive development activities, including mining (Maze, 2003).

Underpinning any effective spatial planning should also be the creation of a reliable land cadastre for the countries in question, which takes into account both traditional/customary and formal land usage and ownership rights. Such a map or survey would commonly include details of the ownership, tenure, precise location, dimensions, cultivation status, and value of individual parcels of land. This would then become a fundamental source of data in any disputes between land owners/users. The only stakeholder that stands to benefit from continued opacity in respect of land tenure is the unscrupulous exploiter, whether a government or an investor. While an enormous undertaking in itself, good old-fashioned land surveys and cadastre preparation would do much to support spatial planning initiatives.

Clearly, the management of forests occurs in complex settings, often on the margins of development, where wildlife conservation and livelihood issues intersect in unusual ways. Growing evidence suggests, for example, that timber concessions will be highly important for long-term orangutan survival (Wich *et al.*, 2012b), and it is well documented that gorillas and chimpanzees can also survive in timber concessions when illegal hunting is low. When ape surveys indicate the importance of certain areas for these populations, it might be possible to set them aside as conservation areas within the concession and left unlogged or unmined. Designating these special conservation zones for wildlife protection and establishing buffer zones around protected areas or reserves may enhance wildlife protection, as well as potentially reducing human–wildlife conflict outside. Special measures could also be implemented to further reduce the impact of resource exploitation on apes in these particularly sensitive areas. Survey results can be shared with government officials to assess the possibility of obtaining formal protected status for such important regions and/or obtaining economic incentives (i.e. alleviation of taxes) for abstaining from extraction within them. If such management decisions are made in areas where there are human communities, then strategic spatial planning undertaken in a participatory fashion could help inform these decisions.

Key challenges of/to mitigation strategies
Knowledge deficits

Land tenure is a critical issue not only for the protection of biodiversity, but also for any incentive-based policy instruments that aim to safeguard public goods found in tropical forests. Conflict and disagreement over who should control and manage a country's forests and forestlands underlie many existing tensions, and the structure of incentives can lead stakeholders to operate in ways that are detrimental to sound forest management and thus biodiversity conservation.

In the case of Indonesia, for example, this disagreement lies in part in simplistic interpretations of the definition and location of both forests and the jurisdiction of the Department of Forestry. Different interpretations lead to radically different levels of control over forest resources by different actors and institutions (Contreras-Hermosilla and Fay, 2005). Remote-sensing data have revealed that significant areas of what Indonesia's Department of Forestry legally defines as the "Forest Zone" are in fact community-planted agroforests (fruit, resin-producing, and timber trees), agricultural lands, or grasslands. These areas are currently regulated as if they still are natural forests or lands to be reforested for timber production; an approach that often results in conflict (Contreras-Hermosilla and Fay, 2005). In a context like this, disagreements over the control of land and natural resources due to uncertainty of ownership (state or community) are only likely to be remedied by a serious effort to rationalize state zoning policies in a clear action strategy that provides all stakeholders with a clear understanding of the respective limits to their access.

Trade-offs with industry

While the issues surrounding stakeholder engagement, capacity building, policy change, land-use planning, and corporate responsibility should be considered as achievable and realistic objectives, it is important not to underestimate some of the complex problems for conservationists or indigenous people. One of the key risks facing those engaging with industry is that they become "green-washers" for the companies and governments involved – promoting the positive potential, while tending to sweep over the complex trade-offs and contradictions that may occur in practice. As a partnership develops, the initial good intentions of the parties concerned can fall victim to the desire/need for profit, contradictory objectives, and the lack of capacity/willingness to invest long term so as to understand and find solutions to these complex and interrelated socioenvironmental issues. As divergences increase over time, some of these partners may find themselves powerless to impose change on either the companies or governments in question owing to the huge power imbalances involved. Examples of this include the much-lauded Noel Kempff REDD (Reducing Emissions from Deforestation and forest Degradation) project in Bolivia, where corporate partners (predominantly from the energy sector) have made huge offsets, while critics claimed deforestation was simply shifted elsewhere

and that there were few sustainable benefits to local communities (Densham *et al.*, 2009). Such partnerships must be promoted responsibly.

It is also important to recognize that there is a huge range of approaches to resource extraction exhibited by different companies in different sectors, and that it is currently only a tiny minority of such firms that seek to achieve sustainable and long-term solutions to the environmental and social impact of their activities. Furthermore, this may translate into fairly simplistic initiatives, such as providing support for basic livelihood activities, especially those that can deliver provisions such as vegetables, fish, and other produce to the exploration camp (McNeely, 2005). A discourse that uncritically presents any extractive industry or major infrastructure project as "development" may obscure the fact that in reality such development may be disproportionately enjoyed by national elites, while those local inhabitants (both animal and human) most affected by the company's activities get little if any return, and mostly lose far more than they ever gain.

In some cases, exploration companies may not be interested in strengthening local institutions, or in trying to improve the service and support link between communities and government. This could be a reflection of short-term perspectives and does not bode well for other concerns, such as biodiversity protection and conservation. Nevertheless, as the YTS case study showed, properly managed exploration can make a relatively small impact on the environment and on local biodiversity while at the same time strengthening community relationships. And if the company has a broader vision and a social conscience, then it can provide a useful entry point and platform for initiating programs that are aimed at wider issues, which can include protecting great apes if they occur in the area of operation.

Customary tenure and the "commons"

Historically, the agencies and ministries governing land use have prioritized financial revenue over the rights and interests of the peoples living in areas containing valuable resources. In many instances, these individuals lack even basic recognition from government, such as citizenship – and are therefore not considered when regulations are implemented, even those that are meant to protect indigenous cultures. Customary land tenure is as much a social system as a legal code and from the former obtains its enormous resilience, continuity, and flexibility. Of critical importance to modern customary landholders is how far national law supports the land rights it delivers and the norms operated to sustain these (Alden Wiley, 2011). It is not just a question of who owns the land, but how this ownership might be secured.

This issue is particularly invasive in Africa. With community-governed commons being converted into private property traded on the market, local people can lose their main or only source of income generation. In areas of the DRC, for example, the government does not recognize or protect the rights of indigenous peoples to own, enjoy, control, or use their communal lands. As a result no effective measures guaranteeing and securing their rights are in place, and these people have become squatters on their own land and are often disenfranchised from customary and communal use of natural resources (IWGIA, 2007). While land reforms are taking place around the globe, communal rights are often overlooked, with the result that laws end up either ineffective or with unintended consequences that further negatively impact local communities. Furthermore, such legal frameworks and limited interagency coordination within governmental ministries can also lead to weak oversight and a lack of enforcement of the necessary protections and safeguards. Changes in customary land tenure also exacerbate already inequitable trends, including accelerating class formation and the concentration of landholding. Such trends, which jeopardize the rights of the majority poor, are increasingly having a direct effect on precious local common resources such as forests, as well as on their ape populations.

International mechanisms

The international mechanisms relating to tenure and rights come into effect through international and national political, legal, and financial institutions. In the face of weak governance and regulations to hold companies to account within both host and home governments, international financial institutions play a critical role by requiring companies and governments who wish to borrow funds to comply with set conditions. The World Bank Group (WBG) – and particularly the International Finance Corporation (IFC), the private-sector lending arm of the Group – is seen globally as the standard-setter for corporate behavior. However, there is scope for confusion in how to interpret FPIC, and the language in the IFC's draft Performance Standards leaves much of the interpretation of what FPIC comprises, and whether it has been obtained, to the discretion of companies (Weitzner, 2011). There is also little in the way of penalties for non-compliance, suggesting that voluntary initiatives cannot take the place of strong protection, regulation, and enforcement by host and home governments.

In the past, the WB has successfully helped countries promote investment to stimulate development. However, in keeping with their remit, the focus of this development is on economic development and on strengthening the private sector. With increasing awareness of the importance of promoting biodiversity conservation,

> In the face of weak governance and regulations to hold companies to account within both host and home governments, international financial institutions play a critical role.

alongside the need to maintain underlying ecosystem goods and services, the WB could play a role in helping governments integrate the public into development decision-making processes, and in the promotion of more equal partnerships between the private and public sectors. This could help mitigate the power imbalances of what Randeria (2003) calls the "cunning state," one which primarily promotes the interests of political elites and capitalizes on the government's perceived weaknesses to render itself unaccountable to both its citizens and international institutions. Many administrations deliberately tinker with terms such as indigenous or marginalized, and consent or consultation, to concurrently please donors and circumvent international legal responsibilities attached to the concept of indigenous rights or FPIC. As some of the examples in this chapter have illustrated, the inclusion of civil society in monitoring, forestry information systems, management plans, and public–private alliances (e.g. to combat illegal resource extraction) can provide a critical means of increasing community development and stakeholder participation. If land registration schemes and the formalization of tenure rights for indigenous communities can create an incentive to defend resources, then they might also benefit sympatric great ape populations at the same time. This might also provide clarity for the private sector regarding who to negotiate with, thereby reducing much of the conflict that can arise over competing claims to resources.

> " The interplay between extractive industries, local communities, and conservation is complex and demands a multi-level response. "

Conclusion

It is recognized in the Convention on Biological Diversity (CBD) that biodiversity will not be conserved without a far greater understanding of how humans interact with the natural world (CBD, 2012). But the interplay between extractive industries, local communities, and conservation is complex and demands a multi-level response. With areas of HCV shrinking, the need for a network that includes both adequately protected areas and carefully managed production forests seems self evident.

Worldwide, communities manage and conserve a minimum of 3 600 000 km² (360 million hectares – or as much as the areas in the formal protected area systems), and it is claimed more effectively and without substantive government support (Contreras-Hermosilla and Fay, 2005). However, socio-political and spatial asymmetries or inequalities in these management systems can play a key role in forming the patterns of access to benefits obtained from the environment. At the center of conflict over resources lie notions of tenure, and as the case of oil exploration in the Virungas shows, without the support of all stakeholders to promote sustainable use, moves to protect community rights and conserve biodiversity are likely to be underachieving.

However, such alliances stand a far greater chance of securing both the forest and forest peoples' sustainable livelihoods than an approach in which the extractive, developmental, and conservation sectors regard each other as enemies. Collaboration requires the careful navigation of numerous conflicts of interest. At the corporate level, clearer legal obligations for consultation, cooperation, and social responsibility might help corporations attain this. By drawing on good practices in this field, it might be possible to determine a minimum contribution to both biodiversity conservation and local development (jobs, education, health, infrastructure, etc.), which could then be taken into consideration when evaluating their tenders. As was illustrated in the case of Kalimantan Gold, the sooner all stakeholders can start a dialog, supplemented with detailed studies, the easier it becomes to facilitate collaboration.

At a local level, policies and programs aimed at legally recognizing customary community land and resource rights, although not free from risks, can offer many advantages in terms of economic efficiency, poverty reduction and environmental impacts. Properly executed, these would also redress past dispossession by the state of an asset that is essential for the livelihoods and economic opportunity of rural people. But while governments and civil society are now looking for solutions to threats to ecosystem services and biodiversity, clear tenure arrangements must form the backbone of future strategies. Anything less will fall far short of a scenario in which industry, human communities, and great apes can co-exist together in a working landscape.

Acknowledgments

Principal author: Adam Phillipson

Contributors: Marcus Colchester, FPP, Global Witness, Matthew Hatchwell, Justin Kenrick, Bardolf Paul, Edward Pollard, James Tolisano, Ray Victurine, Ashley Vosper, WCS, and YTS

CHAPTER 3

Ecological impacts of extractive industries on ape populations

Introduction

This chapter explores the significant threats and risks to apes, and their habitat, that result from the activities of extractive industries. All apes are protected by national and international laws throughout their geographic range. It is therefore illegal to kill, capture, or trade in either live apes or their body parts. It is important to understand where and how extractive industries affect great apes and their habitat during each phase of a project. In mining, oil, and gas projects (Chapter 5), these phases include exploration and evaluation, preliminary engineering and alternatives analysis, final engineering and site selection, construction and commissioning, operation, closure, and post-closure phases. All phases of all extractive industries are likely to have some impact on resident apes, although the scale and severity are likely to vary. Generally speaking, the behavior and physiology of wildlife are known to be impacted by human activities (Griffiths and van Schaik, 1993; Kinnaird and O'Brien, 1996; Woodford, Butynski, and Karesh, 2002; Blom *et al.*, 2004a; Wikelski and Cooke, 2006; Rabanal *et al.*, 2010; Ruesto *et al.*, 2010; Chan and Blumstein, 2011). Species' responses to environmental disturbance will, however, vary according to their biological dispositions and the type and scale of disturbance. For example, species with highly specialized requirements may manifest significant adverse impacts, as found in studies looking at the impact of logging on terrestrial and bark-gleaning insectivorous birds or bats, while those with more general requirements may be less affected (Putz *et al.*, 2001; Peters, Malcolm, and Zimmerman, 2006).

The list of potential impacts of extractive industries on ape populations is extensive and diverse: (1) Habitat loss from large-scale clear-fell logging and opencast mining will result in total loss or displacement of resident ape populations. (2) Habitat disturbance and degradation from selective logging, subterranean, and smaller-scale mining operations will likely impact the home range and resource use of resident apes, potentially resulting in additional knock-on effects. Changes in resource abundance could, for example, drive changes in activity patterns and energy budgets. These changes may be adaptive, but in some circumstances lowered energy budgets may lead to increased mortality through starvation, stress, and lowered fertility, ultimately reflected in lowered carrying capacity in affected habitats. Indeed, reduced population densities in forests degraded through selective logging are a common theme discussed below. Habitat fragmentation caused by infrastructure development and general reduction in forest quality may also have long-term effects, including the isolation of sub-populations and a reduction in long-term population viability (see Box 3.1). Social effects may also be expected as habitats are impacted, forcing groups into neighboring areas and increasing contact with conspecifics, potentially causing loss of social cohesion in groups and increased aggression, conflict, and mortality. All of these factors may also increase levels of stress on ape populations with impacts potentially including altered energy budgets, changes in social behavior, higher mortality rates, immunosuppression, lowered growth rates, and reduced reproductive success (Woodford *et al.*, 2002; Wikelski and Cooke, 2006).

In addition to the direct impacts of extractive operations, some impacts will be indirect consequences of other subsistence or commercial activities that have been put in place as a result of the work or economic activity generated by extractive industries. The often more significant indirect impacts result from the opening up of forests to people, driven by increased population size and wealth, and accessibility (to forests and markets) through the development of transport routes into once remote areas. Threats that are indirectly associated with logging and other extractive industries include increased targeted hunting (i.e. poaching) of apes and indirect hunting, where other species are targeted but apes are unintentionally caught and killed. This is for commercial and subsistence bushmeat consumption, perceived medicinal properties, and live animal trade. Further habitat degradation and fragmentation, land conversion for agriculture, the potential introduction of human diseases, and increased spread of diseases between resident apes can adversely affect their populations (Chapter 7). Forests overly degraded by timber extraction or mining become more prone to drought and fires, and other stochastic events, which can in turn have disastrous consequences for ape survival. Increasingly, these direct and closely linked indirect consequences are further intensified by the cumulative impacts resulting from multiple industries and activities operating within the same landscapes (Chapter 7).

Despite the large list of potential impacts that extractive industry operations may have on apes, many are speculative in that causal links have not been demonstrated. However, we can extrapolate from what is known about the processes of extraction and the extensive information available on ape socioecology (see "Potential long-term impacts and future studies" on page 93). Other impacts have been documented in the relatively small number of studies that have followed ape populations from pre-extraction to post-extraction. In this chapter, we draw on a large body of literature to come to conclusions about ape responses to the activities of extractive industry. We address the issues

BOX 3.1

Can great apes survive in forest fragments?

As Southeast Asia's forests are cleared, orangutans are seeking refuge in surrounding areas. They may return as forest regenerates, but degraded forests do not meet all of the orangutan's biological requirements. They need a mosaic of habitat types, as in the highly fragmented Kinabatangan floodplain of Malaysia, where riparian and mixed lowland dipterocarp forest can still be found along the riverbanks (Ancrenaz et al., 2010). Orangutans are also known to persist in acacia and eucalyptus plantations (Meijaard et al., 2010), although the long-term viability of these individuals is uncertain.

In Africa, great ape populations outside the central basin are greatly threatened by habitat fragmentation, and much of East and West Africa has been deforested by human activities, principally slash-and-burn agriculture (e.g. Brncic, Amarasekaran, and McKenna, 2010). Chimpanzees and bonobos are capable of occupying a wide range of habitat types, so they are not confined to dense forest. Chimpanzees inhabit mosaics of savanna–woodland, gallery forest, and relatively impoverished dry forests in Guinea, Mali, Senegal, and Tanzania; some bonobos occur in mosaics of swamp forest, dry forest, marshy grassland, and savanna–woodland. Nonetheless, chimpanzees and bonobos are heavily dependent on any available tree cover for shade and nesting in these open environments. In Gabon, chimpanzee densities have been found to be similar in fragmented forest patches and swaths of continuous forest, whereas gorilla densities were much lower in fragmented than in continuous forest because of their general reluctance to cross large unforested gaps (Tutin, White, and Mackanga-Missandzou, 1997).

Studies of habitat fragmentation as a result of logging suggest that the impacts on great apes depend on the species (Tutin and Fernandez, 1984; Plumptre and Reynolds, 1994; Hashimoto, 1995). Onderdonk and Chapman (2000) studied primate occupation and the characteristics of forest fragments outside Kibale National Park, Uganda. Evidence of chimpanzee presence was found in 9 of 20 fragments, some as small as 0.008 km² (less than 1 hectare). However, the authors had

the impression that chimpanzees were foraging in these localities for short periods only and frequently moved between patches. They did not find a relationship between primate presence and specific patch characteristics (size of the patch, distance to the next nearest patch, distance to the national park, or number of food trees present). Chimpanzees in Bulindi, also in Uganda, survive in fragmented riverine habitat comprised of markedly different food sources to those in nearby Budongo. Apparently, those resources are sufficient for the chimpanzees to survive and may even be a direct result of persistent human disturbance (McLennan and Plumptre, 2012). Similarly in Gabon, chimpanzees and gorillas visited natural forest fragments but did not continuously occupy these small patches of forest, which were surrounded by savanna grasslands (Williamson, Tutin, and Fernandez, 1988; Tutin, 1999).

A recent survey in Sierra Leone (Brncic et al., 2010) revealed that approximately 2000 chimpanzees are living outside officially protected areas, travelling between the remaining forest patches, feeding in regenerating farmbush and secondary forest, but relying heavily on crops grown for human consumption. It is not yet clear if these individuals will survive into the long term or if they are remnants of a dwindling population. Chimpanzees seemed to have managed to survive in fragmented forests in Nigeria, but sites surveyed recently are losing their remaining chimpanzees (Greengrass, 2009).

According to Harcourt and Doherty (2005), 65% of forest fragments where primates are found have an area of less than 1 km², which is too small to support great apes in the long term unless connected to other suitable habitats. These habitats can be natural or human modified, such as the forest–farm mosaics that are typical of East and West Africa and frequently used by great apes (Hockings and Humle, 2009). The critically endangered Cross River gorilla persists in a largely fragmented landscape; however, habitat and dispersal corridors are extensive (Bergl et al., 2012). So it seems that great apes in modified habitats are dependent on resources elsewhere in the landscape, and that habitat connectivity via networks of forest corridors must be maintained if they are to survive.

faced by apes from the extractive industries of logging and mining separately. We also split analysis along taxonomic and geographical lines, and consider the great apes – orangutans and African apes (gorillas, chimpanzees, and bonobos) – and gibbons separately owing to their differing ecological requirements and threats posed by different extractive industries and regional standards. We begin by describing the apes' socioecology to provide a backdrop to the documented and potential ecological impacts on these species. We then review studies that have detailed the impacts of extractive industries on apes and speculate on impacts that additional study may reveal.

Key findings:

- Clear felling is incompatible with ape persistence and it results in their total absence.

- Ape tolerance of selective or responsible logging is not fully understood, but over-harvesting of timber can lead to a significant reduction in population densities.

- Changes in ape behavior as a result of logging are poorly understood, but could lead to a negative energy balance in apes in logged forest owing to changes in the availability of food.

- Clear themes on the impacts of logging on gibbon persistence are difficult to isolate, especially given the family's large geographic range.

- Crucial information on the impacts of mining on all apes is lacking.

- There is a clear and pressing need for education in extractive industries, so that they understand the importance of early stage (baseline) ape population studies.

- There is a need for legal requirements in all ape countries to adopt wildlife-friendly best practices before, during, and after exploration/extraction have occurred.

> There is a need for legal requirements in all ape countries to adopt wildlife-friendly best practices before, during, and after exploration/extraction have occurred.

Ape socioecology
Great ape socioecology

There are six species of great ape: two orangutans (Bornean and Sumatran), two gorillas (eastern and western), the chimpanzee, and the bonobo. Here we present an overview of the aspects of great ape socioecology and the basic requirements for their survival that are important in the context of this book. There is considerable variation among species and even among populations of the same subspecies. For more detailed information on orangutans see the volume by Wich *et al.* (2009b) and for recent syntheses on African great apes see Emery Thompson and Wrangham (2013), Reinartz, Ingmanson, and Vervaecke (2013), Williamson and Butynski (2013a, 2013b), and Williamson, Maisels, and Groves (2013).

Social organization and structure

Social organization differs considerably among the three great ape genera: orangutans are semi-solitary, gorillas live in stable mixed-sex groups, and chimpanzees and bonobos form dynamic (fission–fusion) communities. The chimpanzee and bonobo communities are multi-male/multi-female closed social networks, which fission into smaller parties according to food availability and presence of cycling females (e.g. Wrangham, 1986), or come together (fusion) at large food sources. The average size of a chimpanzee community is 35 individuals, although one especially large community of 150 members is known in Uganda (e.g. Mitani, 2009). In forest habitats, party size is usually 5–10 individuals; in the savanna–woodlands of Fongoli, mean party size is 15 (Pruetz and Bertolani, 2009). Bonobo communities comprise 10–120 individuals. When foraging on the ground, bonobo social units splinter into mixed-sex parties that are larger and more cohesive than chimpanzee parties, averaging 5–23 individuals. In both species, party sizes tend to be smaller when fruit is scarce (e.g. Mulavwa *et al.*, 2008).

Large body size and folivorous (leaf-eating) tendencies enable gorillas to cope with fruit shortages and reside in cohesive social units. Gorillas live in relatively stable groups with one or more adult "silverback" males, several females, and their offspring. Group size, composition, and patterns of dispersal are similar across all gorilla taxa; median group size of both species is 10 individuals. One of the main roles of the dominant male is to use his strength, size, and intimidating displays to defend females from other males. Among female great apes, only gorillas live in permanent association with males, relying on males to protect their infants against infanticidal attacks by other males (Robbins *et al.*, 2004). A female who transfers to another group with an infant faces the risk of her offspring being killed by the dominant male in her new group (Watts, 1989; see also "Reproduction").

Orangutans have loosely defined communities in which residents are familiar with other orangutans in their neighborhood. Most flanged adult male orangutans lead a semi-solitary existence, while the smaller unflanged adult males are comparatively tolerant of other males (some adult male orangutans increase in size and develop cheek flanges, linked to increases in testosterone levels (Emery Thompson, Zhou, and Knott, 2012)). Adult female orangutans are more gregarious than adult males and related females sometimes travel together. Unflanged males will travel with females and off-spring, and this gregariousness significantly impacts their habitat requirements and ranging behavior. The forests of Sumatra are more productive than on Borneo (Wich *et al.*, 2011c) and Sumatran orangutans congregate when food is abundant (Wich *et al.*, 2006). Sumatran orangutans also have slightly larger party sizes (1.5–2.0 individuals; Mitra Setia *et al.*, 2009).

Reproduction

Great apes reproduce very slowly. Gestation length in gorillas and orangutans is about the same as for humans, i.e. 9 months; it is slightly shorter in the smaller chimpanzees and bonobos at 7.5–8.0 months. Females usually give birth to just one infant at a time, although twin births do occur. In those cases, it is often not possible for the mother to keep both infants alive (e.g. Goossens *et al.*, 2011). There are no birth seasons; however, because the female's reproductive cycle is energetically demanding and requires her to be in good health, conception will be determined by food availability and this may be seasonal (Emery Thompson and Wrangham, 2008). Number of births may peak during particular months in relation to resource availability. Bornean orangutans living in highly seasonal dipterocarp forests are most likely to conceive during mast fruiting events, when seeds high in fat are plentiful (Knott, 2005). Sumatran orangutans do not face such severe constraints (Marshall *et al.*, 2009a). Gorillas are somewhat less dependent upon fruit and there is no seasonality in their reproduction. However, chimpanzee and bonobo females are more likely to ovulate when fruit is abundant, so in some populations there are peaks in numbers of females conceiving, with contingent peaks in birth rates (e.g. Anderson, Nordheim, and Boesch, 2006).

Young great apes develop relatively slowly and are dependent on their mother for several years, sleeping in her nest either until they are weaned or the next sibling is born. Much of what is known about the age at which weaning is completed is preliminary, but estimates range from 4–5 years for African apes, 5–6 years for Bornean orangutans, to 7 years for Sumatran orangutans. Weaning marks the end of infancy for African apes, but orangutan infants do not become fully independent of their mothers until 7–9 years of age (van Noordwijk *et al.*,

2009). Resumption of a female's reproductive cycle is inhibited by lactation, so while her infant is nursing, she cannot become pregnant (e.g. Stewart, 1988). As a result, births are widely spaced, averaging 4–7 years in African apes, 6–8 years in Bornean orangutans, and 9 years in Sumatran orangutans. The orangutans' exceptionally long interbirth intervals are thought to be a consequence of their more solitary lifestyle. This investment by orangutan mothers results in lower mortality and about 90% survival of infants, compared to 73% in mountain gorillas and as low as 50% for some chimpanzee populations, such as those in western Tanzania (Wich et al., 2004, 2009a).

Interbirth intervals can be shortened by a phenomenon common throughout the animal kingdom and significant in the context of behavior resulting from external impacts: infanticide is the killing of unweaned offspring by a member of the same species (Harcourt and Greenberg, 2001). In great apes this is typically an unrelated adult male and results in early resumption of the mother's reproductive cycle (since the infant is no longer suckling). Infanticide has been documented among gorillas and chimpanzees, but has not been observed in orangutans – due in part to their more solitary lifestyle (Beaudrot, Kahlenberg, and Marshall, 2009). Some female great apes adopt tactics to "create confusion" about paternity by mating with multiple males. Bonobo males have no indication of whether or not they sired any particular offspring, and infanticide seems to be absent in their communities (Furuichi, 2011).

Slow rates of reproduction are common to all great apes, due to the mother's high investment in a single offspring and the infant's slow development and maturation. Male bonobos reach sexual maturity by 10 years of age, and male chimpanzees mature between the ages of 8 and 15 years (Emery Thompson and Wrangham, 2013). Male eastern gorillas mature at 15 years;

male western gorillas reach full maturity at 18 years (Breuer et al., 2009). Male orangutans reach sexual maturity between the ages of 8 and 16 years, but may not become flanged until they are at least 35 years old (Wich et al., 2004). Orangutans and gorillas are among the most sexually dimorphic of primates, reflecting intense physical competition between adult males. Some flanged male orangutans are extremely aggressive and are able to monopolize an area into which they attract receptive females (Delgado, 2010).

Female great apes reach maturity at similar ages: orangutan females begin to display sexual behavior at 10–11 years, chimpanzees 7–8 years, bonobos start cycling at 9–12 years, gorillas at 6–7 years. Age of giving birth for the first time in orangutans is 15–16 years, 10 years in gorillas (range of averages 8–14 years), 13.5 years in chimpanzees (mean at different sites 9.5–15.4 years), and 13–15 years in bonobos. Mean birth rate in gorillas and chimpanzees is 0.2–0.3 births/adult female/year, or one birth per adult female every 3.3–5.0 years. Female lifetime reproductive success has been estimated for mountain gorillas and chimpanzees: on average, chimpanzee females give birth to four offspring during their lifetime, but only 1.5–3.2 survive beyond infancy (e.g. Sugiyama and Fujita, 2011); mountain gorilla females produce an average of 3.6 offspring during their lifetime (Robbins et al., 2011). Orangutans have the slowest life history of any mammal, with later age at first reproduction, longer interbirth intervals, and longer generation times than the African apes (Wich et al., 2009a). Generation time in the great apes is between 20 and 25 years (IUCN, 2013).

Habitat preferences and nest building

Most great apes live in closed, moist, mixed tropical forest, and they occupy a range of forest types, including lowland, swamp, seasonally inundated, gallery, coastal, sub-montane, montane, and secondary regrowth. Eastern and western chimpanzees also occur in savanna-dominated landscapes. The largest great ape populations are found below 500 m elevation in the vast *terra firma* and swamp forests of Africa and Asia (e.g. Morrogh-Bernard *et al.*, 2003; Stokes *et al.*, 2010) although eastern gorillas range up to 3800 m altitude. Gorillas, chimpanzees, and bonobos are rarely found in monodominant stands of *Gilbertiodendron dewevrei* where the herb layer is sparse, except during mast fruiting that occurs every 4–5 years in Central Africa (e.g. Blake and Fay, 1997).

African great apes are semi-terrestrial. Orangutans have been assumed to be almost exclusively arboreal, but recent studies show that Bornean orangutans use terrestrial locomotion (Loken, Spehar, and Rayadin, 2013). Nevertheless, orangutans are not adapted to travel on the ground and they depend more heavily on lianas to help them move through the canopy without descending to the forest floor than the other great apes (Thorpe and Crompton, 2009). Great apes not only feed but also rest, socialize, and sleep in trees, although gorillas and chimpanzees often rest on the ground during the daytime. Being large-brained mammals, they need to sleep for long periods. A behavior that is partially innate to all great apes is that they build nests to spend the night in; each weaned individual makes a new nest almost every night (e.g. Tutin *et al.*, 1995). Gorillas often nest on the ground, building cushions of vegetation, usually from herbs. In some populations, chimpanzees occasionally sleep on the ground (e.g. Koops *et al.*, 2007). To build nests, great apes need access to trees sturdy enough to support their weight, yet flexible enough that the branches can be bent and secured, and with abundant foliage to provide a cushion against hard

Photo: To build nests, great apes need access to trees sturdy enough to support their weight, yet flexible enough that the branches can be bent and secured, and with abundant foliage to provide a cushion against hard surfaces.
© Kathelijne Koops

surfaces. These beds are constructed high in the trees, generally 10–30 m above the ground (e.g. Morgan *et al.*, 2006). Orangutans choose to nest in trees with a large diameter and other features that increase stability, such as buttresses, in a position that will offer protection from wind and rain (e.g. Prasetyo *et al.*, 2009; Cheyne *et al.*, 2013).

Nests provide comfort and support that improves the quality of sleep. A recent study comparing the nesting habits of chimpanzees in Senegal and Tanzania has shown that nests have multiple functions, which include providing insulation and simply preventing a fall from a tree while asleep, but that predation is also an important factor for nest-building above ground (Stewart and Pruetz, 2013). Nesting in trees is a way to avoid predators and large forest mammals that are active at night, such as pigs and elephants. Sleeping location is critical for populations vulnerable to poaching: western lowland gorillas in Cameroon and Grauer's gorillas in eastern DRC (Democratic Republic of Congo) are known to nest at steep locations that humans would find difficult to reach (E.A. Williamson, personal observation). Various anti-parasite and anti-disease functions have been ascribed to nest building, particularly as nest reuse is uncommon (e.g. Fruth and Hohmann, 1996; McGrew, 2010). It is evident, therefore, that the structure of the habitat and diversity of tree species are critical to great apes.

Foods and feeding

Great apes are not strictly vegetarian, as all taxa consume insects and some eat meat; however, they are all adapted to a diet of plant parts that are easy to digest: succulent pulp, new leaves, petioles, buds, shoots, and herbs. Ripe, sugary fruits produced by forest trees are their primary source of nutrition, with the sole exception of mountain gorillas, which live at high altitude where few suc-

culent fruits are available (Watts, 1984). The other African apes average 62–85% fruit in their diet, with marked seasonal variation (e.g. Rogers *et al.*, 2004). Bornean orangutans are less frugivorous than Sumatran orangutans as they experience months when almost no fruit is available (Russon *et al.*, 2009). The great apes' frugivorous nature is an important factor in maintaining forest diversity as they are important seed dispersers (e.g. Tutin *et al.*, 1991; Gross-Camp, Masozera, and Kaplin, 2009; Beaune *et al.*, 2013).

Even the largest of the apes occasionally climb to heights of 30 m or more when feeding. They do not forage randomly, but are selective feeders, tending to choose items from relatively few of the wide range of foods available (e.g. Leighton, 1993). Although much of their food is harvested in the canopy, African apes forage at all levels of the forest, and most also specialize on the abundant terrestrial herbs that are available all year round in more humid forested areas.

During periods of food scarcity, dietary flexibility is crucial. "Fallback foods" are food items that are always available but which are "not preferred" and are usually poor quality, such as bark and unripe fruit (Marshall and Wrangham, 2007). When succulent fruit is rare, bonobos, chimpanzees, and gorillas eat more herbaceous and woody vegetation, such as shoots, young leaves, and bark (e.g. Rogers *et al.*, 1994); at many sites, chimpanzees eat more figs when preferred alternatives are rare. Similarly, orangutans may consume large quantities of bark and figs, which are produced in abundant crops year-round. Some Bornean orangutan populations live in such highly seasonal habitats that they experience periods of negative energy balance during food shortages (Knott, 1998a, 2005).

Ranging

Great apes travel through the forest in daily searches for food. Their movements are not

> The great apes' frugivorous nature is an important factor in maintaining forest diversity as they are important seed dispersers.

random and are generally restricted to a particular location, an area of forest that the ape or group of apes knows well. Foraging in complex forest environments requires spatial memory and mental mapping, and it has been demonstrated that chimpanzees are capable of memorizing the individual locations of thousands of trees over many years (Normand and Boesch, 2009). The other great ape species are likely to possess similar mental capacities.

More or less restricted to the canopy, orangutans do not travel long distances: Bornean adult females and flanged adult males move 200 m to 1 km each day. The lighter and more agile unflanged adult males are able to move faster and usually double the distance. Sumatran orangutans move farther, but still average less than 1 km each day (Singleton et al., 2009). The semi-terrestrial African apes range considerably longer distances and the most frugivorous roam several kilometers each day: chimpanzees 2–3 km, with occasional 10 km excursions; and bonobos and western lowland gorillas average 2 km, but sometimes 5–6 km (e.g. Doran-Sheehy et al., 2004). Habitat and season affect day length as well as home-range use.

The size of the area used habitually by an individual, group, or community (depending on the species) is called the home range. This averages 4–8 km² for male Bornean orangutans, which is small compared with Sumatran males, whose home ranges in swamp forest may exceed 25 km² (Singleton and van Schaik, 2001). Orangutan home-range overlap is usually extensive. High-status flanged males are to some degree able to monopolize both food and females, and so may temporarily reside in a relatively small area (e.g. Delgado and van Schaik, 2000). Establishment of a circumscribed home range helps secure access to resources within it (e.g. Delgado, 2010), and a male's home range may encompass several (smaller) female home ranges. Flanged male orangu-

tans do not tolerate one another, but rather than using active defense, they establish personal space by emitting long calls. Unflanged Sumatran males occasionally congregate around a favored food source where a flanged male may also be present and as long as distance is maintained, physical conflicts are rare; however, close encounters between adult male orangutans trigger aggressive displays that sometimes lead to fights (Knott, 1998b). When males do battle and inflict serious injuries on their opponent, infection of the wounds can result in casualties. Such deaths have been known amongst male Bornean orangutans (Knott, 1998b).

Eastern gorillas range over areas of 6–34 km² (Williamson and Butynski, 2013a). Western gorilla home ranges average 10–20 km², although Head et al. (2013) reported a home range size of over 50 km² in coastal Gabon. Gorillas are not territorial and range overlap between neighboring groups is substantial. Encounters between groups using the same area can occur without them being able to see each other, due to the poor visibility in dense forest. Instead, dominant males may exchange vocalizations and chestbeats, sometimes for hours, until one or both groups move away. Groups ignore each other under particular conditions, such as in the large swampy clearings found in northern Congo, where good visibility allows adult males to monitor potential competitors from a safe distance (Parnell, 2002). These males may display, but physical contact between them is rare. In contrast, in a study of mountain gorillas, adult males engaged in contact aggression during 17% of group encounters (Sicotte, 1993). Serious aggression between gorillas is rare, but when contests escalate, fighting can be intense and the outcome fatal. Deaths from septicemia have followed injuries sustained during intergroup interactions (Williamson, in press).

The home ranges of chimpanzees living in forest habitats vary between 7 and 41 km²

> The structure of the habitat and the diversity of tree species are critical to great apes.

(e.g. Emery Thompson and Wrangham, 2013), but are larger in drier habitats (e.g. over 65 km², Pruetz and Bertolani, 2009). Females have small "core" areas within a community home range defended by the males. Males are highly territorial and patrol the boundaries of their range, especially if it borders that of another community's range. Groups of males may attack members of neighboring communities and some populations are renowned for their aggression (Williams *et al.*, 2008). Wilson *et al.* (2012) reported that most attacks are launched by communities and patrols with large numbers of males, and that victims are usually adult males and infants. The protagonists benefit by gaining females or increasing the size of their range. Bonobo communities share home ranges of 22–58 km² and the overlap between community ranges is 40–66% (e.g. Hashimoto *et al.*, 1998). Bonobos exhibit neither territorial defense nor cooperative patrolling. Encounters between bonobo parties from different communities are frequent and characterized by high-pitched excitement rather than conflict (e.g. Hohmann *et al.*, 1999). Some encounters are aggressive, but thus far no lethal incidents have been recorded (e.g. Hohmann *et al.*, 1999).

Where gorillas and chimpanzees are sympatric, the two species occasionally meet at the same fruiting trees. In most circumstances, there is dietary partitioning between chimpanzees and gorillas to avoid direct competition over food sources. If the area of available habitat is restricted, such mechanisms for reducing competition will be compromised. Observations of interactions between the two species are rare, and encounters can either be peaceful or result in agonistic contests. In Uganda, a gorilla was seen feeding in a fig tree within a few meters of several adult male chimpanzees, although at the same site a party of chimpanzees temporarily prevented a gorilla group from entering the tree they occupied (Stanford,

2006). Co-feeding has also been witnessed in the Republic of Congo. Aggressive encounters between gorillas and chimpanzees have not been observed and it is thought that both species may be more tolerant when they are mutually attracted to a highly preferred food source, especially in times of fruit scarcity (Morgan and Sanz, 2006).

Two key points to be noted here are:

1. that documenting the biology of these long-lived species takes decades of study due to their slow rates of reproduction; and

2. that a great ape population that has been reduced in size is likely to take several generations to recover.

These factors make great apes far more vulnerable to threats than smaller, faster breeding species. The orangutan's rate of reproduction is the slowest of all and they are, therefore, the most susceptible to population losses. Also significant is that great apes have large brains and rely heavily on social learning. Populations and individuals exhibit differences in learned behavior and different ways to exploit their natural habitat. Based on these observations, we can expect great apes to adapt to habitat changes to a certain degree and therefore to show some resilience to habitat degradation and exploitation.

Gibbon socioecology

Gibbons (Family Hylobatidae) are the most widely distributed of ape taxa, occurring from Assam, India, eastwards through Bangladesh, Myanmar, Thailand, Southwestern China, Cambodia, Laos, and Vietnam, and southwards through Malaysia and Indonesia. Currently 19 species in 4 genera are recognized; *Hylobates* which contains 9 species, *Nomascus* the next most speciose with 7 species, *Hoolock* with 2 species, and the monospecific *Symphalangus*

(IUCN, 2013). Indonesia holds the most gibbon taxa with 8, followed by Laos, Vietnam, and China with 6 each. Sympatry between species occurs between some taxa in generally narrow bands with the exception of the ecologically distinct siamang and white-handed gibbon species *Hylobates lar* and *H. agilis,* which may be sympatric.

Gibbons are highly threatened, and have been referred to as the most threatened of primate families (Melfi, 2012) with four species critically endangered, 13 endangered, one vulnerable, and one not yet assessed (*Nomascus annamensis*) on the IUCN Red List of Threatened Species (IUCN, 2013). The urgent nature of this conservation situation has been driven by large-scale habitat loss and fragmentation, and hunting. Drivers for these threats and their relative severity are variable given the wide distribution of the Hylobatidae across ten countries with variable ethnological and legislative environments, levels of forest dependency of rural communities, and commercial forest exploitation. Hunting of gibbons occurs largely for subsistence, traditional Chinese-based medicine, and for the pet trade, while habitat loss and degradation is driven by conversion of forest for small-scale and industrial-scale agriculture, infrastructure development and of specific relevance to this publication, logging and mining operations (see Chapter 7 for more information on indirect impacts).

The Hylobatidae occur across a wide range of habitats, including predominantly lowland, sub-montane, and montane broadleaf evergreen and semi-evergreen forests, as well as dipterocarp dominated and mixed deciduous forests. Some members of the *Nomascus* genus also occur in limestone karst forests and some populations of the *Hylobates* genus occur in swamp forest. Gibbons may occur from sea level up to around 1500–2000 m asl (above sea level) although this is taxon and location specific. *Nomascus concolor* has been recorded up

to 2900 m asl in China, for example. Being strictly arboreal (Bartlett, 2007) (with the exception of the rarely recorded behavior of moving bipedally and terrestrially across forest gaps or to access isolated fruiting trees in more degraded and fragmented habitats) the Hylobatidae are intimately impacted by the extent and quality of forest.

Gibbons are also reliant on forest ecosystems for sourcing food. Gibbon diets are generally characterized by high levels of fruit intake, with figs dominating in some studies, supplemented with young leaves and, to a lesser extent, mature leaves as well as flowers (Bartlett, 2007; Elder, 2009). Reliance on other protein sources such as insects, birds' eggs, and small vertebrates has been recorded but is likely underrepresented in the literature. The gibbons' frugivorous nature is also significant in maintaining forest diversity as they are important seed dispersers (McConkey, 2000, 2005; McConkey and Chivers, 2007).

Gibbons are territorial, with each family group maintaining a territory defended from other groups. Territories average about 0.42 km² (42 ha) across the family (Bartlett, 2007) but there is considerable variation and there is some indication that the more northerly *Nomascus* taxa may maintain larger territories, possibly related to lower resource abundance at some times of year in these more seasonal forests. Gibbons are also generally typified as forming socially monogamous family groups. More recent studies, however, have revealed they are not necessarily sexually monogamous (Palombit, 1994). Some notable exceptions include extra-pair copulations (mating outside of the pair-bond), individuals leaving the home territory to take up residence with neighboring individuals, and male care of infants (Palombit, 1994; Reichard, 1995; Lappan, 2008). It also appears that the more northerly *N. nasutus*, *N. concolor*, and *N. haianus* commonly form polygynous groups composed of more than one breeding female (Zhou *et al.*, 2008; Fan

> Gibbons are highly threatened, and have been referred to as the most threatened of primate families.

Peng-Fei *et al.*, 2010; Fan Peng-Fei and Jiang Xue-Long, 2010). There is still no conclusive argument regarding these variable social and mating structures, but they may be natural or a by-product of small population sizes, compression scenarios, or sub-optimal habitats.

Both males and females disperse from their natal groups (Leighton, 1987), at approximately 9 years of age, based on limited data (Brockelman *et al.*, 1998), and set up their own territories. They generally have their first offspring at around the same age. Data from captive settings, however, suggest gibbons may become sexually mature much earlier than this, as early as 5.5 years of age (Geissmann, 1991). Interbirth interval is in the range of 2–4 years, with a gestation period of approximately 7 months (Bartlett, 2007). Although captive individuals have been recorded living upwards of 40 years of age, gibbon longevity in wild conditions is unknown and thought to be considerably shorter. Due to the gibbons' relatively late age of maturation and long interbirth intervals, reproductive lifetime may be only 10–20 years (Palombit, 1992). Population replacement in gibbons is therefore relatively slow.

Studies of the direct impacts of logging on ape populations

Commercial and artisanal logging cause changes in both forest composition and structure, ranging from degradation to elimination of habitat. As forest dependent species, the magnitude of negative impacts on apes is greatest in the case of clear felling as this results in the removal of most if not all trees. Clear felling and ape persistence are incompatible. Since it results in the total absence of apes, we do not consider clear felling in this section and focus instead on selective logging. There are differences between selective logging and responsible logging (reduced-impact logging (RIL), as described in Chapter 4). Selective logging is a forestry technique devised to mimic at some level natural rates of tree fall through the removal of only a percentage of commercially saleable trees (Okimori and Matius, 2000). Theoretically this allows for the sustainable use of forests, as natural regeneration is allowed before logging is recommended (Rijksen, 1978). Even at low levels of removal, however, significant damage to forest can be expected, with extraction machinery and falling trees causing additional damage to standing trees (Mittermeier and Cheyney, 1987). It has been variously reported that even with the removal of only 10% of trees in an area, 55% of other trees were lost (Rijksen, 1978), or that with removal of only 3.3% of trees, 50.9% of trees with a diameter at breast height (DBH) $\geq$ 30 cm were also destroyed (Johns, 1986b).

Over the last 10–20 years, much research has been directed towards understanding the effects of logging activities on wildlife in tropical forests. This is a particularly challenging area of research and it has proven difficult to draw conclusions regarding the impact of specific logging practices that are broadly applicable across the sector. This is partly due to the sheer complexity of life found in tropical forests, compounded by the innate variability between study sites, logging techniques used, species responses, as well as study methods. Disentangling the interactions between these and the potential direct and indirect impacts is problematic. Survey results do not reflect solely the impact of forestry practices, but a myriad of indirect or collateral impacts that make it difficult to isolate response patterns in relation to the specific logging disturbances. Methodological issues have also hampered efforts to identify generalities and achieve consensus among scientists regarding the impacts of logging on apes (Plumptre and Grieser Johns, 2001).

Three main considerations will determine how seriously wildlife populations are impacted by logging operations. First, that populations are able to survive the logging process itself, second that they are able to survive and reproduce successfully on the resources remaining after logging, and third that recolonization and population stabilization post-logging are possible (Grieser Johns and Grieser Johns, 1995). Assessment is limited by the fact that there are very few studies of change in populations from pre-logging through the logging process to regeneration. A common approach has been to compare logged and unlogged sites, and while we draw information from these studies, it should be noted that results may be confounded due to lack of information on original pre-logging population densities, which may be variable over even small areas.

Further, a temporal effect can be seen whereby patterns in responses observed immediately following logging may change as time passes. A study in East Kalimantan, Indonesia, showed that, after an initial decline related to the disturbance of the logging process, primates in general seem to cope relatively well, particularly those with a generalist diet, although it should be noted that these changes are confounded in the face of hunting (Meijaard *et al.*, 2005). Clark *et al.* (2009) sought to tease apart the direct and indirect impacts of logging on the abundance of a suite of species in northern Congo. They reported a pattern similar to that noted by Meijaard and colleagues, in that many species increased in abundance after the initial disturbance of logging had passed, linked perhaps to the opening up of the canopy stimulating new growth, and numbers returning to previous levels with time.

Although many primates are relatively tolerant of habitat disturbances, others are negatively affected, and different species may be variably impacted at a single site (Johns and Skorupa, 1987; Weisenseel, Chapman,

and Chapman, 1993; Plumptre and Reynolds, 1994; Chapman and Lambert, 2000; Paciulli, 2004; Stickler, 2004). Logging is likely to change both the abundance and the distribution of food sources in the apes' home ranges, which in turn will impact feeding strategies. These changes will alter the efficiency of foraging, which will be reflected through changes in activity budgets, the way the animal spends its time foraging, moving or resting on a daily, seasonal or other basis. For example, primates may have to forage more intensively in logged over forests to find resources (Johns, 1986b) or, alternatively, primates may adopt an energy conservation strategy, limiting activity as a result of lowered energy budgets brought about by lower resource abundance. This has been found in orangutans in monocultural acacia plantations where they feed on low-quality bark and rest much more than orangutans in natural forest (S. Spehar, unpublished data). Such effects can be identified through changes in daily ranging distance and amount of time spent feeding versus other activities.

While early studies suggested that frugivorous species are most likely to be negatively impacted by logging (Johns and Skorupa, 1987), which is particularly important given the generally frugivorous nature of the apes, a simple relationship between fruit abundance and ape persistence is unlikely to be found in most instances. For example, a meta-study of nine primate species (not including any member of the Hylobatidae) found that there was only a weak and inconsistent correlation between mortality and resource abundance and that, contrary to the results of Johns and Skorupa (1987), this was more pronounced in folivores than in frugivores (Gogarten *et al.*, 2012). This lack of a simple relationship between mortality and resource availability is likely to be because mortality is regulated by many factors, including resource abundance, disease, parasitism, and stress-related reduction in immune function. All of

> Although many primates are relatively tolerant of habitat disturbances, others are negatively affected, and different species may be variably impacted at a single site.

these factors act synergistically to impact animal abundance (Chapman, Lawes, and Eeley, 2006; Gogarten *et al.*, 2012), further confounding attempts to draw hard and fast conclusions about the impacts of resource extraction.

In the following sections, we summarize what is known to date of the impacts of logging on orangutans, African apes, and gibbons, and the possible mechanisms driving any changes in population density and persistence. We highlight some information gaps and provide recommendations based on this assessment.

Logging and orangutans

In Borneo and Sumatra, damage from timber harvesting is generally severe, with up to 80% damage to the canopy and potentially large ecological impacts on the apes living in these forests (Husson *et al.*, 2009; Ancrenaz *et al.*, 2010; Hardus *et al.*, 2012). Studies on Borneo show that over-harvesting of timber significantly degrades orangutan habitat and results in reduced population densities (Husson *et al.*, 2009; Ancrenaz *et al.*, 2010), and that the higher the intensity of logging, the greater the decrease in orangutan density (see Figure 3.1). Nonetheless, orangutans can survive in logged areas (Felton *et al.*, 2003; Knop, Ward, and Wich, 2004; Husson

FIGURE 3.1

Orangutan densities for Borneo under different logging intensities

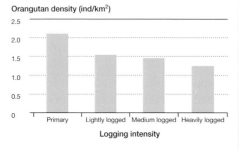

Based on Husson *et al.*, 2009.

et al., 2009) and orangutan densities can be maintained with appropriate management (Marshall *et al.*, 2006; Ancrenaz *et al.*, 2010). In fact, Ancrenaz and colleagues found higher nest densities in logged forests than in nearby primary forests.

A recent large-scale nest survey on Sumatra (S.A. Wich, unpublished data) shows similar results to those from Borneo, with transects in primary forests having a higher mean number of nests per kilometer than transects in forests that have been logged. The effects of logging intensities and duration after logging could not be quantified, but, in several cases, the transects were in concessions where logging had ceased more than 20 years previously, indicating that orangutans are able survive in such areas in the long term (Knop *et al.*, 2004). However, surveys carried out in the late 1990s recorded some transects that had been heavily logged and did not contain any orangutan nests, while adjacent primary forests still contained orangutans (S.A. Wich, unpublished data). It is difficult to be certain, but it appears that after heavy logging Sumatran orangutans disappear from logged areas. Although speculative, observations indicate that some males might move away, but that females remain and would die if food availability decreased to a level that cannot support them anymore (van Schaik, 2004; S. Wich, personal observation, 2013).

Although there is now a reasonable amount of data on changes in orangutan density associated with logging, there are fewer data on behavioral change. Some studies have assessed activity budgets during and after logging. Rao and van Schaik (1997) showed that there were more feeding bouts on leaves in the logged forest than in the primary forest. More time was spent feeding on fruits in primary than in logged forest. Both studies also showed a difference in locomotion styles between logged and unlogged, indicating that in logged forest

more energetically expensive styles of locomotion are used. More recently, a long-term
study of the effects of logging on Sumatra
orangutan behavior showed that orangutans
spend more time travelling and less time
resting in logged than in primary forest
(Hardus *et al.*, 2012). Such energetically more
expensive locomotion in combination with
less time spent feeding on fruits could
potentially lead to negative energy balances
in orangutans living in logged forest, as
described for the fruit-scarce periods between
mast-fruiting periods in primary forest at
Gunung Palung in Borneo (Knott, 1998a).
There is some evidence that orangutans are
traveling on the ground more frequently in
logged forests, thus potentially addressing
those energy imbalances (e.g. Loken *et al.*,
2013). However, a follow-up study for all of
Borneo indicated that although the degree
of forest disturbance and canopy gap size had
an influence on terrestriality, orangutans
were recorded on the ground as frequently
in primary forests as in heavily degraded habitats (M. Ancrenaz, unpublished data).

No other studies have been able to make
such direct comparisons of behavior in
logged and unlogged forest, but an alternative approach is to do a cross-site comparison and assess whether differences in activity
budgets and diet between logged and unlogged sites exist. It appears that activity patterns do not show clear differences between
logged and unlogged sites (see Figure 3.2);
however, this rough comparison does not
take into consideration potential age or sex
differences, subspecies variation, or whether
the sites were in dryland forests, peat swamp
areas, or a mixture of the two. Nor does
comparing diet across sites reveal clear differences between logged and unlogged sites
(see Table 3.1), but, again, caution should
be taken when comparing mean and range
data without carefully controlling for the
above-mentioned confounding variables.
Nonetheless, both activity and diet in these

logged areas seem to be comparable to the
patterns seen in orangutans in primary forests. It is also worth mentioning that the sites
labeled as unlogged in the cross-site comparison have been logged since those studies
took place. Consequently, Ketambe, Suaq
Balimbing, Gunung Palung, Mentoko, and
Ulu Segama are now sites that have undergone logging at various intensities and where
data were collected when the forest was
still primary. Thus, in the coming years we
can expect behavioral data to come out of
these sites that will allow for pre- and post-
logging comparisons.

Photo: Orangutans spend more time travelling and less time resting in logged forest, which could potentially lead to a negative energy balance. © Perry van Duijnhoven

TABLE 3.1

Orangutan diets in logged and unlogged forests

Site and range	Fruits	Flowers	Leaves	Bark	Invertebrates	Other
Suaq Balimbing (S)						
mean	66.2	–	15.5	1.1	13.4	3.8 (inc. flowers)
low fruit–high fruit	*62.7–69.6*	*–*	*18.3–12.7*	*0.8–1.4*	*14.6–12.2*	*3.6–4.1*
Ketambe (S)						
mean	67.5	3.5	16.4	2.7	8.8	1.3
monthly range	*57.5–71.5*	*–*	*10.6–20.1*	*2.2–3.3*	*5.7–11.7*	*–*
Batang Toru (S)						
mean	73.7	5.3	6.8	2.9	2.9	8.4
Sabangau (B-L)						
mean	73.8	9.0	5.1	1.5	8.6	2.0
monthly range	*24.4–91.9*	*0.0–60.2*	*0.3–17.4*	*0.0–9.1*	*0.7–28.0*	*0.1–4.9*
Tuanan (B-L)						
mean	68.6	5.9	17.2	1.0	6.3	0.6
monthly range	*26.3–88.0*	*0.0–5.1*	*4.5–49.5*	*0.0–5.9*	*0.3–24.1*	*0.0–2.5*
Tanjung Puting (B)						
mean	60.9	3.9	14.7	11.4	4.3	4.0
monthly range	*16.4–96.1*	*0.0–41.1*	*0.0–39.6*	*0.0–47.2*	*0.0–27.2*	*0.0–21*
Gunung Palung (B)						
mean	70.0	5.1	13.4	4.9	3.7	2.9
monthly range	*25.8–99.0*	*0.0–49.6*	*0.1–41.1*	*0.0–30.9*	*0.0–14.0*	*0.0–9.2*
Kinabatangan (B-L)						
mean	68.0	1.3	22.9	6.7	1.2	–
Mentoko (B)						
mean	53.8	–	29.0	14.2	0.8	2.2 (inc. flowers)
monthly range	*25.7–89.0*	*–*	*5.3–55.6*	*0.0–66.6*	*0.0–11.1*	*0.0–2.5*
Ulu Segama (B)						
mean	51.5	–	35.6 (inc. flowers)	11.2	2.1	–
monthly range	10.0–90.0	–	8.3–75.0	0.0–36.7	0.0–8.3	–

Note: Mean values and ranges are presented. For Suaq Balimbing monthly ranges were not available, but low and high fruit availability values were available so these are reported. For Batang Toru, the "other" category includes pith and stem. Due to the preliminary nature of the Batang Toru data monthly ranges are not yet known. Data were not available from some sites for some food items. S = Sumatra, B = Borneo, L = logged. Based on Morrogh-Bernard et al. (2009) and Wich et al. (2013).

If forests are allowed to regenerate, the longer-term impacts of unsustainable logging can be limited as long as the logged area is adjacent to forest where orangutans still exist. Recolonization can even occur in cases where the logging intensity was at such a level that it led to the complete disappearance of orangutans (e.g. Knop *et al.*, 2004). With time, orangutan populations are able to recover to pre-logging densities if the volume of timber harvested was low and residual forest damage was limited. However, in Southeast Asia, the level of damage that occurs during the logging process is usually significant and, as a result, orangutan densities tend to be much lower.

Overall, the findings of recent studies indicate that conventional logging practices will cause decreases in orangutan density (but see Marshall *et al.*, 2006), although these decreases are likely to become less marked as the forests have time to regenerate and densities gradually increase again through recovery or recolonization. In addition, conventional logging seems to have no large effects on activity budgets and diet once logging has ceased. Both these findings argue that logging concessions have an important potential role in orangutan conservation as long as they are well managed in regards to both their direct and indirect impacts, where, for the latter, the control of hunting and poaching is vital (Meijaard *et al.*, 2012; Chapter 6). Concessions where RIL (as opposed to conventional) practices have been used tend to have higher orangutan densities (Ancrenaz *et al.*, 2005, 2010). For the survival of orangutans, it is therefore not of crucial importance whether or not logging occurs, but whether this logging uses reduced impact methods and how much time a forest is given to recover following logging.

FIGURE 3.2

Orangutan activity budgets in a 12-hour day

Key: ● Feed ● Rest ● Travel ● Other
S = Sumatra, B = Borneo, L = logged

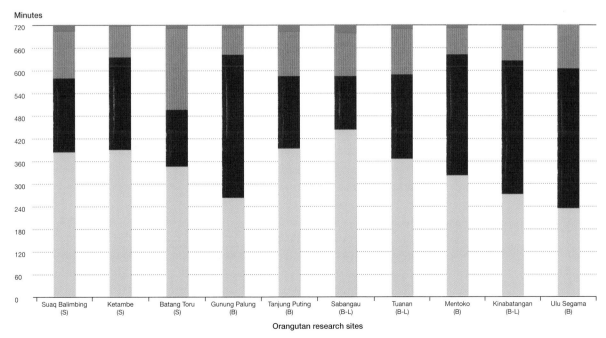

Based on Morrogh-Bernard *et al.*, 2009; Wich *et al.*, 2012.

Logging and African apes

Studies of the African apes in logged forests thus far have produced ambiguous results and have failed to identify consistent patterns of impact. Whilst conventional logging has definite negative impacts on ape populations (Morgan and Sanz, 2007), the impacts of selective logging are less clear. Bonobos have not been studied in logging concessions, whereas some gorilla and chimpanzee populations in logging concessions have been monitored for more than a decade. Some nest-count surveys have indicated that gorillas are relatively unaffected by logging once the initial disturbance has passed (White and Tutin, 2001; Arnhem *et al.*, 2008) and, indeed, longer-term studies have found gorillas occurring at fairly high densities in concessions in northern Congo that are considered to be well-managed (Morgan and Sanz, 2006; Stokes *et al.*, 2010). Nonetheless, gorilla densities decline in proximity to the roads and human settlements throughout logging concessions (Poulsen, Clark, and Bolker, 2011; see also Chapter 6), indicating possible variability in population responses within active or previously logged concessions.

For chimpanzees, the picture is less clear; an early investigation in Uganda demonstrated an inverse relationship between logging intensity and chimpanzee density, and identified the degree of habitat disturbance as a key factor in determining chimpanzee abundance in post-logged forests (Skorupa, 1988). Subsequent nest-count surveys at various sites found no consistent response: some chimpanzee populations decreased, others increased or showed no change (Plumptre and Reynolds, 1994; Hashimoto, 1995; White and Tutin, 2001; Dupain *et al.*, 2004; Matthews and Matthews, 2004; Arnhem *et al.*, 2008). The accuracy of nest counts can differ, depending on survey intensity and ability to assess nest decay rates. However, long-term monitoring of chimpanzees in logged and unlogged habitats in

northern Congo has been able to detect preferences for less disturbed forest and suggests that chimpanzees are more adapted to mature forest (Stokes *et al.*, 2010; D. Morgan, C. Sanz, S. Strindberg, J. Onononga, C. Eyana-Ayina, and E. Londsorf, personal communication, 2013). Even if they avoid human contact and favor mixed mature forest for nesting, chimpanzees seem to be able to slowly restore a stable population in regenerating forest on logging concessions if hunting pressure is controlled. Over the long term, chimpanzee densities in forests logged 15 years prior remained low compared to unlogged habitat in Congo (Stokes *et al.*, 2010). Similarly, a 28-year study of primates in Uganda has shown that chimpanzees consistently occur at lower densities in logged areas than in unlogged areas (Chapman and Lambert, 2000).

Apes generally move away from operational areas and their forced migration into adjacent home ranges will stress both immigrant and resident apes. It has been suggested that, in the short term at least, chimpanzees appear to be more negatively impacted than gorillas by the disturbance associated with logging (e.g. Arnhem *et al.*, 2008). A plausible explanation for this is that chimpanzees are territorial and incursions into another chimpanzee community's home range are generally hostile (Mitani, Watts, and Amsler, 2010). Logging activities will displace resident chimpanzees and may force them to encroach on a neighboring community's home range, resulting in social upheaval and sometimes in lethal conflict: females might be able to transfer between groups, but males are likely to be attacked and possibly killed. Aggressive intercommunity interactions in association with logging are thought to have reduced chimpanzee densities at Lopé in Gabon (White and Tutin, 2001). Gorillas are not territorial and it has been suggested that they do not have the same constraints on their movements as chimpanzees, and this may help them to resist the impacts of forestry

> " Logging activities will displace resident chimpanzees and may force them to encroach on a neighboring community's home range, resulting in social upheaval and sometimes in lethal conflict. "

activities. However, the vulnerability of gorilla group stability should not be overlooked: extreme social disruption leads to higher rates of infanticide in mountain gorillas (Kalpers *et al.*, 2003).

To date, there has been little research on how changes in forest productivity may ultimately affect the demography and density of ape populations. However, rare insights into the impacts of logging on chimpanzee ecology and reproductive fitness come from ongoing studies at Kibale in Uganda, where logging took place in the 1960s, with the intensity of timber extraction varying between logging compartments. Female chimpanzees had lower reproductive success with longer interbirth intervals and higher infant mortality in areas with outtake rates of 17.0 m³/ha (50.3% of basal area reduction) and 20.9 m³/ha (46.6% basal area reduction) than females residing in less disturbed forests (Emery Thompson *et al.*, 2007). One might conclude that more intensive logging regimes had reduced the food resource base for chimpanzees. However, more recent research indicates that the explanation may be more complex because the impact of logging on the chimpanzees' diet was low, even in cases where preferred food items had been exploited (Potts, 2011). In Potts' study, chimpanzee abundance did not appear to be related to logging history, highlighting the fact that previously logged forests may still retain resource attributes important for ape survival. However, it is important to consider the difference in spatial and temporal scales of these investigations and that indirect impacts could also be influencing chimpanzee densities (see Chapter 7).

The density data compiled in Annex II show that both chimpanzees and gorillas are able to persist in timber production forests, but with varying degrees of success and undetermined prospects for long-term survival. Studies in northern Congo indicate that Forest Stewardship Council (FSC) cer-tification processes have positively benefitted conservation in the context of timber exploitation (Stokes *et al.*, 2010; Morgan *et al.*, 2013); however, it has not yet been determined if and how specific low-impact logging practices are affecting gorillas and chimpanzees. See also the Goualougo Triangle case study and the Wildlife Wood Project (WWP) case study in Chapter 4 (pages 117 and 120).

Logging and gibbons

As with the great apes, the impacts of logging on gibbons are somewhat equivocal. There are doubtless numerous variables which interact to determine how well gibbons are able to persist and recover after logging. These variables include the intensity and extent of logging operations; the incidental damage incurred to habitats during operations; the time since the logging event; the silvicultural techniques used before, during, and after logging; the species of tree targeted for extraction, and the resident population's reliance on them as keystone species or fallback resources; the taxon's dietary flexibility; how marginal the site was for gibbon persistence pre-logging; degree of competition with sympatric taxa; and the severity of any additional anthropogenic impacts such as hunting, road access, human influx, and agricultural expansion. It is therefore not surprising that clear themes on the impacts of logging on gibbon persistence are difficult to isolate, especially given the family's large geographic range.

Within the Hylobatid family, the genus *Hylobates* is the best studied in terms of impacts of logging on population densities. The most comprehensive study to date was conducted on *Hylobates lar* in Peninsula Malaysia and tracked gibbon density prior to logging through the logging process and followed up post logging, spanning a research period of over 12 years. Johns and colleagues (Johns, 1986b, 1992; Grieser Johns and Grieser Johns, 1995) found that there were no clear trends in density of gibbons at the site over this period, including no sign that the population had decreased post logging, despite increased mortality during the logging process itself. Conversely, Southwick and Cadigan (1972) found in their study of *H. lar* that group densities were marginally higher in primary forest (0.43 groups per km²) than disturbed or secondary forests (0.34 groups per km²) caused by selective logging in the past. Pileated gibbon (*Hylobates pileatus*) in Thailand have lower densities and tend to avoid selectively logged areas and even areas of undisturbed forest nearby (Brockelman *et al.*, 1977). Gibbon densities in areas which had not been logged since the 1970s were almost three times higher than those logged in the 1990s but still lower than those in pristine conditions, suggesting some recovery over long time periods but probably restricted by lower resource abundance (Brockelman and Srikosamatara, 1993; Phoonjampa *et al.*, 2011).

Studies of Müller's gibbon (*Hylobates muelleri*) on Borneo are contradictory. One study showed no difference in group density between primary forest and low intensity, selectively logged forest (Wilson and Wilson, 1975). A second study showed decreases in group density from 7.3 groups per km² in primary forest, 5.0 groups per km² in forest logged three to five years previously, and 2.3 groups per km² in forest logged one week previously, suggesting populations go through a bottleneck caused by mortality, or possibly migration out of the area, at the time of logging with subsequent recovery still not complete five years later (Wilson and Johns, 1982). Another Bornean gibbon species, the Bornean white-bearded gibbon (*Hylobates albibarbis*), living in peat-swamp forest in the Sabangau catchment, Central Kalimantan, Borneo, has been shown to have densities correlated with canopy cover and

tree height and it has been surmised that, at one site, 30 years of logging had negatively impacted gibbon densities (Buckley, Nekaris, and Husson, 2006; Hamard, Cheyne, and Nijman, 2010). Conversely, a study on Kloss's gibbon (*Hylobates klossii*), a species endemic to the Mentawai Islands, Indonesia, showed no difference in densities between unlogged forests and those logged 10–12 years and 20–23 years earlier (Paciulli, 2004). Paciulli (2004) surmised that this lack of relationship between density and logging may be because tree species targeted by loggers are dipterocarps, which are not used by *H. klossii* as a feeding resource (Whitten, 1982), suggesting that the resource base was not impacted by the logging regime. However, this hypothesis disregards the likely significant incidental damage caused by the logging process.

Information from the other three genera of the Hylobatidae is generally lacking, being largely comprised of anecdotal observations. For example, the siamang (*Symphalangus syndactylus*) reportedly occurs in lower densities in logged over forests in southern Sumatra (Geissmann, Nijman, and Dallmann, 2006), an observation apparently borne out by lower recorded densities in forest disturbed by logging (0.20 groups per km²) compared to undisturbed habitats (0.42 groups per km²) (Southwick and Cadigan, 1972). Qualitative observations suggested that the northern yellow-cheeked gibbon (*Nomascus annamensis*) was absent in several areas that had been subjected to logging in southern Laos (Duckworth *et al.*, 1995; Evans *et al.*, 1996). However, high hunting pressure may have confounded these assessments (Duckworth *et al.*, 1995) as they probably do for all *Nomascus* species (Duckworth, 2008; Rawson *et al.*, 2011). Large home range size in the eastern black-crested gibbon (*Nomascus nasutus*) was anecdotally attributed to forest degradation caused by logging, specifically loss of fruit trees.

Where detected, changes in population density may be driven by a number of factors including direct and indirect mortality, changes in resource abundance and habitat fragmentation. Gibbons, due to their territorial and strictly arboreal nature, may be more affected by the immediate impacts of logging regimes than many other wildlife species. Gibbons have been shown to stay in their home ranges during logging activities because of their territoriality, maintaining distance from areas actively being logged by staying in unlogged or already logged areas within their home ranges, and only marginally travelling outside the home range to skirt logging activities if necessary (Wilson and Johns, 1982; Johns, 1986b). It is surmised that in instances where gibbons are forced from their home ranges during logging operations, high levels of mortality will result (Johns and Skorupa, 1987), with constant displacement by resident gibbon groups, unfamiliarity with the distribution of resources, and stress all playing a role. Additionally, their arboreal nature coupled with fragmentation of home ranges by logging roads and tree falls may also limit their ability to effectively avoid logging operations (Meijaard *et al.*, 2005) and may also result in increases in fatal falls. These factors may result in the complete loss of groups from areas during the logging process (e.g. Fan Peng-Fei, Jiang Xue-Long, and Tian Chang-Cheng, 2009).

Increases in infant mortality for resident gibbons may also occur during the logging process. Infant mortality in all primates commonly increases at times of environmental stress and resource shortages (Dittus, 1982; Hamilton, 1985; Gould, Sussman, and Sauther, 1999), and pregnancy and lactation are particularly energetically expensive for female mammals (Clutton-Brock, Albon, and Guiness, 1989; Rogowitz, 1996; Lee, 1998). Displacement and stress caused by logging, plus changes in the abundance and

distribution of resources within a home range may negatively impact females' energy budgets, with subsequent nutritional impacts on dependent infants. Significantly, Johns (1986a) found that, when subjected to selective removal of timber, infant mortality in

Photo: Gibbons, due to their territorial and strictly arboreal nature, may be more affected by the immediate impacts of logging regimes than many other wildlife species. © Terry Whittaker

a population of *H. lar* was 100%. Although the cause of this was not described, it was likely through abandonment and infant malnutrition (Meijaard *et al.*, 2005).

Finally, an indirect impact of the logging operation itself on gibbons can be increased levels of hunting (Bennett and Gumal, 2001; see also Chapter 7). It is quite common for logging crews, for example, to be involved in hunting activities during operations and some reports suggest the volumes of bushmeat consumed can be staggeringly large, for example, 29 086 kg, including 445.5 kg of primates, in one year for one logging camp in Sarawak (Bennett and Gumal, 2001). For hunters using guns to take species such as deer and bearded pigs, gibbons can make relatively easy targets, particularly because of gibbons' proclivity to vocalize loudly in the morning from fixed locations (Bennett and Gumal, 2001). Areas with high hunting pressures may have localized extirpation of gibbon populations (Duckworth, 2008; Rawson *et al.*, 2011), and even low levels of off-take can impact population viability in already small and vulnerable populations (e.g. Waldrop *et al.*, 2011). As such, control of hunting, specifically with guns, during logging may be an important determinant of gibbon persistence and recovery.

While it appears clear that increases in mortality occur during the logging process, as described above, the ability of gibbons to adapt to and recover in forests post logging is less conclusive. Johns and Skorupa's (1987) review of the literature relating to impacts of logging on primates showed that a primate species' degree of frugivory was negatively correlated to persistence in recently logged forests, in contrast to more recent meta-studies (Gogarten *et al.*, 2012). This relationship is especially relevant for gibbons given their large reliance on fruit sources both as primary food sources and fallback resources (Bartlett, 2007). Some commentators have maintained that selective logging

will have little effect on gibbon populations as gibbon diets are relatively flexible so the removal of food trees either deliberately or incidentally will only change relative species utilization in the diet (Chivers, 1972; Wilson and Wilson, 1975). Gibbon responses to this relatively quick change in the availability of food resources, specifically fruit, will likely depend on behavioral and dietary flexibility, including the ability to rely on low quality leafy matter. Gibbons possess simple stomachs, thus do not have the same ability to digest foliage as the often sympatric colobine monkeys, such as leaf-monkeys or langurs (e.g. *Trachypithecus* and *Presbytis* species), which possess specialized stomachs and symbiotic bacteria which break down and aid in digestion of leaf cellulose (Raemaekers, 1978; Chivers and Hladik, 1980; Chivers, 1994; Caton, 1999). As fruits generally have more free sugars available than leafy matter (Raemaekers, 1978; Johns, 1986b) this may in turn impact energy budgets and, potentially, mortality and fertility.

Existing evidence suggests that gibbons are likely to change behavior in response to changes in resource availability brought about by logging events. Gibbons commonly reduce ranging behavior and other activities in times of low resource abundance under natural conditions, for example when fruit is not seasonally available (Chivers, 1974; Raemaekers, 1980; Gittins, 1982; Fan Peng-Fei and Jiang Xue-Long, 2008). In his comparison between pre- and post-logged forest, Johns (1986b) found that gibbons responded similarly, with significant reductions in activity levels post logging. These changes in activity patterns in response to changes in resource abundance may be functional, however if there are insufficient resources, this may result in negative energy budgets, resulting in increases in mortality through starvation and associated factors. Lowered energy budgets will have different impacts on different age and sex classes in gibbons.

During pregnancy and lactation, adult females have considerably higher metabolic requirements per unit body weight, as do juveniles due to growth trajectories. Juveniles are also less efficient foragers and may suffer displacement from preferred food resources (e.g. Fan Peng-Fei and Jiang Xue-Long, 2010). Thus, under conditions of sub-optimal food availability, we may predict increased mortality in juveniles and infants (O'Brien *et al.*, 2003; Meijaard *et al.*, 2005; Rawson, 2012). This may also result in declines in birth rates and/or infant survival as females may not be able to maintain pregnancy or lactation on a low energy diet; both possible outcomes would impact the demographic structure of the population.

One study on gibbons does bear out a direct link between lowered resource abundance and increased mortality in infants and juveniles that may be applicable to logging scenarios. O'Brien *et al.* (2003) studied siamang in forest areas subjected to severe fires in 1997 and compared them to those in forests which did not experience fires. Areas subjected to fire suffered mortality of 25% of trees including the loss of almost half of the population of strangling figs, a key siamang resource, followed by ongoing high levels of tree mortality. Infant and juvenile mortality in groups living in fire-impacted areas was significantly higher, with 30% fewer infants, 24% fewer small juveniles, and 39% fewer large juveniles. After several years, groups in fire-impacted areas had declined in number compared to control groups. The impacts on infant and juvenile survival, leading to changes in the demographic structure of the population, were attributed to a reduction in the availability of food resources. This was brought about by tree mortality and may therefore provide some proxy for initial impacts in a logging scenario.

Here we suggest that while responses by gibbons to logging operations will not be uniform, there is potential for them to impact long-term viability of resident populations. Increased levels of mortality, especially amongst infants and juveniles, appear to be likely, which may have long-term impacts on the demography and therefore viability of the population. Populations which are already suppressed due to hunting are likely to be particularly vulnerable due to gibbons' slow reproductive rates. We also suggest that the dietary flexibility of gibbons in response to logging events may not always be sufficient to overcome impacts on energy budgets, and increased mortality, again, especially in infants and juveniles, and lowered fertility may also result in some circumstances. Comparative ecology also suggests that some gibbon taxa may be more affected by changes in resource abundance than others. For example, it has been noted that siamang (*Symphalangus syndactylus*) densities may be reduced less by logging than the densities of sympatric agile gibbons (*H. agilis*) owing to the former's naturally more folivorous diet (Geissmann *et al.*, 2006). Additional longitudinal studies following a population from pristine to post-logged forest are likely needed to tease out the full impacts on resident gibbon populations.

As discussed above, recovery of gibbon populations post logging is likely to be linked to the impacts of logging on key-stone food resources and the demographic profile of the populations, particularly where populations are already suppressed. In addition, changes in forest structure caused by selective logging practices and infrastructure for timber removal are likely to impact resident gibbon populations after the logging teams leave. Logging and associated infrastructure may cause habitat fragmentation, where a formerly contiguous area of forest becomes discontinuous sections (see Chapter 7 for more information on habitat fragmentation). Under these circumstances demographic variability, natural stochastic events such as disease and natural disaster, inbreeding depression, as well

> "Recovery of gibbon populations post logging is likely to be linked to the impacts of logging on key-stone food resources and the demographic profile of the populations."

as anthropogenic influences may make small populations in forest fragments more susceptible to localized extinction than those in larger areas with larger populations (Fahrig and Merriam, 1994).

As gibbons can become isolated by even small openings in the canopy (Johns, 1986b; Choudhury, 1990; Sheeran, 1995), fragmentation must be considered a potentially significant issue. The isolation of populations from one another may lead to prevention or retarding of gene flow between populations. Recolonization of fragments where local extirpations have occurred, which may be vital for species conservation at the landscape level (Fahrig and Merriam, 1994), will also be problematic in highly fragmented landscapes. At a more local level, isolation may also impact dispersal of gibbons. Gibbons generally leave their natal territory upon reaching maturity to form their own group; however, fragmentation may prevent this dispersal (Kakati *et al.*, 2009). Despite their acrobatic nature and apparent comfort brachiating through a complex three-dimensional environment, gibbons are subject to high levels of injury, and presumably mortality, through falls. Schultz (1939) found that 36% of gibbons in his sample of 118 wild caught individuals had long-bone fractures (some more than one) which had subsequently healed and were likely attributable to falls (Gibbons and Lockwood, 1982). It is logical that incidences of falls may be exacerbated by reduced availability of supports for arboreal travel, increased canopy gaps and the unfamiliarity of routes associated with habitat fragmentation caused by logging. One solution which has been successfully tested for gibbons is the construction of canopy bridges which may reduce incidences of falls and the need for terrestrial travel (Das *et al.*, 2009).

The minimum fragment size for maintaining gibbon populations has been assessed in two taxa with similar results. Gray *et al.* (2010) modeled minimum fragment size of

evergreen forest for southern yellow-cheeked gibbon (*Nomascus gabriellae*) persistence in a naturally fragmented landscape in Cambodia, finding that areas > 15 km² were required to maintain a viable population. Kakati *et al.*'s (2009) assessment of western hoolock (*Hoolock hoolock*) in a fragmented landscape in India suggested that populations in areas < 5 km² had smaller group sizes and higher mortality and were more likely to suffer localized extirpation than those in larger fragments > 20 km². This suggests that fragmentation of habitat, when severe enough to reduce forest patches to < 20 km², may be highly detrimental to the long-term persistence of gibbon populations. Yanuar and Chivers' (2010) study in five sites in Indonesia suggests that for the agile gibbon (*Hylobates agilis*) and the siamang (*S. syndactylus*), fragmentation of the forest leads to behavioral changes, such as reduction in home range size and change in diet due to changes in forest composition, which may also impact the long-term viability of these groups.

Only one case study of the impacts of logging on forest fragmentation and persistence in gibbons is available, that of the eastern hoolock (*Hoolock leuconedys*) in China, which has been heavily impacted by commercial-scale logging. Road networks and extraction of timber have resulted in severe fragmentation of gibbon habitat, with the total population now residing in 17 fragments and none having more than five groups (Fan Peng-Fei *et al.*, 2011b). A 50% decline occurred between 1994 and 2009 in five sites and extirpation in nine sites has been recorded, including the country's previously largest population (Fan Peng-Fei and Huai-Sen Ai, 2011; Fan Peng-Fei *et al.*, 2011b). Logging operations and effects from fragmentation are thought to be significant factors, although hunting has played a confounding role.

While demographic composition and general population health may return to pre-logging levels despite increases in mortality at the time of logging, populations which are already heavily impacted by other processes, such as hunting or habitat fragmentation, may not recover. Gibbons have long interbirth intervals and late sexual maturity resulting in low lifetime reproductive output (Palombit, 1995; Bartlett, 2007; Reichard and Barelli, 2008) and as such, even small increases in mortality in small populations may lead to loss of population viability (Waldrop *et al.*, 2011). Logging in areas with small vulnerable gibbon populations, especially those taxa that are highly globally threatened and/or range restricted, should therefore be conducted only with considerable assessment of the potential impacts.

Studies of the direct impacts of mining on ape populations

Mineral and hydrocarbon developments result in broad-scale changes to habitat structure and composition as a direct result of activities during the different phases of mining, oil, and gas projects (see Chapter 5 for more information on these phases). Seismic surveying and exploratory drilling require the clearing or disruption of only a few hectares of vegetation in each site, but there could easily be hundreds of such sites scattered across the landscape, and infrastructure development will fragment the habitat. Further, noise associated with seismic surveys has been shown to displace wildlife (Rabanal *et al.*, 2010). Displacement and disturbance also occur as the number of people in the forest increases during exploratory operations (Chapter 7).

The implementation phase of a project typically results in the most dramatic ecological changes and greatest period of disturbance for biodiversity in general. Implementation activities may include more complete devel-

opment of a transportation network; construction of drilling and extraction sites; and construction of facilities. The operation phase generally results in continuous day-to-day production; maintenance of facilities; and transport of the extracted materials via pipelines and export terminals. Although the ultimate impacts of these activities on biodiversity are often similar, they may differ in source, area affected, scale, intensity, and boundaries of responsibility.

The study of the impacts of extractive industry on wildlife is still nascent and is yet to provide a detailed picture of the consequences of mining operations or of the cumulative impacts that may occur. Research is needed to assess the impacts of each phase of project development, both in mine site areas and along key sections of the transport corridor. However, the above observations suggest that the risks and threats to apes are potentially very high over the life of a resource extraction project, and severe negative impacts may occur, increasing in intensity unless appropriate impact avoidance, minimization, and compensation measures are implemented early in a project's life.

Mining and orangutans

The impacts of mining activities on orangutans have been studied in much less detail than those associated with timber extraction. Although no comprehensive studies have been conducted on the impact of mining on orangutans, it is obvious that the mining industry is a potential threat to orangutan habitat in a number of important areas. Anecdotal information and observations suggest that where open-pit mining and orangutan habitat overlap, orangutans are generally ignored, but some are translocated (relocated) during mine development, with likely detrimental outcomes for the orangutans. This is primarily a concern where coal and bauxite deposits significantly overlap

> The study of the impacts of mining on wildlife is still nascent and yet to provide a detailed picture of the consequences of mining operations.

Photo: The establishment of mine sites, roads, and associated infrastructure in natural forest has a direct impact on orangutans and other biodiversity. © HUTAN – Kinabatangan Orangutan Conservation Project

with orangutan habitat and open-pit mining is practiced.

Mining concessions often cover large areas of prime orangutan habitat. The establishment of mine sites, roads, and associated infrastructure in natural forest has a direct impact on orangutans and other biodiversity. There are no scientific publications in the peer-reviewed literature that report on the impacts of mining on orangutans. At least one company, however, reports its own findings with regard to forest and orangutan management. Kaltim Prima Coal (KPC) reported in their 2010 Sustainability Report (KPC, 2010, p. 63) that "fauna monitoring in 2010 was done to inventorize the orangutan as a protected endangered species. [...] The conclusion of this activity is that the orangutan uses vegetation resources in the mining reclamation area as its source of food and trees as nests, this is shown by the many nests and scratches in the tree trunks in the reclamation area." This company also relocates orangutans found at their mining sites to safer locations; however, no popula-

tion trends or success rates of the translocations are known.

The establishment of opencast mines and access roads generally results in clear cutting of much of the vegetation. This leaves little habitat in which orangutans can survive, nor the opportunity to successfully manage any orangutans that do survive in such areas. In many cases, the only option has been to translocate orangutans from these cleared areas to nearby forests with the help of government agencies and orangutan welfare organizations. However, translocation can create ecological problems (e.g. orangutan numbers exceeding the carrying capacity of the area into which they are moved, introduction of disease, disruption of the original social network) and only offers a partial solution to the problem of keeping orangutans out of operational areas. This suggests that large-scale mining is of most concern with regard to orangutans. However, a World Bank study in 2000 suggested that artisanal and small-scale mining (ASM) might be more harmful to the environment (McMahon *et al.*, 2000). For more information on ASM see Chapter 6.

Unfortunately, there are hardly any data on the potential impacts of the exploration phase on orangutans. The only dataset we are aware of comes from southwestern Sumatra. Here, the impact on orangutans of drilling activity during the exploration phase was assessed in the Batang Toru area. Standard line transects were conducted in this area and orangutan densities were determined for each phase. Drilling intensity for each transect was determined by assigning a drilling intensity category to each transect (ranging from none to high, based on the number of drill holes per unit area). These results show that there is a significant negative effect of drilling intensity on orangutan density (Figure 3.3). Thus, high intensity drilling negatively impacts orangutan density, whereas low and medium intensity exploration does not significantly decrease orangutan density. In this case, there were no access roads in the forest and physical damage to the forest was limited. As a result, it is likely that orangutans in this area shifted location within their home range during the drilling phase and that there were no actual long-term decreases in orangutan density.

FIGURE 3.3

Boxplot showing the orangutan density (ind/km^2) for three categories of drilling intensity and one area without drilling

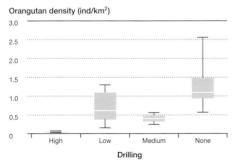

Orangutan density (ind/km^2)

Adapted from S. Wich and M. Geurts in PT Newmont Horas Nauli (2003). Courtesy of S. Wich.

Orangutans are ecologically relatively versatile and can be expected to recover to some extent following high-quality land rehabilitation after mining, especially if this is done with native species that provide food to orangutans. However, they are not expected to attain the same densities in rehabilitated areas as in primary forest, partly because human disturbance is likely to be high in such former mine areas. A good example is the KPC mine in East Kalimantan, where orangutans still occur after decades of coal mining, although apparently at low densities. This mine borders Kutai National Park, which could provide a refuge. For more information on Kutai National Park and the KPC mine see the case study in Chapter 2 (page 43).

Mining and African apes

Despite numerous environmental impact assessments (EIAs), there have been very few studies of African apes at mining sites. Such studies have been implemented only relatively recently, because baseline data often do not exist or, if they do, data sharing is restricted by confidentiality clauses. Rabanal *et al.* (2010) reported that noise associated with seismic surveys in Gabon displaced gorillas and chimpanzees for many months after operations had been completed, which could result in increased inter- and intra-specific conflict as animals are forced into neighboring home ranges or feeding and nesting sites within their range are disrupted. Observational and conjectural data derived from recent field studies carried out in the vicinity of extractive industry sites provide some insight into probable risks and threats to apes during the extractive industry life cycle. Ecologically, great apes and the habitat they depend on appear to be experiencing a two-fold threat in both mining sites and transport corridors. Table 3.2 summarizes some of the potential impacts on apes for each phase of mine development.

Mining and gibbons

The extent and impacts on gibbons from mining operations are poorly understood and documented. Of the Hylobatid taxa currently listed on the IUCN Red List of Threatened Species (IUCN, 2013), mining is only mentioned as a potential threat to two species, *Hoolock hoolock* and *H. leuconedys*. A trawl of the literature on the Hylobatidae comes up similarly short. While mining is occasionally mentioned as a potential threat, information as to the extent, intensity or nature of the threat is unavailable.

For example, opencast mining and oil drilling were identified as a threat to *Hylobates* species on Indonesian Borneo, Sumatra, and Java but the threat was not quantified or qualified because information is generally lacking, and perhaps as such in a ranking exercise it was listed as priority 19 of 20 for gibbon conservation (Campbell *et al.*, 2008a). Likewise, opencast coal mining, limestone mining, and oil drilling and exploration are mentioned in the literature as having impacted western hoolock (*H. hoolock*) gibbon habitats in northern India (Choudhury, 2006, 2009), but how and to what extent is not detailed. It appears based on the evidence, or lack thereof, that either mining poses a minimal threat to gibbons relative to other threats or that the degree of threat is not yet appreciated by those engaged in gibbon conservation.

However, mining operations and gibbon distribution do co-occur in many landscapes. A recent analysis (UNEP-WCMC, 2012) found that only two Hylobatid taxa did not have mining operations within their global ranges: *Nomascus nasutus* and *N. hainanus*. This is perhaps not surprising given that these species have a global area of occurrence of only a few thousand hectares with global populations of approximately 130 and 23 individuals, respectively. However, this initial analysis (UNEP-WCMC, 2012) also found that no more than 0.02% of any

of the 16 taxa of gibbons' assessed global range fell within known areas of mining and the number of 1-km² pixels occurring within any taxon's range was under 60 in all instances. This represents a very small proportion of global ranges for most taxa (see Chapter 5 for more detail). Those species which were predicted to be most impacted by mining operations, based on (1) the overlap between mining activities and global range; (2) a large proportion of mines in what may be core areas; and (3) productive mines in the protected area network, were *H. lar* and *H. muelleri* (UNEP-WCMC, 2012).

Impacts of these extractive industries on gibbon ecology will however depend on the scale and nature of operations. Surface mining projects such as opencast mining and strip mining are, of course, highly disruptive for gibbons as the forest is clear-felled in order to remove the overburden. Given gibbons' arboreal nature and reliance on forests, surface mining and gibbon persistence are clearly incompatible (Cheyne *et al.*, 2012). Gibbons, under these circumstances, may be forced from the area, despite their territorial nature. As discussed in the logging section, this may cause high rates of mortality and is likely to create increased competition for remaining resources and the possibility of a future population reduction.

In addition to the direct impacts on habitat of mining operations themselves, associated infrastructure development including access roads and provision of power supply may have detrimental impacts on gibbons. Most significantly these may fragment the landscape, provide improved access for hunters and permit access into remote regions for in-migration and conversion of forest for agriculture (see the earlier logging section for a discussion of the implications of these impacts and Chapter 7 for more information on indirect impacts).

Anthropogenic sound generation has been shown to have potentially negative impacts on a wide range of wildlife species

> In addition to the direct impacts of mining operations, associated infrastructure development including access roads and provision of power supply may have detrimental impacts on gibbons.

due to its ability to mask calling behaviors, induce stress, displace animals, change behavior, for example increasing vigilance activities, and distract animals, resulting in predation or a reduction in time available for other important activities (see Chan and Blumstein, 2011 for a review). This is likely to apply to gibbon groups living in association with mining operations or result in displacement from territories. For example, Delacour's langur (*Trachypithecus delacouri*) groups reportedly changed their home range in response to nearby blasting of limestone (Nguyen Vinh Thanh and Le Vu Khoi, 2006) while a range of taxa, especially wide ranging taxa, changed their behaviors in response to noise associated with oil prospecting (Rabanal *et al.*, 2010); however, this remains supposition at this time.

ASM has larger environmental impacts per unit of production than industrial-scale mining; however, these impacts are largely spatially restricted owing to their smaller operation sizes (Hentschel, Hruschka, and Priester, 2002). ASM is a recognized driver of deforestation, and may act to fragment the landscape at the local scale (Hentschel *et al.*, 2002), with impacts on gibbons as discussed under habitat fragmentation in the logging section. However, the most significant impacts on biodiversity are the result of pollution in waterways but how seriously this influences gibbon ecology is unclear, though the effects is likely to be small.

Mining impacts on the Hylobatidae, both in terms of severity and extent, represent a large information gap. It has been noted that there is very little conservation work with gibbons in mining or logging concessions in Indonesia. A barrier is the lack of engagement of the companies in conservation issues and the fact that the conservation threats to the gibbons can be overshadowed by other high profile taxa, such as the orangutans (S.M. Cheyne, personal observation, 2013). Raising the profile of gibbons as a threatened taxon, which is potentially neg-

atively impacted by mining operations and other extractive industry, may prove beneficial in addressing these information gaps and gaining an improved understanding of the relative threats, as well as approaches for mitigation.

Potential long-term impacts and future studies

The impacts of extractive industries on ape populations are likely to be severe and long lasting, but thus far few studies have been able to detect, let alone measure them beyond changes in population densities. Surveys of apes generally use proxies for the animals rather than direct observations, for example nest counts for great apes and point count vocal surveys for gibbons. Approaches commonly vary between studies, which limits comparability of the data (Kühl *et al.*, 2008). However, a fundamental issue in determining how extractive industry impacts animal density is that most studies involve comparison of population density in theoretically matched exploited and unexploited areas rather than longitudinal studies at a single site. As densities may vary naturally over small spatial scales, such approaches further confound efforts to determine the impacts of extraction on resident ape populations. Additional long-term studies which use uniform methods for determining density from pre- to post-extraction at the same site are needed to elucidate the long-term impacts of the various extractive industries on apes. New techniques, such as the ability to ascertain population size and structure by genotyping DNA extracted from feces that have been collected non-invasively (e.g. Arandjelovic *et al.*, 2011), will improve the reliability of future surveys of ape population size estimates.

Measuring specific impacts on apes is problematic for a number of reasons, and the complexity of trying to isolate specific

94

factors in any ecosystem is mentioned above, however, a major obstacle to behavioral observations is that apes are extremely wary and generally flee when they see, hear, or smell a human. Therefore studies of ape behavior, particularly in low visibility environments, generally require that animals become habituated to human observers. With orangutans, this process is rapid, but it can take several years with African apes (Williamson and Feistner, 2011). In addition, to calibrate change linked to extraction, habituation should be initiated before the onset of industrial activities. Such foresight led to the establishment of the Goualougo Triangle Ape Project, where researchers began to habituate and study gorillas and chimpanzees in a pristine habitat years before it was destined to be logged (Morgan *et al.*, 2006). Several orangutan studies were established in primary habitat that has since been logged, allowing retrospective analysis (e.g. Hardus *et al.*, 2012). However, habituation is not usually feasible or desirable in areas that are to be exploited on an industrial scale.

While our understanding of the general ecology of apes is good, being some of the best-studied taxa globally, the details of how resource extraction impacts ape ecology are still poorly known. Based on current knowledge of the behavior and ecology of apes in undisturbed natural environments, we are able to predict that extractive industries cause behavioral changes with subsequent physiological changes, but the impacts of these changes are hard to quantify. This is due to the complex relationships between extractive industry activities, their impact on resident apes' resource base, and the adaptive flexibility of each ape taxon to that impact within a specific environment. Thus these issues will be industry, site, and species specific, making it difficult to draw general principles. However, it is generally accepted that reductions in resource abundance are likely to, at best, drive changes in behavior of resident apes as they adapt to the changed quality, quantity, and distribution of resources. At worst we could expect increased levels of stress, reduced energy budgets, immuno-

Photo: While our understanding of the general ecology of apes is good, being some of the best-studied taxa globally, the details of how resource extraction impacts ape ecology are still poorly known. © Takeshi Furuichi, Wamba Committee for Bonobo Research

suppression, and increases in disease and parasite loads, leading to increased mortality and lower fertility. These impacts, together or independently, if sustained, are likely to be detrimental to the long-term viability of ape populations. Our understanding of recovery post-extraction is also poor, but it is clear that recovery will be determined by the ecology of the resident ape taxon, as well as extraction history, and the restoration regime.

Getting a better understanding of the complex socioecological responses of apes to resource extraction will require focused research using emerging techniques. The practical challenges of assessing the physical condition of apes in their natural habitat are enormous and until recently many of the physiological changes we might expect, stress in particular, could only be measured using invasive techniques. However, during the past decade huge strides have been made in the development of non-invasive sampling techniques and state-of-the-art diagnostics. Hormones, ketones, antibodies, pathogens, and parasites can now be extracted from feces and urine (e.g. Leendertz *et al.*, 2004; Gillespie, 2006; Masi *et al.*, 2012), making research on stress, reproductive endocrinology, diet, and nutritional status of wild animals feasible (e.g. Bradley *et al.*, 2007; Deschner *et al.*, 2012; Muehlenbein *et al.*, 2012; Murray *et al.*, 2013). Nonetheless, it will take studies of several generations of apes to elucidate how the stress, ranging variations, and behavioral changes induced by extractive industries impact their health and ultimately determine the survival, fecundity, stability, and maintenance of their populations.

Conclusion

Beyond broad generalities, little precise information exists on the ecological needs of apes in relation to specific forest attributes, as little is known of the normal or stochastic variations in the distribution and abundance of most ape species. Also, few detailed quantitative data are available on how direct impacts differ, other than scale, therefore no simple inferences can be drawn about the impacts of extractive industries on apes. Specific studies are needed to establish baselines against which to assess impacts. These will include, but not be limited to, surveying ape populations at regular intervals to detect changes in their abundance and distribution. Targeted and frequent monitoring should produce the data needed to support more effective decision-making and adaptive management in concessions and surrounding buffer zones.

Carrying out baseline studies of ape populations often requires considerable support from the extractive industry. This, in turn, requires the industry to be either willing or coerced to provide such support, particularly during the early stages of a project when financial resources are limited as company investment is tied into exploration activities to ensure there is a profitable resource for exploitation. Logging is different but again, company investment is frequently channeled into infrastructure for extracting logs rather than carrying out surveys or EIAs. Thus there is a clear and pressing need for (1) education of the extractive industries, so that they understand the importance of early stage studies, and (2) enforced regulatory regimes or incentives which actually encourage companies to implement the recommended studies and mitigation measures. Voluntary action is not sufficient, therefore laws or incentives intended to change company behavior are a key missing element. As with the indirect impacts of the extractive industry, key issues are weak governance, inconsistent government policies, insufficient resources, a lack of enforcement, and corruption. The allocation of permits for exploration and extraction must include legal requirements for the adoption of wildlife-friendly and social best practices before, during, and after exploration/extraction has

TABLE 3.2

Potential impacts of extractive industries on apes

Industry: project phase	Expected responses	
	Chimpanzees and bonobos	**Gorillas**
POTENTIAL IMPACT: Large-scale loss of habitat (expected in cases of open cast mining and logging)		
LSM: I, O	High death rates, especially infants and weaker individuals, due to starvation or reduced food intake	High death rates, especially infants and weaker individuals, due to starvation or reduced food intake
ASM: E, I, O	Limited, restricted and reduced feeding opportunities	Limited, restricted and reduced feeding opportunities
O and G: I, O	Elimination of nesting sites	Reduction in number and quality of nesting sites (ground and trees)
SL:	Breakdown or total collapse of community structure	Females possibly integrated into other groups
	Destabilization of surrounding communities	Destabilization of groups with silverback males fighting for dominance as group is displaced
	Integration of females into other communities	Possible increase in disease as animals are weakened by hunger
	Death of males (especially the alpha male) due to intercommunity conflict (less likely with bonobos)	
	Increased conflict over reduced resources	
	Possible increase in disease as animals are weakened by hunger	
POTENTIAL IMPACT: Partial loss and fragmentation of habitat		
LSM: E, I, O, C	Limited, restricted and reduced feeding opportunities	Limited, restricted and reduced feeding opportunities
ASM: E, I, O, C	Degradation/reduction of home range	Degradation/reduction of home range
O and G: E, I, O, C	Breakdown and possible fragmentation of community	Breakdown or possible fragmentation of group
SL:	Elimination of nesting sites	Reduction in number and quality of nesting sites (ground and trees)
	Breakdown or total collapse of community structure	Females possibly integrated into other groups
	Destabilization of surrounding communities	Destabilization of groups with silverback males fighting for dominance as group is displaced
	Integration of females into other communities	Possible increase in disease as animals are weakened by hunger
	Death of males (especially the alpha male) due to intercommunity conflict (less likely with bonobos)	
	Increased conflict over reduced resources	
	Possible increase in disease as animals are weakened by hunger	
POTENTIAL IMPACT: Habitat degradation/reduction (e.g. noise, reduced air or water quality, change in habitat composition)		
LSM: E, I, O, C	Disruption of home range delineation	Disruption of home range delineation
ASM: E, I, O, C	Possible reduction in food sources due to invasive species and loss of total habitat area	Reduction in food sources due to invasive species and loss of total habitat area
O and G: E, I, O, C		
SL:		

Industry: project phase	Expected responses	
	Gibbons	**Orangutans**
POTENTIAL IMPACT: Large-scale loss of habitat (expected in cases of open cast mining and logging)		
LSM: I, O	High death rates, especially infants, juveniles, and weaker individuals, due to starvation or reduced food intake	High death rates, especially infants and weaker individuals (particularly females because they are more philopatric), due to starvation or reduced food intake
ASM: E, I, O	Limited, restricted and reduced feeding opportunities	Reduced feeding opportunities (change in diet, likely less caloric intake)
O and G: I, O	Reduced population density	Reduction in number of nesting sites (trees)
SL:	Changes in ranging behavior	Males moving out of cleared areas
	Changes in activity budgets to an energy conservation strategy	Possible increase in disease as animals are weakened by hunger
	Increased conflict with neighboring groups if displaced during operations	Shifts in home range use
	Possible increase in disease as animals are weakened by hunger and increased stress	Increased conflict over reduced resources (predominantly between females)
		Reduction in female reproductive rates due to lower food availability
		Reduction in home range size
		Change in time budget (more travelling, less feeding, less resting)
		Reduction in social behavior due to fewer opportunities for large party sizes due to reduced food
POTENTIAL IMPACT: Partial loss and fragmentation of habitat		
LSM: E, I, O, C	Limited, restricted and reduced feeding opportunities	Reduced feeding opportunities (change in diet, likely less caloric intake)
ASM: E, I, O, C	Reduced population density	Reduction in home range size
O and G: E, I, O, C	Degradation/reduction of home range	High death rates, especially infants and weaker individuals (particularly females because they are more philopatric), due to starvation or reduced food intake
SL:	Increased mortality from falls	Reduction in number of nesting sites (trees)
	Population isolation and loss of population viability in smaller fragments	Males moving out of cleared areas
	Reduced dispersal options	Possible increase in disease as animals are weakened by hunger
	Possible increase in disease as animals are weakened by hunger	Shifts in home range use
		Increased conflict over reduced resources (predominantly between females)
		Reduction in female reproductive rates due to lower food availability
		Change in time budget (more travelling, less feeding, less resting)

Industry: project phase	Expected responses	
	Gibbons	Orangutans
POTENTIAL IMPACT: Habitat degradation/reduction (e.g. noise, reduced air or water quality, change in habitat composition)		
LSM: E, I, O, C	Disruption of home range delineation	Reduced feeding opportunities (change in diet, likely less caloric intake)
ASM: E, I, O, C	Possible reduction in food sources due to invasive species and loss of total habitat area	Reduction in home range size
O and G: E, I, O, C		High death rates, especially infants and weaker individuals (particularly females because they are more philopatric), due to starvation or reduced food intake
SL:		Reduction in number of nesting sites (trees)
		Males moving out of cleared areas
		Possible increase in disease as animals are weakened by hunger
		Shifts in home range use
		Increased conflict over reduced resources (predominantly between females)
		Reduction in female reproductive rates due to lower food availability
		Change in time budget (more travelling, less feeding, less resting)

Notes:

Extractive industry: LSM = large-scale mining, ASM = artisanal and small-scale mining, O and G = oil and gas development, SL = selective logging

Project phase: E = exploration, I = implementation, O = operation, C = closeout

occurred (see Chapter 7 for more information and examples).

Nearly a decade of continuous research in the Goualougo Triangle has demonstrated that gorillas and chimpanzees can co-exist with RIL (D. Morgan, C. Sanz, S. Strindberg, J. Onononga, C. Eyana-Ayina, and E. Londsorf, personal communication, 2013). Likewise, one detailed longitudinal study on gibbons suggests that gibbon populations can persist and rebound in selectively logged areas under particular circumstances (Johns, 1986a; Johns and Skorupa, 1987; Grieser Johns and Grieser Johns, 1995); however, the conditions required for population persistence remain unknown. A few studies have noted that Sumatran orangutans are less tolerant of logging, possibly due to their more specialized dietary requirements (Husson et al.,

2009; Hardus et al., 2012). Bornean orangutans appear to survive outside protected areas such as in the FSC certified concession, Dermakot in Sabah, Malaysia, at the present time or at least in the short term (see also Marshall et al., 2006; Ancrenaz et al., 2010).

However, it is too soon to comment on long-term survival in timber estates with respect to this long-lived, slow-reproducing species. Of all the forms of mechanized logging, certified timber operations seem to be the most compatible with the persistence of apes for a variety of reasons. Ensuring the long-term viability of apes requires greater emphasis to be placed on maintaining the quality and quantity of their food and nest resources in relation to forestry treatments.

Overall, the available evidence suggests that conventional logging negatively impacts biodiversity, but that sustainably managed forests can maintain viable populations of apes and therefore contribute to their conservation. However, it is important to stress that concessions are not a substitute for unlogged primary forests and the protected area network (Clark *et al.*, 2009; Gibson *et al.*, 2011; Woodcock *et al.*, 2011). Consequently, proximity of unlogged suitable habitat plays a vital role in both the short- and long-term survival prospects of apes in modified habitats. Such areas provide "refuge" and effectively buffer some animals from negative impacts, although details such as optimal distance to refuge areas or characteristics signifying the quality of these habitats are unknown.

Despite the variability observed, severity of the impacts of logging on apes seems to be a factor of (1) type of logging practice, (2) availability of adequate undisturbed and suitable habitat adjacent to logging sites, (3) intensity of logging, and (4) control of associated activities, such as hunting and clearing of land for agriculture. Ape populations appear to be able to recover if the right mitigating factors can be assured. Additionally, shifts in resource use and behavior observed across a continuum of human influence highlight the flexibility of these apes in adapting to environmental changes and opportunities (Hockings, Anderson, and Matsuzawa, 2006, 2012; Meijaard *et al.*, 2010; D. Morgan, C. Sanz, S. Strindberg, J. Onononga, C. Eyana-Ayina, and E. Londsorf, personal communication, 2013). Such observations are encouraging.

In the long term, the impacts of extractive industries on apes will depend on how well a company: (1) understands the ecological and behavioral requirements of resident apes, especially for shelter, food, both social structure and social dynamics, and space; (2) recognizes the potential threats to resident apes from logging or the operational practices during all phases of a mining/oil and gas project; and (3) identifies and manages potential biodiversity risks and opportunities during the relevant phases of the project. These are described in more detail in both Chapters 4 and 5.

It is incredibly important for industries to recognize the immediate and enduring impacts that individual projects can have on ape populations and associated biodiversity. Avoidance and mitigation of negative impacts is always more effective and less costly than repair or offsets. RIL and certification of logging operations are examples of effective approaches that may reduce the negative impacts on apes. The actions already being taken by some companies to apply technologies to anticipate and reduce potential impacts and to carry out mitigation measures that will avoid and minimize the negative impacts must be applauded and held up to serve as essential lessons to guide ape conservation strategies.

Acknowledgments

Principal authors: Elizabeth A. Williamson, Benjamin M. Rawson, Susan M. Cheyne, Erik Meijaard, and Serge A. Wich

Contributors: Eric Arnhem, Laure Cugnière, Oliver Fankem, Matthew Hatchwell, David Morgan, Matthew Nowak, Paul De Ornellas, PNCI, Chris Ransom, Crickette Sanz, James Tolisano, Ray Victurine, and Ashley Vosper

Photo: Reduced impact logging establishes limited extraction rates and minimum stem diameter whilst minimizing the collateral damage associated with the removal of larger, more valuable trees. © ZSL

CHAPTER 4

Avoiding the chainsaws: industrial timber extraction and apes

Introduction

Industrial timber extraction is dominated by the removal of timber for round wood. It is considered a serious threat to biodiversity with significant repercussions, particularly for forest-dependent species such as the great apes and gibbons, who rely on the forest and its resources for survival. Most of the tropical forest zone is covered with logging concessions and will likely be logged unless there is a change in land-use allocation. As different types of logging have emerged, so too have their impacts on the environment. In particular, selective logging, although extensive in nature, has relatively less impact. However, if the long-term impacts on the fate of the great apes and gibbons of old-growth habitat transformation to secondary forests and further degradation by repeated logging are to be significantly reduced, harvesting intensity must remain low and over longer time frames.

Current knowledge on the effects of logging on gibbons is outlined in Chapter 3; however, because of the lack of information on conservation efforts with gibbon species in logging concessions, this chapter focuses on the interface of logging with great apes only.

The initial section of this chapter presents detail on the various forms of industrial logging with particular emphasis on sustainable management and its uptake and impact on the environment. Section two focuses more specifically on the interface of great apes and industrial logging. Two case studies from Central Africa, Cameroon and the Republic of Congo, highlight initiatives where conservationists are engaging with logging companies to secure positive outcomes for ape conservation. Key findings of the chapter include:

- The prohibitive cost of implementing sustainable forest management (SFM) is cited as a key reason for lack of uptake within the tropical forest context;

- Although SFM is incorporated into policy and legislation of many producer countries, implementation is often weak, rendering the regulatory frameworks redundant;

- Evidence that current SFM practice is not sustainable owing to short cutting cycles is currently not incorporated into species-specific conservation strategies;

- Much conservation action is based on the premise that logging is an unavoidable reality for tropical forestry and conservation groups and organizations are engaging with industry to mitigate its impacts;

- There is a lack of clarity on the compatibility of ape conservation with industrial logging as a result of unresolved research findings on the impacts of sustainable forest management on ape behavior.

Industrial logging in tropical forests

This section initially presents an overview of the different types of logging followed by a more detailed treatment of sustainable logging practices and the viability of this approach for the conservation of biodiversity. The purpose of timber production is to harvest trees from forest landscapes to produce wood and wood products. Three types of logging practice dominate the industry:

- **Clear felling**, which is often associated with the conversion of forests to plantation or some other land use or associated with the harvesting of fiber for pulp and paper mills. This form of clear–fell–replant is not compatible with managing forest biodiversity.

- **Selective logging**, which removes specific valuable species from a forest but with no regard for the environmental effects of extraction.

- **Reduced impact logging** (RIL) is also considered a form of selective logging but limited extraction rates and stem diameters are maintained. This is done in conjunction with minimizing the collateral damage associated with the removal of larger, more valuable trees. The intention is to enable the forest to naturally rejuvenate from young trees that were growing prior to logging or from the seeds of the remaining trees (van Kreveld and Roerhorst, 2009). While reduced impact logging has been found to maintain some ecosystem services such as carbon (Putz *et al.*, 2008), it does not address some key issues related to biodiversity conservation largely linked to the indirect impacts of tropical forestry.

" Although SFM is incorporated into policy and legislation of many producer countries, implementation is often weak, rendering the regulatory frameworks redundant. "

Sustainable forestry management (SFM)

The potential impacts that forestry operations can have on forests, biodiversity, and the associated ecosystem functions they provide have been recognized for some time. Actions to try to mitigate these impacts while also utilizing the forest as an economic resource have also been implemented and are commonly defined under the term SFM; however, there is no clear consensus on the definition of the term. The International Tropical Timber Organization (ITTO) encourages its members, who represent over 90% of the tropical timber trade, to manage their operations in such a way as to provide, "a continuous flow of desired forest products and services without undue reduction of its inherent values and future productivity and without undue undesirable effects on the physical and social environment" (ITTO, 2013).

Whereas a more holistic definition of SFM is provided by the UN: "Sustainable forest management as a dynamic and evolving concept aims to maintain and enhance the economic, social and environmental value of all types of forests, for the benefit of present and future generations" (UN (2008), Resolution 62/98, p. 2).

Despite a broadly agreed international consensus that SFM should be the vision that guides forest managers, SFM has gained limited traction in tropical forests to date. Only 7% of permanent forest estates within the ITTO's member countries are considered to be responsibly managed (Blaser and Sabogal, 2011), although there is no clarity as to whether this means that sustainability has been achieved. Conventional/intensive logging is still therefore the predominant choice in a majority of forestry operations which gives little priority to long-term sustainability (Putz, Dykstra, and Heinrich, 2000; Shearman, Bryan, and Laurance, 2012). One of the main reasons cited by timber companies as preventing them from adopting an SFM approach is the prohibitive cost of implementation and a corresponding lack of realistic incentives to do so (Putz *et al.*, 2000). There is an acknowledgment that this issue must be addressed if SFM, especially in the tropical forest context, is to become the norm; companies are businesses that must remain economically viable if they are to succeed.

A number of options exist that seek to increase and guide the implementation of SFM within tropical forests. These range from the development of voluntary guidelines through to market-linked certification systems to the establishment of policy or legislative instruments.

Voluntary guidelines

A number of trade organizations exist to promote the development of the tropical timber sector and over the last 10–15 years they have moved towards incorporating sustainability as a goal. These organizations help develop technical guidelines, training and financial support for countries and industry to support the implementation of more sustainable practices in the sector.

The ITTO was established in 1986 to promote the protection and sustainable management of tropical forests and looks to balance the need for economic development with environmental and social safeguards. The ITTO is a voluntary organization that develops and promotes better trade practices in the use and management of tropical forest. In 1993, following the development of the Convention on Biological Diversity (CBD), ITTO produced *Guidelines on the Conservation of Biological Diversity in Tropical Production Forests*. Since then the ITTO has collaborated with the IUCN (International Union for Conservation of Nature), revising the ITTO guidelines and providing additional protocols to forestry companies

> Only 7% of permanent forest estates within the ITTO's member countries are considered to be responsibly managed.

for conservation management (ITTO and IUCN, 2009).

The Association Technique Internationale des Bois Tropicaux (ATIBT) (www.abtibt.org) supports the development of and capacity building in the tropical timber industry in Central Africa. Formed in 1951, it has increasingly adopted an approach that is grounded in SFM.

A fundamental problem across tropical forest countries is the permissive and corrupt jurisdictional environments that result in weak law enforcement of illegal logging and practice. This means that implementing responsible logging practice imposes a high opportunity cost, which is likely to be a key factor in the poor uptake of SFM in the tropical forest context. The implication is that the level of support provided by these industry organizations is not sufficient incentive to drive widespread change in the sector.

Certification

Forest certification is a market-based mechanism that incentivizes timber producers to implement more sustainable practices. However, certification does not indicate that sustained yields have been achieved – it certifies compliance with a number of best practices, and thereby commands either a market premium, or in other cases market access. There are at least seven voluntary, independent certification bodies worldwide with the Forest Stewardship Council (FSC) as the key international certification scheme in the tropics. It provides standard setting, trademark assurance, and accreditation to companies, organizations, and communities interested in responsible forestry. The FSC is an independent non-profit NGO and the only truly global certifier of tropical forests that carries the support of a broad

Photo: For many tropical timber producing countries sustainability underpins legislation behind the management of their national forest estate . . . however, implementation is often weak.
© Chloe Hodgkinson, FFI

TABLE 4.1

Summary of extent of FSC-certified forest in Congo basin and Southeast Asia

Region	Area of FSC-certified forest	
	10 km²	Proportion total forest
Congo basin[1]	44 610	0.02
Southeast Asia[2]	22 880	0.01

1. Cameroon, Republic of Congo, and Gabon
2. Cambodia, Indonesia, Laos, Malaysia, and Vietnam

Data from FSC (2013) and FAO (2010b, 2011b).

base of environmental NGOs (Gullison, 2003; Nussbaum and Simula, 2005). Since its foundation in 1993, the FSC has certified over 1.8 million km² of forest, in 80 countries (FSC, 2013). While this represents the equivalent of 4.5% of the world's forests, uptake in tropical forests has been significantly less extensive (Table 4.1).

Although certification uptake in tropical regions has been increasing over the last few years, it still represents a tiny fraction of overall production forest area. Perceptions related to the lack of sufficient demand for certified products, combined with front-end costs associated with achieving certification, are possible reasons for this. Despite this, FSC certification has been more successful to date in improving management practices than any other improved forestry model, particularly in regards to biodiversity, and has encouraged many stakeholders to modify their approach to logging (Sheil, Putz, and Zagt, 2010). In fact, Principle 6 relates directly to conservation of biodiversity and states "Forest management shall conserve biological diversity and its associated values, water resources, soils, and unique and fragile ecosystems and landscapes, and, by so doing, maintain the ecological functions and integrity of the forest" (FSC, 2012). While there is a trend of increasing demand for FSC products on the international market (FSC, 2013), the impact on tropical forests has been minimal.

Consumer country measures

Controls at the purchasing end of the timber supply chain have recently been developed. The EU Forest Law Enforcement, Governance and Trade (FLEGT) Action Plan, which was designed to stop illegal timber entering the region's markets, is an example of this and is enforced through bilateral agreements between the EU and producer countries (see Chapter 1).

Although not a consumer nation policy per se, the Convention on International Trade in Endangered Species of Wild Fauna and Flora (CITES) is increasingly utilized by countries to ensure that trade in listed timber species is legal, sustainable, and traceable. Around 350 tree species are listed under CITES Appendices (CITES, 2013a), and trade in their products is therefore subject to regulation to avoid utilization that is incompatible with their survival (see Box I.2 in the Introduction).

CITES works with the ITTO to promote sustainable forest management and to build the capacity of developing states to effectively implement the Convention as it relates to listed tree species. However, it is not considered to be an effective strategy for curbing the trade in illegal logging as the number of important timber species listed is considered to be insignificant to the volume of timber traded (S. Lawson, email communication, July 27, 2013).

Producer country measures

For many tropical timber producing countries sustainability underpins legislation behind the management of their national forest estate. In Cameroon the adoption of the 1994 forestry laws meant that forestry concessions have to be managed on the basis of approved "Forest Management Plans" (FMPs) that should ensure sustainable use of the resource and avoid social and environmental damage. The laws detail a forest zoning system within which a forest management unit (FMU) represents the "concession" allocation within the permanent forest estate. Large-scale timber production typically operates within the FMU. FMUs are leased at public auction and although limited harvesting can begin immediately, an FMP must be submitted to the Ministry of Forestry and Wildlife (Ministere des Forets et de la Faune – MINFOF) within 3 years. The FMP is envisaged as a document outlining how the FMU will be sustainably managed and should include an assessment of the potential social and environmental impacts of harvesting and how these will be minimized and mitigated to ensure the forest resource is maintained (République du Cameroun, 1994).

Similar measures exist in other countries and although over 140 000 km² (14 million hectares) of forests in Central Africa have management plans (Bayol et al., 2012), implementation is weak. In the Cameroon context for example, these policies do not ensure the application of SFM and improved outcomes on the ground (Cerutti and Tacconi, 2008).

Can sustainable forest management contribute to tropical forest bio-diversity conservation?

The increasing encroachment of industrial timber extraction in ape habitats and the documented increasing impact on their socio-ecology raises a number of crucial questions about the compatibility of this form of resource extraction on ape and broader biodiversity conservation. Does the application of SFM practices in relation to industrial logging reconcile profitable utilization of the resource with "maintaining and enhancing the economic, social and environmental value of the forest" (UN (2008), Resolution 62/98, p. 2)? Is there evidence that responsible logging maintains or enhances biological diversity in tropical forests and thereby can contribute to ape conservation and be truly sustainable?

Timber production in tropical forests has a range of effects on their biodiversity. The complexity of understanding these impacts is reflected in the lack of consensus from research at this interface over the last 10–20 years. For example, studies that have focused on responses in species' population parameters depend very much on the traits of the studied species. Studies looking at the impact of logging on terrestrial and bark-gleaning insectivorous birds or bats showed a significant adverse impact (Putz et al., 2000; Peters, Malcolm, and Zimmerman, 2006) whereas those looking at impacts on species with more generalist needs observed less of a negative effect (Johns, 1997).

Similarly a temporal effect can be seen whereby patterns in responses observed immediately after logging can change as time passes. After an initial decline related to the disturbance of the logging process in Indonesia, primates seem to cope relatively well, particularly if they have a generalist diet. The critical factors determining a species' ability to recover are often tied to duration of logging disturbance, as well as time passed since logging took place. Sun bears, however, suffered if fruiting tree diversity was not maintained and most of their recorded range is therefore within primary non-logged forest. Ungulates, on the other hand, as generalist herbivores, seem to be able to adapt to the change and partially benefit from the increase of grazing areas as the canopy opens up (Meijaard *et al.*, 2005). Studies that look at changes in measures of diversity or species richness overall also present conflicting trends with no change, for example, observed in the diversity and structure of butterfly assemblages in logged areas in Belize (Lewis, 2001) while marked differences have been documented between logged and undisturbed forests amongst moths in North American forests (Summerville and Crist, 2001). To some extent the patterns associated with observed impacts on species depend on where, how, and when you look.

Findings in relation to the impact of different management systems on biodiversity support the concept that populations of many species are significantly lower in conventionally logged concessions than those that are selectively logged, of which the best model is certified forest. The findings of a long-term study in Northern Congo sought to tease out the different effects of the direct and indirect impacts of logging on the abundance of a number of species. Significant populations of wildlife were observed in the logged forests, although these were still less than in unlogged areas (Clark *et al.*, 2009). A similar pattern was observed in Borneo, where many species increased in abundance after the initial disturbance of logging had passed, linked perhaps to the opening up of the canopy and new growth, with numbers returning to previous levels over time (Meijaard *et al.*, 2005).

Several additional factors influence species abundance, namely proximity to protected areas and distance from roads and settlements, reflecting the impact of hunting pressure (Fa, Ryan, and Bell, 2005). Illegal and unsustainable hunting indirectly linked to logging operations represents a far greater threat to species conservation than the direct impact of tree removal (Milner-Gulland and Bennett, 2003; Meijaard and Sheil, 2007, 2008). The opening up of forests for logging with associated roads and expansion of local human populations is linked to increased pressure on wildlife from hunting (Wilkie *et al.*, 2001; Fa *et al.*, 2005; Laporte *et al.*, 2007). Indirect impacts of logging and other extractive industries are explored in more depth in Chapter 7.

Photo: The opening up of forests for logging with associated roads and expansion of local human populations is linked to increased pressure on wildlife from hunting.
© GTAP/D. Morgan

Wildlife population density is reported to be higher in certified forests than in any other logging system and, in some rare instances, wildlife density is higher in certified forest than some protected areas (Clark *et al.*, 2009; van Kreveld and Roerhorst, 2010). The Deramakot FS concession in Sabah, Malaysia, is an example of this where the density of large mammals is higher within the concession than in the surrounding protected areas. A contributing factor is likely to be improved law enforcement on the concession (e.g. effective patrols and guarded roads). This, however, highlights both the need for better management of protected areas and the positive contribution that responsible management of timber forests can effect on conservation (van Kreveld and Roerhorst, 2010). The control of hunting is therefore considered to be a critical aspect of certification and the FSC, in response to criticisms from civil society, updated their standards to make this explicit (FSC Watch, 2008).

Overall, evidence suggests that implementing the principles of sustainably managed forestry can make a contribution to conservation relative to the impact of conventional logging. The application of SFM principles in tropical forests is not however considered to be a viable alternative to unlogged primary forests and an effective protected area network where no extraction maintains the full ecological function of these areas (Clark *et al.*, 2009; Gibson *et al.*, 2011; Woodcock *et al.*, 2011).

> Wildlife population density is reported to be higher in certified forests than in any other logging system.

Viability of current industrial logging and relevance for ape conservation

To maintain or enhance timber yields, a minimum cutting cycle of 50–100 years would be required (Brienen and Zuidema, 2007). In some of the larger sized concessions, felling cycles range from 10–20-year intervals with a period of about 30–40 years to allow the timber to regenerate before felling is resumed. These re-entry schedules are considered to be far too premature because they do not allow adequate forest recovery with evidence that depletion, and in some cases extirpation of most timber species, occurs within three cutting cycles (Hall *et al.*, 2003; Shearman *et al.*, 2012; Zimmerman and Kormos, 2012).

Tropical timber producing countries in Asia-Pacific are therefore believed to be reaching "peak timber" exploitation levels (Shearman *et al.*, 2012) due to continued depletion of native top-quality timber species at "unsustainable" cut levels, implying a "timber famine" is imminent. While the necessary data are lacking to provide a comprehensive assessment detailing the number of times concessions throughout tropical Africa and Asia have been repeatedly exploited, it is reasonable to assume that many concessions are likely to be second and third growth forests since the 1950s (ITTO, 2006). Concessions closer to human population centers are generally small artisanal managed forests with a longer history of more intensive exploitation than larger scale industrial concessions, due to factors such as market demands and access (Pérez *et al.*, 2005). As it is likely that those smaller artisanal managed concessions were initially intensively exploited, they have already incurred steep and detrimental changes in forest structure as the volume and dimensions of trees dramatically diminish with subsequent exploitation (Hall *et al.*, 2003). Further, evidence has led to contrasting views on the possibility and feasibility of natural regeneration techniques and the merits of SFM in general (Shearman *et al.*, 2012; Zimmerman and Kormos, 2012). These concerns about the overall sustainability of large-scale logging are further compounded by the failure of World Bank funded development in this sector to achieve reductions in poverty and environmental destruction (IEG, 2012).

These arguments are countered by claims that there are trade-offs to be made and that subsidizing industry action towards managing timber concessions in a more ecologically friendly manner will be of benefit to conservation initiatives. Secondary forests have been characterized as a "middle way" towards ensuring conservation of biodiversity across mosaic landscapes that consist of highly degraded human-modified habitats to those important enough to be left intact and strictly off-limits to extraction (Putz *et al.*, 2012). The current conservation paradigm has in large part broadened from the protection focused approach of the 1980s to also emphasize securing species survival prospects beyond the boundaries of reserves and within the heterogeneous matrix of single and multi-use forests.

To attain success beyond the confines of areas established for strict protection, initiatives require safeguards to protect biodiversity and improve the economic lives of human populations living in proximity to the permanent forest estates (PFE). PFE incorporate land for production and protection (Blaser *et al.*, 2011). Although participation in such initiatives has been slow to gain traction across great ape ranges, there are multiple indications that trends are on the rise:

- A growing number of concessionaires across the African sub-regions have started adopting SFM practices and certification schemes (Table 4.2). Just over 140 000 km² (14 million hectares) or 8.2% of forested area are under formal management (Bayol *et al.*, 2012). Production PFE categorized under SFM across Africa totaled roughly 66 000 km² in 2010, which is an increase of 23 000 km² since 2005. Similarly certified forest in African ITTO producing countries more than tripled from 14 800 km² to 46 300 km² between 2005 and 2010 (Blaser *et al.*,

2011). Certified forests however accounted for just 2.8% of the production PFE in African ITTO member states. Most progress towards implementing certification standards on the African continent has occurred in the Congo Basin (van Kreveld and Roerhorst, 2009), where the Republic of Congo leads in total area of concessions certified by FSC, notably between two companies, followed by Gabon (Nasi, Billand, and van Vliet, 2012).

- Timber companies that take their environmental responsibilities seriously are increasing across the orangutan range, as indicated by increased certification through Indonesian timber certification (*Lembaga Ekolabel Indonesia,* LEI) (Muhtaman and Prasetyo, 2004) and the FSC. However, it remains to be seen whether those commitments translate into reduced forest loss in timber concessions that contain wild orangutans.

- The Sabah Government at the Rio Earth Summit in 1992 indicated its long-term commitment to maintain 50% of its state as natural forest (Embas, 2012, p. 3), and aims to ensure FSC certification of all its remaining natural forest concessions by 2014 (REDD Desk, 2011). There is acknowledgement by the government that it will take several decades of minimal revenues from timber extraction until forests have recovered to a productivity level that again allows for timber extraction.

- The Indonesian government has made similar commitments, for Kalimantan at least, by promising to retain a minimum of 45% of the land area as forest (President of the Republic of Indonesia, 2012) – note that the definition of forest in this context remains to be clarified and it is unclear whether "forest" would also include timber plantations. The mechanisms to do so, however, remain unclear,

> To attain success beyond the confines of protected areas, initiatives require safeguards to protect biodiversity and improve the economic lives of human populations.

TABLE 4.2

Attributes of permanent forest estate within the range countries of African apes

Country	Permanent forest estate attributes Natural forest (10 km²)										
	Total available for harvesting		Management plan		Certified		Sustainably managed		Total area production forest		Total area protection forest
	2005	2010	2005	2010	2005	2010	2005	2010	2005	2010	2010
Cameroon	4,950	6,100	1,760	5,000	0	705	500	1,255	8,840	7,600	5,200
Central African Rep.	2,920	3,100	650	2,320	0	0	186	0	3,500	5,200	560
Rep. Congo	8,440	11,980	1,300	8,270	0	1,908	1,300	2,494	18,400	15,200	3,650
Dem. Rep. Congo	15,500	9,100	1,080	6,590	0	0	284	0	20,500	22,500	25,800
Gabon	6,923	10,300	2,310	3,450	1,480	1,870	1,480	2,420	10,600	10,600	2,900
Ghana	1,035	1,124	1,150	774	0	150	270	155	1,150	774	396
Liberia	1,310	1,000	0	265	0	0	0	0	1,310	1,700	194
Côte d'Ivoire	1,870	1,950	1,110	1,360	0	0	277	200	3,400	1,950	2,090
Nigeria	1,060	1,060	650	na	0	0	na	33	2,720	2,720	2,540

Note: modified from ITTO (2011). Courtesy of David Morgan and Crickette Sanz.

and insufficient engagement between different government departments is not conducive for developing optimal trade-offs between economic, social, and environmental goals.

However, any potential benefits derived from SFM and its trade activities risk being undermined by unchecked or illegal logging practices, which are a pressing threat, as well as illegal allocation of logging permits that not only undermine the ecology of the forest but also the associated social benefits (Smith, 2004; Blaser et al., 2011; Global Witness, 2012a; see Box 4.1). Economic development patterns in Africa have also become increasingly diverse and the trade in African timber faces increasing competition from a range of non-timber commodities (aluminum, steel, plastic) and non-native crops that threaten to replace the very existence of naturally regenerating forests. It appears that the only way towards securing a viable future for natural forest-based trop-

ical wood products is emphasizing SFM and adoption of certification standards to ensure growth and persistence in the forestry sector. However, there is poor understanding of the low uptake of certification schemes in tropical forests despite financial investments in this direction. Furthermore, if prospects for wildlife conservation are to be truly considered more needs to be done in the overall process to resolve impacts such as bushmeat hunting. In order to achieve this, greater efforts would be required by conservation scientists to aid forestry managers in identifying site-specific needs that they can act upon (Bennett, 2004).

Considering that large areas of ape habitat are logging concessions (see subsequent sections), the likelihood of their conversion to formal protection has been greatly diminished. Voluntary independent certification has the best potential to improve practice in the short term as the standard, expert independent auditors and transparency coupled with the involvement of stakeholders such as conservation organizations and local communities have proved an effective way to influence logging practice. The case studies towards the end of this chapter outline how this has been achieved in two sites in Central Africa. Perhaps most significant to the survival prospects of great apes is that certified forestry practices also strive to ensure that exploited tree species are managed as renewable resources. This principle is largely overlooked by ape conservationists who usually view these criteria solely as forestry standard and less as a tool for assessing and managing ape survival prospects. However, African tropical hardwood trees are currently central to forestry discussions of renewable resources and debates on sustainability. Based on available growth ecologies of timber species, most ecologists advocate a "precautionary approach" so that unrealistically optimistic felling cycles are avoided.

Logging and great apes

This section presents detail on the overlap of great apes with logging concessions. It further presents two case studies from Central Africa where conservationists are engaging with the timber industry to mitigate impacts on great apes through the use of sound science, dialog, and partnership.

Logging and orangutan distribution

A recent study (Wich *et al.*, 2012b) showed that an estimated 29% of the current orangutan distribution in Borneo is found in natural forests exploited for timber, where logging is allowed but forest conversion is prohibited. A smaller proportion (21%) of orangutan distribution lies within protected areas where logging and conversion are prohibited. In these forests, despite logging

BOX 4.1

Illegal logging

Illegal logging encompasses a number of activities that include the removal of timber from protected areas, harvesting in excess of concession permit limits or outside concessions, and violating export bans, international trading rules, or CITES. Although no clear definition exists, it significantly undermines responsible logging operations and threatens the integrity of forest ecosystems. It also represents lost revenue for countries where it is on-going and is considered to contribute to a 7–16% reduction in world timber prices, as trading prices are compromised due to the availability of illegal wood (Seneca Creek Associates and Wood Resources International, 2004).

It is estimated that in 2007, approximately a quarter of Cameroon's timber production was illegal, and the figure for Indonesia stood at 40% in 2005. Furthermore, the figures for Indonesia do not include questionable allocation of licenses for clearance to make way for agricultural plantations, at the expense of the natural forest (Lawson and MacFaul, 2010). The equivalent of 50 000 km² of forest was destroyed as a result of over 100 million cubic tons of illegal timber being felled globally in 2009. Declines in these trajectories prior to 2009 have been attributed to the global financial crisis and actions by some producer countries, such as Indonesia where, in 2005, a Presidential Instruction on Illegal Logging was issued (Lawson and MacFaul, 2010). More recently, trade agreements under frameworks such as FLEGT and the Lacey Act hold some promise for further changes in illegal logging rates as long as they are effectively enforced.

Photo: "Considering that large areas of ape habitat are logging concessions, the likelihood of their conversion to formal protection has been greatly diminished." © Alison White

prohibition, illegal activities can still occur due to ineffective protection on the ground. An almost equal percentage (19%) overlaps with undeveloped industrial oil palm concessions, and 6% overlaps with undeveloped industrial timber plantations. Although these concessions are still forested they are expected to be converted to plantations in the near future. Finally, an estimated 25% of the orangutan distribution range occurs outside of protected areas and outside of concessions, with 13% and 12% on conversion forests and in production forests, respectively. Conversion forests include forested regions allocated explicitly for non-forest purposes such as oil palm plantations (see Figure 4.1).

FIGURE 4.1

Orangutan habitat in Borneo and the land use to which it has been allocated

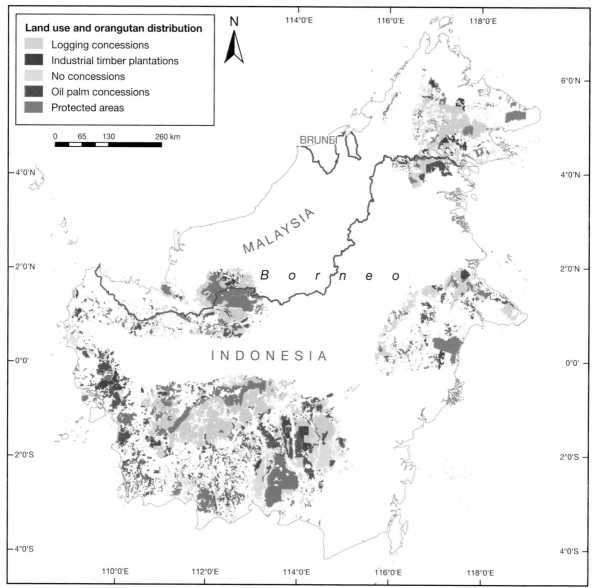

ITP= industrial tree concessions and IOPP = industrial oil palm concessions (Wich *et al.*, 2012b)

On Sumatra almost equal percentages of orangutan distribution are found within protected areas (43%) and outside protected areas and concessions (41%) (Wich *et al.*, 2011b; Figure 4.2). Protected areas were defined as those areas that fall under management by the Ministry of Forestry and are strictly protected. They therefore do not include the Leuser Ecosystem area outside of the Gunung Leuser National Park in Aceh, which has been designated as a National Strategic Area. Including this area in the protected area category would increase the percentage of orangutans in protected areas, but would also create considerable overlap between the concessions and protected area category.

The overlap of orangutan distribution with logging concessions is much less than on Borneo at only 4%. The overlap with plantation concessions (almost exclusively oil palm) is 3%, and 9% of orangutan distribution is under mining concessions (Figure 4.2).

A specific problem associated with unsustainable timber extraction is that it leaves natural forest concessions with limited economic potential to generate revenues. The next step often chosen is to convert these natural forest stands into more intensively managed plantations of one or a few tree species. This pattern of conversion from natural forest to logging concession to managed plantations highlights the risks of engagement in any form of industrial logging. As the timber value of the forest decreases, alternatives to selective logging become attractive and increase the likelihood of conversion away from natural forests. Even though such plantations provide some habitat for orangutans, carrying capacity appears to be far lower than in natural forests, while human–orangutan conflicts due to crop damage further limit their chances of survival (Campbell-Smith, Sembirang, and Linkie, 2012). The implementation of sustainable forest management (SFM) in

FIGURE 4.2

Orangutan habitat in Sumatra and land-use allocation

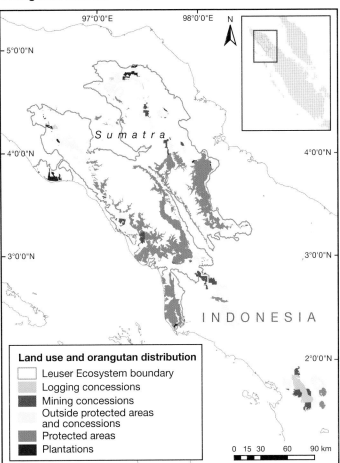

Note: Multiple boundaries of Gunung Leuser National Park exist and the SK 276 are used in this analysis. Courtesy of S. Wich.

natural forest concessions is thus considered to be a key strategy in orangutan conservation.

Logging and African apes

Using data on land use provided by the World Resources Institute (WRI, 2012) and the latest data on the distribution of great apes in Africa provided by the A.P.E.S. (Ape Populations, Environments and Surveys) database, distribution range map polygons for each species/subspecies were overlaid on data for both the protected area network and forest concessions to produce maps

TABLE 4.3

The estimated range within protected areas and timber concessions of great ape taxa found in Central Africa

Great ape species/subspecies	Total range, km² (Congo Basin only)	Range within protected areas, km² (proportion)	Range within timber concessions, km² (proportion)
*Gorilla beringei beringei** (mountain gorilla)	259	259 (1.00)	0 (0.00)
Gorilla beringei graueri (Grauer's gorilla)	64 860	23 719 (0.37)	0 (0.00)
*Gorilla gorilla diehli** (Cross River gorilla)	2414	998 (0.41)	76 (0.03)
Gorilla gorilla gorilla (western lowland gorilla)	691 277	99 722 (0.14)	338 114 (0.49)
Pan paniscus (bonobo)	420 018	63 163 (0.15)	56 698 (0.13)
Pan troglodytes ellioti (Nigeria-Cameroon chimpanzee)	123 672	17 949 (0.15)	11 144 (0.09)
*Pan troglodytes schweinfurthii** (eastern chimpanzee)	886 103	131 553 (0.15)	45 311 (0.05)
Pan troglodytes troglodytes (central chimpanzee)	712 951	101 727 (0.14)	336 555 (0.48)

* Estimates do not include range outside of Central Africa, defined here as Cameroon, CAR, Gabon, Equatorial Guinea, Republic of Congo, and DRC.

TABLE 4.4

Estimated area of priority sites for conservation of western lowland gorilla and central chimpanzee within protected areas and timber concessions in the Congo Basin

Site name	Priority level	Total area, km²	Area in timber concessions, km² (proportion)	Area in protected areas, km² (proportion)
Odzala complex	Exceptional	39 694	24 116 (0.61)	15 257 (0.38)
Lac Télé complex	Exceptional	26 550	1715 (0.06)	4494 (0.17)
Sangha Trinational	Exceptional	27 811	16 964 (0.61)	7388 (0.27)
Loango-Gamba complex*	Exceptional	13 062	2593 (0.20)	12 208 (0.93)
Dja	Exceptional	6238	140 (0.02)	5864 (0.94)
Boumba Bek/Nki	Exceptional	6110	343 (0.06)	5599 (0.91)
Lopé/Waka	Exceptional	7434	1656 (0.22)	5703 (0.77)
Ivindo	Important	2989	112 (0.04)	2842 (0.95)
Rio Campo complex	Important	5843	1511 (0.26)	2486 (0.43)
Belinga-Djoua	Important	3453	2443 (0.71)	0 (0.00)
Mengamé	Important	1220	27 (0.02)	1027 (0.84)
Conkouati/Mayumba*	Important	7066	5517 (0.78)	3508 (0.50)
Ebo-Ndokbou	Survey	1426	0 (0.00)	0 (0.00)
Maiombe	Survey	7999	3286 (0.41)	0 (0.00)

* Both Loango-Gamba complex and Conkouati/Mayumba contain sites classed as both forest concessions and protected areas, meaning total proportion > 1.00

FIGURE 4.3

Great ape distribution and overlap with protected areas and timber concessions

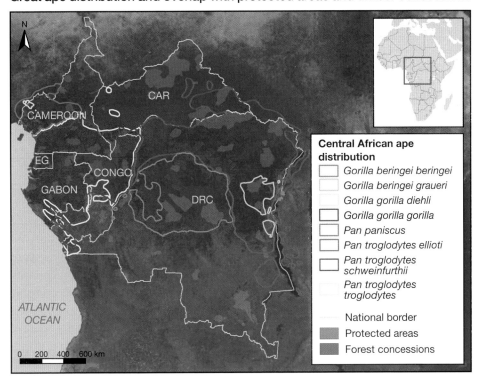

Map layers derived from World Resources Institute (www.wri.org), A.P.E.S. database, and Environmental Systems Research Institute (www.esri.com). Courtesy of ZSL

FIGURE 4.4

Priority conservation areas for great apes in West Central Africa* related to protected areas and timber concessions

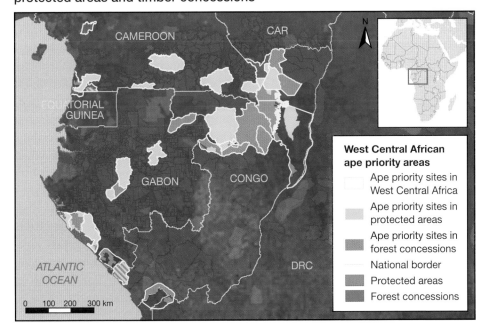

Map layers derived from WRI, A.P.E.S. database, and ESRI. Courtesy of ZSL.
* Tutin *et al.*, 2005

representing the portion of each species' range located within these two land classes (Figure 4.3). Proportions of ape ranges in protected areas and timber concessions were then assessed and tabulated (Table 4.3). Data on forest concessions in Tanzania, Uganda, Rwanda, and Nigeria were not available so the analysis focused purely on the eight ape species/subspecies found within the Central African region (encompassing Cameroon, Central African Republic (CAR), Gabon, Equatorial Guinea, Republic of Congo, and Democratic Republic of Congo (DRC)). This also represents the area in which tropical forestry operations are most extensive. The results demonstrate that for three of the African great ape subspecies over 10% of their remaining range is within timber concessions and for two of those, the sympatric central chimpanzee (*Pan troglodytes troglodytes*) and western lowland gorilla (*Gorilla gorilla gorilla*), this rises to almost 50% of their total range. This represents a major proportion of both subspecies' ranges and conserving them within timber concessions is therefore considered to be crucial to securing their future.

A second analysis focused on existing conservation planning efforts for these two widely distributed great apes. Following an expert-led assessment process, 12 priority areas were identified as key to securing the future for the great apes of the western Congo region (Tutin *et al.*, 2005). Some of these areas are wholly contained within protected areas but to explore the role that timber concession management might play in securing these sites a similar analysis to that conducted for distribution was carried out (Figure 4.4 and Table 4.4). For certain priority sites such as the Dja and Boumba Bek/Nki the vast majority of the zone is within the protected area network and only a tiny fragment is contained within timber production forest; however, Dja is surrounded by timber concessions. For a number of other key sites, such as the vast Sangha and Odzala complexes, timber concessions encompass over 60% of the total area as well as significant portions in other priority sites. Management of the timber concessions is therefore considered to have a significant bearing on the conservation status of the site itself and conservationists working in this region are increasingly engaging with the timber production industry as part of a strategy to conserve the great apes of the Congo basin.

Best practice guidelines for logging and apes

Best Management Practices for Orangutan Conservation: Natural Forest Concessions (Pedler, 2010) presents best practice guidelines for orangutans developed under the auspices of the USAID-funded Orangutan Conservation Services Program (OCSP). It outlines four key commitments for companies to embrace to meet their corporate social responsibilities. They encompass: articulating a corporate commitment to protect orangutans; adhering to laws and regulations; implementing management planning and monitoring of orangutans; and engaging in landscape-level collaborative management.

Great Apes and FSC: Implementing "Ape Friendly" Practices in Central Africa's Logging Concessions (Morgan *et al.*, 2013) was prepared by the IUCN Species Survival Commission (SSC). It outlines a framework within which logging companies adhering to FSC certification can incorporate the long-term preservation of great apes into their activities; providing practical considerations for collaboration between forestry and conservation practitioners in maintaining wildlife.

© USAID. http://pdf.usaid.gov/pdf_docs/ pnady484.pdf

© Ian Nichols and IUCN/SSC Primate Specialist Group. http://www.primate-sg. org/storage/pdf/Great_apes_and_FSC.pdf

Evaluating the effects of logging on great apes: Goualougo Triangle case study

The Nouabalé-Ndoki National Park (NNNP) in northern Republic of Congo (2°05'–3°03' N; 16°51'–16°56' E) is part of the larger transboundary Sangha Trinational (TNS) forest conservation area, extending over approximately 35 000 km² and comprising of a vast stretch of lowland Guineo-Congolian forest in Republic of Congo, CAR, and Cameroon. The NNNP was founded in 1993 and, while rich in wildlife and world-renowned for conservation efforts, this protected region lies at the center of a landscape that since the 1990s has become dominated by commercial forestry concessions.

In an effort to initiate more effective conservation activities around the core conservation area encompassing the NNNP, the Project for Ecosystem Management in the periphery of NNNP (PROGEPP – *Projet de Gestion des Ecosystémes Péripheriques du Parc*) was signed in 1999 between the Wildlife Conservation Society (WCS), *Congolaise Industrielle du Bois* (CIB), and the Congolese government's *Ministere de l'Economie Forestiere* (MEF). This agreement aimed to establish management systems that would maintain the long-term integrity of the forest ecosystem in the context of commercial forest exploitation for the Kabo–Pokola–Loundougo logging concessions (Elkan *et al.*, 2006). To date, the CIB is one of only ten companies in the Congo Basin to adopt and adhere to formal measures of sustainable development (Bayol *et al.*, 2012). In 2006, the Kabo forestry concession was the second FSC-certified concession in all of Central Africa. Initial surveys in the Kabo concession indicate that gorilla densities are comparable to those in NNNP (Stokes *et al.*, 2010), implying that FSC certification processes have produced positive results and benefited conservation in the context of timber

FIGURE 4.5

Goualougo Triangle study area

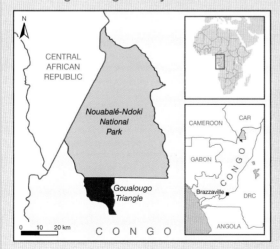

© GTAP

exploitation However, it had not been determined if and how low impact logging practices affect gorillas and chimpanzees.

A study was therefore initiated by the Goualougo Triangle Ape Project (GTAP) of Lincoln Park Zoo to evaluate the effects of selective timber harvesting on wild gorilla and chimpanzee populations, with an additional aim of then developing initiatives to mitigate any negative impacts so as to contribute to the conservation of these endangered species. The study employed a multi-faceted approach incorporating detailed knowledge about species-specific habitat preferences, ecological needs, and ape behavior. Utilizing data collected along standardized line transects before, during, and after timber operations, ape distribution in relation to increasing human influence was mapped and a model for monitoring at-risk ape populations in production forests was developed.

The study was conducted in the Goualougo Triangle, located between the Ndoki and Goualougo Rivers, an area that was recently annexed to the NNNP (Figure 4.5).

The study area was divided into zones to systematically evaluate changes in ape abundance and distribution as related to protection status, forestry activities, and other factors.

- Zone A is a pristine forest in the National Park that serves as a control condition for analytical studies of anthropogenic disturbance.

- Zone B is also a pristine forest in the National Park. It has been further subdivided into Zones B1 and B2 because the apes in these areas are expected to be affected differently by future logging activities in Zone C. Zone B1 is where the Goualougo Triangle Ape Project focuses efforts to study habituated chimpanzees and gorillas.

- Zone C is comprised of the pristine forest along the southeastern boundary of the NNNP. It is part of an FSC-certified logging zone (Kabo Forestry Management Unit) attributed to CIB. The first harvest of this forest is scheduled to begin by early 2015.

- Zone D is adjacent to the southwestern border of the NNNP. It is part of the Kabo Forestry Management Unit. The area was previously exploited for timber between 1971 and 1972 by the Société Nouvelle des Bois de la Sangha (SNBS), and subjected to a second harvest cycle from 2005 to 2009.

During the second cycle of logging activities in Zone D, abundance and spatial distribution of apes were monitored via repeated surveys of ape nests along line transects. Between October 2004 and December 2010, 11 passages of line transect surveys were repeated in the Kabo forestry concession. The first survey passage was conducted after logging activities had been dormant for more than 30 years. All subsequent surveys were conducted during active timber prospection, exploitation, and post exploitation.

In the active logging zone of the Goualougo Triangle, an inverse relationship between ape presence and human hunting and gathering activities was observed, suggesting that chimpanzees and gorillas became more cryptic in response to human contact (Morgan *et al.*, 2013). This occurred despite

FIGURE 4.6

Chimpanzee and gorilla density estimates in pristine and logged forests, Goualougo Triangle study zones

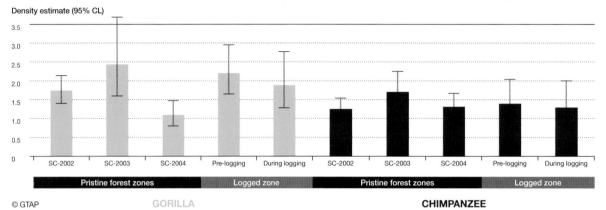

© GTAP   GORILLA   CHIMPANZEE

the fact that forestry activities and staff were often focused on particular areas for only days or weeks before moving to another section of the zone.

Within the active logging zone (Zone D) of the Goualougo Triangle, the study documented the arrival of forestry teams into a landscape. Gorilla and chimpanzee signs were significantly more frequent than human signs during the baseline surveys in 2004 and were similar to neighboring pristine forests located in the NNNP (Morgan et al., 2006). During the course of timber exploitation, no dramatic fluctuations in ape abundances were observed. Density estimates in Zone D remained similar over the 8-year study period. In fact, densities of both ape species remained relatively stable during and after logging had been active in the area (Figure 4.6). However, long-term monitoring is still required to establish the impacts of logging into the future.

Spatial shifts in habitat use

Although the abundances of apes remained stable, there were indications that both species were impacted by the disturbance associated with the arrival and activities of forestry teams. While global density estimates for each zone were stable, there were changes in the way the apes occupied their ranges. Prior to the arrival of forestry teams, chimpanzees and gorillas were concentrated in habitats predicted to have the highest foraging value for each of these respective species. Over the course of this study, both species shifted away from areas of highest human disturbance and into neighboring forests with lower forage quality but less human disturbance. It seems that both gorillas and chimpanzees were driven away from active logging, with pre-exploitation levels of ape abundance not reaching normally expected levels until 2 km distant from the areas of greatest disturbance. These results support previous assertions that gorillas and chimpanzees seek neighboring "refuge" areas during periods of active disturbance (Hashimoto, 1995; Matthews and Matthews, 2004; Arnhem et al., 2008). Importantly, the apes were displaced within the normal ranging distances for both species.

The responses of both species supported species-specific predictions, with gorillas dispersing considerably further in reaction to disturbance and chimpanzees contracting rather than expanding their ranging, presumably to avoid potential conflicts with neighboring groups.

Disturbance associated with forestry activities may have resulted in decreased access for chimpanzees to preferred and assumed high quality habitat over the course of the study. Availability of the most suitable forest patches for chimpanzees was significantly reduced in 2009 when compared to pre-exploitation or baseline levels (Figure 4.7). It is considered that shifts in great ape distribution therefore seem to represent a trade-off of optimal resource use and decreased contact with human disturbance. Assessing ape spatial distribution in different logging conditions and environments to more precisely define their ecological needs and interspecies interactions is required so that it can be communicated to forestry managers to ensure the preservation of key resources for ape survival within concessions.

Present-day changes in ape behavior were examined and interpreted in reference to past logging. The research demonstrated a legacy effect from previous logging on the nesting behavior of both gorillas and chimpanzees. The change in nesting behavior is believed to be due to past and recent timber exploitation rather than underlying ecological factors that predate timber extraction. The results indicate that gorillas and chimpanzees adjust their nesting patterns to cope with potential changes in forest structure, abundance, and diversity associated with timber exploitation. The consistency in behavioral responses between past and present logging regimes implies enduring impacts that may be due in part to similar silviculture techniques, tree species removals, and overall disturbance regimes employed in the 1970s and during the more recent logging cycle. RIL practices and adherence to FSC certification standards are likely to have decreased the direct impacts on ape numbers, but environmental changes in the forest ecology nonetheless elicited significant behavioral responses. Given the recurrent nature of timber exploitation, such behavioral alterations are likely to increase.

FIGURE 4.7

GTAP study Zone D in the Kabo logging concession, a mosaic of suitable and non-suitable habitats for chimpanzees

 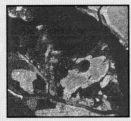

Before   After

Green filled areas represent the location of most preferred habitat for chimpan-zees, with yellow areas decreasing in chimpanzee preference. Red filled areas represent the least suitable habitat for chimpanzee nesting and foraging. Blue areas represent rivers and streams. Our results indicate that accessibility to particular areas changes due to logging disturbance. The panel on the left depicts habitat available to chimpanzees in 2004, representing the pre-logging phase in this study. The panel on the right represents a time when logging had been underway for 3 years. As logging advanced, the availability of chimpan-zee preferred habitats decreased owing to human occupation and disturbance.

© GTAP/E. Lonsdorf

Implications for ape conservation locally and regionally

The origin of NNNP and recently granted protected status of the Goualougo Triangle were the result of a forward-looking approach, which took into consideration scientific studies of great apes as well as local societies' needs (Ruggiero, 1998; der Walt, 2012; Elkan and Elkan, 2012). The Goualougo Triangle was known to be of exceptional conservation value during the initial planning of the NNNP, and WCS actively lobbied the Congolese Government for inclusion of the area within the pro-tected area boundary in 1992. However, the National Park was created without inclusion of the Goualougo Triangle and the long-term protection of the apes in this region remained uncertain for two decades. Subsequent discussions between the Congolese Government, WCS, and the local logging com-pany CIB were focused on sparing the intact forests of the Goualougo Triangle from timber exploitation. After several years of debate, a flexible land-use planning approach resulted in an agreement that recognized the biological value of the Goualougo Triangle and recommended that it should be main-tained in its pristine state via formal protection. However, obtaining official protected status was a long-term process. In 2003, a positive step towards protection occurred when the Congolese Government announced that the Goualougo Triangle, comprising 250 km^2 of pristine forest, would be officially annexed to the National Park. While this proclamation received a great deal of public attention the area remained unprotected for another 9 years. The official decree from the President of the Republic of Congo modifying the boundaries of the NNNP to include the Goualougo Triangle finally occurred on January 20, 2012.

Discussions with the logging company about the Goualougo Triangle led to identification of other important conservation areas within the active logging concessions surrounding NNNP. As part of its FSC certification process, CIB announced two additional important conservation set-aside areas in the Kabo Forestry Management Unit. The two areas, the Djéké Triangle and the Bomassa/Mombongo zone, comprise over 150 km^2 and are located in the Bomassa Triangle. The Bomassa Triangle provides an important conservation conduit in the Sangha Trinational protected area network by connecting national parks in the Central African Republic (CAR) and the Republic of Congo. The Djéké Triangle is a pristine forest block located within the Republic of Congo between NNNP and Dzanga-Ndoki National Park. Both areas contain important complexes of bais and yangas (natural clearings frequented by large mammals) and are the subject of long-term ecological research programs. The set-aside agreement recognized the conservation and scientific value of the region and its potential for ecotourism development and was reached after stakeholder discussions between CIB, WCS, and the Government of Congo.

A further significant step was recently taken in 2012 when the Sangha Trinational conservation complex was named a World Heritage Site by the United Nations Educational, Scientific and Cultural Organization (UNESCO). The site consists of a 25 000 km^2 contiguous area across the Republic of Congo, Cameroon, and the CAR and marks the first World Heritage site that spans three nations. The core of the Sangha Trinational conservation complex is formed by three contiguous national parks connected by the Sangha River.

The preservation of the Goualougo and Djéké Triangle forests was a landmark conservation initiative that continues to have far reaching impacts. Thriving research (GTAP and the Mondika Research Center) and ecotourism projects (Mondika, and Djéké Triangle Ecotourism Project), which are compatible with regional conservation planning strategies, have been estab-lished in these areas.

At the same time, these sites continue to facilitate advocacy for ape conservation through education programs and sup-port of Congolese nationals in continuing research and grad-uate education. The success of these projects relies upon the involvement and support of stakeholders from the local vil-lages. The economic dimensions of sustainable forestry have led to opportunities for employment and access to health programs for local Ba'Aka staff in the periphery of the NNNP. These efforts are considered both to promote alternative activ-ities to unsustainable hunting and to address current gender and ethnic imbalances in development opportunities.

The research conducted by GTAP not only furthered under-standing of the interaction of African great apes and SFM but also enabled further identification of important conservation areas to be set aside and not utilized for industrial exploita-tion. This arguably enhanced the conservation status of these species in this landscape; however, significant alterations in the nesting behavior of the ape species as a result of long-term logging raise a number of unresolved questions regarding the compatibility of industrial logging and ape conservation.

Wildlife Wood Project – Cameroon

The Wildlife Wood Project (WWP) was initiated by the Zoological Society of London (ZSL) as a way to assist the tropical timber industry to achieve more sustainable practices that contribute to conserving the biodiversity of the Congo basin. Initially they sought to develop pilot models to show how FSC certification principles and criteria and SFM could be implemented and used to ensure sustainable wildlife management in working timber concessions.

ZSL's goal was sustainable wildlife management within timber production landscapes using the WWP as a mechanism to provide timber companies with the capacity to achieve this goal as part of their standard operating practices. For this to succeed their industry partners had to commit to four key elements:

■ To work with ZSL to develop and implement the necessary monitoring and management systems to ensure that wildlife populations are not significantly impacted by their activities.

■ To take suitable steps to ensure that illegal activity, and in particular illegal and unsustainable hunting, are not taking place within their area of operation.

■ Engage with other stakeholders, in particular local forest communities, to meet project objectives, and, crucially, to ensure that they are not adversely affected by the timber enterprise.

■ And finally, and in the longer term perhaps most significantly, to commit to develop the necessary capacity in terms of human resources and logistics to sustain on-going delivery of project objectives.

Many of these objectives are part of a company's obligations under Cameroonian forestry law and FSC certification standards; however, the tools and approaches to realize these obligations are often lacking or not implemented.

Identifying willing, suitable partners to develop long-term working relationships within a supportive national context was the first step. Following consultations with a number of companies, two were identified as suitable and willing to partner on WWP: Pallisco and SFID-Rougier.

FIGURE 4.8

Wildlife Wood Project area of intervention, bridging the landscape between the Dja Biosphere Reserve and Boumba Bek National Park

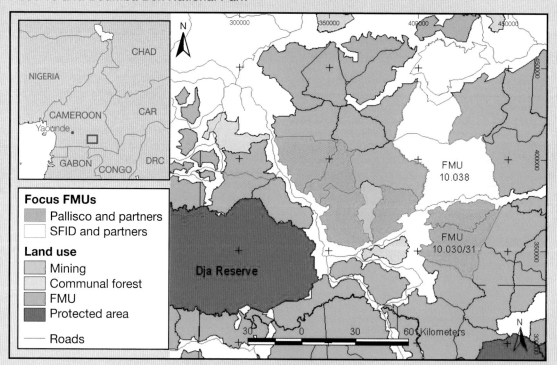

The forestry concessions highlighted are managed by company partners and encompass almost 7000 km².

Courtesy of ZSL

The initial focus for WWP activities extended over Pallisco's and SFID's allocated FMUs in the eastern region of Cameroon, in the landscape between Dja and Boumba bek/Nki (Figure 4.8). This production forest block of almost 6500 km² is an area larger than the nearby Dja Faunal Reserve World Heritage Site. These FMUs are located in the transition zone between the mixed moist semi-evergreen Guineo-Congolian rainforests and the evergreen forests of the Congo Basin. They are a mosaic of mixed mature forests without predominant species and secondary forests at different succession stages. Three main timber species account for the majority of timber harvested in these concessions:

- the sapele or sapelli (*Entandrophragma cylindricum* – sometimes called "poor man's mahogany");
- the ayous or abachi or obeche (*Triplochiton scleroxylon* – African whitewood); and
- the tali or missanda (*Erythrophleum ivorense* – sasswood tree).

From a biodiversity perspective, these concessions are located at the northeastern border of the Tri-national Dja-Odzala-Minkébé (TRIDOM) landscape, a high priority conservation zone spanning the borders of Cameroon, the Republic of Congo, and Gabon. They are home to remarkable forest wildlife, such as the western gorilla, common chimpanzee, and forest elephant, including populations within or bordering areas of highest priority for the conservation of these species.

The Cameroonian legal context and certification

The management of all forests in Cameroon comes under the legislative framework outlined by the 1994 forestry laws, which enshrine the principles of SFM.

For FSC-certified companies and those seeking certification, the principles and criteria (Box 4.3) are amongst the strongest incentives in timber production forests for sustainable forest management and, in particular, actions that favor wildlife conservation. Several of the principles and criteria agreed for the Congo Basin region are explicit regarding the impacts of logging operations on wildlife populations and the responsibilities of companies to mitigate them.

The effects of logging on mammals

Wildlife monitoring programs were designed and implemented in two concessions managed by Pallisco and SFID, FMU 10.030 (1180 km²) and FMU 10.038 (1520 km²), to assess the response of wildlife populations to logging activities.

In each concession four permanent biomonitoring stations were established, including one "impact station," where logging operations were in effect during the time of the study, and three "control stations," where no logging took place in their immediate surroundings (> 2 km), with data collected by the timber companies' wildlife monitoring teams. The results of this study provide a baseline for future monitoring and allowed for exploration of the immediate effects of logging on the study species that included forest elephant, yellow backed duiker, western lowland gorilla, and common chimpanzee. Trends in abundance of these species showed a different

BOX 4.3

FSC principles relating to wildlife

"Principle 1: Forest management shall respect all applicable laws of the country in which they occur, and international treaties and agreements to which the country is a signatory, and comply with all FSC Principles and Criteria." (FSC, 2002, p. 4)

It should be noted that under this principle the forest manager is obliged to be aware of and contribute towards national biodiversity strategies. The manager is also obliged to ensure that no illegal or unauthorized activities take place within the concession and to liaise with the national authorities to achieve this.

"Principle 2: Long-term tenure and use rights to the land and forest resources shall be clearly defined, documented and legally established." (FSC, 2002, p. 4)

"Principle 3: The legal and customary rights of indigenous peoples to own, use and manage their lands, territories, and resources shall be recognized and respected." (FSC, 2002, p. 5)

A key element of this principle, in relation to forest conservation, is the obligation to engage with local forest dependent communities and ensure that they maintain their customary rights and resource access and that those resources are maintained.

"Principle 6: Forest management shall conserve biological diversity and its associated values, water resources, soils, and unique and fragile ecosystems and landscapes, and, by so doing, maintain the ecological functions and the integrity of the forest."(FSC, 2002, p. 6)

Under this principle are criteria that oblige the organization to identify potential impacts and take steps to preserve ecosystems and threatened species. This includes controlling hunting and ensuring company staff are not involved in production, consumption or trade of wild meat.

"Principle 7: A management plan – appropriate to the scale and intensity of the operations, shall be written, implemented, and kept up to date. The long-term objectives of management, and the means of achieving them, shall be clearly stated." (FSC, 2002, p. 7)

The management plan referred to under this principle should detail objectives relating to, amongst others, identifying and protecting rare, threatened, or endangered species, and including explicit reference to the High Conservation Value Forest (HCVF) framework (see Box 4.4 for detail on Principle 9 relating to HCVF). The HCVF concept is of particular importance to wildlife conservation as it obliges the concession manager, in consultation with relevant stakeholders, to identify, monitor, and manage areas of high conservation value to maintain and/or enhance them.

The High Conservation Value Forest concept (HCVF)

"Principle 9: Management activities in high conservation value forests shall maintain or enhance the attributes which define such forests. Decisions regarding high conservation value forests shall always be considered in the context of a precautionary approach."
(FSC, 2002, p. 9)

Six classes of social and environmental HCVF values (FSC, 2008, p. 1) have been established that forest managers are obliged to take account of:

"1. Forest areas containing globally, regionally, or nationally significant concentrations of biodiversity values (e.g. endemism, endangered species, refugia).

2. Forest areas containing globally, regionally, or nationally significant large landscape-level forests, contained within, or containing the management unit, where viable populations of most if not all naturally occurring species exist in natural patterns of distribution and abundance.

3. Forest areas that are in or contain rare, threatened, or endangered ecosystems.

4. Forest areas that provide basic services of nature in critical situations (e.g. watershed protection, erosion control).

5. Forest areas fundamental to meeting basic needs of local communities (e.g. subsistence, health).

6. Forest areas critical to local communities' traditional cultural identity (areas of cultural, ecological, economic, or religious significance identified in cooperation with such local communities)."

Before logging can begin, forest managers are obliged to engage with other stakeholders in a participatory process to assess, identify, and map areas of HCVF within their concession. These assessments must then be made publically available. Once identified, the concessionaire must work with these stakeholder groups to agree a monitoring and management system to maintain and/or enhance these values. It is noteworthy that, under this principle, criterion 9.4 requires a specific data collection protocol to be developed and annual monitoring to verify the status of the HCVF that feeds into adaptation of the FMP.

pattern in each of the two logging concessions. In FMU 10.030, logging activities were observed to have no impact on chimpanzees as no significant changes in abundance were detected before and after logging. There was also no difference in abundance between the impact station and control stations. This seems to indicate that chimpanzees in this FMU did not move away from the impact station during logging operations and one might conclude on this basis that the species is tolerant of the logging practices at the site. In FMU 10.038 however, a significant drop in relative abundance was detected at the impact station after logging, evidenced by a lower encounter rate with chimpanzee signs than for those found in the two control stations. On the basis of the data from this concession one might draw the opposite conclusion: that chimpanzees are adversely affected by logging activities and move away from the associated disturbance.

The study did not identify any significant changes in population size of chimpanzee or of the sympatric western lowland gorilla as a consequence of logging operations across all sites. It is possible that in subsequent years different trends might become apparent, although the literature tends to suggest that the immediate post-disturbance phase is when wildlife are most impacted (White and Tutin, 2001; Arnhem et al., 2008). Thus the target species assessed in this study seem to have mostly been able to cope with the direct impacts of selective logging activities as they occur in Pallisco and SFID's FMUs. This is likely partly due to the low extraction rates of one stump per hectare ($0.01 \text{ km}^2/10\,000 \text{ m}^2$) and subsequent low levels of disturbance in these concessions and suggests that RIL associated with SFM is consistent with maintaining populations of large mammals.

Adapting logging to mitigate impacts on great apes

The identification and management of HCVF is a key concept in the FSC certification standard (Box 4.4). This is a potentially invaluable tool for wildlife conservation in the timber production landscape and has also been adopted as an industry standard in other sectors such as the Roundtable for Sustainable Palm Oil (RSPO).

HCVFs are perhaps more easily understood when they represent spatially discrete areas such as cultural sites for local people or riverine forest that maintain ecosystem functions. Identifying areas vital for threatened species, particularly for mobile larger mammals, can prove more challenging.

ZSL promotes the concept that the core territories of chimpanzee communities represent refuges for the species and should be viewed as HCVF. These should be identified, mapped, and logging practices adapted in these areas to minimize their impacts. To identify the core areas, timber company wildlife teams use an adaptive sampling method, developed by ZSL, to more efficiently survey large blocks of production forests by concentrating survey effort in areas where apes are more abundant. Adaptive Recce Transect Sampling (ARTS) involves walking "recce" transects, taking the easiest path along a pre-planned route and whenever a chimpanzee nest is encountered, cutting a cross of more rigorous straight line transects to identify additional nests and inform the core territory mapping process. In the example below, in SFID's FMU 10.056 (76 660 ha/767 km²), two areas with a high concentration of nest sites were identified using the ARTS method suggesting the presence of at least two chimpanzee communities in the logging block (Figures 4.9a and b).

On this basis a number of recommendations were made for the management of the forest block:

- To organize tree cuts to enable chimps to retreat to these core areas, i.e. to cut towards the core area, to alternate the cutting blocks in such a way as to avoid splitting the community, and to avoid erecting barriers that the chimps will not cross as harvesting approaches the core area.

- To establish annual monitoring of the HCVF areas and carry out surveys to identify core chimpanzee areas during the annual tree inventory prior to each annual allowable cut (AAC).

- To complement this with strategies to reduce poaching in the concession and in particular in the vulnerable areas when harvesting approaches the chimpanzee HCVF.

- To incorporate these recommendations into the overall forest management plans.

These recommendations have already begun to be implemented although proof of the efficacy of the management of these chimpanzee HCVFs will only be seen in the monitoring program over the coming years.

While not elaborated on here, other aspects of the WWP that are part of the holistic approach to improving the management of logging concessions for the benefit of conservation include:

- mitigating disease transmission through the development of health protocols for company staff (see Chapter 7 for more information on the dangers of disease transmission),

- developing management strategies to mitigate unsustainable and illegal hunting that not only involve the private sector but also local communities (see Chapter 7). In fact, engagement with local communities is an explicit action that considers them an essential component of the forest ecosystem. Engaging communities is considered essential to empower them to play a role in managing their resources.

FIGURE 4.9

(a) Density of chimpanzee signs observed within one active five-year logging block, collected using ARTS methodology

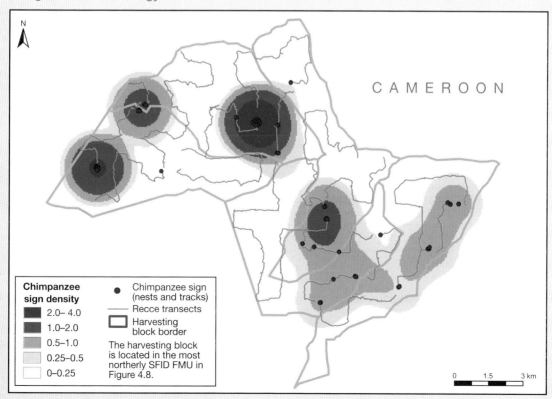

FIGURE 4.9

(b) Data from (a) enable core areas of use for chimpanzees to be identified and mapped and for logging regimes to be adapted to mitigate their impacts

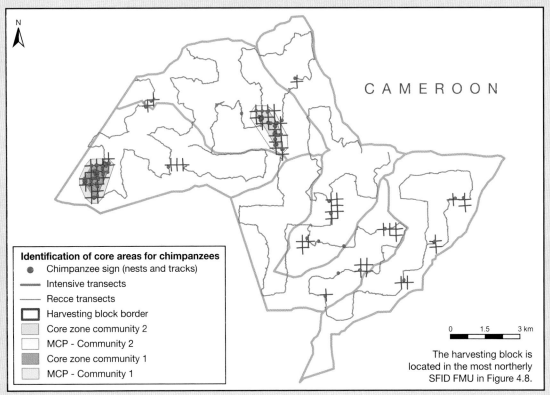

CAMEROON

Identification of core areas for chimpanzees
- ● Chimpanzee sign (nests and tracks)
- ━━ Intensive transects
- ── Recce transects
- ▢ Harvesting block border
- ▢ Core zone community 2
- ▢ MCP - Community 2
- ▮ Core zone community 1
- ▢ MCP - Community 1

0   1.5   3 km

The harvesting block is located in the most northerly SFID FMU in Figure 4.8.

MCP (minimum convex polygon) indicates the boundaries of the community's home range.
© ZSL.

When viewed together, the FSC principles and criteria, forestry laws, and other guidelines appear to comprehensively address the issues relating to sustainable forest management and ensuring good outcomes for wildlife. They explicitly state the criteria that a forestry operation must meet and in the case of the FSC they include both indicators and means of verification for demonstrating that they have been achieved.

These case studies demonstrate that initial research at the interface of responsible logging and great apes indicates that they can co-exist, however only a very small number of companies are applying the techniques outlined in these contexts. Further to this, the costs of engaging logging companies to implement more ecologically friendly practices have been borne by conservation organizations, raising questions about the viability of this approach at a wider scale.

Conclusion

Insights from the Goualougo Triangle and the WWP have illustrated the importance of collaboration between the logging industry, conservationists, and local governments to address the environmental dimensions of sustainable forestry that can mitigate the

impacts on apes. Engagement beyond areas of strict protection becomes a necessity when attempts at conservation have failed and logging is moving forward. Developing more efficient and informative ways of assessing ape habitat and designing actions that protect ape resource needs in the context of timber exploitation then becomes an important way to mitigate the impacts of logging.

However, research that focuses on the broader impacts of current SFM practice on forest ecology points to wider repercussions to biodiversity beyond single species such as apes, highlighting the need for additional research on the interaction between the broader impacts of logging on forest ecosystems and local communities. Without a better understanding at this interface, current SFM practice is likely to be inadequate to meaningfully reconcile conservation and industrial logging. Furthermore initial exploitation of primary forest by selective logging is linked to an increased probability of these areas being converted to plantations or agroforestry areas. This further diminishes biodiversity stock and eliminates options for meaningful SFM. Additional analysis of the policy and legislative environments can provide some insights into the causes of this trajectory and represents an added gap in current understanding.

Although there is an acknowledgment that strict protection is always the preferred course of conservation action, pressures on tropical forest ecosystems are unlikely to diminish in the foreseeable future. Local and global demand for the resources that forests provide, alongside competition for the forested land itself from agriculture, agroforestry, urbanization, and mining are on-going and are crucial factors for increasing engagement by a range of stakeholders. Unless other models are developed that move beyond private logging concessions, such as timber plantations in degraded lands, encroachment of logging into primary forest and ape habitats will continue. Ultimately, it appears that SFM benefits great ape conservation within the current context of poor environmental management in many ape range states, but this does not necessarily assure longer-term benefit. In addition, there need to be greater incentives, through fund-ing and other mechanisms, to encourage change in practice and behavior by logging companies. At present, best practice is not generally the standard that is adhered to.

Acknowledgments

Principal author: Helga Rainer

Contributors: Eric Arnhem, Laure Cugnière, Oliver Fankem, Global Witness, Erik Meijaard, David Morgan, Paul De Ornellas, PNCI, Chris Ransom, Crickette Sanz, Serge Wich, and ZSL

Photo: Extractive industries (mining, and oil and gas) have undergone notable growth in Asian ape states, and now pose a threat to several species. Opencast coal mine in Vietnam. © Terry Whittaker

CHAPTER 5

Mining/oil extraction and ape populations and habitats

Introduction

The extractive industries overlap extensively with ape habitat across Asia and Africa. In both regions, these industries are growing in intensity and scale, with increasing amounts of exploration and development/production in areas of land previously unexploited. Africa, in particular, is experiencing an unprecedented surge in mineral and hydrocarbon development, and the landscape is quite literally being turned upside down in search of the materials and energy that drive the global economy. The significant peak in exploration in the past decade was from 2000–08, with a gradual but significant slowdown over the past 5 years (J. Suter, personal communication, 2013). Although the mineral and hydrocarbon industry directly affects the landscape at a different scale to that of the forestry industry, broad-scale changes to habitat structure and composition can result from both direct and indirect impacts generated during the project exploration, development, operation, and closeout phases of mineral/hydrocarbon projects.

Far less is known about the impacts of mining and hydrocarbon project development (including exploration, analysis, site selection, construction, operations, closure, and post-closure) than about the impacts of logging. Chapter 4 explores the impacts of logging in greater detail. There are few published studies on the impacts of mining, oil, and gas projects (exploration and development) on African or Asian ape populations (Kormos and Kormos, 2011b). It is evident, however, that mining and hydrocarbon exploration and development processes are impacting the habitats and populations of all taxa of apes both directly and indirectly. Across Africa and Asia, extractive industries are affecting the social, cultural, and ecological fabric of the region. The extractive industries can be an economic engine with valuable local and regional benefits for both local people and national economies. However, mining cannot be done without negative social and environmental impacts in localized areas. The challenge is to find the "best balance" for co-existence.

To fully understand and address the threats to apes, a range-wide analysis of the overlap between ape range and extractive industries is needed. The range of each ape species should be compared with the known areas of potential mineral distribution. Once the oil, gas, and/or mining lease is issued, the land can be exploited. However, if the review is done before leases are issued, so that they avoid the most important conservation areas, then reserves and set-asides can be designated. A review of ape habitat compared with areas designated as exploration and exploitation leases for mining, oil, and gas would help identify what proportion of each species range is in areas

designated for industrial activities, and provide information for conservation practitioners on strategies to avoid and mitigate damage. Support for best practices can then be targeted towards concessions of high value for apes.

In conjunction, long-term longitudinal studies are needed to understand more completely the impacts of all extractive industries (logging, mining, and oil and gas) on apes. Such studies would enable mining companies and national governments to be more effective in avoiding negative impacts throughout the project cycle by carefully locating concessions and associated operations. These should start with the establishment of accurate biodiversity baselines before any industrial activities have taken place, and track the impacts on ape populations in the same location over time. Ideally, such studies would be completed before an area is opened to mineral exploitation, and therefore would need to be funded and implemented by a government/nongovernmental organization (NGO) collaborative effort, rather than mining companies. It could be an impact-offsetting action for industry to support future offsite studies such as these, as part of their mitigation commitments. Although these currently happen on a site-specific basis within the mineralized area footprint, they need to happen across a broader landscape, as it is likely that the effects of the project will cover a much larger area. Such studies would provide a more appropriate understanding of the impact of industrial activities, and the effectiveness of mitigation techniques. It is also important, however, to study the broader landscape so that areas that will not be impacted by the project can be enhanced and protected, rather than just the area that will in all likelihood be significantly impacted/destroyed.

As described below, a number of strategies exist to ensure that the negative impact of extractive industries is minimized to the extent practical, and these are described as part of the "mitigation hierarchy." In summary, these are described as prevention, avoidance, minimization, and reduction, and then reparation and restoration. Only finally are biodiversity offset strategies developed to ensure that harm to ape populations in one area is offset by enhanced ape conservation impact in another area. If any biodiversity offsets are established it is essential that research and monitoring are carried out into their effectiveness for ape conservation. A critical research question that remains is whether or not offset strategies actually achieve a net gain. This would most simply be measured as whether population losses at the impact site are more than compensated for by conservation gains at the offset site (Chapter 1).

Based on experience where industry has partnered with conservation agencies to identify and implement best practices, it is recommended that:

- The conservation community works with the private sector to assist responsible and willing companies to implement and share experience of best and leading-edge practices, including but not limited to certification, and appropriate use of the mitigation hierarchy including biodiversity offsets (with reference to the Business and Biodiversity Offset Programme (BBOP) principles).

- Conservationists and the private sector lobby governments to establish a policy environment that at a minimum removes disincentives for best practice, and where possible supports best practice; for example, exemption of land tax on conservation set-asides in mining concessions, clear offset policies, and legislation that supports retiring unallocated land (land that is currently not assigned for exploration or mine development lease or concession) from mining activities.

- All stakeholders support and promote the enforcement of existing laws, par-

ticularly in relation to illegal logging, illegal mining, hunting, and agricultural encroachment.

- Independent Environmental and Social Impact Assessments (ESIAs) and Strategic Environmental Assessments (SEAs) should be carried out, which include detailed examination of the direct, and the indirect, impacts of development on people and biodiversity.

- All best practice management systems should include a rigorous monitoring program to evaluate the effectiveness of ape conservation measures. This must be linked to a system of adaptive management whereby lessons are learned and actions improved.

- Conservationists and industries should be more proactive in raising awareness of guidance and management tools which are already available to support best practice, for example the Orangutan Conservation Services Program (OCSP) Best Management Practice (BMP) tools, Business and Biodiversity Offsets Program (BBOP) publications, and the International Council on Mining and Metals (ICMM) guidelines, such as the independent report on biodiversity offsets (ICMM and IUCN, 2012).

Annex III provides a more detailed overview of specific recommendations for the responsible management of apes in the extractive industry sector.

Overview of impact of mining/oil on ape habitats and populations

A global, broad-scale analysis conducted by the UNEP World Conservation Monitoring Center (WCMC) of all apes across their range, including gorillas, chimpanzees, bonobos, orangutans, and gibbons, indicates that only five of the 27 ape taxa analyzed have no mining projects within their range. This survey examined the overlap of ape ranges from the International Union for Conservation of Nature (IUCN) Red List (in some cases refined by more recent, peer reviewed data from the A.P.E.S. Portal[1] and other publications), with mining data from the Mine-Search database of the Metals Economic Group.[2] The MineSearch database covers projects with a focus on a set of 37 core commodities, including coal, iron ore, and other minerals and metals. The taxa with no mining projects within their range are also the species with some of the smallest ranges, namely mountain gorillas (*Gorilla beringei beringei*), Cross River gorillas (*Gorilla gorilla diehli*), Nigerian–Cameroon chimpanzees

(*Pan troglodytes ellioti*), Hainan black-crested gibbons (*Nomascus hainanus*), and eastern black-crested gibbons (*Nomascus nasutus*).

For the majority of taxa, where mining projects in the various phases of their implementation do overlap with the habitat of apes, it is important to note that the spatial scale of ape ranges is significantly different to the footprints of mining operations. Ape ranges generally cover thousands of kilometers, while mining operations are represented in this analysis with a spatial resolution of 1 km². As a consequence of these significantly different spatial scales, less than 0.02% of each taxon's range is spatially coincident with points (mining pixels) identified as containing one or more mining projects. However, as well as the possibility

FIGURE 5.1

Great ape action plan sites (priority areas) and their spatial coincidence with mining pixels

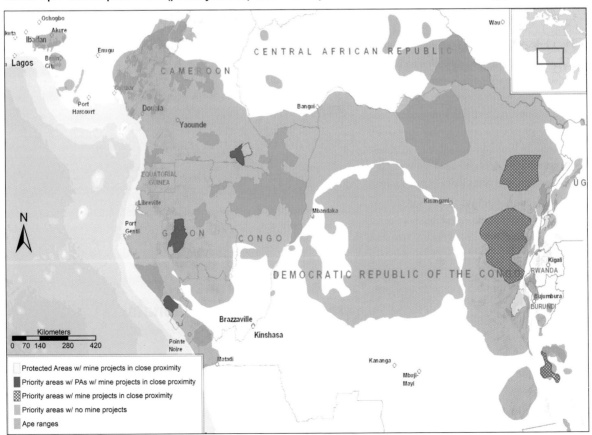

of significant localized impacts, the mining pixels that do contain mining projects at one or more stages of their development and operation could potentially have a much more extensive impact on the forest – such as from roads, infrastructure, etc. – than is indicated by the specific point of the operation. Species with only one mining project within their range are the bonobo (*Pan paniscus*), Kloss' gibbon (*Hylobates klossii*) and pileated gibbon (*Hylobates pileatus*). In each of these taxa, a single mining project is currently undertaking development activities. This statistic does not preclude the presence of artisanal operations within the species range but is indicative of no (or a low number of) corporate operations within the range of these taxa.

A key characteristic of all ape taxa analyzed is the predominance of activities that are part of the exploration and evaluation phase of the mining project within their ranges. This identifies the potential future threats from mining operations, and allows these potential threats to be flagged. It should be noted, however, that the number of exploration and evaluation projects is not necessarily indicative of the level of future threat from operational mines. Only a very small proportion of exploration licenses actually develop into commercially profitable mines. However, a concentration of development activities suggests the existence of commodity reserves within ape ranges and the potential for future issues/conflicts in relation to resource exploitation.

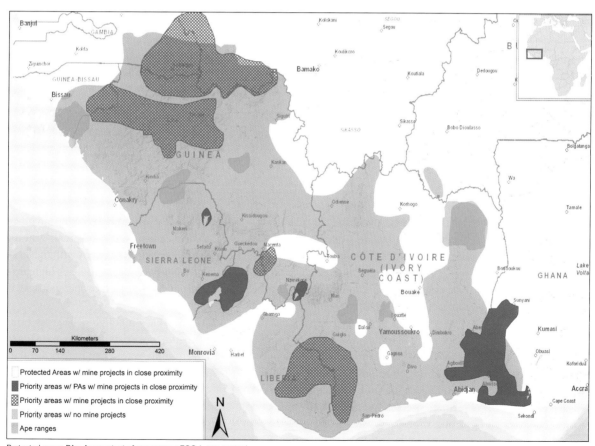

Protected areas: PAs. Apes extent of occurrence: EOO (= ape ranges).

Courtesy of UNEP-WCMC.

Data sources: Kormos and Boesch, 2003; Tutin *et al.*, 2005; Plumptre *et al.*, 2010; Morgan *et al.*, 2011; ESRI, 2012; IUCN, 2012c; IUCN and UNEP-WCMC, 2012; SNL, 2012

FIGURE 5.2

Asian protected areas which coincide with the range of one or more ape species and contain, or are in close proximity to, mining pixels (split according to their development stage)

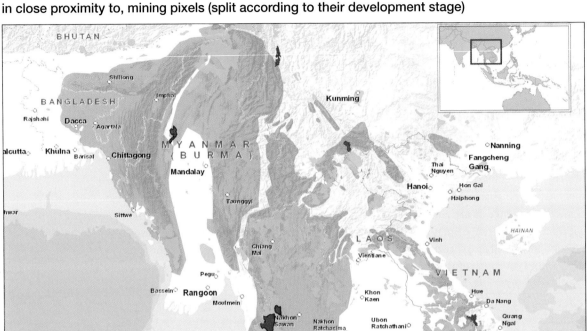

The two taxa that have the most notable overlap with mining operations are the Bornean orangutan (*Pongo pygmaeus*) and western chimpanzee (*Pan troglodytes verus*). Five percent of protected areas within the range of *Pongo pygmaeus* contain, or are in close proximity to, mining operations. The range is spatially coincident with 17 mining projects of which four are producing operations and 11 are development activities. Such high spatial coincidence between the refined species range and mining is a strong indication that this species has a high interaction with mining operations. *Pan troglodytes verus* is also identified as having a significantly higher number of mining activities present within its range than other taxa. The range of the Bornean gibbon (*Hylobates muelleri*) overlaps with the largest number of productive mines, a high proportion of which are surface operations, such as open-pit mines.

The overview highlights the cross-taxa, cross-regional overlap between ape ranges and the mining sector. Both in Africa and in Asia, mining operations overlap the ranges of apes and indicate significant potential conflict. It is difficult, however, to rank the impacts of mining operations on the different taxa analyzed without more detailed information on taxa-specific sensitivities to different mining activities.

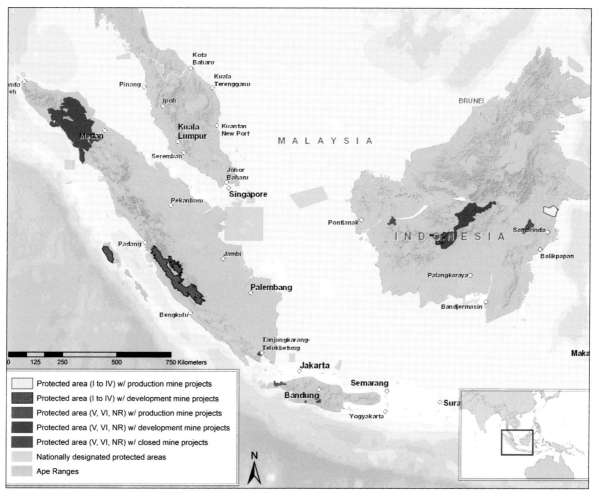

Courtesy of UNEP-WCMC.

Data sources: ESRI, 2012; IUCN, 2012c; IUCN and UNEP-WCMC, 2012; SNL, 2012; Wich *et al.*, 2012b).

Extractive industry processes and potential impacts on habitat and species populations

Extraction of the Earth's mineral resources inherently causes environmental and social impacts. This is an especially sensitive issue when exploration prospects are identified within high-biodiversity areas, or suitable habitat for great apes. The accumulations of the Earth's natural resources often occur in some of its most underdeveloped regions, where people are poor, lack cultivable food sources, and have extensive subsistence cultural practices. Yet when mineral resources are discovered in economic quantities, they represent an extremely significant engine for economic development in the region, and potentially a mechanism to improve people's livelihoods and welfare. Despite significant advances to improve the terms of mining contracts and transparency of benefit/wealth sharing, many challenges still exist that have continued to exclude rural indigenous communities from the economic benefits of mineral development contracts. Considering the current uncertainties about energy supply and the expected rise in future demand for hydrocarbons and other minerals, particularly due to global economic growth and technology development in Asia and Africa, there is an urgent need to develop strategies to ensure that development in this sector can be conducted in a way that does not require a sacrifice of natural and social capital.

Prior to moving forward with conservation responses it is important to recognize where and how extractive industries affect apes and their habitat during each phase of a project development cycle:

- **Phase 1:**
  Exploration and evaluation
- **Phase 2:**
  Preliminary engineering and alternatives analysis
- **Phase 3:**
  Final engineering and site selection
- **Phase 4:**
  Construction and commissioning
- **Phase 5:**
  Operation, closure, and post-closure.[3]

Some of these impacts are a direct consequence of industry actions, while others are the indirect consequences of other subsistence or commercial activities that have been put in place as a result of the work or financial activity generated by extractive industries. Increasingly, these direct and closely linked indirect consequences are further intensified by the cumulative impacts resulting from multiple industries operating within the same landscapes. While it is often difficult to isolate specific impacts as being the sole responsibility of one actor, it is still crucially important to recognize where and how extractive industries may be contributing to threats through their project life cycles. Identifying and acknowledging these contributions becomes the first critical step in formulating truly effective mitigation responses and, ideally, can form the basis for more effective *ex-ante* planning.

While there are few specific studies on the impacts of mining on Asian and African apes, they can be inferred from studies on

Photo: Mining impacts may be relatively localized, but extremely intensive. Aerial shot of a drill pad in cleared forest, Indonesia.
© Bardolf Paul

other taxa elsewhere. In contrast to forestry, which typically causes extensive degradation over a wide area, mining impacts may be relatively localized, but extremely intensive. Logging operations might take place across almost all of a 2000 km² concession, whereas even a large open-pit mine (and ancillary facilities) might have a footprint of only 30 km². This footprint, however, will involve complete destruction of all ape habitat. The impacts of mining on biodiversity fall into two categories, direct and indirect (ICMM, 2006; TBC, 2012). Direct impacts include: habitat loss from mines, roads, processing facilities, tailings dams, etc.; and potential pollution from fugitive chemicals, noise, and dust. Mines use extensive and costly tankage and liner systems to contain process fluids to the maximum practical extent, and apply a variety of noise and dust mitigation strategies. Environmental assessments evaluate the risk of potential accidents and failures on the various receiving resources. Indirect impacts may include: building of roads allowing access to the forest for hunting, logging, and agricultural encroachment; and hunting and logging by company staff. Chapter 4 describes the impacts of logging on apes, based on extensive and long-term research. The indirect impacts of mining are often comparable to those of logging, leading to very similar effects on ape populations, and are likely to be comparable in significance in terms of ape and habitat loss (for more information on indirect impacts, see Chapter 7).

Potential cumulative impacts of extractive industries during the project life cycle and action to address them

The study of impacts of extractive industries on wildlife is still too incomplete to provide a definitive picture of the consequences of each phase of project development, or of the cumulative impacts that may occur. Observational and conjectural data derived from recent field studies carried out in the vicinity of extractive industry sites do provide some insight into probable risks and threats to apes during the extractive industry life cycle. Chapter 3 outlines some of these impacts on apes.

Most oil and mining projects proceed through a similar set of phases (Figure 5.3) implemented over the course of the project life cycle, which for small projects may only be a few years, but for larger ones, could be many decades. Each stage of the development process can be expected to raise the threat of distinct impacts, whose intensity, scale, and duration will vary, and on occasion accumulate over time.

Phase 1

Prospecting

Before committing to the development of a concession, most of the more reputable companies will carry out a series of preliminary studies to evaluate the potential financial, social, and environmental risks, as well as the institutional risks to future company operations and reputation that the project may incur. These studies are generally conducted as desk exercises, but may occasionally include limited field activities. Much exploration is carried out by smaller companies, without the resources or incentive to do this screening, and who may only have the incentive to do this once exploration has demonstrated the presence of a valuable resource that can be sold to a larger company, to recoup the initial exploration investment. Few impacts typically occur during this phase of the project life cycle unless actual field studies are carried out.

FIGURE 5.3

Typical development cycle for a mineral prospect

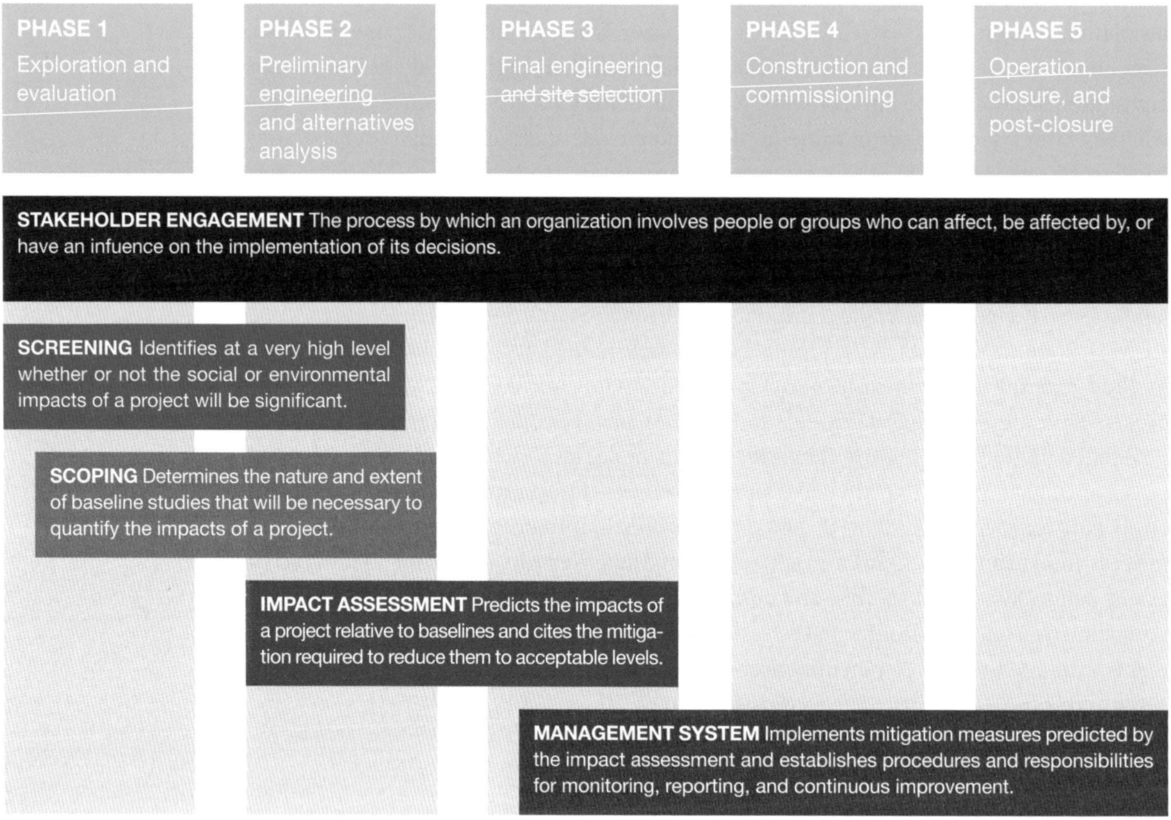

PHASE 1	PHASE 2	PHASE 3	PHASE 4	PHASE 5
Exploration and evaluation	Preliminary engineering and alternatives analysis	Final engineering and site selection	Construction and commissioning	Operation, closure, and post-closure

STAKEHOLDER ENGAGEMENT The process by which an organization involves people or groups who can affect, be affected by, or have an infuence on the implementation of its decisions.

SCREENING Identifies at a very high level whether or not the social or environmental impacts of a project will be significant.

SCOPING Determines the nature and extent of baseline studies that will be necessary to quantify the impacts of a project.

IMPACT ASSESSMENT Predicts the impacts of a project relative to baselines and cites the mitigation required to reduce them to acceptable levels.

MANAGEMENT SYSTEM Implements mitigation measures predicted by the impact assessment and establishes procedures and responsibilities for monitoring, reporting, and continuous improvement.

Courtesy of B. Filas

Exploration and appraisal

A commitment to acquire a concession requires companies to carry out field studies to gain a more thorough understanding of the extent, quality, and marketability of subsurface resources, and of the social and environmental risks that may be associated with their extraction. Seismic surveying and exploratory drilling are likely to be carried out during this phase with the objective of proving or disproving the presence of commercially viable quantities of exploitable metals, minerals, or hydrocarbons. Most survey sites and drill pads will typically be small in area, often requiring the clearing or disruption of only a few hectares of vegetation, or less, in each site. However, there could easily be hundreds of such sites scattered across the landscape with an elaborate network of secondary and tertiary roads and access trails constructed or rehabilitated to service each site. The transport infrastructure may begin to fragment available habitat, and species such as gorillas that are reluctant to stray far from home territories may become isolated. Many ape groups may also be severely disrupted by the significant increase in noise and disturbance of traditional feeding and nesting sites, and of other habitat within their range.

A centralized field station will also likely be established to service prospecting and exploration teams. Such stations frequently cover large areas, and inject significant amounts of capital into local economies.

This new capital can result in a dramatic rise in bushmeat hunting to meet increased demand as locals and industry workers can now afford to buy bushmeat with their salaries. The new influx of human residents also increases the risk of disease transmission to apes and the possible introduction of exotic species, which can reduce or compete for food supplies. In many cases the new human residents have come from far afield in the hope of employment, so that even if the local community has a taboo against eating apes (such as along the southern Congo and Gabon coastline), the new arrivals may not. This can further result in a weakening of local tradition. Finally, new residents are sometimes driven to clear forest in order to cultivate staple food crops, thus further reducing the area available to wildlife and native vegetation. For more information on these indirect impacts, see Chapter 7.

Screening: Once a company receives authorization to conduct exploration activities within a given area by the host country government, a preliminary exploration program is planned. High-level screening (Figure 5.3) is typically initiated prior to the initial field activities to determine if development of the prospect may result in social, environmental, or other impacts that could affect project viability or be a fatal flaw to development. Local and regional stakeholders are identified during this phase and relationship development is evaluated.

Scoping: To understand scoping (Figure 5.3), a definition of common mining development terms may be helpful. "Resource discipline" means areas of expertise in the fields of minerals, air, surface and ground water, land, humans, and flora and fauna. "Project alternatives" means the identification of various methods and/or locations of development investigated and preliminary assessment of potential mitigation and types for each

option. Scoping provides the background required to design the impact assessment in detail and to determine the nature and scope of specialist studies that will be required. It is at this stage that site-specific baseline studies are laid out for each of the potentially affected resource disciplines relative to the footprints of the more probable project alternatives. It is also a phase when estimates of the cost of the impact study are compiled.

It is important to keep in mind that screening, and to a lesser extent scoping, activities occur very early in the project cycle, when little or no subsurface exploration has been conducted. The company does not yet know if the geologic indications they have identified on the ground will prove commercially feasible for development.

Phases 2 and 3

Preliminary engineering and alternatives analysis and final engineering and site selection

During these phases, efforts are focused on determining whether or not the mineral resource is worth pursuing further. Hence, land disturbance associated with initial exploration activities will usually be limited. Small excavations, pit digging, and/or drilling activities may unavoidably involve opening up corridors through the forest to access mineralized zones. Early-stage exploration is typically systematically widely spaced to determine the extent of the mineralization. Advanced-stage exploration will then involve infill drilling between the wider-spaced excavations undertaken for those preliminary investigations, to more clearly define the specific nature and extent of the deposit.

Impact assessment: Most companies will typically prepare the comprehensive impact assessment (Figure 5.3) during this phase of the project cycle. The ESIA is the process by which the impacts that project development, operation, and closure will have on the local environment and people are assessed. It includes the collection of detailed site-specific data that characterize potential impacts for all resource disciplines. Ideally, baseline data are collected for at least 1 year in order to adequately characterize the seasonal variation in certain resources, and may require longer periods depending on site-specific circumstances. In particular, surface water and groundwater and flora and fauna species are usually subject to seasonal variation so it is important that the characterization study period is sufficient to adequately document these variations. This is an area, however, where weakness often comes up, as the baseline data are often absent, weak, or of far too short a duration to illustrate the reality (see Chapter 8). The process and methods of the ESIA are often not transparent, and independent, qualified evaluation by an internationally recognized body with ape expertise is recommended (e.g., International Association of Impact Assessment or IUCN Primate Specialist Group/Section on Great Apes (SGA)).

Once the baseline conditions are characterized, discipline-specific resource experts will "superimpose" or model the development, operating, and closure plans onto the resource baseline conditions and predict the impacts associated with the development over the life of the project. Depending on impact significance, experts will identify mitigation measures that can reduce predicted impacts to acceptable levels. That is not to say that project impacts are eliminated; mining results in short- and long-term impacts, both positive (economic development) and negative (affected resources). The impact assessment is the means by which that "best balance" can be found between the positive and negative effects.

Note that mining industry professionals and the consultants involved become keenly aware, through the scoping and impact assessment research they conduct, that not developing a mineral resource can be a negative impact of its own. Ape habitat protection is directly affected by the lack of any type of economic opportunity for local impoverished people with steadily increasing protein food source needs that exacerbate the pressure on the bushmeat trade. The questions are:

1. Can the impact mitigation measures adequately balance the economic development needs so that over the long term ape population numbers and habitat are better protected? and

2. Will the local people develop better protein sources and move away from historical cultural practices that currently have a negative impact on ape populations without development?

The ESIA will often follow national guidelines, if any exist, or those required by lenders or donors, if outside funding has been obtained to advance a project. National requirements in many countries are weak, but Equator Principles, which are embraced by most international lenders financing mining projects, are the main ESIA guidance. The challenge is largely in the interpretation of these guidelines, and the degree of rigor in their application. This has been illustrated in numerous examples, including in the Guinea case study highlighted in Chapter 8. It may therefore be important to include supplemental processes that can support and greatly enhance the ESIA results, as described in Chapter 8.

There is a need for transparency, the sharing of data on impacts and sharing of lessons learned. Studies undertaken as part of the ESIA process result in a wealth of valuable information. However, as previously indicated, this data is generally inaccessible to scientists as it is restricted by confidentiality clauses. Mining companies would contribute significantly to scientific knowledge and understanding and the development of best practice by relaxing or excluding this confidentiality requirement.

Phase 4
Construction and commissioning

If the analysis of appraisal data meets the technical, financial, and corporate policy objectives then the company may decide to develop the resource field, a commitment that may result in the investment of hundreds of millions or billions of dollars over the life of the project, which in some cases may be several decades or more.

This phase of the project typically results in the most dramatic ecological changes and greatest period of disturbance for biodiversity in general and for individual species. Construction and commissioning activities may include more complete development of the transportation network both to move around the extraction area and to connect with regional distribution and shipping centers; construction of drilling and extraction production sites; and construction of facilities, such as pipelines and terminals, processing centers, and lodging and service centers for workers. The ESIA can help anticipate and respond to some of these impacts, although it is unlikely that the prior environmental assessments will take full account of the cumulative impacts likely to occur, or reveal

Photo: Drilling rig core mining for iron ore on Mount Avima in the Republic of Congo.
© Pauwel de Wachter/WWF

the actual magnitude of impacts. Predicting the future with 100% accuracy is unrealistic, and for this reason, management systems are developed alongside impact assessments to implement the mitigation and monitoring programs, and as such include reporting, transparency, and continuous improvement commitments as a fundamental element to enable companies to react in a timely manner to any issues that were not accurately predicted in the EIA. For many species, including apes, the responses to increased noise, habitat degradation or destruction, road and vehicle encounters, and increased hunting pressures may not become fully apparent until project implementation begins. Some unverified observations suggest that, when disturbed, a community of chimps or gorillas will generally migrate to adjacent territories, resulting in stress to both immigrant and resident populations. Females might be able to migrate between groups but males may be killed, form male-only groups, or in a few cases be integrated into a new group. For more details on the ecological impact of extractive industries on apes refer to Chapter 3.

Management systems: Management systems (Figure 5.3) define the specific steps by which the mitigation measures identified in the impact assessment will be implemented on the ground. The management system cites the system philosophy, relevant corporate policies, organization and management responsibilities, and the systems required to identify, organize, manage, and monitor impacts. For some impacted resources, it is necessary to develop discipline-specific management plans to further detail the specific actions and responsibilities for implementing the required mitigation.

The management system also includes provisions for audit, assessment, and continuous improvement of all implementing actions and defines the reporting process and methods for assuring transparency. An important element of the management system is the implementation schedule and budget, which specifically defines the monitoring, additional studies, and future activities to which the company has committed. It includes a capital and operating cost estimate for their implementation throughout the construction, commissioning, operation, closure, and post-closure phases of the project. This allows for all of the environmental and social program costs and the timing of their expenditure to be adequately and accurately factored into the overall project financial evaluation.

Phase 5

Operations

The construction and commissioning phase of an extractive resource development project transitions into the operations phase, and generally results in the continuous day-to-day production of metals, minerals, oil, or gas; maintenance of facilities; and transportation of the exploited materials to market via roads, pipelines, conveyor systems, and export terminals. In some cases, the most dramatic impacts on populations of species such as great apes will already be very apparent, with some individuals lost, groups disrupted or reduced in size, and overall population size and genetics altered.

One challenge for project managers during the operations phase is distinguishing between direct and indirect project impacts and enacting appropriate mitigation measures.

Closure and post-closure

When the commercial life of the extraction project comes to an end, a decommissioning process will typically be implemented to remove facilities and restore project sites to the degree feasible. Restoration work typically includes efforts to reclaim and revegetate the site, usually with the goals of eliminating safety hazards, establishing a stable land form and watershed, and restor-

> One challenge for project managers is distinguishing between direct and indirect project impacts and enacting appropriate mitigation measures.

ing the surface to an acceptable post-mining land use compatible with the surrounding uses. If the surrounding land use is undeveloped forest, the regrading and revegetation programs will strive to enhance the habitat to the maximum practical extent. Industry could benefit from the expertise of ecologists and primatologists to help ensure ape habitat is suitably restored. Mining companies usually have to post a reclamation surety to guarantee that the land will be reclaimed successfully and that surety is not released until after success is demonstrated through post-closure monitoring.

Some infrastructure, such as buildings, conveyors, or railway lines, may also be removed. Open pits or shafts may be filled in and land surfaces recontoured. Industrial wastes (e.g. lubricating oils, hydraulic fluids, coolants, solvents, and cleaning agents) will need to be treated similarly to wastes generated during mining activities, for example by placing them in containers for temporary storage or transport by a licensed hauler to an off-site disposal area.

Direct impacts to great apes from the decommissioning and close-out work may be similar to those experienced throughout the life of the project, as site disturbance levels from noise and physical disruptions are likely to be very high, but they diminish substantially during the closure phase.

Strategies to reduce the impact of mining, oil, and gas extraction on apes and biodiversity

Measures to reduce conflict between apes and industry

This section looks at three key approaches that are rapidly becoming central components in the requirements and practices being adopted by governments, lenders–donors, and companies to protect biodiversity: the preparation of SEAs to provide a cumulative overview of potential impacts across landscapes; the use of spatial planning tools to guide the practical implementation of mitigation hierarchy principles; and the application of the "mitigation hierarchy" as articulated by BBOP and the International Finance Corporation (IFC). In general practice, these three approaches are best combined to generate the data, analysis, and stakeholder response that permits a clear delineation of conservation threats, action targets, and response scenarios.

Strategic environmental assessments

As mentioned previously, most industries prepare a comprehensive ESIA during the exploration and appraisal phase of project development. Unfortunately, there are numerous examples of ESIAs that inadequately analyze the threats to biodiversity and are based on insufficient data and baselines. ESIAs are often prepared for isolated and specific development projects and do not take cumulative impacts into account, including the cumulative impacts from other economic sectors operating in the same landscape. As a consequence, the value of the ESIA is limited and provides poor guidance for mitigating, avoiding, and reducing harm/ threats to populations. Another challenge is the enforcement of the actions included in the ESIA to mitigate identified adverse impacts.

One option for strengthening the outputs and use of the ESIA is to provide a broader framework for viewing all industry developments proposed or taking place across a landscape, and include more specific guidelines and requirements for the ESIA process. Increasingly, governments, lenders–donors, and civil society groups are employing an SEA process to build this framework. SEAs are high-level decision-making procedures used to promote sustainable

> SEAs are high-level decision-making procedures used to promote sustainable development.

development. These assessments take place before decisions about individual extractive industry projects are made, and they generally include entire landscapes or regions as their frame of reference. The SEA can also serve as the mechanism to establish the key questions, criteria, and actions that should be included in a project-specific ESIA.

An SEA should be conducted at the very earliest stages of decision-making to help formulate broad-scale policies, plans, and programs and to assess their potential development effectiveness and sustainability. This distinguishes the SEA from more traditional environmental assessment tools. EIAs and ESIAs certainly have a proven track record in addressing the environmental threats and opportunities of specific projects. However, they are less easily applied to policies, plans, and any broader program. In this way the SEA serves to complement and provide the gateway and guidance for the EIA or ESIA and other assessment approaches and tools.

SEAs require extensive scoping among all groups who may be affected by direct or indirect impacts from regional development scenarios. Scoping sessions generally aim to identify when, how, and where it is best to develop extractive industry projects within the landscape or region in question, involving all the relevant stakeholders. SEAs usually place a great deal of emphasis on identifying information gaps in advance of individual project developments, and in this sense they can result in ESIAs that ultimately fill these gaps through the required research and field studies. SEAs also typically place a strong emphasis on identifying specific geographic areas likely to be highly sensitive to extractive industry projects, and the SEA will frequently include identification of opportunities to strengthen or establish protected areas and no-go zones, along with recommendations for protocols and standards to guide individual project developments (Kloff, Wicks, and Siegal, 2010).

Much of the emphasis in the development of the SEA is on assessing risk and predicting social and environmental effects over broad geographic areas from the potential mix of development actions. Thus scenario analysis and multi-criteria assessments, risk analysis, and the identification of mitigation opportunities become important components of the final SEA product. In this way the SEA provides an important initial step to support the use of more advanced spatial planning tools and the mitigation hierarchy.

The success of SEAs requires stakeholder consensus that absolutely needs to include buy-in by government. Private sector companies can work with technical experts, including NGOs, to explore and develop mutually acceptable solutions. As stated previously, these studies would ideally be carried out before industry comes in and would help identify areas for exploration and for conservation. In-country industry associations are the most likely opportunity for funding these studies.

In Cameroon, for example, there is both an established and active petrochemical industry association and a newly formed mining association. It would be in their interest to contribute to cumulative impact studies like SEAs, as it would contribute data, share costs, and demonstrate good corporate citizenship. Ideally, they would not just look at site-specific cumulative impact evaluations, but also look at it on a regional basis.

Although the IFC's Performance Standard (PS) 6 places the emphasis on site/project impacts (see Chapter 1), there would be significant benefit in examining broader scale impacts to understand how the site/project contributes to them. In the absence of a government-led planning process, a consortium of private sector companies may find it advantageous to engage in broad analysis of this type as a way to anticipate impacts and reduce overall risk.

Spatial data analysis and long-term conservation planning and monitoring

Spatial planning uses existing data to provide an integrated perspective on conditions, threats, and opportunities for improved biodiversity conservation across a specific geographic area, and helps to understand trade-offs in decision-making. The use of spatial planning tools typically includes measures to coordinate the spatial impacts of sectoral policies in order to achieve a more even distribution of economic development across a region or between regions than would otherwise be created by market forces, and to regulate the conversion of land and property uses (Economic Commission for Europe, 2008; Moilanen, Wilson, and Possingham, 2009).

Some of the decisions and actions that spatial planning typically seeks to support include:

- More socially and economically balanced development within regions, and improved competitiveness;
- Enhanced transportation and communication networks;
- Greater access to information and knowledge by affected stakeholders;
- Reduced environmental damage from all infrastructure as well as extractive development;
- Enhanced protection for biodiversity, ecosystem services, and natural heritage;
- Enhancement of cultural heritage as a factor for development;
- Development of energy resources while maintaining safety; and
- Limits to the impact of natural disasters.

Since most of these issues are cross-sectoral in nature, effective spatial planning should help to avoid duplication of effort by

Photo: Mine employee testing stream water, Indonesia. © Bardolf Paul

all actors engaged in development across a region or landscape, including governments, industry, civil society, communities, and individuals (Economic Commission for Europe, 2008).

Spatial planning processes thus become a potentially valuable tool for anticipating and responding to threats (in this case to great apes) by understanding trade-offs, and may incorporate a variety of methods and outputs. Its ultimate goal in this context would be to identify the optimal scenarios, decisions, and actions to reduce risks and maximize benefits for apes and their habitat in the face of impending extractive development proposals. The planning tool currently under development by the Wildlife Conservation Society (WCS) offers one perspective of how the spatial planning process can contribute to reducing threats from extractive industry developments.

Spatial planning processes, like the tool being developed by WCS, can provide an opportunity for government, industry, lender–donors, NGOs, and civil society to anticipate and prepare for potential adverse impacts early in the project life cycle. Like the SEA, they can provide a broader and richer understanding of direct and indirect cumulative impacts across a larger area than the project development site. Other tools that are used by the mining industry include the ICMM Sustainable Development Framework,[4] Good Practice Guidance for Mining and Biodiversity (ICMM, 2006), and Good Practice Guide for Indigenous Peoples and Mining (ICMM, 2010a), the IPIECA (global oil and gas industry association for environmental and social issues) Good Practice Standards and guidance documents,[5] and the International Association for Impact Assessment.[6] See Chapter 7 for information on how some of these voluntary guidelines address the indirect impacts of extractive industries.

The mitigation hierarchy: biodiversity offsets and compensation

The mitigation hierarchy is a best practice approach to managing biodiversity risk. The approach advocates applying efforts early in the development process to prevent or avoid adverse impacts to biodiversity wherever possible; then minimize and reduce impacts that cannot be avoided; and then repair or restore impacts that cannot be avoided, minimized, or reduced. Only after these initial actions to avoid, minimize or reduce, and repair or restore adverse impacts have been completed do project developers respond to any remaining residual effects. This is achieved through compensation measures for those residual impacts, or ideally and where feasible, creating a "biodiversity offset" through the process of the mitigation hierarchy. If an offset is not possible, some other form of compensation may be needed (see Figure 5.4).

The mitigation hierarchy forms a part of the IFC's Performance Standards and, for some industry representatives, it is the language of PS6 that states "the goal of biodiversity offsets is to achieve no net loss[7]" that presents a real challenge (B. Filas, personal communication, May 2013). The area

BOX 5.1

What are "biodiversity offsets"?

Biodiversity offsets are measurable conservation actions designed to respond to significant residual adverse impacts to biodiversity from project development. Offset actions are proposed and implemented after appropriate prevention and mitigation measures have already been applied. The goal of biodiversity offsets is to achieve **no net loss** (NNL) and preferably a net gain of biodiversity on the ground, with respect to species composition, habitat structure, ecosystem function, and people's use and cultural values associated with biodiversity.

While biodiversity offsets are defined here in terms of specific development projects (such as a road, mine, or well field), they can also be used to compensate for the broader effects of programs and plans.

Courtesy of WCS

FIGURE 5.4

The mitigation hierarchy and biodiversity impact

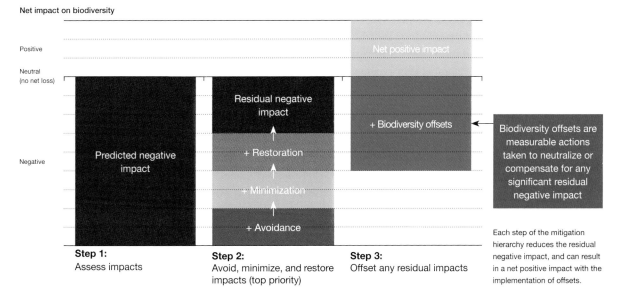

Net impact on biodiversity

Step 1:
Assess impacts

Step 2:
Avoid, minimize, and restore impacts (top priority)

Step 3:
Offset any residual impacts

Biodiversity offsets are measurable actions taken to neutralize or compensate for any significant residual negative impact

Each step of the mitigation hierarchy reduces the residual negative impact, and can result in a net positive impact with the implementation of offsets.

of impact identified by the IFC's PS6 is typically considered the area within which the company has control, which by definition is the mineralized area. Offsite areas can be of equal value, or even preferred habitat for species being offset, but the "no net loss" circle is typically drawn around the area under company control. Industry, government, and stakeholders need to work together here to identify the best offset areas and come up with accurate means to demonstrate no net loss.

The mitigation hierarchy process distinguishes between actions to "compensate" for residual impacts, and those to "offset" residual impacts. Compensation for residual impacts can take a variety of forms, including financial payments or funds established and managed over the life of a project to cover recurrent costs for conservation management. Offsets typically involve specific actions designed to ensure that an equal or greater area of identical habitat is protected or improved to compensate for an area destroyed or degraded as a result of residual project damage (Figure 5.5). It can also refer to individuals of a population, as well as habitat.

Examples of possible offset activities that may be included as a form of compensation include:

- Strengthening ineffective protected areas by investing in capacity building and other management activities for staff;
- Establishing new protected areas or no-go zones in collaboration with communities and government in order to conserve particular species and increase available habitat;
- Establish movement and dispersal corridors for wildlife;
- Establish or strengthen buffer zones adjacent to protected areas;
- Work with communities to develop alternative livelihoods that can reduce or eliminate unsustainable activities and hunting pressures.

Biodiversity offsets and other compensatory projects hold great potential to significantly reduce the impact of extensive commercial activities such as those inherent in large-scale extractive industry projects.

They are not a panacea, however, and must be designed to take into consideration the cumulative threats across the landscape or region to be effective. Offset projects that are designed for individual projects or in isolation from other planned or active developments in a region could result in an incomplete response to risks and threats that accumulate from multiple projects and industries across large geographic areas. In some cases, individual offset proposals will be too small to affect the landscape scale impacts facing a species at risk. There is also a risk that poorly coordinated offset projects omit to account for other regional or national conservation strategies, and thereby negate or fail to support conservation priorities, and represent a lost opportunity for greater conservation impact (Kormos and Kormos, 2011b). There are significant methodological challenges, costs, and time associated with NNL and *net positive impact* (NPI) for great apes. Generating population estimates within relevant geographic areas is difficult and time consuming, and should include both directly affected areas as well as surrounding areas into which the apes may migrate, or potential offset areas. These challenges are described in greater detail in Chapter 8.

Ideally, offsets should be designed and implemented as part of a national planning effort taking into account the cumulative impacts of development in the country, and contributing to and nested in existing national conservation strategies, including recovery plans for IUCN-recognized threatened and endangered species and protected area strategies (Kormos and Kormos, 2011a, 2011b). It is very likely that government-endorsed national offset and compensation strategies would be more effective if supported and overseen by transparent institutions (including conservation trust funds), to ensure permanent funding to deliver conservation outcomes over the long term.

A key factor in the development of any compensation or offset strategy is the assurance that investments in conservation or offset activities do not simply provide a mechanism to allow inappropriate developments to move forward. This is particularly true in areas of rare, unique, or highly threatened species and ecosystems, and it may be distinctly true in the last areas harboring the world's great apes. Thus all compensation and offset strategies proposed in great ape habitat must ensure that appropriate monitoring, planning, and management mechanisms are in place and secure over the

FIGURE 5.5

The role of offsets in a biodiversity compensation strategy

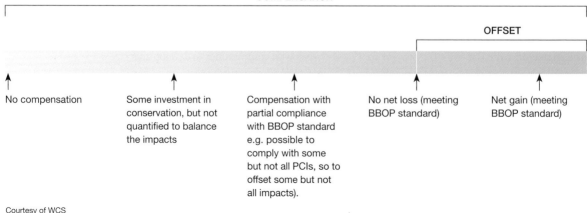

Courtesy of WCS

long term to guarantee that the compensation objectives are achieved (Carroll, Fox, and Bayon, 2009).

Optimally, the collective process of avoiding, minimizing, repairing, and compensating or offsetting will produce NNL of biodiversity. The concept of NNL and NPI for biodiversity is a central principle in the mitigation hierarchy process, and often raises concerns as a risky or impractical goal for extractives. There is an implicit assumption that the implementation of an extractives project always results in some biodiversity loss. Changes in populations, composition or structure of biodiversity could very well occur, particularly in the immediate site of a mining, oil, or gas development project. In some cases, such as in the immediate vicinity of a large, open-pit mine, these changes are unavoidable; however, the NNL principle requires industry to identify actions that can lead to a situation where targeted conservation actions can result in gains in population, composition, and structure for species and ecosystems that will match (NNL), or in the case of NPI, exceed any losses incurred. To accomplish this it is necessary to establish a wide enough geographic sphere of influence to permit populations to disperse or relocate, and a time frame of reference that will permit the recovery or expansion of disturbed groups. This requires collaboration between the company, with limited land under its control, and the government, which manages the extended lands. When this point is achieved, field assessments are necessary to confirm that the "quantity" and "quality" of biodiversity present in the defined affected area remain relatively constant over space and time.

There will unquestionably be instances where NNL may be extraordinarily difficult, if not impossible to attain. In such cases a like-for-like offset of the residual impacts on biodiversity may be beyond reach and a project would be restricted to implementing compensation actions that strive to incur the least amount of biodiversity loss possible, while accepting that some loss will occur. It is essential for projects employing the mitigation hierarchy to acknowledge these risks and possibilities at the outset. This may be particularly important in situations where great apes occur, since the potential impacts of extractive industries on apes can be severe and long lasting.

The aim of achieving NNL is based on two important concepts: first is that the entity causing the impacts is responsible for paying for that compensation, and second, that the compensation financing will be put in place for at least as long as the impacts last, or ideally in perpetuity, to ensure the permanence of conservation outcomes. If an SEA has been completed in advance of a company obtaining a mineral concession, they have the information needed to make informed decisions and estimates on the level of effort and cost of compensation before major investment in a project is made, which can then be factored into the feasibility analysis. Although some companies may be concerned with the costs, they will be able to assess them up front, allowing them to make important informed decisions before making significant investments. Ideally this should lead to increased additional financing for conservation of key habitat and species. Further, it is essential to demonstrate that mitigation actions are additional to already planned conservation actions, and that proposed conservation measures are not duplicative or redundant. Mitigation is generally far more expensive than avoidance. As a consequence, industry and ape experts must work together from the outset, rather than after the fact. Ape "experts" must also be credible and have real expertise. It is challenging for industry to distinguish between the real experts and less qualified

scientists just looking for income. An international certification scheme, set up by the IUCN SGA, for example, could provide credible recommendations of ape experts to industry.

Integrating SEA, spatial planning, and mitigation hierarchy into broad conservation planning

As mentioned earlier, the application of the SEA, spatial planning, and mitigation hierarchy tools at a program or project scale can typically become a closely integrated process that produces the data, analysis, and stakeholder response that permits a clear delineation of conservation threats, action targets, and response scenarios. These steps are proving to be essential to achieve realistic and long-term conservation outcomes. Even in those cases where it is not possible to achieve NNL or NPI, there exists the ability to explore compensation actions that deliver the best possible conservation results on the ground. Table 5.1 provides a concise overview of how these approaches can be seamlessly integrated.

The mitigation hierarchy is endorsed by an increasingly wide body of business, government, lenders, donors, NGOs, and civil society groups, and can provide important principles and protocols to guide the application of these actions on the ground. However, the mitigation hierarchy differs from the SEA and spatial planning in one very important respect – it can be applied on a site-specific level. A company or producer can decide to apply the mitigation hierarchy as part of a voluntary determination to apply best practice and reduce its biodiversity risk. Thus the mitigation hierarchy could be relegated to project- or site-specific concerns, which could prevent the recognition and mitiga-

TABLE 5.1

Applying an integrated process of SEA, mitigation hierarchy, and spatial planning

At a landscape or project scale:
Government commissions an SEA *to review policies and programs* that will influence extractive industry development strategies across a landscape or region.
Spatial planning tools applied to *reveal impact threats and identify mitigation solutions.*
Develop baseline data and ongoing monitoring programs to *quantify biodiversity values* at the site and landscape level.
Use species distribution models and systematic conservation planning tools to *produce best practice mitigation measures and biodiversity offset plans.*
Build the technical and management expertise to *implement offsets.*
Ensure the permanence of implemented offsets by establishing resilient legal and financial mechanisms for offset management.
At a global, regional, and national scale:
Ensure the availability of technical support to lenders, companies, and governments to *establish regulatory and voluntary standards and policies for the development and delivery of NNL of biodiversity or NPI.*
Generate lessons learned from *a portfolio of site-based biodiversity offset and compensation projects and distribute them to all stakeholders.*

Courtesy of WCS

tion of critical indirect or cumulative impacts. It therefore becomes essential to determine where, in the planning and management process, tools such as the SEA, spatial planning, and the principles of the mitigation hierarchy are best applied.

SEA and spatial planning have such strong political dimensions that, in most circumstances, government must play a key role in initiating, steering, and validating the process, although there is also an important role for lenders and donors to play in supporting this process. Both sectors have a great deal to gain from the results provided from the SEA and spatial planning tools. The data- and stakeholder-verified scenarios and objectives which can ensue from these processes provide a valuable framework from which to adapt policies and standards for industry development across a landscape. The business sector also gains immensely from this process as the outputs can help to define the rules under which they will operate. Thus, industries would do well to

be engaged throughout the spatial planning and SEA process since their readiness to respond to predicted impacts and preferred scenarios can provide them with a competitive advantage in eventual concession awards and project development. Establishing such a level playing field between extractive industries is of paramount importance to companies seeking to address their biodiversity impacts responsibly. The SEA is a tool to enable that and as such is fundamental to improving the extractive industry's environmental and social performance. However, in places where the political will or understanding is absent, it may only be possible to increase the application of SEA and spatial planning tools once the government has understood their importance and adopted them. Capacity building is a critical tool for donor governments, the private sector, and NGOs, to assist in developing these skills. Wider adoption and use of SEAs, spatial planning tools, and more cumulative benefits from the guidance of the mitigation hierarchy will likely depend on provision of this capacity building and the subsequent dialog necessary to mainstream and institutionalize it.

Despite these constraints and concerns, the number of extractive industry development projects benefiting from increased use of an integrated approach to SEA, spatial planning, and mitigation and compensation processes continues to grow worldwide. Mining and oil and gas associations can play a significant role.

Changing rules of the game: regulating and incentivizing industry for conservation gain

The dramatic growth in investments in the energy and minerals sector is resulting in ever-growing threats to biodiversity, ecosystem services, and communities that depend on natural resources for their livelihoods. This growth is encouraging a unique four-pronged response by governments, lenders, conservation experts, and the companies themselves. Cumulatively, these actors could produce a set of policies, standards, requirements, and practices to incentivize all extractive industries to do much more than just account for their adverse impacts. If enacted, enforced, and applied, these measures could result in extractive processes that significantly reduce impacts on biodiversity.

National policies and standards

Governments are slowly starting to respond and, together with civil society, are looking for solutions to these threats to ecosystem services and biodiversity. Requiring companies to follow strict mitigation requirements and then offset their impacts may provide one of the most immediate and effective options. Practical applications of these

changes in ape range states are still few and far between. Some initiatives are starting to be seen, however. The government of Gabon is exploring measures to mitigate and offset the negative impacts of extractive industries, which is discussed in greater detail in Chapter 8, and initial conversations have also taken place in Uganda. The policy paths being pursued by these and other countries have the potential to create a momentum that can grow substantially as a result of cumulative exchanges and the growing pressures to respond to the pace of investment. Many of the challenges, however, in Gabon, Guinea, the Democratic Republic of Congo and other parts of Africa, as well as Indonesia and much of Asia, occur because the enforcement of existing regulations is weak, and the capacity of organizations to assess and develop integrated approaches is also very weak. This can lead to the agreement of policies, but inadequate implementation and control, leading to the loss of habitats and species, as well as marginalization of communities.

Funding sources and lender policies and standards

Government changes are being further enhanced by increasing pressure from lenders and donors to mitigate and offset adverse impacts to biodiversity. A mining project is capital intensive to build and start up. Most companies do not have the financial resources available from investor proceeds to fund the development of a project internally. Typically they turn to lending institutions to invest in the project, and/or in project development financing. Companies often build their projects on borrowed money until such time as the mine is producing saleable products. This then allows the company to re-pay the bank loans from the proceeds from product sales before and/or concurrent with providing returns to the stockholding investors.

> The dramatic growth in investments in the energy and minerals sector is resulting in ever-growing threats to biodiversity, ecosystem services, and communities that depend on natural resources.

Most of the lending institutions that are big enough to finance a mining project are signatories to the Equator Principles (www.equator-principles.com). Equator Principles are a credit risk management framework that cross-reference and incorporate the environmental and social PSs of the IFC (www.ifc.org). The IFC is the private investment arm of the World Bank Group. Financial institutions signatory to the Equator Principles apply the principles to all transactions exceeding US$10 million. Because nearly all mining projects exceed US$10 million in capital investment and require external financing, mining companies will typically conform to both Equator Principles and IFC PSs as an inherent part of their project planning. This conformance obliges rigorous social and environmental impact assessment and the implementation of detailed management systems to reduce project impacts to acceptable levels.

The most significant influence from lender policies is the IFC's PS6 that has now been adopted by 76 Equator Bank financial institutions responsible for more than 70% of project financing in developing countries. The IFC's PS6 requires funding recipients to demonstrate NNL for impacts in natural habitat and NPI for biodiversity as a result of project implementation activities in critical habitat. PS6 recognizes that protecting and conserving biodiversity, as defined in the Convention on Biological Diversity (CBD), is fundamental to sustainable development and to all of its investments. The applicability of this Performance Standard is established during the ESIA process, while implementation of the actions necessary to meet the requirements of PS6 is managed through the client's Social and Environmental Management System (SEMS) (see Chapter 1).

Unfortunately, few lenders have biodiversity specialists working within their organization, and a recent study has identified that most bankers are not equipped to identify biodiversity risks. There is now a pressing need to help financial institutions to develop this technical capacity or ensure that they have easy access to it. In addition, most Chinese banks that lend to mining projects (China Development Bank (CDB), Export–Import Bank of China (China EX–IM), Industrial and Commercial Bank of China (ICBC)) are not Equator Principle signatories. China has become a leading developer of extractive projects in Africa. Many Chinese investors do not even seek project finance, as it is not generally their preferred funding option. So the Equator Principles are becoming increasingly marginalized for many Chinese-led investments in Africa.

Internal corporate policies and standards

The emerging government and lender–donor trends are further complemented by a growing corporate interest in adopting environmental and social best practices to manage project risk and highlight corporate social responsibility (CSR). More and more natural resource extraction companies are creating voluntary internal responses to environmental and social risks through policies and protocols designed to avoid adverse impacts wherever possible, and otherwise minimize, mitigate, restore, or offset them in all other cases.

The incentives driving this behavior are largely market-based and institutional. Companies with a proactive vision of future markets realize that their readiness to comply with government, lender, or shareholder mandated requirements gives them a leading edge in obtaining and following through on the development of concessions. Companies without this readiness may be poorly positioned to participate in the growing natural resource development markets.

> The IFC's PS6 recognizes that protecting and conserving biodiversity is fundamental to sustainable development and to all of its investments.

152

CASE STUDY 1

The XYZ iron ore mine in Central Africa

In 2012, a major international mining company embarked on the early stages of planning the development of a proposed iron ore mine ("the XYZ project") in central Africa (Figure 5.6).[8]

The proposed XYZ mine will be located in a core area of the Guineo-Congolian Forest in an area known to contain biodiversity of global significance, including significant populations of lowland gorillas and chimpanzees. The source of a major river situated adjacent to the mine site has been identified by the IUCN as critical for the conservation of forest ecosystems in this basin. The national government recognizes the conservation importance and ecological sensitivity of this region, and established an operating national park immediately adjacent to the proposed mine site in the 1990s. The government has now also proposed the establishment of a protected area contiguous to the existing national park, to further ensure the long-term ecological viability of this area. The two parks will form an

FIGURE 5.6

Location of the XYZ mine project and a proposed resource transport corridor route

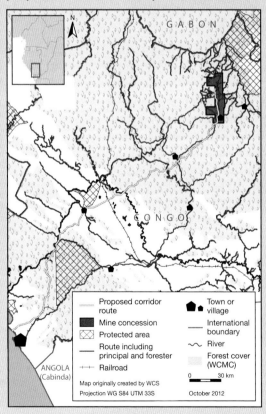

Courtesy of WCS

FIGURE 5.7

Location of XYZ mine concession and proposed protected area in relation to logging concessions

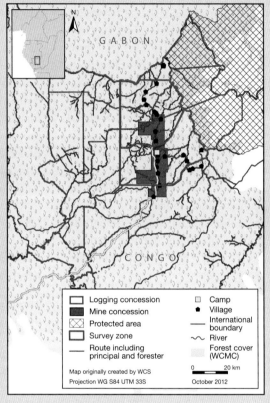

Courtesy of WCS

important contiguous transboundary protected area of over 5000 km² once protected area establishment and development is complete.

The current mine concession overlaps with part of the western section of the proposed new protected area by an estimated 125 km² (although the ore body itself is located outside the boundary). The subsurface rights granted to the mine concession further overlap with surface rights granted in three forest concessions, all of which are being actively logged (Figure 5.7).

Following earlier reconnaissance work, XYZ was awarded exploration rights for approximately 1000 km² after submitting a research permission application. The extracted ore will be transported via a buried slurry pipe network that travels southwest from the mine site more than 400 km to a coastal port facility.

An Order of Magnitude (OoM) work program as part of pre-feasibility studies indicated that the XYZ mine had the potential to become a world-class iron ore operation and, when fully operational, could be capable of exporting 45–50 million tons of iron ore per year for approximately 25–30 years.

As part of its ongoing pre-feasibility work, the mining company has undertaken detailed investigations to determine the engineering feasibility and economic viability of exploiting the iron ore resource. An ESIA is on-going. More specific studies to establish biodiversity baselines and carry out monitoring of biodiversity in the mine site area and along key sections of the transport corridor have also been on-going since 2009.

Direct and indirect threats to great apes

Particular attention has been placed by the mining company on potential impacts to great apes and their habitat. Although exact population numbers are unknown for the mine site or the transport corridor, it is evident that western lowland gorilla (*Gorilla gorilla gorilla*) and western chimpanzee (*Pan troglodytes troglodytes*) do occur in the project area, although in lower numbers than are found elsewhere in the region (Figure 5.8).

FIGURE 5.8

Great ape sign density in the area of the proposed XYZ mine project, 2012 surveys

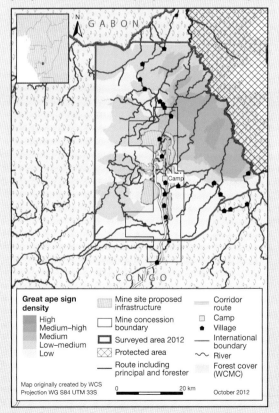

Courtesy of WCS

FIGURE 5.9

Hunting sign density in the vicinity of the proposed XYZ mine project, 2012 surveys

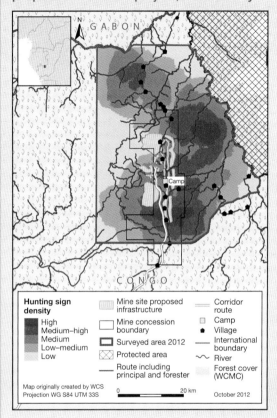

Courtesy of WCS

Field surveys to estimate great ape relative abundance indicated an estimate of 75.7 (45.35–126.33) nests per km^2, which suggests an approximate number of 900 individuals in the mine site area. While this reveals the presence of a reasonably healthy population, it is noticeably lower than similar areas surveyed elsewhere in the country with a density estimate of 234 (185–299) nests per km^2, suggesting an estimate of 68 000 great apes across 27 000 km^2 of rainforest.

Ecologically, great apes and the habitat they depend on appear to be experiencing a two-fold threat in both the mine site and transport corridor. On the one hand commercial and artisanal loggers are quickly degrading and eliminating habitat. They are also greatly increasing access opportunities for hunters through new road and trail construction. At the same time, the new employment opportunities available from the logging companies and at the mine site have significantly increased some local incomes and available revenue, which, in turn, is increasing hunting incentives as hunters seek to take advantage of the increased demand and purchasing power for bushmeat.

154

Surveys carried out in 2012 show a significant increase in hunting across a large part of the mine site and transport corridor areas compared to previous surveys carried out in 2009–10 (Figures 5.8 and 5.9). Hunting signs were recorded over almost all of the surveyed area in 2012. There also appears to be a strong correlation between the increased hunting pressures and a dramatic increase in logging operations in the mine site area. Field observations indicate that the loggers consume significant quantities of bushmeat, and do not restrict access to the logging roads or trails to enter the forest. This suggests a strong correlation between expanded logging operations and increased hunting pressures, and this can be expected to further intensify as previously inaccessible areas are opened to new logging operations.

Thus the increasing threats to great apes in this area appear to be principally indirect ones related to the proposed mine project. The rehabilitation or construction of new roads and access routes in the forest is certainly assisting increased hunting, both subsistence and commercial. However, the logging companies have contributed to this growing transport infrastructure and disposable income for the local population, and thus hold significant responsibility for this impact. Separating out the sources and responsibilities for responding to these growing impacts thus becomes a highly complicated task.

Commitment to the mitigation hierarchy: the future for great apes in the vicinity of the XYZ mine

The XYZ mine is sensitive to these overlapping responsibilities and recognizes that the threats to wildlife being experienced in the mine site area and transport corridor are severe, possibly some of the most intense in the country. However, the mine is also committed to contributing what it can to try to mitigate its share of the impacts through improved natural resource management practices, with a particular attention to monitoring of wildlife populations and enforcement of laws and codes to protect them.

The mining company has expressed a voluntary commitment to follow the guidelines of the IFC's PS6, and the XYZ project is now completing its comprehensive ESIA process. More detail on these guidelines is provided in Chapter 8. However, the spatial planning has been limited to the distinct boundaries of the mine site in the concession area, and a narrow width of the proposed pipeline transport corridor extending to a coastal port. No assessment of possible indirect impacts outside of these mine site areas or of adjacent developments has been considered in these spatial analyses.

The ESIA and spatial planning work completed to date has suggested several possible measures that can be implemented to mitigate and offset direct and indirect adverse impacts from further mine development, including support for the establishment of new protected areas, improved management of existing ones, and more effective land-use practices outside of protected areas. Some of the initial actions being considered by the mine project that could benefit great apes include:

- Carry out semi-annual monitoring of large mammals, including great apes, in the wet and dry seasons to verify on-going changes in the relative abundance and distribution of mammal, avifauna, reptile and amphibian, and selected aquatic species now known to inhabit the mine site area.

- Develop education and public awareness campaigns to ensure that local residents have the information necessary to make responsible decisions on land and resource uses. It will be particularly important for residents to understand the benefits from the ecological services provided by mammals, birds, bats, and invertebrates, including such roles as insect control, pollination, and seed dispersal.

- Continue assessments of the frequency, intensity, and duration of hunting expeditions, and development/ enforcement of mechanisms to halt or reduce access for hunters, including more detailed analyses of the drivers of bushmeat hunting.

- Implement a hunter education program to empower local communities to reduce their take to scientifically determined sustainable levels, and to assist in the enforcement and prosecution of non-sustainable and illegal hunting practices. Hunter education programs can inform hunters of BMPs to reduce harvests during important reproductive and migratory periods, control the number of species taken, and result in more responsible game management.

- Provide support to government and NGO groups to enforce existing wildlife conservation laws through trained and equipped teams that are empowered by local community councils and government agencies. Enforcement would also include monitoring of hunters and harvests, and the sale of meat in markets.

- Fund and implement existing draft natural resource management and economic development plans. Preliminary community-endorsed plans have been prepared for several communities in the area of the proposed mine, and include a wide range of activities that could help reduce bushmeat demand.

- Increasing the availability of domestic meat supplies could reduce the severe price difference that now exists in local markets. Supplies of domestic meat are often sold at logging concession markets, but the market price is often higher for domestic meat than for wild caught/ bushmeat.

- Design a biodiversity offset and compensation plan. The tentative options for a compensation plan include the possibility of providing the financial and technical support for the establishment and management of the proposed new protected area contiguous to the existing national park. Consideration is also being given to providing long-term financial and technical support to another existing protected area located adjacent to parts of the proposed transport corridor. While the results from the proposed offset mechanism at the mine will not necessarily resolve all impending risks and threats to biodiversity, the implementation of the mitigation hierarchy for a project of this type would constitute significant progress in the efforts to reconcile extractive exploitation projects in Africa with significantly improved safeguards for biodiversity and the ecosystem services upon which local human populations depend.

If applied, these actions could collectively result in greatly reduced impacts to great apes, in particular, and local biodiversity, in general. Some gorilla and chimpanzee groups should benefit from the establishment of new protected areas and connecting corridors, and improved management in existing ones.

The proposed mitigation and compensation actions are, however, unfortunately limited in geographic and institutional scope. They will principally respond to the voluntary commitments of the mining company, and are designed to reduce or compensate for direct impacts expected from the mining activities. Other indirect and cumulative impacts are not likely to be fully resolved by this mitigation and compensation process, including the dramatic impacts being incurred by intensified logging and hunting throughout the affected environment, and the limited capacity and weak political will of national and local government agencies to enforce existing policies, or forge and implement much needed new ones. Without immediate action to control logging and commercial hunting outside of the mine site the end result over time is likely to be a continued decline in the size, integrity, and health of great ape populations in the immediate mine site and surrounding areas.

Indonesia

Mining and orangutan distribution

Mining concessions overlap with orangutan habitat in both Kalimantan and Sumatra (Figure 5.10, and Figure 4.2 on page 113). In Sarawak and Sabah, the situation is less clear because no data on official mine concessions could be obtained for this study. On the basis of the presence of coal and mineral deposits, the threat of mining to orangutans in these Malaysian states appears limited. Mining concessions in Borneo overlap with other concessions, thus this chapter focuses on the extent of orangutan distribution shared with mining concessions. The results of these analyses show that 15% of orangutan distribution overlaps with mining concessions (Figure 5.10). For Sumatra the same analysis showed that 9% of orangutan distribution overlaps with mining concessions (Figure 4.2, page 113).

Mining concessions often cover large areas that may include either prime orangutan habitat such as natural forest or more marginal habitat such as degraded forest and agricultural mosaics. The impact of mining on orangutans and their habitat is both direct and indirect (see Chapters 3 and 7 for more information).

Typically, an exploration lease covers a much larger area than the area that will ultimately be mined. Following a set timeline, the original lease area is relinquished back to the government and can be re-issued as a new lease to another company. In reality, mining companies therefore only have management rights over a relatively small area (typically a few thousand hectares), which is known as the borrow-use area. These borrow-use areas, especially those on state forest land, are usually much smaller than the operational areas of pulp and paper and oil palm plantations, or timber concessions. It is thus important to understand that many of the mining exploration leases that overlap with orangutan habitat may not actually be mined. Mining exploration leases are therefore not a good indicator for the potential impact mining activities will have on orangutans for the following reasons: (1) many areas leased for exploration will have low economic potential and will not be developed; (2) only a section of an exploration lease area will ultimately be used for mining.

Kaltim Prima Coal (KPC) in Kalimantan has worked with ecologists to identify ways to enhance its reclaimed mine sites with local tree species and species that provide food for orangutans. Some of these older rehabilitated sites now provide habitat for orangutans (KPC, 2010). The key now is to ensure these areas are linked through habitat corridors to the wider forested landscape so that orangutans can move away from operational areas without becoming cut off or isolated from suitable habitat.

FIGURE 5.10

Mining concessions in Kalimantan* in relation to orangutan habitat

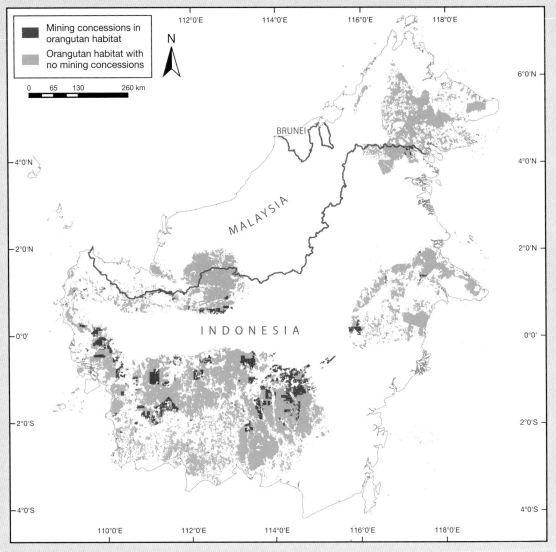

* No data available for Malaysian Borneo

Courtesy of E. Meijaard and S. Wich

Mining laws and their implications for orangutan habitat

Indonesia's forests are split into the following categories: (1) Conservation Forest including National Parks; (2) Protection Forest; and (3) Production Forest. All mining activities are forbidden in Conservation Forest. Forestry Law no. 41/1999 strictly prohibits open-pit mining in Protection Forest, but the development of underground mines is still permitted under this law. Presidential Decree no. 41/2004 and Ministry of Forestry Regulation no. 14/2006 give legal exemption to 13 companies, because their mining concessions within Protection Forest were awarded before the regulation came into force. Among these are two coal-mining companies, namely PT Indominco Mandiri with an area of 251.2 km² (25 121 ha) in East Kalimantan, and PT Interex Sacra Raya, which has 156.5 km² (15 650 ha) of coal-mining concessions in East and South Kalimantan. As mentioned above, the former company operates in orangutan habitat.

Investors can apply for a Forest Land Borrow and Use Permit (*Izin Pinjam Pakai Kawasan Hutan* – IPPKH) for the development of mining activities in forest that is officially classified as a Production Forest. This permit provides the right to use the designated forest area for non-forestry development interests, without changing the status and designation of the land as being forest (Ministry of Forestry Regulation no. 43/2008). Depending on whether the total forest area in the province concerned is more or less than 30% of the total land area, either Non-Tax State Revenue (*Penerimaan Negara Bukan Pajak* – PNBP) is paid or the company compensates by reforesting another area of land. Moreover, Forest Resource Provision (*Provisi Sumber Daya Hutan* – PSDH) and a reforestation fund (*Dana Reboisasi* – DR) have to be paid. Mining within forest land without the obligatory IPPKH is considered illegal under the Forestry Law. However, the Ministry of Forestry does not have the authority to revoke licenses in the case of non-compliance.

According to the IPPKH, the land should be returned to the same state as it was when the permit was issued. Ministerial Decree 43/2008 suggests this can be achieved through reclamation and the planting of forest species in 4 m × 4 m spacing. In the third year after planting, at least 80% of the plants should be in a healthy state. However, the ease of issuance of permits for forests protected under such permits, and the rudimentary state of reclamation plans and their implementation, challenge the credibility of large tracts of land actually being returned to their original forested state (McMahon *et al.*, 2000).

The impacts of mining operations on Asian apes, and particularly the gibbons, have been much less widely studied than the impacts of forestry. Why this is so is not clear, but could be due to a perception that other activities (e.g. plantations, forestry) are much more widespread and therefore have a more significant impact on ape populations. Historically, this may have been the case, but in recent years the extractive industries (mining, and oil and gas) have undergone notable growth in Asian ape states, and now pose a threat to several species (IUCN, 2012b, 2012c). What is important to note is that the impacts of logging (as described in Chapter 4) are likely to be similar in terms of disturbance and certainly in terms of indirect threats associated with the activity.

Market incentives for low impact methods such as those of the Forest Stewardship Council (FSC) have driven best practice in forestry for many years. Very few similar incentives exist in the mining industry and implementation of leading edge practices in biodiversity management has lagged behind forestry. In recent years, however, some companies and operations have begun to implement voluntary commitments to improve practices and reduce their impacts on biodiversity and specifically on endangered species like great apes. This is being driven by several factors including: CSR, regulatory pressure, and investor pressure.

Leading edge practices in the mining industry

Lao People's Democratic Republic (Lao PDR) still retains approximately 68% of its forest cover (FAO, 2011b), which is habitat for six species of gibbon (Duckworth, 2008; MAF, 2011). All of these gibbon species are under threat, principally from high levels of hunting for food and trade, and the conversion and degradation of their forest habitat. The 2011 Gibbon Conservation Action Plan for Lao (MAF, 2011) identifies mining as a development activity that can cause major impacts on biodiversity, including gibbons. Mining is central to the economy of Lao PDR however. A 2011 report (ICMM, 2011) concluded that mining contributed 45% of all exports, 12% of government revenue, and 10% of GDP. Almost all of this derives from only two mines, the PBM Phu Kham mine, and the Sepon gold and copper mine. Funds from mining operations could be used to support gibbon conservation elsewhere in the country, as proposed by the Gibbon Action Plan (MAF, 2011).

The Sepon mine is located in northern Savannakhet Province, in central Lao (Figure 5.11). The mine was originally developed as an open-pit copper and gold mine by the Australian company Oxiana. Gold production started in 2002, and copper in 2005 (MMG, 2012). After a series of mergers most of what was then known as OZ Minerals was bought by the Chinese company Minmetals Resources

FIGURE 5.11

Location of Sepon mine in Lao PDR

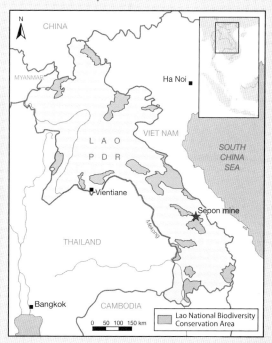

Developed from IUCN and UNEP-WCMC, 2013

Ltd in 2009, which operates mines through its subsidiary Minerals and Metals Group (MMG). Since taking over, MMG have expanded operations and extended the estimated life of the mine. They now predict that gold extraction will continue until at least 2013 and copper until at least 2020.

MMG controls a lease area, known as a Mineral Exploration and Production Agreement (MEPA), of approximately 1300 km². The mine is located in the central Annamite mountains, an area renowned for its high levels of endemism and the relatively recent scientific discovery of several new mammals, including the critically endangered saola (*Pseudoryx nghetinhensis*), and annamite striped rabbit (*Nesolagus timminsi*) (IUCN, 2012b, 2012c). Gibbons are known to occur within the lease area, but it is still not known how many, and which species are present. The lease is located in the area thought to be at the possible boundary between two species, the endangered southern white-cheeked gibbon (*Nomascus siki*) (IUCN, 2012b, 2012c) and the newly described northern yellow-cheeked gibbon (*N. annamensis*) (Thinh *et al.*, 2010; MAF, 2011). It is possible that both species are found in the lease area, and that it could be a zone of hybridization (C. Hallam, personal communication, July 2012).

MMG is now attempting to implement leading edge practice in the management of biodiversity at the Sepon mine. Leading companies in the mining sector aim to follow the mitigation hierarchy to manage impacts on biodiversity (BBOP, 2012). As stated earlier in this chapter, this approach places emphasis on first implementing measures to avoid, then minimize, then restore, and only as a last resort to offset impacts with conservation actions leading to biodiversity gains elsewhere (BBOP, 2012). MMG is collaborating with the WCS Lao Program to implement a biodiversity strategy that follows the mitigation hierarchy. The key elements of this strategy are:

- **Avoidance:** WCS and MMG have mapped and modeled biodiversity features, and threats across the wider landscape. From this they have identified areas of higher biodiversity value. To date the mine has not cleared any forest holding extant gibbon populations. As the mine expands, high biodiversity forest areas, including those with gibbon populations, will be avoided where possible.

- **Minimization:** MMG has strict bans on hunting, and collection of forest resources by staff and contractors. This program is supported by training and awareness raising in environmental issues. Where possible, road widths are kept to a minimum, minimizing forest loss and barriers to gibbon movement.

- **Reinstatement:** Pits are back-filled where possible and native flora re-established. Rehabilitation also occurs in other disturbed areas, for example along roadsides.

Photo: Tin mining tailings ponds in Vietnam. The residual ore and water from the processing plant is dumped into large ponds. The contaminated water drains into the environment. Thai Nguyen province. © Terry Whittaker

Offsets: The mine ESIA includes a program of "Partnerships with wildlife conservation groups and government authorities to develop offset programs outside the project area" (C. Hallam, personal communication, July 2012). MMG is working with WCS to quantify the biodiversity losses from future work, and develop an offset for residual losses leading to a net gain for biodiversity, including improving the conservation status of gibbons. To compensate for existing operations MMG supports a variety of other conservation efforts in Lao including those for Asian elephants (*Elephas maximus*) and Siamese crocodiles (*Crocodylus siamensis*).

The approach taken by MMG stands in clear contrast to practices by many other operations that pay little regard to the management of biodiversity impacts. This is particularly clear with illegal or artisanal mining, which occurs in many parts of Asian as well as African ape ranges (Global Witness, 2003; Laurence, 2008). This is described in greater detail in Chapter 6 of this volume. Phnom Prich Wildlife Sanctuary (PPWS) in eastern Cambodia, for example, is home to a population of approximately 150 groups of southern yellow-cheeked gibbons (*Nomascus gabriellae*) (Channa and Gray, 2009). These gibbons are part of a much larger metapopulation including around 1000 individuals in the neighboring Seima Protected Forest (Pollard *et al.*, 2007). Despite its protected status, exploration for gold has been allowed in PPWS and illegal mining for gold is occurring in several locations. Illegal mining has led to clearance of forest within gibbon home ranges, and illegal miners are known to be hunting in the forest (Channa and Gray, 2009). Gibbons are threatened from this through habitat loss and degradation, and hunting. The continued spread of illegal mining in this area could threaten an important population of this globally endangered gibbon (IUCN, 2012b, 2012c).

Conclusion

The impacts of mining on ape populations and their habitats have not been studied extensively. They can be understood, however, in terms of the direct and indirect effects of operations throughout all stages of project development. Significant gaps still exist in the information and analysis required for both policy-makers and practitioners to determine if it is truly possible to achieve profitable extractive projects together with NNL/effective ape conservation, which is also respectful of social and environmental priorities. Efforts to follow the mitigation hierarchy (avoid, minimize, restore, and compensate) have, to date, shown partial success with respect to biodiversity targets, but they insufficiently address the cumulative impacts of human land use and economic activities. It is likely that leadership from governments at national and regional levels, as well as commitment from leaders in industry, based on strong conservation science and input from civil society (including marginalized, indigenous communities) is required for the extractive industries to be compatible with environmental and social objectives. The case studies show that this is patchy, and specifically for apes, too little data exists to accurately assess and predict the impact of mining on ape survival.

Clearly, there is much work to be done to help mainstream the application of the measures and methods outlined in this chapter, which are now being considered by governments, lenders–donors, and companies as part of the broader solutions toolbox. A pressing task for decision-makers in the next decade will be to lead the work that can demonstrate where and how these new practices can be best applied, and to create the lessons learned that will lead to more and better conservation, with sustainable financing provided directly by the private sector. Essentially, industry can and should work with national governments to ensure that SEAs are carried out over a large enough area, and that measures put in place to avoid, mitigate, and compensate for impacts are effective. Industry associations are probably better than individual companies to take on these possibilities, as well as other mechanisms, such as land disturbance taxes.

It will also be essential for practitioners to ensure that the two key prerequisites for achieving NNL of biodiversity are included in the growing corporate, government, and donor policies, namely that the funds for compensation actions come from the entity causing the impacts, and that the compensation financing is ensured for at least as long as the impacts last, or ideally in perpetuity to ensure the permanence of conservation outcomes. Compensation funding must be sufficient to finance the management of offsets and dedicated to sustain conservation areas and actions that are not already financed. Certification schemes could certainly filter some of that cost to the growing urban middle classes that are driving much of the consumption.

As these demonstrations and lessons grow it will become possible to provide a tangible response to one of the key constraints affecting great ape and broader biodiversity conservation: the lack of sufficient financing to ensure long-term support for areas identified for conservation and/or sustainable management of working landscapes, including protected areas.

At the present time these methods are frequently applied in a piecemeal manner with little integration or coordination across regions or landscapes. More significantly, the institutional support for the use of these methods, and their ability to enforce and monitor them, is also inconsistent and incomplete. Most applications of spatial planning and the protocol of the mitigation hierarchy occur through voluntary conditions established by companies in collaboration with NGOs or civil society. In those

> Leadership from governments and commitment from leaders in industry, based on conservation science and input from civil society is required for extractive industries to be compatible with environmental and social objectives.

instances where government standards are in place or in process, there are significant questions remaining about the long-term enforcement, and thus the effectiveness, of these standards. The end result for great apes and other associated biodiversity is uncertain in all of these cases, but certainly not encouraging.

Acknowledgments

Principal author: Annette Lanjouw

Contributors: Liz Farmer, Barbara Filas, Global Witness, Matthew Hatchwell, Cecilia Larrosa, Erik Meijaard, Chloe Montes, Bardolf Paul, PNCI, Edward Pollard, James Tolisano, Melissa Tolley, UNEP-WCMC, Ray Victurine, Ashley Vosper, WCS, and Serge Wich

Endnotes

1   http://mapper.eva.mpg.de/

2   http://www.metalseconomics.com

3   B. Filas, 2013

4   For more information go to http://www.icmm.com/our-work/sustainable-development-framework

5   For more information go to http://www.ipieca.org/focus-area/biodiversity

6   For more information go to http://www.iaia.org/

7   Taken from "a biodiversity offset should be designed and implemented to achieve measurable conservation outcomes that can reasonably be expected to result in no net loss and preferably a net gain of biodiversity" PS6 page 2 footnotes (IFC 2012)

8   The XYZ project is an actual project in development. However, the name and location of this project have been changed to respect the privacy of the implementing company

CHAPTER 6

Artisanal and small-scale mining and apes

Introduction

The term "artisanal and small scale mining" (ASM) describes the use of manual labor and low-level technologies that characterize the activity (Hruschka and Echavarría, 2011), as opposed to the capital-intensive and high technological input of industrial, large-scale mining (LSM). ASM is often an informal activity and artisanal miners' lack of recognition, formal rights, and support creates a structural inability that can make it difficult for them to move out of poverty. Described as being amongst the poorest members of society, their trade is often fraught with dangerous practices and, in conflict and post-conflict countries, can have serious implications for security (Hayes and Wagner, 2008). At the local level, however, and in contrast to other subsistence-based livelihoods, artisanal miners are often better off than their neighbors, as their income can enable them to invest in their families' health care and education, buy consumables, and better cope with shocks. But while ASM is an important and increasingly popular livelihood for tens of millions of people around the world, bringing in needed income to rural communities, it is also a serious and growing threat to biodiversity and the integrity of protected areas due to the extraction methods and the livelihood practices that support mining populations (Villegas *et al.*, 2012).

This chapter attempts to integrate the extent of artisanal mining activity within previously identified ape habitats with those mitigation strategies currently in existence, alongside the emerging lessons and knowledge gaps. In the context of conservation, economic activity, and human rights, it illustrates just how dire the environmental impacts of uncontrolled ASM can be, as well as highlighting the importance of this sector as an economic force that requires better regulation and understanding. Critical issues to be addressed include:

- An overview of the structure of ASM activity in protected areas and critical ecosystems (PACE) around the world;

NOTE

Protected areas and critical ecosystems

Protected areas have been defined according to the IUCN definition of a "clearly defined geographical space, recognized, dedicated, and managed, through legal or other effective means, to achieve the long-term conservation of nature with associated ecosystem services and cultural values" (Dudley, 2008, pp. 8-9). Different notions of how to classify which of the world's ecosystems should be considered "critical" exist, but for the purposes of this chapter, they include Areas of Zero Extinction (of which there are only 587 in the world), in which endangered or critically endangered species of mammals, birds, amphibians, reptiles, plants, and reef-building corals are known to reside, and the Global 200 Priority Ecoregions as described by Olson and Dinerstein (2002).

- The policy and regulation of artisanal mining;
- The nature of ASM experiences in ape range states, illustrated through case studies of artisanal mining in ape habitats, focusing primarily on central Africa;
- Mitigation strategies and their challenges.

Key findings:

- The presence of ASM in PACE can have a devastating impact on local biodiversity and thus apes, through obvious, direct activities such as habitat destruction, degradation, and fragmentation, but also no less significantly through a multitude of indirect impacts such as water pollution, soil removal, and the increase in hunting pressure that accompanies migration to mining sites (see Chapter 7).
- ASM activities increase the risk of the spread of diseases to ape populations due to poor sanitation and poor hygiene within mining communities, as well as zoonotic disease transmission from animal to human populations due to increased contact through habitat intrusion (see Chapter 7).
- The role of LSM as a magnet in drawing ASM into these areas (as they are seen as viable for exploitation) is complex and misunderstood, and with current mitigation thinking generally focused at the site level, an analysis of markets at both the supply and demand ends also requires further investigation.

Both political perceptions and attitudes towards the ASM sector are central to progressive policy processes. But while it remains poorly understood, with this knowledge deficit reflected in weak or non-existent legislation, so too have recent management options been few in number and with little analysis as to what extent they have either succeeded or failed. While existing programs are slowly beginning to rectify this situation, the often immature and corrupt governance structures found in many ape range states exacerbate ASM's environmental and social impacts. With increased encroachment on ape habitat, there is now a recognized need amongst conservationists to focus on the opportunities for not only mitigating the environmental impacts of the sector, but also improving the social impacts, through better regulation and the formalization of tenure rights. In areas considered critically important for ape conservation there may also be the need to ban mining altogether, and this will require interventions supported by more robust law enforcement. As long as ASM remains an economically rational choice for often chronically poor individuals, the ultimate aim will be to find ways of navigating these complex conservation and development trade-offs that it produces in sites of high conservation value. Some of the shortfalls apparent in existing management strategies highlight how integrated interventions that include policy and legislative development in traditional spheres of control, coupled with poverty alleviation measures, are more likely to mitigate the impacts of ASM on great apes and gibbons than efforts that focus on any one of these alone.

The structure of artisanal mining

There are four main types of ASM (Hruschka and Echavarría, 2011):

- **Permanent**: refers to ASM as a full time, year round activity. Mining is frequently the primary economic activity and is sometimes accompanied by other activities such as farming, herding, or other localized extractive practices.

> **BOX 6.1**
>
> ### Overview of ASM sites and the key minerals obtained through them
>
> Artisanal mining primarily depends on the most basic tools (hammers, picks, shovels, buckets, wheelbarrows, etc.) and manual labor for excavation. More advanced organization and production methods – such as the use of bulldozers and advanced mechanization – can also be referred to as small-scale mining. The term 'ASM' is thus used to describe a sector that is in fact quite diverse. Different types of ASM include: recovery of alluvial material from river beds or banks; recovery of tailings from old processing plant discharges or rejected material; open-pit mining, with or without benches to stabilize the pit walls; vertical or inclined shafts, of which tunnels or galleries may be excavated; irregular tunnels into hillsides following mineral veins; extraction from abandoned industrial mines, whether open pits or underground mines, which can include removal of ore-bearing pillars and other supports for underground galleries or destabilization of pit walls; and appropriation from large-scale mine stockpiles of rejected or prepared materials (Hayes and Wagner, 2008).
>
> Using data collected by the German Federal Institute for Geosciences and Natural Resources (BGR), Figure 6.1 shows the contribution of ASM to the global production of minerals, including those commonly extracted in or adjacent to protected areas or critical ecosystems (and thus great ape habitats).
>
> Many other minerals are also mined (both artisanally and otherwise). These include bauxite, different gemstones, iron ore, marble, limestone, and other construction materials.

FIGURE 6.1
ASM share of global production (%)

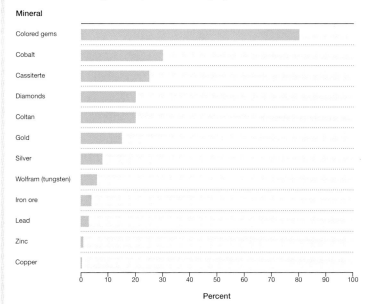

Villegas *et al.*, 2012, p. 9, courtesy of ASM-PACE.

- **Seasonal**: refers to ASM taking place during specific seasons owing to seasonal alternating of activities or seasonal migration of people into artisanal mining areas during idle agricultural periods, for example, to supplement their annual incomes.

- **Rush-type**: massive migration of artisanal miners to an area, based on the perception that the expected income opportunity from recently discovered deposits far exceeds the current actual income of those people who are lured into it.

- **Shock-push**: refers to when ASM is a poverty-driven activity emerging after recent loss of employment in other sectors, often as a result of conflict or natural disasters.

ASM can impact and become a threat to endangered species when initially temporary mining sites become increasingly permanent, in turn bringing affiliated serv-

ice industries, increasing associated livelihood activities (hunting, forest clearing for mining or agriculture, etc.), or through the mining techniques themselves (use of toxic chemicals, dynamite, forest clearing, diversion or dredging of rivers and streams). However, given that the processes involved in preparing the terrain, and extracting and processing the materials, differ greatly, there are differing degrees of impact on humans, wildlife, and the environment.

Driving factors behind artisanal mining

There are many reasons why people undertake ASM. Often the primary motivation is that, although extremely physically demanding, and physically and financially risky, ASM is an economically rational choice for chronically poor individuals in a context of limited options. People generally undertake ASM because it offers:

Photo: An artisanal miner holding his find of alluvial gold in Buheweju, Uganda. © Estelle Levin

- Immediate cash, which is otherwise difficult to acquire in rural, subsistence-farming contexts (Villegas *et al.*, 2012).

- Potential relief during difficult circumstances in fragile societies that have undergone or are undergoing deepening poverty, natural disasters (e.g. in Mongolia), economic transition or collapse (e.g. in Zimbabwe), or civil conflict or post-conflict reconstruction (e.g. in Sierra Leone and Liberia) (Villegas *et al.*, 2012).

- Opportunity to earn higher income for unskilled or illiterate individuals (Villegas *et al.*, 2012).

- Subsistence for people who are desolate and mine in exchange for food or other basic provisions (Villegas *et al.*, 2012).

- Emancipation from traditional hierarchies and social structures; artisanal mining economies (especially in rush situations) are often highly individualistic and provide scope for young people to organize and discipline themselves as they see fit (King, 1972; Levin, 2010, cited in Villegas *et al.*, 2012).

- Hope that mining will help them break free of poverty and bring them increased dignity and respect from their community (Levin, 2005; Zoellner, 2006, cited in Villegas *et al.*, 2012).

ASM is an economic activity that rises and falls with global mineral prices and shifts production of certain minerals in accordance with local or global demand. For example, Nyame and Grant's (2012) analysis of the recent shift from artisanal diamond production to artisanal gold mining in Ghana emphasizes the fact that artisanal miners would rather adapt their activities to the extraction of other minerals (sometimes at great environmental cost, e.g. the use of mercury) rather than return to traditional activities. In the context of high mineral prices, ASM is a rational economic choice for people seeking to escape absolute poverty or improve their lives. In Uganda, for example, the average miner contributes almost 20 times more to GDP than the average woman or man in farming, forestry, or fishing (Hinton, 2009, p80; Hinton, 2011). In Liberia, the average artisanal digger working north of Sapo National Park has the potential to make 17 to 50 times more than the average Liberian per day (Small and Villegas, 2012).

Unfortunately, the increasing price of precious minerals has launched rushes on all continents. More often than not, these rushes are attracting people to relatively undisturbed places that are important conservation sites, including protected areas and other critical ecosystems (Villegas *et al.*, 2012). Furthermore, it is also important to note that if and when miners decide to move to other livelihoods, these might be more damaging to ape populations and their habitat than mining alone (e.g. hunting, charcoal making, slash and burn agriculture, etc.).

The complex, market-based forces that drive ASM can be further exacerbated by the following factors:

- **An increase in Foreign Direct Investment (FDI) in the extractive industries.** While governments can gain needed income from FDI, this may in practice have detrimental impacts on miners, pushing them to mine in ever more remote areas. There is some awareness of this physical and economic displacement phenomenon and pressure on companies to create displacement plans. However, instead of being seen as an economic asset, artisanal miners are often seen as an impediment to development in spite of the fact that ASM can be a force for local economic development (albeit founded on a largely informal activity). There is often a misperception that LSM is more 'developmental' (Villegas *et al.*, 2012).

- **Impact of international legislation aimed at increasing transparency in the "conflict minerals" sector**. In response to the perceived connection between mining and armed rebel activity in the eastern Democratic Republic of Congo (DRC), there have been a series of initiatives aimed at so-called "conflict minerals," including tin, tantalum, tungsten, and gold ("3TG") originating from this or any adjoining country. This has served to further stigmatize and marginalize the sector, in some cases taking away ASM buyers for fear of being the target of conflict-minerals-inspired consumer campaigns. This has the outcome of pushing it further underground without constructive restructuring of legislative environments to be supportive of formalizing existing practices in the sector.

- **Large-scale land-use change**. Commercial or industrial agricultural activities may drive local farmers out of business or deprive them of land, and could then push them towards ASM as an alternative means of business.

- **The effects of climate change** may make traditional livelihood activities less viable, and there is a great deal of uncertainty as to whether and how this might impact future ASM scenarios.

FIGURE 6.2

Sample supply chain of tin, tantalum, or tungsten from a mine in the DRC

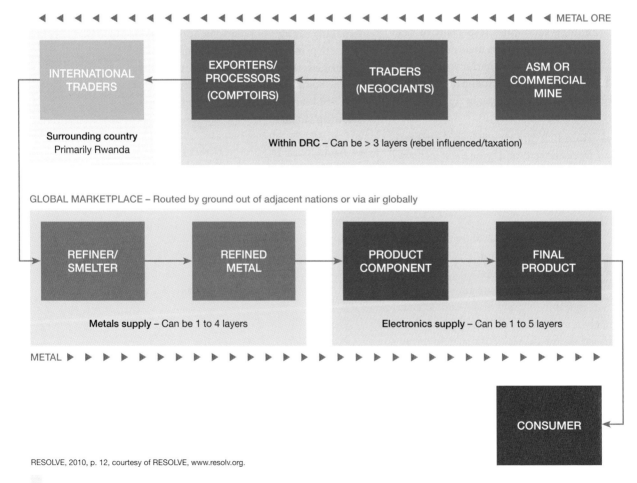

RESOLVE, 2010, p. 12, courtesy of RESOLVE, www.resolv.org.

The supply chain

The nature of the commodity chain itself also plays an important role in defining ASM. Much of artisanal mineral trading is informal. There is not usually any type of paper trail during the early stages of the commodity chain, making transactions vulnerable to smuggling, money laundering, or other types of illegal trade. Thus the ability of miners to receive a "fair price" for their mineral varies considerably. In some cases, they do not know the true value of their goods, are innumerate or illiterate, or do not have transparency on where their mineral goes and the costs of getting it to the international trader, so cannot judge if a price is fair or not. In addition, the need for immediate cash to continue living and mining often outweighs the effort of selling the product further up the chain or stockpiling it to sell in larger quantities, even though they would be likely to get a higher price were they to do so. In other cases, however, miners are able to achieve prices that are close to or even above the international reference price. This occurs when a trader is buying gold either to launder money or to use the mineral as a financial instrument to limit costs associated with his/her primary economic activity (e.g. importing food or goods from a neighboring country that works with a different currency).

As is the case with many resource commodity chains, there can be multiple levels or layers of buyers and sellers (see Figure 6.2). These can include locals, residents from urban areas, foreigners, and the military and government agents, with mined products being exchanged for both cash and in trade. It is usually at the point of export (when the international trade occurs) that the paper trail begins and the trade becomes formal or legal. The lack of price transparency, the lack of value addition early on in the chain, the multitude of middlemen, and the convoluted (and often corrupted) path to market leave miners in a vulnerable economic position, whereby miners capture little value of the end product (such as with diamonds), thus fuelling a cycle of poverty.

The relationship between artisanal and large-scale mining

Recent research undertaken for this publication on the spatial overlap between mining activity and 27 ape taxa indicates that only six have no commercial mining projects within their range (see Chapter 5), and that the remaining taxa ranges are characterized by a predominance of development stage mining projects. While these activities are not necessarily a direct indicator of the future threat from mining operations, their concentration is indicative of potential commodity reserves within ape ranges, which may lead to future conflict in relation to resource exploitation at both the large and the artisanal scale.

One of the reasons why ASM is a growing phenomenon in areas of suitable environmental conditions for apes is due in part to the fact that the rush for minerals by large-scale corporate miners may lead to a gradual squeeze of ASM off land where industrial mining companies have achieved statutory prospecting, exploration, and/or mining rights (e.g. in DRC and Sierra Leone), thus potentially pushing artisanal miners towards other more remote sites. While large and small mining actors come into contact with each other extremely frequently, with LSM following ASM (which may have been on site for decades) or ASM following LSM (anticipating the economic boom or hoping for employment generated by the LSM's presence), the nature of this relationship is complex. The presence of alluvial gold or diamond mining, for example, can suggest the presence of a larger subsurface resource that is amenable to LSM, but resources amenable to LSM may be wholly unsuited to

170

ASM because they occur at depth and/or are low grade and/or are metallurgically complex. LSM may attract ASM where excavations create access to otherwise inaccessible ore (e.g. illegal miners underground at the Obuasi gold mine in Ghana) or where it creates waste dumps that can be picked over by individuals (e.g. coltan/tin in the DRC, diamonds at the Williamson mine in Tanzania). However, given this complexity, and multi-scale patterns in the spatial variability of the potential impacts from mining operations on great ape and gibbon taxa ranges needs to be further investigated.

Given that ASM and LSM can often occur side by side, and that there now appears to be increased recognition that large mining companies should engage with artisanal miners and their dependents, the particular sustainable development challenges of ASM – including security, human rights, and relocation programs – need specific consideration. However, the fact that much of

ASM occurs outside regulatory frameworks can present significant challenges for companies and regulators. This relationship has also been troubled by a mismatch of expectations between the two sectors, which in some cases can lead to mistrust and conflict. This might include potential competition over the same minerals, impacts on livelihoods if access to resources is limited, and changing social conditions, including between host communities and companies (IFC, unpublished data).

ASM in protected areas and critical ecosystems (PACE) around the world

An appreciation of this complex economic and social context is essential in attempting to understand why ASM is increasing in areas of high biodiversity. The ASM–PACE

FIGURE 6.3

Map of countries with ASM in PACE

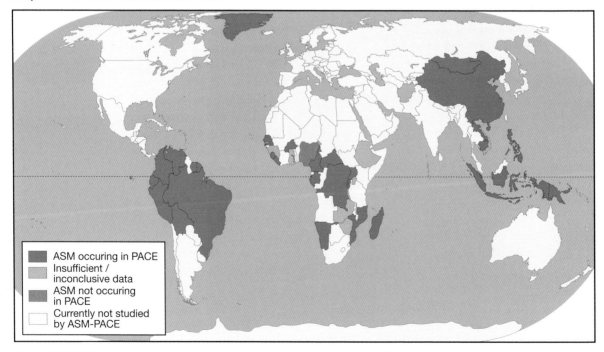

Courtesy of ASM–PACE.

State of the Apes 2013 Extractive Industries and Ape Conservation

FIGURE 6.4

Map showing the overlap of ape countries with ASM

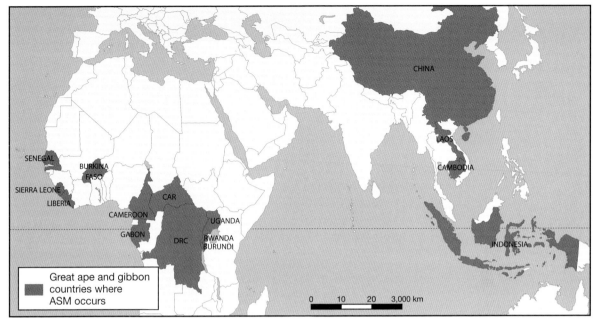

Courtesy of ASM–PACE.

Global Solutions Study (Villegas *et al.*, 2012) provides the following analysis on the scope and scale of ASM encroachment into PACE and thus the habitats of endangered species, including great apes and gibbons.

- ASM is occurring in or around 96 of 147 protected areas evaluated in the Global Solution Study, and in 32 of 36 countries studied (Figure 6.3).

- Affected sites include at least seven natural World Heritage Sites and at least 12 World Wildlife Fund (WWF) Priority Landscapes.

- ASM is occurring in or impacting a wide range of critical ecosystems, not only tropical rainforests in Central Africa and South Asia, which are typical ape habitats (Figure 6.4), but also arctic landscapes (Greenland) and coral reefs (Philippines).

- On a global scale, ASM of gold has the most significant negative environmental impacts; however other minerals have

significant localized impacts within specific ecoregions or countries, such as tin, tantalum, and tungsten in the DRC; colored gemstones in Madagascar, and diamonds in West Africa.

There are many "push" and "pull" factors behind why men and women choose to mine in or around protected areas in particular. Often they are seen as untouched, virgin areas, or they have not been mined in living memory (e.g. Liberia). Many colonial governments created forest reserves (which later became protected areas) in places where rich mineral deposits were known to exist, and there may also be a lack of recognition or knowledge of park borders amongst the local population (e.g. in Sapo National Park in Liberia and the Kahuzi-Biéga National Park in DRC). In some parts of the world, protected areas are perceived as common land, in which there is no statutory or customary landowner to whom one must pay for access rights (e.g. mining

TABLE 6.1

Impact and mitigation of ASM

ASM activity	Examples of observed or anticipated ecological impact	Recommended mitigation options
Clearing vegetation, and harvesting timber and non-timber forest products	■ Ape food sources diminished, including fruit trees and terrestrial herbaceous vegetation. ■ Habitat and migration paths are blocked by mining camps. ■ Habitat loss due to deforestation. ■ Increased vulnerability of forest ecosystems to invasive plant and animal species. ■ Erosion of unsecured soil during rains, sometimes resulting in landslides. ■ Soil degradation leading to changes in vegetation, including food sources. ■ Extensive use of tracks both on foot and by cars leads to additional habitat loss, migration range disruption, and increased vulnerability to commercial bushmeat trade (D. Greer, personal communication, 2012), markets for ape infants, and hunting for ivory and animal parts used in traditional medicine. ■ Important non-timber forest products used in food preparation and house construction, like leaves from the Marantaceae (and to a lesser extent, Zingiberaceae), are also staples for lowland gorillas (D. Greer, personal communication, 2012).	■ Only buy local supplies of firewood, timber, or charcoal from certified ASM suppliers, i.e. other areas where wood is grown commercially and sustainably (Cook and Healy, 2012). ■ Restrict access/usage to miners with mining identification cards for the specific site (Cook and Healy, 2012). ■ Strict regulation and enforcement together with sensitization and education campaigns. ■ Foster an environment of close cooperation between ASM, nongovernmental organizations (NGOs), and government experts to understand which plants/animals can or cannot be used, by explaining economic and environmental motivation of so doing (D. Greer, personal communication, 2012).
Physical removal of soil and rock to access the deposit	■ Release and dispersal of corrosive dusts (such as lime dust). ■ Oxidation of soil piles leading to the release of toxic metal ions. ■ Leaching of toxic minerals through erosion or water seepage can impact groundwater and surface water quality. ■ Air-borne or water-borne toxins can detrimentally impact soils, water quality, vegetation, and human and animal health. ■ Destruction of riverbanks and riverbeds impacts hydrological systems and aquatic ecology. Gorillas are known to consume the aquatic herbs *Hydrocharis* and *Scleria*, but it is not known if the impacts of mining methods affect these plants significantly or not (D. Greer, personal communication, 2012).	■ Conduct studies to understand the chemical composition of soil, characterize the risk of contamination, and take appropriate steps for containment (Villegas *et al.*, 2012). ■ Introduce alternative techniques and technologies that target known deposits and impact a less extensive area (Villegas *et al.*, 2012). ■ Do not allow mining in highly sensitive erosion areas, i.e. steep slopes and fragile soils (Cook and Healy, 2012).
Mining in or near rivers and streams	■ Siltation reduces light penetration into water bodies, causing reduced photosynthesis in aquatic plants, depleting oxygen levels in the water.	■ Conduct a thorough evaluation of endemic aquatic biodiversity and identification of potentially important aquatic habitats.

	▪ Direct (tailing, diesel from pumps) and indirect (turbidity) pollution of water sources for humans, apes, and other wildlife ▪ Smaller streams and waterways can cease to flow due to numerous open pits and clogging of springs. ▪ Erosion of unprotected earth during rains leading to landslides, additional sediment release, and riverbank deterioration. ▪ Loss and degradation of aquatic herbaceous vegetation through riverbank impacts, some of which can be important seasonal gorilla foods.	▪ Conduct statutory environmental studies in PACE sites (Cook and Healy, 2012). ▪ Minimize extraction for mine sites and conserve/recycle water (Cook and Healy, 2012). ▪ Create dedicated sites for washing/panning with settlement holes or tanks to reduce waste-water flowing into watercourses with high sediment loads (Cook and Healy, 2012).
Use of toxic chemicals in gold processing	▪ Risk of "dead zones" and localized death of animals (including birds and fish) exposed to unmanaged cyanide releases. ▪ Aquatic faunal and other animals' health affected by mercury in air or water (including great apes).	▪ UNEP promotes a two-step approach to reduce mercury use in ASM: ▪ Step 1: Reduce mercury use and emissions through improved practices, which use less mercury. ▪ Step 2: Eliminate mercury use by using alternative mercury-free technologies that increase (or at least maintain) income for miners, and are better for health and the environment (UNEP, 2011b).

Ancillary/support services

Hunting of animals for bushmeat for personal consumption or sale Opportunistic and deliberate poaching of endangered species for trade	▪ Population decline of critically threatened and endangered species due to hunting (including great apes). ▪ Animals maimed or mortally wounded after escaping from snares (including great apes). ▪ Disturbance of wildlife habitats and migration routes due to large number of people resident in and moving through forest, as well as light and sound pollution of mining activities.	▪ Ban commercial hunting as part of a mining permit, but allow closely monitored subsistence hunting (Cook and Healy, 2012). Include artisanal miners in the creation of park patrols and ecoguards where possible (Hollestelle, 2012). ▪ Restrict access to the ASM site to reduce pressure on the biodiversity and the site's environmental impact (D. Greer, personal communication, 2012).
Establishment of permanent and semi-permanent camps, villages, and towns	▪ Enlarged settlements may result in reduced great ape home ranges and increased resource competition, resulting in lower quality of diet and increased great ape interactions (D. Greer, personal communication, 2012). ▪ Noise may alter great ape home-range movement. ▪ Increased human–wildlife conflict.	▪ Population monitoring (pre-, during, and post-mining activity) and habitat quality preservation completed in association with relevant ministries, NGOs, universities, etc. ▪ Initiate education programs tailored to ASM to minimize human–wildlife conflict (e.g. what to do or not do when animal approaches, etc.)

Larger ecosystem impacts

	▪ Ecological changes due to loss of keystone species such as elephants and apes. ▪ Long-term changes in watershed due to rapid run-off in deforested areas. ▪ Downstream hydrological impacts with respect to water quality and flow due to widespread siltation and pollution of rivers and streams.	▪ Create a cordon sanitaire or buffer zone (min. 500 m) between ape-critical habitat and the ASM, and clearly mark it. The buffer must be recognized and respected by the miners and the ASM management authorities (Cook and Healy, 2012).

license, surface rent). Gazetting of protected areas can also stimulate ASM activities by making other livelihoods less viable owing to the limited availability of land for farming and other activities (e.g. Uganda).

The closure of industrial mining sites can also create a surge of impoverished and out-of-work miners in rural areas who migrate towards protected areas in order to maintain their livelihoods (e.g. in Ecuador and the DRC). Furthermore, protected areas offer a variety of livelihood options that complement ASM in a logical livelihood strategy for individuals or households, for example timber extraction, bushmeat and other wildlife products, and charcoal making (Villegas et al., 2012).

The impact of ASM activities in ape habitats

While the scale of ASM will impact ape populations in different ways, as with timber extraction, it can disrupt behavior, alter habitat, reduce food resources, disperse populations, and increase exposure to hunting pressures (see Chapters 3 and 7). According to Hruschka and Echavarría (2011):

> [M]ost artisanal miners have little knowledge or awareness about the environmental impact of their activity; their main concern is the subsistence of their family [...] The economic situation of artisanal miners forces environmental protection issues to be secondary concerns as expenditure on environmental protection remains a lesser priority as long as basic needs are not satisfied.

A number of these impacts are given as examples in Table 6.1, alongside potential mitigation options. It is necessary to bear in mind, however, that limited research has been done on both the direct and indirect impacts of ASM on ape populations, especially in Asia.

Thus some of the following assumptions about anticipated outcomes warrant further investigation.

Policy and regulation of artisanal mining

The recognition of ASM as a potentially important part of the economy and an engine for poverty alleviation has led many countries to draft specific laws for its management. However, often these mining laws and policies do not adequately define and give recognition to the sector. In the Tapajos River Basin of the Brazilian Amazon, for example, assessments indicate that around 99% of miners operate without the environmental and mining permits required by law (Sousa et al., 2011). This is a result of a combination of unrealistic and/or ineffectual policies and regulations, lack of political will, lack of infrastructure to enforce the existing regulations, and lack of incentives to miners to comply with legal requirements. Artisanal miners operate in vast and remote areas and the government lacks the resources (personnel, vehicles, information, and materials) to enforce the laws. Furthermore, idiosyncrasies in the regulation of over 20 laws, decrees, and resolutions relating to ASM reveal massive gaps between policy and reality (Sousa et al., 2011). The slow evolution of appropriate and effective policy tools has been hindered by a number of more general, contextual issues that often reoccur in the regulation and formalization of ASM in ape range states.

Land-rights issues

Mineral resources are often owned by the state, which then issues permits or licenses to private entities to start the process of exploration and exploitation of these sub-surface resources. But while in many countries the

law defines how artisanal miners can acquire rights to exploit the resource, the majority of artisanal mining is either conducted *a-legally* (outside of the law) or *illegally* (in violation of the law). A-legal mining means that the law either does not provide for artisanal mining or the state does not put in place the structures necessary for miners to comply with the law, so it is not possible for miners to be legal. This is commonly known as informality, which must be understood as being distinct from illegality.

In some cases, there may also be an ethnic dimension to ASM, with certain ethnic groups traditionally being artisanal miners, with the activity now a part of their herit-

age, and not just a source of revenue (Lahm, 2002). Furthermore, ASM is often conducted in line with customary practices around land tenure, which may have been in place for many decades or more (see Chapter 2). This means that the miners follow regulations and customs set by traditional authorities including paying taxes, following site rules, and so on, even where they are not compliant with what is required in national law. In these circumstances, miners view their practices as *formal* to some degree as they are compliant with local regulations, even where they may be in violation of national ones. This is especially common in places where the state has limited reach and influence in rural areas.

Photo: While the scale of ASM will impact ape populations in different ways, as with timber extraction, it can disrupt behavior, alter habitat, reduce food resources, disperse populations, and increase exposure to hunting pressures.
© Gustave Mbaza/WWF

In these settings, conflict between miners and the state and between local authorities and the state can occur where the state chooses to clamp down on what it judges to be illegal activities but what locals consider to be legitimate. For example, miners may be mining illegally within a protected area whilst respecting the rules and regulations of the traditional landowners who held ownership rights before the land was gazetted. Conflict may also occur when the local authorities and/or communities and/or miners specifically see park boundaries as illegitimate, or where the precedence of national over local regulations is not accepted, or when massive rush-type migrations take place (Villegas *et al.*, 2012).

Institutional or structural discrimination

Artisanal miners are often not capable of meeting legal requirements set by governments and other governmental agencies (Hruschka and Echavarría, 2011). This is due to various factors: for example, miners are often illiterate and unaware of their rights and responsibilities under the national mining law and policies; often legislation is designed with large-scale industrial mining in mind and miners are therefore structurally unable to fulfill the requirements (e.g. South African mining law). In other cases, miners are institutionally prevented from formalizing due to the stigma and negative connotation of the activity. In some countries, like Gabon, artisanal mining is not a nationally recognized "profession" (although miners do have some status in the government's Mining Code), therefore miners lie about their real profession, obscuring the scale and scope of the activity, and the need for developmental, legal, and financial support (Hollestelle, 2012).

Such structural issues can bind ASM activities to its informal and illegal status,

making it vulnerable to violence, corruption, exploitation, and also exacerbating its negative environmental and social impacts due to a lack of state support or services that could otherwise mitigate some of its impacts (Hruschka and Echavarría, 2011). It can also leave ASM camps vulnerable to influence by persons engaged in illegal activities such as hunting elephants for ivory, with ASM camps used to disguise activities. There is thus a key need to be clear about stakeholder roles and responsibilities among actors and ensure a coherence of policy and governance across sectors in order to create structures that facilitate this.

Lack of good governance and conflict among government agencies

The institutions, polices, and processes that influence livelihoods in the ASM sector vary significantly both from country to country and within different regional contexts. Even in countries where ASM is a formalized activity, there might still be discrepancies and conflict over who can and cannot get rights to use a resource or carry out an economic activity. In many countries where ASM occurs, contradictions between mining, forestry, and/or environmental laws and/or poor coordination across the various agencies responsible for enforcing these creates confusion and unpredictability in how the law should be applied. Likewise, at the local level, a range of different public institutions (often tiers of institutions) influence or are influenced by ASM policy. Local government-district assemblies (Ghana, Guinea, Gabon) also influence land use and local development policy, although evidence suggests that grassroots tiers of government are under-resourced and have different priorities to those of central government (Lahm, 2002; Centre for Development Studies, 2004).

Case studies

The following are a set of case studies examining the specifics of ASM in ape habitats, focusing primarily on central Africa. For each there is a brief situational summary, a discussion of ASM's known or presumptive impacts on ape populations, and a summary of previous intervention attempts to manage ASM's environmental impacts.

Central African Republic (CAR)

Spanning the northern edge of the Congo Basin rainforest in the south all the way up to the Sahel, CAR has a wealth of natural resources and biodiversity, including significant populations of western lowland gorilla (*Gorilla gorilla gorilla*), central chimpanzee

(*Pan troglodytes troglodytes*), and the eastern chimpanzee (*Pan troglodytes schweinfurthii*). ASM, primarily in diamonds, represents a key threat to CAR's great apes. Addressing ASM's impact is complicated by the extreme poverty in the country; it ranks 180 out of 187 on the Human Development Index (UNDP, 2012) and exploitation of resources like diamonds offers a critical opportunity not only for national income, accounting for 40–50% of all export revenue, but also constitutes a fundamental livelihood strategy for over 10% of the country's population of 5.2 million people. Indeed, ASM is both poverty-driven and poverty-alleviating, and taking this into account is both challenging and essential to protecting its wildlife (Tieguhong, Ingram, and Schure, 2009).

FIGURE 6.5

ASM in CAR

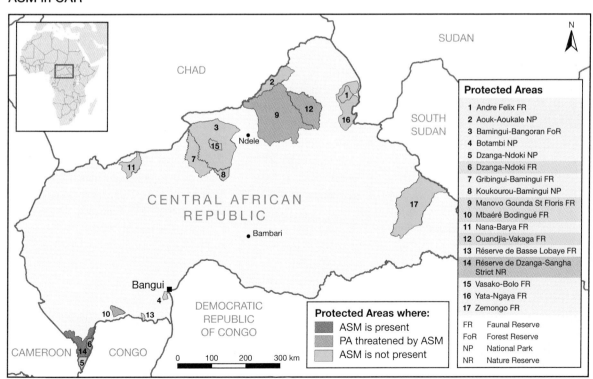

Using data provided by PRADD/WWF-CARPO/GTZ (Chantiers d'exploitation miniere (diamants) dans la Reserve Speciale de Dzanga-Sangha) the CAR map shows where known ASM occurs. By cross-referencing known diamond deposits with protected areas, a list of protected areas threatened by ASM has been produced.

Courtesy of ASM–PACE.

Overview of the ASM sector and its impact on critical protected areas

The ASM sector dominates the CAR extractive industry, particularly in the diamond field, and brings with it a host of social issues. As in other countries, exploitative labor relationships, smuggling, and links to armed groups have been documented (ICG, 2010). Despite ASM being a fundamental livelihood activity for thousands of people, most are unable to escape poverty. In addition, ASM activity in a number of protected areas, including Mbaére-Bodingué National Park, Manovo-Gounda-Saint-Floris National Park, and near Dzanga-Sangha National Park, poses an environmental threat and negatively impacts apes (Figure 6.5).

This network of protected areas in the CAR together makes up more than 10% of the national territory (World Bank, 2010). However, one-third of these areas have been deemed 'paper parks', in the sense that they afford little protection owing to a lack of resources and enforcement (Blom, Yamindou, and Prins, 2004). The parks in the southwest are the only ones located in dense closed Guineo-Congolian rainforest, which makes up about 15% of the country's environment (de Wasseige et al., 2009). This northern part of the Congo basin is great ape habitat, and Dzanga-Sangha in particular has important populations of western lowland gorillas and chimpanzees, among a total of 16 species of primates (Tieguhong et al., 2009). Gorilla concentrations in the Dzanga sector of the park were estimated at 1.6 km^{-2} in 1996–97 (CARPE, 2010), and even higher in the Ndoki section. A more recent study from 2005 estimated concentrations in the park at around 1 km^{-2} (MIKE, 2005). Another important attribute of the area is its inclusion in the transboundary Sangha Trinational Landscape (TNS), one of 12 priority ecological landscapes identi-

fied in 2000 by the Congo Basin Partnership Facility. Overall, TNS has some of the healthiest populations of great apes in Central Africa, making this accord particularly important, as it enables cross-border patrols and harmonization of laws and regulations. Indeed, the principal threats to the TNS landscape include hunting and commercial bushmeat trade, but also unsustainable commercial logging, the ivory trade, the capture of grey parrots, and uncontrolled ASM (de Wasseige et al., 2009).

Mining activity was first observed in the Dzanga-Sangha area during a patrol in 1997 (CARPE, 2009). While most of the activity is located in the special reserve, surveys conducted in 2002 and 2006 show a steady movement towards the Dzanga sector of the park, in some places coming within 2 km of the boundary (Tieguhong et al., 2009). Characterizing the ecological impact of ASM, however, requires looking at the specific impact, and its geographical as well as temporal scale (DeJong, 2012a). While a single miner may destroy plenty of vegetation, the severity of an impact cannot be assessed without looking at the cumulative effect of many miners, as well as to what extent regenerative capacity naturally reverses the effects through time (World Bank, 2008).

The most significant impacts on protected areas, however, are indirect. The worst impact is from poaching (as opposed to legal, but often excessive hunting), which often accompanies mining (World Bank, 2010) and increases as miners penetrate or set up camps in or near protected areas (CARPE, 2010). There is at least one mining camp that has become a town in the special reserve (DeJong, 2012a) and the associated human pressures that result from this development are perhaps more significant than the direct impacts of digging holes. However, the only study to look specifically at mining in the TNS landscape concluded that despite these impacts, the cumulative effect represents a

Photo: Since mining is the most important source of revenue for many people, working in unexploited areas known to have deposits is worth the risk of some harassment and the hardship of living for weeks or months as far as 50 km from home.
© Micha Hollestelle

minimal negative impact on the environment, given the small geographical scale and the fact that many of the effects, such as forest degradation, are reversible (Tieguhong *et al.*, 2009). Nevertheless, the largest direct threats to great apes besides habitat loss, including disease outbreak and poaching, are exacerbated by their proximity to humans, and ASM brings hunters and disease-carriers closer to gorillas and chimpanzees (see Chapter 7).

Motivations of miners

While CAR's mining communities are often refugees and have come from elsewhere (Freudenberger and Mogba, 1998), diamond mining near Dzanga-Sangha is not a "rush" situation, but instead has a long and gradual history of advancement. Indeed, socio-economic studies reveal that diamonds have been the primary livelihood for the majority of people for many years (DeJong, 2012a). In this sense, pull factors appear to be less prominent. Instead, push factors seem to be at work, including the fact that many of the best claims near villages are either already mined out or belong to someone else, which pushes people towards new territory (DeJong, 2012a). However, there is also evidence that people have customary claims in areas in the special reserve that go back many years, perhaps pre-dating the park's creation (DeJong, 2012a) . However, most are aware that they are operating in or near the park, suggesting that poorly understood limits are not an issue. In addition, miners report on confrontations with state authorities, including ecoguards (Tieguhong *et al.*, 2009), which suggests that enforcement is not enough to deter people from working. At a most basic level, since mining is the most important source of revenue for many people, working in unexploited areas known to have deposits is worth the risk of some harassment and the hardship of living for weeks or months as far as 50 km from home.

Attempts to mitigate the impact of ASM in the CAR

A number of mitigation techniques to reduce the impact of ASM on protected areas have been suggested in the case of the CAR.

Enforcement

Effective enforcement requires sensitization, establishing a clear and accepted understanding of park boundaries, and building positive relationships with surrounding communities. These have all been important cornerstones of the strategy in Dzanga-Sangha (CARPE, 2010). However, perceptions by miners of unwarranted harassment by guards (DeJong, 2012a) and the fact that guards continue to confiscate mining material (DeJong, 2012b) show that this tactic may be too narrow in scope.

Alternative livelihoods

Understanding how mining fits into an overall livelihood picture is needed for any "alternative" livelihood to succeed. According to WWF, the problem of mining in Dzanga-Sangha will not be resolved unless the would-be miners can make a decent living outside the park doing other activities (J. Yarissem, personal communication, 2012). However, it is difficult to find activities that can provide better financial prospects than artisanal mining (Tschakert, 2009).

The Property Rights and Artisanal Diamond Development (PRADD) program is a joint US State Department and USAID initiative aimed at increasing the amount of diamonds entering the legal chain of custody. Its objectives are to:

- Clarify and formalize rights to land and natural resources;
- Improve monitoring of the production and sale of diamonds;
- Increase the benefits accruing to mining communities;
- Strengthen capacity to mitigate environmental damage; and
- Improve stakeholders' access to crucial information.

While new mines are continually being established, others are inherited, purchased, or given as gifts. Through the clarification of these customary means of acquisition, and by focusing specifically on claimant identity, land transactions, and mining documentation PRADD has been able to take advantage of opportunities present in the current Mining Code for registering legitimate claims. The environmental rehabilitation program includes the provision of technical assistance to miners to convert mined-out pits into fishponds, agroforestry plots, and vegetable gardens. The program is a unique attempt to meld together livelihood diversification with environmental rehabilitation, and stands out from other regulatory-driven attempts which have had limited success (DeJong, 2012a). It has also proved popular, with at least 381 rehabilitated sites being counted in under a year (DeJong, 2012a).

While this approach is not directly relevant to protected areas, since both mining and agriculture are illegal in most of them, there is some evidence that for a number of small-scale miners, revenue from fish farming has surpassed revenue from diamonds. This raises the possibility of finding activities that might provide sufficient incentives to keep miners closer to home and away from protected areas, although PRADD's aim was never to foster alternative livelihoods, but rather to promote complementary ones while strengthening the legal and fiscal regimes that underlie ASM.

Sustainable development policies

It is possible that a sustainable development of the diamond economy could in fact have a positive long-term effect on great ape conservation, provided it leads to economic growth, stronger institutions, and greater respect for the rule of law. CAR is still far from reaching this point, considering its extreme poverty, lack of institutional coordination, limited capacity, and the recent uptick in industrial mining deals. However, the holistic approaches being piloted, like land-use planning and property rights clarification (e.g. PRADD), offer a glimpse of strategies that stand a good chance of enabling both people and primates to thrive.

The Democratic Republic of Congo (DRC)

Environmental impacts of ASM and associated threats to apes

The DRC is a unique region for biodiversity in Africa and the only country on earth to have three species of great ape (Draulens and Van Krunkelsven, 2002), the mountain gorilla (*Gorilla beringei beringei*), Grauer's gorilla (*Gorilla beringei graueri*), bonobo (*Pan paniscus*), central chimpanzee (*Pan troglodytes troglodytes*), and eastern chimpanzee (*Pan troglodytes schweinfurthii*). ASM and associated activities such as wildlife hunting and the bushmeat trade are known to occur in many of the DRC's protected areas and critical ecosystems (Figure 6.6). However, judging the relative significance of ASM as a threat to protected areas and apes against other activities is not a simple task because they often occur in tandem,

rather than being independent of one another. Moreover, many of the threats are less obvious as they relate to habitat destruction or reduction. Major threats include: logging (legally and illegally), large-scale extractive projects, the presence of refugees and/or armed groups, and the site-specific particularities of mining, charcoal making, agricultural conversion, and bushmeat hunting and other illegal wildlife trade. An additional ring of environmental degradation is created by the construction of access routes for miners allowing other people to penetrate further into remote areas well beyond the time frame of direct mining activity.

Bushmeat hunting and the illegal wildlife trade is a case in point of ASM occurring in conjunction with, and often inciting, other human activities that have a detrimental impact on the environment. Hunting for ivory, and the capture of birds and baby chimpanzees, often takes place at artisanal mining sites, as the buyers of minerals are likely to engage in other lucrative activities as well. In the southern Congo alone, 300 gorillas were estimated to have been killed in 2009 to supply the local bushmeat markets (Endangered Species International, 2009). Concurrent with the invasion of the Bili–Uéré Domaine de Chasse by approximately 3000 gold miners in June 2007, a five-year survey documented expansion of the bushmeat trade to the south of the Uélé River, linked to the artisanal diamond and gold mining industries and centered on Buta (Hicks *et al.*, 2010). By contrast, in areas where there was no ASM, they found no snares and limited evidence of bushmeat and related trades (e.g. skins) in nearby forest zones. While researchers found that the miners consumed primate bushmeat, and that a higher proportion of miners admitted to hunting and eating chimpanzees than did villagers (Darby, Gillespie, and Hicks, 2010; L. L. Darby, unpublished data), it should be noted that a 2012 ASM–PACE study

> " Judging the relative significance of ASM as a threat to protected areas and apes against other activities is not a simple task because they often occur in tandem. "

FIGURE 6.6

ASM occurring in DRC

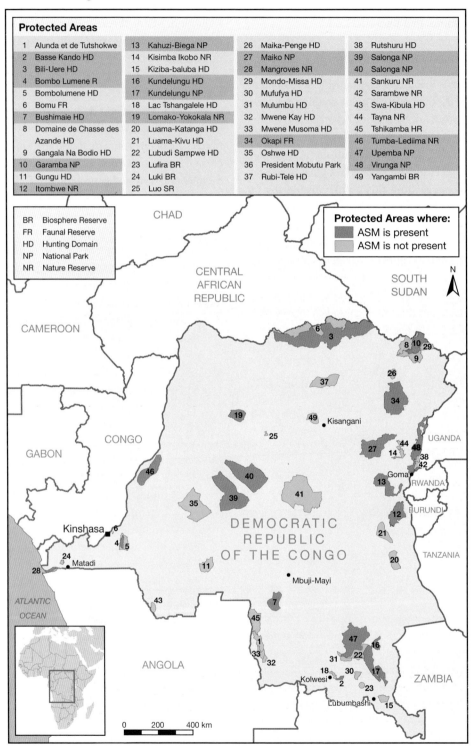

found this not to be the case in the eastern part of the Itombwe Reserve where cultural beliefs kept people from consuming apes (Weinberg *et al.*, 2012, 2013).

Kahuzi-Biéga National Park (KBNP): co-existence and conflict between conservation and the ASM sector

Located in South Kivu, near the DRC's border with Rwanda, the Kahuzi-Biéga National Park (KBNP) was founded in 1970 and became a World Heritage Site in 1980 (Walker Painemilla *et al.*, 2010). Its status was upgraded to World Heritage Site in Danger in 1997 (Plumptre *et al.*, 2009), and it is now managed by the Congolese Wildlife Authority (ICCN – *Institut Congolais pour la Conservation de la Nature*), with support from a host of international organizations. The park forms a part of the Congo Basin ecosystem as well as the Albertine Rift. With an area of 6000 km², it boasts a wide array of dense primary tropical forests, montane forests, and bamboo galleries. The high mountains in the east, including the non-active volcanoes Mount Kahuzi (3308 m) and Mount Biéga (2790 m), are connected by a corridor to the lower altitude tropical forests of the west (D'Souza, 2003). This critical ecological corridor is one of the most conflicted parts of the park, with tensions especially high between local communities and park authorities as those communities which were originally located within park boundaries seek to regain access to the land.

The high and low altitudes serve as the habitat for 136 species of mammals, including 13 species of primates: the endangered Grauer's gorilla, chimpanzees, baboons, three different colobus species, and five different guenon species (D'Souza, 2003). Studies at the end of the twentieth century estimated eastern lowland gorilla populations to be at 17 000 (plus or minus 8000 gorillas) with 86% of the populations living in KBNP and the adjacent Kasese Forest (Hall *et al.*, 1998). The population has seen a significant decline in the last decade, and in 2010 UNEP reported that the surviving population is likely to be below 5000; yet regional insecurity makes accurate surveying difficult (UNEP, 2011b).

ASM has been occurring in KBNP since the 1970s (Steinhauer-Burkatt, Muhlenberg, and Stowik, 1995); the dramatic population movement and the global coltan boom only enhanced an already existing phenomenon. As of March 2011, people were mining gold, tantalum, and tin on the outskirts of the KBNP and occasionally within the park as well (Debroux *et al.*, 2007), especially in the lowland sector (UNEP and McGinley, 2009). As of 2006, there were an estimated 9000 to 12 000 miners living in the park, although this number will have fluctuated since (Durban Process, 2006). This population has been connected with hunting, deforestation, and clearing for subsistence agriculture, as well as poaching for ivory, wood for cooking fires, human waste, and many more pressures to the park (UNEP and McGinley, 2009; Conservation International, 2010). The Ministry of Mines also found that artisanal gold miners in the park were using mercury to wash the gold they extracted (Mazina and Masumbuko, 2004). Likewise, coltan miners use a great deal of water to wash the mineral (D'Souza, 2003). Some of the silt enters the rivers and streams and ends up polluting entire water supplies and causing long-term changes in the watershed, especially since run-off can be considerably fast in deforested areas (D'Souza, 2003). Heavy mining adjacent to rivers and streams has also led to soil erosion and landslides (D'Souza, 2003).

One of the reasons why the KBNP is a contested conservation space is a result of its recent history of changing boundaries and the subsequent (and controversial) resettlement of different groups of people living in its conservation zones. In 1975, the ICCN and then *Deutsche Gesellschaft für Technische Zusammenarbeit* (GTZ, German Technical Cooperation enterprise) increased the lowland area of the park's boundaries from 750 km² (UNEP-WCMC, 2011) to 6000 km², culminating in an official extension of the park (UNEP-WCMC, 2011). The 13 000 people of the Shi, Tembo, and Rega tribes who were living in the extension zone were told to move outside of the new conservation zone (Barume, 2000). These tribes had practiced agriculture, cattle grazing, and mining on the land years before these lands became protected.

As the population was unwilling to move after the decision to extend the national park, authorities used force and destroyed farms and cattle that remained in the extension zone. People retaliated by setting fire to hundreds of hectares of the park (Barume, 2000). By 1995, there were still 15 000 people living inside, despite the ICCN's efforts to negotiate compensation for their cooperation in resettlement. It was not until 2007 that the KBNP, with support from partners, engaged with these communities in a lengthy negotiation over the demarcation.

Programs offering an alternative way forward in dealing with ASM in the DRC's conservation areas

There are a number of examples of on-going programs and initiatives in the DRC that engage with ASM on environmental concerns. Some of these include:

Central African Regional Program for the Environment (CARPE)

CARPE began operation in 1997 and is currently under consideration for extension into 2016 (CARPE, 2011). It is a USAID-funded consortium focusing primarily on "reducing the rate of forest degradation and loss of biodiversity [in the Congo Basin forest of which the DRC forms a large part of the landscape] by supporting increased local, national, and regional natural resource management capacity"(IUCN, 2011). Through CARPE funding NGOs such as WWF have been able to engage with ASM.

Growth with Governance in the Mineral Sector Project (PROMINES)

PROMINES is an integrated, multi-sectorial and multi-component program initiated by the Government of the DRC, the World Bank, and the UK Department for International Development (DFID) to provide technical assistance to the mining sector, as well as improve its governance, efficiency, and future growth. The objective of the artisanal mining component of PROMINES is to improve the legal status, working practices, and economic return of artisanal mining in the DRC whilst establishing mechanisms to sustainably reduce its negative impacts on society, security, and the environment. This project has a multi-million dollar component to tackle some of the key issues in the DRC's ASM sector, including:

- Improving environmental and social management aspects of ASM and mining sector legislation as a whole;
- Helping to ensure that the revenues from ASM contribute to local and regional development;
- Recommending an extensive environmental impact assessment of the mining sector.

Mining and mindful conservation planning in the Itombwe Nature Reserve

This is premised on the observation that many of the difficulties in addressing ASM in

PACE are being neglected or underestimated early in planning processes. ASM–PACE, a joint program founded by Estelle Levin Ltd. and global conservation organization WWF, is working with WWF DRC and other conservation stakeholders focused on the Itombwe Nature Reserve (RNI), where final demarcation is still awaiting approval by the State (Weinberg *et al.*, 2012, 2013). Conservation and local CSOs (civil society organizations) have proposed the RNI be split into three zones: a human habitation zone, a resource-use zone, and a core protected zone. While it is in its early stages, this process aims to take into account existing mining activities in the proposed protected area and plan conservation strategies accordingly.

Gabon

Looking for a green future and balancing conservation and development

ASM in Gabon (Figure 6.7) is currently regulated by the Mining Code (Law N° 5/2000 of 12 October 2000), two additional texts, and a Presidential Decree fixing the conditions of application of law. Permission to engage in artisanal mining is granted by the Ministry of Mines in the form of a card for artisanal exploitation, the *Carte d'Exploitation Artisanale* (Hollestelle, 2012). By law, the Ministry of Mines can support small-scale operators in improving existing technologies or introducing new techniques with regard to artisanal mining, but there remain several weaknesses in the law. For example (Hollestelle, 2012):

- Legal artisanal miners are not bound by environmental or health regulations. The only mention of health is in an article that states that the Ministry of Mines needs to inform relevant local authorities of concentrations of human beings in artisanal mining camps as a means of preventing epidemics such as cholera, AIDS, and Ebola.

- Neither the Code nor the Decree mentions any environmental obligation with respect to the practice of artisanal mining other than the aforementioned support to technology improvement.

- Technically the government requires artisanal miners to sell mined gold at fixed prices that may be uncompetitive with the black market rates available. This requirement – if and when enforced – may have the unintended consequence of exacerbating smuggling operations in the country.

- There are also currently problematic definitions in the government's classification of "artisanal" and "small-scale" mining. Owing to imprecise language, there is a legal 'gray' area for certain types of ASM, specifically those artisanal sites that employ fewer than 70 people.

- There is currently very little incentive to formalize activities. Indeed, artisanal miners gain little with the purchase of a Carte d'Exploitation. If anything, it puts them on the radar of the government when they are already in a weak negotiating position, even if legal.

Minkébé National Park – Government interest in finding "common ground": using ASM as a force for conservation

The environmental stakes are particularly high in Gabon. It has the highest forest cover as a proportion of national surface area in any African country, its pristine forests have brought attention from global conservation organizations, and it has been dubbed the "Green Heart of Africa." Indeed, Gabon is home to five of the world's 200 Global ecoregions, which together cover the entirety of the country, and its national parks contain important populations of western lowland gorillas and western chimpanzees. Thus far,

> " The environmental stakes are particularly high in Gabon. It has the highest forest cover as a proportion of national surface area in any African country. "

186

low population density, government stewardship, and a case of 'Dutch disease' (due to its large dependence on the petroleum industry and mainly offshore wells) has meant that Gabon's precious forests are largely intact.

"Dutch Disease implies declining competitiveness and structural change across sectors, normally triggering 'deindustrialisation' in developed countries and 'de-agriculturisation' in developing countries. Yet, this de-agriculturisation also tends to significantly reduce pressures to convert land for agricultural uses, which globally is the principal direct cause of deforestation" (Hollestelle, 2012).

However, since oil production "peaked" in the late 1990s in Gabon, there have been few major oil discoveries, and logging and mining have steadily increased in importance as sources of revenue (Lahm, 2002). A series of oil palm plantations is currently under development in the country as a means of further diversifying the economy and several large mining projects have commenced or are planned, including in neighboring areas of Cameroon and Republic of Congo, with associated regional infrastructure projects.

For years, ASM was a relatively overlooked sector at the national level, although gold panning has been a major source of

FIGURE 6.7

ASM in Gabon

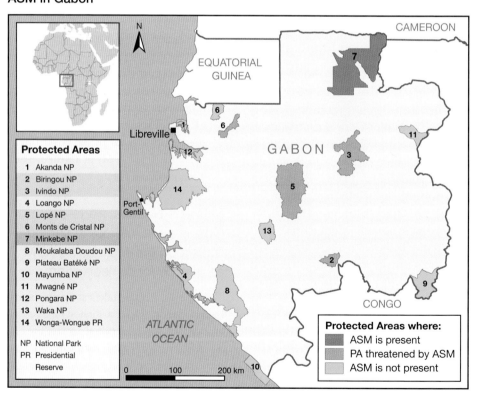

Minkébé National Park is the only protected area in Gabon where ASM is known to be occurring with a significant numbers of miners, and thus where it is likely to have significant impacts on apes. ASM is also known to have taken place in Moukalaba Doudou National Park and Monts de Cristal National Park; however those in Moukalaba Doudou areas were inactive at the time of writing, and the ASM within Monts de Cristal is deemed manageable due to the low number of miners present. The map derives from a sketch map of Gabonese Greenstone belts and major banded iron formations (Hollestelle, 2012). Where these formations overlap PAs, they are considered at risk of ASM activities. Indeed, Ivindo National Park is known to have ASM activity on its outskirts.

Courtesy of ASM–PACE.

revenue for many families in northeastern Gabon since the 1940s (Lahm, 2002). While artisanal and small-scale gold mining in the buffer zone of Minkébé National Park has long been a source of tension, in 2008 the situation became significantly worse in terms of the large number of miners present in the Minkébé camps following the climb in global gold prices. This was facilitated by the sparse presence of national park guards and monitoring teams in the park. A combination of local discontentment with the view that foreigners were financially benefitting from uncontrolled illegal ASM, concern by the State as to the illegality and lack of revenues from the gold sector in Minkébé, and concerns that poaching for bushmeat, ivory and other illegal activities were increasing at an alarming rate, led the government to evict all miners from Minkébé in June 2011 (Koumbi, 2009; Mbaza, 2011). The purge led to between 2000 and 5000 mainly Cameroonian illegal immigrants leaving the Minkébé ASM zone. The Gabonese military personnel have remained in the area, also evicting illegal fishing and hunting camps, and they still occupy these camps to prevent the miners from returning (Hollestelle, 2012).

However, there is now significant government and local interest in re-opening the Minkébé camps to local Gabonese miners. The forced exit of illegal Cameroonian miners has apparently been welcomed by local miners, but they too lost their livelihoods and personal property as a result of the mass eviction. Though outnumbered in recent years, the Minkébé zone was historically populated with Gabonese miners, pit owners, and predominantly foreign traders, while most Gabonese traders were ambulant (Lahm, 2002). Gabonese miners who engaged with the different conservation initiatives have often been keen for the government to step in, a sentiment likely to have been shared by other miners. As a

matter of fact, throughout the last decade reports on Minkébé and other mining camps consistently show a desire of Gabonese miners for their trade to be formalized and for the government to address the influx of foreigners. Combined with the government's desire to control the gold trade and coupled with the Park Authorities' desire to safeguard the park for conservation purposes, the notion of economically and socially responsible artisanal and small-scale mining (ESER-ASM) gold seems appealing to all parties as a viable solution. The government has received support from donors to do a national scoping of ASM in PACE locations as a first step to this larger vision of having ASM develop in line with the government's vision of a "Green Gabon." When examples of "best practice" are few and far between, signals of pragmatism in solutions, constructive attention to the sector, and a desire to capitalize on its potential benefits and minimize its environmental impacts are a welcome change.

Management options for mitigating the impacts of ASM in protected areas

While ASM practices are on the rise around the world, including within protected areas, there has been little coordinated or systematic effort to curb their environmental impacts until quite recently (Villegas *et al.*, 2012). Furthermore, recent attempts to incorporate the critically important social impacts of ASM in management practices have been hindered by the fact that the extent of ASM as both an economic and developmental force is not well understood and thus requires further investigation at a variety of different scales. What is evident, however, is that one of the major constraints is the lack of adequate enforcement

of existing national laws, due to low human capacity, insufficient budgets and equipment, corruption, and inadequate training or technical knowledge; something that is particularly relevant for many ape range states. Whether or not all of the stakeholders involved (miners, government agencies, international NGOs and governmental organizations) work together on a long-term strategy and have enough funding to finance the longevity of the strategy also has a major influence on policy success (Tranquilli *et al.*, 2012). Whatever the extent of such collaboration, population increases and pressures associated with greater development will likely increase over time, thus paying attention to the mining sector now will likely yield more fruit than paying attention when the threat becomes more severe. The following list of the most widely adopted policy strategies to contain ASM in PACE provides a limited overview of their successes and constraints.

Eviction

To clear miners from a specified area by use of force, or threat of force

This appears to be the most commonly used strategy, although it is more likely to be successful if coupled with alternative livelihood programs and improved park security. The risks with taking this approach include:

- worsening relations with forest-adjacent communities;

- the interruption of mining-dependent rural economies;

- the potential for human rights abuse if eviction is done by undisciplined military (or risk of military involvement in mining sector), and

- pushing miners into increasingly remote and sensitive ecosystems, which has significant and deleterious effects for biodiversity.

Furthermore, a long-term security strategy must be in place in order to prevent miners from re-entering the area in question. Without a robust program offering them an economic stake in respecting the border areas of the park, eviction is likely to fail and ultimately, perhaps, be a waste of time and resources.

Recent examples in ape range states include Sapo National Park in Liberia and Gola Forest Reserve in Sierra Leone. In Gola, the reason for eviction was given as the need to establish both the rule of law and the primacy of conservation priorities in the contested national park. In Liberia, the official rationale for the 2011 "voluntary departure" was for conservation. Other reasons suggested included an upcoming presidential election, the park's remote location near an international border yet with access to roads leading to the capital city, and the profile of miners as ex-combatants. In the short-to-near term, the "voluntary departure" process seemingly left people economically worse off than before because of the disruption of the local economy and livelihoods, and alleged actions by the enforcement agencies to maintain the eviction of all persons from the national park. Furthermore, LSM in the south of the park was due to begin soon after, and the potential for displacing ASM participants back towards the national park was high. It was likely that due to insufficient government monitoring, LSM push factors, and poor knowledge of park boundaries by ASM participants that miners/diggers would soon once again be active in the park (Villegas *et al.*, 2012).

Negotiated access

To allow conditioned access to protected areas where limited ASM is permitted under agreed conditions

The aim of this is to regulate and limit ASM in PACE, and is more likely to be successful in long-established mining sites with strong local community connections and the potential for collaborative efforts to fulfill the agreement. In Brownsberg National Park in Suriname, a 2010–11 agreement was negotiated between park authorities, a facilitating NGO, and local gold miners. In exchange for legal access, the miners would help maintain the road leading up to the tourist lodges in the park. This agreement mutually broke down, however, when authorities failed to clearly delineate the park boundaries and the miners did not fix the road within the desired time frame. Ultimately, the dialog appears to have stopped and the miners continue to work as before. While the potential for this to either be reinitiated in Brownsberg National Park or replicated elsewhere is currently unclear, it is evident that without the necessary trust-building, accountability, and arbitration methods, conditions for negotiated access are unlikely to be met. Indeed, since 2011, the government has returned to a policy of no artisanal gold mining in protected areas.

Geographically based multi-stakeholder supply chain initiatives

To use a participatory method to engage all stakeholders in developing a sustainable supply chain

In areas where there is sustained interest and investment by stakeholders, this may be an effective means of addressing ASM's environmental impacts. An excellent example of an attempt at conservation engagement with ASM is the Gorilla Organization's Durban Process in the Kahuzi-Biéga National Park. The Durban Process was driven by an alarming number of deaths of eastern lowland gorillas in the KBNP, caused in part by the spike in global prices for coltan – and the ensuing increase in ASM – and the on-going conflict in Eastern DRC. The Durban Process was launched in 2003 at a multi-stakeholder meeting in Durban, South Africa, organized by the Dian Fossey Gorilla Fund (Europe) to address the issue of coltan mining in the KBNP. The majority of the people working on the Durban Process were Congolese and the aim was to make it as participatory as possible, managed by the stakeholders through a monitoring committee – the *Comité de suivi du processus de Durban* (CSPD). Chosen according to their role in the KBNP coltan supply chain, the stakeholders included miners, indigenous people, customary authorities, members of the various militias occupying the park, mining officials, and politicians.

"Even small adjustments to mining techniques can vastly ameliorate negative impacts."

Members compiled a list of objectives that would come to be known as the central strategies through which the Durban Process would reduce the environmental, social, economic, and political ramifications of ASM in the KBNP. While utilizing many best practices, by 2009, the Durban Process began to wind down, likely due to several factors, namely donor fatigue, a decrease in funding available generally due to the global economic downturn that began in 2008, and the shifting priorities of the Gorilla Organization. While the Durban Process ended prematurely, with a slow return to a "business-as-usual" scenario, the experience revealed much about the challenges of attempting to address the issue of ASM in PACE in this part of the world.

The complexity of resource governance in a context of state fragility is particularly relevant for ape conservation in the DRC. Informal mining and the illicit trading of minerals has long been associated with violent conflicts in the Kivu provinces of eastern Congo, for example, with the DRC military involved in at least some of the mining as well as the systematic elimination of regional elephant populations, and remains a significant hindrance to conservation interventions in the area. While the situation does not lend itself to quick and easy recommendations, the fact that miners receive little state support, while economic operators invest little in their social needs, suggests that the creation of formal structures for coordination between provincial governments and the mining sector is required. The formation of artisanal and trader representation groups (whether cooperatives, associations, or others) would be an important contribution to the engagement of stakeholders and thus the evolution of better governance of the sector (Spittaels, 2010).

The incentivization of responsible mining in PACE

To use a toolbox of political, financial, and social incentives to encourage positive change in the mining sector

This approach recognizes that even small adjustments to mining techniques can vastly ameliorate negative impacts. It is more likely to succeed in areas where eviction is inappropriate, and where miners are unlikely to transition into alternative livelihoods, or where de-gazettement is to be carried out but ASM is still occurring in a critical ecosystem. Examples include the Sustainable Management of Mineral Resources Project funded by the World Bank in Uganda (2003–11) to improve ASM areas and sector governance, and the Global Mercury Project, which worked to encourage mercury management and elimination in eight countries around the world.

The Oro Verde (Green Gold) Project, which was launched in 2000 in the Chocó Bioregion of Colombia, and uses ASM to benefit Afro-Colombian communities through sustainable, environmentally friendly mining and the utilization of social, economic, environmental, and labor standards, also inspired the creation of the Alliance for

Responsible Mining (ARM) in 2004. ARM's mission is to set standards for responsible ASM and to support and enable producers to deliver fair-mined certified metals and minerals through economically just supply chains to markets. As it continues to evolve, it aims to develop a diversified strategy combining communications, applied research, capacity building, networking, partnership, and lobbying activities, involving stakeholders from all sections of the metals and minerals supply chain.

ARM also previously partnered with Fairtrade International under a joint "Fairtrade/Fairmined" program. In April 2013, the partnership ended and both initiatives have continued independently. The new standards, due to be finalized by the end of 2013, incorporate a more nuanced consideration of how to manage ASM in protected areas, with provisions for allowing it under certain circumstances (E. Levin, email communication, August 5, 2013). The Fairtrade and Fairmined programs are considered to be moderate and pragmatic in their approach to help transform ASM into a more socially and environmentally responsible activity, with improvements in the quality of life of marginalized artisanal miners, their families, and communities. However, the pragmatism of their approaches means, inevitably, that there are trade-offs between environmental protection and economic benefit. For example, both allow for the managed use of mercury and cyanide, which can have long-term impacts on the health of human communities, wildlife, and the environment, but whose exclusion would lead to lower adoption of Fairtrade and Fairmined standards by miners around the world, thereby sacrificing the other environmental benefits they garner (e.g. tailings management and rehabilitation).

More generally, there is also a need for programs that educate miners on their environment, the ecosystem, its ecology, and ecosystem services, as a means of poten-

tially engendering a sense of stewardship. If advocated, this approach might stimulate engagement *with* miners rather than reinforcing the traditional paradigm of pitting them *against* environmental protection.

Alternative livelihoods programs

To incentivize participants away from ASM by offering jobs with fewer negative impacts

ASM is often a highly dangerous practice with a variety of health risks for those involved, and raising awareness of these could encourage a change in income generating activity. There may be more potential to introduce new livelihoods when miners are from the local area and have permanent settlements. In Sierra Leone, for example, an international consortium has had apparent success bringing ASM within the Gola Forest National Park under control. ASM was banned from the park and this has been enforced with robust security using locally-recruited forest guards. The Gola Forest Program has been paying compensation packages to land-owning families, the paramount chiefs of the seven chiefdoms constituting the area, and undertaking infrastructural developments like building schools and health centers, as well as giving scholarships to local school and college students.

Following the aforementioned eviction of miners from Sapo National Park in Liberia in 2005, it was found that in practice the alternative livelihoods offered were simply not robust enough, so that those with the requisite equipment, skills, and desire recommended mining in the Park, suggesting that ASM is an integral part of the local economy. In areas comprising large numbers of economic migrant miners, be they from the same country or foreigners, this model has proven less effective owing to

> " There is a need for programs that educate miners on their environment, the ecosystem, its ecology, and ecosystem services, to potentially engender a sense of stewardship. "

the population's impermanent status, lack of cohesive social capital, and disinterest in long-term collective enterprises. In many areas ASM's main appeal is how lucrative it is with minimal prerequisite skills. As was seen in Sapo, matching the economic weight with alternative livelihoods can be difficult and might even require unsustainable subsidization, a significant hindrance in the more impoverished ape range states.

Selected de-gazettement

To strategically exempt certain parts of an area from PA status during the gazetting process

If established communities are willing to work with the government and respect the established boundaries, then this method can be an effective way of taking into consideration historic mining sites and local community livelihoods. In Uganda, artisanal salt mining has been taking place for hundreds of years on the Katwe Crater Lake surrounded by the Queen Elizabeth National Park. When the Park was being gazetted, Katwe and 12 other towns – mainly fishing villages – were demarcated to protect existing industry and livelihoods. Thanks to that strategic demarcation, Katwe's artisanal salt mining was allowed to continue even though it was physically in the park area.

However, communication and commitment with the relevant communities must be strong in case they are tempted to move into the protected areas. Likewise, when the mining in the exempt portion runs out, the same thing may happen. There is also the possibility that environmental impacts of

Photo: Artisanal miners pan for diamonds in Sierra Leone. © Estelle Levin, 2007

mining may not be contained in the exempt area and could have negative impacts on the neighboring PA. The reconfiguration of hydrological systems, for example, and the loss of spawning grounds for fish through increased sedimentation, can threaten both the human communities that rely on these resources, and the wildlife that they share them with.

Conversion to a protected area

To obtain or strengthen significant government protection

The ultimate aim of ceasing all mining in a given area is only likely to work in places with strong rule of law, political will, and sufficient resources. In Colombia, protected areas have heightened constitutional protection, enjoy a complete ban on mining, and are managed by the Colombian Park Service. The actual (versus theoretical) legal protection is so strong that some indigenous communities are voluntarily converting their lands into protected areas in order to stop encroachment by both industrial and artisanal mining. For such a move to be effective, sufficient trust must exist that the government will not steal or redistribute the land nor exploit it for its own benefit. Unfortunately, few of the most vulnerable protected areas are in countries able to maintain this level of protection.

"Mining mindful" conservation strategies

To consider on-going and potential ASM when planning or discussing protected areas

Many of the difficulties in addressing ASM in PACE are neglected or underestimated early in planning processes. In areas that are candidates for protected area status, and have on-going ASM or substantial exploitation potential, there may be the possibility of initiating such a strategy. Although it is still awaiting final approval by the state, the Itombwe Nature Reserve in the DRC could become a good example of this, if mindful management strategies succeed in taking into account existing mining activities in the proposed protected area and thus plan conservation projects accordingly. However, it takes considerable forethought and cooperation between government, conservation stakeholders, and mining stakeholders to reach consensus. Mining and critical wildlife habitat might overlap in inconvenient but real ways, resulting in a choice having to be made between conservation and mining activity, and significant enforcement resources deployed if the former is chosen. In Itombwe, for example, a major constraint to successful implementation has been rebel activity within the reserve.

Conclusion

As illustrated, current strategies for mitigation of ASM's impact on PACE and great apes include better enforcement of park boundaries, the promotion of alternative livelihoods, the adoption of land-use planning frameworks, clarification of property rights, the formalization of the ASM economy, and the adoption of larger sustainable development initiatives. However, one of the key difficulties with engaging the sector is its huge diversity (e.g. between and within countries, type of mineral, modes of extraction and processing, marketing arrangements, political economy, socio-economic organization, etc.). Thus strategies to reduce vulnerability and improve livelihood security for artisanal and small-scale miners need to be context-specific at both the country and local levels if they are to have a positive impact on biodiversity conservation.

Some of the management options presented in this chapter suggest that, in order to maximize the chances of sustainability, processes should be:

- **Locally owned and driven**. Projects have a much better chance of survival if local stakeholders are committed to their aims and are involved in all stages of design and implementation. Participation encourages ownership and, with it, a sense of accountability for project outcomes.

- **Informed on robust research data**. In order to both tailor and legitimize policy, any change needs to be based on transparent research data, thus ensuring that a link can be made between micro realities and macro policy. While research can play a valuable role in articulating some of the social aspirations of ASM operators, in the past it has failed to put these needs in the context of the relevant environmental legislation. Building trust between ASM operators and the policy process (of which robust research is a crucial part) is essential to navigating the complex trade-offs that exist between the sector and the landscapes in which it works.

- **Strategic, and link to other key policy initiatives/sectors.** Isolated initiatives rarely have impact on deep and complex environmental and economic issues.

However, the situation in areas of high conservation value is not likely to improve unless there is a global drop in mineral prices or miners are incentivized either financially or by increased protected area security not to mine there or – if allowed – to be incentivized to do so in a responsible manner. This is also the case for areas outside of protected areas. Indeed, recent research on the overlap between orangutan distribution and a variety of land-use categories in Kalimantan suggests that while 22% of this

distribution lies in protected areas, 29% lies in natural forest concessions (Wich *et al.*, 2012b). One of the key dilemmas from a conservation point of view concerns areas that might be considered so precious that perhaps mining should not be permitted in them at all. While the direct environmental effects of artisanal mining may be limited in themselves (as seen in the CAR), the sheer size of the sector and its related activities scale up the environmental impacts to alarming proportions. Furthermore, implying that people ought to be compensated financially for leaving an area that they should not have been in, in the first place raises a number of complex ethical questions. This might be the case where miners were present before a protected area was proclaimed, but would certainly not apply in most rush situations like those in DRC or Madagascar. In a context such as this, where mining is opportunistic and out of control, strong enforcement of the law is also needed.

The complex nature of environmental factors, the limited legislation involved, and the lack of knowledge on the interface of these with ape conservation require further investigation. Ultimately, whether or not great apes manage to survive within these human-modified landscapes depends on whether protected areas are large enough and, more importantly, adequately protected (Tranquilli *et al.*, 2012). Given that diverse interests, goals, and agendas for each stakeholder converge when considering ASM in protected areas and critical ecosystems, accompanying policy changes may also be necessary to support their conservation, and these require political will and, ideally, enthusiasm. While ASM needs to be integrated with institutional change, with legislators, governments, multilateral organizations and industry collaborating, there is no global solution to the problem. Consequently, the need to formalize the sector and protect PACE must be reconciled in a way that brings all stakeholders together. ASM goes beyond individual livelihoods, and while vast deposits of mineral wealth remain undiscovered and unexploited, and markets continue to fluctuate, there needs to be a recognition that this is not just an economic issue, but also a social, ethical, political, ethnic, and environmental one, too.

Acknowledgments

Principal authors: ASM–PACE and Adam Phillipson

Contributors: Alessandra Awolowo, Terah DeJong, David Greer, Estelle Levin, Erik Meijaard, PNCI, Cristina Villegas, Ruby Weinberg, and Serge Wich

Photo: Deforestation brought about through a rise in mechanized logging, and the expansion of mining and oil and gas extraction, has increased in many tropical forest areas. © Global Witness

CHAPTER 7

The bigger picture: indirect impacts of extractive industries on apes and ape habitat

Introduction

As illustrated in the preceding chapters, clear standards exist to regulate the direct impacts of extractive industries. However, responsibility and management for the indirect impacts caused by natural resource extraction are mostly absent. Yet, these often pose the greatest threats to natural habitats as well as to indigenous territories. Although mining and oil/gas extraction have significant localized impacts on the surrounding environment, their indirect impacts can also be substantial and reach beyond the immediate exploitation areas. This is relevant to even extensive logging activities, especially where sustainable management practices are in place. Logging, as with mining and oil and gas extraction, results in infrastructure development that is often accompanied by the growth of human population centers and marketplaces, dependent upon the exploitation of land, forests, and wildlife. Evidence from remote sensing indicates that infrastructure created for extractive industry operations causes widespread changes in regional land use. These changes can have long-term effects on forest ecosystems and forest-based livelihoods (Asner *et al.*, 2009). In this chapter, we describe such impacts on apes and their habitats, present options for their mitigation, and examine some of the challenges faced.

The first section focuses on the indirect impacts of extractive industries on apes and ape habitats. Although all indirect impacts are important, in this chapter we concentrate on those that are most pressing at this time.

- **Increased hunting and poaching**: the opening up of forests for extractive industries facilitates the expansion of associated roads and thus access to markets. Settlements associated with extractive industries can also increase demand for bushmeat if the industry does not supply employees with imported domestic animal meat. The lack of alternative domestic protein tacitly encourages employees and their families to feed off the forest. All hunting of apes is illegal and thus classified as poaching, however, apes also fall victim to hunting methods used for other species.

- **Habitat degradation and land conversion**: although humans have always had an impact on ape habitats, more recently, deforestation brought about through a rise in mechanized logging, and the expansion of mining and oil and gas extraction, has increased in many tropical forest areas.

- **Probable introduction of infectious pathogens**: habitat fragmentation, as well as industrial expansion, may force ape populations into greater contact with one another, creating pockets of artificially higher ape densities that can trigger disease outbreaks. Disease cross-infection between humans and apes (e.g. influenza, measles) is known to occur. Thus, increased proximity of people and apes may have significant implications for the health of both species through the spread of infectious pathogens.

The second section examines ways for preventing or reducing the impact of indirect effects by focusing on management practices and corporate policies, compliance with national policies and regulations, certification, and the uptake of voluntary guidelines. Since translation of policy into practice remains a major challenge, primarily because of the lack of technical and human capacity for implementation on the ground, we investigate how some extractive companies, and other stakeholders, have addressed the challenge of reducing and/ or mitigating their impacts on wildlife populations. We identify what actions they can and should take to ensure illegal hunting does not take place within their concessions, and also establish how best to engage with other stakeholders.

Of particular importance is how indirect impacts affect areas and wildlife populations beyond concession boundaries, alongside the potential for cumulative impacts from multiple industrial and development projects within a specific area.

In the third section we address the challenges involved in curbing the indirect impacts of extractive industries. Since some impacts triggered by the presence of the extractive industry extend beyond the concessions' boundaries and may not be directly associated with their activities, ascertaining the burden of obligation can be complicated. There is also the challenge of ensuring that the rights of traditional communities to continue to benefit from their natural resources are not affected by any policies or practices put in place to address the indirect impacts of these industries.

The complexity and extent of the issues around indirect impacts mean that the cost of addressing them can be high. Currently, there is a lack of realistic incentives for companies to make this investment. Weak governance, inconsistent government policies, insufficient resources, a lack of capacity, poor enforcement, and corruption further exacerbate the stakeholders' ability to address the indirect impacts of extractive industries.

Key findings include:

- Significant increases in the hunting and poaching of wildlife as a result of the physical presence of extractive industries have been observed.

- Indirect impacts of extractive industries are likely to have a more significant impact on ape conservation than localized direct impacts, particularly in relation to mines and oil and gas wells.

- Illegal and unsustainable hunting indirectly linked to logging operations represents a far more important threat to species conservation than direct logging impacts (Milner-Gulland and Bennett, 2003; Meijaard and Sheil, 2008).

- The extent to which individual mining companies can reduce their impact from haul roads, exploration drilling, and concentrations of large numbers of employees once mines become operational will determine their overall impact on ape habitat and unsustainable and illegal hunting and snaring.

- Some guidelines for industry practice exist; however, critical issues remain unresolved, such as the extent to which industry and/or government is responsible for managing their impacts beyond the concession borders.

- There is lack of clarity regarding responsibility, and there is a poor capacity of national and sub-national governance structures to respond to indirect impacts.

- If the indirect impacts of extractive industries are not addressed, the on-going survival of many, if not all, ape populations is at risk.

Indirect impacts: the primary threat to apes and ape habitats?

Extractive industries in tropical forests have a range of effects on biodiversity. These are classified as the direct impacts associated with the operation of extraction, or the indirect impacts that happen as an unintended consequence of the extractive enterprise. For example, with artisanal and small-scale mining (ASM) environmental impacts can include deforestation and improper management of mining and human waste leading to water and soil pollution. Equally, demand increases for specific plant and animal species for mining inputs such as tools, food, and medicines (Pact, 2010). Other human activities supporting ASM populations which have a detrimental impact on the environment include bushmeat hunting and poaching, tree cutting for timber, and slash-and-burn agriculture. An additional ring of environmental degradation is created by the construction of access routes allowing the wider population to access and exploit more remote areas well beyond the time frame of direct mining activities. Of all the indirect impacts, increased hunting and poaching, habitat degradation, fragmentation, and loss, and the threat of infectious diseases are widely considered to be the most pressing.

Indirect impacts arise from the activities but also from the mere presence of extractive industries. Crucially, immigration of

> If the indirect impacts of extractive industries are not addressed, the ongoing survival of many, if not all, ape populations is at risk.

people into emerging satellite communities linked to these industries, alongside their greater access to remote areas (through road networks, other transport routes, and the opening up of pipeline tracts and industry transects), promotes higher levels of hunting for bushmeat and the live animal trade. There is also the potential for intraspecies and interspecies disease transmission due to the greater proximity of ape populations to each other and to human and other animal vectors. Moreover, habitat loss and fragmentation are exacerbated through infrastructure development for power supplies, such as dams and power lines and the development of satellite communities, which also result in agricultural expansion, the introduction of exotic species and livestock, which can reduce or compete for available food supplies, personal logging, and so on (Asner *et al.*, 2009; Laurance, Goosem, and Laurance, 2009).

Increased hunting and poaching

The hunting and sale of wild animals for their meat or for the live animal trade is unsustainable in many parts of the world and is widely recognized as the primary threat to wildlife in tropical forests. This situation is often linked to the increase in demand for animal protein by the burgeoning human populations in many tropical regions, and the rise in access by hunters to remote forest regions. The latter has been possible through the expansion of road networks and other access routes into remote forests. Infrastructure development, such as the building of new roads associated with industries such as logging and mineral extraction, opens up the forests to commercial hunting, and workers associated with these industries often turn to hunting to supplement their diets or to sell within and outside the concessions (Wilkie *et al.*, 2001; Fa,

Ryan, and Bell, 2005; Laporte *et al.*, 2007). These factors, alongside improved hunting technology and efficient and affordable communications, all contribute to what many believe is widespread unsustainable hunting pressure on tropical wildlife (Robinson and Bennett, 2000).

In general, hunting pressure in tropical forests worldwide has increased because of the introduction of modern firearms and stronger materials (wire cables and, more recently, nylon string) for snaring animals. The distribution of firearms is facilitated in areas of civil unrest/war, as well as through purchase, and there is a wide range of available sources of stronger materials, such as telephone cables and rice sacks. As a consequence, current hunting pressure on tropical wildlife is unsustainable and very likely to cause the local extinction of more vulnerable species (Robinson and Bennett, 2000). This is because the hunting of wild animals for bushmeat is rampant throughout many tropical regions (Milner-Gulland and Bennett, 2003), even within certified logging concessions (Poulsen, Clark, and Bolker, 2011). The latter is in spite of the fact that if ape hunting occurs in certified concessions they are not compliant with Forest Stewardship Council (FSC) standards. Unchecked, current levels of wildlife extraction will lead to an "empty forest syndrome" (Redford, 1992), whereby forests are stripped of their medium- and large-bodied fauna, left standing but empty.

Clark *et al.* (2009) report findings of a long-term study that sought to tease out the effects of direct and indirect impacts of logging on the abundance of species in northern Congo. They found significant populations of wildlife in logged forests, though in lower numbers than in unlogged areas. They noted a similar pattern to that observed by Meijaard *et al.* (2005) in that many species increased in abundance after the initial disturbance of logging had passed. This initial response is probably linked to the opening up of the canopy stimulating new growth, with numbers returning to previous levels over time. Other factors influenced species abundance, namely proximity to protected areas and distance from roads and settlements. This likely reflects a widely recognized feature for wildlife conservation in tropical forests – that hunting pressure is a crucial determinant of species persistence (Fa *et al.*, 2005).

Extractive industries in the oil and gas, and timber subsectors operate and/or develop camps normally established to service centralized field stations. Such activities may include facilities for exploration and extraction of key products; installation of extraction and processing equipment; as well as being centers for data gathering activities in the field (such as exploration

lines). Often, these properties cover large areas, employ large numbers of people and inject significant amounts of capital into local economies. This rise in the number of humans inhabiting relatively undisturbed forest regions can result in a dramatic increase in bushmeat hunting. This is to meet not just growing local demands, but also increased demand from industry workers, who can now afford to buy bushmeat with their larger salaries. In a study in Gabon, where gorillas are eaten, Harcourt and Stewart (1980) reported that employees at a small iron mine in Belinga consumed 24 tons of meat from the forest in one year. As mentioned in Chapter 6 (page 181), the bushmeat trade rose dramatically to the south of the Uélé River in the Democratic Republic of Congo (DRC) following the invasion of the Bili–Uéré

Photo: In the southern Congo alone, 300 gorillas were estimated to have been killed in 2009 to supply the local bushmeat markets. Confiscated gorilla hands, Yaounde, Cameroon. © LAGA & The EAGLE Network

Domaine de Chasse (hunting reserve) by approximately 3000 artisanal miners (Hicks *et al.*, 2010). The miners relied more on primate bushmeat and admitted to hunting and eating chimpanzees (Darby, Gillespie, and Hicks, 2010; L.L. Darby, unpublished data). By contrast, forest areas near sites with no ASM show less evidence of bushmeat hunting or skin trade (Hicks *et al.*, 2010). However, further studies that allow quantification of the threat hunting poses to, or impact hunting will have on, the long-term survival of ape populations (and other primates) are urgently needed (see Coad *et al.*, 2013). What is patently clear from the published literature is that harvest rates do not have to be high before declines pose a serious threat to ape populations. The apes' slow development and long interbirth intervals, which determine their relatively low densities compared to other species, as described in Chapter 3, mean that even small losses of individuals can significantly reduce a population's survival prospects very quickly.

Monitoring studies of commerce and trade of bushmeat in parts of the Congo Basin indicate low amounts of ape meat on sale (Wilkie, 2001; Fa *et al.*, 2006). Although this may be a function of the relatively low abundance of gorillas and chimpanzees, researchers caution on drawing firm conclusions of hunting pressure on specific species, particularly protected wildlife, from data gathered further down the bushmeat commodity chain. Market-based surveys can be biased as they may not provide an accurate depiction of the volume and taxa harvested, particularly for species that are illegal to hunt, such as great apes (Auzel and Wilkie, 2000; Cowlishaw, Mendelson, and Rowcliffe, 2005; Allebone-Webb *et al.*, 2011). Regional variation is found in amounts of ape meat traded, though gorillas and chimpanzees are more likely to be consumed in Cameroon, Republic of Congo, and Gabon,

> The hunting of apes for food, due to human–wildlife conflict, or for the pet trade are exacerbated by the presence of extractive industries.

which still have important populations (Caldecott and Miles, 2005; Tutin *et al.*, 2005). However, as van Vliet, Nasi, and Taber (2011) report, across the Congo Basin apes may not constitute more than 0.5% of animals sold in bushmeat markets. In general other primates rarely exceed 20% (van Vliet *et al.*, 2011); Bowen-Jones and Pendry (1999) estimated that primates accounted for 8–22% of hunted animals in West and Central Africa. In Asia, few data exist compared to that available for West and Central Africa to calculate the percentage of total bushmeat attributable to apes. In a large-scale analysis of hunting in Kalimantan, Meijaard *et al.* (2011) estimated that 1970–3100 orangutans were being killed every year, with the highest losses recorded in Central Kalimantan. Such high hunting levels may be responsible for gaps in orangutan distribution on Sumatra and Borneo (Rijksen and Meijaard, 1999), and orangutans are susceptible to extinction even at low hunting intensity (Marshall *et al.*, 2009b).

Reasons for the hunting of orangutans, gibbons, and siamangs, which include for food, human–wildlife conflict, or for the pet trade, are all intricately linked (Nijman, 2005; Meijaard *et al.*, 2011). All these factors, however, are exacerbated by the presence of extractive industries. Despite this, most studies have focused on the trade in live apes in the region, which has been more visible, therefore easier to measure. Export of wildlife to the United States alone was estimated at over 500 000 shipments of more than 1 480 000 000 live animals between 2000 and 2006 (Duckworth *et al.*, 2012). Of these, most (92%) were for commercial purposes, largely the pet trade, and over 69% of these live animal imports originated in Southeast Asia (Duckworth *et al.*, 2012).

In remote regions of the Congo Basin range states, forest-dependent as well as indigenous peoples rely on protein from wild meat (Hart, 2000; Wilkie, 2001; Fa,

Currie, and Meeuwig, 2003). Over 100 different species, mostly mammals, are consumed as bushmeat (Fa and Peres, 2001). However, a study of hunting dynamics in southwestern Gabon suggested that apes were more at risk from commercial than subsistence hunting (Kuehl *et al.*, 2009). Commercial hunters typically do not hunt in village hunting areas because only the smaller, more resilient species remain. Thus, commercial hunters tend to prefer relatively pristine forest with abundant large mammals – these are often logging concessions. Most bushmeat killed by commercial hunters in concessions is exported to urban centers where prices are higher than in concession camps.

Hunting of apes throughout their ranges can be influenced by cultural traditions (Kuehl *et al.*, 2009). Although bushmeat hunting is common throughout sub-Saharan Africa, there are some communities where hunting of large animals has been eliminated, as is the case in communities of artisanal miners in and around the Itombwe Reserve (DRC) (Weinberg *et al.*, 2013). There are also examples where cultural taboos impose restrictions on the killing of monkeys and apes, as seen in the Kema clan of Baka hunter-gatherers in Cameroon (Nelson and Venant, 2008). However, commercial hunting and the role extractive industries play in enabling the bushmeat trade currently supersede any of the positive effects of a few local hunting prohibitions.

Off-take of bushmeat species varies according to the hunting history of the exploited areas (Muchaal and Ngandjui, 1999), alternative employment opportunities (Gill *et al.*, 2012), local hunting controls (Eves and Ruggiero, 2000), accessibility to markets (Dupain *et al.*, 2012), as well as hunting technology used (Alvard, 2000; Hart, 2000). Given the choice, hunters will take larger-bodied mammals, such as ungulates and primates, because the return for effort invested is higher for these species

(Juste *et al.*, 1995; Fa and Brown, 2009; van Vliet *et al.*, 2012). But, extensive use of snares to hunt a variety of ground-living species is typical throughout tropical forests in Africa and Asia. In southwestern Central African Republic (CAR), for example, Noss (2000) found that a total of 18 different mammal species were captured with snares, and in some cases with nets. Snaring is effective for hunting forest antelopes and other smaller prey, but gorillas and chimpanzees do inadvertently fall victim to this indiscriminate prey capture technique (Waller and Reynolds, 2001; Quiatt, Reynolds, and Stokes, 2002). Some apes succumb to injuries from snares; in other cases, they may survive without a limb (Robbins *et al.*, 2011b).

Snare hunting is pervasive and can contribute to the decline in wildlife. Equally, gun hunting of large vertebrate species is just as concerning. Both methods are widely used in any area accessible to hunters. Moreover, previously unexploited regions can be opened up to hunters by the extensive road networks and other infrastructure developed by extractive industries. These networks facilitate migration of hunters into once isolated areas, leading to increased hunting and poaching (Auzel and Wilkie, 2000; Wilkie *et al.*, 2001; Poulsen *et al.*, 2009). Logging roads and secondary access routes, including tracts cleared along pipelines, enable hunters to quickly and efficiently set and subsequently check snares, and shoot animals. A logging concession in the Republic of Congo, which had a staggering 3000 km of tree inventory transects (established in a single year), enabled hunters to reduce travel time from what was once a four-day journey to a one-day event (Wilkie *et al.*, 2001). Concession roads, and vehicles, dramatically reduce transport logistics – walking into the forest limits hunting area and how much bushmeat can be head-carried to the road. Driving into the deepest reaches of the forest brings down the cost of hunting and

> Previously unexploited regions can be opened up to hunters by the extensive road networks and other infrastructure developed by extractive industries.

the challenges of transporting bushmeat to markets (Fimbel, Grajal, and Robinson, 2001). Even roads in national reserves have been found to assist poaching and hunting in Bolivia (Townsend, 2000) and South Africa (Kotze, 2002).

There are few studies that provide specifics on temporal and spatial dynamics of hunting in relation to logging activities. One study indicated that once harvest rates start to decline and economic returns dwindled, hunters within logging concessions would abandon these catchment areas for neighboring, less-hunted patches, where abundant prey were perceived more likely (Wilkie et al., 2001). In these previously unhunted areas, some species may be more vulnerable to hunting, given their limited exposure to hunters (Allebone-Webb et al., 2011). "Naïve" apes are highly vulnerable to hunters due to their easy detection (Morgan and Sanz, 2003; Werdenich et al., 2003). Hunters who specifically target apes can swiftly deplete local populations and the density of chimpanzees and gorillas within 1–5 km of human settlements is exceedingly low, suggesting that even local hunting for the table can extirpate great apes from forests close to settlements (Tutin and Fernandez, 1984). In a nationwide ape survey in Gabon, researchers reported that heavy hunting pressure may have contributed to the reduction of chimpanzee densities by 57%, and gorilla densities by as much as 72% (Tutin and Fernandez, 1984). Subsequent surveys suggest that hunting may have led to the extirpation of apes in some of these forests (Lahm, 2001).

Opening of previously inaccessible forest areas results in movement and colonization by people, which can cause dramatic increases in resident human populations (Poulsen et al., 2009). Rising incomes and improving socioeconomic conditions, often stimulated by extractive industries, augment local markets by changing hunting dynamics (Eves and Ruggiero, 2000). In northern Republic of Congo, for example, demand for bushmeat increased 64% with the arrival of industrial logging operations, with likely negative consequences on ape populations (Poulsen et al., 2009). In the case study presented in Chapter 5 on the XYZ iron ore mine in central Africa, hunting increased dramatically within the mine site and transport corridor, as a consequence of the increase in logging activities (for full details of this case study, go to page 152). Indeed, uncontrolled hunting and habitat conversion reduced chimpanzee populations in Ivory Coast by more than 90% over a 20-year period (Campbell et al., 2008). Similarly, ape populations in Gabon declined by over 50% between 1983 and 2000 (Walsh et al., 2003, p. 611). Commercial hunting was identified as the primary cause of this significant drop in ape numbers, in part facilitated by the rapid expansion of mechanized logging.

Although direct impacts cease when extractive industries withdraw from a site, indirect ones can persist. Transport routes continue to provide access to the forest. However, after withdrawal from a site additional indirect impacts may result from the significant economic downtrend in the region from reduced investment in the local economy, loss of employment, and the decline in demand for services. Under a best-case scenario for the environment, the departure of extractive industries may promote the relocation of many residents, which may result in the reduction of human pressures on apes and other hunted species, allowing their populations to recover. In contrast, if residents remain, hunting pressures and habitat alterations may intensify as these human populations turn to the available natural capital to make up for lost revenue from the closed project. This is clearly depicted in the case study of Bayanga in the CAR opposite.

Increased hunting pressure has immediate devastating effects on wildlife populations, but as a consequence of the loss of seed dispersers in particular, hunting can have long-term impacts on the ecology of tropical forests. In southeastern Nigeria, a recent study compared mammalian communities and forest structure in three well-protected, unhunted sites with three others with no protection. The protected sites had more than three times as many primate groups (including the Cross River gorilla, *Gorilla gorilla diehli*), and more than twice the number of fruit-tree seedlings as the hunted sites. From these findings, the researchers concluded that in areas with fewer primates eating fruits and dispersing their seeds (by spitting and defecation), the regeneration of fruit trees is limited and forest composition will change. Dying fruit trees will be replaced by non-fruiting trees that disperse by other means, thus reducing food supply in forests. Primates (and humans) may not be able to find sufficient food to eat, leaving the forest uninhabitable for apes, even if hunting is later controlled (Effiom *et al.*, 2013).

Habitat degradation and fragmentation

Changes in ape habitats (degradation and fragmentation) result from both direct and indirect impacts of extractive industries. Moreover, synergetic and cumulative effects of a number of indirect impacts also occur. The scale of degradation and fragmentation of habitats by logging activities depends on method of harvesting, transportation of timber, and associated management practices, as discussed in Chapter 4. At one extreme, clear felling of trees is a forestry practice in which most or all trees in an area are uniformly cut down. Selective logging, on the other hand, is a practice of specific tree spe-

CASE STUDY

Bayanga, the Dzanga-Sangha landscape, and logging

In southwestern CAR, the Dzanga-Sangha landscape consists of a national park surrounded by production forests of high biodiversity. In 1972, a logging concession was awarded to Slovenia Bois (Blom, 1998) and a sawmill established in Bayanga, at the time a small fishing village. By 2005, the Dzanga-Sangha landscape had a population of approximately 6850 people, with 57% living in Bayanga, the largest of 12 villages. The original inhabitants, BaAka pygmies (hunter-gatherers) and Sangha Sangha Bantu (fishers) made up just one-third of the current population, the rest were Bantu immigrants.

Between 1972 and 2004, the logging concession changed hands four times, each company staying only a short time due to the high production and transport costs in such a remote area. Employees were often dismissed without notice and left unpaid. Moreover, the concession would remain unallocated for periods of 1–4 years. Many of the workers, however, remained in the concession, hoping for their back-pay and re-employment. When the new companies moved in, they would re-employ only some, with the remaining roles filled by new migrants. When the sawmill eventually closed in 2004, the number of households practicing agriculture rose from 39% to 76%. Many also turned to hunting, which had already increased with the onset of logging activities (Sandker et al., 2011).

cies selection though others may be affected in the process. Mining operations also result in the clear felling of forest areas for drill site location, open-pit mining, and infrastructure development. However, although oil and mining industries can have variable impacts, often smaller surface areas are affected compared with commercial timber extraction. Oil and mining operations may affect ape populations at a more local level compared with the larger land area often impacted by commercial logging (or plantation development). There is evidence that oil production activities are less impactful, with lower deforestation rates reported, as can be seen from studies in Indonesia (Wunder, 2003). But, the indirect impacts are similar for all extractive industries and just as devastating, through the development of transport networks, particularly roads, and the influx of human populations.

As indicated above, in mining, survey sites and drill pads may typically be small in the surface area affected, often forest clearing or disruption only occurs over a few hectares of vegetation, or less, in each site. Yet, because there are often a multitude of such sites (possibly in their hundreds) scattered across the landscape and inter-connected by an elaborate network of sec-ondary and tertiary roads and access trails to service each site, the infrastructure may begin by fragmenting available habitat; whereby, species such as gorillas, reluctant to move out of their home ranges, may become isolated. Apes may also be severely disrupted by the significant disturbance of feeding and nesting sites within their range.

Indirect impacts will occur during all phases of a mining project. During Phase I, exploration of mining operations, roads can be constructed into areas that may previously have been relatively inaccessible. Even if the project does not proceed to Phases 4 and 5, construction, operation and closure, the roads will remain, enabling access for hunters, loggers, and agricultural encroach-ment. If a project proceeds to construction and operations, the mine footprint might be relatively small, but mine leases are often much larger and indirect impacts occur across a wider landscape. Mines in remote areas lead to a considerable rise in the human population. Mine workers often move with their families to the area. Other people follow to provide services to mine families, or with the expectation of finding work. Mines can attract thousands of house-holds to areas that have previously had low human populations. This in turn leads to a significant increase in demand for food and, associated with this, the development of more extensive agricultural areas. The latter may involve forest clearance, and alongside this, increased levels of hunting. This has been observed in the Rio Tinto mining oper-ations in Madagascar, started in the 1990s, where road construction encouraged and accelerated the conversion of the remaining forest to agricultural land (Virah-Sawmy and Ebeling, 2010).

In Indonesia, oil and gas industries have enabled the building of roads, bridges, and other infrastructure, thereby supporting eco-nomic development in their exploitation areas which has encouraged deforestation (Wunder, 2003). In addition to this, during the oil-boom periods of 1973–81, Indonesia's significant revenues from oil and gas pro-duction were spent on physical and social infrastructure, agricultural investments and subsidies, strategic investments, and pres-tige projects, as well as public employment, administration, and the military (Wunder, 2003). All these have indirectly boosted agri-cultural expansion and provided funding for further development of the forestry industry.

Photo: A remote mining camp in the Indonesian forest. © Serge Wich

Although ASM occurs at much smaller scales than commercial, large-scale mining (LSM), without road construction, it does encourage the influx of people to an area. Any analysis of the ecological impacts of ASM must be examined in relation to their specific geographical and temporal context (DeJong, 2012a). A single miner may remove much vegetation in his own right; however this is nothing in comparison to the cumulative impact of many miners (World Bank, 2008). One development project in two mining provinces in the CAR documented at least 3.67 km² (367 hectares) of mined-out land (DeJong, 2012a), with miners moving closer to the Dzanga-Sangha protected area; in 2006 there were between 9000 and 12 000 artisanal miners living in the Kahuzi-Biéga National Park (KBNP) in the DRC – down from 10 000–15 000 in 2000, at the height of the coltan boom (Redmond, 2001). For more details on ASM, refer to Chapter 6.

Numerous social, economic, political, and policy-driven motives may act separately or in concert, and lead to extensive forest clearance and subdivision, affecting ape populations. But, forest conversion for agriculture or plantation, not logging, is in fact the leading cause of deforestation in Equatorial Africa (Achard et al., 2002; FAO, 2005; Gibbs et al., 2010). Further, there is a strong relationship between logging and deforestation owing to other land uses. Numerous examples from East and West Africa indicate that, post timber extraction, degradation of remaining habitat continues as a result of intensification of other land uses (Kormos et al., 2003; FAO, 2010b; Norris et al., 2010). Hence, even though reduced-impact logging may lessen the direct effects of the industry on ape habitats, indirect ones can still have a major impact on biodiversity if left unchecked.

Fragmentation of ape habitats occurs after the initial establishment of a logging concession. As with mining, shifting agri-culture, opening of pastures, and land clearance for farming often follow logging activities. In some regions, apes visit and may be able to persist between fragments. However, unless connected to other suitable habitats, most habitat patches are too small to provide the long-term ecological requirements of chimpanzees or gorillas. As previously highlighted in Chapter 3, Harcourt and Doherty (2005) reported that over 65% of forest fragments in Africa where primates are found are less than 1 km². Fragments may vary in habitat quality, and thus may range from being relatively undisturbed to human modified to differing degrees, for example the typical forest–farm mosaics of West and East Africa. Such landscapes are frequently utilized by great apes (Kormos et al., 2003; Hockings and Humle, 2009; Brncic, Amarasekaran, and McKenna, 2010; Plumptre et al., 2010). But, because agricultural expansion involves the planting of palatable crops, depending on proximity to neighboring forests and the particular species of cultivar, apes may adapt these items into their diets and, when close to remaining ape habitat, apes will crop raid (Hockings and Humle, 2009; Hockings and McLennan, 2012). This leads to serious conflict between people and apes, extending the impact of habitat degradation and loss.

In Sumatra and Borneo, large-scale deforestation and agricultural expansion since the 1960s threatens the survival of orangutans, particularly when logged forests are then replaced by oil palm plantations. Killing of orangutans because of their (perceived) impact on crops is rampant (Meijaard et al., 2011; Wich et al., 2012a). Hence, it is no surprise that orangutan density increases with distance from the forest edge (Wich et al., 2012a). This observation, derived from questionnaires, was linked to the fact that hunting pressure drops with distance from settlements; with 76% of people's trips into the forest lasting less than a day, limiting distance of travel. As forest fragmentation increases, distance from the forest edge will no longer be a hindrance as all areas become easily accessible, putting orangutans and other wildlife at risk. Little is known about the behavior and long-term population stability of apes living in forest fragments. The smaller the habitat fragments left, the more difficult it may be for viable ape populations to survive. In Asia, orangutans have been translocated from habitat patches to nearby forest areas. These operations have involved government agencies, industry, and orangutan welfare organizations, e.g. Kaltim Prima Coal (KPC) with the Natural Resource Conservation Institute and BOSF (Balikpapan Orangutan Survival Foundation) (e.g. KPC, 2010), and IndoMet Coal/BHP Billiton with BOSF (ICMM, 2010b). However, translocation offers only a partial solution since apes are removed from operational areas but are exposed to other threats. Not only is the actual process stressful to the group, but additional threats and changes in the dynamics of ape behavior, such as the introduction of diseases, numbers that exceed the carrying capacity of the area that groups are moved to, and territorial in-fighting, further extend the impacts of habitat degradation and loss rather than addressing them (Dennis *et al.*, 2010a).

The threat of infectious pathogens

Infectious diseases, alongside unsustainable hunting, and habitat loss and fragmentation, are now synergistic threats to the long-term survival of apes and their habitats. Ape range states are rapidly converting into a mosaic of human settlements, industry concessions, agricultural land, forest fragments, and increasingly isolated protected areas. The result is that ape populations are in closer and more frequent contact with one another and with people. This increased proximity may have significant negative implications for the health of both apes and humans, given the possibility of zoonotic and anthropozoonotic disease transmission between them (e.g. Homsy, 1999; Hahn *et al.*, 2000; Woodford, Butynski, and Karesh, 2002; Rouquet *et al.*, 2005; Leendertz *et al.*, 2006; Goldberg *et al.*, 2007; Gillespie and Chapman, 2008; Köndgen *et al.*, 2008; Locatelli and Peeters, 2012). The close genetic relatedness between humans and non-human primates (in particular, great apes) facilitates the cross-species spread of pathogens. Outbreaks of human diseases can potentially affect ape populations, as the latter have not developed antibodies to even the more common human pathogens (Homsy, 1999). Thus, a variety of human viruses and bacteria, including influenza, adenovirus, rhinovirus, respiratory syncytial virus, pneumococcal pneumonia, herpes viruses, measles, polioviruses, *Shigella*, and gastrointestinal parasites may cause severe infection in apes (Morgan and Sanz, 2007). At the same time zoonotic diseases may pose a threat to people who live and work in the forest, and ape populations may be more exposed and/or vulnerable to infections passed between them (Table 7.1).

The Nahua, inhabitants of a reserve in Peru, offer an example of vulnerability of immunologically naive populations to disease (FPP, 2012). In May 1984, this hunter-gatherer group experienced their first contact with extractive industry personnel when a small Nahua group were captured by loggers attempting to access the valuable timber in their territory. Within only a few months, the Nahua population had been reduced by almost 50% due to outbreaks of respiratory infections to which they had no immunity. The diseases and resulting dependency on loggers for humanitarian aid meant they were unable to prevent their territory from being overrun by loggers. As

TABLE 7.1

Parasites exchanged between humans and apes: the route and direction of exchange

Parasite	Route of exchange	Direction of exchange
Polio virus	Fecal, oral	Human to non-human primate
Tuberculosis	Respiratory droplet	Human to non-human primate
Dracunculiasis	Water mediated	Human to non-human primate
Gastrointestinal parasites	Fecal	Both directions
Malaria	Vector	Both directions
Filaria	Vector	Both directions
Yellow fever	Vector	Both directions
Mycobacterium leprae	Nasal secretion	Among primates
Herpes B	Animal bite	Non-human primate to human
Monkey pox	Animal bite	Non-human primate to human
Ebola	Hunting and butchering	Non-human primate to human
Schistosomiasis	Water mediated	Non-human primate to human
Simian virus 40 (SV40)	Vaccinations	Non-human primate to human

From Chapman *et al.* (2005, p. 135, this material is reproduced with permission of John Wiley & Sons, Inc.)

extractive industries continue to reach into more remote habitats and ape populations are forced into closer human proximity, we take a step towards the level of duration and intimacy of contact that resulted in the transmission of "new" pathogens to the Nahua.

Anthropogenic habitats are also associated with an increase in the prevalence of gastrointestinal parasites (Gillespie, Chapman, and Greiner, 2005; Gillespie and Chapman, 2006, 2008). Parasitic infection from humans to wildlife, and vice versa, may occur when apes range into forests that have become logging or mining concessions, which were formerly part of their home range, and where there is inadequate sanitation and sewage disposal. In areas where local human populations consume foods also preferred by apes, not only are they competing over resources, but parasite cross-contamination from feces can occur, especially during peak fruiting periods where both humans and apes coincide at

these resources. Feces contain micro- and macro-parasites that are generally more resistant to environmental degradation compared to viruses. Moreover, apes and people are not only vulnerable to infections through close contact, some, particularly gastrointestinal parasites, survive in water and may be water-borne and transported into ape habitats and villages via streams and rivers (Ryan and Walsh, 2011).

The Ebola virus, probably the best-known pathogen to recently threaten African apes, was first identified in 1976 and since then has killed hundreds of people. The Zaire Ebola strain has also killed around 30% of the world's gorilla population and almost the same number of the world's chimpanzees (Ryan and Walsh, 2011). In the Minkébé region of northeastern Gabon, for example, lowland gorilla and chimpanzee populations almost disappeared during the Ebola outbreaks of 1994 and 1996 (Chapman *et al.*, 2005). Morvan *et al.* (1999, in Chapman *et al.*, 2005) found that Ebola is more common at the periphery and in fragments than in deep forest. As forests become increasingly fragmented owing to human activities, more outbreaks are likely, which may significantly impact both human and ape populations.

Disease results in higher mortality levels in wild animal populations, which has an equivalent impact on the populations' time to recovery. Population resilience in apes is particularly affected by unnatural population losses as these species are slow to mature and have low breeding rates. The combination of infectious disease and unsustainable hunting, both leading to higher levels of mortality in apes, could have significant consequences for the viability of these species (Walsh *et al.*, 2003; Walsh, 2006).

Ways to prevent or reduce indirect impacts

Management practices and corporate policies

All great ape populations are at risk, and threats to the remaining populations from logging, and mineral and hydrocarbon exploitation become an even more dangerous mix, which will jeopardize the long-term survival of apes throughout the world. To mitigate these threats, a number of businesses are working with governments, nongovernmental organizations (NGOs), planners, and field scientists to explore management practices that attempt to first avoid and minimize adverse consequences, and then compensate for any residual impacts. The ultimate goal of any mitigation process for great apes and other threatened species is to produce a net positive gain by bringing more exploited areas under enhanced conservation management and contributing to protected area networks and their management.

We have discussed in earlier chapters how management practices, such as Environmental and Social Impact Assessments (ESIAs), Strategic Environmental Assessments (SEAs), spatial planning, and the mitigation hierarchy can become best practice to managing biodiversity risk. The principle here is to avoid and minimize adverse impacts from the start of operations. Compensation should also be contemplated as a means of restitution for any residual impacts using biodiversity offsets (see Guinea case study in Chapter 8) and direct payments. More proactively, some companies have already committed to stand out as leaders in best practice, enhancing their local, national, and international public reputation through visible corporate social responsibility practices.

There are examples of industry commitment to best management practice and policy development, including the logging company Congolaise Industrielle des Bois (CIB) which has been working in partnership with the Wildlife Conservation Society (WCS) and the Ministry of Forest Economy (MFE) of the Republic of Congo on the Project for Ecosystem Management in the periphery of Nouabalé-Ndoki National Park (PROGEPP) (Poulsen and Clark, 2012); and Pallisco-CIFM, logging companies in Cameroon. Pallisco-CIFM have worked with the Zoological Society of London (ZSL) under their Wildlife Wood Project (WWP) to establish a wildlife policy and associated adaptive wildlife management plan by moving beyond business-as-usual, by adhering to an ethical, long-term arrangement to serve the environment, encourage responsible sustainable development, promote social welfare and conserve forest ecosystems (see Box 7.1). Although critics argue that this policy in itself does not improve conservation outcomes in the forest (logging still continues), it does represent a tangible commitment, a public declaration of intent above

Pallisco-CIFM: Responsible Management of Wildlife Policy extract*

Recognizing that industrial logging operations have an impact on wildlife in production forests, noting that, because of their large surface areas, forest concessions play an important role in preserving forest ecosystems, and adhering to the principle of sustainable management of forest resources for the benefit of future generations, the societies of Pallisco and CIFM make a public commitment to responsibly manage the wildlife of the forest that has been allocated to them. Therefore, Pallisco and CIFM will:

- Implement a set of actions for wildlife upheld in a management plan for which the human, logistical, and financial resources are made available.

- Adopt a system of adaptive management based on comprehensive knowledge of animal populations and the risks they face. This knowledge is acquired through periodic monitoring of the effects of logging on wildlife and continuous collection of information about wildlife threats.

- Reduce the direct impact on biodiversity resulting from their presence and activities. This involves, in particular, implementing rules prohibiting the involvement of the employees of Pallisco and CIFM in the trade in bushmeat and poaching of protected species. Access to alternative sources of quality protein, in sufficient quantity, for their workers is ensured through commissaries and canteens. Techniques for reduced-impact logging are applied in forest operations and particular care is given to the potential effects of these on wildlife and habitat quality in order to minimize negative impacts.

- Minimize the indirect effects of logging on wildlife. Poaching of protected animals is not tolerated in the timber concession. Pallisco and CIFM will address this by systematically exposing any illegal activities to Justice Camerounaise, and through effective implementation of laws protecting wildlife. However, the rights of local communities in the concession are fully respected. The access of motorized vehicles in the concession is limited to the vehicles of Pallisco, CIFM, and their collaborators.

- Contribute to the efforts of local, national, and global wildlife conservation and position themselves as stakeholders in the various initiatives to this end. Therefore,

the recommendations of experts for the preservation of biodiversity are applied following approval by Pallisco-CIFM and, in general, the requirements for management of protected areas adjacent to the concession are met.

Pallisco Adaptive Wildlife Management Plan*

The management plan used by Pallisco is based on the model developed by ZSL under WWP and includes specific goals, objectives, and indicators, such as:

Goal: To ensure that Pallisco's forestry operations conserve biological diversity and its associated values, in line with FSC principles (for more information on FSC principles, see Chapter 4).

Based on an analysis of the context of Pallisco's forestry operations and baseline data, objectives are agreed that help meet the goal. An example of how the plan links monitoring and management to these objectives is given below.

Objective 4. A significant decrease evidenced in commercial hunting and poaching of elephants, great apes and other class "A" protected species within the concessions.

Management activities are detailed in the plan (with methodologies where appropriate) that contribute to meet this objective including: preventive action (controlling access to the concessions, closing secondary roads, education, etc.); affirmative action (providing cheap, good quality sources of alternative protein for workers, providing employment for local community members, etc.); and enforcement (patrols, joint operations with the Ministry of Forestry and Wildlife (MINFOF), supporting prosecutions, etc.).

A suite of complementary indicators is established to measure progress towards meeting the objective and assess the efficacy of management actions. Implementation indicators such as verifying the establishment and maintenance of roadblocks confirm that actions have been taken as planned, whilst performance indicators link management performance to outcomes (Table 7.2).

These management performance indicators are matched with biological indicators tracking population trends in the suite of ten Class "A" protected species found within the concessions. Together these provide a quantitative measure of the levels of illegal activity and status of the target species linked to management performance in meeting the objective.

* Pallisco and CIFM, 2013. Courtesy of Pallisco and CIFM.

TABLE 7.2

Management performance indicators

Indicator	Not achieved	Part achieved	Achieved	Means of verification
At least four cases of poaching of Class A species reported to the authorities and lead to a prosecution annually	No cases reported	1–3 cases	4+ cases	Database records, reports, and legal record
A 6% decrease from baseline in the number of commercial hunting signs (relative to patrol effort) found during patrols year on year	No reduction or increased	1–5% reduction	6%+ reduction	Database records and reports

and beyond the legal or certification requirements to which the company can be held accountable. There is no doubt that this represents a replicable model of how a company can signal its commitment to wildlife conservation and sustainable development, while responsibly exploiting a natural resource.

Although hunting has been the indirect impact that has received the most attention, it is crucial to understand the different impacts that affect ape populations. As shown above, apes may also be susceptible to many human pathogens as a result of increased human presence and disturbance in ape habitats. Concurrently, humans are vulnerable to pathogens carried by apes and other animals. It is essential therefore that part of the operation policies and practice of extractive industries is to ensure employees

are aware of and implement safe hygiene measures. These are often simple and easily carried out measures related to washing, disposal of waste, and avoiding contact with dead animals. This is another example of where an NGO partner can provide support to implement improved management on the ground. The WWP, working with its partners, developed protocols for "best forest practice" containing information on the potential risks of disease transmission between wildlife and humans, and good sanitation and hygiene for those who spend long periods of time in forest camps. The protocol "10 Basic Rules to Avoid Zoonotic Disease Transmissions in Forest Camps" was produced in the form of leaflets distributed to logging staff and local communities as part of an outreach campaign (Figure 7.1).

Photo: Apes may also be susceptible to many human pathogens as a result of increased human presence and disturbance in ape habitats. Satellite settlement near an extractive industry.
© Pauwel de Wachter/WWF

See also Morgan *et al.* (2013). Although these tools will be of limited value to some groups such as the Baka, Biaka, Babongo, Efe, and Mbuti hunter-gatherers who spend many months in the forest without soap, pit latrines, and other basic hygiene essentials, it will have value to groups who can access some of the necessities to avoid disease transmission.

The result of the adherence to best practices by extractive industries can stimulate examples of how economic development can proceed without completely sacrificing biodiversity and ecosystem services, which are, after all, the essential "natural capital" of all nations. In Kalimantan Gold's Kalimantan Surya Kencana (KSK) concession (exploration and evaluation phase) there is no outside road access to the site. All materials, goods, and personnel are transported into the concession by helicopter. This minimizes the risk of outside incursion by roads. Because movement of workers and transport of materials inside the concession is also by helicopter, there is no clearing of forest to build roads for ground transportation (B. Paul, personal communication, 2013).

Although examples of good practices are growing in number, biodiversity mitigation and compensation by extractive industries are still nascent. Moreover, the results are not yet conclusive enough to verify that the practices adopted to mitigate impacts are the most suitable to maintaining viable ape populations. Much more widespread adoption and testing of mitigation measures is essential to ensure the long-term protection of apes. The mitigation of indirect impacts must take into account not just concession areas and offset or compensation zones. To be truly effective, any such initiative needs to take into account the wider landscape, neighboring industrial and development projects, and community rights and needs, and to involve all of the relevant stakeholders.

Compliance with national policies and regulations

Extractive industries are obliged to reduce illegal activities, including hunting, in their concessions but should also contribute to wider efforts to reduce illegal and unsustainable hunting. To achieve this involves the implementation of activities at site level, but also actively engaging with other stakeholder groups, such as local communities, NGOs, national authorities, and other extractive industries. It is essential to ensure

FIGURE 7.1

WWP leaflet explaining the "10 Basic Rules to Avoid Zoonotic Disease Transmissions in Forest Camps"*

* Only available in French.

214

that company employees tasked with stopping commercial hunting do not simply burn camps, and stop and arrest marginalized subsistence hunters rather than commercial hunters who may be better connected. Mechanisms need to be put in place to ensure that processes do not simply target poorer subsistence hunters over commercial hunters who are known to hunt protected species.

The control of illegal activities in concessions requires:

1. prevention of incidents;
2. identification of illegal activities that actually take place; and
3. enforcement of sanctions.

Actions undertaken by some companies include:

- Ensuring their own employees are not implicated in the bushmeat trade through developing and enforcing policies that ban them from hunting and trading bushmeat. Where relevant, certification standards also oblige companies to ensure that firearms are not carried on company vehicles. To bolster this, companies provide alternative supplies of reasonably priced sources of meat and fish for their employees.
- Control of entry points to the concession to prevent poachers gaining access. A key activity is erecting and manning barriers at active logging and access roads and carrying out searches of vehicles for bushmeat and firearms. It is important to ensure that the firearms carried by employees manning these entry points are controlled and cannot be used for hunting. These control activities also need to be undertaken whilst acknowledging and exploring how to build on the needs, rights, and knowledge

of local communities. Alongside this, roads that are no longer used are rendered permanently impassable to vehicles.

- Initiating an illegal activity monitoring program within their concessions, as detailed in the Pallisco example in Box 7.1. An important aspect of this is that patrol plans are informed by a risk assessment as part of an adaptive approach: responding to findings, intelligence, or simply ensuring that patrol activities are not predictable. For more information on WWP, see Chapter 4.

Collaborative actions:

- Extractive industries are typically not mandated to arrest or prosecute and therefore must work with the national authorities to ensure that laws are enforced in their concessions and with people whom they employ. For example, in mining concessions access control by a company is sometimes made very difficult by the fact that the company only has the right to exploit the subsurface resource, and does not actually own or hold exclusive land usage rights over the land surface. This means the company is legally unable to stop hunters and poachers from entering the concession. Only the government and/or private land owners have this right. This issue can be partly resolved by granting companies specific rights in their concession agreements to "police" their concession area, subject to close cooperation with the law enforcement agencies.
- In the Congo Basin, forestry agencies often lack the capacity and resources to respond efficiently, at the same time the judicial process can be subject to influence and inefficiencies which all serve to hinder effective enforcement of national laws. Extractive industries can work with

other stakeholders to assist this process. By coordinating with local communities, government agents, and NGOs an effective model for enforcement can be implemented. Well-organized company monitoring systems complemented by co-managed patrols can engender wide support as well as improve detection of illegal activities. Logistic support can be provided to government agents to enable them to respond effectively to incidents whilst the understanding of legal procedure that some NGOs can provide ensures that cases are properly pursued. Extractive industries can also use their influence to press for the proper process to be followed through.

- Coordinated efforts between neighboring companies in controlling illegal activities will maximize efficiencies and improve the efficacy of actions such as road barriers and patrolling, as well as sharing information on poaching. Efforts to coordinate these activities should be a priority and could be an area of opportunity for NGO facilitation.

A role that an outside NGO can play, such as the one assumed by ZSL as part of the WWP model, is to facilitate the development of these systems, linking the various stakeholders and associated protocols for both identifying and responding to illegal activities.

Certification

Market-linked certification systems are becoming commonplace in the logging industry. However, these are still lacking for other extractive industries. There are at least seven certification bodies worldwide, which provide incentives to timber producers to implement more sustainable practices by complying with a designated set of standards.

BOX 7.2

FSC criteria and hunting

"FSC Criterion 1.5 Forest management areas should be protected from illegal harvesting, settlement and other unauthorized activities." (FSC, 2002, p. 4)

Obliging the forest manager to take measures to control illegal activities as well as establish systems to detect, document, and report them to the national authorities.

"FSC Criterion 6.2 Safeguards shall exist which protect rare, threatened and endangered species and their habitats (e.g. nesting and feeding areas). Conservation zones and protection areas shall be established, appropriate to the scale and intensity of forest management and the uniqueness of the affected resources. Inappropriate hunting, fishing, trapping and collecting shall be controlled." (FSC, 2002, p. 6)

Illegal hunting in the concession is forbidden as is the transport and trade of bushmeat in company vehicles. The concessionaire is obliged to develop and demonstrably enforce a hunting policy on site and to take action to protect rare or threatened species. The company is also obliged to provide adequate supplies of alternative sources of protein for employees at a price equal to or less than that of wild meat.

Certified products command either a market premium or, in other cases, market access. The FSC is the key international certification scheme in the tropics and it is supported by a range of environmental NGOs. FSC standards take the form of ten principles and associated criteria and indicators, developed through a multi-stakeholder process, that relate to explicit legal, operational, social, and environmental targets that forest management must meet. These include criteria relating to hunting and forest incursion (see Box 7.2). For more information on certification and the FSC, go to Chapter 4.

Uptake of voluntary guidelines

There are a number of voluntary guidelines that have been developed to assist extractive industries and other stakeholders, including governments, to implement best practice, some of which include guidance on addressing indirect impacts, such as:

International Council on Mining and Metals

(ICMM, 2006)

Good practice guidance for mining and biodiversity

This guidance document developed out of the IUCN–ICMM Dialogue and includes a section on "non-mining related threats to biodiversity," which identifies the four types of threat (p. 76) as:

- "conversion of natural habitat to cropland, urban areas or other human-dominated ecosystems;

- overexploitation or overharvesting of commercially important species;

- introduction of invasive species, including pests and pathogens; and

- climate change, pollution and other environmental changes external to the area of interest."

It also presents recommended practices for limiting impacts on biodiversity (p. 27), which include:

- "limiting land clearing by using technologies and mining practices that minimize habitat disturbance;

- avoiding road building wherever possible by using helicopters or existing tracks – if roads are to be constructed, use existing corridors and build away from steep slopes or waterways;

- removing and reclaiming roads and tracks that are no longer needed; and

- using native vegetation to revegetate land cleared during exploration."

Under "mitigation, rehabilitation and enhancement tools," it is suggested that a way in which companies can address one of the underlying threats to biodiversity is by engaging in alternative livelihoods initiatives to substitute for existing unsustainable economic activities such as overharvesting of biodiversity resources and illegal hunting.

United States Agency for International Development
(USAID, 2010)

Best management practices for orangutan conservation in mining concessions

This document puts forward a number of corporate commitments, one of which is to ensure that orangutans are sensitively managed within the concession by consulting with experts, NGOs, and other stakeholder groups (p. 9) to:

- "Implement silvicultural and other types of habitat management approaches and techniques to minimize the impact of these activities on areas used by orangutans;
- Protect key ecological resources for orangutans in both conservation set-asides and habitat corridors; and
- Work to prevent hunting of orangutans by company employees, contractors and others."

International Tropical Timber Organization (ITTO) and International Union for the Conservation of Nature (IUCN)
(ITTO and IUCN, 2009)

ITTO/IUCN Guidelines for the conservation and sustainable use of biodiversity in tropical timber production forests

These guidelines advise that a number of the threats to biodiversity in tropical production forests, such as illegal mining and agriculture, hunting, and the unregulated exploitation of other forest species, can be detected by patrolling or use of remote sensing and that a field presence is essential for their control. Other impacts, such as the introduction of invasive species and disease, can be harder to recognize and their control will likely require specialized support (p. 48). They present priority actions under the various guidelines, which are grouped for the different stakeholders, which include the timber companies:

- Provide forest employees with meat and fish that are obtained from sustainable sources.

Banks, credit facilities and multilateral financial institutions:

- Take biodiversity conservation values into account in financial analyses of forest-related investments.
- Create special credit programs with simplified rules to encourage biodiversity conservation in forest management projects.

As well as actions for the authorities, timber companies, conservation NGOs, and other relevant stakeholders to undertake in partnership, such as (p. 56):

- Compile information and data on globally, nationally or locally threatened species that are commonly hunted or gathered in forests and make it available in appropriate formats and in local languages and dialects.
- Determine the drivers of the bushmeat trade at national and international levels and increase consumer access to domestically raised meat.
- Through participatory processes, establish hunting zones and employ local people and private companies to help control these areas.

IUCN

(Morgan *et al.*, 2013)

Great Apes and FSC: Implementing 'Ape Friendly' Practices in Central Africa's Logging Concessions

These guidelines cover the FSC Certification System, FSC Principle 6 – environmental values and impacts, and identifying and managing risks and threats to environmental values, and look at the scientific justification for enforcing health and safety of employees and their families (FSC Principle 6); subsidized anti-poaching teams; an employee code of conduct (FSC Principles 6 and 7); monitoring threatened species in logging concessions (FSC Principle 8); and the adaptive exploitation and protection of resources important to great apes (FSC Principle 9). There are three key recommendations presented in the conclusion (p. 31):

- **"Decrease the risk of ape–human disease transmission** in concessions through educational campaigns and by implementing worker health programmes and field protocols.

- **Strengthen law enforcement within concessions and address poaching** through the designation of controlled hunting zones. Fund well-trained and supervised teams of eco-guards and support strict compliance of judiciary laws for those convicted of poaching.

- **Implement the High Conservation Value (HCV) approach and monitor ape populations in concessions.** Refine the High Conservation Value approach through studies of the abundance and distribution of tree species that are important to apes. Execute standardized surveys and establish long-term monitoring of great apes in concessions, preferably in collaboration with conservation biologists or ape experts."

International Finance Corporation

(IFC, 2009)

Projects and People: A Handbook for Addressing Project-Induced In-Migration

Although not specifically aimed at extractive industries, the IFC's *Handbook* identifies large extractive industry projects as those best known for serious negative impacts from in-migration.

The *Handbook* presents:

- The business case for addressing project-induced in-migration.

- An overview of the issue, including the dynamics of project-induced in-migration and the potential environmental and social impacts, looking in detail at issues of in-migration in relation to ASM, resettlement, indigenous peoples, areas of high biodiversity value, and cultural heritage.

- How to assess the probability of project-induced in-migration and the associated risks.

- Potential management approaches to reduce in-migration, enhance the positive impacts, and prevent and mitigate the negative impacts.

- The development of influx management strategies and how to integrate them into a project.

There are a number of other guidelines (see Chapter 4), checklists, and best practice manuals, both general and specialized, such as IUCN's guidance on World Heritage Sites and the extractive industries (Turner, 2012), and the sample set in Annex III.

However, little detail or attention has been given to managing landscapes post closure of a project and what additional rehabilitation strategies should be employed beyond the actual site of extraction, except for the ICMM's *Planning for Integrated Mine Closure: Toolkit* (2008). One general recommendation, however, is that roads in concessions should be blocked once projects have ended, to increase transportation costs and challenges for hunters and poachers.

Key challenges

There are a number of factors that make it difficult to achieve a reduction in indirect impacts of extractive industries on apes and ape habitats. There are also additional factors that have to be taken into account. These include the differing needs and goals of the various stakeholders; communication barriers; lack of inclusion in some guidelines, and limited uptake of all voluntary guidelines and certification schemes; lack of technical capacity within government ministries, lenders, and industry; economics, a lack of will, and the complex linkages

and extended geographical reach of indirect impacts. The last blurs boundaries of responsibility for implementing and facilitating any strategies to reduce them. The main challenges are discussed below.

The question of responsibility

A primary challenge is the question of who is responsible? Direct impacts resulting specifically from project development are normally limited to the exact boundaries of the project area, and will decline and cease at the end of the project's life. Some of these impacts can be minimized or mitigated through good management practices. However, indirect impacts may not even be closely associated with project activities. Instead, they can result from the actions and decisions made by people with little or no association with the project, and are simply triggered by the project's presence. For example, a logging concession, mine, or oil

Photo: ESIAs and spatial planning are generally limited to the boundaries of the concession, and, for oil extraction, the narrow width of any pipeline corridor. © Jabruson, 2013. All Rights Reserved. www.jabruson. photoshelter.com

resource development project may result in a dramatic influx of new settlers into a previously sparsely populated area, with only a small portion of the new residents actually working for the extractive company. Most will seek employment through existing or new service sectors, or simply try to benefit from the increased cash flow generated by the company. Deforestation resulting from the development of new settlements and associated agricultural expansion, and increased hunting pressures from subsistence or commercial hunting ventures, as discussed above, are examples of indirect impacts that may be out of the immediate control of the extractive company, but are unquestionably a consequence of its presence and driven by it. The cumulative results from such indirect impacts can be far more severe than the direct impacts of project development and have a greater geographic reach. Although it may be difficult to determine who is responsible for addressing and mitigating such indirect impacts, they are just as likely to disrupt a project as direct impacts (Energy and Biodiversity Initiative, 2003).

Although most extractive companies undertake ESIAs and spatial planning, as in the XYZ case study on page 152, the planning is generally limited to the boundaries of the mine site and/or the concession area, and, for oil extraction, may include a narrow width of any pipeline transport corridor extending to a coastal port; the mitigation strategies are limited to the concession and, in some cases, distinct areas outside of the concession, such as newly created protected areas. There is no assessment of indirect impacts outside of these areas, or of the cumulative impact of adjacent development. Separating out the sources and responsibilities for responding to growing indirect impacts would be a highly complicated task, possibly with limited results, as apportioning blame does not make for a constructive environment in which to address

> Effectively addressing the indirect impacts of extractive industries needs an integrated landscape-level collaborative management approach that involves and is facilitated by all stakeholders.

the issues at hand. Effectively addressing the indirect impacts of extractive industries needs an integrated landscape-level collaborative management approach that involves and is facilitated by all stakeholders. This is highlighted in the IFC Handbook (2009, pp. V–VI):

> Although a project cannot be held wholly responsible for in-migration associated with the broader economic development of the region, the project should assume primary responsibility for project-induced in-migration within the project area of influence. The project should assume responsibility for areas within its direct control and seek the agreement, coordination, and collaboration of all stakeholders, including the government, non-governmental organizations, community-based organizations and project-affected communities, for management of other areas lying outside of its control.

Traditional communities and scale of action

Traditional resource use

Traditional forest dwelling communities rely on their natural resources for food, medicine, tools, craft materials, and so on. When areas are designated as industry concessions or protected areas the local communities are generally excluded from the forests that they may have depended on for generations. Although it is clear that unsustainable commercial and illegal hunting must be addressed it is vital that this is grounded in a good understanding of local forest dependent communities' reliance on bushmeat, to ensure they are not adversely impacted. Socioeconomic surveys carried out by ZSL to explore bushmeat consumption patterns in communities around two large logging concessions estimated that 20 000 animals were captured per year by all the hunters interviewed. The majority of prey items were smaller mammals and duikers, and no protected species were reported to be hunted (although it is likely this reflected reluctance to report what was known to be an illegal activity). These levels of off-take represent a major resource for local communities as a substantial portion was sold and represented a significant amount of income for hunter families. Irrespective of the ethnic background of the hunters, the incentives for hunting were both economic and nutritional. This study illustrates what can be achieved in a rapid assessment as well as providing baseline data against which to measure the impact of subsequent activities. It highlighted the importance of hunting for the local communities and the consequent need to take that into account when developing strategies for reducing hunting pressure.

Lack of alternative livelihoods

Tropical forests have supported the livelihoods of people for thousands of years and in the Congo Basin, for example, more than 90% of the people living in the region depend to varying extents directly on forest resources for food, fuel, income, timber, and medicine (FAO, 2011b). The forestry sector is a significant employer: globally over 2 million people are estimated to be employed in the tropical timber sector, over half of these in Southeast Asia (FAO, 2011a). In this region, forestry contributes almost US$20 billion to the region's economy annually. For the Congo Basin, the figure is US$1.8 billion which although less than that for Southeast Asia, represents a similar proportion of GDP (FAO, 2011b).

ASM is a key sector for alleviating poverty and diversifying local economic opportunity in many rural areas in ape range states, as it is viable in remote locations that have minimal infrastructure, which restricts the development of other industries. ASM and other extractive industries provide relatively high incomes compared to those from agriculture and construction and ASM often provides a livelihood for workers from large-scale mines when operations are down-sized or decommissioned (Hilson, 2002).

When looking specifically at the indirect impacts of extractive industries, particularly in remote rural areas, there is a lack of alternative livelihood opportunities other than hunting and poaching for bushmeat and the live animal trade, tree cutting for timber, and slash-and-burn agriculture. Essentially, the commercialization of bushmeat and harvesting of forest resources has become the challenge. The presence of infrastructure and demand, as well as opportunity, through extractive industries, enables subsistence practices to be amplified through commercialization. Unless action is taken to provide viable alternative livelihoods, possibly through employment as ecoguards or the establishment of cooperatives providing protein sources through fishing and traditional animal-husbandry practices, as well as new initiatives, such as fish-farming, improved chicken farming, and beef importation (Elkan *et al.*, 2006), the local population is left with little option but to continue.

Scale of the issue

Bushmeat hunting is a complex problem with impacts from site level up to the broader forest landscape and for some species the issue is linked to global criminal trade. Thus strategies to address it must also act at this range of scales and link to a wide group of actors and stakeholders. Extractive industries cannot be held solely responsible for addressing the challenges of hunting, harvesting of timber, extensive agriculture, and other destructive practices both inside and

> "Unless action is taken to provide viable alternative livelihoods for the local population, indirect impacts will continue."

222

outside their concession areas. The responsibilities are shared by government and numerous other actors to ensure that protective measures for the environment and social needs for the local forest-dependent people are met. This is a challenging problem relating to jurisdiction, responsibility, and capacity as well as being a livelihood and rights issue for those forest communities who depend on bushmeat and forest products.

Photo: Development projects and conservation projects have traditionally been viewed as juxtaposed, there is a growing understanding that they are actually closely linked, which highlights the need for integrated planning.
© Pauwel de Wachter/WWF

Cost of addressing indirect impacts and competition for funds

One of the main reasons cited by timber companies, preventing them from adopting a sustainable forest management (SFM) approach, is the prohibitive cost of imple-

mentation and a corresponding lack of realistic incentives to do so (Putz, Dykstra, and Heinrich, 2000). For example, it costs the PROGEPP project in the Republic of Congo approximately US$1 per hectare/year for up to 3000 km² (300 000 hectares) and US$0.75 up to 10 000 km² (1 000 000 hectares) to reduce unsustainable and illegal hunting in CIB's logging concessions (Aviram, Bass, and Parker, 2003, p. 9). The funds for this came from CIB, the government and international aid from WCS, USAID, Central African Regional Program for the Environment (CARPE), ITTO, United States Fish and Wildlife Service (USFWS), and Columbus Zoo. This investment was possible as CIB's concessions are very large, in areas of low population density and close to an ecologically valuable protected area containing threatened species, which attracted

State of the Apes 2013 Extractive Industries and Ape Conservation

international support (Aviram *et al.*, 2003). Given the additional costs of adopting wildlife-friendly and social best practices, the obligation should not be a voluntary one but an obligatory condition for concessions to be allocated. If nations mandated adoption of wildlife standards for extractive industries and required conservation bonds to ensure compliance, this would level the playing field and all private sector companies would adopt wildlife-friendly best practices or risk losing their operating license. Currently the costs and lack of commercial incentives apply for most activities to minimize and mitigate the indirect impacts of all extractive industries.

Linked to the actual cost of minimizing and mitigating indirect impacts, another factor that affects the commitment of both government and industry to dedicate people and resources to these actions is the relative poverty, population growth rates, and development needs of ape range states. There is national, regional, and international pressure to improve the standard of living of the poorest peoples, and governments see forests as a valuable resource to be utilized. Southeast Asia is very densely populated compared to the Congo Basin countries (121 people/km² compared to 24 people/km²), although the African region has a significantly higher population growth rate at 2.7% pa (Southeast Asia 1.2% pa) (FAO, 2011a, p. 12). Both regions also have a similar proportion of rural people (54% and 61%, respectively, p. 58) with substantially below average per capita incomes by global standards (US$4742 and US$1865 per person per year contrasting with a global mean of US$10 384) (FAO, 2011a, p. 12). This pressure is also felt by industry, which, as well as wanting to support human development, also looks to foster positive relations with local communities. This results in competition for industry funds to support social and development projects. Although social/

development projects and conservation projects have traditionally been viewed as juxtaposed, there is a growing understanding that, when taking a more holistic view, they are actually closely linked, which again highlights the need for integrated planning that involves the active participation of all stakeholders. In the mining sector there is the additional issue that exploration companies, particularly the smaller ones, may not be inclined to invest time and money to strengthen local institutions, support human development or participate in long-term conservation projects due to their short-term perspective – no viable deposit may be found. Although private sector companies cannot be held responsible for the provision of social services and development investments that the state has failed to provide, they are one of the actors that have enormous influence over the landscape and the movements of people, and as such need to be part of the integrated planning process and responsible for playing their part in implementing social, development, and conservation strategies.

Weak governance frameworks

Weak governance, inconsistent government policies, insufficient resources, a lack of enforcement, and corruption further exacerbate the ability to address the indirect impacts of extractive industries. For example, in CAR, the Ministry of the Environment and Ecology (MEE) is responsible for the country's environmental policy and law enforcement, but it carries less weight than the mining ministry, getting only 0.2% of total government spending (World Bank, 2010). The Ministry of Water, Forests, Hunting and Fishing has relatively more influence, being in charge of granting and regulating forest concessions, among other resources. Additionally, the MEE was only recently created, its precise mandate is not yet clear (World Bank, 2010) and a poor definition of the respective roles and responsibilities of the different ministries and directorates has been cited as an institutional weakness (World Bank, 2010). Subsequently, the status of mining in CAR's protected areas in both law and practice is muddled. For example, mining was explicitly outlawed in one of the decrees establishing usage guidelines in the Dzanga Sangha Special Reserve, promulgated in 1992, but this document also gave authority to the government to offer exemptions (CARPE, 2010), and there are two exploitation permits in the northwest of the reserve (CARPE, 2009, 2010). This is only one example of many. The issue of extraction in a protected area is further discussed in the case study on the Virunga National Park on page 44 a World Heritage Site which is "protected" under national law and international conventions, but is still under threat.

This limited national and sub-national capacity often results in the government and communities relying on companies to take the lead and provide services in relation to social and environmental factors.

Conclusion

For all extractive industries, the indirect impacts, such as illegal and unsustainable hunting, and clearing of forest for building and agriculture, both by people associated with the project and those who are drawn to the location simply by its presence, are the most complicated and challenging to address, but also the most threatening to apes and ape habitat. If in-migration is minimized, the root cause of most of the indirect impacts would be addressed. Without strategies to reduce and/or mitigate the three primary impacts of increased hunting and poaching, habitat degradation and fragmentation, and the spread of

infectious pathogens, then the survival of apes is at serious risk.

Extractive industries can actively mitigate their direct and indirect impacts by establishing and implementing best practices for biodiversity management at all stages of project and site development. The adoption of best management practices for biodiversity, including apes, can present opportunities for positive biodiversity outcomes both at the immediate site and concession level and in the wider landscape through external engagement with local and national government, conservation experts, NGOs, local communities and their representatives, and other relevant stakeholders.

To address the threats and sustainably manage the forest in extractive industry concessions there must be incentives for the sectors to act; relying on business practice to change simply because it's "the right thing" is not always realistic. There is also a need to increase capacity and awareness across the sectors and initialize a shift in thinking and attitudes to alter what the sectors view as the essential activities involved in extraction and concession management. Some of the examples above and throughout this publication show that apparently conflicting goals – biodiversity conservation and maximizing economic benefits from extractive industries – can be reconciled and ultimately met by shared objectives that can become part of core operational practices.

Conservation organizations have been making great strides toward recognizing that protected areas must respect the rights of indigenous peoples as enshrined in international law, including the right to give or withhold their free prior and informed consent (FPIC) to the establishment of new protected areas in their customary territories, as discussed in Chapter 2. The World Wildlife Fund's (WWF) Statement of Principles on Indigenous Peoples (2008) makes very clear that this is not only a question of respecting their fundamental human rights, but also a question of recognizing that such people have been at the forefront of conservation for millennia. In the preamble WWF states that:

> Most of the remaining significant areas of high natural value on earth are inhabited by indigenous peoples. This testifies to the efficacy of indigenous resource management systems. Indigenous peoples, their representative institutions and conservation organizations should be natural allies in the struggle to conserve both a healthy natural world and healthy human societies. Regrettably, the goals of conserving biodiversity and protecting and securing indigenous cultures and livelihoods have sometimes been perceived as contradictory rather than mutually reinforcing. (2008, p. 1)

If these efforts are to be truly effective, industry and government also need to follow suit and recognize the rights and harness the expertise of local communities, bringing all stakeholders together to develop and work towards integrated landscape management that strives towards economic development and effective conservation of their heritage and natural resources, including apes.

Acknowledgments

Principal authors: Alison White and John E. Fa

Contributors: Eric Arnhem, ASM–PACE, Marcus Colchester, Laure Cugnière, Oliver Fankem, FPP, Matthew Hatchwell, Josephine Head, Justin Kenrick, Erik Meijaard, David Morgan, Paul De Ornellas, Bardolf Paul, PNCI, Chris Ransom, Crickette Sanz, James Tolisano, Ray Victurine, Ashley Vosper, WCS, Serge Wich, and ZSL

Photo: There is no evidence that Indonesia's forest moratorium has effectively reduced the conversion of forest in Indonesia to non-forest/degraded forest land. © Serge Wich

CHAPTER 8

Case studies of national responses to the impacts of extractive industries on great apes

Introduction

There is increasing recognition in ape range states of the importance of ensuring that environmental considerations are emphasized in both national policies and legislation. While this demonstrates an evolving acknowledgment of the importance of the environment, this shift in focus has not always been driven from within countries. This chapter provides examples of how national governments in emerging economies are responding to the environmental impacts of economic development. It demonstrates how these responses were influenced by global processes, financial institutions and international organizations and thus the role of outside influences in catalyzing the response within three great ape range states: Guinea, Gabon, and Indonesia.

228

The first section presents details on an on-going process in the Republic of Guinea to develop a national strategy for biodiversity offsets. The strategy will be developed to offset the impact of extractive industries on critically endangered (CR) and endangered (EN) species. It will be supported by a conservation trust fund to provide resources to manage biodiversity offset projects in perpetuity. The second section presents detail on the evolution of Gabon's leading legislative and regulatory frameworks that prescribe industry behavior in relation to tropical forest conservation. The final section looks at Indonesia's recent decision to implement a national logging moratorium and places it within the context of the evolution of forest management in relation to orangutans.

Offsetting mining impact in the Republic of Guinea – protecting chimpanzees

The Republic of Guinea is situated on the West African coast, between Sierra Leone,

FIGURE 8.1

The Republic of Guinea

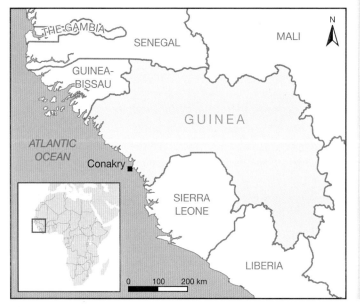

Liberia, Côte d'Ivoire, Mali, Senegal, and Guinea Bissau. Guinea has a human population of approximately 11 million (CIA, 2013c), with an enormous wealth of mineral and other natural resources. It has one-third of the world's known bauxite reserves (aluminum ore) and significant iron ore, gold, diamond, and uranium reserves. In spite of the country's mineral wealth, hydropower, and agricultural resources, it is a poor country that has struggled with political instability, a weak economy, and the impacts of long-term political instability in neighboring Liberia and Sierra Leone. It is estimated that 47% of the population fall below the poverty line, and the country is ranked 178 out of a total of 187 countries in the world with comparable data for human development (UNDP, 2013).

This section describes an approach that national and international environmental nongovernmental organizations (NGOs) are urging the Government of Guinea, and private sector companies, to undertake that will maintain a focus on conservation objectives when the country's mineral reserves are exploited. It presents details of an innovative process to develop a national strategy for biodiversity offsets to compensate for the residual impacts of extractive industries on biodiversity in Guinea. This approach would also include an endowment fund to finance the implementation of a national strategy for biodiversity offsets. The concept for this approach was first launched in a report funded by the Arcus Foundation entitled "Towards a strategic national plan for biodiversity offsets for mining in the Republic of Guinea, West Africa With a Focus on Chimpanzees" (Kormos and Kormos, 2011b). The approach was subsequently summarized in a report to the World Bank in 2012 proposing a strategy for great ape conservation in Africa (Kormos et al., 2012).

The main findings, summarized from this chapter, show that:

- There is interest from large mining companies based in developed countries in a national-level biodiversity offset strategy that provides clear guidelines, and in designing and implementing biodiversity offsets, but they require further details before they are willing to fully engage in the process.

- Working in partnership with the private sector does not ensure that investments, available funding streams, or activities are predictable.

- Private sector financing for an endowment is likely, but providing full funding for an endowment up front may prove challenging.

- The Government of Guinea favors a national strategy for biodiversity offsets focusing on all EN and CR species rather than a separate strategy exclusively for chimpanzees.

- The private sector often needs to offset residual damage from their activities on more than one EN or CR and so they also prefer a strategic national plan for biodiversity offsets in general and not just one CR or EN species.

Offsetting extractive industry impact at the macro level

Widespread mineral extraction activities in Guinea are threatening key habitats and species including chimpanzees. Several companies operating in Guinea are applying for funding from the International Finance Corporation (IFC) and Equator banks, and are therefore exploring ways to meet IFC Performance Standard 1 (PS1[1]; regarding management of environmental and social risks) and Performance Standard 6 (PS6[2]; regarding biodiversity and sustainable management of living natural resources), as well as meeting their own commercial targets. Offsetting

EN and CR species is considered a last resort to compensate for residual impacts to species after all other mitigation measures have been exhausted. Species offsets are nevertheless being considered by almost all companies working in chimpanzee habitat in Guinea since environmental impact assessments (EIA) have determined that there will be residual impacts of mining on chimpanzees, in most cases.

The IFC's reviewed PS1 (see Chapter 1) allows for the offset option to be applied to project areas that include CR and EN species, whereas PS6 provides the framework for responding to the risks and impacts to biodiversity identified by the assessments required under PS1. However, developing offsets on a project-by-project basis without an overarching national framework and strategy guiding biodiversity offset projects, and without taking into account the cumulative impacts of development activities, could lead to a series of uncoordinated, isolated, and ineffective conservation projects (C. Kormos, unpublished data).

Offsets are designed to ensure that any residual loss of EN or CR species that occurs despite an industrial development project's best efforts at mitigation is fully compensated through an off-site conservation project protecting an equivalent number of species elsewhere. PS6 notes that offsets should achieve conservation outcomes that can "reasonably be expected" to achieve no net loss of biodiversity, though in the case of Critical Habitat, offsets must not only achieve no net loss, but must achieve a net gain (see Chapter 1 and Annex I).

However, if the offset needs are assessed solely on the basis of a particular development project's footprint, the offset project may fail to take into account the cumulative impacts caused by other development projects in the area. For instance, a development project may calculate an offset based on the assumption that remaining habitat outside their project area will be able to sustain a certain number of EN or CR species displaced by development activity. However, if there are several other development projects planned nearby which may reduce or eliminate that habitat, that assumption may not be valid and an offset would have to be larger. In many countries, extractive industries and infrastructure development are advancing at a fast pace and multiple large-scale projects are being developed in the same area at the same time, sometimes adjacent to each other, so an offset assessment based on impacts from a single project will fail to take into account the cumulative impacts. Offset projects should therefore be based on an assessment of the cumulative impacts from development in the region surrounding the project.

Another risk with a project-by-project approach is a lack of coordination between offset projects and failure to integrate offsets into a broader conservation strategy. Ideally offset design and implementation should be coordinated so that offsets contribute to a recovery strategy for EN and CR species. Such a strategy would aim to target priority sites within a recovery strategy first. It would aim to create connectivity between conservation sites so that larger and therefore more robust areas are protected. It could also aim to protect sites that complement each other and are strategically placed in areas representative of the nation's biodiversity. The end result of implementing offsets on a project-by-project basis without a framework for coordination could be protection of multiple smaller, isolated offset projects that are not viable in the long term. A strategic plan for offset sites has the additional benefits of being more efficient; this avoids duplication of efforts in conducting inventories and other biological studies, increasing impact of funding through joint finance mechanisms (such as conservation trust funds).

> An offset assessment based on impacts from a single project will fail to take account of the cumulative impacts from other development in the region.

Towards a national strategy for biodiversity conservation that incorporates mining impacts on species in Guinea

In the Republic of Guinea, mining companies are confronted with the question of how to define critical habitat for chimpanzees, how to mitigate the negative effects of activities on chimpanzees, and how and where to design offsets for residual impacts after all mitigation has been carried out. A number of mining companies are working with conservation organizations and experts to address these issues. They are engaging with different experts and different NGOs on a project-by-project basis.

International and national NGOs proposed a more strategic response to the impacts of industrial activities in Guinea due to the:

- failure to assess the cumulative impacts of mining on biodiversity;
- lack of coordination between biological inventories and site selection for offset projects;
- absence of sharing methodologies for mitigation strategies or offset methodologies; and
- absence of framing offset plans within larger species recovery plans or Guinea's national biodiversity strategy.

Recommendations were made to stakeholders in Guinea for a new approach to offsets in 2011; action was taken to build consensus and seek endorsement for this approach, and to generate donor commitments to fund its implementation. The new approach to offsets has two key components. The first is the development of a national strategy for offsets, based on an assessment of cumulative impacts on great apes and other EN and CR species, including a consensus, peer reviewed and transparent methodology for determining offset needs, prioritizing offset sites, aggregating offsets, integrating offsets with existing biodiversity strategies in the country, and defining "no-go" zones where industrial development should not occur. Chimpanzees have been identified as a useful starting point for the national strategy as they are an important flagship as well as an umbrella species, and they are found on most concessions.

The second component is an independent conservation trust fund to support the national strategy. It would include an endowment, funded by those private sector entities that incur offset obligations due to their development projects in Guinea. The fund is considered critical to the success of the national strategy approach for a number of reasons:

- Funding for conservation offsets must be permanent (because the impact on EN and CR species and their habitat is likely to be permanent) and a trust fund – or a "foundation," its nearest equivalent in civil law countries – is one of the few available financial mechanisms to ensure permanence.

- Conservation trust funds are independent of government (they may have government representation on trust fund boards, but never a majority of government board members). The independence of the trust fund ensures that there is a permanent entity dedicated to overseeing the financing and management of offsets in Guinea. This helps shelter offset projects from political pressure, and also creates a mechanism that the private sector entities can use to avoid having to manage offset projects themselves in perpetuity.

- Conservation trust fund endowments can be registered offshore, with a secretariat located in country.

- Conservation trust funds are a multisector mechanism (thereby increasing transparency), which is useful given that the issues in Guinea relating to development and to EN species also involve multiple sectors (government, NGOs, private sector, multilateral development banks etc.).

Key activities to promote a national offset strategy and finance mechanism in Guinea

The first key activity was to make the case for the need for a national strategy for biodiversity offsets in Guinea. The Kormos and Kormos (2011b) report was circulated in Guinea, and the authors engaged subsequently in a process of consultation, deliberation, and strategizing for the development of the offset strategy and a supporting financing mechanism. This consultation process brought together key stakeholders involved in mining and biodiversity conservation in Guinea at a range of meetings and workshops, including a workshop in Washington DC, meetings in Europe, and a workshop in Conakry in 2012.

The Washington DC workshop provided initial confirmation from a larger group of stakeholders that the national offset strategy/trust fund was worth pursuing. The workshop in Conakry later in 2012 went further in approving recommendations supporting a national offsets strategy and trust fund approach. This approval is "in principle," i.e. non-binding, with no funding commitments but was a necessary first step to open the door for discussions within government and with potential donors on how to advance implementation of this approach.

A number of lessons emerged during workshops and meetings with stakeholders, and several areas were highlighted that will require further investigation and research before all stakeholders are willing to fully commit to this process. These include technical issues with respect to the offsets design and the conservation trust fund, as well as the need to consider unforeseen developments

> Funding for conservation offsets must be permanent and a trust fund is one of the few available financial mechanisms to ensure permanence.

in the region, and globally, that must be taken into account. These lessons learned and areas requiring further work are highlighted below.

Broader biodiversity concerns

The Government of Guinea clearly stated its preference for national offset planning that would extend beyond chimpanzees to include all EN and CR species (while acknowledging the importance and usefulness of a chimpanzee focus). Government officials from the Ministry indicated that a broader planning exercise was necessary to ensure that this work would be fully consistent with and nested in Guinea's national biodiversity strategy. They suggested that an entirely chimpanzee focused approach would not be received well by the Guinean public, creating the perception that chimpanzees are more important to the government than social issues. The sense was that this concern could be alleviated by a broader focus on biodiversity, which is generally important for human wellbeing. Mining companies also emphasized their preference for a multispecies plan for potential biodiversity offset locations given that they often have requirements to offset their residual impacts on more than one species and would prefer to choose sites where they can manage these multiple offsetting needs.

The Government of Guinea was also interested in broadening the scope of the conservation trust fund so that it covers all conservation efforts in country, including the entire protected areas network. Broadening the scope of the fund's mission is feasible. However, narrowly focusing the conservation trust fund's activities early on to supporting offset projects would give the fund the greatest likelihood of success, both in terms of maintaining a clear operational and strategic focus and in terms of raising the financing from the private sector. Broadening the

fund's activities beyond offsets would be more appropriate once the success of the fund has been established.

Legal frameworks

Guinean officials informally considered whether offsets should be a requirement under Guinean law. The impetus for offsets is currently generated by the IFC performance standards (and potentially by requirements from other development banks/aid agencies), Equator banks and their performance standards, and the internal standards of individual companies. Companies that do not have internal requirements or that choose not to borrow from a bank that has an offset requirement currently have no obligation to offset in Guinea. As highlighted in Chapter 1, in relation to the review of the PS6, the IFC retains considerable discretion as to when to apply their offset requirement. Companies need not apply to the IFC for funding nor are internal corporate safeguard policies binding. As a result, offsets are currently more of a voluntary undertaking than a truly binding requirement.

Financial concerns

One question raised by the workshop in Conakry had to do with the tax implications of a mining company's contribution to a conservation trust fund. Participants noted that tax implications would differ depending on whether the contribution was deemed a business expense or a charitable contribution, and, depending on how the contribution was considered, could reduce the Guinean government's revenues. Clarifying this point would be important as trust fund planning goes forward.

Partnerships

Both bilateral and multilateral development organizations play a critical role in this ini-

> Offsets are currently more of a voluntary undertaking than a truly binding requirement.

tiative. At a political level they provide a measure of political risk insurance to private sector borrowers. At a financial level they have the capacity to provide critical seed money to develop this initiative. While the private sector can and should support this initiative, development agencies have a clear role in supporting both capacity building and national strategic planning in Guinea. Development agencies can thus be leveraged to complement the private sector funding, creating a productive public–private partnership.

A number of bilateral and multilateral funding agencies, including the Agence Française de Devéloppement (AFD) and the Fonds Français pour l'Environnement Mondial (FFEM), and the Global Environment Facility (GEF) of the World Bank, have expressed interest in this work. AFD and FFEM are exploring funding to develop a national offset policy in Guinea. Although discussions with funding agencies are still preliminary, financial institutions are watching this process with interest.

NGO presence in Guinea is very limited: Guinée Ecologie is the only domestic civil society organization with a clear biodiversity conservation focus. Together with the international NGOs working in Guinea, they have been leading much of the impetus to develop a national offset strategy.

Although a number of the world's largest mining companies have shown interest in the idea of a national offset strategy, support for this approach in smaller or less high profile mining companies is untested. The theory is that a strong partnership consisting of the Government of Guinea, NGOs, development agencies, and very large companies could work to raise standards for all development projects and provide the institutional framework to make it easier for the private sector as a whole to comply (e.g. by helping to fund the implementation of a national strategy). Whether

this bears out will only become clear as the project progresses.

Private sector response, risk, and predictability

While this is still somewhat speculative, it appears from communications with mining companies that they appreciate the greater efficiency of a national planning approach given that it avoids a certain amount of redundancy in the conservation planning and analysis they have to do and can help develop common environmental performance standards for the entire mining sector, therefore creating a more level playing field and increasing transparency. Large mining operations in developing countries are inherently complex undertakings and large-scale problem solving is a perpetual challenge for these operations. Mining companies seem to appreciate that a national approach is designed to address a conservation problem at scale, rather than making short-term marginal contributions such as a grant for a three- to five-year conservation project that is not likely to continue when funding ends. This initiative therefore appears to resonate with mining companies in that it attempts to take a larger scale view of the conservation challenge.

Even after all mitigation has taken place, there will be unavoidable residual impacts on endangered species from mining operations in Guinea, especially for great apes. To achieve best practice, permanent funding for an offset project should be in place at the time the development project begins, or soon thereafter. Mining companies may be understandably reluctant to provide an endowment to fund their offset projects before they commence mining and generate a revenue stream. This could be resolved by mining companies making a binding commitment to fully fund their offset project costs on an annual basis for a predetermined

> A national planning approach can help develop common environmental performance standards for the mining sector, creating a more level playing field and increasing transparency.

234

234
234

period, such as three to five years, and to fully fund the endowment at the end of that period.

Conclusion – Guinea

No country has yet implemented a national biodiversity strategy to offset the impact of extractive industries on wildlife. However, as a result of the launch of this approach in Guinea, consensus is emerging that the concept has value across a range of actors that include financial institutions, government, NGOs, and the private sector. The process of developing a national biodiversity offset strategy in Guinea has highlighted a number of unresolved issues and areas needing further work. Nonetheless, interest from the private sector and multi- and bilateral funders has been significant, and, with continued effort, Guinea could be the first nation to develop a comprehensive biodiversity offset strategy for CR and EN species. Such a strategy would be part of a broader national biodiversity plan, and present a strategy for one of the options for achieving conservation targets.

FIGURE 8.2

Gabon

Evolving environmental policies in Gabon that influence extractive industry practice

Gabon is situated along the western coast of Central Africa, bordering Cameroon, the Republic of Congo, and Equatorial Guinea. Gabon's low human population (approx. 1.6 million in July 2013) and extensive mineral and oil reserves have enabled it to achieve relative wealth in comparison to other sub-Saharan countries. It enjoys a per capita income four times that of most sub-Saharan African nations; however, high income inequality prevails with a large proportion of the population living below the poverty line. In 2010, the economy was reliant on oil for about 50% of its GDP, about 70% of revenues, and 87% of goods exports (CIA, 2013b). Gabon harbors 13% of the African tropical forest belt and its combination of low human population and natural mineral and oil wealth have been cited as reasons for why it has maintained high forest coverage and biodiversity (CIA, 2013b).

This case study presents an overview of the evolution of environmental and protected area legislation as it pertains to extractive industries and business-as-usual models of economic development. It also outlines more recent moves by the Gabonese government to incorporate green macroeconomic models as it looks to diversify its economic development away from oil and mineral extraction. Key findings indicate that:

- Scientists and international conservation organizations have been instrumental in informing the development of a biodiversity conservation policy framework.

- High political support has been critical in the establishment of protected areas and a protected area authority, as well as for the promotion of a green economy.

- Creation of a protected area network resulted in the cancellation of logging concessions.

- Iterative changes in implementation of legislation and importance of the environment within government structures were a product of intervention at the highest political levels influenced by international press, public relations, and conservation organizations.

- Despite strong legislation and pro environmental policies, there have been significant declines in key mammal populations across their ranges, primarily as a result of poaching.

The case study also provides details on the evolution of the legislative framework that culminated in the creation of a national parks law, how interaction with extractive industries influenced the creation of this policy environment, and how this ultimately in turn impacted extractive industry practice. This is then followed by detail on the creation of a policy direction for Gabon that incorporated green economic development models and presents some of the emerging impacts of this relatively recent move.

Establishment of a legislative framework for conservation of biodiversity in Gabon

In 1993, after the Earth Summit held in Rio de Janeiro in 1992, the government of the late President Omar Bongo passed an Environment Law obliging all major industrial and development projects to undertake EIAs. This was further strengthened in 2001 when a new Forestry Code was signed into law. The new Forestry Act made it obligatory for all forestry permits to develop sustainable harvest management plans along the lines of the norms being promoted at the time by the Forest Stewardship Council

(FSC, see Chapter 4). This was followed in July 2002 by the creation of 13 national parks, covering 11% of Gabon's terrestrial ecosystems. The decision by President Bongo to create the national parks estate was considered significant by conservation organizations because it was perhaps the first time in history that a nation had decided to establish such an extensive and well-planned network in one go. Second, the parks had been designed by scientists to optimize the protection of Gabon's vast intact ecosystems and its exceptional biodiversity, ensuring that areas of the highest and most significant biodiversity were protected.

The decision also resulted in the cancelling of 13 000 km^2 of logging concessions in order to convert them to protected areas for conservation. While the role of conservation organizations in lobbying the highest levels of government to protect important ecosystems is considered to have been critical, it is likely that the decision was also influenced by the fact that Gabon's oil reserves had peaked by 2002 and the government had to consider alternative sustainable sources of funding. With ecotourism cited as a potential and significant source of economic development, the importance of protecting potentially lucrative tourism sites would not have been lost on the President.

The Gabonese government consolidated its commitment to biodiversity conservation in 2007 with the passing of a National Parks Law that created a National Parks Agency – *Agence Nationale des Parcs Nationaux* (ANPN) and built on the provisional legislation passed in 2002. This unusual step for a Central African country means that any modifications in park boundaries need to be approved by Gabon's Parliament and Senate, as well as by the Cabinet (La Republique Gabonaise, 2007). The law defines the rules and regulations regarding land use as it relates to national parks. It describes the conditions under which mining and oil exploration

236

are possible, as well as the procedure for
declassification should it be decided that it is
in the national interest to undertake mining
or oil exploration in an area that falls within
a park. It also provides for the definition of
buffer zones where any anthropogenic activity requires authorization by ANPN, as well
as peripheral zones. ANPN has the power of
veto over projects supported by EIAs undertaken by extractive industries within these
peripheral zones, if there are likely to be
negative impacts on the national parks.

Although no other Gabonese law is so
prescriptive regarding relations with other
land-use options, making it much easier to
manage parks than forestry, agriculture,
mining, or oil concessions, the government
maintained the right to allow extraction of
mineral wealth and to degazette protected
areas if it were in the national interest.

Oil exploration, dam building, and the creation of robust national parks legislation

The content of the national parks law in
relation to extractive industries was likely
influenced by the actions of a Chinese oil
company, Sinopec. In the summer of 2006,
Sinopec moved into the northern section of
Loango National Park to undertake seismic
surveys. Authorization for the exploration
had been issued by the Ministry of Mines,
Petroleum, and Hydrocarbons, with some
agreement from the Ministry of Environment,
although it is not clear whether the person in
the Ministry of Environment had the authority to allow exploration in a national park.
The Wildlife Conservation Society (WCS),
who were working in the area at the time, not
only informed the President of the presence

of the oil company in a national park, but were also able to ascertain that an EIA had not been conducted. The attention of the international press (Haslam, 2006) and an appeal to the highest levels of government were factors that resulted in a presidential order halting the exploratory work by Sinopec until an EIA had been completed. Changes in government, notably the appointment of the Deputy Prime Minister in charge of environment, elevated the importance of the Ministry of Environment. This created a more balanced dynamic between the Ministry of Environment and what had been considered to be the traditionally richer and more powerful Ministry of Mines, Petroleum, and Hydrocarbons.

The initial EIA that Sinopec completed was presented at a public hearing, implementing for the first time the EIA conditions outlined in the 1993 Environment Law. However, it lacked detailed assessments of potential impacts of seismic activities and did not present any concrete mitigation actions in its Environmental and Social Management Plan. The subsequent rendition was developed in partnership with two international conservation NGOs – WCS and the World Wide Fund for Nature (WWF) who had been asked by the Director General of the Environment to work with Sinopec to conduct an adequate EIA. The final EIA included unprecedented detail in the Environmental and Social Management Plan. It resulted in the first on-shore seismic campaign in a Central African rainforest that did not use chainsaws to cut seismic lines or helipads – rather field teams on foot used machetes to trace lines just 1 m wide, cutting nothing above a 10 cm diameter. They avoided areas used by gorillas in the dry season by delaying their work in these areas until the gorillas had moved out, and the impact of operations was evaluated by independent scientists (Rabanal *et al.*, 2010; Wrege *et al.*, 2010).

The ongoing evolution of the Gabonese government's reconciliation of biodiversity conservation and economic development was highlighted when the President convened a conference, attended by the entire government, including Parliament, Senate, and also civil societies, to resolve the actions of extractive industries in areas of important biodiversity already under protection. The conference focused on the actions of SINOHYDRO, another Chinese company contracted to assess the possibility of building a hydroelectric power dam to provide electricity to the planned Belinga iron ore mine in northeast Gabon. In 2008, SINOHYDRO constructed a road to the Koungou waterfalls on the Ivindo River, in the Ivindo National Park. This site had previously been the focus of a campaign spearheaded by an Italian NGO "Trust the Forest" and the Gabonese NGO "Brain Forest" to preserve the waterfalls from logging by Rougier Gabon.

The laterite road was built without an EIA. Promoters of the dam claimed the Belinga Iron Mining Project was important for the future economic development of Gabon, and would create thousands of jobs for the region as a whole. Detractors of the project, namely national and international conservation organizations and environment agencies, highlighted how studies conducted by the French in the 1960s identified alternative sites that were far better suited for dam construction, would result in a smaller environmental footprint, and would preserve what is considered to be the most spectacular waterfall in Central Africa. As the EIA did not consider these other options, the Director General of the Environment blocked the project pending further work and the Deputy Prime Minister, as head of the Environment Ministry, personally visited the site to ensure that any further construction was halted. These actions have been attributed to the initiation of a national debate that culminated in the conference called by the President. SINOHYDRO's perceived attack on Ivindo National Park was actually no more than a feasibility study and resulting tensions would likely have been avoided through the systematic application of the environmental and park laws. A decision was taken to stop the work at Koungou, underlining that the implementation of these laws was a reality. This incident highlighted the tension created by poor implementation of legislation, and how the engagement by senior government officials and politicians to enforce legislation was necessary to ensure that due process was followed. The ensuing national debate served to strengthen environmental law implementation. Despite these successes in ensuring the enforcement of environmental legislation, there continue to be wildlife losses.

Green Gabon

In 2009, presidential candidate Ali Bongo Ondimba made sustainable development one of three pillars of his election campaign. "Green Gabon," a catchphrase in his election manifesto, encompasses all that Gabon has done in the years and decades after Rio. It presents a novel integrated long-term vision to develop Gabon sustainably, by finding a balance between Industrial Gabon, Services Gabon, and Green Gabon (Republic of Gabon, 2013). Immediately after the elections, President Bongo Ondimba created an interministerial Climate Council that the President personally chairs. The Ministry of Economy was transformed into the Ministry of Economy and Sustainable Development, further emphasizing the shift in focus with respect to the economic development of Gabon.

The National Climate Change Plan integrates climate/low carbon emission considerations into the 26 sectorial development plans that were developed on the back of the 2009 election manifesto. Carbon emission savings that have resulted from the political decisions to oblige forestry companies to adopt sustainable harvest practices (Government of Gabon, in press), as well as from the creation of the national parks, are considered to be about 350 million tons lower over the 2000–10 period compared to the 1990–2000 period (Government of Gabon, in press). Conservative values assigned to emissions reductions in voluntary schemes such as the Amazon Fund indicate that this represents a contribution of around US$2 billion to the global efforts to mitigate climate change (Government of Gabon, in press). The climate plan not only integrates climate/low carbon emission considerations into 26 sectorial development plans, it also acknowledges that a national land-use plan is critical to ensuring Gabon continues to develop sustainably. This plan was under development at the time of writing and is intended ultimately to define national land-use strategy by law. The plan is expected to indicate areas to be set aside for conservation, forestry, agriculture, mining, infrastructure, and urban expansion. The General Secretary of the Government is overseeing the development of the plan with technical aspects managed by the Climate Council and the National Parks Agency. The first draft of the national land-use plan is due for release by early 2014.

In February 2013, Gabon passed a Sustainable Development Law that was inspired by the work of Australia and the UK to develop biodiversity and ecosystem services offsets, by Costa Rica and Botswana's efforts to integrate natural capital into economic accounting systems, and by Prince Charles' (Rainforest Project) work on Community Capital. Considered to be progressive legislation, it strengthens the Environment Law, particularly through legislation governing EIAs, making it obligatory for all companies and government departments,

including all extractive industries, to do an annual sustainable development report and to offset any negative impacts on carbon emissions, biodiversity, and ecosystem services and community capital. A new agency will be created to ensure adequate implementation of this law. Examples of companies applying the draft law as they develop new projects include Olam, who are developing a series of oil palm and rubber plantations in Gabon. A specific agreement with the Gabonese Government obliges Olam to obtain certification from the Round Table on Sustainable Palm Oil (RSPO) for their entire Gabonese oil palm plantation estate, and this signals the commitment of both parties to move towards more environmentally responsible action. Olam have, in partnership with the government, selected low carbon/low biodiversity areas for plantation development; calculated carbon emissions and undertaken voluntary offsets. They have engaged

PROFOREST to undertake high conservation value forest (HCVF) assessments resulting in the allocation of over 40% of their concessions to conservation areas, and have solicited full prior informed consent from local populations before initiating their projects (Rainforest Foundation, 2012). Today, all industrial projects undergo an effective impact assessment and all of Gabon's planned oil palm developments will be RSPO compliant and will include HCVF evaluations and set-asides as well as ape management plans.

Conclusion – Gabon

Today Gabon has 30 000 km² of FSC certified forestry permits and annual deforestation rates are less than 0.01% (Bayol *et al.*, 2012). National parks cover 11% of the country and a further 10% of the land surface area has protected status in the form of wildlife reserves and Ramsar sites. The government

Photo: Today Gabon has 30 000 km² of FSC certified forestry permits and annual deforestation rates are less than 0.01%. Lopé timber yard on the edge of Lopé National Park, Gabon.
© Jabruson, 2013. All Rights Reserved. www.jabruson.photoshelter.com

has a stated policy of zero tolerance for wild-life crime but, despite this, there has been a decline in forest elephants of 18% between 2002 and 2011 (Maisels *et al.*, 2013). As a result of much higher elephant declines in other regions of the tropical forest belt, in the DRC in particular, Gabon is now home to over half the surviving population (Maisels *et al.*, 2013). Apes have also suffered over the last two decades from population decline, linked primarily to Ebola (Walsh *et al.*, 2003) and hunting for bushmeat, current estimations place populations of gorillas at 20 000 (F. Maisels, personal communication, 2013). These declines raise questions about the capacity to implement legislation effectively, a common problem across all ape range states.

However, the robust policy environment provides the framework for operation, and the intervention and involvement of the highest levels of politics and lobbying by international conservation agencies were key factors in its evolution. The modification of industry behavior, reassigning logging concessions to areas of lower biodiversity importance, and consideration of the development of a national green economy frame-work point to some of the successes of this process. It is, however, too early to ascertain whether the recently developed sustainable development framework will become the main driver of economic development. Unless economic returns become the reality, political support may turn back to business as usual models of operation to ensure Gabon generates the necessary revenue for its future development. Emphasis is being placed on opportunities that arise from climate change. How centrally wildlife conservation, and ape conservation in particular, factor into this scenario, considering the current lack of substantial return from tourism, is still to be seen.

The case of logging and implementing a forestry moratorium in Indonesia

Indonesia is an archipelago in Southeast Asia comprising 17 508 islands, the largest of which are Borneo (shared with Malaysia and Brunei) and Sumatra. Indonesia has a human population density of 251 million over 1.8 million km² (CIA, 2013a). Its primary exports are oil and gas, timber/plywood, and manufacturing products. Indonesia is considered to be the third largest emitter of greenhouse gases (GHG). Eighty percent of those emissions are due to deforestation. The Norwegian government embarked on a process to support Indonesia in reducing its GHG; establishing and implementing a two-year logging moratorium (May 2011) was part of a deal in which Indonesia would receive US$1 billion from Norway. During a CNN interview in June 2011, President Susilo Bambang Yudhoyono reiterated his commitment and that of his government to protecting Indonesia's remaining forest and preventing further destruction. "Our philosophy is that we can achieve both, economic growth and environmental protection, and

FIGURE 8.3

Indonesia

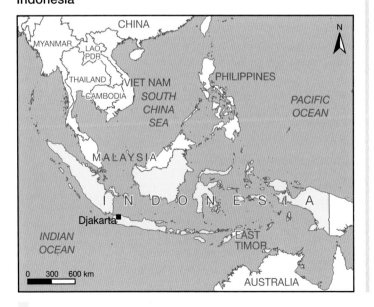

my government is committed to doing that" (CNN, 2011).

His acknowledgement of the importance of reconciling two disparate issues was further reinforced by Indonesia's commitment to reduce its GHGs by 26% by 2020 as outlined in a presidential decree in September 2011 (Presidential Regulation, September 20, 2011). The logging moratorium was extended for another two years on May 15, 2013 (*Inpres 6/2013*). This case study examines the experience of implementing the forestry moratorium, highlighting the complexity of such an undertaking in a context that has traditionally exploited its forest resource through extraction. Key findings include:

- There is no evidence that Indonesia's forest moratorium has effectively reduced the conversion of forest in Indonesia to non-forest/degraded forest land.
- The Indonesian forest moratorium has not led to any significant reduction in either loss of orangutan habitat or loss of orangutan populations.

It goes on to present details on the trajectory of forest loss and degradation over the last decades in the context of the political changes. It subsequently covers the evolution of the logging moratorium and outlines some of the challenges to its effective implementation.

The evolution of forest management in Indonesia

Forest management in Indonesia is strongly influenced by the political dynamic and changes in the country's development strategy aiming to boost the national economy. During the last 50 years forest management policies can be divided into three main periods, each with distinct priorities and approaches. Until the rise to power of

President Soeharto (apparently his preferred spelling, 'Suharto' is more commonly used in the international English press) in 1966 the focus was on agricultural expansion that had limited impact on forest areas in Indonesia. The following period, which ended with the fall of the Soeharto regime in 1998, was earmarked by extensive forest exploitation and the development of timber and oil palm plantations as well as increased mining operations. The year 1998 was the beginning of a new era in Indonesia – the so-called Reformation era – that has been marked by the decentralization and deconcentration of authority to manage natural resources, including forest resources, from central to local government.

The period until 1998

Up until 1966, *circa* 77% (1 470 000 km²) of Indonesian land was covered by dense tropical rain forest. The rise of the late President Soeharto (New Order Regime) in 1966 changed the situation dramatically. Triggered by the Agrarian Act 1960 and the Forestry Act 1967 that declared almost all forests as state property under the full control of the Indonesian Government (Simorangkir and Sardjono, 2006), and the Forest Investment Law 1967 that enabled foreign companies to operate in Indonesian forests, the so-called "timber boom" era started with the expansion of large-scale logging operations all across the country. This period lasted for around two decades and reached its peak in the early 1980s when the country became one of the largest producers and exporters of tropical timber/logs worldwide. By 1983, the government had granted concession permits totaling 651 400 km² of forest[3] to 560 logging concessions (World Rainforest Movement, 1998).

Extractive logging operations continued into the following years. During this period, however, the forest development strategy shifted from the primary product (timber/log) to "higher-value" secondary products, particularly plywood. The promotion of the plywood industry that was supported by the log export ban (established in 2001) was triggered by the increasing world demand for plywood, particularly from East Asia. Until that time, the Philippines had been the main source for plywood, but had lost most of its forest owing to overexploitation. Plywood production increased rapidly over a very short period of time, and Indonesia became the world's largest plywood producer, with a 75% global market share by the late 1980s. The contribution of the plywood sector to Indonesia's exports increased significantly from almost nil in 1977 to 54% by the beginning of the 1990s (Manurung, 2002).

The latter half of the 1980s was characterized by the development of large-scale industrial timber plantations (HTI, *Hutan Tanaman Industri*) for producing both hardwood and softwood for the pulp and paper industry. The Government of Indonesia pushed towards the target of establishing 62 500 km² of plantation forest by 2000 (Handadhari *et al.*, 2002), which was influenced by three factors. First, after decades of over-logging of the natural forest there was an acute shortage of timber as raw material for plywood. A study disclosed that acute timber shortages encouraged many companies to use timber from illegal sources from 1985–97 (Kartodihardjo and Supriono, 2000). Second, since the 1970s there has been increasing global demand and price

Photo: The extensive use of fire in land conversion and clearance, alongside poor forest logging practices, has had a devastating effect on the forests of Indonesia.
© Serge Wich

for pulp; and third, planting fast-growing tree species was seen as the "right" strategy for "regreening" vast areas of degraded and bare land caused by extensive logging operations. In less than a decade (1991–98) the plantation forest area extended from 2000 to 19 000 km² (Ministry of Forestry, 2013).

During the 1980s Indonesia also saw the beginning of massive forest conversion into oil palm plantations that was driven by strong global demand. The government eagerly supported oil palm expansion as a strategic way to support the development of remote inland regions and to improve the livelihood of rural populations (Bangun, 2006). Planting oil palm was also meant to "re-green" unproductive and bare land exposed by logging and other extractive industries. Until the early 1970s, palm cultivation was primarily carried out by large plantation companies. In 1974, however, the price and demand for palm oil in the international market peaked and efforts were made to increase production by attracting small private companies and farmers into this business through a scheme called the Nucleus Estate Scheme, where state-owned plantation companies helped farmers to grow oil palms and provide access to processing mills. This led to a significant increase in the number and size of oil palm plantations across Indonesia. From the end of the 1970s to 1997, the area of oil palm plantation increased from c. 4000 to 22 500 km², with the largest expansion through forest clearing in Sumatra and Kalimantan (Susila, 1998; Bangun, 2006). The clearing of natural forest for oil palm and HTI intensified with the issuance of Government Regulation No. 7/ 1990 that allows plantation companies to convert "unproductive forest areas" into new plantation areas and harvest the timber during the land clearance. As the definition of "unproductive" was very vague and technically difficult to determine in the field, this regulation perversely encouraged the plan-

tation companies to expand their concession areas – more than they could manage – by clearing relatively good forest areas to reap the benefit of harvested timber and then abandon the land without replanting it (Kartodihardjo and Supriono, 2000).

Deforestation resulting from plantations, large-scale agriculture, and mining was exacerbated by the extensive use of fire in forest clearance, particularly in plantation development. Forest and land fires are challenges Indonesia has struggled with for centuries, resulting from human activities such as slash-and-burn agriculture. However, before the 1980s, even in dry periods, the scale and intensity of forest and land fires was limited with minimal environmental impacts. In subsequent decades, the extensive use of fire in land conversion and clearance and poor forest logging practices[4] have changed the situation dramatically (Bappenas, 1999; Gouyon and Simorangkir, 2002). Especially during the El Niño events in 1982/83, 1987, 1991, 1994, and 1997/98, widespread forest and land fires broke out, devastating 10 000 km² of forest (Simorangkir and Sumantri, 2002). The 1997 fires were considered the worst in Indonesia (and the Southeast region) over the last 15 years, resulting in 100 000 km² of forest being burnt. The fires burning in 2013, primarily in peat swamps and the burning of the peat itself, and for the clearing of land for oil palm plantations, were considered the worst since 1997 (which caused an official state of emergency in Sarawak as well as the Malaysian peninsular) and caused health hazards in cities around the Malaysian peninsula (Vidal, 2013a).

Reformation era

The sociopolitical situation in Indonesia changed fundamentally with the economic crisis that hit Asia in 1997 and the fall of Soeharto in 1998. Up until 1998, natural resource management was fully controlled

244

by the central government in Jakarta and the profits from resource exploitation were mainly diverted to the central government and powerful individuals.

Following the collapse of the New Order Regime in 1998, provinces and districts started to voice their disagreement and disappointment with the system and demand more independence and rights in governing their natural resources. The issuance of Act No. 22/1999 and Government Regulation No. 25/2000 paved the way for decentralization and the devolution of authority and

responsibility for natural resource management from central to regional (provincial and district) government. This was done in the belief that decentralization would strengthen local government, improve the livelihoods of rural people in the provinces, and lead to better governance of natural resources. The reality, however, was a dramatic acceleration of uncontrolled logging, both legal and illegal, the encroachment and conversion of forestland into plantations, forest clearance for mining operations, the creation of road networks through large areas of tropical rainforest and extensive use of fire in land clearance across Indonesia.

In part, this can be attributed to a lack of capacity and preparation for the changes. More importantly, however, decentralization created perverse incentives that led to further acceleration of environmental degradation and land conversion as provinces and districts were now expected to generate their own revenues. Increasingly they have been forced to turn to the exploitation of forests, creation of large-scale oil palm plantations, and expansion of mining operations. Data from the Ministry of Forestry show that the HTI area increased between 1995–2007 from 11 300 to 70 700 km², while another study estimated that, up to 2009, 99 700 km² of HTI had been established (Forest Watch Indonesia, 2011).

The decades-long overexploitation, followed by the clearance and degradation of natural forests, has resulted in immense destruction of natural forests in the last 50 years. In total, since the beginning of the "timber boom" in the 1960s more than 963 000 km² of Indonesian forestland has been degraded, of which 546 000 km² is within state forest areas, including production forests and conservation and protection forests, and 417 000 km² is outside of state forest areas (Nawir, Murniati, and Rumboko, 2007). It is estimated that Indonesia has one of the highest rates of deforestation in the world and loses 18 700 km² of forest each

FIGURE 8.4

Diminishing forest coverage in Indonesia

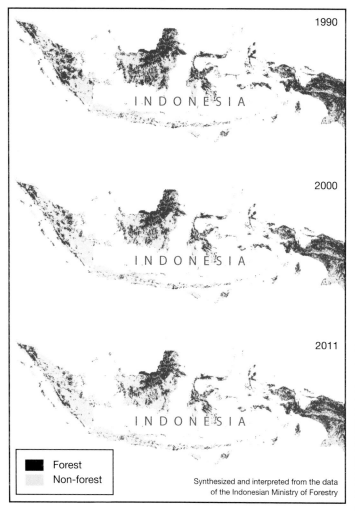

Synthesized and interpreted from the data of the Indonesian Ministry of Forestry

Courtesy of Charites Institute.[5]

State of the Apes 2013 Extractive Industries and Ape Conservation

year to logging, agriculture, settlement and infrastructure development, and fire (FAO, 2006). The rapid deforestation in Indonesia can clearly be seen by comparing forest coverage over time as presented in Figure 8.4.

Forest loss and orangutans

Forest loss negatively impacts orangutans both directly and indirectly. Orangutans are often killed during logging activities as well as during land clearance operations, especially when fire is used. Forest clearance also leads to complete loss of orangutan habitat, resulting in their death or forcing groups to migrate to other areas.

Over the past 20 years, 40 000 km² (from a total of 130 000 km²) of orangutan habitat has been destroyed or converted for other purposes (Nellemann *et al.*, 2007), and the annual rate of habitat loss in Sumatra and Kalimantan runs at 1–1.5% and 1.5–2%, respectively (Singleton *et al.*, 2004). UNEP studies, illustrated in Figure 8.5, show that between 1930 and 2004 large areas of critical orangutan habitat were lost and the fragmented forests that remain are becoming increasingly isolated (Nellemann *et al.*, 2007).

The opening of the forest increases the vulnerability of orangutans to illegal hunting for consumption and commercial trade, as further discussed in Chapter 7. Orangutans are often killed/captured opportunistically when loggers are clearing the forest. Moreover, as the forest becomes increasingly degraded and food becomes scarce, the apes start to enter villages or plantations around the degraded forest, where they are killed by villagers or farmers that perceive orangutans as crop raiding pests (Meijaard *et al.*, 2011). This has contributed significantly to the sharp decline of orangutans.

It is estimated (Nellemann *et al.*, 2007; Meijaard *et al.*, 2011) that, in the last 35 years, about 50 000 orangutans have been lost as their habitat has been destroyed. Currently only 6650 Sumatran and around 55 000 Bornean orangutans remain in the wild. Of these populations, approximately 70% live outside of protected areas (WWF, 2013). Although the species are classified by the IUCN as EN and CR, respectively, and are listed on CITES Appendix I (see the Introduction), and therefore benefit from legal protection, the laws are inadequately enforced and their habitats continue to be destroyed.

FIGURE 8.5

Change of orangutan habitat distribution and size in Borneo 1930–2004

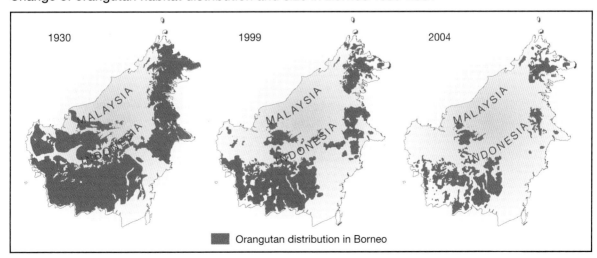

Orangutan distribution in Borneo

The logging moratorium in Indonesia: *quo vadis*?

With the extensive forest destruction and land-use transformation that has taken place in Indonesia over the last few decades, alongside the increasing global awareness of climate change, Indonesia has been branded as one of the largest GHG emitters in the world. The country has been under severe international and domestic pressure to improve their land-use management practices.

Within this context, the Indonesian President announced, in 2009, a voluntary commitment to reduce the country's carbon footprint by 26%, whilst achieving 7% economic growth.[6] In May 2011 the commitment was put into action with the issuance of the Presidential Instruction (*Inpres*) No. 10 for the Suspension of Granting New Licenses and Improvement of Natural Primary Forest and Peatland Governance, effective until May 2013, and renewed for another two years until May 2015. The *Inpres*, or more commonly called "the Moratorium," aims to cut the country's emissions by reducing the conversion of primary forest and peatland for other purposes, particularly monoculture plantations. It is not intended to stop the future exploitation and use of peatland and forest areas, but rather to give the government time to evaluate and reorganize its development strategies. The area to be excluded from conversion is specified in an indicative map – as part of the Moratorium – that was prepared collaboratively by key government agencies under the coordination of the Ministry of Forestry and is revised at least every six months. Between June 2011 and January 2013 the indicative map was revised three times.

The implementation of the Moratorium, though, faces serious challenges (Murdiyarso *et al.*, 2011; Wells, Neil, and Paoli, 2011; Wich, Koh, and Noordwijk, 2011a).[7] First, from a legal point of view the Moratorium is a non-legislative document and simply provides a set of presidential instructions to concerned government agencies. As such, there are no legal consequences if the instructions are not implemented. Moreover, the Moratorium includes almost all key government agencies (three ministries, five agencies) and provincial and district heads but excludes the Ministry of Agriculture and the Ministry of Energy and Mineral Resources, both of which are engaged in deforestation. The exclusion of these ministries obviously limits the effectiveness of the Moratorium. Second, the definition of forest types and the scope and areas included under the Moratorium are not clear:

- The Moratorium is limited to the "state forest area" (*kawasan hutan*) and applies only to "primary forests," defined as "natural forests untouched by cultivation or silvicultural systems applied in forestry." This means that all forested areas outside of the state forest area, as well as logged-over and secondary forests within state forest areas – some of which have high biodiversity – are exempt from the Moratorium and can be converted into new plantations. In fact, the establishment of industrial timber plantations through the conversion of secondary forests is perceived by the Ministry as forest improvement. As of 2009, Indonesia had a total of 866 000 km² of state forest areas, of which 452 000 km² are primary forest and 414 000 km² secondary forest. There are also 53 000 km² of forested areas outside the state forest area (Ministry of Forestry, 2009a) and, as stated earlier, 70% of orangutans live outside protected forests.

- With regard to peatlands, it is prohibited to undertake new conversion of any peatlands deeper than 3 m, either within or outside of state forests. Yet, this is actually redundant as the exclusion of such peatlands was already stipulated in other government regulations before the Moratorium was put in place. Currently there is talk of changing the threshold from 3 m to 0.5 m, which will be very difficult to apply as the maps showing peat-depth are inaccurate and for many parts of the country do not actually exist. Clarifying this issue is critical as peatland covers huge areas across all of the Indonesian islands, which are partly forested or covered by woody vegetation.

- The indicative map includes protection and conversion forests, which is redundant as they are already protected under other regulations (e.g. Forestry Law 41/ 1999). Of the 664 000 km² covered by the first indicative map, around two-thirds (439 000 km²) are already protection and conservation forests (see below) (Ministry of Forestry, 2008; Murdiyarso *et al.*, 2011).

Third, the Moratorium excludes certain activities that are potentially destructive, as it only applies to applications for new concession areas and:

- still allows the clearance of forest areas by companies that already have a "principal permit" (*ijin prinsip*) to develop a plantation;[8]
- permits companies to apply for an extension of concession permits that are close to expiration;
- allows for the expansion of existing plantations into new forest areas, without applying for a new concession permit, under "special conditions" that are not clearly defined; and
- the use and conversion of primary forest and peatlands for activities related to mineral mining and other strategic industries, such as oil and gas, energy, rice, and sugar cane is exempted from the

Moratorium. Although this is economically and socially understandable and perhaps justifiable, it could seriously undermine the Moratorium in its application. In the past, such development activities have often led to the destruction of huge forest areas and/or peatland with disastrous consequences to the environment.

When the Moratorium was issued, the number of companies that already held a principal permit and those that had applied for expansion was unknown. It is commonly believed that in the months before the Moratorium came into force many principal permits were issued, particularly by district governments.

These challenges, together with a lack of reliable and accurate data and insufficient coordination and agreement between key government agencies, have led to continued debate over the areas to include in the indicative map and how to enforce the commitments made. Many environmental groups support strict implementation of the Moratorium and even a total ban on forest and peatland conversion. Conversely, there are strong lobbies from the forest and tree plantation industries that are advocating for easing the Moratorium. This has significant support from local governments who argue that they need to use the forest resources within their districts/provinces to achieve economic development.

One of the earliest analyses of the Moratorium, and perhaps one of the few reliable ones (Murdiyarso *et al.*, 2011), estimated the spatial extent of the Moratorium as 664 000 km², of which around 439 000 km² are protection and conservation forests. Since the latter are already protected by other laws, in reality the Moratorium provides additional protection to only 225 000 km² of forest areas, of which only 72 000 km² are primary forests (others are peatlands).

> " The Moratorium allows for the use and conversion of primary forest and peatlands for activities related to mineral mining, oil and gas. "

There is no evidence that the Moratorium has effectively reduced the conversion of forest in Indonesia. By January 2013 little sign of improvement and improved transparency in the process of granting permits and forest governance was discernible. The constant changes to the indicative map continue to create strong business uncertainties and have reportedly enabled many companies to continue their practice of clearing and converting forested areas to do so. Many violations have been observed in the field, such as opening and converting peatlands that are included in the indicative map (Forest Watch Indonesia, 2012).

Conclusion – Indonesia

Ultimately, the Moratorium has not improved conservation of the orangutan. It does not impact orangutans in conservation areas, as these were legally protected before the Moratorium, and the lack of law enforcement means that there has been no change in their conservation in these areas.[9] With respect to the protection of orangutans outside conservation areas, particularly secondary forest and other forests outside the state forest areas, the Moratorium does not offer any protection.

Although the Indonesian government's recognition of the importance of environmental protection demonstrates an awareness of the role of conservation, this commitment does not translate easily to effective policy development and implementation. The creation and implementation of the forestry moratorium highlights the interaction of international environmental considerations, business interests, and political process, and has resulted in little change to rates of deforestation across Indonesia. Effective policy implementation requires a combination of law enforcement and recognition of the importance of environmental protection across Indonesia's entire political spectrum.

> Environmental protection needs to be considered as a central component of all economic development strategies and initiatives, and not as an add-on or a secondary consideration.

Conclusion

All ape range states are at various stages of dynamic economic transformation. The conflict that often arises between the drive for economic development and the importance of environmental conservation is particularly challenging considering the limited resources, capacity, and data available to not only inform but also implement meaningful policies. The conflicting time frames of often short-term economic gains versus the environmental benefits that can be felt over the long term are also difficult to reconcile.

In Indonesia and Gabon the interventions of the heads of state were significant factors in enabling the creation of the policy framework and the debate for attaining both environmental protection and economic development. The potential for meaningful implementation of policy is significantly hampered, however, when loopholes and weak enforcement are exploited by government agents and the private sector, or when inadequate and poorly planned measures are adopted. This disconnect points to a fundamental aspect of natural resource protection in ape range states that needs to be addressed. Environmental protection needs to be considered as a central component of all economic development strategies and initiatives, and not as an add-on or a secondary consideration handed to less powerful departments or organizations to enforce.

It could be argued that the role of external partners, working together with local agencies, is to provide data and monitor and leverage change in implementation, while providing a level of transparency that can help reduce potential corruption. The impact of international conservation organizations on the evolution of Gabon's environmental protection legislation continues to inform and influence subsequent implementation. The critical impact of the changes to PS6 of the IFC to the initiation of a national biodiversity offset planning process will impact, on an on-going basis, the availability of nations to safeguard and finance conservation of areas that include CR and EN species. Monitoring the impacts of legislation, policy, and law enforcement on biodiversity and conservation areas is critical for a balance between exploitation and conservation of natural resources to be found and maintained, to keep a balance between the often conflicting activities. Finally, the on-going global process of climate change, payment for ecosystem services, and other mechanisms to finance the protection of forests and peatlands will continue to influence environmental protection action at state level.

It is clear, however, that the on-going loss of forest cover, increase in pressure on natural resources, and decline in ape populations and other species highlight the importance of resolving the challenges to effective management of these areas. It is critical that all partners work together to:

1. find the appropriate strategies and mechanisms for reconciling economic development and environmental conservation;

2. empower stakeholders at national and regional level to implement those strategies; and

3. enable those strategies and mechanisms to be sustained, through broader engagement beyond the confines of nation states.

Nations, and specifically weak government departments responsible for forest conservation and management, cannot be held responsible alone for the protection of fragile resources and ecosystems. This must be brought into a much broader consideration of the consequences of extractive industries on economies and environment, and thus include multiple players with engagements and responsibilities.

Acknowledgments

Principal authors: Helga Rainer and Annette Lanjouw

Contributors: Cyril Kormos, Rebecca Kormos, Niel Makinuddin, Erik Meijaard, PNCI, Dicky Simorangkir, and Serge Wich

Endnotes

1   PS1 Assessment and Management of Environmental and Social Risks and Impacts: http://www1.ifc.org/wps/wcm/connect/3be1a68049a78dc8b7e4f7a8c6a8312a/PS1_English_2012.pdf?MOD=AJPERES

2   PS6 Biodiversity Conservation and Sustainable Management of Living Natural Resources: http://www1.ifc.org/wps/wcm/connect/bff0a28049a790d6b835faa8c6a8312a/PS6_English_2012.pdf?MOD=AJPERES

3   Based on Consensus Forest Land Use Plan/TGHK in 1987 the 1.47 million km2 forestland was divided into permanent forestland (75.49%) and conversion forest (24.51%). From the permanent forestland 19.95% was protection forest, 13.08% conservation areas, 22.44% production forest, and 20.02% limited production forest. The conservation areas and protection forest cannot be used for any kind of exploitation, while the production forest mainly for timber harvesting, and conversion forest can be converted for other purposes, such as plantation.

4   Forest exploitation does not lead directly to fire outbreak. Poor logging practices, however, will degrade forest areas into very poor, light dense secondary forests and grass/bushland, making them more susceptible to fire.

5   Maps produced by Indrawan Suryadi, December 2012, based on satellite imagery interpretation and official data about forest coverage from the Indonesian Ministry of Forestry.

6   Many suspected that the announcement was rather a populist one. Prior to the announcement, the commitment had never been discussed, and scientifically and technically there is no solid basis that supports and justifies the level of commitment. The announcement surprised even top-level government officers who represented the country at the international climate change negotiations.

7   There are many problems that are related more to the emission issue rather than to deforestation and forest degradation. For example, the exclusion of large peatland areas on deforested areas outside

250

of state forest area will reduce the effectiveness of the moratorium in reducing emissions but will not affect the effort to reduce the deforestation. As this chapter focuses on deforestation and forest degradation issues, such problems are not discussed here.

8   From obtaining a principal permit up to field operational activities, i.e. obtaining a concession permit and planting the concession area, a company has to go through a long and complicated process and undertake specified activities; however, once the a principal permit has been issued the company can start to clear the forest and/or dry out the peatland.

9   Data from the Ministry of Forestry in 2008 indicated that encroachment of conservation areas occurred at an estimated annual rate of 2000 km^2.

252

Photo: There has been a continent-wide decline in suitable environmental conditions within the geographic range of African apes. © Takeshi Furuichi, Wamba Committee for Bonobo Research

State of the Apes 2013 Extractive Industries and Ape Conservation

CHAPTER 9

The status of apes across Africa and Asia

Introduction

This chapter provides information on the conservation and welfare of great apes and gibbons. It focuses on the distribution and environmental conditions in which apes live in both Africa and Asia. The information presented is drawn from various sources, especially from the A.P.E.S. Portal (http://apesportal.eva.mpg.de), and can be used by decision-makers and stakeholders to contribute to the development of informed policies and effective planning. Although reference is made to particular great ape and gibbon taxa in some parts of the report, discussions are tailored to address issues about apes in general (not necessarily species specific). Because data quality and availability are not uniform across all ape taxa, regions, or

FIGURE 9.1 Ape distribution in Africa

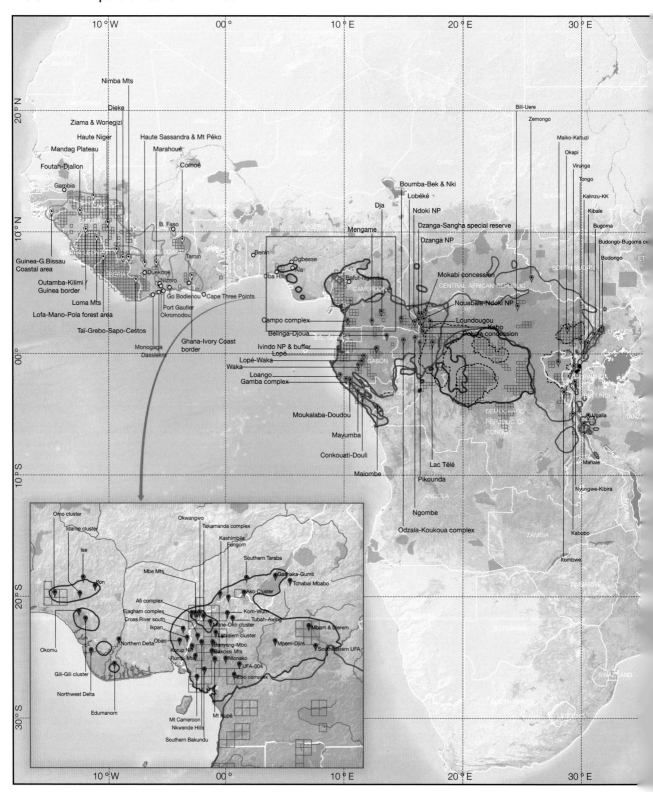

LEGEND

- ○   Apes locally extinct
- ☗   Central chimpanzee priority sites
- ☗   Nigeria–Cameroon chimpanzee priority sites
- ☗   Western chimpanzee priority sites
- ☗   Eastern chimpanzee conservation units
- ⬚   Bonobo conservation landscapes
- ⬚   A.P.E.S. Database survey data coverage
- ▨   Protected areas (IUCN categories I-IV)

APE RANGE DISTRIBUTION

- ⬚   Eastern Chimpanzee (*Pan troglodytes schweinfurthii*)
-     Grauer's gorilla (*Gorilla beringei graueri*)
- ⬚   Bonobo (*Pan paniscus*)
- ⬚   Western lowland gorilla (*Gorilla gorilla gorilla*)
- ⬚   Central chimpanzee (*Pan troglodytes troglodytes*)
- ⬚   Nigeria–Cameroon chimpanzee (*Pan troglodytes ellioti*)
- ⬚   Mountain gorilla (*Gorilla beringei beringei*)
- ⬚   Western chimpanzee (*Pan troglodytes verus*)
- ⬚   Cross River gorilla (*Gorilla gorilla diehli*)

HOMINOIDEA
- humans (genus *Homo*)
- chimpanzees (genus *Pan*)
- gorillas (genus *Gorilla*)
- orangutans (genus *Pongo*)
- gibbons (family Hylobatidae)

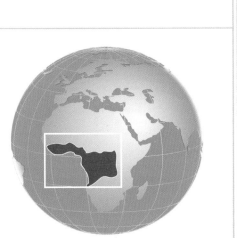

SPECIES INFORMATION

CENTRAL CHIMPANZEE
Pan troglodytes troglodytes
Population in the wild: c. 70 000 - 117 000
Current range size: 811 425 km²
IUCN Redlist Classification: EN
Range size distribution
Angola: 0.79% range
Cameroon: 23.22% range
Central African Rep.: 4.87%
Congo: 32.72% range
Equatorial Guinea: 3.43% range
Gabon: 33.20% range
DR Congo: Present

WESTERN CHIMPANZEE
Pan troglodytes verus
Population in the wild: c. 23 080
Current range size: 771 975 km²
IUCN Redlist Classification: EN
Range size distribution
Burkina Faso: 0.42% range
Sierra Leone: 10.04% range
Senegal: 3.17% range
Mali: 2.97% range
Liberia: 11.64% range
G. Bissau: 1.88% range
Ghana: 2.55% range
Guinea: 33.77% range
Ivory Coast: 33.60% range
Population estimate source: Kormos et al., 2012.

WESTERN LOWLAND GORILLA
Gorilla gorilla gorilla
Population in the wild: c. 150 000
Current range size: 791 425 km²
IUCN Redlist Classification: CR
Range size distribution
Angola: 0.58% range
Central African Rep.: 2.64% range
Eq. Guinea: 3.54% range
Gabon: 36.66% range
Cameroon: 23.34% range
Rep. of Congo: 33.23% range

MOUNTAIN GORILLA
Gorilla beringei beringei
Population in the wild: c. 880
Current range size: 785 km²
IUCN Redlist Classification: CR
Range size distribution
Uganda: 47.07% range
Rwanda: 20.76% range
DR Congo: 32.23% range
Population estimate source: Gray et al., 2013.

NIGERIA–CAMEROON CHIMPANZEE
Pan troglodytes ellioti
Population in the wild: c. 3 500 - 9 000
Current range size: 193 475 km²
IUCN Redlist Classification: EN
Range size distribution
Cameroon: 72.55% range
Nigeria: 27.45% range
Population estimate source: Morgan et al., 2011

EASTERN CHIMPANZEE
Pan troglodytes schweinfurthii
Population in the wild: c. 200 000 - 250 000
Current range size: 1105 675 km²
IUCN Redlist Classification: EN
Range size distribution
DR Congo: 82.49% range
Burundi: 0.65% range
Central African Rep.: 9.38% range
Rwanda: 0.20% range
South Sudan: 3.58% range
Tanzania: 1.71% range
Uganda: 1.97% range
Population estimate source: Plumptre et al., 2010.

BONOBO
Pan paniscus
Population in the wild: c. 15 000 - 20 000*
Current range size: 47 925 km²
IUCN Redlist Classification: EN
Range size distribution
DR Congo: 100% range
*Bonobo population is MINIMUM Estimate
Population estimate source: IUCN and ICCN, 2012.

CROSS RIVER GORILLA
Gorilla gorilla diehli
Population in the wild: c. 200 - 300
Current range size: 12 000 km²
IUCN Redlist Classification: CR
Range size distribution
Cameroon: 66.08% range
Nigeria: 33.92% range
Population estimate source: Oates et al., 2007.

GRAUER'S GORILLA
Gorilla beringei graueri
Population in the wild: c. 2 000 - 10 000
Current range size: 75 225 km²
IUCN Redlist Classification: EN
Range size distribution
DR Congo: 100% range
Population estimate source: Maldonado et al., 2012

SCALE: 1:35 000 000

Km
0   500   1 000   1 500

There is active, ongoing data collection to gather details about population numbers for apes in various locations across their entire range. Updated information will be made available on the A.P.E.S. Portal. Visit this portal at http://apesportal.eva.mpg.de for regular updates.

FIGURE 9.2 Ape distribution in Asia

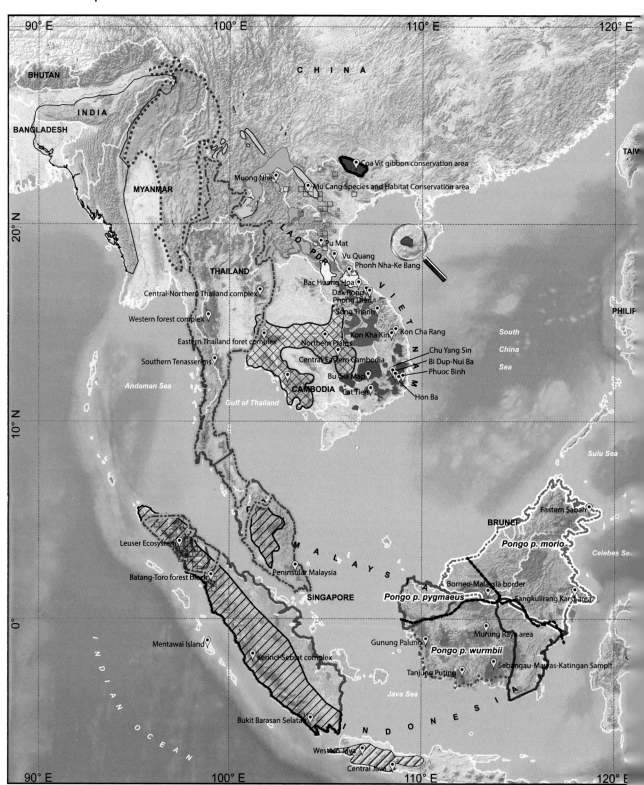

LEGEND

- ⚲ Priority ape conservation sites
- ▪▪▪▪ Bornean orangutan subspecies boundaries
- ⊞ A.P.E.S. Database survey data coverage
- ▨ Protected areas (IUCN categories I-IV)

APE RANGE DISTRIBUTION

GIBBONS

- *Hoolock hoolock*
- *Hoolock leuconedys*
- *Hylobates abbotti*
- *Hylobates agilis*
- *Hylobates albibarbis*
- *Hylobates funerus*
- *Hylobates klossii*
- *Hylobates lar*
- *Hylobates moloch*
- *Hylobates muelleri*
- *Hylobates pileatus*
- *Nomascus annamensis*
- *Nomascus concolor*
- *Nomascus gabriellae*
- *Nomascus hainanus*
- *Nomascus leucogenys*
- *Nomascus nasutus*
- *Nomascus siki*
- *Symphalangus syndactylus*

ORANGUTANS

- *Pongo abelii*
- *Pongo pygmaeus*

N

SCALE: 1:35 000 000

Km
0   500   1 000   1 500

SPECIES INFORMATION

SUMATRAN ORANGUTAN
Pongo abelii
Population in the wild: c. 6 660
Current range size: 8 641 km²
IUCN Redlist Classification: CR
Range size distribution
Indonesia (Sumatra)

SIAMANG
Symphalangus syndactylus
IUCN Redlist Classification: EN
Range countries
Thailand, Malaysia, and Indonesia

WHITE-HANDED GIBBON
Hylobates lar
IUCN Redlist Classification: EN
Range countries
Indonesia, Lao PDR, Malaysia, Myanmar, China, and Thailand

JAVAN GIBBON
Hylobates moloch
IUCN Redlist Classification: EN
Range countries
Indonesia

BORNEAN WHITE-BEARDED GIBBON
Hylobates albibarbis
IUCN Redlist Classification: EN
Range countries
Indonesia (Borneo)

AGILE GIBBON
Hylobates agilis
IUCN Redlist Classification: EN
Range countries
Indonesia, Malaysia, and Thailand

MÜLLER'S GIBBON / BORNEAN GRAY GIBBON
Hylobates muelleri
IUCN Redlist Classification: EN
Range countries
Indonesia, and Malaysia

ABBOTT'S / WEST BORNEAN GRAY GIBBON
Hylobates abbotti
IUCN Redlist Classification: EN
Range countries
Brunei Darussalam, Indonesia, and Malaysia

PILEATED GIBBON
Hylobates pileatus
IUCN Redlist Classification: EN
Range countries
Cambodia, Lao PDR, and Thailand

KLOSS' GIBBON
Hylobates klossii
IUCN Redlist Classification: EN
Range countries
Indonesia

EASTERN BORNEAN GRAY GIBBON
Hylobates funerus
IUCN Redlist Classification: EN
Range countries
Malaysia, and Indonesia

BORNEAN ORANGUTAN
Pongo pygmaeus
Population in the wild: c. 54 000
Current range size: 155 106 km²
IUCN Redlist Classification: EN
Range size distribution
Indonesia (Borneo)

WESTERN HOOLOCK GIBBON
Hoolock hoolock
IUCN Redlist Classification: EN
Range countries
Bangladesh, India, and Myanmar

EASTERN HOOLOCK GIBBON
Hoolock leuconedys
IUCN Redlist Classification: VU
Range countries
China, India, and Myanmar

NORTHERN YELLOW-CHEEKED GIBBON
Nomascus annamensis
IUCN Redlist Classification: Not assessed
Range countries
Cambodia, Lao PDR, and Viet Nam

WESTERN BLACK-CRESTED GIBBON
Nomascus concolor
IUCN Redlist Classification: CR
Range countries
China Lao PDR, and Viet Nam

EASTERN BLACK-CRESTED / CAO VIT GIBBON
Nomascus nasutus
IUCN Redlist Classification: CR
Range countries
China, and Viet Nam

SOUTHERN YELLOW-CHEEKED GIBBON
Nomascus gabriellae
IUCN Redlist Classification: EN
Range countries
Cambodia, and Viet Nam

HAINAN GIBBON
Nomascus hainanus
IUCN Redlist Classification: CR
Range countries
China

NORTHERN WHITE-CHEEKED GIBBON
Nomascus leucogenys
IUCN Redlist Classification: CR
Range countries
Lao PDR, China, and Viet Nam

SOUTHERN WHITE-CHEEKED GIBBON
Nomascus siki
IUCN Redlist Classification: EN
Range countries
Lao PDR, and Viet Nam

HOMINOIDEA
- humans (genus *Homo*)
- chimpanzees (genus *Pan*)
- gorillas (genus *Gorilla*)
- orangutans (genus *Pongo*)
- gibbons (family Hylobatidae)

There is active, ongoing data collection to gather details about population numbers for apes in various locations across their entire range. Updated information will be made available on the A.P.E.S. Portal. Visit this portal at http://apesportal.eva.mpg.de for regular updates.

even countries, we refer to specific cases for which data are available and reliable. The current chapter has not yet been expanded to fully include the gibbons and, as such, data mining for this family is still limited; however, additional data collection will occur in between this and the subsequent edition of *State of the Apes* to ensure that gibbons are well represented in future.

The body of the report is organized into four parts (plus an online-only section):

BOX 9.1

Map commentary

The maps included in this report combine information from the literature with more recently documented information, with the intention of providing the reader with an overview of the distribution and status of all ape species, across Africa and Asia. The majority of the information presented in these maps is drawn from the Ape Populations, Environments and Surveys (A.P.E.S.) Portal (apesportal.eva.mpg.de). The portal holds some of the most up-to-date spatial and non-spatial information on great apes, either contributed by experts working in the field or obtained by permission from other credible sources (research and conservation institutions and organizations around the world).

The maps show some sites identified in various Regional Action Plans for ape conservation as priority sites for conservation and/or surveys. Given that these regional action plans are collated by experts with the best knowledge of each ape species, information gleaned from them is considered to provide the most accurate information, which reflects the opinions of hundreds of experts and stakeholders.

Caveat

While information presented on the maps is considered highly informative and valuable for ape conservation, it should be noted that gaps do exist.

- Only protected areas categorized under the International Union for Conservation of Nature (IUCN) categories I–IV are shown on the maps. Protected areas with lower/unclassified protection levels are not included for map clarity, and to eliminate the effect of poor quality data in some protected sites.

- Figures on total species abundance presented on the maps are by no means absolute values. These are estimates based on current and past field surveys and in some cases extrapolations based on density estimates at selected sites. Providing absolute values for any population would be highly misleading, but the figures cited on the maps represent the best current estimates.

- Ape geographic ranges do not represent strict boundaries of ape occurrence. While these range boundaries represent the best current representation of ape existence, they may be larger or smaller in some places than current knowledge suggests.

- **Spatial distribution.** This section comprises two maps showing ape distribution and other relevant baseline information about the different subspecies.

- **Suitable environmental conditions for African apes.** In this section, statistics on modeled Suitable Environmental Conditions (SEC) for great apes in Africa are presented, first at the species level and then at the country level. These statistics were computed from models calibrated using ape survey data drawn from the A.P.E.S. Portal, covering eight of the nine African ape taxa (mountain gorillas not included).

- **Apes in human-dominated landscapes.** This section addresses and attempts to simplify the complexity of the interaction of factors that affect ape population abundance and survival in the wild. It presents a model flowchart highlighting some of the pathways through which factors interact to influence ape distribution and survival. This is further illustrated by charts showing the effects of selected factors on ape abundance in selected countries (based on availability of reliable ape abundance estimates at country level), or rate of change in suitable environmental conditions in range countries.

- **Areas of high ape density and contiguous populations.** Maps showing spatial distribution gradients of ape abundance by region are presented in this section. These are interpolated surfaces generated from site-level population estimates, and relevant for identification of important populations of apes.

- **Site-level ape abundance estimates.** This section presents known ape sites (locations where apes are currently known to exist) by country (for which data are currently available) and population abundance estimates for each site. Here ape abundance is categorized by definition of abundance classes.

Environmental conditions and great ape survival: models from Africa

Species-level assessment

The suitability of environmental conditions for African great ape survival within their range was recently assessed by Junker *et al.* (2012), constituting the first ever continent-wide model for African apes. This assessment suggests a continent-wide decline in suitable environmental conditions within the geographic range of African apes between the 1990s and 2000s (Figure 9.3).

With an approximately 61.3% loss in the proportion of suitable environmental conditions within its geographic range, the Cross River gorilla (*Gorilla gorilla diehli*) records the highest decline of all ape species studied between the 1990s and the 2000s, while the eastern chimpanzee (*Pan troglodytes schweinfurthii*) records the least decline with

less than 1% loss. Other species fall between these extremes. This decline is a result of complex interaction between various human and environmental factors (Junker *et al.*, 2012). For various reasons, however, the direct interpretation of this trend and pattern must be undertaken with caution (see notes in Box 9.2 on p. 260).

Country-level assessment

In this section, African ape range countries are grouped by three regions: West, Central, and East Africa.

In West Africa, environmental conditions have deteriorated severely in Burkina Faso for *Pan troglodytes verus* by over 70% (Figure 9.4). The chimpanzee is actually suspected to be extinct in this country. Nigeria also presents a case for concern, where the Cross River gorilla appears to have lost over three-quarters of the proportion of suitable

FIGURE 9.3

Suitable Environmental Conditions for African apes at species level (excluding mountain gorillas), expressed as percentage of total range size

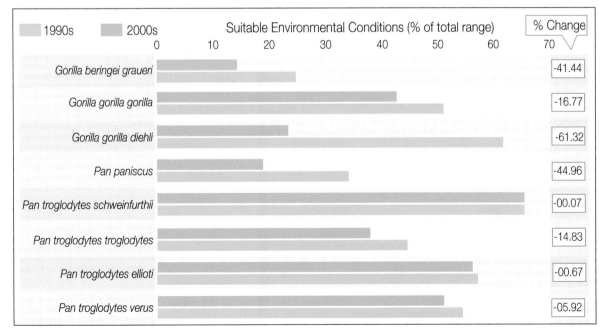

Source: Junker *et al.*, 2012.

BOX 9.2

The concept of Suitable Environmental Conditions (SEC)

The concept of Suitable Environmental Conditions (SEC) is used to represent modeled environmental suitability for great ape survival. It uses sophisticated statistical techniques, based on survey data and carefully selected environmental factors that are known or hypothesized to influence ape survival. The results of these models indicate the probability of ape occurrence at every point in space within its range.

SEC is valuable in assessing the availability of potentially suitable habitat for apes. There is a highly complex interaction between factors that affect ape survival, and putting this combination of factors together in sound statistical models is certainly the best way to evaluate their contribution to ape occurrence because it unveils the effect of highly complex interactions between factors, which otherwise would remain unnoticed. An area may be regarded as good habitat with enough food and shelter to theoretically sustain a healthy ape population, but if human pressure such as hunting is high, such an area does not constitute a suitable environment for apes. Therefore the word "environment" describes not only the physical factors within a species' range but also anthropogenic influence and the interactions between them.

The SEC statistics presented here cover all African ape taxa except mountain gorillas. These are the first ever continent-wide models calibrated for apes, and have been peer-reviewed by the scientific community. Data used for this assessment were drawn directly from the IUCN/SSC A.P.E.S. database. For details on the methodology applied and in-depth discussion, see Junker et al. (2012). For reasons stated in the original publication, the models were computed with a 100 km buffer outside each ape range (10 km for Cross River gorillas), but for the purpose of this report, statistics have been extracted only within the ape range, excluding this buffer. There are, therefore, slight variations between the figures stated here and those reported by Junker et al. SEC models for Asian apes (orangutans) are still in development and not reported in this volume.

Caveat

While results from SEC models contain information relevant to the understanding of ape conservation status, it is important to note that:

■ SEC models provide an assessment of environmental conditions (anthropogenic and physical), but do not directly translate to ape abundance. Therefore the SEC percentage stated for each species or country should not in any way or for any reason be interpreted as population size. High environmental suitability does not imply high ape density, but means that there is room for population expansion.

■ Like any spatial model, SEC models can be highly affected by various factors such as the spatial resolution at which models are calibrated and predictions made, species range size, and the availability and quality of survey data. Therefore, while these continent-wide statistics are useful for portraying general range-wide trends, results from site-focused analyses will be useful for more detailed, local trends if they are available.

environmental conditions. Interestingly, the Nigeria–Cameroon chimpanzee (*Pan troglodytes ellioti*) has witnessed an increase in SEC in this country, implying that the percentage deficit in SEC for *Pan troglodytes ellioti* presented in Figure 9.3 is accounted for on the Cameroonian side of the range.

Note should be taken of the fact that this is not a reflection of ape abundance, neither is it of habitat occupancy. Many suitable habitat patches are uninhabited, and the connectivity of suitable patches is a very important requirement for ape populations expanding to these uninhabited patches. Ivory Coast for instance records only 11.4% decline in proportion of SEC, but a site-based assessment by Campbell et al. (2008b) suggested about 90% decline of chimpanzee population nationwide resulting from various factors, among which human population explosion (about 50% increase between the 1990s and 2000s) and political unrest seem to stand out.

The period between the 1990s and the 2000s witnessed a general decline in SEC in the Central African sub-region (Figure 9.5). Cameroon is one of two African countries where four ape taxa occur – Cross River gorilla, western lowland gorilla, central chimpanzee, and Nigeria–Cameroon chimpanzee. All four subspecies have witnessed a decline in suitable environmental conditions in the country, with highest decline rate recorded for Cross River gorillas. This puts Cameroon in the lead in SEC loss of all countries in the Central African region, with an average SEC loss of over 20%.

Gabon closely follows Cameroon with approximately 17% mean decline rate in SEC, while Equatorial Guinea records the lowest mean decline rate in the region (5.7%) (likely because in this small, quite densely populated country, conditions were already poor in the 1990s). While there was a slight gain in SEC for the Nigeria–Cameroon chimpanzee on the Nigerian side of its geographic

FIGURE 9.4 SEC for West African apes at country level, by decade

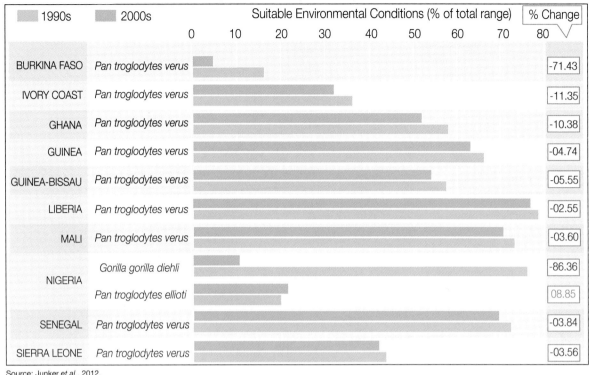

Source: Junker *et al.*, 2012.

FIGURE 9.5 SEC for Central African apes (excluding Angola and DRC) at country level, by decade

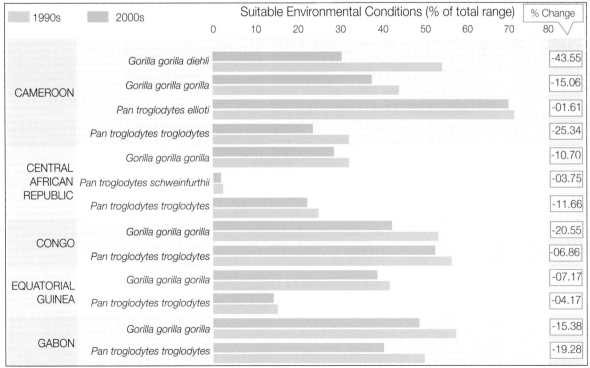

Source: Junker *et al.*, 2012.

range, the Cameroonian side accounted for a higher loss, causing an overall decline for the subspecies.

Trend figures from East Africa also show a general decline. However, SEC has been more stable for the eastern chimpanzees (*Pan troglodytes schweinfurthii*) during this period, especially in DRC and Uganda (Figure 9.6). The biggest losses in this region are recorded within the ranges of bonobos (*Pan paniscus*) and Grauer's gorilla (*Gorilla beringei graueri*), both in DRC.

Statistics for Angola, Burundi, Rwanda and central chimpanzees in DRC have been excluded here because those countries contain relatively small areas of great ape range. Given the (coarse) spatial resolution at which the SEC models were computed (500 m resolution), figures in such small areas are most likely to be a result of model error (see Box 9.2 for caveats).

Apes in human-dominated landscapes

Interactions between human and biophysical factors

Human encroachment into forests is one of the main factors causing wildlife population crashes. However, the relationships and interactions between an array of many human and biophysical factors vary over space, taxon, and time. Sometimes just one or two factors are responsible for a reduction in an ape population; for example, the combination of hunting and the Ebola virus in western equatorial Africa almost halved gorilla populations in Gabon (Walsh *et al.*, 2003). Ebola alone killed thousands of gorillas in one area of northern Congo (Bermejo *et al.*, 2006). Factors can, however, be highly complex where, for example, a single factor

FIGURE 9.6

SEC for East African apes at country level, by decade (excluding Burundi, Rwanda and *Gorilla beringei beringei*)

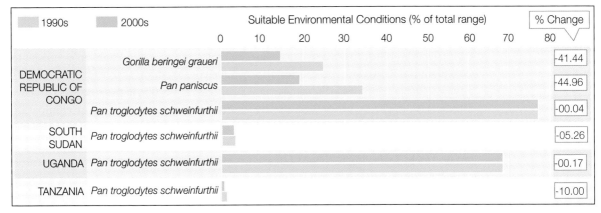

Source: Junker *et al.*, 2012.

FIGURE 9.7

Representation of factors influencing ape abundance

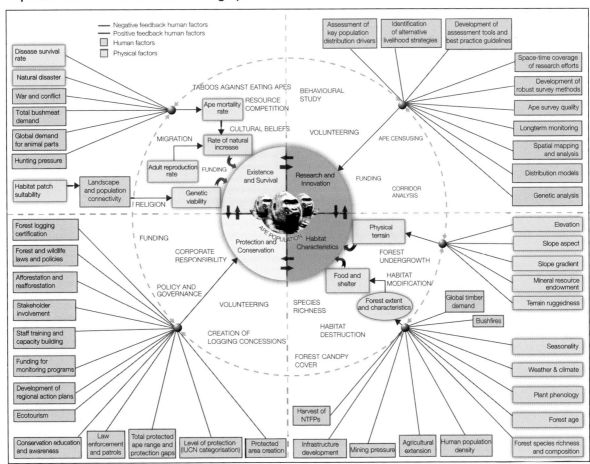

acts through a multitude of pathways or is driven by many other causes. At best, factor effects in such complex scenarios can be estimated through statistical models, and the ability of such models to disentangle these complex relationships and quantify their effects is at the crux of ape conservation planning. Different ape species also possess variable responses to the same magnitude of factor effects, hence the necessity of carrying out assessments at species level.

The complex web of anthropogenic and physical factors working to shape both ape occurrence and abundance can ideally be represented in a simple flowchart (Figure 9.7). These factors are sub-categorized into broader, interrelated themes – *Ape Existence and Survival, Conservation and Protection, Habitat Characterization*, and *Research and Innovation*. In no way is this representative of all factors affecting ape populations, and factor interaction can in some cases form an endless loop. In any case, factors can have negative or positive feedback, and the net balance between the negative and positive determines the size of any given population.

Apes and human activities

In this section, the effects of various anthropogenic factors on ape population and survival are demonstrated through descriptive surface and bubble graphics. In each case, two factors are considered as predictors, while estimated country- or site-level ape abundance, or rate of SEC loss are used as response variables. Considering that variables are computed at the country level and that some ape populations have not been assessed at the country level in most regions, only selected countries for which these data are available are used in plots based on country-level data. However, on a broad scale, the effects of particular variables are expected to be similar across countries, permitting illustrated plots for these selected

case studies to be generalized across different ape range countries.

Effects of range protection and range size on ape abundance

Protection of natural habitats is crucial to ape conservation, as it is for most wildlife species. Protection in this case refers to activities aimed at minimizing or eliminating threats to species of flora and/or fauna, while range size is defined as the area of occupancy for each species. Human pressure on natural resources is accelerating globally (see Chapter 1), and like most other wildlife species, apes must compete for space and resources with humans (Gils and Kayijamahe, 2009; Etiendem *et al.*, 2013). Enforcing laws that protect as much ape range as possible directly favors the maintenance, or even growth, of ape population density (Figure 9.8) in the form of reduced human impact (only protected areas under IUCN categories I–IV are considered here). Analyzing the effect of conservation efforts on ape populations across Africa, Tranquilli *et al.* (2012) make a clear case for the need for effective law enforcement. Law enforcement was the best predictor of ape survival above the other conservation factors considered (including research and tourism).

Protecting a natural habitat does not entirely eliminate the impacts of human activities, but if the areas have effective guards, it does reduce the effects. In the forests of Central Africa, where most African apes occur, the probability of human presence decreases with increasing distance from major roads, but is much lower in protected than in unprotected areas (Blake *et al.*, 2007). In the Sumatran region of Indonesia, some of the largest populations of orangutans occur in the Leuser Ecosystem and other protected lands around it, and deforestation is significantly lower in protected areas and up to 10 km of surrounding matrix. In

Viet Nam, the largest contiguous gibbon populations are recorded in protected forests (Rawson *et al.*, 2011). In Borneo, recent studies suggest that about 49% of orangutan range stands the risk of being lost as this proportion lies outside protected lands (Wich *et al.*, 2012b). A recent global study of 60 tropical forest sites showed that effective on-the-ground protection both in parks and in their buffer zones was one of the most important factors in maintaining biodiversity (Laurance *et al.*, 2012). The importance of forest protection and law enforcement to ape population abundance and viability cannot therefore be overemphasized.

Although the existence of protected areas generally has a positive effect on ape abundance, the level or category of protection also matters. The IUCN World Commission on Protected Areas (WCPA) has defined categories for classification of protected areas, taking many factors into consideration. The categories range from one (strictly protected) to level six (less strictly protected) (see Dudley, 2008, for details). The question of whether strict protection yields better results in keeping nature intact over forests managed by local communities is subject to much controversy and debate. Some researchers strongly support the need for strict national laws on protected area management (Terborgh, 1999; Bruner *et al.*, 2001), while others have argued for a more social conservation approach where the socio-economic needs of local people are taken into account (see Chapter 2). Some case studies have demonstrated reduced deforestation and increased nature protection in community-managed forests while sustaining the livelihoods of local people (Olsen and Helles, 2009; Porter-Bolland *et al.*, 2011). However, looking at trends in deforestation, the effectiveness of government and community-based forest management vary by region and continent. For instance, between 2000 and 2010 the highest deforestation rates recorded

Photo: The importance of forest protection and law enforcement to ape population abundance and viability cannot be overemphasized. © Perry van Duijnhoven

in Asia were attributed to expansion in large-scale commercial agriculture, but in Africa the root cause was conversion of forestland to small-scale subsistence agricultural lands by local communities (DeFries *et al.*, 2010; Fisher, 2010; Hansen, Stehman, and Potapov,

2010; Doug *et al.*, 2011). The effectiveness of different types of forest protection should therefore be treated on a case-by-case basis, and in spite of these controversies, one fact remains: any protection is better than no protection at all.

Of course, no factor works in isolation to determine ape abundance. In Figure 9.8, range size is considered in combination with proportion of range protected, and both factors are positively correlated to ape abundance. Therefore, protecting total ape range and preventing range loss and constriction are likely to lead to sustained ape populations.

Trends in West Africa show the relationships between the proportion of range under protection, geographic range size, and human population density (Figure 9.9).

Geographic range sizes in West African countries are generally small, with low rates of protection and high human population density, coinciding with generally low (and decreasing) ape populations nationwide. Nigeria records the highest average human population density within its ape range (*c.* 142 inhabitants/sq. km), and harbors two ape taxa (Nigeria–Cameroon chimpanzee and Cross River gorilla). Ape populations in this country persist in protected areas (national parks and forest reserves). With relatively low human population density in its ape range (*c.* 40 inhabitants/sq. km) and large range size (*c.* 219 532 sq. km), Guinea holds the largest estimated ape population in West Africa (*c.* 10 000 individuals). This population persists despite its lower proportion of protected range. Other factors such as intensive conservation activity, religion, and culture are possibly in play here, but these await assessment.

It is worth noting that in West Africa the majority of ape sites (that is, locations where apes are known to exist) are designated Classified Forests. These are forest areas with legal protection for the trees, but not necessarily for fauna. There has been a rapid

FIGURE 9.8

African ape range protection and ape abundance

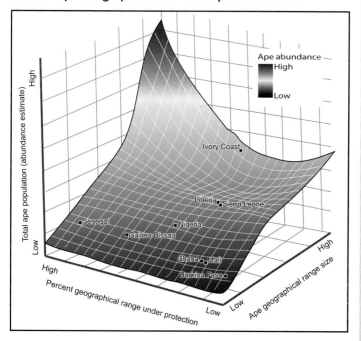

FIGURE 9.9

Ape abundance, range size, percent of range that is protected, and human population density in West Africa

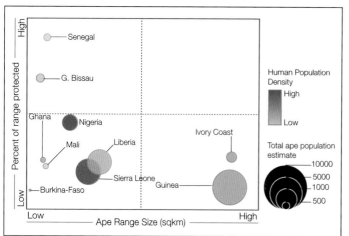

decline in ape numbers across this region, and total extirpation in some of these Classified Forests (Campbell *et al.*, 2008), further highlighting the importance of protection. Given the general importance of protected areas to ape abundance and distribution, it is likely that if current human threats persist, apes will only exist in protected areas in the near future.

While creating more protected areas is without doubt very important for great ape survival, their effectiveness can be compromised by various threats (poaching, illegal logging, agricultural encroachment, artisanal mining, infrastructure development, corruption, etc.). In Viet Nam, the northern white-cheeked gibbon (*Nomascus leucogenys*) is already locally extinct in several protected areas (Rawson *et al.*, 2011), while expansion of oil palm plantations is increasingly taking over protected lands in Malaysia and Indonesia (Buckland, 2005). This suggests, too, that it is not only the existence of protected areas that is crucial, but also addressing and understanding the sociopolitical conditions required for their effective management.

Human economic welfare and ape welfare

The Human Development Index (HDI) is a measure derived by the United Nations Development Programme (UNDP) and is based on various socioeconomic indicators in countries worldwide. Ideally, the HDI can be used as a measure of welfare and prosperity at country level. The index ranges between 0 and 1, signifying lowest–highest, respectively. All apes occur in countries identified by international standards as low-income (poor) economies. Using the HDI as a direct measure of poverty, Gabon, which harbors two ape taxa (*Gorilla gorilla gorilla* and *Pan troglodytes troglodytes*) is the most affluent of all African ape range countries, ranking 106 of 187 countries assessed globally,

TABLE 9.1

HDI values and world ranks (2011) for ape range countries in Africa and Asia

Country	HDI	World rank (out of 187 countries)	Number of ape species
Africa			
Angola	0.486	148	1
Benin	0.436	166	1
Burkina Faso	0.331	181	1
Burundi	0.316	185	1
Cameroon	0.482	150	4
Central African Republic	0.343	179	3
Congo	0.533	137	2
Côte d'Ivoire	0.400	170	1
DRC	0.286	187	4
Equatorial Guinea	0.537	136	2
Gabon	0.674	106	2
Ghana	0.541	135	1
Guinea	0.344	178	1
Guinea-Bissau	0.353	176	1
Liberia	0.329	182	4
Mali	0.359	175	1
Nigeria	0.459	156	2
Rwanda	0.429	166	2
Senegal	0.459	155	1
Sierra Leone	0.336	180	1
South Sudan	n/a*		
Tanzania	0.466	152	1
Togo	0.435	162	0
Uganda	0.446	161	2
Asia			
Brunei	0.838	33	1
Cambodia	0.523	139	3
China	0.687	101	6
India	0.547	134	2
Indonesia	0.617	124	11
Laos	0.524	138	6
Malaysia	0.761	61	6
Myanmar	0.483	149	3
Thailand	0.682	103	4
Viet Nam	0.593	128	6

Note: * South Sudan not ranked on the Human Development Index due to data constraints.

Source: UNDP (2011)

FIGURE 9.10

Ape abundance, range size, HDI, and human population density in West Africa

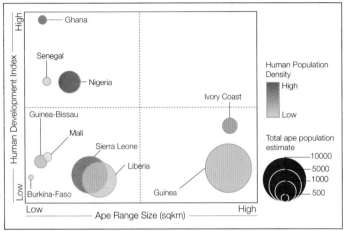

while DRC, home to four ape taxa (*Gorilla beringei beringei, Gorilla beringei graueri, Pan paniscus, Pan troglodytes schweinfurthii*) is the poorest, ranking 187 globally (Table 9.1). In Asia, except for Malaysia and Brunei, eight ape and gibbon range countries rank above 100 in terms of global HDI.

These statistics clearly indicate that apes occur in landscapes dominated by some of the poorest people in the world. Such poor economies, especially in the humid forested tropics, are ecosystem dependent, with few options except to hunt and gather non-timber forest products for cash income, food, and medicine (FAO, 1995; Falconer, 1996; Ros-Tonen, 1999; Ndumbe, 2010). Unlike some of the extremely poor areas in India,

Photo: Large ranges with low percentage of tree cover are of little use to apes, while high tree cover even amidst relatively small range sizes is more important. © Ian Nichols

where millions of people have been culturally vegetarian for centuries, meat is considered vital for human survival in most of Africa. As domestic meat production is low in much of forested Africa, meat comes from wildlife (and indeed in many languages the words for "animal" and "meat" are one and the same).

In West Africa, the countries with the largest total ape populations (such as Liberia, Sierra Leone, and Guinea) have the lowest HDI (Figure 9.10). However, human population density is relatively low and area of ape occupancy is greater in these countries than in more affluent economies such as Ghana and Senegal.

The competition between apes and humans for forest resources and space is one of the driving forces behind other factors that directly affect ape survival. This is particularly true of West Africa and Asia, where small-scale subsistence farming, habitat destruction, and modification remove large areas of suitable forest (especially oil palm plantations in Asia) (Wich *et al.*, 2008).

Figure 9.11 shows an inverse relationship between HDI and ape abundance, showing that most apes occur in poor countries. This is hardly surprising, as apes are essentially tropical species, and most of the worlds' tropical countries are on the low side of the HDI.

The spatial overlap of ape range and poor economies is one reason why conservation practice and planning must be a careful initiative. While maintaining stronger protected areas to keep apes alive is a plausible option (and may be the best option in the midst of rapid ape decline), there is also a need to consider the livelihoods of the local people whose economic lives are rooted in the forest. This is a challenging task for conservationists, and in a bid to alleviate poverty while conserving apes and protecting their habitats, the Poverty and Conservation Learning Group (PCLG) of the International Institute for Environment and

FIGURE 9.11

Relationship between HDI, ape range size, and African ape abundance

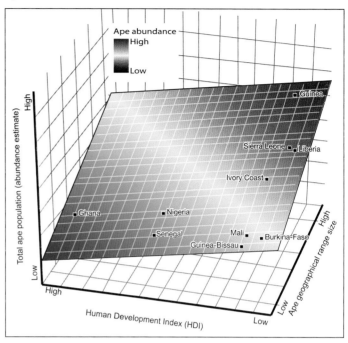

Development (IIED) has organized workshops to seek ways to address this issue and promote conservation approaches that integrate economic welfare of local populations at every level possible. In 2010, a workshop focused specifically on great apes was organized in Uganda and followed by a second workshop hosted by the Centre for International Forestry Research (CIFOR) in Indonesia, 2012. Although these workshops drive towards developing best practice guidelines for poverty alleviation in ape conservation and in promoting integrated conservation and development projects (ICDPs), it should be noted that ICDPs are not a novel idea. In fact, ICDPs have been largely criticized for their failure in many cases; (Kiss, 2004; McShane and Newby, 2004; McShane and Wells, 2004). However, this approach may still be valid for countries where there is competition for land between apes and humans. In Central Africa, where land is in use the most common activity is

FIGURE 9.12

Relationship between forest cover, range size, and ape abundance in Africa, computed at country level

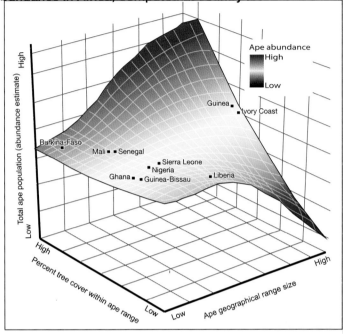

FIGURE 9.13

Relationship between forest cover, range size, and ape abundance in Africa, computed at site level

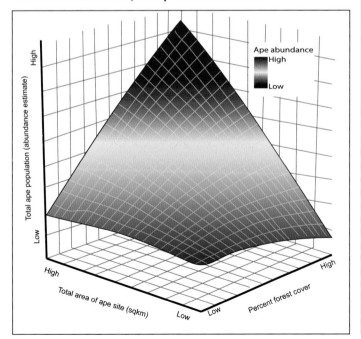

industrial logging. With appropriate and strictly enforced regulations, including control of hunting, it has been shown that ape survival and reduced impact logging (RIL) can be compatible (Stokes *et al.*, 2010). See Chapter 4 for additional information on this topic.

Effects of forest cover, forest loss, and human population density on ape abundance and survival

Apes are forest dwellers and their existence depends largely on the total extent of forest. Based on country- and site-level statistics from Africa and Asia, Figures 9.12, 9.13, and 9.14 illustrate the strong positive relationship between forest cover, area of ape occupancy, and ape abundance.

Large ranges with low percentage of tree cover are of little use to apes, while high tree cover even amidst relatively small range sizes is more important. This underscores the need to consistently map and update deforestation trends across the entire ape geographic range using robust scientific methods and techniques, such as remote sensing.

Over the past 5000 years, the world is estimated to have lost over 18 million km² of forest, yielding approximately 3600 km² per year (Williams, 2002). Among the key factors that fuel this destruction, human population growth and increasing demand for and pressure on natural resources are principal drivers (FAO, 2010b). Ape occurrence in Africa and Asia coincides strongly with countries recording some of the highest human population growth rates and population densities in the world. The direct result of this is high loss of forestland owing to expanding agricultural activities, expansion of human settlements, infrastructure development, and logging.

The implication of human encroachment into natural forests on apes is habitat loss and degradation (see Chapter 7). Figure 9.15 illustrates the combined impacts of growth in human population density and forest loss on rate of decline in suitable environmental conditions for apes in African range countries. It should be noted that the two countries (Congo and Gabon) harboring most of the worlds' gorillas and central chimpanzees, and the country (DRC) with all of the bonobos, probably most of the eastern chimpanzees, and all the Grauer's gorillas, have extremely low rates of forest loss (Figure 9.15).

In figures 9.4–9.6, we presented country-level statistics of decline in SEC between the 1990s and 2000s. Two of the important variables that defined SEC for almost all ape taxa were human population density and the Human Influence Index (HII). The latter is essentially an amalgam of several different spatially explicit human factors, including roads, human density, settlements, and global lights (WCS/CIESIN, 2005). Thus, as human populations grow and/or forest is increasingly lost, SEC for apes will be further reduced. High human population density may also increase the risk of infectious disease transmission between humans and apes.

Open issues

There still exist gaps in current knowledge of how apes survive in the wild amidst human influence, and how effective current protective measures are in maintaining long-term population survival. This chapter therefore serves as a pointer to some of the open issues pertaining to ape conservation.

Effectiveness of local community forests and government-protected areas

In areas where local communities have claims to areas that harbor apes, it is important to determine whether or not community forests

are more effective in protecting natural areas than strict, government-designated protected areas, and whether a top-down approach to protected area management works better

FIGURE 9.14

Percent tree cover, ape range size, human population density, and ape abundance in West Africa

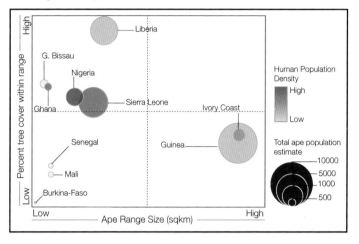

FIGURE 9.15

Human population density, rate of forest loss, and SEC for African apes

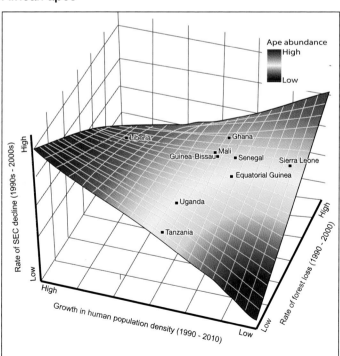

272

than a bottom-up approach (Naughton, 1993; Malla, Neupane, and Branney, 2003; Gibson, Williams, and Ostrom, 2005; Hayes and Wagner, 2008; Gibson *et al.*, 2011). Despite different arguments and views, there is currently no statistically measured and quantified study addressing this issue. The opposing views presented in current research seem to suggest that this issue needs to be addressed on a case-by-case basis, but rigorous statistical measurements need to be carried out to quantify the effects of different protection categories on ape existence and survival. In terms of a more general approach, a review of over 60 alternative livelihood community projects in Africa, including an in-depth review of 15 of them, was unable to find compelling evidence of conservation success (Wicander and Coad, 2013).

Photo: Gaps still exist in the current knowledge of how apes survive in the wild amidst human influence, and how effective current protective measures are in maintaining long-term population survival.
© Zhao Chao

Assessment of different type of governance

The type of governance that is put in place to manage conservation areas is crucial to the effectiveness of conservation efforts. A governance system that diffuses authority to multiple institutions (polycentric governance) will have different management effects than a system where authority is consolidated to a single or limited number of bodies. If, hypothetically, a single organization is in charge of a highly important conservation site, management of the site will become ineffective if the organization decides, for any reason, to withdraw from the site. A polycentric system of management may potentially also make local governments and other actors feel involved in the conservation process, but at the same time runs the risk of misalignment of responsibilities between the various stakeholders for management of the area and implementation of the laws. This is an open issue waiting to be addressed through in-depth field research.

Global indicators of threats and conservation status

In order to keep track of trends in ape populations and threat levels, it is important to develop standard statistical indicators of ape conservation status and threats to their survival. This could involve the computation of Ecological Index Scores at site and country levels, using a combination of relevant factors, including conservation effort, research coverage, sign encounter rates, species richness, and SEC. Such indicators will be valuable for assessing temporal trends in ape conservation.

Active contribution to the A.P.E.S. Portal

The A.P.E.S. Portal project is one recent step towards long-term conservation and monitoring of ape populations throughout the world. Developed by the Department of Primatology at the Max Planck Institute for Evolutionary Anthropology (MPI-EVA), A.P.E.S. is a collaboration between the IUCN/ SSC Primate Specialist Group (PSG), the Jane Goodall Institute, the United Nations Environment Programme World Conservation Monitoring Centre (UNEP-WCMC), and numerous other organizations/institutions involved in ape conservation and research. The Portal is a one-stop website where the most up-to-date information about great ape status and conservation is cataloged. It also provides a centralized platform for great ape survey data collected in Africa and Asia over the last 20 years, as well as valuable contextual information and tools relevant for ape conservation. Currently, this platform houses limited information on the small apes; however, it is a work in progress. The long-term usefulness of the Portal depends on the active participation and continued contribution by different actors involved in ape conservation around the world, in providing new survey data, site population estimates, information on existing research and conservation sites, and using the dashboard and other tools provided for conservation planning.

Ape abundance: population concentrations and largest contiguous populations

Ape population concentrations are identifiable by applying basic spatial interpolation[1] methods to site location and ape population estimates at each site. Whether or not a site can be considered a population concentration is contingent on its total ape population as well as on its proximity to other ape sites. Through site-level population estimates, large potentially contiguous populations can

be mapped, and identifying such concentrations and contiguous populations is crucial for site prioritization, creation of conservation landscapes and conservation/research resource allocation. While such concentrations are presented below, it is worth noting that they are based on currently available site abundance estimates (total number of apes estimated for each site). If there were no data gaps, it is possible that the trends would differ slightly from those presented in this section.

Ape abundance in West Africa

Alarming decline rates in ape populations in West Africa have been reported over the past decade (Campbell *et al.*, 2008b), suggesting that firm conservation measures need to be taken to protect the remaining populations. Recent estimates suggest that the Foutah Djallon region of Guinea supports the largest remaining western chimpanzee population (see Annex IV, Table 2),

FIGURE 9.16

Ape population abundance in West Africa

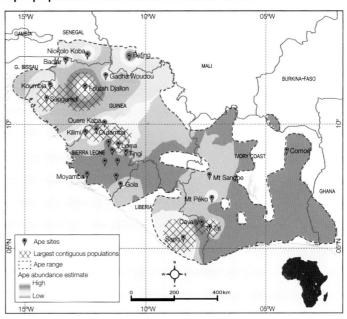

274

while the population gradient decreases towards the eastern part of their geographic range (Figure 9.16).

Amidst this general pattern, some large contiguous populations are identifiable, such as Foutah Djallon-Koumbia-Sangaredi, Outamba-Kilimi-Loma Mountains, and Sapo-Grebo-Taï. These regions coincide with the efforts of the Wild Chimpanzee Foundation (WCF) to protect apes and their habitats, in collaboration with local organizations and mining companies. Mont Peko and Mont Sângbé in Ivory Coast and Gola in Sierra Leone also constitute western chimpanzee population concentrations.

Ape abundance in the Nigeria–Cameroon sub-region

Cameroon and Nigeria host two ape taxa: the Nigeria–Cameroon chimpanzee (*Pan troglodytes ellioti*) and the Cross River gorilla (*Gorilla gorilla diehli*). The total ape population for each site is the sum of pop-

ulations for both subspecies. The isolation of ape populations in this region is glaringly depicted in Figure 9.17.

The high–low distribution of ape populations in Nigeria and Cameroon follows an east–west gradient, with especially small site-level populations in Nigeria, which also contains a relatively small percentage of ape geographic range. The large contiguous populations identifiable are the Ebo Complex; Gashaka-Gumti and neighboring forests; the Lebialem Complex-Banyang Mbo; Mbam and Djerem and neighboring forests northwest of the Sanaga River; and Takamanda-Mone-Mbulu. Working closely with organizations such as San Diego Zoo Institute for Conservation Research and World Wildlife Fund (WWF), the Wildlife Conservation Society (WCS) has been carrying out research and conservation in this region since 1988.

Ape abundance in western equatorial Africa

Western equatorial Africa covers five countries in the Central African sub-region – Cameroon, Central African Republic (CAR), Congo, Gabon, and Equatorial Guinea (here we exclude Angola because it contains a relatively small area of ape range). Two ape subspecies are found in this area – the central chimpanzee and the western lowland gorilla.

Ape populations at known ape sites in this region are generally much larger than in other parts of Africa, but they face severe hunting pressure, a greater likelihood of Ebola virus outbreaks and, in the next decade, habitat loss due to expanding industrial agriculture is a very real possibility. Gabon and Congo support the largest ape populations in Africa (Figure 9.18).

Here, very large potentially contiguous populations cut across vast landscapes, such

FIGURE 9.17

Ape population abundance in Nigeria–Cameroon

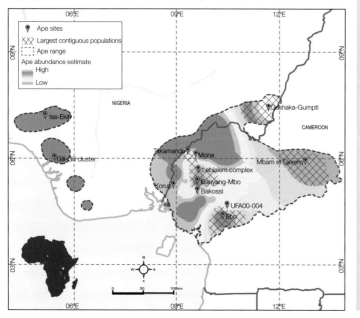

as Lopé-Waka in Gabon, and the Odzala National Park which is contiguous with Ngombe and other surrounding logging concessions (Pikounda, Ntokou) in Congo. Another contiguous block is found on the east side of the Sangha River, where ape populations in Dzanga-Sangha National Park, Nouabalé-Ndoki National Park, and Lac Télé Community Reserve are connected by selectively logged timber concessions.

The maintenance of such large ape populations in forest concessions indicates that with good management and planning, apes can survive amidst industrial extraction of forest resources (Stokes *et al.*, 2010; Maisels *et al.*, 2012). See chapters 4, 5, and 6 for more information in relation to the different extractive industries.

A vast area of ape range in western equatorial Africa, cutting across Gabon and Congo, was struck by an Ebola virus outbreak in 1994, which is estimated to have wiped out approximately 90% of western lowland gorillas in northern Congo and Gabon (Walsh *et al.*, 2003; Bermejo *et al.*, 2006). WCS and WWF, in partnership with a number of local and international organizations and research institutes, run strong conservation programs in this region, protecting ape habitat to sustain healthy populations of wildlife.

Ape abundance in East Africa (including DRC)

Four ape taxa are found in East Africa: bonobos (*Pan paniscus*), one chimpanzee subspecies (*Pan t. schweinfurthii*), and two eastern gorilla subspecies (*Gorilla b. beringei* and *Gorilla b. graueri*).

The region stretching from Bili-Uere to the Okapi Reserve in DRC harbors some of the largest remaining eastern chimpanzee populations (Figure 9.19). The largest bonobo populations have been recorded in Salonga

National Park (both northern and southern sectors); this taxon occurs in DRC only. Many conservation organizations and research bodies are active in this region.

FIGURE 9.18

Ape population abundance in western equatorial Africa

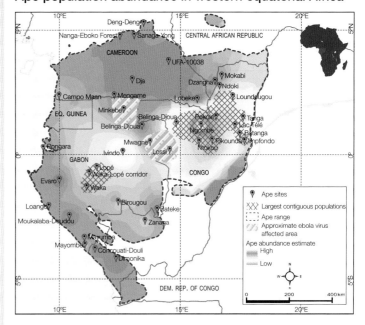

FIGURE 9.19

Ape population abundance in East Africa

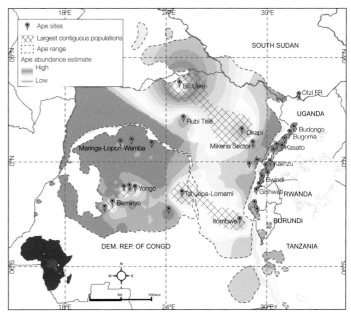

Ape abundance in Borneo (Southeast Asia)

Figure 9.20 shows great apes (Bornean orangutans), but not small apes (gibbons) due to the current scarcity of data for this Family

FIGURE 9.20 Ape population abundance in Borneo

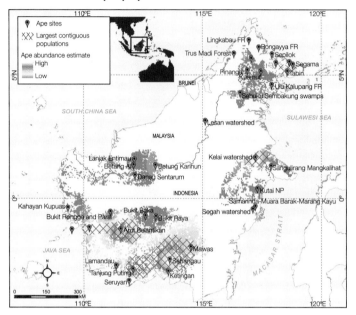

FIGURE 9.21 Ape population abundance in Sumatra

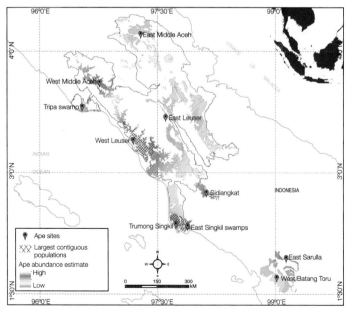

Based on Wich *et al.*, 2012b

in the IUCN/SSC A.P.E.S. database. Extensive data collection is on-going and will be presented in subsequent editions of *State of the Apes*. Three orangutan subspecies occur on the Bornean island of Indonesia, Malaysia, and Brunei. The largest populations occur in the southwestern part of the island: the region stretching from Tanjung Puting through Sebangau to Mawas harbors a large orangutan population. Other notably large populations are found in Gunung Palung-Arut Belantikan, the Kelai watershed (including Gunung Gajah, Wehea, and many logging concessions), and Tabin-Segama in the northeast.

Ape abundance in Sumatra (Southeast Asia)

There remain an estimated 6660 Sumatran orangutans (*Pongo abelii*) on the Indonesian island of Sumatra (Wich *et al.*, 2008). This species is mostly located within the protected Leuser Ecosystem in the province of North Sumatra and Aceh (Figure 9.21). A smaller population exists further south, in the forests of West Batang Toru and East Sarulla. Surveys show that the largest surviving populations (> 1500 individuals) are in West Leuser and Trumon-Singkil, but they face high levels of threat from humans. Conservation and research efforts are active throughout the Sumatran orangutan range, led by the Sumatran Orangutan Conservation Programme (SOCP), a partnership of four organizations – Directorate General of Forest Protection and Nature Conservation (PHKA), PanEco Foundation, Yayasan Ecosistem Lestari, and Frankfurt Zoological Society – in collaboration with several academic institutes.

Ape abundance estimates

Ape abundance estimates at site level, where "site" is a protected area and its buffer zone, or a logging concession or group of concessions, or any discrete area where a survey has taken place in the last two decades (a few sites were last surveyed in the 1980s), are presented in Annex IV, available on the State of the Apes website: www.stateoftheapes.org. The list of ape sites in the Annex is not in any way exhaustive and updates (to both sites and survey data) will be made available in digital format via the A.P.E.S. Portal.

Conclusion

■ This chapter summarizes current knowledge of the status of ape populations. The information presented reveals the gaps in our knowledge of great ape distribution, abundance, and population trends. It is hoped that these will be filled in the coming years and complemented with additional data on small ape populations.

■ The majority of all ape populations are found in forested areas. Effectively protected areas generally have a positive effect on maintaining ape abundance; however, the level or category of protection is also important. Range size must be considered in combination with proportion of range protected, and both factors correlate positively with ape abundance.

■ The proportion of ape populations found outside the system of protected areas is a cause for concern. This highlights that effective conservation of apes not only requires the establishment and maintenance of protected areas, but also involves understanding and addressing the sociopolitical conditions required for the effective management of both protected areas and the unprotected matrix in which so many apes still occur.

■ Apes in Southeast Asia and West Africa occur in landscapes dominated by some of the world's poorest people and the competition between apes and humans for space and resources is one of the driving forces behind other factors that directly affect ape survival. This competition between apes and poor people needs to be taken into account in planning ape conservation strategies/initiatives.

■ The effectiveness of community-managed forests in comparison with government-protected areas is a subject of much debate and is beyond the scope of this report; rigorous testing of the validity of these approaches is clearly overdue.

■ Most African apes live in the vast, relatively intact forests of Central Africa, where there is no competition for resources between humans and apes, because the human population density is very low.

Conservationists, researchers, and industry environment programs are encouraged to engage with the A.P.E.S. project by contributing data on ape abundance, distribution, and changes in land use (if available), to contribute to both conservation planning and practice.

Acknowledgments

Principal authors: Neba Funwi-Gabga, Hjalmar S. Kuehl, Fiona G. Maisels, Susan M. Cheyne, Serge A. Wich, and Elizabeth A. Williamson

Contributors: Genevieve Campbell, Jessica Junker, Benjamin M. Rawson, Ian Singleton, and Suci Utami Atmoko

We gratefully acknowledge all organizations and individuals who have contributed data to the IUCN/SSC A.P.E.S. database, and from whose publications and reports some of the estimates have been extracted.

Endnotes

1   Spatial interpolation is a statistical procedure for estimating values for unsampled locations or sites based on values of known sites.

Photo: A key part of protecting wild apes is combating illegal trafficking to provide apes as pets, as performers in exhibits and entertainment, and for unscrupulous zoos. © Jurek Wajdowicz, EWS

CHAPTER 10

Status of captive apes across Africa and Asia: the impact of extractive industry

Introduction

The lives of apes in their natural habitats and in captivity are inextricably intertwined. Policy and practice focused in one arena can and will have impacts in others. For example, allowing for the commercial uses of apes for entertainment purposes or as pets to private owners can create or sustain the illegal trade in these animals in range states and elsewhere in the world. Thus, the status of captive apes in non-range states bears upon efforts to conserve and manage apes globally, in terms of both public perception and the expansion of political will to save them from extinction. A key part of protecting wild apes is combating illegal trafficking in response to demands for apes as pets, as performers in exhibits and entertainment, and for unscrupulous zoos (Stiles *et al.*, 2013). How apes are treated and portrayed can influence public perceptions (Schroepfer *et al.*, 2011), and thus markets driven by human choices.

The status of captive apes is not only a policy or conservation issue; the captive apes themselves are impacted directly as well. Apes in captive environments can suffer from a number of diseases, injuries, and other factors leading to poor welfare. Detrimental effects can be long lasting; studies have found that apes living in captivity are sensitive to trauma and stress, experiencing both acute and chronic effects that can impact their lives and need for specialized care (e.g. Brüne, Brüne-Cohrs, and McGrew, 2004; Brüne *et al.*, 2006).

The association between extractive industries, the illegal trade in apes, and demand for sanctuary care is widely appreciated – from sanctuary employees and law enforcement officials, to ministry officials and international leaders. In a 2012 statement, Mr. John Scanlon, the Secretary General of CITES (Convention on International Trade in Endangered Species of Wild Fauna and Flora) emphasized the severity of the problem and the responsibility of industries: "Illegal trade is clearly a threat to great apes. [. . .] We must remain vigilant. Illicit trade is a problem particularly in respect to timber and minerals" (GRASP, 2013).

When extractive industries and associated activities result in the deaths of adult apes either directly or indirectly, the subsequent increase in the number of orphans drives demand for rescue centers and sanctuaries in which to home these apes. Just as regional and continental issues highlight the need for transboundary cooperation to protect ape populations, sanctuaries must be responsive to both local and national drivers as well as to other external pressures.

This chapter attempts to put ape welfare in the context of the global status of apes. It starts by providing a fundamental background on general issues of welfare and captivity, with results discussed in relation to the best available science on ape welfare and ethical considerations. It then focuses more explicitly on the impact of extractive industries on sanctuaries and rescue centers. Case studies from Africa and Asia illustrate evolving theory and practice on the linkages between apes in sanctuaries and rescue centers and ape conservation. The conclusions explore suggestions for engaging with the sector in ways that benefit extractive industries and apes, and thus reduce the pressure on sanctuaries.

The welfare status of captive apes: examples from non-range states and global implications

How and where are apes in captivity?

Apes are found in a variety of captive settings in both range and non-range states. A substantial number of international, national, state/regional, and municipal laws and regulations that vary widely determine where, why, and how apes may be held in captivity. For example, EU law severely limits testing on apes to cases of unusual emergency [2010/63/EC Article 55(2)], and there are currently no apes in European laboratories. Non-range states generally allow captive apes in accredited zoos or similar public or private facilities subject to limits specified by international agreements such as CITES. Though apes are sometimes used in entertainment, appearing in live performances, advertisements, television, and movies in some jurisdictions, the legal status of this practice varies and is subject to on-going legal and policy challenges (Stiles *et al.*, 2013). In some jurisdictions, apes are sold by commercial breeders and exotic animal dealers

> The association between extractive industries, the illegal trade in apes, and demand for sanctuary care is widely appreciated.

or are owned as private pets. Sanctuaries and rescue centers may be permitted to house captive apes for rehabilitation or maintenance care. Apes at such facilities are often confiscated by authorities, but can also be relinquished voluntarily.

Origins of captive apes in non-range states

Most captive apes in non-range states were born in captivity. Where it is permitted by law, some captive breeding programs are for commercial purposes, while others were designed to manage captive populations of endangered species. These are typically operated by zoos that maintain studbooks and manage the reproduction of captive apes according to conservation and genetic priorities as well as criteria such as funding and other resources (WAZA, n.d.).

A small proportion of captive apes in non-range states were captured in the wild and imported before CITES and national laws such as the US Endangered Species Act (ESA) restricted such trade. As a result, wild-caught apes in captivity are now generally over the age of 30. Younger, wild-caught apes can be associated with fraud or other illegal trade, as highlighted by recent cases involving China and Egypt (Ammann, 2012; Tanna, 2012; Stiles *et al.*, 2013).

Status and welfare of captive apes: policy and practice

Any form of captivity comes with some risks for ape welfare, which can vary in form and severity depending on species, captivity type, facilities, and what people do to and for the apes in their charge. The general concept of animal welfare informs a number of policies and practices that directly and indirectly influence captive apes. There have been many efforts to define adequately the

concept of welfare, ranging from broad and simple, such as the absence of debilitating disease, to the very specific, such as a welfare matrix with 15 dimensions (Broom and Kirkden, 2004). A general definition of welfare from the World Organisation for Animal Health (OIE – *Office International des Epizooties*), for all terrestrial mammals is:

> how an animal is coping with the conditions in which it lives. An animal is in a good state of welfare if (as indicated by scientific evidence) it is healthy, comfortable, well nourished, safe, able to express innate behaviour, and if it is not suffering from unpleasant states such as pain, fear, and distress. (OIE, 2012, section 7.1)

Notably, the OIE definition includes both positive and negative criteria, i.e. criteria that must be present and others that must be absent in order to achieve the state of "welfare" or "wellbeing."

Both social attitudes and science influence animal welfare. For example, strong public support can influence funding, policy, and even the practices of private companies. Laws and other policies on animal welfare are common, ranging from international agreements to codes in a specific city or town. Examples noted elsewhere in this chapter highlight how welfare policies inform which captive settings are permitted for apes, what minimum standards are in place where apes are captive, and which organizations or people are responsible for the care and welfare of apes in captivity. A vital consideration is that welfare laws and other legal protections and practices vary widely. Whether governed by laws or by organizational policies and procedures, welfare practices can range from the most basic protections aimed at preventing abuse and neglect to exemplary standards that aim for comprehensive individual welfare.

The law in a particular jurisdiction can impose positive and/or negative standards

> Welfare practices can range from the most basic protections aimed at preventing abuse and neglect to exemplary standards that aim for comprehensive individual welfare.

on the captive environment. These may be minimal, determining whether or not there is even a duty to avoid harming apes (or animals in general). In the places where such laws do exist, generic animal cruelty and welfare laws can include apes. Some jurisdictions may have laws or welfare standards that are specific to apes. There are few regulatory standards and the welfare of captive apes is determined by the practices of a given industry, institution, or individual.

BOX 10.1

Positive and negative lists

Eighteen EU member states have negative lists of animals (including great apes) that are (un)suitable to be kept as pets, i.e. they identify prohibited rather than permitted species, usually based on health and safety reasons/risks or restrictions on international trade for conservation purposes. However, these lists allow for unrestricted trade in the species that are not listed, until enough evidence is presented to elicit inclusion on the list and/or the implementation of additional controls. Negative lists can be long and need updating regularly as new species enter the pet trade.

Currently, Belgium is the only EU member state that has a positive list of animals that are suitable to be kept (mammals only). This is a concise list of 42 permitted species, which was developed using the following criteria:

- the animal must be easy to keep in respect of its physiological, ethological, and ecological needs;
- it must not be aggressive and/or dangerous nor represent any other public health hazard;
- it must not be a threat to the native environment/indigenous fauna if it escapes or is released;
- detailed information concerning the care of the species in captivity must be available;
- and, where there is any doubt as to the suitability of the species as a "pet," the benefit of the doubt must be given to the animal and it be excluded from the list.

In addition to this, each person must also prove s/he has the knowledge and equipment to care for the animal.

Implementation of the positive list has resulted in a significant reduction in the illegal trade in wildlife, impulse purchases of exotic pets, and unwanted animals entering shelters. It has also gained support from the Belgian public who assist the government by reporting prohibited species being kept illegally (Endcap, 2012, p. 2).

In June 2013, the Dutch Minister for Agriculture presented a positive list of exotic and non-exotic mammals that may be kept by private individuals. The list will come into force in January 2014.

Eurogroup for Animals, 2011; Endcap, 2012

Welfare concepts

A basic framework often used in animal welfare is the Five Freedoms (FAWC, 2009):

1. Freedom from hunger, thirst, or malnutrition;
2. Freedom from discomfort;
3. Freedom from pain, injury, and disease;
4. Freedom to express normal patterns of behavior;
5. Freedom from fear and distress.

The Five Freedoms emphasize essential biological functions and physical health and are largely freedoms from environmental drivers of poor physical welfare. The development of the Five Freedoms has roots in industrial animal agriculture, where the social and psychological complexity of farmed animals has historically been less readily acknowledged than among primates or apes per se. While the Five Freedoms are necessary for welfare, they are not sufficient to ensure positive welfare for captive apes. With respect to good practices in ape welfare, the Five Freedoms are most useful and appropriate as one component in the foundation of a more comprehensive welfare framework.

Welfare indicators and standards

A first step toward good welfare practice is defining standards and metrics that can demonstrate legal compliance or other standards of performance. Experts generally agree that injury, disease, malnourishment or other unhealthful states substantially decrease general welfare (e.g. Broom, 1991; Dawkins, 1998). The welfare of apes held in captivity depends partly on the current environment and the risks and protective factors it affords. For example, an evaluation of the suitability of primates as pets in terms of primate health and welfare reached a clear position

TABLE 10.1

Potential welfare risks for the various forms of captivity where apes are found

Captivity type	Examples of potential welfare risks
Zoos	Varying quality of facilities and care programs (resources), contact with crowds of people (noise, sanitation)
Sanctuary or rescue center	Ape residents arrive with varying histories of injury, illness, abuse, and neglect that can be difficult to treat or manage. Varying quality of facilities and care programs (resources)
Exhibition and entertainment	Maternal and social deprivation, untrained handlers/personnel, harsh physical training techniques, poor access to veterinary care, poor facilities, nutrition, and care programs. Unpredictable environment as apes are sold and traded. Apes abused/neglected after infancy because of aggression and other conflict, untrained handlers/personnel
Breeders and dealers	Maternal and social deprivation, untrained handlers/personnel, poor access to veterinary care, poor facilities, nutrition, and care programs. Unpredictable environment as apes are sold and traded. Apes abused/neglected after infancy because of aggression and other conflict, untrained handlers/personnel
Pets	Complete social isolation from conspecifics is common, animals abused/neglected after infancy because of aggression and other conflict, untrained handlers/personnel, poor access to veterinary care, poor facilities, nutrition and care programs
Laboratories and testing facilities	Maternal and social deprivation, induced illness or injury through experiments and testing procedures, illness or injury untreated as part of experiments and testing procedures, depauperate, sterile environments used for some testing

against the practice (Soulsbury *et al.*, 2009). In addition to the welfare considerations for apes, there are a number of health and safety risks for humans who keep apes as pets, as well as for public safety. See Box 10.1 for information on "positive" and "negative" lists of animals that individuals may keep.

While some of the welfare risks documented for apes kept as pets generalize to other forms of captivity, risk factors can vary owing to the resources committed to care and the knowledge of the people who are in charge of ape welfare. For example, some zoos have dedicated welfare staff and veterinary care, whereas circuses typically do not. Examples of potential welfare risks for the various forms of captivity where apes are found are given in Table 10.1.

In addition to needs that stem from basic biology, some individuals in captivity have special needs owing to past experience, for

example developmental conditions, injuries, or disease owing to natural causes or intentional exposure in a laboratory environment. It is important to emphasize the difference between sanctuaries and zoos, as sanctuaries have developed specialized services to deal with physically injured and psychologically traumatized animals. Those responsible for the welfare of these individuals must provide for special needs requiring additional or individualized care.

Ethology and the welfare of captive apes

The presence of abnormal behavior is widely accepted as evidence of poor welfare. Importantly, these pathologies can be influenced by genetics, illness, or injury, or previous experience, including cruelty, neglect, and trauma. Behavioral pathologies have been reported among apes in captivity (Yerkes, 1943), and recent studies have found that these can range from common to nearly ubiquitous in some populations of captive apes (e.g. Hook *et al.*, 2002; Birkett and Newton-Fisher, 2011). Behavioral and psycho-pathologies are not common among apes in the wild (Walsh, Bramblett, and Alford, 1982), and the natural behavioral repertoires of animals and behavioral diversity observed in the wild can act as benchmarks for creating and optimizing captive care programs.

Photo: The presence of abnormal behavior is widely accepted as evidence of poor welfare. Behavioral pathologies have been reported among apes in captivity for nearly a century. © Terry Whittaker

Apes tend to show strong motivation and preference for certain behaviors and exhibit signs of stress when they cannot engage in these behaviors. Drawing from concepts of natural behavior, some welfare practices have refocused on how captive environments and practices can offer opportunities suited to the needs and capabilities of a given species. Some environments fail to provide the means and opportunity for such behaviors. However, merely providing opportunities does not guarantee welfare, and detailed programs that specify practices and outcomes are vital. For example, following a mandated review of US policy that began in 2010 (Altevogt *et al.*, 2011b), a working group recently assembled by the US government defined ten recommendations for ethologically and socially appropriate environments, which included issues of group size, space requirements, outdoor access, diet, enrichment, and the appropriate training of personnel (NIH Chimpanzee Working Group, 2013).

Current and emerging practices that emphasize needs and opportunities are positive steps forward for the welfare of apes in captivity. Lingering limitations for an opportunities-based approach stem from the continued emphasis on environmental features such as furnishings and behavioral management. Where standards and performance are founded on the environment rather than on the apes per se, minimum standards and box-ticking could take center stage for implementation and compliance. By incorporating animal-centric metrics and outcomes, standards and practices can go beyond basic needs to account for supportive care and positive welfare for individual apes.

Another remaining challenge for the welfare of apes in captivity concerns the affective or emotional components of well-being. A comprehensive framework for ape welfare necessarily includes attention to the affective realm that goes beyond "freedom from fear." Not only does fear miss a full range of negative emotional states with legitimate welfare implications, such as sadness or distress, fear fails to address any neutral and positive emotional states, which are important and oft-neglected components of wellbeing (Balcombe, 2006, 2009, 2010).

Comprehensive frameworks for ape welfare: where do we go from here?

Welfare policies and practices lag behind the evidence that has emerged from a range of disciplines. One valuable trend is a more holistic view; instead of thinking of each behavior or trait in isolation, a broader framework can be used for considering clusters of related behaviors that comprise wellbeing or the lack thereof. A synthetic, ape-centered welfare practice must draw from knowledge across many disciplines and achieve multiple aims as shown in Figure 10.1 and in the following list.

1. Specific behaviors or biomarkers of poor welfare (Walsh *et al.*, 1982; Wobber and Hare, 2011; Lopresti-Goodman, Kameka, and Dube, 2012; Rosati *et al.*, 2012);

2. Cognitive skills and capabilities (Tomasello, Call, and Hare, 2003; Hare, Call, and Tomasello, 2006; Savage-Rumbaugh

et al., 2007; Fay, 2011; Hill, Collier-Baker, and Suddendorf, 2011);

3. Normal and abnormal development (Bloomsmith, Pazol, and Alford, 1994; Nash *et al.*, 1999; Van Noordwijk and Van Schaik, 2005; Matsuzawa, Tomonaga, and Tanaka, 2006);

4. The role of experience in behavior and social relationships (Reimers, Schwarzenberger, and Preuschoft, 2007; Kalcher-Sommersguter *et al.*, 2011);

5. Emotion and personality (Kano, Yamanashi, and Tomonaga, 2012; Weiss *et al.*, 2012);

6. Specific psychological symptoms and disorders (Brüne *et al.*, 2004, 2006; Bradshaw *et al.*, 2008, 2009; Ferdowsian *et al.*, 2011, 2012);

7. Other indicators of wellbeing (Weiss, King, and Enns, 2002; King and Landau, 2003; Weiss, King, and Perkins, 2006).

Number and status of captive apes in select non-range states

Assessments of the number of apes in captivity and the conditions under which they are captive are vital for understanding the status of captive apes globally. With respect to captive apes in non-range states, such information bears upon a range of issues

FIGURE 10.1

Schema showing a building-block system for welfare practices that starts with a minimal Prevent Harm block (left), adding core components with each block to the right for Provide Basics, Support Needs, Promote Wellbeing and Assure Welfare

PREVENT HARM	PROVIDE BASICS	SUPPORT NEEDS	PROMOTE WELLBEING	ASSURE WELFARE
■ Cruelty	■ Food	■ Rehabilitation	■ Behavioral	■ Evaluation programs, individuals
■ Neglect	■ Water	■ Treatment	■ Emotional	
■ Exploitation	■ Shelter	■ Training	■ Social	
■ Disease & injury	■ Environment	■ Equipment	■ Developmental	■ Infrastructure
	■ Care	■ Accommodation	■ Cognitive	■ Systems
				■ Culture

from international policy and harmonizing captive care practices to bioethics and deliberations regarding the funding of captive care.

Methods and reporting

The geographic sites used in the analysis were chosen because data on captive apes were available in government reports and other published sources. The type and amount of data available varied geographically, and also by captivity type. Some data were voluntarily reported and published, while other data were drawn from compulsory government reports that are available to the public. Other information has been aggregated from published studies and reports, media sources, or direct communications, which are cited accordingly. Where possible, multiple sources of information were cross-referenced to identify gaps in coverage and the reliability of figures reported, but some potential sources, such as legal cases or unpublished data, were not pursued. Thus, the information reported here represents best estimates based on the sources cited.

The best data coverage was found for the United States. Results from the United States are compared with figures available for the European Union (EU). Some sources were limited to a particular taxonomic group or to a particular type of captivity, which is noted in the text for each geographic region. For example, no figures are reported for non-accredited zoos, pets, or other forms of private ownership in the EU. Data were

not obtained for apes in any form of captivity not mentioned explicitly.

Since some variation in the number of individuals or the types of captivity reported could reflect differences in the law, some basic legal context for each geographic region in the analysis is provided. Following a description of specific data sources, the number of apes is reported by taxonomic class. Generally, data were aggregated at the level of the genus. However, figures for all species of gibbons and the siamang were aggregated into a single class, *Hylobatidae*. The number of individuals is also reported by captivity type together with other variables affecting welfare where applicable. The types of captivity found in each of the selected regions and data coverage are summarized in Table 10.2.

Captive apes in the EU, the political context and lawful types of captivity

The EU member states are parties to CITES and other multilateral agreements governing trade and other activities involving apes. There are a number of EU laws related to compliance with CITES, especially as it pertains to permitted uses and conditions for endangered fauna, including apes. For example, facilities must apply for exemptions under the law to pursue activities such as research, education or breeding for reintroduction (Council of the European Union,

TABLE 10.2

Forms of ape captivity found in reviewed sites.

	Zoos	Ent	Sanc	Other	Test	Pet	Deal
EU	Y	YND	Y	YND	N	?ND	?ND
USA	Y	Y	Y	Y	Y	Y	Y

Ent = entertainment and performing acts; Sanc = sanctuary and rescue centers; Test = invasive laboratory testing; Pet = privately owned pets not exhibited to the public; Deal = commercial dealers and breeders. For further explanations of each type, refer to text. Y = practice present; N = practice not present; YND = practice present, but no data available; ?ND = status of practice unknown, no data available.

1992, 1997). Zoos are further mandated under 1999/22/EC to meet standards including providing species-specific enclosures, suitable veterinary care and nutrition, along with provisions for licensing and inspection by member states (Council of the European Union, 1999).

Though it has been 10 years since the zoo directive was to be fully implemented, a recent report found that many member states did not have laws that fully satisfied the mandates, that many zoos still failed to meet minimum standards in practice or were altogether unlicensed, and work is still being done on developing guidelines for this directive (Born Free Foundation, 2011). Variation in the standards of the national laws governing zoos is considerable, including provisions that directly impact apes. For example, the minimum outdoor enclosure space for chimpanzees is 400 m² per five chimpanzees in Austria versus 40 m² per four chimpanzees in Lithuania with considerable variation in between. In some member states there are no explicit standards at all (Born Free Foundation, 2011).

Enforcement and inspection are also an on-going concern. Analysis of zoo inspection reports from 2005–08 found that approximately 9% of British zoos were graded as substandard, with another 8% lacking documentation of an inspection for the period studied (Draper and Harris, 2012).

In 2006–08 the Environmental Directorate of the EU undertook a series of evaluations regarding directive 86/609/EEC (Council of the European Union, 1986) governing the use of animals, including apes, in experiments and testing. Citing exceptional welfare risks for apes and finding no evidence for impact on competition or scientific capacity (Gramke et al., 2007, p. 237; see also Resolution 18, 2010/63/EC), new language on ape experiments was adopted in 2010. While the new language in 2010/63/EC is not an outright ban, all future research

on great apes is prohibited (Article 8(3)) with the sole exception provided under a "safeguard clause" (Article 55(2)) that may be requested only to save an ape species from extinction or under exceptional circumstances with an "unexpected outbreak" of disease among humans (European Parliament and Council, 2010).

EU data by captivity type

Laboratories

As a consequence of both EU law and the national laws of member states, there are no apes used in laboratory testing at this time. Apes previously used in testing have been transferred to zoos or sanctuaries (see next section).

Sanctuaries

Apes previously used in testing before the various laws were enacted were transferred to other captive settings. For example, in the Netherlands, chimpanzees previously used in disease experiments were transferred to a specialized sanctuary for exotic animals, while apes with no health conditions were transferred to zoos (van den Berg, 2006). Austria adopted a national ban on the use of apes in research in 2006 (Knight, 2008), but the path from laboratory testing to retirement was more complex. A small number of captive apes in the EU are housed in sanctuaries that provide care for apes formerly used in research, entertainment, or held as pets or in other private ownership. While some transfers to the sanctuary are made voluntarily (e.g. laboratories in Netherlands and Austria), others involve legal actions or seizures (e.g. AAP, 2011, 2012). The number of apes is reported for each sanctuary in Table 10.3. For information on sanctuaries and rescue centers both published sources and personal communications were used as cited.

TABLE 10.3

Number of apes in EU sanctuaries by country and taxonomic group (where available)

Sanctuary name	Country	Taxon	Number
AAP (AAP, 2012)	Netherlands	Chimpanzee	44
Gut Aiderbichl (Gut Aiderbichl, 2011)	Austria	Chimpanzee	37
Mona Foundation (MONA Foundation, 2013)	Spain	Chimpanzee	12
Monkey World (Monkey World, 2012)	UK	Chimpanzee	59
		Orangutan	16
		Hylobatidae	23
Primadomus (AAP, 2013)	Spain	Chimpanzee	8
Wales Ape and Monkey Sanctuary (Wales Ape and Monkey Sanctuary, n.d.)	UK	Chimpanzee *Hylobatidae*	10 2

TABLE 10.4

Number of apes in EU zoos based on figures reported by ISIS

Taxon	Male	Female	Unknown	Taxon total
Orangutan	113	177	16	306
Gorilla	164	239	5	408
Chimpanzee	273	465	3	741
Hylobatidae	355	275	89	719
Grand total				**2174**

Zoos

Between October and December 2012, census data were requested for all ape genera from the International Species Information System (ISIS), which aggregates census figures voluntarily reported by member zoos (ISIS, 2012a). The ISIS website indicated that some data may be missing or out of date as they transition to a new software system (ISIS, 2012b). Since membership and reporting are voluntary, not all zoos are necessarily included. The ISIS data contained records for 2174 apes in Europe. The number of male, female, and unspecified sex individuals for each taxon is shown in Table 10.4.

Discussion and specific welfare risks raised by EU data

Evidence of rescues and sanctuary transfers from circuses and other private ownership within the EU indicates on-going challenges with variation in legal standards and enforcement within the Union. There is a lack of animal welfare consideration in the EU for captive wild animals, as it is seen as a national and not regional issue for member states to implement. Adoption of EU-wide standards for zoos could address some of these problems, and coordinated reporting and law enforcement will also be critical. The political will and legal mechanisms for enforcement might benefit from advocacy and other forms of public awareness, and the European Alliance of Rescue centers and Sanctuaries (EARS) is currently being developed to support and represent rescue centers and sanctuaries in Europe (EARS, 2013).

A main concern arising from the ISIS data is the 77 solitary apes in the record. Most of the isolates were *Hylobatidae* (49, 63.6%), followed by 19 chimpanzees (24.7%, one bonobo), seven orangutans (9.1%) and just two gorillas. Six facilities with solitary apes exhibit no other ape taxon. As noted earlier, the legal standards and practices for zoos vary widely across the EU, with evidence that welfare is lacking at many locations, especially newer member states. *National Geographic* recently published an extensive report on the welfare of great apes in German zoos (Nakott, 2012), which included an infographic highlighting some key facts, including:

■ Of the 40 zoos exhibiting about 450 apes, ten of the zoos exhibited great ape isolates or pairs only.

■ Of the zoos considered, only six met the highest standards and international best practices consistent with the needs and capabilities of great apes.

■ Eleven chimpanzee exhibits and four other ape exhibits at 13 zoos were classified inappropriate for on-going ape exhibition and recommended for closure. The remaining exhibits were found in need of varying degrees of improvement to realize minimum standards.

As the EU moves forward with a review of zoo standards, and member states evaluate policy and practice, a long-term view is critical, in part because of the long lifespan of apes. The *National Geographic* article, for example, pointed out that captive breeding could affect when individual zoos or countries could phase out ape exhibitions. Likewise, it suggested that a network of "havens" or sanctuaries could be a suitable alternative for apes housed in isolation or other inappropriate settings (Nakott, 2012). For any system of sanctuaries or other "havens," the age structure of the ape population to be served, including future births, strongly influences the demand for space and for care services over time.

The United States and its legal context

The United States is also party to CITES and other treaties covering trade in apes. Testing on apes is subject to US regulations regarding housing and other conditions in laboratories and other standards under the Animal Welfare Act (AWA). What laboratories may do with individual apes once they are deemed "surplus to need" is governed by the Chimpanzee Health Improvement and Maintenance Act (CHIMP Act). In 2011, the US government undertook a formal review of ape testing with the National Academies of Science, which recommended several changes, including reducing the number of individuals used (Altevogt *et al.*, 2011b). A working group recently evaluated the new requirements put forward by the Academies for biomedical and behavioral research using chimpanzees and suggested a number of standards for housing and care practices (Box 10.2).

US law allows individuals and organizations to exhibit apes subject to licensure and standards with the United States Department of Agriculture (USDA). If properly registered, it is lawful to sell captive-bred apes, or to buy and privately own apes purchased from such dealers. State and local laws may also govern these activities. Depending upon the jurisdiction, these range from outright prohibition, to negative or positive standards, to an absence of any law specifically addressing apes. Where these activities are legal, state and local licenses can also be required and local authorities may pursue legal action against violating parties.

BOX 10.2

Breakthrough NIH decision 2013

Although invasive biomedical research protocols have decreased in US laboratories over the past decade, a significant number of chimpanzees have continued to be held in laboratories and holding facilities for potential future need. Signaling a major shift on the part of the government, on June 26, 2013 the National Institutes of Health (NIH) announced a decision to accept the vast majority of recommendations made in the Council of Councils Working Group on the Use of Chimpanzees in NIH supported Research Report.[1]

Among other things, the newly announced policy will permanently retire hundreds of chimpanzees now held in laboratories. The NIH decision stipulates that all but 50 chimpanzees owned and supported by the government shall be transferred to the federal sanctuary system in the near future. There, individuals will live the rest of their lives in specialized sanctuary settings, with proper nutrition, preventative veterinary care, enriching stimulation, and a social environment appropriate for chimpanzees.

The new NIH plan followed from a review process that was initiated by members of Congress and culminated in a December 2011 report by the Institute of Medicine (IOM), entitled "Chimpanzees in biomedical and behavioral research: assessing the necessity" (Altevogt et al., 2011a). The IOM made strong recommendations after determining that the US chimpanzee research program was largely unnecessary. As a result of the IOM study, NIH Director Collins requested that a special Working Group of experts develop a plan to implement the IOM's guiding principles and criteria for chimpanzee research, analyze the current use of chimpanzees in research, assess the placement and size of chimpanzee populations, and review potential future use.

The NIH announcement came on the heels of a Proposed Rule by the United States Fish and Wildlife Service (USFWS) to list US captive chimpanzees as endangered, alongside their wild counterparts.[2] (See sub-section entitled 'Transparency and regulatory practices impacting ape welfare' in the Discussion section below for further detail.)

Photo: On June 26, 2013 the National Institute of Health (NIH) announced its decision to permanently retire hundreds of chimpanzees now held in US laboratories. © Jurek Wajdowicz, EWS

Analysis of data sources, limitations, and results

Data on ape sanctuaries were collated from external sources and from sanctuary materials or direct communications. Some figures were drawn from government records, published sources and personal communications as cited. For chimpanzees only, independently vetted data from the ChimpCARE project (ChimpCARE, 2013) served as the authoritative data source. Official USDA data for registrations for breeders, dealers, exhibitors, federal research, and research using captive apes were used to assess the number of sites and number of individuals by taxon, and frequency of animal welfare citations were obtained from the agency's public records database (USDA, 2012). Not all entities that house captive apes are required to register with the USDA. Data were obtained on December 28, 2012 for the period 2010–12.

The number of apes in US sanctuaries is shown by species in Table 10.5. A notation of where these data are also counted in other sections is indicated.

ChimpCARE, established by Lincoln Park Zoo, uses different categories than the USDA for most site types, and allows for

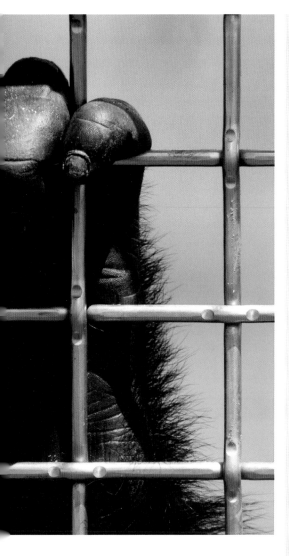

TABLE 10.5

Apes in US sanctuaries by taxonomic group with reference to appearance in other sections of the report dataset

Sanctuary name	Taxonomic group					In other data?	
	B	C	G	O	H	USDA	ChCare
Center for Great Apes		29		15		x	x
Chimp Haven		123				x	x
Chimpanzee Sanctuary NW		7				x	x
Chimps Inc.		8				x	x
CA Black Beauty Ranch		3		4		x	x
Gorilla Haven			1			x	
Great Ape Trust	6					x	
International Primate Protection League					33		
Primarily Primates		47		4			x
Primate Rescue Center		11		1		x	x
Save the Chimps		267				x	x
Wildlife Waystation		48					x

B = bonobo; C = chimpanzee; G = gorilla; O = orangutan; H = *Hylobatidae*; ChCare = ChimpCARE Project.

more nuanced consideration of patterns across site type. ChimpCARE does not geo-reference or break out distinct sites for private parties such as pet owners, providing a total of 60 chimpanzees (3% PRIV) in this category. Chimpanzees were most frequently reported for laboratories (962, 49.3% LAB) followed by sanctuaries (522, 27.9% SANC), and AZA zoos (261, 13.4% AZA). Fewer chimpanzees are designated as being in non-accredited facilities (106, 5.4% NON) and entertainment (20, ~1% ENT). The number of chimpanzees by ChimpCARE site type is shown in Figure 10.2, and to facilitate comparison with USDA figures and interpretation of data, a matrix is also provided in Figure 10.2.

From 2010 12, 239 bodies registered with the USDA were reported to hold captive apes. Accounting for registrants who held more than one certificate type, cancellations and revocations (1 only), 224 entities were active in 2012: 201 exhibitors, 8 research laboratories, 9 dealers, 4 breeders and 2 federal research facilities (see Figure 10.3).

USDA data for inventory by taxonomic class were drawn from the most recent report for each ACTIVE registrant (see Table 10.6). If a registrant went from ACTIVE to CANCELLED status during 2012 AND had

FIGURE 10.2

Number of chimpanzees reported by Project ChimpCARE for six site types relative to those used by the USDA to classify official federal licenses and registrations. See text for abbreviations

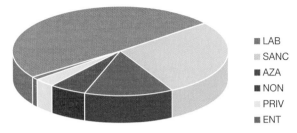

- LAB
- SANC
- AZA
- NON
- PRIV
- ENT

FIGURE 10.3

Number of 2012 USDA registrations with apes, by certificate type. The single-letter code is assigned by the USDA for use in its official records

- Exhibitor (C)
- Research (R)
- Dealer (B)
- Breeder (A)
- Federal research facility (F)

TABLE 10.6

Apes inventory by taxonomic group*

Registration type	Number of apes
Hylobatidae	
Breeder	17
Dealer	35
Exhibitor	567
Federal Research	5
Research	0
Total for *Hylobatidae*	624
Gorillas	
Exhibitor	310
Total for gorillas	310
Orangutans	
Federal Research	1
Exhibitor	245
Total for orangutans	246
Chimpanzees	
Federal Research	172
Research	777
Exhibitor	977
Total for chimpanzees	1926
Grand total of apes	3106

* As reported for USDA active registrants in 2012

a 2012 inspection, those data were included in the analysis. If an ACTIVE registrant had no 2012 inspection, the most recent, from 2011 or 2010, were used. Data are collated by certification type.

Discussion and specific welfare risks and violations

The USDA enforces the AWA, but the agency does not technically issue "violations" when registrants do not meet AWA standards. The USDA calls such instances "non-compliance items" (NCIs). There are a number of caveats for interpreting what the USDA data mean for the health and welfare of apes.

- The NCIs reported for facilities with apes may or may not impact the apes present. The electronic query data do not provide details about the number

or species of animals impacted, except where certain sections of the law are themselves species specific.

- At minimum, compliance failures at a site could represent increased risk for the apes, increasing in severity across a range of welfare effects. For example, some cases are merely administrative (e.g. out of date health certificates), while others involve poor welfare or even death (e.g. lack of routine veterinary care or treatment of acute injury resulting in premature death).

- It is not always clear whether an NCI represents acute or chronic welfare concerns, or some combination thereof.

- Inspection data only provide some of the story on welfare: just as the absence of disease is distinct from excellent health, the absence of NCIs on an inspection is distinct from a certification for welfare best practices or evidence of positive welfare status among apes.

During 2010–12, there were 1344 NCIs at USDA registered sites where captive apes were held. More than 42% of these were in reference to housing and facilities. The frequency of USDA inspections varied across sites; for example, not all sites were inspected in all years while other sites were inspected multiple times per year. This can pose a risk for welfare, in that pain and suffering or the risk thereof are not identified and mitigated, or cited with the potential of punitive actions by the agency, as early as possible.

Apes as pets

Both the ChimpCARE and the USDA data revealed that apes are still kept in private ownership as companion animals, particularly chimpanzees and gibbons. The number of apes kept as pets varied by state, perhaps as a result of variation in legal requirements. As noted earlier, though this may be legal in some jurisdictions, the practice is subject to regulation under a number of federal laws.

Public knowledge and opinions on the keeping of apes as pets varies considerably. For example, a recent experiment examined how people perceived the keeping of chimpanzees as pets after viewing either entertainment or educational videos (Schroepfer et al., 2011). Among those watching entertainment, 35% of people reported that they were in favor of the right to keep chimpanzees as pets. Even after viewing an educational video about chimpanzees, approximately 10% of people surveyed stated that they were in favor. In the entertainment group, the authors attributed greater support for allowing chimpanzees to be pets to misinformation about factors such as "size, desirability, and abundance" of chimpanzees portrayed in entertainment settings (Schroepfer et al., 2011).

Discussion

The data that are available on the welfare of apes in captivity in these representative non-range states can, to an extent, aid in estimating welfare status elsewhere. As gaps regarding the number of apes in captivity are filled, there is no doubt that efforts are needed to expand the number of apes receiving high-quality captive care. A scientific approach that is grounded in best-available evidence regarding ape ethology, natural history, needs, and capabilities will provide a critical foundation for future efforts both to establish welfare programs where they do not exist and to improve existing welfare practices globally. The use of strong evidence and vetted model programs can serve practical implementation as well as monitoring and evaluation activities.

Transparency and regulatory practices impacting ape welfare

Some evidence suggests that many people living in the United States are unaware that all apes, including chimpanzees, are at risk of extinction. It turns out that when seeing chimpanzees in artificial, unnatural settings where they wear clothes, and especially if they are seen posing with people, people mistakenly think chimpanzees are abundant and safe (Schroepfer et al., 2011). These misconceptions can be hard to set straight. For example, some people surveyed had misconceptions about the status of chimpanzees, even after passing through a zoo exhibit with signs that explain the plight of wild chimpanzees (Ross et al., 2008). These studies demonstrated that people use their experiences with captive apes as a basis for drawing conclusions about wild apes. Even when those conclusions conflict with facts presented in scientific or educational contexts, personal experience and cultural context affected conclusions such that many people were unconvinced that chimpanzees needed protection in the wild. There could be analogous impacts for education and sensitization projects in range states that stem from local or international drivers.

These personal, albeit indirect experiences with apes have proven to be so influential that it would be risky to ignore social practices and regulations that influence apes in captivity. Under the ESA, the US government has long considered the chimpanzee under a "split" listing where wild animals are *Endangered*, but captive individuals are only recognized as *Threatened*. Under this lower risk designation, it is legal to use chimpanzees for a variety of commercial purposes within the United States so long as the proper permits are in place.

For example, chimpanzees can be forced to perform in circuses, film, and television and kept in commercial exhibit centers, zoos, and laboratories. To one extent or another, all of these practices hinge on the split-listing status under the ESA.

Some scientists and organizations contend that the split-listing status in the United States is harmful because it creates markets for chimpanzees and it sends contradictory messages about the impetus and urgency for protecting them (USFWS, 2013). Such a policy could undermine conservation and protection efforts, including those undertaken by sanctuaries in range states. Indeed, calling on range states to protect wild chimpanzees and enforce laws that prohibit keeping chim-

Photo: Orphaned apes may be seized from hunters, markets, or private dealers, whether obtained indirectly, as a secondary effect of the bushmeat trade, or directly, as products for sale. The illegal trade in live apes, affecting thousands of apes each year, is currently growing. © Alison White

panzees as pets or using them for private commercial exhibition is potentially less compelling when coming from a government that allows those same practices to occur within its own borders.

The US government announced, in June 2013, a Proposed Rule that would enable the FWS to address the inconsistency of the split-listing of chimpanzees (USFWS, 2013). The agency cited increased threats to chimpanzees throughout their range and a lack of evidence that these patterns would change in the near future. While the agency noted that domestic use of chimpanzees in entertainment or other commercial activity could lead to misperceptions that may impact conservation negatively, these practices were not deemed a "significant" driver for threats to the chimpanzee, where habitat loss, hunting, disease, and illegal trade have been on the rise and have direct effects on wild chimpanzee populations (Federal Register, 2013, pp. 35211–14). For these and other reasons detailed by the agency, the FWS determined that the ESA "does not allow for captive held animals to be assigned separate legal status from their wild counterparts on the basis of their captive state" (Federal Register, 2013, p. 35202). Following a mandatory public comment period, the FWS will make a final determination regarding the Proposed Rule and address remaining questions about its implementation.

More generally, and as both international and intergovernmental organizations implore private and public institutions to give funding for ape conservation, there are also calls on range states to adopt stronger legal frameworks and enforcement, accountability, and even to fund these efforts. Wild chimpanzee populations are declining, and a unified, global effort is needed to save the species from extinction. Consistent conservation policy at the national level is an integral part of the larger global efforts, a subject explored in greater detail in the next section.

The impacts of extractive industries on sanctuaries and rescue centers

Range state sanctuaries and rescue centers

After the bushmeat trade, habitat loss and fragmentation, and disease, the illegal trade in live apes is considered to be one of the most pressing threats to the survival of apes in the wild. Orphaned apes may be seized from hunters, markets, or private dealers, whether obtained indirectly, as a secondary effect of the bushmeat trade, or directly, as products for sale. The illegal trade in live apes, affecting thousands of apes each year, is currently growing (Stiles *et al.*, 2013).

In range states, a number of different facilities may offer care to orphaned apes and other individuals that are taken into captivity, including sanctuaries, rehabilitation centers, and rescue centers. Rescue centers and rehabilitation centers typically focus on shorter-term residency, for example for recovery from an injury or until a release site can be finalized. By contrast, sanctuaries typically house long-term residents and even provide lifetime care that can span decades in some cases. While some sanctuaries do have reintroduction programs, these run in parallel with long-term housing. Zoos sometimes provide short- or long-term care in ape range states, and where no such facilities exist, such housing and care must be improvised. While there are distinctions between facility types, for the purposes of this chapter the term "sanctuary" shall be taken as an inclusive term that covers all such facilities, unless an exception is explicitly noted.

The most obvious impact on sanctuary capacity in both the short and long term is arrival rate: the more apes that are orphaned, the greater the number of potential rescues and residents at the facilities. In fact, demand for sanctuaries in ape range states has been substantial since at least the 1990s (Farmer, 2002). A comparison of data from 2001 and 2009 (Faust *et al.*, 2011) reveals that the total population size across 13 Pan African Sanctuaries Alliance (PASA) sanctuaries housing apes increased nearly 60% overall (479 to 855). A detailed analysis of arrivals at 11 PASA sanctuaries reported that the growth rate from 2000–06 was approximately 15% (Faust *et al.*, 2011), though it has slowed over time (Stiles *et al.*, 2013). Models of future growth that account for various re-release and arrival scenarios estimate the population will grow to between 550 and 1800 individuals in the next 20 years (Faust *et al.*, 2011). A summary of sanctuary information gathered from 2009 to 2012 is shown in Table 10.7 (Africa) and Table 10.8 (Asia). The number and location of ape sanctuaries and the number of present residents shown were drawn from a number of sources, including published articles, websites, and

personal communication. Although an effort has been made to update and confirm these data, figures might not account for the most recent rescue arrivals in residence, births, transfers, reintroductions, or deaths, especially those taking place since March 2011.

The pattern for ape sanctuaries in Asia is different (Figure 10.8). Not only is the sanctuary population substantially bigger, but growth due to arrival rates is accelerating (Stiles *et al.*, 2013). For orangutans, the situation has been especially dire for years. The Great Apes Survival Partnership (GRASP) sent a technical mission to Indonesia to evaluate the situation in 2006 (CITES and GRASP, 2006). Trade and weak CITES enforcement were viewed as significant drivers. The mission report concluded:

> Whatever form the trade takes and whatever motivates it, the overwhelming evidence of the scale and seriousness of the problem is

TABLE 10.7

Number of apes in African sanctuaries in 2011 by country

Country	Range state?	# Sanc	B	C	G
Cameroon	Yes	4	0	244	33
Congo (ROC)	Yes	3	0	156	5
DRC	Yes	6	55	85	30
Rwanda*	Yes	0	0	0	0
Gabon	Yes	3	0	20	9
Gambia	Yes	1	0	77	0
Guinea	Yes	1	0	38	0
Nigeria	Yes	1	0	28	0
Sierra Leone	Yes	1	0	101	0
Kenya	No	1	0	44	0
Uganda	Yes	1	0	45	0
Zambia	No	1	0	120	0
South Africa	No	1	0	33	0

Sanc = number of sanctuaries reported for country; B = bonobo; C = chimpanzee; G = gorilla. *The Mountain Gorilla Veterinary Project (MGVP) runs a rescue program with joint operations in Rwanda and the DRC, which is reported only in this cell ("Rwanda").

TABLE 10.8

Number of apes in Asian sanctuaries in 2011 by country

Country	Range state?	# Sanc	O	H
Cambodia	Yes	1	0	9
Indonesia	Yes	16	1208	293
Malaysia	Yes	3	400	0
Taiwan	No	1	0	0
Thailand	Yes	4	0	182
Viet Nam	Yes	2	0	17

Sanc = number of sanctuaries reported for country; O = orangutan; H = *Hylobatidae*.

the number of orangutans in "rescue" and "rehabilitation" centers. In Kalimantan alone, [...] Indeed, it is hard to view this figure as anything other than an indictment against the law enforcement efforts of the relevant agencies in Indonesia. (CITES and GRASP, 2006, p. 11)

In Africa and Asia, the demand for sanctuary space far exceeds both supply and funding. Furthermore, whilst reintroduction might be a long-term goal for many facilities, arrival rates can outpace the rehabilitation training and/or exceed the release capacity of sanctuaries and rescue centers. The sheer number of apes entering these centers is not the only challenge facilities face. Responsible reintroduction involves a variety of complex factors including financial cost, disease risk, post-release monitoring, and securing suitable release sites (Beck, Rodrigues, and Unwin, 2007). Whether sanctuaries and rescue centers undertake reintroduction or not, essentially all of the work they do can be impacted by extractive industries.

Potential impacts of extractive industry on ape sanctuaries

In part, the impacts of extractive industries on sanctuaries are shaped by complex ecological and socioeconomic factors, in addition to the specifics of the industries themselves. Impacts can range in severity (mild to severe) and interval (immediate to delayed) and can be either positive or negative for the sanctuaries and ape residents. The case studies presented later in this chapter illustrate how relationship building with the sector (in the case of Best Management Practices (BMPs) or other partnerships) can help to mitigate negative impacts. These voluntary practices are not, however, a complete solution; as long as competing economic interests for resources exist, wild apes will still face risks owing to industrial expansion, and sanctuaries will continue to be impacted.

Impacts to operations

By their nature, extractive industries clear land, convert land from one use to another, or otherwise modify landscapes. Habitat loss and degradation reduce the area that might be available for sanctuary locations, for sanctuary programs of managed rehabilitation of semi-free ranging individuals, as well as the creation or the expansion of reintroduction sites that can be used by sanctuaries.

Operational impacts can also be administrative and logistical in nature. For example, if roads and vehicles operated by a private company facilitate the illegal transport of apes from one country to another, seizing individual apes, transferring them to a rescue facility, and potentially repatriating them to the country of origin becomes more complex legally and thus administratively. The laws of the country of seizure and the country of origin are involved, as well as CITES authorities. Some of these challenges have been recognized, and experts have called on CITES to be responsive to the special needs of such cases (Wolf, 2009). Where nationals of other countries are involved in illegal activities, those laws could come into play as well, as has been seen in a number of recent high-profile international cases in Egypt, Guinea, and China (Ammann, 2012; Stiles *et al.*, 2013).

If the country of seizure is not a range state or is not equipped to handle the necessary testing for transport or to handle ape care during law enforcement, permitting or planning, outside experts or resources are usually necessary. For example, special expertise, testing equipment, and transport were necessary for sanctuary transfer to Uganda when four chimpanzees from the Democratic Republic of Congo (DRC) were seized in Sudan (CS and WCT, 2011; PASA, 2011). A charter flight was also necessary to airlift another chimpanzee from Sudan to a sanctuary in Kenya (Maina, 2009).

Impacts to resident ape health and wellbeing

In extractive industries, work sites, roads, and other business activities often take place in remote areas where the natural resources are found. Some of these areas are also ape habitat. By nature, such sites and operations are difficult to police and illegal activity can thus be easier to conceal. Increased access and reduced risk could make illegal activities such as keeping apes as pets on private company property easier or more attractive.

There are many health and welfare risks for apes kept as pets. Even in the absence of abuse or neglect, inadequate nutrition or veterinary care, close confinement and other risks can impact health, welfare, and ultimately survival. For example, in April 2013, an orangutan rescued by a sanctuary in Indonesia was found at a plantation with no cage or other housing at all; the infant was simply kept tied up in a bag (SOS, 2013). Where there is frequent transport from industrial sites to urban centers or across borders, these apes could easily become victims of the illegal trade, transported under poor conditions with associated health risks. If these infants are ever seized or rescued, they can require extensive veterinary care and rehabilitation that could last for many years. Specialized needs owing to injury or illness increase the pressure on sanctuary services and resources.

Impacts to rescue, rehabilitation, and related community programs

Sanctuaries are often involved in programs that require the permission of, or cooperation with, government authorities or local communities – including conservation programs focused on wild apes. Where those same authorities and/or communities have relationships with industry and the needs of sanctuaries or rescue organizations are at odds with those interests, organizations involved with protection of apes in captivity and in the wild can face challenges working with government and/or communities as well as with the industries themselves.

In the extreme, these challenges could take the form of conflict. Such competition between sanctuaries and industry might be direct, as in the case of land rights to a specific area pursued by both parties. The competition could also be indirect. For example, a private landowner might be convinced to protect ape habitat under a payment-for-ecosystem-services (PES) model that benefits apes. However, if there are faster or more lucrative returns from renting out land rights or extracting and selling natural resources to a commercial buyer, one or many landowners might forgo PES options. The government or its agents could also be involved in such scenarios by virtue of authority to grant or deny permits to sanctuaries and rescue centers or to private companies. Where interests differ greatly, there is the potential for legal action or other conflict between parties.

Spatial effects, the catchment area, and law enforcement

For apes in their natural habitats, the impacts of extractive industries are expected to have strong spatial relationships, i.e. the strongest impacts are more likely to come from extraction near them than distant from them. The same is not always true for the association between extractive industries and sanctuary populations. Sanctuaries and rescue centers can be influenced by localized and distant drivers because they can serve as a "catchment" for other geographic areas, either (1) where orphaned apes arriving at the sanctuaries originate or (2) where orphaned apes are confiscated. Catchment areas can be synonymous with the home country, or, in the case of sanctuaries in non-range states, such as South Africa, be exclusively outside the home country.

While customs, laws and other risks in catchment areas can differ from those operating locally, increasing arrests, prosecutions, and penalties are priorities for combating the illegal trade in apes (Stiles *et al.*, 2013). One fundamental challenge is that law enforcement capacity is often insufficient to counter the volume of the bushmeat and illegal live animal trades (Drori, 2012; Stiles *et al.*, 2013). However, it has been recognized that if there is no sanctuary in a given area then there is no real incentive for confiscations. Indeed a range of factors can delay the law enforcement needed to seize an

ape held captive illegally for months or years (Teleki, 2001). Even where enforcement challenges are largely administrative, such as coordination between government agencies, the availability of sanctuary space and services could impact enforcement actions.

Beyond a lack of incentives, confiscations could be disincentivized where stakeholders perceive potential costs for initiating enforcement owing to a lack of accessible sanctuary space. For example, informants or officers could be concerned that they might be compelled to provide care for or to obtain veterinary services for the confiscated apes despite a lack of resources. The effect could also work the other way, where access to a sanctuary is a driver. The availability of sanctuary capacity, funding, and political will for protecting apes theoretically could prompt a surge in enforcement and confiscations. In so doing, initial access to a sanctuary could further increase demand for it, potentially beyond capacity. The evidence for a variety of enforcement–sanctuary interdependencies warrants careful consideration by those managing and financing the expansion of enforcement because sanctuary capacity can impact activities as well as outcomes.

The involvement of international law enforcement where repatriation is mandatory or preferable provides a stark example of how broad a catchment area can be, from transcontinental to several continents away, and also sends a strong message to those involved in the trade (Stiles *et al.*, 2013). Such confiscations can be local, where individuals are found near the site where they once lived freely, or regional, where some cross-border coordination is required. However, enforcement actions can also involve a much larger geographic net spanning continents, disparate legal frameworks, and complicated logistics that bear directly upon sanctuaries. Proving the provenance and origins of illegally traded animals has

> Sanctuaries and rescue centers can be influenced by both localized and distant drivers because they can serve as a "catchment" for other geographic areas.

become a sticking point, repatriating individuals is controversial, and DNA testing may be required. Furthermore, if the apes are to be returned, they would require both sanctuary space and services, at least for rehabilitation, although possibly for lifetime care.

Temporal relationships

Whether industry drivers have immediate or delayed repercussions for sanctuaries can be influenced by a number of factors, such as local cultural practices, corruption, and the history and capacity of law enforcement. Beyond arrival rates, the demographic traits of new residents can also be influenced, and sanctuaries have to respond accordingly. For example one analysis reported that 100% of gorillas and bonobos, as well as the majority of chimpanzees (80%), were estimated under 4 years of age upon arrival, while some chimpanzees were estimated to be 5–11 (16.6%) or even more than 12 years of age (2.8%) (Farmer, 2002). A subsequent analysis of demographics at sanctuaries indicates that average age at arrival decreases over time (Faust *et al.*, 2011). Such a pattern appears to reflect the history of law enforcement and the population of apes being rescued.

When a sanctuary becomes operational, local rescues might include individuals used in exhibitions or privately owned for an extended time. As most animals in that category are successfully rescued, arrivals gradually shift towards newly orphaned apes and lower median age (Faust *et al.*, 2011). Where catchment areas are large and enforcement is unpredictable, such a shift could take more time or result in periodic increases in median age at arrival. Likewise, with complex, lengthy repatriation cases, age at arrival would likely be above the median. Increased age at arrival is likely associated with both longer histories of captivity and weaker temporal relationships

between sanctuary demands and their drivers, including extractive industries. Importantly, the longer histories of captivity associated with illegal trade have direct implications for the health and welfare of individual apes and the care that they need after arrival at a sanctuary.

Socioeconomic factors influencing extractive industry impacts

The influence of extractive industries on ape sanctuaries and their residents is determined by socioeconomic factors within their country and by variables associated with catchment countries. Some sanctuary programs are directly affected by poverty and other socioeconomic variables. For example, household poverty in an area could affect the motivation of stakeholders to participate in community programs such as PES or the sustainability of programs to reduce human–wildlife conflict (HWC) through insurance or incentives. Land conversion to cash crops or agroforestry might also impact sanctuary programs or the availability of land for facilities or release sites. In many countries where household poverty rates are high, the concentration of natural resources is also high, a phenomenon called the "resource curse" (Kolstad, Søreide, and Williams, 2008). Not surprisingly, these same countries and resources also attract extractive industries.

The available evidence does not indicate that illegal trade is linked to poverty per se, but rather that the income and power disparities that occur in many developing countries are the drivers (Stiles *et al.*, 2013). More directly, factors such as weak governance or corruption could undermine sanctuary efforts to prevent illegal ape trade or impede the enforcement actions necessary to rescue an ape.

Governance

Poor governance and corruption are recognized risks with natural resources and may serve to weaken other governance structures in the countries affected (Layden, 2010). Likewise, governance is also a critical variable that can influence how extractive industries impact sanctuaries. For example, when governments are corrupt, laws that are intended to protect apes and ensure that nongovernmental organizations (NGOs) and civil society organizations operate effectively can be undermined by competing interests or ignored altogether.

The forestry sector has proven to be vulnerable to corruption, though scale can be hard to estimate (Layden, 2010). Some evidence suggests there is a relationship between rate of deforestation, prevalence of illegal logging, and weak governance and corruption; for example, at a time when illegal logging was estimated to account for more than half of all logging in Indonesia, the country also ranked high on the Corruption Perceptions Index (2009: 111 of 183 (Layden, 2010, p. 2)). Recognized risk factors may increase vulnerabilities in the natural resources sector and make it harder to combat the effects of corruption, including industries where existing corruption levels are high and existing governance and regulation are poor (Kolstad *et al.*, 2008, p. 4). With the complex relationships between governance and extractive industries in mind, it is clear that these are also risks for sanctuaries and rescue centers.

Potential for positive impacts through private sector partnerships

While there is ample evidence of the risks and negative impacts on ape populations and ape sanctuaries from the presence of extractive industries, it is vital to remember that opportunities also exist for engagement with the sector. Even while policy reforms are sought to strengthen ape protection, including those that curb extractive industries, ape conservation and sanctuary organizations can also seek collaboration. Partnerships that emphasize mutual benefit and obviate harm are also instructive (see the Wildlife Wood Project case study in Chapter 4). Two case studies from Uganda and Indonesia are presented here.

Photo: Rescued chimpanzees from within Uganda demonstrate that illegal trade is an on-going risk; whilst chimpanzees with origins outside Uganda reflect the regional risk associated with illegal trade and the significance of sanctuaries for transboundary enforcement and long-term chimpanzee care. © LAGA & The EAGLE Network

CASE STUDY 1

Chimpanzee Sanctuary and Wildlife Conservation Trust, Entebbe and Ngamba Island, Uganda

In 2010, approximately 9.7% of Uganda's land (19 981 km²) was officially protected (FAO, 2012). Wild populations of both chimpanzees and gorillas are found in Uganda, with chimpanzees living both within and outside of protected areas and gorillas ranging outside of protected areas. In addition to these ape populations, two facilities house rescued chimpanzees from both within and outside of the country. Rescued chimpanzees from within Uganda demonstrate that illegal trade has occurred in the recent past, and is an on-going risk. Similarly, chimpanzees with origins outside Uganda reflect the broader regional risk associated with illegal trade as well as the significance of sanctuaries for both transboundary enforcement and long-term chimpanzee care.

The Chimpanzee Sanctuary and Wildlife Conservation Trust (CS and WCT) established the Ngamba Island Sanctuary (NIS) in 1998, and is a founding member of PASA. The project was undertaken in cooperation with the Uganda Wildlife Education Center (UWEC) and the Uganda Wildlife Authority (UWA), both of which continue to serve as Trustees. The founding of NIS coincided with a wave of new enforcement actions that resulted in a number of chimpanzee confiscations and even some successful prosecutions. Since NIS was established, a greater number of confiscated and/or surrendered chimpanzees have been placed at Ngamba Island (28) than the original facility at Uganda Wildlife Education Centre (UWEC) (12).

Most individuals arrived at Ngamba when they were 2–4 years of age (26; see Table 10.9). The number of very young individuals under 2 years of age at arrival is over 20% overall, with the average age of new arrivals decreasing over time. As NIS has approached maximum physical capacity, annual arrival rates have also declined, with approximately ten arrivals since 2004. Though some chimpanzee residents at NIS are of Ugandan origin (18), the majority are from the DRC (27). The precise origins of the residents belie a much larger area in terms of catchments, as some residents arrived following enforcement efforts in Burundi (2), Tanzania (1), and Sudan (4).

Natural forest accounts for a relatively small (29 880 km²), rapidly declining (-2.3% p.a. 2000–10 (FAO, 2010b)) proportion of land in Uganda. Although forest extraction and exporting of timber and other forest products is limited under law, the Ugandan government has acknowledged illegal logging as a major challenge, noting that constraints on measuring or estimating these activities are impediments to enforcement and to realizing sustainable development objectives linked to forestry (Ssekika, 2012). In the context of impacts for chimpanzees, CS and WCT, together with partners and collaborators, have undertaken a number of activities to slow rates of loss through protection and to accelerate reforestation. The project has contracted 342 forest owners who are conserving and reforesting a total of 15.9 km² in designated areas within the Semliki-Murchison landscape (P. Hatanga, personal communication, 2013). While this is a fraction of the total private forestland in the area, the pilot project has gained traction in the community and has achieved important milestones for the project plan (P. Hatanga, personal communication, 2013).

Oil exploration is also on-going in the area around CS and WCT forest projects that include a PES component. The CS and WCT and its partners have taken an active role in engaging representatives of the sector, adding Tullow Oil to the technical steering committee that guides and monitors PES implementation (P. Hatanga, personal communication, 2013). Through this partnership, Tullow Oil has expressed interest in conservation initiatives, specifically buying carbon credits, supporting biomass energy efficiency projects, and other potential forms of financial support (P. Hatanga, personal communication, 2013).

TABLE 10.9

Summary data for chimpanzee residents at Ngamba Island Sanctuary, 2012

Gender of residents		Year of arrival		Country of origin		Age at arrival		Catchment source	
Males	20	Before 1998	19	DRC	27	0–1*	11	Uganda*	35
Females	28	98–99	4	Uganda*	18	2–4	26	Sudan	4
Total	48	00–01	8	Rwanda	1	>4	10	Europe	3
		02–03*	6	Unknown	1			Burundi	2
		04–05	0					DRC	2
		06–07	4					Tanzania	1
		08–09	2						
		10–11	0						
		2012	4						

* Does not account for one live birth on site

CASE STUDY 2

Borneo Orangutan Survival Foundation (BOSF), Central and East Kalimantan, Indonesia[3]

Forest accounts for a significant (approx. 50%, 937 500 km²), but declining (-1.13% p.a. 2000–10), proportion of land in Indonesia. It has been an important part of the economy for many years, although patterns of extraction and trade have changed over time. Both legal and illicit markets have major impacts on forest cover and land use more generally, and thus the orangutans residing in affected habitats (Robertson and van Schaik, 2001; Nellemann et al., 2007; Lawson and MacFaul, 2010; Felbab-Brown, 2011; Wich et al., 2011; Felbab-Brown, 2013; Stiles et al., 2013; Vidal, 2013b). Importantly, deforestation is tied to multiple extractive industries in Indonesia, making it difficult to link larger trends to any single sector.

Wild populations of orangutans are found both within and outside of protected areas in Indonesia (Nellemann et al., 2007), and direct HWC involving orangutans is a well-known problem that has received considerable international media attention around conservation and consumer habits (Wich et al., 2011; Meijaard et al., 2012). Orangutans displaced by habitat conversion are often treated as pests, and may be trapped and brought to rescue centers or sanctuaries. Orangutans captured by workers or residents of nearby communities following conflict are subject to seizure by authorities, and if they survive, would be candidates for placement at a sanctuary if they cannot be re-released immediately. In addition to wild populations, some facilities house rescued orangutans where they undergo veterinary care and rehabilitation for re-release. In cases of injury or illness that prevents reintroduction, specialized facilities and programs provide long-term care (e.g. BOSF, 2012).

Indonesia's strategic plan aims for the re-release of all orangutans (Ministry of Forestry, 2009b). While some animals might be able to return to the wild right away or after minor veterinary care, others require a period of more extensive rehabilitation or skills training to ensure that they can survive in the wild. BOSF was established in the 1990s with the primary aim of keeping orangutans in their natural habitat. BOSF also operates rehabilitation and reintroduction programs that return confiscated or surrendered orangutans to the forest through translocation or reintroduction programs. Only a small number of orangutans are long-term residents; those orangutans that are ineligible for release because of their health status are provided with lifetime care.

A 2012 report on BOSF's Samboja Lestari orangutan re-release program emphasized three criteria for successful release (Preuschoft and Nente, 2012):

1. That the orangutans have learnt the skills needed to survive and thrive in the forest. These skills are not instinctual for the orangutan; they must be learnt.

2. That the released orangutans will not infect the wild population with dangerous transmittable diseases, including diseases that can affect both humans and orangutans (zoonoses).

3. That the forest they are released into is secure and the orangutans can remain safe from further human threat in the future.

Between 1991 and 2012, more than 650 orangutans were released or translocated from BOSF rehabilitation centers. The smaller program at Nyaru Menteng released 44 orangutans and translocated an additional 190 orangutans. The larger program, Samboja Lestari, released 422 orangutans and translocated 41 orangutans. In accordance with the strategic plan, release efforts have been building momentum in recent years. In 2012 BOSF re-released 44 orangutans in Central Kalimantan and another 6 in East Kalimantan. As of February 2013, 20 more orangutans had been re-released, with plans for 100 more within the year. Efforts to ensure safety are enhanced via post-release monitoring, which is becoming an increasingly important component of the BOSF programs.

Even with this ambitious re-release schedule, demand for sanctuary space and services is substantial. In early 2013, approximately 820 orangutans were present in the BOSF reintroduction programs in Central and East Kalimantan. Arrival rates at orangutan sanctuaries have been a concern for many years and currently far outpace those at sanctuaries for African apes (Farmer, 2002; Stiles et al., 2013).

For BOSF and its facilities, a primary strategy for working with extractive industries is the promotion of BMPs, which include oil palm, forestry, and mining sectors. The BMPs address both prevention and mitigation efforts that ideally are undertaken in cooperation with other companies and with conservation organizations, such as BOSF. Some BMPs include land and wildlife management efforts, such as:

- Surveying private concessions and locating areas supporting significant biodiversity. Such areas should be allocated and restored if necessary to serve as conservation areas protecting viable habitat for wildlife, including orangutans.

- Collaborating with neighboring companies and organizations to maintain or create corridors, connecting conservation areas with those in other concessions, as well as with nearby protected areas.

If a private company has intact forest BOSF could partner with the company to evaluate the habitat and determine if it is possible for resident orangutans to remain in the forest over time (J. Sihite, personal communication, February 2013). If there are no resident orangutans in a private forest, but that habitat is suitable for orangutans, there is the potential to use BMP to re-introduce orangutans into the forest. The aim is to have the companies voluntarily implement BMP and work in partnership with rescue centers and other industry and conservation partners to sustain orangutan populations on private land.

While BMPs can potentially prevent or reduce impacts on orangutans, this is not always possible. For example, there can be concessions where there is no suitable area for conservation, where the resident orangutan population is not viable, and/or pressure from surrounding communities is not sustainable. In such cases, a company would conduct rescue and translocation of those individuals to ensure their introduction into safe, suitable natural habitat at some other location, potentially after seeking input from the government or in consultation with government officials (J. Sihite, personal communication, February 2013).

Where these cases are directly linked to a particular company, involvement can entail more than the voluntary BMPs. For example, if orangutans arrive from a specific company at one of the BOSF centers, the company could offer to pay for care and treatment costs (J. Sihite, personal communication, February 2013). Such support can be temporary, i.e. lasting until the orangutans are re-released. If individuals are ineligible for re-release because of health status or other factors and long-term residency is required, company financial support could also take the form of lifetime care costs. This sort of financial support is viewed as a company's responsibility to the orangutans. Importantly, support for specific displaced orangutans is distinct from voluntary donations through adoptions (BOSF, 2012) or other charitable giving by companies and individuals who do not have a direct role in habitat conversion or HWC (J. Sihite, personal communication, February 2013).

Sanctuary challenges specific to Indonesia

Site selection for the final re-release of rehabilitated orangutans is especially impacted by extractive industry vis-à-vis the availability of habitat. As forest is shrinking, there are fewer and fewer options for such sites because of the two-fold space requirement:

- First, there must be a pre-release area without resident orangutans for outgoing quarantine to manage the risk to the re-release candidates.
- Second, there should be a distinct release forest for post-quarantine animals to minimize infection risk from re-release candidates.

The present rates of habitat conversion are so extreme that it will become increasingly difficult to find new sites that can provide optimal size and configuration for both pre-release health quarantine and re-release forest areas.

The mining of coal, for example, provides an illustration of how extractive industry could have a wide range of effects relevant for apes: immediate–long-term, localized–international, and direct–secondary–indirect. Through various direct and indirect effects associated with water – demand on water resources, flooding secondary to deforestation, and pollutants such as sulfates that pose risks to people and/or animals – coal mining operations can impact both the immediate vicinity and wider surrounding areas (Voorhar and Myllyvirta, 2013, pp. 45–46; Van Paddenburg et al., 2012). In the long term, the effects of increased CO_2 emissions from growing coal consumption (domestic and exports), which is expected to increase dramatically in Indonesia by 2020 (Voorhar and Myllyvirta, 2013), could be further compounded by deforestation from other mining and other extractive industries.

Conclusion

The patterns and impacts of extractive industries are complex. While direct and indirect effects for wild populations have been documented, and research continues to suggest where the greatest challenges and opportunities lie for industry partnerships to serve conservation, few studies have been undertaken on the impacts of extractive industries on sanctuaries per se. Given their vital role in combatting the illegal ape trade – education, prevention, alternative sustainable livelihoods, law enforcement partnerships, ape care and rehabilitation, and even re-release to the wild – such data gaps could slow progress in the long run.

A growing body of data indicates that the illegal ape trade is associated with extractive industries, and that these same industries can take a proactive role in reducing harm and protecting apes if they so choose or where such efforts are mandated or incentivized. This is not to say that the solutions are simple. More data are needed, and it is imperative to make progress on implementing BMPs with a wide range of extractive industries (e.g. Morgan and Sanz, 2007; Morgan et al., 2013). Evaluation and monitoring will continue to be vital tools for linking these practices to outcomes that are positive for ape conservation and protection.

Wildlife conservation organizations have called for greater involvement of CITES (e.g. TRAFFIC, 2010) and appear to envision an even larger role for the future (CITES, 2013b). Multilateral agreements and resolutions on ape protection vis-à-vis extractive industries do not always acknowledge the value and growing role of sanctuaries, while others do so explicitly. For example, key sections of the 2009 Frankfurt Declaration on Gorilla Conservation directly and indirectly impact sanctuaries. The role of mining, energy and other extractive industries is highlighted throughout the Declaration, with the most significant item involving explicit demand for sanctuary space and services:

> 5. Call upon states to combat illegal trade through the confiscation of illegally held live gorillas and ensure their repatriation into sanctuaries in their country of origin in cooperation with CITES. (Frankfurt Declaration, p. 3)

Thus, as range and donor states and industries respond to calls for action, sanctuaries need to be at the table as vital stakeholders. The impacts on and the needs of sanctuaries are vital for planning, logistics, and funding of such programs. One risk is in failing to anticipate and plan for the impacts on sanctuaries as a distinct component in overall conservation and protection planning. For example, a failure to provide for the capacity of sanctuaries or inadequate accounting for space and services could be detrimental to rescue as well as larger protection efforts. While animal rescue and welfare has not been a traditional conservation concern, it nevertheless has a role that must be appreciated, supported, and acknowledged, with the facilities themselves seen as a tool for conservation goals.

For policy, law enforcement, and rapid change in industry practices to turn things around, rescue centers and sanctuaries also need to be strong. These facilities and organizations need sustainable funding and other support to expand their capacity – infrastructure, human capacity, systems – to serve the apes in their charge and be a partner in the preservation and protection of apes. Sanctuaries and rescue centers also need and deserve a seat at the table wherever the future of apes is on the agenda; as stakeholders in the protection of apes and their habitats, they have invaluable insight and knowledge to share and they are an essential part of the solutions.

Whether we consider a population of apes losing the last of their habitat, an isolated individual hidden away as a pet, or a sanctuary full of rescued apes, our ultimate goal is to protect them. Protection requires a shared, global ethos that values apes and is based on respect for apes in their own right wherever they happen to be. Emphasizing the intrinsic value of the apes in captivity, and the interdependencies and shared risks facing apes in captivity and in their natural habitats positively reflects such an ethical foundation.

Acknowledgments

Principal authors: Debra Durham and Adam Phillipson

Endnotes

1   http://dpcpsi.nih.gov/council/working_group.aspx

2   https://s3.amazonaws.com/public-inspection.federalregister.gov/2013-14007.pdf

3   All data in this section via J. Sihite, personal communication, February 2013 or BOSF, 2012 except as cited

Annex I

Summary of PS6 Habitat types (IFC, 2012)

Modified habitat

The IFC defines modified habitat as habitat with a large proportion of non-native species and areas whose ecological functions and species composition have been substantially modified by human activity. PS6 will apply to modified areas only if they contain biodiversity "of significance to conservation" as identified under PS1. PS6 requires clients to "minimize impact" and implement mitigation measures on modified habitat "as appropriate."

Natural habitat

PS6 defines natural habitat as areas with "viable assemblages of plant and/or animal species of largely native origin, and/or where human activity has not essentially modified an area's primary ecological functions and species compositions." Clients operating in Natural Habitat must not "significantly convert or degrade" the area unless no other viable project location exists in the region, stakeholder consultations have been held regarding the degradation, "adequate" conservation measures will occur on the project site, and conversion or degradation is mitigated according to the mitigation hierarchy. The objective for natural habitat is to achieve no net loss of biodiversity "where feasible."

Critical habitat

Critical Habitat (CH) is the most important designation from the perspective of protection of critically endangered and endangered species. CH can exist in either natural habitat or modified habitat and is defined as those areas that are of "significant importance to Critically Endangered and/or Endangered Species." PS6 establishes that a client will not implement project activities in CH unless there will be net gains in the biodiversity values for which the CH was designated and the project will not lead to "a net reduction in the global and/or national/regional population of any Critically Endangered or Endangered species over a reasonable period of time." Clients may use the mitigation hierarchy, including offsets to satisfy the "net reduction" requirement.

Annex II

Summary of reported great ape densities and forest management policies across equatorial Africa (courtesy of D. Morgan and C. Sanz)

	Indicators of forest management			Ape indicators		
Location Logging concession	Implementation of RIL practices/timber removed (m³/ha or stems/ha)	Hunting pressure (signs/km)	Pristine forest (ind/km²)	Production forest (ind/km²) (* = no hunting)	% Difference in ape density
Campo, Cameroon[a]	No (1.9–4.8 m³/ha)	High (0.93–2.9)	1.1 chimpanzees –	0.54 chimpanzees 0.2 gorillas	-51% chimpanzees
Ntonga, Cameroon[b]	No	Low	–	1.1 chimpanzees 3.8 gorillas	
Dzanga, CAR[c] Sylvico	No (1–2 stems/ha)	Medium (1.6)	–	1.67 gorillas	
Kabo, Rep. of Congo Kabo UFA[d]	Yes	Low (0.2)	1.4 chimpanzees 1.8 gorillas	1.3 chimpanzees 1.8 gorillas	-7% chimpanzees 0% gorillas
			1.03 chimpanzees 1.02 gorillas	0.39 chimpanzees 2.16 gorillas	-62% chimpanzees +112% gorillas
			6.2 chimpanzees 3.1 gorillas	1.7, 1.9* chimpanzees 1.7, 2.4* gorillas	-73%, -69% chimpanzees -45%, -23% gorillas
			0.29 chimpanzees 1.92 gorillas	0.24 chimpanzees 1.57 gorillas	-17% chimpanzees -18% gorillas
Lopé, Gabon[e] Soforga–Lutexfo	No (2 stems/ha)	Low	1.1 chimpanzees 0.4 gorillas	0.2 chimpanzees 0.7 chimpanzees 0.3 gorillas 0.5 gorillas 0.3 gorillas	-82% chimpanzees -36% chimpanzees -25% gorillas +25% gorillas -25% gorillas
Petit Loango, Gabon[f]	No	Low	0.97 chimpanzees 0.05 gorillas	0.52 chimpanzees 1.25 gorillas	+46% chimpanzees +2400% gorillas
Budongo, Uganda[g] N15, KP11–13 (pristine) B4, N3,N11,W21,B1,K4 (production)	No (19.9–80.0 m³/ha)		3.0 chimpanzees 2.8 chimpanzees 1.7 chimpanzees 3.2 chimpanzees	1.5 chimpanzees 1.5 chimpanzees 1.1 chimpanzees 2.3 chimpanzees	-47% chimpanzees -46% chimpanzees -35% chimpanzees -28% chimpanzees
Kibale, Uganda[h]	No (14.4–20.9 m³/ha)		1.9 chimpanzees	0.9 chimpanzees (9.5–11 years since logging) 0.4 chimpanzees (10–13 years since logging) 0.1 chimpanzees (11–16 years since logging)	-53% chimpanzees -79% chimpanzees -95% chimpanzees
Kalinzu, Uganda[i]		Low	3.46 chimpanzees 2.28 chimpanzees 4.19 chimpanzees	4.92 chimpanzees 3.74 chimpanzees 5.70 chimpanzees	+43% chimpanzees +64% chimpanzees +36% chimpanzees

[a] Matthews and Matthews (2004)

[b] Dupain *et al.* (2004)

[c] Remis (2000)

[d] This study, Clark *et al.* (2009), Poulsen *et al.* (2011), Stokes *et al.* (2010)

[e] White (1992), White and Tutin (2001)

[f] Furuichi *et al.* (1997)

[g] Plumptre and Reynolds (1996)

[h] Skorupa (1988), Johns and Skorupa (1987)

[i] Hashimoto (1995).

Note: Percentage difference in ape density was calculated by dividing the density estimate in production forest by the density estimate in pristine forest, and subtracting the resulting percentage from 1. Negative values indicate percent decrease in ape density between pristine and secondary forest. Positive values indicate increases in ape density within secondary forests compared to logged forests.

For Campo, density estimates for pristine forest are represented by NP 2 (southeastern part of the National Park) and NP DI (Dipikar Island in the National Park), with production forest represented by surveys in Lc 1–4 (logging concessions) and NP 1 (southwestern part of the National Park). Also, the gorilla density estimate for Campo represents surveys conducted within the national park and the adjacent logging concession.

Hunting sign encounter rates and density estimates for Dzanga are represented by the Mabongo Reserve estimates.

Density estimates from Loango include both coastal and interior habitats. Gorilla density estimates are based on 53.6-day lifespan of nest. Although the increase in gorilla density at Loango is dramatic (2500%), the resulting density estimate of 1.25 gorillas per square kilometers is within the range of gorilla densities reported from the region (Morgan *et al.*, 2006).

The four density estimates from Budongo represent the standing crop (exponential and standard methods), marked nest method, and chimpanzees seen.

Density estimates from Kalinzu represent different sampling methods (Methods I, II, and III as described in Hashimoto, 1995).

Annex III

Specific recommendations for responsible management of apes in the extractive industry sector (after Dennis *et al.*, 2010a, 2010b)

These recommendations were developed specifically for orangutans and gibbons, however they are applicable to all apes in relation to extractive industries and have therefore been edited for the management of all ape species.

The overall objectives of these recommendations are improved prospects for ape survival in mining concessions and enhanced business value for companies. Companies should seek to minimize their impact on apes in their sphere of influence. This can be achieved through careful planning and application of best management practices (BMPs), improving and increasing ape habitat set-asides within concessions and offsets outside their concessions, and participation in conservation efforts in the greater landscape in collaboration with other local, regional, and national actors. The threats to apes are very similar and mitigation efforts should, therefore, apply to all species with minimal need for adaptation.

Positive and negative impacts on apes in the long term will depend on how well a company:

■ Understands the ecological and behavioral requirements of the relevant ape species, especially for shelter, space, food, and both social structure and space.

■ Recognizes the potential threats to apes from operational practices during phases of exploration, construction, production and closure.

■ Identifies and manages potential biodiversity risks and opportunities during project development, implementation and closure.

Ideally, operations should be planned to avoid disturbance of ape habitat, including corridors that are used to connect areas of natural forest within the concession. However, these practical and technical considerations may result in the realization that disturbance is recognized but unavoidable. For example, a concession may have a few apes remaining in patches of vegetation that are too small and are unconnected to other patches of habitat suitable for apes. In these situations, apes will not survive within the concession. This may lead to the conclusion that the least favored solution may have to be applied to conserve them, namely to have them translocated to another area. Responsible companies may then consider purchasing suitable land for these apes near their concessions as a conservation offset and translocating the surviving apes to this offset area. In this way, companies will help ensure that overall numbers of apes are not diminished in their general area of operations.

Corporate commitments

Commitment #1: corporate commitment to protect apes

A company requires support at all levels to achieve best management practices that ensure the long-term survival of apes in its concession. To assist with this, it should:

1.1 Commit to the goals and objectives of the government regulations, legislation, and objectives with regard to ape conservation

Scope

Governmental legal frameworks, such as the Orangutan Action Plan in Indonesia, are the basis for activities to conserve apes. These require all companies with a stake in the management of apes to support actions for the conservation and management of apes and their habitats.

Actions recommended

A company should commit to the goals and objectives of national ape commitments and any government policies that follow from that. The company should incorporate its commitment to the government goals into its policy, procedures, and operational management plans by taking the following actions:

- Develop and implement an ape-sensitive conservation management plan within its concession.
- Develop standard operating procedures for the protection of apes and their habitats (including habitat management, rescue activities, conflict mitigation, and community involvement).
- Contribute to community education and development activities that are conducive to the conservation of apes and ape habitat.
- Build and maintain corridors between fragmented patches of ape habitat within and adjacent to its concession, where possible.
- Develop a monitoring and evaluation system to assess the impact of its conservation management plan.
- Ensure operations minimize negative impacts on apes and their habitat.
- Collaborate with other stakeholders to conserve apes at the landscape level.

1.2 Make a publicly available policy statement for the protection of apes

Scope

A company should demonstrate full transparency in the implementation of its ape-sensitive conservation management plan by publicly demonstrating that it is adhering to the principles of best management practices.

Actions recommended

- Commitment to minimize impacts on apes in the landscape.
- Commitment to adhere to national and internationally binding regulations.
- Commitment to make public its data and information on apes, and its monitoring and operational actions to conserve apes.
- Commitment to respect customary indigenous rights and legal requirements.
- Commitment to engage with communities and stakeholders in a fair and transparent manner.
- Commitment to identify and consider all threats to apes that may result from the company's strategic management decisions.

1.3 Ensure that apes are sensitively managed within the concession

Scope

A company should consult with experts, nongovernmental organizations (NGOs) and other stakeholder groups to work towards maintaining the ape populations within its concession.

Actions recommended

- Implement silvicultural and other types of habitat management approaches and techniques to minimize the impact of these activities on areas used by apes.
- Protect key ecological resources for apes in both conservation set-asides and habitat corridors.
- Work to prevent hunting of apes by company employees, contractors, and others.

1.4 Report to international standards on ape status and management in concessions

Scope

A company should employ transparent and timely reporting to demonstrate to stakeholders and the environmental community that biodiversity within the scope of its management area is monitored, evaluated and protected. A company should include information on apes in its environmental reports where its operations are located in ape sensitive areas. While adherence to these standards is voluntary, compliance with these standards enhances a company's external transparency and responsibility in managing its impacts on apes, and serves as an internal guide on its performance against stated corporate ape policies. Reporting to these guidelines is in addition to any formal government environmental reporting requirements. For example, all mining companies that adhere to the International Council for Mining and Metals (ICMM) Sustainable Development Framework resolve to follow the Global Reporting Initiative (GRI) standards on sustainability reporting (http://www.icmm.com/our-work/sustainable-development-framework/public-reporting).

Actions recommended

A company should comply with internationally accepted standards for biodiversity reporting, namely:

- Collect all information on its concession relevant to the development of BMPs.
- Document and describe significant threats to biodiversity within its concession. Gather and make publicly available information on locations where apes occur, using GPS if possible. This should include relative abundance estimates, and their key ecological resources and nest sites. Information on habitat types should be divided between natural, created and enhanced, and artificial (new habitats), by area and known ape presence.
- Detail strategies, current actions, and future plans for managing threats to biodiversity and apes.

Commitment #2: compliance with laws and regulations

A company should demonstrate compliance with laws (both statutory and customary), regulations, international treaties, and agreements to which the relevant ape range state is a signatory. To demonstrate this, a company should:

2.1 Respect national and local laws and administrative requirements related to biodiversity protection

Scope

A company should comply with relevant laws and regulations that have implications for apes and their habitats. In addition, a company should be aware of any provincial or district laws and regulations that apply in the location of its operations. A company should also ensure that all required permits are obtained and updated. For example, the national laws of Indonesia and Malaysia that are relevant include, but are not limited to, the following recommended actions.

Actions recommended

- Be familiar with and make available a document summarizing central government, provincial, and district laws and regulations relevant to apes and their habitats, and possible implications of these on planning and operational decisions, and on the conduct of employees and contractors.
- Conduct a communication program to ensure that senior management is in a position to consider these legal issues and comply with the law when making decisions.
- Conduct a communication program for employees and contractors that ensures that their actions when dealing with apes and their habitat comply with the law.
- Develop a documented system to identify, track, close out and report on issues relating to potential legal non-compliance by the company, employees, and contractors.
- Ensure all permits that relate to activities that may impact ape habitat are maintained in a permits register.
- Publicize legal requirements and obligations to all employees and contractors on an annual basis as part of work reviews.
- Develop procedures for compliance assessments and demonstrate internal enforcement and penalties in the event of identified breaches of law.
- Instigate an internal reward and punishment system for employees and contractors to promote compliance.

2.2. Comply with the provisions of all binding international agreements that relate to ape protection

Scope

A company should not only be in compliance with national laws and regulations but also meet the intent of international agreements and conventions to which the relevant ape range state is a signatory. For example, the international agreements that relate to the protection of orangutans are as follows:

- Convention on Biodiversity (ratified through Act No. 5 of 1994).
- Kinshasa Declaration of Great Apes.
- CITES.
- Tropical Timber 83.
- Tropical Timber 94.
- Ramsar Convention.

Actions recommended

A company should disseminate requirements within these conventions and international agreements to all employees and contractors where relevant, and should demonstrate how these provisions have been incorporated within operational planning and management, namely:

- Be familiar with and make available a document summarizing international conventions relevant to apes and their habitats and possible implications of these on planning and operational decisions, and on the conduct of employees.
- Ensure that all employees and contractors are aware of and understand the legal and administrative obligations in respect to relevant international agreements to which the relevant ape range state is a signatory.
- Conduct a communication program to ensure that senior management is in a position to consider these issues when making decisions.
- Conduct an employee communications program that ensures that their actions when dealing with apes and their habitat comply with these conventions.

2.3 Ensure that ape habitat is protected from illegal and unauthorized activities

Scope

A company should protect its ape habitat from unauthorized harvesting and other activities in the concession. It should strive to have sufficient security and protection systems, and capacity to support compliance with its ape-sensitive conservation management plan. Conservation set-aside areas should be delineated from operations at the planning stage due to the presence of rare, threatened, or endangered plant and/or animal species.

Actions recommended

- Identify and assess threats and practical interventions to reduce or eliminate threats.
- Standardize approaches for demarcation of conservation set-asides and notify local stakeholders of these boundaries.
- Consider the establishment of forest patrols by local community members and forest police across the concession. This is to identify and combat encroachment, fire risk, illegal activities, and other issues.
- Ensure a system exists for monitoring, documenting, and reporting to appropriate authorities any instances of illegal harvesting, settlement, occupation or other unauthorized activities.

2.4 Clearly document local communities' long-term legal or customary ownership and use rights to the land, where these rights exist

Scope

A company should show commitment to long-term ownership and use rights of local communities to the land and forest resources inside or bordering concessions. The land use rights should be clearly defined, documented, and respected.

Actions recommended

- Document evidence of legal, long-term rights to manage lands and to utilize forest resources over any part of the concession.

- These rights should be agreed to by local communities with evidence of this consent.

- To ensure cooperation of local communities and secondary stakeholders is maintained, a mechanism should be employed to resolve disputes which also documents the nature of the dispute and its resolution, particularly as it relates to apes and their habitat.

2.5 Respect local communities' legal or customary ownership and use rights while protecting apes

Scope

A company should respect the rights of local communities with legal or customary ownership or use rights to maintain control over these aspects in concessions, to the extent required for them to protect these rights and meet their economic and cultural needs. Where possible, a company should engage these communities in forest management and protection of apes.

Actions recommended

- Identify and support sustainable use of resources by local communities and take steps to ensure that customary and other rights are upheld.

- Recognize and support these use rights, which should be clearly identified, demarcated and recorded using participatory approaches.

- Support formalization of use rights through a local decree.

- Give free, prior, and informed consent (FPIC) to use rights of local communities or affected parties.

- Where appropriate, include participation of local communities or parties with legal or customary tenure or use rights in the management planning of concession forests.

- Create mechanisms for resolving disputes over land use claims and use rights that respectfully involve disputants so as to reduce the risk of conflicts endangering apes.

Commitment #3: management planning and monitoring of apes

A company should ensure that apes within the concession are sensitively managed. This requires the development, implementation and monitoring of an ape-sensitive conservation management plan. This plan should be integrated and form part of the overall environmental management plan. This will ensure that the long-term objectives of management, and the means of achieving them, will be clearly stated and monitored. To this end, a company should:

3.1 Ensure that a comprehensive ape conservation management plan is developed that is in line with best management practices

Scope

The basis for a good extractive industry operation is a well-planned and comprehensive conservation management plan that addresses the need to maintain, enhance, and protect conservation set-aside areas and general biodiversity values. The general guidelines for best practice in environmental management systems are covered by ISO 14001. A company's ape conservation management plan is considered satisfactory if corporate policy and objectives on ape protection are incorporated into environmental policy and management systems that strive for this standard. The conservation management plan needs to be appropriate to the scope and scale of operations and should clearly explain the long-term objectives of management, and the means of achieving them. One of the long-term objectives should be the protection of apes and their habitat in the area surrounding the concession.

Actions recommended

A conservation management plan should be developed that includes but is not limited to the following:

- The aim, goals, and objectives of the plan should be clearly described in relation to the conservation of apes.
- The plan should include a clear description of the forest areas to be managed, environmental issues, land-use patterns, ownership status, socioeconomic conditions, and a profile of adjacent lands.
- The long-term silvicultural and other management systems should be clearly described and justified in relation to the requirements of any resident apes.
- The plan should clearly show how rare, threatened, and endangered species and/or their habitat are to be identified and protected. It should include all measures planned for the protection of apes in a concession, and identify habitat corridors to facilitate movement of apes around the edge of a concession (if possible) and to and from the greater landscape.
- The plan should have a full complement of maps. These maps need to describe the forest resources including forest types, watercourses and drains, compartments/blocks, roads, log landings and processing sites, protected areas, unique biological or cultural resources, and other planned management activities. They should also clearly map the distribution of apes in the concession and the immediate adjacent forest, food sources, key ecological resources such as old fruiting trees and mineral licks, and identification of biological corridors.
- The plan needs to cover all environmental safeguards that will be used to ensure the integrity of the forest concession and apes in the concession. These safeguards need to be based on a process of environmental assessments (in Indonesia referred to as the AMDAL (*Analisis dampak lingkungan*)), with clear reference as to how any adverse impacts on apes will be mitigated through management practices. Special attention should be paid to measures undertaken to reduce human–wildlife conflict.
- The plan needs to have a robust monitoring strategy for all aspects of management, including apes. Where appropriate, all monitoring results specifically relating to apes should be reported back to the government so that its databases can be kept up-to-date, and to allow the government to assess progress, in Indonesia for example, in the Orangutan Action Plan.
- There should be detailed emergency response procedures for issues concerning ape encroachments, conflicts, disease, and other possible incidents. A hazard/incident reporting system should be established that documents issues, actions, follow-up, and closeout of ape matters.
- The plan needs to include a full budget for all operations and planning. The budget needs to include a sufficient allocation to cover the cost of operations to conserve apes.
- The plan should be linked to a database system for storing information on apes. Preferably, this should be a map-based system to enable comparisons of locations of apes so that their movements within the concession can be mapped. It is important that the results of ape monitoring are incorporated into the implementation and revision of the plan. Non-confidential elements of the plan should be made public.

The plan should detail rehabilitation of ape habitat both inside the concession and in surrounding areas, which should be undertaken where possible. Other ecological and operational measures should include:

- Retention of large trees, for nesting and fruit, in areas surrounding planted parts of a concession.
- Closure of canal systems in rehabilitation sites and canals that bisect conservation areas.
- Monitoring of permanent sample plots for edge impacts within conservation set-asides.
- Monitoring of community access.
- Monitoring of rehabilitation planting through permanent sample plots.
- Monitoring of external boundaries of conservation areas, and of boundaries adjoining harvesting locations.
- Expansion of riparian habitats to a minimum of 500 m either side of river banks (mineral soil sites) in locations inhabited by apes, and linking them to conservation set-asides and adjacent forest outside the concession.

When planning for rehabilitation, additional actions for land preparation may have to be conducted due to compaction or degradation as a result of infrastructure development. Due to the time delay in fruiting from seedling stock, the use of cutting stock is recommended, where feasible. Many tree species used by apes for food, however, are non-commercial and may not be available. Monitoring should be instigated to support management objectives. This will be particularly important when trees are producing fruit to prevent conflict between humans and apes over the harvest of such fruit.

Selection of species for rehabilitation of important ape habitat should be based on ecological characteristics (e.g. known ape food source, food source for other species, fast growing, native to area, and soil type). Generally, rehabilitation planting should use mixed tree species spaced at intervals of approximately 2–5 m. However, in some instances planting of trees unpalatable to apes may be required as a barrier to deflect them from moving deeper into a plantation. This may also include plantings trees that are particularly favored as nesting sites by apes. All available open areas should be investigated for rehabilitation, including but not limited to:

- Roadsides of access and operational roads.
- Drainage system edges.
- Post-operational log landing sites, sites used for vehicle turning, etc.

3.2 Identify a point person or team to take the lead in coordinating activities related to the management of apes

Scope

A company should elect one person or a team to take responsibility for the management of all ape conservation activities. This person or team needs to be placed within the management structure and should have sufficient authority to influence crucial management decisions.

Actions recommended

- Clearly assign roles and responsibilities for information dissemination and the implementation of management strategies to conserve apes.
- Develop job descriptions that state the roles and responsibilities for internal and external communications.
- Ensure that the person or team responsible for ape management has access to all key information regarding concession planning, and is involved in management decisions regarding activities or plans that potentially affect apes.

3.3 Create and conduct a training and education program for all employees and contractors on the importance of conservation of apes

Scope

A company should ensure that responsibility for conservation of apes and their habitat is the collective responsibility of management and all employees and contractors. To achieve this there is a need to disseminate this notion through direct education. The company should conduct awareness raising and educational actions with employees and contractors on the importance of ape conservation and management. These approaches should include but not be limited to information on legal status and penalties within employment contracts and contract agreements for identified breaches of contract; the natural history of the relevant ape species and its/their ecological requirements; company policy on the conservation of apes and wider biodiversity; and HR policy and disciplinary processes and procedures in place for operational requirements to mitigate risks to apes from operational workers.

Actions recommended

- Identify training needs to ensure the competencies of employees and contractors with responsibilities related to apes.
- Prepare and periodically conduct training for responsible employees and contractors, including community relations staff.
- Identify and train, in collaboration with qualified wildlife management personnel, specific personnel who have responsibility for emergency responses to ape issues. Ape issues, actions, and responsibilities should also be included in the induction for employees, contractors, and visitors.

■ Develop information and brochures for use by all employees, contractors, and visitors identifying the company's responsibilities, strategies and actions with regard to ape conservation. All employees and contractors should have a copy of such standard operational procedures (for details, see 3.5) and be instructed in the use of these procedures.

3.4 Ensure that all monitoring and evaluation is incorporated into a long-term adaptive conservation management plan

Scope

A company should demonstrate the operation of management review systems to ensure that lessons from past actions and experiences, or external factors such as new scientific knowledge on the relevant ape species, are incorporated into updated conservation management plans.

Actions recommended

■ Establish a mechanism to review the company's ape policy and management systems regularly so that they may be adapted to any changes in perceptions or circumstances.

■ Develop a program and procedure for periodic audits of the ape management systems. This would be incorporated into the certification process of companies complying with ISO 14001. Companies not certified to this standard can follow self-assessment guidelines based on ISO principles.

■ Seek new information from all stakeholders, including security agencies, local communities, local government agencies, and the scientific community, to ensure that revised conservation management plans incorporate the best technical practices, knowledge and experiences.

■ Carry out a periodic review of the plan, its objectives, systems and results, to ensure its appropriateness and effectiveness in ape conservation, both on site and within the greater landscape.

■ Identify any changes required to policies and procedures in light of any developments in technical or scientific issues in conservation of the relevant ape species, changes in species viability at the landscape level, and any other legal, business, or financial considerations.

■ Update policies and procedures to accommodate the findings of such a review so as to ensure continual improvement in approaches to conserve apes, and enhance corporate environmental responsibility.

■ Incorporate any results of this review into the planning and operational management of the concession, including review of closure plans and actions.

■ Document and communicate to employees any changes to the conservation management plan and operational procedures.

3.5 Develop standard operating procedures, work instructions and guidelines to support implementation of the conservation management plan for apes

Scope

A company should develop a clear and concise set of Standard Operating Procedures (SOPs) for individual activities in line with the principles and guidelines of its management. It should, at a minimum, ensure that SOPs are developed to encompass all operational actions that have a potential impact on apes and their habitat. This is required because generic company principles and guidelines are not in themselves sufficient to ensure that all operational activities are carried out consistently and in the manner required by the company.

Actions recommended

■ SOPs for operational activities that include dissemination of information to operation planners.

■ SOPs for standardized pre-operational assessment process (pre-land disturbance/land clearing) and post-operational assessment process (monitoring).

■ SOP for land disturbance and clearing to minimize forest damage during land clearing, road construction, and all other mechanical disturbances; and to protect water resources.

- SOP for routine biodiversity monitoring.

- SOP for managing and maintaining voluntary conservation set-aside areas and water resources within the concession, including guidance on retaining groves or individual large trees for nesting or fruiting.

- SOP for establishing and operating forest patrols in the concession.

- SOP for conducting environmental inductions for all employees, contractors, and casual staff.

- SOPs for community engagement and communication protocols, especially with regard to recognizing conflicts between communities and apes, and having standard practices to deal with these conflicts.

- SOPs for the issuance of information, and verification of information to operational planners, field staff and teams tasked with impacting operational activities.

- SOPs for rehabilitation and restoration of degraded areas.

- SOPs about what to do when ape encounters or incidents occur during land clearing, felling, road building, or other activities. These should include recommendations for staff behavior to prevent harm to the apes such as no unnecessary disturbance, no feeding, no felling of trees with apes in them, etc.

- SOPs for land swaps.

3.6 Communicate to local communities the importance of ape conservation and ways to mitigate threats to the species

Scope

A company should be proactive in its communications with communities that have settled within its concession and/or access biodiversity areas, corridors, or controlled habitats. It needs to work with communities to identify consensus-based mitigation or conflict resolution. For example, Indonesia's Orangutan Action Plan 2007 – 2017 (Ministry of Forestry, 2009b), section C1, clearly states that the inclusion of communities and their institutions and customary laws is paramount for the protection of orangutans.

Actions recommended

- Review the community development program to ensure that ape education and awareness activities are included, and that programs are included to take pressure off apes and their habitats through alternative livelihoods and economic activities.

- Prepare a documented process within the company's community development department to identify and engage with communities on ape matters, which should include a register of meetings, issues, agreements, actions, and follow-up.

- Develop systems for rapid reporting of conflicts between apes and people, and have management SOPs in place to mitigate these conflicts and prevent harm to apes and people's agricultural crops and gardens.

- Identify community benefits from ape conservation.

- Provide education to communities on how to mitigate perceived risks from apes.

3.7 Collaborate with conservation scientists and seek technical advice from them when required

Scope

A company should engage with conservation scientists and groups, or seek technical expertise from recognized academic institutions, qualified consultants, or government departments when decisions regarding interventions to conserve apes go beyond the company's scope of understanding or technical capabilities.

Actions recommended

- Obtain technical support for surveying apes, and store survey results in a Geographic Information System (GIS).

- Develop partnerships to review survey data and assess impacts of conservation actions annually.

- Develop partnerships for review of management planning proposals and gain additional input into that process.

- Facilitate studies of ape ecology in mining concessions by allowing local and international researchers to work in the concession, and use the resulting information to identify key features used by apes (old, large fruiting trees, mineral licks, specific nesting sites, etc.).

- If the apes' home range extends into neighboring concessions, collaborate with the management of these concessions and with ape specialists to develop greater landscape-level management plans to assist their conservation (see below).

Commitment #4: landscape-level collaborative management

A company should collaborate with other stakeholders to achieve improved planning and implementation of conservation management for apes in the greater landscape. To do so, the following are encouraged:

4.1 Participate in a landscape-level collaborative management group to rationalize land-use conflicts, that include apes and their habitat

Scope

Companies are encouraged to support landscape collaborative management groups. In Indonesia, this is also in accordance with Ministry of Forestry regulations. They can achieve this by allocating sufficient staff and financial resources to contribute to the following:

Actions recommended

- Assist in land-use planning for the greater landscape.

- Contribute to demarcation of concession boundaries.

- With other stakeholders, assist in the preparation of risk assessments and an ape conservation management plan for the landscape.

- Ensure that the company's on-site ape management plan supports landscape conservation management.

- Where possible, support scientific research concerning apes in the greater landscape.

- Share data, information, and reports on ape management with other partners.

- Collaborate with law enforcement agencies.

- Where possible, build capacity of partners to fulfill their responsibilities.

- Encourage and participate in the resolution of land disputes between the conflicting interests of other stakeholders in the greater landscape.

- Where possible, explore land swaps as an alternative to natural forest conversion or conversion of degraded forest inhabited by apes.

- With other stakeholders, support public awareness programs for ape conservation.

- With other stakeholders, support district, provincial, and national level planning to help improve biodiversity values in the greater landscape.

Acknowledgments

Authors: Erik Meijaard and Serge Wich

Acronyms and abbreviations

3TG	tin, tantalum, tungsten, and gold
A.P.E.S.	Ape Populations, Environments and Surveys
AAC	annual allowable cut
ACF	African Conservation Foundation
ADB	Asian Development Bank
AFD	Agence Française de Devéloppement
AfDB	African Development Bank
AFLEG	Africa Forest Law Enforcement and Governance
AMDAL	environmental impact assessment process (known in Indonesia as Analisis dampak lingkungan)
ANPN	National Parks Agency, Gabon (Agence Nationale des Parcs Nationaux)
APEC	Asia–Pacific Economic Cooperation
ARF	ASEAN Regional Forum
ARM	Alliance for Responsible Mining
ARTS	Adaptive Recce Transect Sampling
ASEAN	Association of Southeast Asian Nations
asl	above sea level
ASM	artisanal and small-scale mining
ATIBT	Association Technique Internationale des Bois Tropicaux
AU	African Union
AWA	Animal Welfare Act
AZA	Association of Zoos and Aquariums
BBOP	Business and Biodiversity Offsets Programme
BDEAC	Banque de Développement des Etats de l'Afrique Centrale
BMP	best management practices
BP	British Petroleum
BOSF	Borneo Orangutan Survival Foundation (based in Balikpapan)
CAR	Central African Republic
CARPE	Central African Regional Program for the Environment
CBD	Convention on Biological Diversity
CEMAC	Commission de la Communaute Economique et Monetaire de l'Afrique Centrale
CH	critical habitat (IFC definition – see Annex I)
CIB	Congolaise Industrielle du Bois
CICMH	Compagnie Industrielle et Commerciale des Mines Huazhou
CIFM	Mindourou Industrial and Forestry Centre
CIFOR	Centre for International Forestry Research
CITES	Convention on International Trade in Endangered Species of Wild Fauna and Flora
CNT	National Transition Council
Comibel	Compagnie Miniere de Belinga
COMIFAC	Regional support for the Central Africa Forests Commission
CR	critically endangered species (IUCN classification)
CSandWCT	Chimpanzee Sanctuary and Wildlife Conservation Trust
CSPD	Comité de suivi du processus de Durban
CSO	Civil society organization
CSR	corporate social responsibility

320

DBH	diameter at breast height
DFID	Department for International Development
DPD	Dewan Perwakilan Daerah (Indonesian Regional Representative Council)
DR	Dana Reboisasi (reforestation fund)
DRC	Democratic Republic of Congo
EARS	European Alliance of Rescue centres and Sanctuaries
EBRD	European Bank for Reconstruction and Development
ECOWAS	Economic Community of West African States
EIA	environmental impact assessment
EIB	European Investment Bank
EIR	WB Extractive Industries Review
EITI	Extractive Industries Transparency Initiative
EN	endangered species (IUCN classification)
ENAFLEG	Europe and North Asia Forest Law Enforcement and Governance
ENSO	El Niño Southern Oscillation
EOO	extent of occurrence
ESA	US Endangered Species Act
ESER	economically and socially responsible artisanal and small-scale mining
ESIA	environmental and social impact assessment
ESRI	Environmental Systems Research Institute
EU	European Union
FAO	Food and Agriculture Organization of the United Nations
FDI	foreign direct investment
FFEM	Fonds Français pour l'Environnement Mondial (French Global Environment Facility)
FLEGT	Forest Law Enforcement Governance and Trade Action Plan
FLO	Fairtrade International
FMP	forest management plan
FMU	forest management unit
FPIC	free prior and informed consent
FPP	Forest People's Program
FSC	Forest Stewardship Council
GDP	gross domestic product
GEF	Global Environment Facility
GFAS	Global Federation of Animal Sanctuaries
GHG	greenhouse gases
GIS	geographic information system
GPS	global positioning system
GRASP	UNEP's Great Apes Survival Partnership
GRI	Global Reporting Initiative
GTAP	Goualougo Triangle Ape Project
GTZ	Gesellschaft für Technische Zusammenarbeit (German Technical Cooperation enterprise)
HCV	high conservation value
HCVF	high conservation value forest
HDI	human development indicators
HTI	Hutan Tanaman Industri (industrial timber plantation)
HWC	human–wildlife conflict
IBA	important bird area
IBRD	International Bank for Reconstruction and Development (UN agency)
ICCM	International Council on Metals and Mining
ICCN	Institut Congolais pour la Conservation de la Nature (Congolese Wildlife Authority)
ICMM	International Council on Mining and Metals

ICSID	International Center for the Settlement of Investment Disputes
IDA	International Development Association
IDB	Inter-American Development Bank
IFC	International Finance Corporation
IFIA	Association Interafricaine des Industries Forestiéres
IIED	International Institute for Environment and Development
IMF	International Monetary Fund
Inpres	Instruksi Presiden (presidential instruction)
Interpol	International Criminal Police Organization
IOPP	industrial oil palm concessions
IPIECA	global oil and gas industry association for environmental and social issues
IPPKH	Izin Pinjam Pakai Kawasan Hutan (Forest Land Borrow and Use Permit)
ISIS	International Species Information System
ISO	International Organization for Standardization
ITP	industrial tree concessions
ITSO	International Technical Support Organization
ITTO	International Tropical Timber Organization
ITU	International Telecommunication Union (UN agency)
ITUC	International Trade Union Confederation
IUCN	International Union for Conservation of Nature
IUCN/SSC	IUCN Species Survival Commission
JGI	The Jane Goodall Institute
KBA	key biodiversity area
KBNP	Kahuzi-Biéga National Park
KLG	Kalimantan Gold Corporation Limited
KPC	PT Kaltim Prima Coal
KSK	Kalimantan Surya Kencana
Lao PDR	Lao People's Democratic Republic
LEI	Lembaga Ekolabel Indonesia (Indonesian timber certification)
LIPI	Lembaga Ilmu Pengetahuan Indonesia (Indonesian Institute of Sciences)
LSM	large-scale mining
MARPOL	International Convention for the Prevention of Pollution from Ships
MEE	Ministry of the Environment and Ecology, CAR
MEF (also MFE)	Republic of Congo – Ministry of Forest Economy (Ministère de l'Économie Forestière)
MEF	Gabon - Ministry of Water and Forests
MEPA	Mineral Exploration and Production Agreement
MGVP	Mountain Gorilla Veterinary Project
MH	modified habitat (IFC definition – see Annex I)
MIGA	Multilateral Investment Guarantee Agency
MINFOF	Ministry of Forestry and Wildlife (Ministère des Forêts et de la Faune), Cameroon
MMG	Minerals and Metals Group
MMSD	mining, minerals and sustainable development
MPI-EVAN	Max Planck Institute for Evolutionary Anthropology
MPR	People's Consultative Assembly (Majelis Permusyawaratan Rakyat)
MSG	multi-stakeholder group
NCI	non-compliance item
NGO	nongovernmental organization
NH	natural habitat (IFC definition – see Annex I)
NIH	National Institutes of Health

NIS	Ngamba Island Sanctuary
NNL	no net loss (of biodiversity)
NNNP	Nouabalé-Ndoki National Park
NP	national park
NPI	net positive impact (for biodiversity)
NTFP	non-timber forest product
OCSP	Orangutan Conservation Services Program
OIE	Office International des Epizooties (World Organization for Animal Health)
OoM	order of magnitude
PA	protected area
PACE	protected areas and critical ecosystems
PASA	Pan African Sanctuaries Alliance
PCI	Principles, Criteria and Indicators (in relation to BBOP)
PCLG	Poverty and Conservation Learning Group
PES	payment for ecosystem services
PFE	permanent forest estates
PNBP	Penerimaan Negara Bukan Pajak (non-tax state revenue)
PNCI	People and Nature Consulting International
PPP	purchasing power parity
PPWS	Phnom Prich Wildlife Sanctuary
PRADD	property rights and artisanal diamond development
PRI	political risk insurance
PROGEPP	Projet de Gestion des Ecosystémes Péripheriques du Parc
	(Project for Ecosystem Management in the periphery of Nouabalé-Ndoki National Park)
PROMINES	"Growth with Governance" in the mineral sector project
PS	performance standard (relates to the IFC)
PSDH	Provisi Sumber Daya Hutan (forest resource provision)
PSG	Primate Specialist Group
Ramsar	Convention on Wetlands of International Importance
REDD	Reducing Emissions from Deforestation and forest Degradation
REM	rare earth metals
RIL	reduced-impact logging
RNI	Itombwe Nature Reserve
RSPO	Round Table on Sustainable Palm Oil
SEA	Strategic Environmental Assessment
SEC	Suitable Environmental Conditions
SEMS	social and environmental management system
SFM	sustainable forest management
SGA	Section on Great Apes of the IUCN
SNBS	Société Nouvelle des Bois de la Sangha
SOP	safe operating procedure
SSC	Species Survival Commission
TNS	Sangha Trinational forest conservation area
TRIDOM	Tri-national Dja-Odzala-Minkébé landscape
UFA	Unité Forestière d'Aménagement (forest management unit)
UN	United Nations
UNCCD	United Nations Convention to Combat Desertification
UNCTAD	UN Conference on Trade and Development
UNDP	United Nations Development Programme

UNDRIP	United Nations Declaration on the Rights of Indigenous Peoples
UNEP	United Nations Environment Programme
UNESCO	United Nations Educational, Scientific and Cultural Organization
UNIDO	UN Industrial Development Organization
UN-REDD	United Nations Reducing Emissions from Deforestation and forest Degradation program
UNWTO	UN World Trade Organization
USAID	United States Agency for International Development
USDA	United States Department of Agriculture
USFWS	United States Fish and Wildlife Service
UWA	Uganda Wildlife Authority
UWEC	Uganda Wildlife Education Centre
Virunga NP	Virunga National Park
VPA	voluntary partnership agreements
VU	vulnerable
WB	World Bank
WBG	World Bank Group
WCD	World Commission on Dams
WCF	Wild Chimpanzee Foundation
WCMC	UNEP's World Conservation Monitoring Center
WCS	Wildlife Conservation Society
WHO	World Health Organization
WIPO	World Intellectual Property Organization
WRI	World Resources Institute
WTO	World Trade Organization
WWF	World Wide Fund for Nature (formerly World Wildlife Fund)
WWP	ZSL's Wildlife Wood Project
YTS	Yayasan Tambuhak Sinta
ZSL	Zoological Society of London

GLOSSARY

African Development Bank: Regional public bank devoted to developing the economy of countries on the continent.

Amalgamation: Mineral processing method which extracts gold from mined ore using mercury to create amalgam which is then decomposed leaving gold.

Anthropogenic: Resulting from humans or human activities.

Anthropozoonosis: An infectious disease/pathogen that can be transmitted from humans to non-human animals; also called anthroponosis. See also "Zoonosis".

Artisanal and small-scale mining: Mining conducted with rudimentary tools such as picks and shovels or simple machinery, usually informal or semi-formal individuals or small groups of people on a subsistence basis. The authors specifically note where ASM is occurring with more advanced mechanization.

Asian Development Bank: Regional public bank devoted to developing the economy of countries on the continent.

ASM: Artisanal and small-scale mining refers to the use of low-level technology and manual labor to extract minerals; conducted by individuals, groups and communities.

Biodiversity baselines: The synthesis of ecological data and research to form a line that will provide conservationists and policy-makers with a means of measuring future change.

Biodiversity offset: Conservation activities that are designed to give biodiversity benefits to compensate for losses caused by a development damaging an ecosystem in some way.

Bioethics: The study of ethics as it relates to advances in biology and medicine.

Biofuels: Fuels produced from living organisms, most often referring to plants or plant-derived materials; e.g. bioethanol, an alcohol made by the fermentation of carbohydrates in crops such as corn or sugarcane.

Biomarker: A measured characteristic, which may be used as an indicator of some biological state or condition.

Biomass: In ecology, the mass of living biological organisms in a given area of ecosystem at a given time. As a renewable energy source, the term refers to biological material derived from living or recently living organisms (see **Biofuels**).

Brachiate: A form of arboreal locomotion in which primates swing using only their arms.

Bushmeat: Meat from wild animals hunted in Africa and Asia (although particularly used to refer to meat from animals in West and Central Africa).

Cadastre: A comprehensive register of the property of the country, commonly including details of ownership, tenure, location, dimensions, and value.

Commons (short for "Tragedy of the commons"): The depletion of a shared resource by individuals, acting independently and rationally according to each one's self-interest, despite their understanding that depleting the common resource is contrary to the group's long-term best interests.

Conspecific: Member of the same species.

Corruptions Perception Index: An annual score formulated by Transparency International on how corrupt a country's public sector is seen to be.

Critical ecosystems: Ecologically rich areas, which include Areas of Zero extinction – of which there are only 587 in the world; protected areas, categories I to IV under the definitions of the International Union for Conservation of Nature (IUCN) and Ramsar sites; WWF priority landscapes, and the Global 200 Priority Eco-regions as described by Olson and Dinerstein (2002).

Cultural convergence: The notion that cultures will become increasingly similar over time.

Cultural hybridity: The notion that cultures will cross-pollinate upon contact to produce new hybrid forms.

Customary ownership: Land that is owned by local communities and administered in accordance with their customs, as opposed to statutory tenure usually introduced during the colonial periods.

Deciduous: Trees that lose their leaves for part of the year.

Development banks: Public banks set up by single or group of countries to facilitate sustainable development.

Dipterocarp: Trees of the family Dipterocarpaceae (prevalent in Asian tropical rainforests).

Ecosystem goods and services: The multitude of resources and processes supplied by ecosystems that humankind benefits from; e.g. the production of food and water, the control of climate and disease, and nutrient cycles and crop pollination. Such benefits accrue to all living organisms, including animals and plants, rather than to humans alone; however, there is a growing recognition of the importance to society that ecological goods and services provide for health, social, cultural, and economic needs.

Enrichment: The practice of providing animals under managed care with stimuli such as natural and artificial objects.

Equator Principles: A risk management framework, adopted by financial institutions, for determining, assessing, and managing environmental and social risk in projects, and primarily intended to provide a minimum standard for due diligence to support responsible risk decision-making.

Ethnological: Relating to the origin, distribution, and characteristics of human racial groups.

Ethology: The scientific study of animal behavior.

European Bank for Reconstruction and Development: Regional public bank devoted to developing the economy of countries in Europe including ones not part of the EU.

European Investment Bank: Regional public bank devoted to developing the economy of countries in Europe including ones not a part of the EU.

Export Credit Agencies: State agencies devoted to increasing outward investment from their own country through financial assistance.

US Export–Import Bank (Ex–Im Bank): The Export Credit Agency of the United States.

Fairtrade and Fairmined minerals: Refers to minerals that are mined and traded according to standards set by Fairtrade International (FLO) and the Alliance for Responsible Mining. At the time of publishing, these standards apply to gold and associated precious metals. The standard ensures that certified artisanal and small-scale mining associations and cooperatives are democratic and accountable organizations with formalized operations; are using safe working practices including the management of toxic chemicals, such as mercury and cyanide, used in the gold recovery process; are respectful of the environment; recognize the rights of women miners; and do not allow child labor in their operations. Organizations that purchase Fairtrade and Fairmined gold from these certified groups are to establish long-term and stable trading relationships, and pay a minimum price and a Fairtrade premium payment. The premium payment is invested in community projects and improving the mining organization's operations. The end product to consumers can be branded as "Fairtrade and Fairmined."

Fallback foods: Food items that are always available but which are not preferred.

Fission–fusion: Split and merge (a fission–fusion society is one in which size and composition are dynamic; individuals merge (fusion) or separate (fission)).

Flanged: One of two morphs of adult male orangutan, characterized by large cheek pads.

Frugivorous: Animal that eats primarily fruits.

Gazetting: Classifying a place as protected.

GDP (gross domestic product): The market value of all officially recognized final goods and services produced within a country in a given period of time.

Genus (plural: genera): A principal taxonomic category that ranks above species and below family, which groups species that are closely related to each other (the first word of the species' scientific name is its genus).

Globalization: A diverse set of notions based on understandings of new or increased movements of goods, ideas, people, and capital across international borders in recent decades, leading to different understandings of space, time, consciousness, and social relations, and associated with new practices of governance.

Gold-washing: Concentrating the gold using water and gravimetric methods, e.g. with a pan or sluice.

Greenhouse gases: A gas in an atmosphere that absorbs and emits radiation within the thermal infrared range. The primary greenhouse gases in the Earth's atmosphere are water vapor, carbon dioxide, methane, nitrous oxide, and ozone.

Habitat fragmentation: A reduction in the size and continuity of an organism's preferred/required environment, resulting in patches of habitat. Natural fragmentation is generally localized, e.g. storm and fire damage, whereas fragmentation due to human activities can be extensive.

Habitat degradation: A reduction in the quality of a habitat such that it can no longer optimally support the fauna and flora previously living there. Natural degradation is generally localized in time and space, e.g., resulting from an earthquake, flood or landslide; whereas human-caused degradation, e.g. through industrial expansion, can be irreversible and widespread.

Hybrid: Something that is formed by combining different elements.

Hydrocarbon: An organic compound consisting entirely of hydrogen and carbon. The majority of those found on earth naturally occur in crude oil

ICSID: The International Center for the Settlement of Investment Disputes is part of the World Bank Group. It mainly hears disputes over projects.

Immunosuppression: Reduction in activity or efficacy of immune system.

Inbreeding depression: Reduced fitness and fertility within a population as a result of inbreeding.

Infanticide: The act of killing an infant.

Inter-American Development Bank: Regional public bank devoted to developing the economy of countries of Latin America.

International Monetary Fund (IMF): Post-World War II institution devoted to ensuring the financial integrity of the global economy. Well-known for its bailouts, often conditional.

Jurisprudence: The study and theory of law.

Keystone species: A species that plays a crucial role in the way an ecosystem functions, and whose presence and role has a disproportionately large effect on other organisms within the ecosystem, relative to its abundance.

Longitudinal studies: A type of observational study that involves repeated observations of the same variables over long periods of time, often many decades, to assess trends.

LSM: Large scale mining/formal mining/industrial mining typically involves capital intensive and high technological input to extract minerals; conducted by mining companies.

Mast fruiting: A phenomenon where large numbers of trees come into fruit simultaneously, without any seasonal change in temperature or rainfall; this does not happen every year but at 2–10 year intervals.

Metapopulation: A group of spatially separated populations of the same species that interact at some level.

Mineral: An element or chemical compound that is normally crystalline and that has been formed as a result of geological processes.

Miners and diggers: In the context presented here, the term "miner" refers to any person involved in ASM. However, there is an important distinction between these terms on the ground. Particularly in African contexts, "miner" usually refers to the legal license holder of the artisanal mining concession or the mine manager (foreman), and "digger" typically refers to the person who does the physical labor to recover the mineral and is either employed by the miner or works informally as an individual or in small gangs.

Mining Mindful Conservation Strategy: When planning or discussing protected areas, consider on-going and potential ASM. This type of strategy possesses the following attributes:

- Sound conservation and mining policy and enforcement.
- Leverages education and capacity building to create incentives for best practice mining and conservation outcomes.
- Embraces all stakeholders.
- Engages local communities to find ways to balance their present livelihood needs with their role as stewards of critical ecosystems for the sake of future generations in the PACE in question and around the world.
- Engages in the update of the national mining code.

Mitigation hierarchy: A tool that guides users towards limiting as far as possible the negative impacts on biodiversity from developmental projects. Often used as a precursor to **biodiversity offsets**.

Monodominant: Dominated by a single species.

Morph: Distinct form of an organism or species.

Multilateral Investment Guarantee Agency (MIGA): The World Bank Group includes this Agency. It is charged with providing insurance to medium and large projects and pursuits. Private investment often depends upon the Agency offering insurance.

Negative externalities: The indirect costs of a transaction among producers and consumers borne by those not involved in that transaction, e.g. food scarcity suffered by populations whose food sources are destroyed through logging that benefits logging companies and consumers overseas.

Neoimperialism: New forms of domination by one state over another that take territorial, political, economic, or cultural forms.

Neoliberalism: A liberal political movement and set of theories that favor the reduction of state interference in markets, such as through tariffs and subsidies (free trade) and argue for greater privatization, the shrinking of state bureaucracy, and expenditure on social provision.

Old-growth habitats: Unlogged primary forest.

Open-pit/opencast/open-cut mining: Surface mining that consists of the removal of minerals from a pit or burrow, e.g. quarries.

Ore: Mineral (rock or gravel) which contains gold at an economic concentration (grade) and that is therefore suitable to be processed.

Pathogen: A microorganism that causes sickness and/or disease.

Payment for ecosystem services (PES): Incentives offered to farmers or landowners in exchange for managing their land to provide some sort of ecological service, thereby promoting the conservation of natural resources in the marketplace.

Petiole: The stalk that joins a leaf to a stem.

Polygynous: A mating system involving one male and two or more females.

Population/species resilience: The ability of a population or species to respond to a disturbance event, including loss of individuals, and return to the same levels as previous to the event.

Prospecting: The first stage of geological analysis undertaken by mineral resource companies as a means of identifying areas where there may be commercially viable ore deposits.

Scoping: A study that helps create a general understanding of an ore body as a means of outlining the processes that could be used to extract the minerals within.

Screening: The separation of particles according to their size in mineral processing.

Sexually dimorphic: Males and females of the same species have different forms (external appearance).

Silviculture: The growing and cultivation of trees.

Slurry pipe: Used in mining to transport mineral concentrate from a mineral processing plant near a mine, or to transport waste after processing.

Spatial planning tools: Used to create a comprehensive picture of where and how an area is being used and what natural resources and habitat exist, and can include information gathering workshops, geographic information systems (GIS), and various other mapping tools.

Stochastic: Occurring in a random pattern.

Strip mining: Surface mining that consists of the removal of strips of surface layers to expose the minerals underneath.

Studbook: A species breeding registry, referring specifically to a list of male animals actively breeding.

Sympatric: Where two species or populations occupy overlapping geographic ranges without breeding.

Synergistic threats: Threats that have a far greater impact in combination than they would in isolation.

Tailings: Leftover material/waste from the mining process.

Tankage and liner systems: Container installations used in the extraction and processing of mineral ore.

Taxon (plural: taxa): Any unit used in the science of biological classification or taxonomy.

Temporal and spatial dynamics: The interaction of multiple factors over time and space.

Terra firma: Dry land.

3TG: Refers to the conflict minerals named in the Section 1502 of the Dodd-Frank Act. The minerals are tin, tantalum, tungsten, and gold.

Vector: An organism, such as a mosquito, ape, or human, that passes disease-causing microorganisms from one host to another.

Zoonosis: An infectious disease that is transmitted between species, from non-human animals to humans, or vice versa. See also "anthropozoonosis".

References

AAP (2011). *Former Circus Ape Regina Can Finally Live an Ape's Life.* AAP Rescue Center for Exotic Animals. Available at: http://www.aap.nl/english/news/news/former-circus-ape-regina-can-finally-live-an-apes-life.html. Accessed March 14, 2013.

AAP (2012). *Chimpanzee Stuck on Canary Islands for 22 Years.* AAP Rescue Center for Exotic Animals. Available at: http://www.aap.nl/english/news/news/press-release-chimpanzee-stuck-on-canary-islands-for-22-years.html. Accessed March 14, 2013.

AAP (2013). *AAP Foundation - Group chimpanzees living at Primadomus.* AAP Rescue Center for Exotic Animals. Available at: http://www.aap.nl/english/group-chimpanzees-on-the-way-to-primadomus.html. Accessed March 27, 2013.

Achard, F., Eva, H.D., Stibig, H.J., *et al.* (2002). Determination of deforestation rates of the world's humid tropical forests. *Science*, 297, 999–1002.

African Union (2009). *Africa Mining Vision.* February 2009. Addis Ababa, Ethiopia: African Union.

Agrawal, A. (2001). Common property institutions and the sustainable governance of resources. *World Development*, 29, 1649–72.

Alden Wiley, L. (2011). *Customary Land Tenure in the Modern World. Rights to Resources in Crisis: Reviewing the Fate of Customary Tenure in Africa. Brief 1 of 5.* Washington DC: Rights and Resources Initiative.

Allebone-Webb, S.M., Kuempel, N.F., Rist, J., *et al.* (2011). Use of market data to assess bushmeat hunting sustainability in equatorial Guinea. *Conservation Biology*, 25, 597–606.

Altevogt, B.M., Pankevich, D.E., Shelton-Davenport, M.K., and Kahn, J.P. (2011a). *Chimpanzees in Biomedical and Behavioral Research: Assessing the Necessity.* Washington DC: Institute of Medicine and National Research Council of the National Academies, The National Academies Press. Available at: http://www.iom.edu/Reports/2011/Chimpanzees-in-Biomedical-and-Behavioral-Research-Assessing-the-Necessity.aspx.

Altevogt, B.M., Pankevich, D.E., Shelton-Davenport, M.K., and Kahn, J.P. (2011b). *Committee on the Use of Chimpanzees in Biomedical and Behavioral Research: Assessing the Necessity.* Washington DC: National Academies Press. Available at: http://www.ncbi.nlm.nih.gov/books/NBK91443/. Accessed March 15, 2013.

Alvard, M. (2000). The impact of traditional subsistence hunting and trapping on prey populations: data from Wana horticulturalists of upland central Sulawesi, Indonesia. In *Hunting for Sustainability in Tropical Forests*, ed. J.G. Robinson and E. Bennett. New York, NY: Columbia University Press, pp. 214–30.

Ammann, K. (2012). *The Cairo Connection Part III. Update on Ape Trafficking In and Out of Egypt and the Guinea Ape Saga, Nanyuki Kenya.* Gerzensee, Switzerland: Pax Animalis.

Ancrenaz, M., Ambu, L., Sunjoto, I., *et al.* (2010). Recent surveys in the forests of Ulu Segama Malua, Sabah, Malaysia, show that orang-utans (*P. p. morio*) can be maintained in slightly logged forests. *PLoS One*, 5, e11510.

Ancrenaz, M., Gimenez, O., Ambu, L., *et al.* (2005). Aerial surveys give new estimates for orangutans in Sabah, Malaysia. *PLoS Biol*, 3, e3.

Anderson, D.P., Nordheim, E.V., and Boesch, C. (2006). Environmental factors influencing the seasonality of estrus in chimpanzees. *Primates*, 47, 43–50.

Arandjelovic, M., Head, J., Rabanal, L.I., *et al.* (2011). Non-invasive genetic monitoring of chimpanzees. *PLoS One*, 6, e14761.

Arnhem, E., Dupain, J., Vercauteren Drubbel, R., Devos, C., and Vercauteren, M. (2008). Selective logging, habitat quality and home range use by sympatric gorillas and chimpanzees: a case study from an active logging concession in Southeast Cameroon. *Folia Primatologica*, 79, 1–14.

Asner, G.P., Rudel, T.K., Aide, T.M., Defries, R., and Emerson, R. (2009). A contemporary assessment of change in humid tropical forests. *Conservation Biology*, 23, 1386–95.

Auzel, P. and Wilkie, D.S. (2000). Wildlife use in northern Congo: hunting in a commercial logging concession. In *Hunting for Sustainability in Tropical Forests*, ed. J.G. Robinson and E. Bennett. New York, NY: Columbia University Press, pp. 413–26.

Aviram, R., Bass, M., and Parker, K. (2003). Extracting hope for bushmeat: case studies of oil, gas, mining and logging industry efforts for improved wildlife management. In *Uncertain Future: the Bushmeat Crisis in Africa*, ed. Problem Solving Team of the Fall 2002 Conservation and Development Course (CONS 680). Washington DC: Bushmeat Crisis Task Force.

Balcombe, J. (2006). *Pleasurable Kingdom: Animals and the Nature of Feeling Good.* Basingstoke, UK: Palgrave Macmillan.

Balcombe, J. (2009). Animal pleasure and its moral significance. *Applied Animal Behaviour Science*, 118, 208–16.

Balcombe, J. (2010). *Second Nature: The Inner Lives of Animals.* Basingstoke, UK: Macmillan.

Bangun, D. (2006). Indonesian oil palm industry. Presented at the National Institute of Oilseed Products Annual Convention, March 21–25, 2006, Sheraton Wild Horse Pass, Phoenix, AZ.

Bappenas (1999). *Planning for Fire Prevention and Drought Management Project. Volume 2. Causes, Extent, Impact and Costs of 1997/98 Fires and Drought.* Jakarta, Indonesia: Bappenas.

Barrow, E. and Murphree, M. (2001). Community conservation from concept to practice. In *African Wildlife and Livelihoods: The Promise and Performance of Community*, ed. D. Hulme and M. Murphree. New Hampshire and Oxford: Heinemann, pp24-37.

Bartlett, T.Q. (2007). The Hylobatidae: small apes of Asia. In *Primates in Perspective*, ed. C. Campbell, A. Fuentes, K.C. MacKinnon, M. Panger, and S.K. Bearder. New York, NY: Oxford University Press, pp. 274–89.

Barume, A. (2000). *Heading Towards Extinction?: Indigenous Rights in Africa: The Case of the Twa of the Kahuzi-Biéga National Park, Democratic Republic of Congo. Document No. 101.* Copenhagen: IWGIA (The Forest Peoples Programme).

Bayol, N., Demarquez, B., de Wasseige, C., *et al.* (2012). Forest management and the timber sector in Central Africa. In *The Forests of the Congo Basin: State of the Forest 2010*, ed. C. de Wasseige, P. de Marcken, N. Bayol, *et al.* Luxembourg: Publications Office of the European Union, pp. 43–61.

BBC (2013). *Panorama*. July 22, 2013. BBC.

BBOP (2012). *Business and Biodiversity Offset Programme (BBOP). 2012. Standard on Biodiversity Offsets.* Washington DC: Forest Trends. Available at: http://bbop.forest-trends.org/guidelines/Standard.pdf.

Beaudrot, L.H., Kahlenberg, S.M., and Marshall, A.J. (2009). Why male orangutans do not kill infants. *Behavioral Ecology and Sociobiology*, 63, 1549–62.

Beaune, D., Bretagnolle, F., Bollache, L., *et al.* (2013). The bonobo-dialium positive interactions: seed dispersal mutualism. *American Journal of Primatology*, 75, 394–403.

Beck, B., Rodrigues, M., and Unwin, S. (2007). *Best Practice Guidelines for the Re-Introduction of Great Apes.* Gland, Switzerland: IUCN/SSC Primate Specialist Group.

Bennett, E. (2004). *Seeing the Wildlife and the Trees: Improving Timber Certification to Conserve Tropical Forest Wildlife. Discussion Paper.* Washington DC: World Bank.

Bennett, E.L., and Gumal, M. (2001). The interrelationships of commercial logging, hunting, and wildlife in Sarawak. In *The Cutting Edge: Conserving Wildlife in Logged Tropical Forests*, ed. R.A. Fimbel, A. Grajal, and J.G. Robinson. New York, NY: Columbia University Press, pp. 359–74.

Benz, S. and Benz-Schwarzburg, J. (2010). Great apes and new wars. *Civil Wars*, 12, 395–430.

Bergl, R.A., Warren, Y., Nicholas, A., *et al.* (2012). Remote sensing analysis reveals habitat, dispersal corridors and expanded distribution for the critically endangered cross river gorilla *Gorilla gorilla diehli*. *Oryx*, 46, 278–89.

Bermejo, M., Rodriguez-Teijeiro, J.D., Illera, G., *et al.* (2006). *Ebola* outbreak killed 5000 gorillas. *Science*, 314, 1564.

Biermann, F., and Siebenhuner, B. (2009). *Managers of Global Change: The Influence of International Environmental Bureaucracies.* Cambridge, MA and London: MIT Press.

Birkett, L.P., and Newton-Fisher, N.E. (2011). How abnormal is the behaviour of captive, zoo-living chimpanzees? *PLoS One*, 6, e20101.

Blake, S. and Fay, J.M. (1997). Seed production by *Gilbertiodendron dewevrei* in the Nouabalé-Ndoki National Park. *Journal of Tropical Ecology*, 13, 885–91.

Blake, S., Strindberg, S., Boudjan, P., *et al.* (2007). Forest elephant crisis in the Congo Basin. *PLoS Biol*, 5, e111.

Blaser, J. and Sabogal, C. (2011). *Revised ITTO Guidelines for the Sustainable Management of Natural Tropical Forests. Full Report.* Yokohama, Japan: International Tropical Timber Organization (ITTO).

Blaser, J., Sarre, A., Poore, D., and Johnson, S. (2011). *Status of Tropical Forest Management 2011. ITTO Technical Series No. 38.* Yokohama, Japan: International Tropical Timber Organization.

Blom, A. (1998). A critical analysis of three approaches to tropical forest conservation based on experiences in the Sangha region. In *Resource Use in the Trinational Sangha River Region of Equatorial Africa: Histories, Knowledge Forms, and Institutions. Yale F and ES Bulletin No. 102*, ed. H.E. Eves, R. Hardin, S. Rupp, *et al.* New Haven, CT: Yale School of Forestry and Environmental Studies, pp. 208–15.

Blom, A., Cipolletta, C., Brunsting, A.M.H., and Prins, H.T. (2004a). Behavioral responses of gorillas to habituation in the Dzanga-Ndoki National Park, Central African Republic. *International Journal of Primatology*, 25, 179–96.

Blom, A., Yamindou, J., and Prins, H.T. (2004b). Status of the protected areas of the Central African Republic (CAR). *Biological Conservation*, 118, 479–87.

Bloodworth, A., and Gunn, G. (2012). The future of the global minerals and metals sector: issues and challenges out to 2050. *Geosciences*, 15, 90–7.

Bloomsmith, M.A., Pazol, K.A., and Alford, P.L. (1994). Juvenile and adolescent chimpanzee behavioral development in complex groups. *Applied Animal Behaviour Science*, 39, 73–87.

Born Free Foundation (2011). *The EU Zoo Inquiry 2011: An Evaluation of the Implementation and Enforcement of EC Directive 1999/22, Relating to the Keeping of Animals in Zoos.* Horsham, UK: Born Free Foundation. Available at: http://www.bornfree.org.uk/campaigns/zoo-check/zoos/eu-zoo-inquiry/country-reports/eu-zoo-inquiry-pdfs/. Accessed October 18, 2012.

BOSF (2012). *The Borneo Orangutan Survival Foundation.* The Borneo Orangutan Survival Foundation (BOSF). Available at: http://orangutan.or.id/. Accessed February 2, 2013.

Bouamama, L., Sorlozano, A., Laglaoui, A., Lebbadi, M., Aarab, A., and Gutierrez J. (2010). Antibiotic resistance patterns of bacterial strains isolated from *Periplaneta americana* and *Musca domestica* in Tangier, Morocco. *Journal of Infection in Developing Countries*, 4, 194–201.

Bowen-Jones, E., and Pendry, S. (1999). The threat to primates and other mammals from the bushmeat trade in Africa, and how this threat could be diminished. *Oryx*, 33, 233–46.

Brack, D. (2008). *Controlling Illegal Logging: Using Public Procurement Policy.* London: Chatham House.

Brack, D. and Buckrell, J. (2011). *Controlling Illegal Logging: Consumer-Country Measures. Energy, Environment and Resource Governance.* London: Chatham House.

Bradley, B.J., Stiller, M., Doran-Sheehy, D.M., *et al.* (2007). Plant DNA sequences from feces: potential means for assessing diets of wild primates. *American Journal of Primatology*, 69, 699–705.

Bradshaw, G.A., Capaldo, T., Lindner, L., and Grow, G. (2008). Building an inner sanctuary: complex PTSD in chimpanzees. *Journal of Trauma and Dissociation*, 9, 9–34.

Bradshaw, G.A., Capaldo, T., Lindner, L., and Grow, G. (2009). Developmental context effects on bicultural post-trauma self repair in chimpanzees. *Developmental Psychology*, 45, 1376–88.

Bray, D.B., Duran, E., Ramos, V.H., *et al.* (2008). Tropical deforestation, community forests, and protected areas in the Maya Forest. *Ecology and Society*, 13, 56.

Breuer, T., Breuer-Ndoundou Hockemba, M., Olejniczak, C., Parnell, R.J., and Stokes, E.J. (2009). Physical maturation, life-history classes and age estimates of free-ranging western gorillas: insights from Mbeli Bai, Republic of Congo. *American Journal of Primatology*, 71, 106–19.

Brienen, R.J.W., and Zuidema, P.A. (2007). Incorporating persistent tree growth differences increases estimates of tropical timber yield. *Frontiers in Ecology and the Environment*, 5, 302–6.

Brncic, T.M., Amarasekaran, B., and McKenna, A. (2010). *Sierra Leone National Chimpanzee Census.* Freetown, Sierra Leone: Tacugama Chimpanzee Sanctuary.

Brockelman, W.Y., Damman, D., Thongsuk, P., and Srikosamatara, S. (1977). Pileated gibbons survey at Khao Soi Dao Sanctuary, Thailand. *Regional Office for Asia and the Far East Tigerpaper*, 4, 13–5.

Brockelman, W.Y., Reichard, U., Treesucon, U., and Raemaekers, J.J. (1998). Dispersal, pair formation and social structure in gibbons (*Hylobates lar*). *Behavioral Ecology and Sociobiology*, 42, 329–39.

Brockelman, W.Y., and Srikosamatara, S. (1993). Estimation of density of gibbon groups by use of loud songs. *American Journal of Primatology*, 29, 93–108.

Broom, D.M. (1991). Animal welfare: concepts and measurement. *Journal of Animal Science*, 69, 4167–75.

Broom, D.M., and Kirkden, R.D. (2004). Welfare, stress, behaviour and pathophysiology. In *Veterinary Pathophysiology*, ed. R.H. Dunlop, and C.H. Malbert. Ames, IA: Blackwell, pp. 337–69.

Brüne, M., Brüne-Cohrs, U., and McGrew, W.C. (2004). Psychiatric treatment for great apes? *Science*, 306, 2039.

Brüne, M., Brüne-Cohrs, U., McGrew, W.C., and Preuschoft, S. (2006). Psychopathology in great apes: concepts, treatment options and possible homologies to human psychiatric disorders. *Neuroscience and Biobehavioral Reviews*, 30, 1246–59.

Bruner, A., Gullison, R., Rice, R., and Fonseca, G. (2001). Effectiveness of parks in protecting tropical biodiversity. *Science*, 291, 125–8.

Buckland, H. (2005). *The Oil for Ape Scandal: How Palm Oil is Threatening Orang-Utan Survival.* London: Friends of the Earth, The Ape Alliance, The Borneo Orangutan Survival Foundation, The Orangutan Foundation (UK) and the Sumatran Orangutan Society.

Buckley, C., Nekaris, K.A.I., and Husson, S.J. (2006). Survey of *Hylobates agilis albibaris* in a logged peat-swamp forest: Sabangau catchment, Central Kalimantan. *Primates*, 47, 327–35.

Caldecott, J. and Miles, L. (2005). *World Atlas of Great Apes and their Conservation.* Berkeley, CA: University of California Press.

Campbell-Smith, G., Sembirang, R., and Linkie, M. (2012). Evaluating the effectiveness of human-orangutan conflict mitigation strategies in Sumatra. *Journal of Applied Ecology*, 49, 367–75.

Campbell, C., Andayani, N., Cheyne, S., *et al.*, ed. (2008a). *Indonesian Gibbon Conservation and Management Workshop Final Report*. Apple Valley, MN: IUCN/SSC Conservation Breeding Specialist Group.

Campbell, G., Kuehl, H., Kouame, P.N.G., and Boesch, C. (2008b). Alarming decline of West African chimpanzees in Côte d'Ivoire. *Current Biology*, 18, R903-R4.

CARPE (2009). Affectation des terres dans du Tri-national du Sangha: draft management plan prepared for the Central African Regional Program for the Environment (CARPE). Available at: http://carpe-infotool.umd.edu/IMT/LS5_Sangha_Tri-National/Landscape/LS5_MP_TNS_Management_Plan_2010.pdf. Accessed September 26, 2012.

CARPE (2010). République Centrafricaine: Dzanga-Ndoki Management Plan: 2010–2014. Submitted to the Central African Regional Program for the Environment (CARPE). Available at: http://carpe-infotool.umd.edu/IMT/LS5_Sangha_Tri-National/5010001_PA_Dzanga-Ndoki_National_Park/5010001_MP_Dzanga-Ndoki_NP_Management_Plan_2010.doc. Accessed September 27, 2012.

CARPE (2011). *About CARPE*. Central Africa Regional Programme for the Environment (CARPE). Available at: http://carpe.umd.edu/about/index.php Accessed July 26, 2012.

Carroll, N., Fox, J., and Bayon, R. (2009). *Conservation and Biodiversity Banking: A Guide to Setting Up and Running Biodiversity Credit Trading Systems*. London: Earthscan Publishers.

Caruso, E., Colchester, M., MacKay, F., Hildyard, N., and Nettleton, G. (2003). *Extracting Promises: Indigenous Peoples, Extractive Industries and the World Bank: Final Synthesis Report*. Moreton-in-Marsh, UK/Washington DC: FPP/Tebtebba.

Cater, C. (2003). The political economy of conflict and UN interventions: rethinking the critical cases of Africa. In *The Political Economy of Armed Conflict: Beyond Greed and Grievance*, ed. K. Ballentine and J. Sherman. Boulder, CO: International Peace Academy, pp. 19–45.

Caton, J.M. (1999). Digestive strategy of the Asian colobine genus *Tracypithecus*. *Primates*, 40, 311–25.

CBD Secretariat (2010). *Global Biodiversity Outlook 3*. Montreal, Canada: CBD.

CBD (2012). Convention of the Parties 2012: Advance unedited copy of COP-11 decisions. Available at: http://www.cbd.int/cop/cop-11/doc/2012-10-24-advanced-unedited-cop-11-decisions-en.pdf. Accessed November 13, 2102.

Centre for Development Studies (2004). *Livelihoods and Policy in the Artisanal and Small-Scale Mining Sector: An Overview*. Swansea, UK: University of Wales.

Cerutti, P.O. and Tacconi, L. (2008). Forests, illegality, and livelihoods: the case of Cameroon. *Society and Natural Resources*, 21, 845–53.

Chan, A.A.Y.-H. and Blumstein, D.T. (2011). Attention, noise, and implications for wildlife conservation and management. *Applied Animal Behaviour Science*, 131, 1–7.

Channa, P., and Gray, T.N.E. (2009). *Status and Conservation of Nomascus Gabriellae in Phnom Prich Wildlife Sanctuary*. Phnom Penh, Cambodia: Ministry of Environment and WWF Greater Mekong Program.

Chapman, C.A., Gillespie, T.R., and Goldberg, T.L. (2005). Primates and the ecology of their infectious diseases: how will anthropogenic change affect host–parasite interactions? *Evolutionary Anthropology*, 14, 134–44.

Chapman, C.A., and Lambert, J.E. (2000). Habitat alteration and the conservation of African primates: case study of Kibal National Park, Uganda. *American Journal of Primatology*, 50, 169–85.

Chapman, C.A., Lawes, M.J., and Eeley, H.A.C. (2006). What hope for African primate diversity? *African Journal of Ecology*, 44, 116–33.

Cheyne, S.M., Rowland, D., Höing, A., and Husson, S.J. (2013). How orangutans choose where to sleep: comparison of nest-site variables. *Asian Primates Journal*, 3, 13–7.

Cheyne, S.M., Zrust, M., Hoeing, A., *et al.* (2012). Barito River Initiative for Nature Conservation and Communities (BRINCC) preliminary report. Palangka Raya, Indonesia: BRINCC Expedition.

ChimpCARE (2013). *ChimpCARE.org. Lincoln Park Zoo's ChimpCARE*. ChimpCARE. Available at: http://www.chimpcare.org/. Accessed March 15, 2013.

Chivers, D.J. (1972). The Siamang and the gibbon in the Malay Peninsula. In *Evolution, Ecology, Behaviour, and Captive Maintainance*, 1st edn, ed. D.M. Rumbaugh. Basel: S. Karger, pp. 103–35.

Chivers, D.J. (1974). The siamang in Malaya: a field study of a primate in tropical forest. *Contributions to Primatology*, 4, 1–335.

Chivers, D.J. (1994). Functional anatomy of the gastrointestinal tract. In *Colobine Monkeys: their Ecology, Behaviour and Evolution*, ed. A.G. Davies and J.F. Oates. Cambridge, UK: Cambridge University, pp. 205–27.

Chivers, D.J., and Hladik, C.M. (1980). Morphology of the gastrointestinal tract in primates: comparisons with other mammals in relation to diet. *Journal of Morphology*, 166, 337–86.

Choudhury, A. (1990). Popualtion dynamics of hoolock gibbons (*Hylobates hoolock*) in Assam, India. *American Journal of Primatology*, 20, 37–41.

Choudhury, A. (2006). The distribution and status of hoolock gibbon, *Hoolock hoolock*, in Manipur, Meghalaya, Mizoram, and Nagaland in northeast India. *Primate Conservation*, 20, 79–87.

Choudhury, A. (2009). The hoolock gibbon (*Hoolock hoolock*) in Tinsukia and Dibrugarh Districts of Assam, India. *Asian Primates Journal*, 1, 24–30.

Churchill Mining (2012). *East Kutai Coal Project: Indonesia*. Churchill Mining. Available at: http://www.churchillmining.com/projects/. Accessed May 13, 2012.

CIA (2013a). *The World Factbook*. Washington DC: Central Intelligence Agency (CIA). Available at: https://www.cia.gov/library/publications/the-world-factbook/. Accessed May 14, 2013.

CIA (2013b). *The Worldfact Book: Gabon*. Washington DC: Central Intelligence Agency (CIA). Available at: https://www.cia.gov/library/publications/the-world-factbook/geos/gb.html. Accessed April 16, 2013.

CIA (2013c). *The Worldfact Book: Guinea*. Washington DC: Central Intelligence Agency (CIA). Available at: https://www.cia.gov/library/publications/the-world-factbook/geos/gv.html. Accessed July 9, 2013.

CITES (2013a). *Convention on International Trade in Endangered Species of Wild Fauna and Flora. Appendices I, II and III*. CITES. Available at: http://www.cites.org/eng/app/appendices.php. Accessed September 16, 2013.

CITES (2013b). *CoP Doc49: Interpretation and Implementation of the Convention Species Trade and Conservation of Great Apes. Sixteenth Meeting of the Conference of the Parties. Bangkok (Thailand), 3–14 March 2013*. Available at: www.cites.org/eng/cop/16/doc/E-CoP16–49.pdf. Accessed January 17, 2013.

CITES, and GRASP (2006). *CITES/GRASP Orang-utan Technical Mission Indonesia*. CITES Secretariat. Available at: http://www.cites.org/common/prog/ape/ID_mission06.pdf. Accessed December 29, 2012.

Clark, C.J., Poulsen, J.R., Malonga, R., and Elkan, P.W. (2009). Logging concessions can extend the conservation estate for central African tropical forests. *Conservation Biology*, 23, 1281–93.

Clutton-Brock, T.H., Albon, S.D., and Guiness, F.E. (1989). Fitness cost of gestation and lactation in wild mammals. *Nature*, 337, 260–2.

CNN (2011). Interview with President Susilo Bambang Yudhoyono. *Talk Asia*, June 2011. CNN.

Coad, L., Schleicher, J., Milner-Gulland, E.J., *et al.* (2013). Social and ecological change over a decade in a village hunting system, central Gabon. *Conservation Biology*, 27, 270–80.

Colchester, M. (2008). *Beyond Tenure: Rights-based Approaches to Peoples and Forests*. Washington DC: Rights and Resources Initiative.

Colchester, M. and Ferrari, M. (2007). *Making Free, Prior and Informed Consent Work: Challenges and Prospects for Indigenous People*. Available at: http://www.forestpeoples.org/topics/civil-political-rights/publication/2010/making-fpic-free-prior-and-informed-consent-work-chal. Accessed January 2013.

Comeaux, P.E. and Kinsella, N.S. (1994). Reducing political risk in developing countries: bilateral investment treaties, stablilization clauses, and MIGA and OPIC investment insurance. *New York School Journal of International and Comparative Law*, 15, 3–48.

Conservation International (2010). Maiko-Tanya-Kahuzi-Biéga Landscape: landscape land use plan, for the Annual Report 2010 for the CARPE Programme. Available at: http://carpe-infotool.umd.edu/IMT/LS10_Maiko-Tayna-Kahuzi-/Landscape/LS10_MP_Maiko_Tayna_Kahuzi__Management_Plan_2010.pdf. Accessed August 24, 2011.

Contreras-Hermosilla, A. and Fay, C. (2005). *Strengthening Forest Management in Indonesia through Land Tenure Reform: Issues and Framework for Action*. Washington DC: Forest Trends.

Cook, R. and Healy, T. (2012). *Madagascar ASM Rushes in Protected Areas and Critical Ecosystems: National Overview Report*. Cambridge, UK: ASM-PACE Programme. Available at: at asm- pace.org.

Council of the European Union (1986). *86/609/EEC The Protection of Animals used for Experimental and other Scientific Purposes, 0001–0028*. Available at: http://eur-lex.europa.eu/LexUriServ/LexUriServ.do?uri=CELEX:31986L0609:EN:HTML. Accessed March 13, 2013.

Council of the European Union (1992). *92/43/EEC Conservation of Natural Habitats and of Wild Fauna and Flora, 0007–0050*. Available at: http://eur-lex.europa.eu/LexUriServ/LexUriServ.do?uri=CELEX:31992L0043:EN:HTML. Accessed March 12, 2013.

Council of the European Union (1997). *338/97/EEC Protection of Species of Wild Fauna and Flora by Regulating Trade, 0001–0069*. Available at: http://eur-lex.europa.eu/LexUriServ/LexUriServ.do?uri=CELEX:31997R0338:EN:HTML. Accessed March 12, 2013.

Council of the European Union (1999). *1999/22/EC Keeping of Wild Animals in Zoos, 0024–0026.* Available at: http://europa.eu/legislation_summaries/environment/nature_and_biodiversity/l28069_en.htm. Accessed March 11, 2013.

Cowling, P., Wiafe, V., and Brogan, C. (2011). *Mid Term Review of Global Witness' Making the Forest Sector Transparent Programme.* Bristol: The IDL Group Ltd. Available at http://www.foresttransparency.info/cms/file/533. Accessed November 8, 2012.

Cowlishaw, G., Mendelson, S., and Rowcliffe, J.M. (2005). Evidence for post-depletion sustainability in a mature bushmeat market. *Journal of Applied Ecology,* 42, 460–8.

CS, and WCT (2011). Baby chimps rescied from South Sudan. *Ngamba News,* June 12, 2011.

Darby, L.L., Gillespie, T.R., and Hicks, T.C. (2010). Consequences of increased artisanal mining for primates in northern DRCongo (abstract). Presented at the XXIII Congress of the International Primatological Society, Kyoto, Japan.

Das, J., Biswas, J., Bhattacharjee, P.C., and Rao, S.S. (2009). Canopy bridges: an effecive conservation tactic for supporting gibbon populations in forest fragments. In *The Gibbons: New Perspectives on Small Ape Socioecology and Population Biology,* ed. S. Lappan and D.J. Whittaker. Berlin: Springer, pp. 467–75.

Dawkins, M. (1998). Evolution and animal welfare. *The Quarterly Review of Biology,* 73, 305–28.

de Wasseige, C., Devers, D., de Marcken, P., *et al.* (2009). *The Forests of the Congo Basin: State of the Forest 2008.* Luxembourg: Publications Office of the European Union.

Debroux, L., Hart, T., Kaimowitz, D., Karsenty, A., and Topa, G., ed. (2007). *Forests in Post-Conflict Democratic Republic of Congo: Analysis of a Priority Agenda.* A joint report by teams of the World Bank, Center for International Forestry Research (CIFOR), Centre International de Recherche Agronomique pour le Développement (CIRAD), African Wildlife Foundation (AWF), Conseil National des ONG de Développement du Congo (CNONGD), Conservation International (CI), Groupe de Travail Forêts (GTF), Ligue Nationale des Pygmées du Congo (LINAPYCO), Netherlands Development Organisation (SNV), Réseau des Partenaires pour l'Environnement au Congo (REPEC), Wildlife Conservation Society (WCS), Woods Hole Research Center (WHRC), World Agroforestry Centre (ICRAF) and World Wide Fund for Nature (WWF). Washington DC: CIFOR, The World Bank and CIRAD.

DeFries, R., Rudel, T., Uriarte, M., and Hansen, M. (2010). Deforestation driven by urban population growth and agricultural trade in the twenty-first century. *Nature Geoscience,* 3, 178–81.

DeJong, T. (2012a). *Environmental Rehabilitation and Artisanal Diamond Mining: A Case Study of Land and Livelihoods in the Central African Republic.* Washington DC: USAID.

DeJong, T. (2012b). Unpublished field notes from visit to Bayanga, Central African Republic.

Delgado, R.A. (2010). Communication, culture and conservation in orangutans. In *Indonesian Primates,* ed. S. Gursky Doyen and J. Supriatna. New York, NY: Springer, pp. 23–40.

Delgado, R.A. and van Schaik, C.P. (2000). The behavioral ecology and conservation of the orangutan (*Pongo pygmaeus*): a tale of two islands. *Evolutionary Anthropology,* 9, 201–18.

Dennis, R., Grant, A., Hadiprakarsa, Y., *et al.* (2010a). *Best Management Practices for Orangutan Conservation. Mining Concessions.* Jakarta, Indonesia: Orangutan Conservation Services Program (OCSP).

Dennis, R., Grant, A., Hadiprakarsa, Y., *et al.* (2010b). *Best Practices for Orangutan Conservation: Nature Forest Concessions.* Jakarta, Indonesia: Orangutan Conservation Services Program (OCSP).

Densham, A., Czebiniak, R., Kessler, D., and Skar, R. (2009). *Carbon Scam: Noel Kempff Climate Action Project and the Push for Sub-national Forest Offsets.* Washington DC: Greenpeace International.

der Walt, L. (2012). CIB's perspective on the PROGEPP partnership. In *Tropical Forest Conservation and Industry Partnership: An Experience from the Congo Basin. Conservation Science and Practice,* ed. C.J. Clark and J.R. Poulsen. Oxford: Wiley-Blackwell, pp. 36–8.

Deschner, T., Fuller, B.T., Oelze, V., *et al.* (2012). Identification of energy consumption and nutritional stress by isotopic and elemental analysis of urine in bonobos (*Pan paniscus*). *Rapid Communications in Mass Spectromotry* 26, 69–77.

Dittus, W.P.J. (1982). Population regulation: the effects of severe environmental changes on the demography and behavior of wild torque macaques. *International Journal of Primatology,* 3, 276.

Doran-Sheehy, D., Greer, D., Mongo, P., and Schwindt, D. (2004). Impact of ecological and social factors on ranging in western gorillas. *American Journal of Primatology,* 64, 207–22.

Doug, B., Elias, P., Lininger, K., *et al.* (2011). *The Root of the Problem: What's Driving tropical Deforestation Today?* Cambridge, UK: Union of Concerned Scientists Publications. Available at: http://www.ucsusa.org/assets/documents/global_warming/UCS_RootoftheProblem_DriversofDeforestation_FullReport.pdf. Accessed January 31, 2013.

Dowie, M. (2009). *Conservation Refugees: The Hundred-Year Conflict Between Global Conservation and Native Peoples.* Cambridge, MA: MIT Press.

Draper, C. and Harris, S. (2012). The assessment of animal welfare in British zoos by government-appointed inspectors. *Animals*, 2, 507–28.

Draulens, D. and van Krunkelsven, E. (2002). The impact of war on forest areas in the Democratic Republic of Congo. *Oryx*, 36, 35–40.

Drori, O. (2012). Trade in great apes and wildlife law enforcement: Challenges and solutions. Unpublished paper. 2nd Great Apes Survival Partnership (GRASP) Council Meeting. Paris, France. November 6–8, 2012.

D'Souza, K. (2003). Scoping Study on the Artisanal Mining of Coltan in the Kahuzi-Biéga National Park. Prepared for The Dian Fossey Gorilla Fund. Newcastle-under-Lyme, UK: Wardell Armstrong LLP.

Duckworth, J.W. (2008). Preliminary gibbon status review for Lao PDR 2008. Cambridge, UK: Fauna and Flora International. Unpublished report.

Duckworth, J.W., Batters, G., Belant, J.L., *et al.* (2012). Why south-east Asia should be the world's priority for averting imminent species extinctions, and a call to join a developing cross-institutional programme to tackle this urgent issue. *SAPIENS*, 5. Available at: http://sapiens.revues.org/1327.

Duckworth, J.W., Timmins, R., Anderson, G.Q.A., *et al.* (1995). Notes on the status and conservation of the gibbon *Hylobates (Nomascus) gabriellae* in Laos. *Tropical Biodiversity*, 3, 15–27.

Dudley, N. (2008). *Guidelines for Applying Protected Area Management Categories.* Gland, Switzerland: IUCN.

Dupain, J., Guislain, P., Nguenang, G.M., de Vleeschouwer, K., and van Elsacker, L. (2004). High chimpanzee and gorilla densities in a non-protected area on the northern periphery of the Dja Faunal Reserve, Cameroon. *Oryx*, 38, 209–16.

Dupain, J., Nackoney, J., Vargas, J.M., *et al.* (2012). Bushmeat characteristics vary with catchment conditions in a Congo market. *Biological Conservation*, 146, 32–40.

Durban Process (2006). *Campaign Report, June 2006.* Durban Process. Available at: http://www.gorillaland.net/WildLIGHT/Durban_Process_files/Campaign%20Report%20Jun%202006.pdf. Accessed September 8, 2011.

EARS (2013). *What We Do.* European Alliance of Rescue Centres and Sanctuaries (EARS). Available at: http://ears-eu.org/about-ears/what-we-do/. Accessed June 16, 2013.

ECA (2011). *Minerals and Africa's Development: The International Study Group Report on Africa's Mineral Regimes.* Addis Ababa, Ethiopia: Economic Commission for Africa (ECA). Available at: http://new.uneca.org/Portals/15/CrossArticle/1/Documents/ISG_Report_eng.pdf. Accessed January, 2013.

Economic Commission for Europe (2008). *Spatial Planning: Key Instrument for Development and Effective Governance with Special Reference to Countries in Transition.* Geneva: United Nations Publication.

Edmunds, D., Wollenberg, E., Contreras, A.P., *et al.* (2003). Introduction. Local forest management: the impacts of devolution policies. In *Local Forest Management: The Impacts of Devolution Policies*, ed. D. Edmunds, and E. Wollenberg. London: Earthscan Publications, pp. 1-19.

Effiom, E.O., Nuñez-Iturri, G., Smith, H., Ottosson, U., and Olsson, O. (2013). Bushmeat hunting changes regeneration of African rainforests. *Proceedings of the Royal Society B: Biological Sciences*, 280, DOI: 10.1098/rspb.2013.0246.

EITI Secretariat (2012a). *EITI Fact Sheet.* Extractive Industries Transparency Initiative (EITI). Available at: http://eiti.org/files/2012–09–20_Fact_Sheet_0.pdf. Accessed November 7, 2012.

EITI Secretariat (2012b). *Supporters.* Extractive Industries Transparency Initiative (EITI). Available at: http://eiti.org/supporters. Accessed September 2013.

Elder, A.E. (2009). Hylobatid diets revisted: the importance of body mass, fruit availability, and interspecific competition. In *The Gibbons: New Perspectives on Small Ape Socioecology and Population Biology*, ed. S. Lappan and D.J. Whittaker. New York, NY: Springer, 133-159.

Elkan, P.W. and Elkan, S. (2012). WCS's perspective on the BZP partnership. In *Tropical Forest Conservation and Industry Partnership: An Experience from the Congo Basin. Conservation Science and Practice*, ed. C.J. Clark, and J.R. Poulsen. Oxford: Wiley-Blackwell, pp. 33–6.

Elkan, P.W., Elkan, S.W., Moukassa, A., *et al.* (2006). Managing threats from bushmeat hunting in a timber concession in the Republic of Congo. In *Emerging Threats to Tropical Forests*, ed. W.F. Laurance and C. A. Peres. Chicago, IL: University of Chicago Press, pp. 393–415.

Embas, D.S.D.U. (2012). Statement by the Honourable Dato' Sri Douglas Uggah Embas, Minister of Natural Resources and Environment, Malaysia. Presented at the United Nations Conference on Sustainable Development, June 22, 2012, Rio de Janeiro, The Republic of Brazil.

Emery Thompson, M., Kahlenberg, S.M., Gilby, I.C., and Wrangham, R.W. (2007). Core area quality is associated with variance in reproductive success among female chimpanzees at Kibale National Park. *Animal Behaviour*, 73, 501–12.

Emery Thompson, M. and Wrangham, R.W. (2008). Diet and reproductive function in wild female chimpanzees (*Pan troglodytes schweinfurthii*) at Kibale National Park, Uganda. *American Journal of Physical Anthropology*, 135, 171–81.

Emery Thompson, M. and Wrangham, R.W. (2013). Pan troglodytes robust chimpanzee. In *Mammals of Africa. Volume II. Primates*, ed. T.M. Butynski, J. Kingdon, and J. Kalina. London: Bloomsbury Publishing, pp. 55–64.

Emery Thompson, M., Zhou, A., and Knott, C.D. (2012). Low testosterone correlates with delayed development in male orangutans. *PLoS One*, 7, e47282.

Endangered Species International (2009). *The Killing of Gorillas for Bushmeat*. Endangered Species International. Available at: http://www.endangeredspeciesinternational.org/bushmeat2_gallery.html. Accessed November 21, 2012.

Endcap (2012). *The Use of Positive Lists to Identify Exotic Species Suitable to be Kept as Pets in the EU*. Horsham: Endcap. Available at: http://endcap.eu/wild-pet/

Energy and Biodiversity Initiative (2003). *Integrating Biodiversity Conservation into Oil and Gas Development*. Washington DC: Conservation International. Available at: http://www.theebi.org/pdfs/ebi_report.pdf. Accessed May 2013.

ESRI (2012). *Ocean Basemap*. Esri, GEBCO, NOAA, National Geographic, DeLorme, NAVTEQ, Geonames.org, and other contributors. Available at: http://www.arcgis.com/home/item.html?id=6348e67824504fc9a62976434bf0d8d5. Accessed December 2012.

Etiendem, D.N., Funwi-Gabga, N., Tagg, N., Hens, L., and Indah, E.K. (2013). The cross river gorillas (*Gorilla gorilla diehli*) at Mawambi Hills, South-West Cameroon: habitat suitability and vulnerability to anthropogenic disturbance. *Folia Primatologica*, 84, 18–31.

Eurogroup for Animals (2011). *Briefing Paper. Keeping of Exotic Animals: Risks and Related Policies*. Brussels: Eurogroup for Animals. Available at: http://eurogroupforanimals.org/what-we-do/category/wildlife/exotic-pets.

European Commission (2011). *Impact Assessment for Financial Disclosures on a Country by Country Basis*. Brussels, Belgium: European Commission. Available at: http://ec.europa.eu/governance/impact/ia_carried_out/docs/ia_2011/sec_2011_1290_en.pdf. Accessed September 2013.

European Parliament and Council (2010). *Directive 2010/63/EU The Protection of Animals used for Scientific Purposes, 0033–0079*. Brussels: European Parliament and Council.

Evans, T.D., Stones, A.J., Towll, H.C., and Thewlis, R.M. (1996). *A Wildlife and Habitat Survey of Dong Hua Sao National Biodiversity Conservation Area, Champasak Province, Laos*. IUCN Biodiversity Conservation Project.

Eves, H. and Ruggiero, R. (2000). Socioeconomics and sustainability of hunting in the forests of northern Congo (Brazzaville). In *Hunting for Sustainability in Tropical Forests*, ed. J.G. Robinson and E. Bennett. New York, NY: Columbia University Press, pp. 427–54.

Fa, J.E. and Brown, D. (2009). Impacts of hunting on mammals in African tropical moist forests: a review and synthesis. *Mammal Review*, 39, 231–64.

Fa, J.E., Currie, D., and Meeuwig, J. (2003). Bushmeat and food security in the Congo Basin: linkages between wildlife and people's future. *Environmental Conservation*, 30, 71–8.

Fa, J.E. and Peres, C.A. (2001). Game vertebrate extraction in African and Neotropical forests: an intercontinental comparison. In *Conservation of Exploited Species*, ed. J.D. Reynolds, G.M. Mace, K.H. Redford, and J.G. Robinson. Cambridge, UK: Cambridge University Press, pp. 203–41.

Fa, J.E., Ryan, S.F., and Bell, D.J. (2005). Hunting vulnerability, ecological characteristics and harvest rates of bushmeat species in afrotropical forests. *Biological Conservation*, 121, 167 76.

Fa, J.E., Seymour, S., Dupain, J., *et al.* (2006). Getting to grips with the magnitude of exploitation: Bushmeat in the Cross-Sanaga Rivers region, Nigeria and Cameroon. *Biological Conservation*, 129, 497–510.

Fahrig, L. and Merriam, G. (1994). Conservation of fragmented populations. *Conservation Biology*, 8, 50–9.

Falconer, J. (1996). Developing research frames for non-timber forest products. In *Current Issues in Non-Timber Forest Product Research*, ed. M. Ruiz-Perez and J.E.M. Arnold. Bogor, Indonesia: CIFOR, pp. 143–60.

Fan Peng-Fei, Fei Hanlan, Scott, M.B., Zhang Wen, and Ma Changyong (2011a). Habitat and food choice of the critically endangered cao vit gibbons (*Nomascus nasutus*) in China: implication for conservation. *Biological Conservation*, 144, 2247–54.

Fan Peng-Fei, Fei Hanlan, Xiang Zoufu, *et al.* (2010). Social structure and group dynamics of the cao vit gibbon (*Nomascus nasutus*) in Bangliang, Jinxi, China. *Folia Primatologica*, 81, 245–53.

Fan Peng-Fei and Huai-Sen Ai (2011). Conservation status of the eastern hoolock (*Hoolock leuconedys*) in China. *Gibbon Journal*, 6, 22–5.

Fan Peng-Fei and Jiang Xue-Long (2008). Effects of food and topography on ranging behavior of black crested gibbon (*Nomascus concolor jingdongensis*) in Wuliang Mountain, Yunnan, China. *American Journal of Primatology*, 70, 871–8.

Fan Peng-Fei, and Jiang Xue-Long (2010). Maintainence of multifemale social organization in a group of *Nomascus concolor* at Wuliang Mountain, Yunnan, China. *International Journal of Primatology*, 31, 1–13.

Fan Peng-Fei, Jiang Xue-Long, and Tian Chang-Cheng (2009). The critically endangered black crested gibbon *Nomascus concolor* on Wuliang Moujntain, Yunnan, China: the role of forest types in the species conservation. *Oryx*, 43, 1–6.

Fan Peng-Fei, Xiao Wen, Huo Sheng, *et al.* (2011b). Distribution and conservation status of the vulnerable eastern hoolock gibbon *Hoolock leuconedys*. *Oryx*, 45, 129–34.

FAO (1995). *Non-Wood Forest Products for Rural Income and Sustainability Forestry. NWFPs 7.* Rome: Food and Agriculture Organization of the United Nations (FAO).

FAO (2005). *State of the World's Forests.* Rome: Food and Agriculture Organization of the United Nations (FAO).

FAO (2006). *Global Forest Resources Assessment 2005, Progress Towards Sustainable Forest Management.* Rome: Food and Agriculture Organization of the United Nations (FAO).

FAO (2009). *How to Feed the World in 2050.* Rome: Food and Agriculture Organization of the United Nations (FAO).

FAO (2010a). *Asia-Pacific Forests and Forestry to 2020. Asia Pacific Forestry Sector Outlook Study ll. RAP-publication 2010/06.* Bangkok: Food and Agriculture Organization of the United Nations (FAO).

FAO (2010b). *Global Forest Resources Assessment: Main Report. FAO Forestry Paper No. 163.* Rome: Food and Agriculture Organization of the United Nations (FAO). Available at: www.fao.org/docrep/013/i1757e/i1757e00.htm.

FAO (2011a). *The State of the Forests of the Amazon, Congo Basin and South East Asia.* Rome: Food and Agriculture Organization of the United Nations (FAO).

FAO (2011b). *State of the World's Forests 2011.* Rome: Food and Agriculture Organization of the United Nations (FAO).

FAO (2012). *FAOSTAT.* FAOSTAT. Available at: http://faostat3.fao.org/home/index.html. Accessed December 29, 2012.

FAO, and JRC (2011). *Global Forest Land-use Change from 1990–2005.* Rome: Food and Agriculture Organization of the United Nations (FAO).

Farmer, K.H. (2002). Pan-African Sanctuary Alliance: status and range of activities for great ape conservation. *American Journal of Primatology*, 58, 117–32.

Faust, L.J., Cress, D., Farmer, K.H., Ross, S.R., and Beck, B.B. (2011). Predicting capacity demand on sanctuaries for African chimpanzees (*Pan troglodytes*). *International Journal of Primatology*, 32, 849–64.

FAWC (2009). *Farm Animal Welfare Council: Five Freedoms.* Farm Animal Welfare Council (FAWC). Available at: http://www.fawc.org.uk/freedoms.htm. Accessed March 15, 2013.

Fay, E.C. (2011). Great ape cognition and captive care: can cognitive challenges enhance well-being? *Applied Animal Behaviour Science*, 135, 1–12.

Federal Register (2013). Listing all chimpanzees as endangered. *Federal Register*, 78, 35201–17. Available at: http://www.fws.gov/policy/library/2013/2013–14007.pdf. Accessed June 12, 2013.

Felbab-Brown, V. (2011). *The Illegal Logging Trade in the Asia-Pacific Region.* Brookings Institution. Available at: http://www.brookings.edu/research/papers/2011/03/illegal-logging-felbabbrown Accessed June 25, 2013.

Felbab-Brown, V. (2013). *Indonesia Field Report III. The Orangutan's Road: Illegal Logging and Mining in Indonesia.* The Brookings Institution. Available at: http://www.brookings.edu/research/reports/2013/02/07-indonesia-illegal-logging-mining-felbabbrown. Accessed February 13, 2013.

Felton, A.M., Engstrom, L.M., Felton, A., and Knott, C.D. (2003). Orangutan population density, forest structure and fruit availability in hand-logged and unlogged peat swamp forests in West Kalimantan, Indonesia. *Biological Conservation*, 114, 91–101.

Ferdowsian, H.R., Durham, D.L., Johnson, C.M., *et al.* (2012). Signs of generalized anxiety and compulsive disorders in chimpanzees. *Journal of Veterinary Behavior: Clinical Applications and Research*, 7, 353–61.

Ferdowsian, H.R., Durham, D.L., Kimwele, C., *et al.* (2011). Signs of mood and anxiety disorders in chimpanzees. *PLoS One*, 6, e19855.

FIM (2012). *Global Timber: Future Value, December 2012.* FIM Service Limited. Available at: http://www.fimltd.co.uk/downloads/Global%20Industrial%20Roundwood%20Demand%20March%202013.pdf. Accessed September 16, 2013.

Fimbel, R.A., Grajal, A., and Robinson, J.G. (2001). Logging and wildlife in the tropics: impacts and options for conservation. In *The Cutting Edge: Conserving Wildlife in Logged Tropical Forests*, ed. R.A. Fimbel, A. Grajal, and J.G. Robinson. New York, NY: Columbia University Press, pp. 667–95.

Fisher, B. (2010). African exception to drivers of deforestation. *Nature Geoscience*, 3, 375-6.

Forest Watch Indonesia (2011). *Potret Keadaan Hutan Indonesia. Periode Tahun 2000–2009.* Bogor, Indonesia: Forest Watch Indonesia.

Forest Watch Indonesia (2012). *Chaotic Permits and Licensing System Causing Disaster in East Kutai Regency.* Bogor, Indonesia: Forest Watch Indonesia. Available at: http://fwi.or.id/english/.

FPP (2012). *Peruvian Government on Brink of Expanding Oil and Gas Development in Reserve for Isolated Peoples and UNESCO World Heritage Site.* Moreton-in-Marsh, UK: Forest Peoples Programme (FPP). Available at: http://www.forestpeoples.org/topics/extractive-industries/news/2012/07/peruvian-government-brink-expanding-oil-and-gas-development.

Franklin, D. and Andrews, J., eds (2012). *Megachange. The World in 2050.* London: The Economist and Profile Books Ltd.

Freudenberger, M. and Mogba, Z. (1998). *Human Migration in Protected Areas of Central Africa: The Case of the Dzanga-Sangha Special Reserve. Yale F and ES Bulletin No. 10.* New Haven, CT: Yale School of Forestry and Environmental Studies.

Fruth, B. and Hohmann, G. (1996). Nest building behavior in the great apes: the great leap forward? In *Great Ape Societies*, ed. W.C. McGrew, L.F. Marchant, and T. Nishida. Cambridge, UK: Cambridge University Press, pp. 225–40.

FSC (2002). *FSC International Standard: FSC Principles and Criteria for Forest Stewardship: FSC-STD-01–001 (version 4–0) EN.* Bonn, Germany: Forest Stewardship Council (FSC). Available at: https://ca.fsc.org/download.principles-criteria-v4.7.pdf.

FSC (2008). *FSC Certification: Protection of Biodiversity and High Conservation Value Forests (HCVF).* Bonn, Germany: Forest Stewardship Council (FSC). Available at: https://ca.fsc.org/download.high-conservation-values-biodiversity.152.pdf.

FSC (2012). *Forest Stewardship Council Standards for Congo Basin. FSC-STD-CB-01–2012-EN Congo Basin Regional Standard EN.* Forest Stewardship Council (FSC). Available at: http://ic.fsc.org/congo-basin.372.htm.

FSC (2013). *Facts and Figures.* Forest Stewardship Council (FSC). Available at: https://ic.fsc.org/facts-figures.19.htm.

FSC Watch (2008). *Friends of the Earth EWNI: FSC Not Recommended.* FSC Watch. Available at: http://www.fsc-watch.org/archives/2008/09/22/Friends_of_the_Earth.

Furuichi, T. (2011). Female contributions to the peaceful nature of bonobo society. *Evolutionary Anthropology*, 20, 131–42.

Furuichi, T., Inagaki, H., and Angoue-Ovono, S. (1997). Population density of chimpanzees and gorillas in the Petit Loango Reserve, Gabon: employing a new method to distinguish between nests of the two species. *International Journal of Primatology*, 18, 1029–46.

Geissmann, T. (1991). Reassessment of the age of sexual maturity in gibbons (*Hylobates* spp.). *American Journal of Primatology*, 23, 11–22.

Geissmann, T., Nijman, V., and Dallmann, R. (2006). The fate of diurnal primates in southern Sumatra. *Gibbon Journal*, 2, 18–24.

Gibbons, E.F., and Lockwood, R. (1982). One-armed brachiation on gibbons (*Hylobates lar*). *American Journal of Primatology*, 3, 167–77.

Gibbs, H.K., Ruesch, A.S., Achard, F., *et al.* (2010). Tropical forests were the primary sources of new agricultural land in the 1980s and 1990s. *Proceedings of the National Academy of Sciences of the United States of America*, 107, 16732–7.

Gibson, C.C., Williams, J.T., and Ostrom, E. (2005). Local enforcement and better forests. *World Development*, 33, 273–84.

Gibson, L., Lee, T.M., Koh, L.P., *et al.* (2011). Primary forests are irreplaceable for sustaining tropical biodiversity. *Nature*, 478, 378–81.

Gill, D.J., Fa, J.E., Rowcliffe, M.R., and Kumpfel, N.A. (2012). Drivers of change in hunter offtake and hunting strategies in Sendje, Equatorial Guinea. *Conservation Biology*, 26, 1052–60.

Gillespie, T.R. (2006). Noninvasive assessment of gastrointestinal parasite infections in free-ranging primates. *International Journal of Primatology*, 27, 1129–43.

Gillespie, T.R., and Chapman, C.A. (2006). Prediction of parasite infection dynamics in primate metapopulations based on attributes of forest fragmentation. *Conservation Biology*, 20, 441–8.

Gillespie, T.R., and Chapman, C.A. (2008). Forest fragmentation, the decline of an endangered primate, and changes in host–parasite interactions relative to an unfragmented forest. *American Journal of Primatology*, 70, 222–30.

Gillespie, T.R., Chapman, C.A., and Greiner, E.C. (2005). Effects of logging on gastrointestinal parasite infections and infection risk in African primates. *Journal of Applied Ecology*, 42, 699–707.

Gils, H.V., and Kayijamahe, E. (2009). Sharing natural resources: mountain gorillas and people in the Parc National des Volcans , Rwanda. *African Journal of Ecology*, 48, 621–7.

Gittins, S.P. (1982). Feeding and ranging in the agile gibbon. *Folia Primatologica*, 38, 39–71.

Global Witness (2003). *A Conflict of Interests: The Uncertain Future of Burma's Forests.* London: Global Witness.

Global Witness (2008–12). *Making the Forest Sector Transparent Annual Report Card.* London: Global Witness. Available at: http://www.foresttransparency.info. Accessed November 8, 2012.

Global Witness (2009). *How do Report Cards Help?* London: Global Witness. Available at: http://www.foresttransparency.info/cms/file/210. Accessed November 8, 2012.

Global Witness (2012a). *The Art of Logging Industrially in the Congo: How Loggers are Abusing Artisanal Permits to Exploit the Democratic Republic of Congo's Forests.* London: Global Witness. Available at: http://www.globalwitness. org/sites/default/files/library/art_of_logging_lr.pdf Accessed November 6, 2012.

Global Witness (2012b). *Making the Forest Sector Transparent Project Information Note.* London: Global Witness. Available at: http://www.foresttransparency.info/cms/file/535. Accessed November 8, 2012.

Gogarten, J.F., Brown, L.M., Chapman, C.A., *et al.* (2012). Seasonal mortality patterns in non-human primates: implications for variation in selection pressures across environments. *Evolution*, 66, 3252–66.

Goldberg, T.L., Gillespie, T.R., Rwego, I.B., *et al.* (2007). Patterns of gastrointestinal bacterial exchange between chimpanzees and humans involved in research and tourism in western Uganda. *Biological Conservation*, 135, 511–7.

Goossens, B., Kapar, M.D., Kahar, S., and Ancrenaz, M. (2011). First sighting of Bornean orang-utan twins in the wild. *Asian Primates Journal*, 2, 12–4.

Gould, L., Sussman, R.W., and Sauther, L. (1999). Natural distasters and primate populations: the effects of a 2-year drought on a naturally occuring population of ring-tailed lemurs (*Lemur catta*) in southewestern Madagascar. *International Journal of Primatology*, 20, 69–84.

Gouyon, A. and Simorangkir, D. (2002). *The Economics of Fire Use in Agriculture and Forestry: A Preliminary Review for Indonesia.* Jakarta, Indonesia: IUCN/WWF International Project FireFight South East Asia.

Government of Gabon (in press). *Plan Climat.* Government of Gabon.

Gramke, K., Beck, J., Biederman, M., and Klemm, M. (2007). *Study on the Impacts of Different Options for the Revision of the Directive 86/609/EEC on the Protection of Laboratory Animals.* Basel, Berlin, Utrecht: PROGNOS. Available at: ec.europa.eu/environment/.../lab.../prognos_final_report.pdf Accessed April 24, 2011.

GRASP (2013). *Press Release. GRASP Council Counts Toll of Ape Trade.* GRASP. Available at: http://us2.campaign-archive1.com/?u=2a648714f89bd919aa28ee022andid=8098e94e31. Accessed February 12, 2013.

Gray, T.N.E., Phan, C., and Long, B. (2010). Modelling species distribution at multiple spatial scales: gibbon habitat preferences in a fagmented landscape. *Animal Conservation*, 1–9.

Greengrass, E. (2009). Chimpanzees are close to extinction in southwest Nigeria. *Primate Conservation*, 24, 77–83.

Grieser Johns, A. and Grieser Johns, B. (1995). Tropical forest primates and logging: long-term coexistence. *Oryx*, 29, 205–11.

Griffiths, M. and van Schaik, C.P. (1993). The impact of human traffic on the abundance and activity periods of Sumatran rain forest wildlife. *Conservation Biology*, 7, 623–6.

Gross-Camp, N.D., Masozera, M., and Kaplin, B.A. (2009). Chimpanzee seed dispersal quantity in a tropical montane forest of Rwanda. *American Journal of Primatology*, 71, 801–911.

Gullison, R.E. (2003). Does forest certification conserve biodiversity? *Oryx*, 37, 153–65.

Gupta, S., Zomorodi, G., Martinez, A., *et al.* (2011). Promoting natural resource rights: laying the groundwork for sustainable community-led development. American Jewish World Service grantmaking strategy paper presented at Indigenous World 2007, IWGIA, Copenhagen.

Gut Aiderbichl (2011). *Gut Aiderbichl's Sanctuary for Traumatized Chimpanzees and Other Primates: The Opening of Enclosure D.* Austria. Available at: http://www.gut-aiderbichl.at/videos/Schimpansen-Heft%20eng.pdf. September, 2011.

Hahn, B.H., Shaw, G.M., De Cock, K.M., and Sharp, P.M. (2000). AIDS as a zoonosis: scientific and public health implications. *Science*, 287, 607–14.

Hall, J.S., Harris, D.J., Medjibe, V., and Ashton, P.M.S. (2003). The effects of selective logging on forest structure and tree species composition in a Central African forest: implications for management of conservation areas. *Forest Ecology and Management*, 183, 249–64.

Hall, J.S., White, L.J.T., Inogwabini, B.I., *et al.* (1998). Survey of Grauer's gorillas (*Gorilla gorilla graueri*) and eastern chimpanzees (*Pan troglodytes schweinfurthii*) in the Kahuzi-Biega National Park lowland sector and adjacent forest in eastern Democratic Republic of Congo. *International Journal of Primatology*, 19, 207–35.

Hamard, M., Cheyne, S., and Nijman, V. (2010). Vegetation correlates of gibbon density in the peat-swamp forest of the Sabangau catchment, Central Kalimantan, Indonesia. *American Journal of Primatology*, 72, 607–16.

Hamilton, W.J. (1985). Demographic consequences of a food and water shortage to desert chacma baboons, *Papio ursinus. International Journal of Primatology*, 6, 451–62.

Handadhari, T., Sumitro, A., Warsito, S.P., and Widodo, S. (2002). Analisis Pungutan Rente Ekonomii Kayu Bulat Hutan Tanaman Industri di Indonesia. Unpublished study paper.

Hansen, M.C., Stehman, S.V., and Potapov, V. (2010). Quantification of global gross forest cover loss. *Proceedings of the National Academy of Sciences of the United States of America*, 107, 8650–5.

Harcourt, A.H., and Doherty, D.A. (2005). Species-area relationships of primates in tropical forest fragments: a global analysis. *Journal of Applied Ecology*, 42, 630–7.

Harcourt, A.H. and Greenberg, J. (2001). Do gorilla females join males to avoid infanticide? A quantitative model. *Animal Behaviour*, 62, 905–15.

Harcourt, A.H. and Stewart, K.J. (1980). Gorilla eaters of Gabon. *Oryx*, 15, 248–52.

Hardus, M.E., Lameira, A.R., Menken, S.B.J., and Wich, S.A. (2012). Effects of logging on orangutan behavior. *Biological Conservation*, 146, 177–87.

Hare, B., Call, J., and Tomasello, M. (2006). Chimpanzees deceive a human competitor by hiding. *Cognition*, 101, 495–514.

Hart, J. (2000). Impact and sustainability of indigenous hunting in the Ituri Forest, Congo-Zaire: a comparison of unhunted and hunted duiker populations. In *Hunting for Sustainability in Tropical Forests*, ed. J.G. Robinson and E. Bennett. New York, NY: Columbia University Press, pp. 106–53.

Hashimoto, C. (1995). Population census of the chimpanzees in the Kalinzu Forest, Uganda: comparison between methods with nest counts. *Primates*, 36, 477–88.

Hashimoto, C., Tashiro, Y., Kimura, D., *et al.* (1998). Habitat use and ranging of wild bonobos (*Pan paniscus*) at Wamba. *International Journal of Primatology*, 19, 1045–60.

Haslam, C. (2006). *Oil Prospecting in Gabon.* Available at: http://www.wildlifeextra.com/go/news/gabon-oil.html. Accessed April 16, 2013.

Hayes, K. and Wagner, F. (2008). *Regional Workshop. Small-Scale Mining in Africa: A Case for Sustainable Livelihoods.* Amsterdam: Common Fund for Commodities (CFC), CASM, PACT. Available at: http://www.common-fund. org/fileadmin/user_upload/Repository_docs/CFC_Report_Mining_2008_final_2_.pdf.

Head, J.S., Boesch, C., Robbins, M.M., *et al.* (2013). Effective sociodemographic population assessment of elusive species in ecology and conservation management. *Journal of Ecology and Evolution*, 3, 2903-16.

Hentschel, T., Hruschka, F., and Priester, M. (2002). *Global Report on Artisanal and Small-Scale Mining.* London: International Institute for Environment and Development (IIED).

Hicks, T.C., Darby, L., Hart, J., Kanuary, N., and Menken, S. (2010). Trade in orphans and bushmeat threatens one of the Democratic Republic of Congo's most important populations of Eastern Chimpanzee. *African Primates*, 7, 1–18.

Hill, A., Collier-Baker, E., and Suddendorf, T. (2011). Inferential reasoning by exclusion in great apes, lesser apes, and spider monkeys. *Journal of Comparative Psychology*, 125, 91–103.

Hilson, G. (2002). Small-scale mining and Its socio-economic impact in developing countries. *Natural Resources Forum*, 26, 3–13.

Hirst, P., and Thompson, G. (2000). *Globalization in Question.* Cambridge, UK: Polity Press.

Hockings, K.J., Anderson, J.R., and Matsuzawa, T. (2006). Road crossing in chimpanzees: a risky business. *Current Biology*, 16, 668–70.

Hockings, K.J., Anderson, J.R., and Matsuzawa, T. (2012). Socioecological adaptations by chimpanzees, *Pan troglodytes verus*, inhabiting an anthropogenically impacted habitat. *Animal Behaviour*, 83, 801–10.

Hockings, K.J. and Humle, T. (2009). *Best Practice Guidelines for the Prevention and Mitigation of Conflict Between Humans and Great Apes.* Gland, Switzerland: IUCN/SSC Primate Specialist Group. Available at: www.primate-sg.org/best_practice_conflict/.

Hockings, K.J. and McLennan, M.R. (2012). From forest to farm: systematic review of cultivar feeding by chimpanzees: management implications for wildlife in anthropogenic landscapes. *PLoS One*, 7, e33391.

Hohmann, G., Gerloff, U., Tautz, D., and Fruth, B. (1999). Social bonds and genetic ties: kinship, association and affiliation in a community of bonobos (*Pan paniscus*). *Behaviour*, 136, 1219–35.

Hollestelle, M. (2012). *Gabon Case Study: A Situational Analysis of ASM in Protected Areas and Critical Ecosystems and Recommendations for Gabonese Policymakers to Attain Ecologically and Socio- Economically Responsive Artisanal and Small-Scale Mining.* Cambridge, UK: ASM-PACE Programme. Available at: www.asm-pace.org.

Homsy, J. (1999). *Ape Tourism and Human Diseases: How Close Should We Get?* Nairobi: International Gorilla Conservation Programme. Available at: www.primate-sg.org/Homsy.

Hook, M.A., Lambeth, S.P., Perlman, J.E., *et al.* (2002). Inter-group variation in abnormal behavior in chimpanzees (*Pan troglodytes*) and rhesus macaques (*Macaca mulatta*). *Applied Animal Behaviour Science*, 76, 165–76.

Hruschka, F., and Echavarría, C. (2011). *Rock-Solid Chances for Responsible Artisanal Mining. ARM Series on Responsible ASM No. 3.* Medellín, Colombia: Alliance for Responsible Mining (ARM).

Husson, S.J., Wich, S.A., Marshall, A.J., *et al.* (2009). Orangutan distribution, density, abundance and impacts of disturbance. In *Orangutans: Geographic Variation in Behavioral Ecology and Conservation*, ed. S.A. Wich, S.U. Atmoko, T.M. Setia, and C.P. van Schaik. Oxford: Oxford University Press, pp. 77–96.

ICG (2010). *Dangerous Little Stones: Diamonds in the Central African Republic. Africa Report 157.* Brussels: International Crisis Group (ICG).

ICG (2012). *Black Gold in the Congo: Threat to Stability or Development Opportunity. Africa Report 188.* Brussels: International Crisis Group (ICG).

ICMM (2006). *Good Practice Guidance for Mining and Biodiversity.* London: International Council on Mining and Metals (ICMM).

ICMM (2008). *Planning for Integrated Mine Closure: Toolkit.* London: International Council on Mining and Metals (ICMM). Available at: http://www.icmm.com/page/84141/our-work/projects/articles/mine-closure-and-legacy.

ICMM (2010a). *Good Practice Guide: Indigenous Peoples and Mining.* London: International Council on Mining and Metals (ICMM).

ICMM (2010b). *Mining and Biodiversity: A Collection of Case Studies.* London: International Council on Mining and Metals (ICMM).

ICMM (2011). *Utilizing Mining and Mineral Resources to Foster the Sustainable Development of the Lao PDR.* London: Ministry Energy and Mines, NERI and International Council for Mining and Metals (ICMM).

ICMM (2012). *Mining's Contribution to Sustainable Development. InBrief: Trends in the Mining and Metals Industry, October 2012.* London: International Council on Mining and Metals (ICMM).

ICMM (2013). *Indigenous Peoples and Mining: Position Statement May 2013.* London: International Council on Mining and Metal (ICMM).

ICMM, and IUCN (2012). *Independent report on biodiversity offsets.* Prepared by the Biodiversity Consultancy. Available at: http://www.icmm.com/biodiversity-offsets.

IEG (2012). *Managing Forest Resources for Sustainable Development: an Evaluation of World Bank Group Experience.* Washington DC: Independent Evaluation Group (IEG).

IFC (2006). *International Finance Corporation's Policy on Social and Environmental Sustainability.* Washington DC: International Finance Corporation (IFC). Available at: http://www1.ifc.org/wps/wcm/connect/5159190048855a4f85b4d76a6515bb18/SustainabilityPolicy.pdf?MOD=AJPERESandCACHEID=5159190048855a4f85b4d76a6515bb18.

IFC (2009). *Projects and People: A Handbook for Addressing Project-Induced In-Migration.* Washington DC: International Finance Corporation (IFC). Available at: http://www.ifc.org/sustainability.

IFC (2012a). *IFC Articles of Agreement: Article I (amended June 27, 2012).* Washington, DC: IFC. Available at: http://www.ifc.org/wps/wcm/connect/corp_ext_content/ifc_external_corporate_site/about+ifc/articles+of+agreement/about+ifc+-+ifc+articles+of+agreement+-+article+i/. Accessed October 2013.

IFC (2012b). *International Finance Corporation's Guidance Notes: Performance Standards on Environmental and Social Sustainability, 1 January 2012.* Washington DC: International Finance Corporation (IFC). Available at: http://www.ifc.org/wps/wcm/connect/Topics_Ext_Content/IFC_External_Corporate_Site/IFC+Sustainability/Sustainability+Framework/Sustainability+Framework+-+2012/Performance+Standards+and+Guidance+Notes+2012/. Accessed September 2013.

Indufor (2012). *Strategic Review on the Future of Forest Plantations.* Helinski: Indufor.

ISIS (2012a). *International Species Information System.* International Species Information System (ISIS). Available at: http://www2.isis.org/AboutISIS/Pages/About-ISIS.aspx Accessed December 29, 2012.

ISIS (2012b). *ZIMS FAQ.* International Species Information System (ISIS). Available at: http://www2.isis.org/products/Pages/FAQ.aspx. Accessed December 29, 2012.

ITTO (2006). *Annual Review and Assessment of the World Timber Situation 2006.* Yokohama, Japan: International Tropical Timber Organization (ITTO). Available at: http://www.itto.or.jp/.

ITTO (2011). *Status of Tropical Forest Management 2011.* Yokohama, Japan: International Tropical Timber Organization (ITTO). Available at: http://www.itto.int/en/sfm/.

ITTO (2013). *Sustainable Forest Management.* Yokohama, Japan: International Tropical Timber Organization (ITTO). Available at: http://www.itto.int/sustainable_forest_management/. Accessed July 24, 2013.

ITTO, and IUCN (2009). *ITTO/IUCN Guidelines for the Conservation and Sustainable use of Biodiversity in Tropical Timber Production Forests. ITTO Policy Development Series No. 17.* Yokohama, Japan: International Tropical Timber Organization (ITTO).

IUCN (2011). *IUCN Red List of Threatened Species. Version 2011.1.* Gland, Switzerland: IUCN. Available at: http://www.iucnredlist.org. Accessed August 17, 2011.

IUCN (2012a). *IUCN Red List Categories and Criteria. Version 3.1,* 2nd edn. Gland, Switzerland and Cambridge, UK: IUCN.

IUCN (2012b). *IUCN Red List of Threatened Species. Version 2012.2.* Gland, Switzerland: IUCN. Available at: http://www.iucnredlist.org. Accessed 2012.

IUCN (2012c). *IUCN Red List of Threatened Species. Version 2012.1.* Gland, Switzerland: ICUN. Available at: http://www.iucnredlist.org. Accessed June 19, 2012.

IUCN (2013). *IUCN Red List of Threatened Species. Version 2013.1.* Gland, Switzerland: IUCN. Available at: http://www.iucnredlist.org.

IUCN, and ICCN (2012). *Bonobo (Pan paniscus): Conservation Strategy 2012–2022.* Gland, Switzerland: IUCN/SSC Primate Specialist Group and Institut Congolais pour la Conservation de la Nature (ICCN).

IUCN, and UNEP-WCMC (2010). *The World Database on Protected Areas (WDPA).* Cambridge, UK: UNEP-WCMC. Available at: www.protectedplanet.net Accessed May 13, 2012.

IUCN, and UNEP-WCMC (2012). *The World Database on Protected Areas (WDPA).* Cambridge, UK: UNEP-WCMC. Available at: http://www.protectedplanet.net. Accessed November 1, 2012.

IUCN, and UNEP-WCMC. (2013). *The World Database on Protected Areas (WDPA).* UNEP-WCMC. Cambridge, UK. Available at: http://www.protectedplanet.net. Accessed October 2013.

IWGIA (2007). *Indigenous World.* Copenhagen: IWGIA. Available at: http://www.forestpeoples.org/documents/africa/drc_iw_2007.pdf.

Jakarta Globe (2009). The fight over the natural wealth of Kalimantan's Kutai National Park. *Jakarta Globe,* September 15, 2009. Available at: http://www.illegal-logging.info/item_single.php?it_id=3707andit=news. Accessed June 20, 2012

Jenkins, M. (2008). Who murdered the Virunga gorillas? *National Geographic.* Available at: http://ngm.nationalgeographic.com/print/2008/07/virunga/jenkins-text. Accessed October 10, 2010.

Jepson, P., Momberg, F., and van Noord, H. (2002). A review of the efficacy of the protected areas system of East Kalimantan Province, Indonesia. *Natural Areas Journal,* 22, 28–42.

Johns, A.D. (1986a). Effects of selective logging on the behavioural ecology of West Malaysian primates. *Ecology,* 67, 684–94.

Johns, A.D. (1986b). The effects of commercial logging on a West Malaysian primate community. In *Current Perspectives in Primate Social Dynamics,* ed. D.M. Taub and F.A. King. New York, NY: Van Nostrand Reinhold, pp. 206–11.

Johns, A.D. (1992). Vertebrate responses to selective logging: implications for the design of logging systems. *Philosophical Transactions: Biological Sciences,* 335, 437–42.

Johns, A.D., and Skorupa, J.P. (1987). Response of rain-forest primates to habitat disturbance: a review. *International Journal of Primatology,* 8, 157–91.

Johns, A.G. (1997). *Timber Production and Biodiversity Conservation in Tropical Rain Forests. Cambridge Studies in Applied Ecology and Resource Management.* Cambridge, UK: Cambridge University Press.

Junker, J., Blake, S., Boesch, C., *et al.* (2012). Recent decline in suitable environmental conditions for African great apes. *Diversity and Distributions,* 18, 1077–91.

Juste, J., Fa, J.E., Delval, J.P., and Castroviejo, J. (1995). Market dynamics of bushmeat species in Equatorial-Guinea. *Journal of Applied Ecology,* 32, 454–67.

Kakati, K., Raghavan, R., Chellam, R., Qureshi, Q., and Chivers, D.J. (2009). Status of western hoolock gibbon (*Hoolock hoolock*) populations in fragmented forests of Eastern Assam. *Primate Conservation,* 24, 127–37.

Kalcher-Sommersguter, E., Preuschoft, S., Crailsheim, K., and Franz, C. (2011). Social competence of adult chimpanzees (*Pan troglodytes*) with severe deprivation history. I. An individual approach. *Developmental Psychology,* 47, 77–90.

Kalpers, J., Williamson, E.A., Robbins, M.M., *et al.* (2003). Gorillas in the crossfire: assessment of population dynamics of the Virunga mountain gorillas over the past three decades. *Oryx,* 37, 326–37.

Kano, F., Yamanashi, Y., and Tomonaga, M. (2012). Emotion as an intervening variable in understanding the cognitive and social complexity and well-being of chimpanzees. *Psychologia,* 55, 9–20.

Kartodihardjo, H. and Supriono, A. (2000). *Dampak Pembangunan Sektoral terhadap Konversi dan Degradasi Hutan Alam: Kasus Pembangunan HTI dan Perkebunan di Indonesia. Occasional Paper No. 26(I).* Bogor, Indonesia: CIFOR.

Kharas, H. (2010). *The Emerging Middle Class in Developing Countries. Working Paper No. 285.* Paris: OECD Development Centre.

King, J.E. and Landau, V.I. (2003). Can chimpanzee (*Pan troglodytes*) happiness be estimated by human raters? *Journal of Research in Personality,* 37, 1–15.

Kinnaird, M.F. and O'Brien, T.G. (1996). Ecotourism in the Tangkok DuaSudara Nature Reserve: opening Pandora's Box? *Oryx,* 30, 65–73.

Kiss, A. (2004). Making biodiversity conservation a land-use priority. In *Getting Biodiversity Projects to Work,* ed. T.O. McShane and M.P. Wells. New York, NY: Columbia University Press, pp. 98–123.

Kissinger, G., Herold, M. and De Sy, V. (2012). *Drivers of Deforestation and Forest Degradation. A Synthesis Report for REDD+ Policymakers*. Vancouver, Canada: Lexeme consulting.

Kloff, S., Wicks, C., and Siegal, P. (2010). *Extractive Industries and Sustainable Development: A Best Practice Guide*. Zeist, Netherlands: World Wild Fund for Nature.

Knight, A. (2008). The beginning of the end for chimpanzee experiments? *Philosophy, Ethics, and Humanities in Medicine*, 3, 16.

Knop, E., Ward, P.I., and Wich, S.A. (2004). A comparison of orang-utan density in a logged and unlogged forest in Sumatra. *Biological Conservation*, 120, 183–8.

Knott, C.D. (1998a). Changes in orangutan caloric intake, energy balance, and ketones in response to fluctuating fruit availability. *International Journal of Primatology*, 19, 1061–79.

Knott, C.D. (1998b). Orangutans in the wild. *National Geographic*, 194, 30–57.

Knott, C.D. (2005). Energetic responses to food availability in the great apes: implications for hominin evolution. In *Seasonality in Primates Studies of Living and Extinct Human and Non-Human Primates*, ed. D.K. Brockman and C.P. van Schaik. New York, NY: Cambridge University Press, pp. 351–78.

Kolstad, I., Søreide, T., and Williams, A. (2008). *Corruption in Natural Resource Management: An Introduction*. Anti-Corruption Resource Center, Chr. Michelson Institute. Available at: http://www.u4.no/publications/corruption-in-natural-resource-management-an-introduction/.

Köndgen, S., Kühl, H., N'Goran, P.K., *et al.* (2008). Pandemic human viruses cause decline of endangered great apes. *Current Biology*, 18, 260–4.

Koops, K., Humle, T., Sterck, E.H.M., and Matsuzawa, T. (2007). Ground-nesting by the chimpanzees of the Nimba Mountains, Guinea: environmentally or socially determined? *American Journal of Primatology*, 69, 407–19.

Kormos, R., and Boesch, C. (2003). *Regional Action Plan for the Conservation of Chimpanzees in West Africa*. Washington DC: Conservation International.

Kormos, R., Boesch, C., Bakarr, M.I., and Butynski, T.M. (2003). *West African Chimpanzees: Status, Survey and Conservation Action Plan*. Gland, Switzerland: IUCN/The World Conservation Union.

Kormos, R., and Kormos, C. (2011a). *International Finance Corporation Performance Standards 1 and 6: Their Potential Impact on Endangered and Critically Endangered Species with a Particular Focus on Great Apes*. Cambridge, UK: Arcus Foundation.

Kormos, R., and Kormos, C. (2011b). *Towards a Strategic National Plan for Biodiversity Offsets for Mining in the Republic of Guinea, West Africa With a Focus on Chimpanzees*. Cambridge, UK: Arcus Foundation.

Kormos, R., Lanjouw, A., Kormos, C., and Rainer, H. (2012). *The World Bank's Africa Biodiversity Strategy: The Case of the Great Apes*. Consultant report for the World Bank.

Kotze, N.J. (2002). The consequences of road development in the Golden Gate Highlands National Park, South Africa: paradise lost? *World Leisure*, 3, 54–60.

Koumbi, P.A. (2009). *Rapport Sommaire sur L'Evaluation de l'Impact de l'Activité d'Orpaillage sur le Parc National de Minkébé*. Libreville, Gabon: WWF Gabon.

KPC (2010). *PT Kaltim Prima Coal. Sustainabilty Report 2010. Expansion for Sustainability*. Sangatta, Indonesia: Kaltim Prima Coal (KPC). Available at: http://www.kpc.co.id/pdf/SR2010FinalEng.pdf.

KPC (2012). *Environment*. Sangatta, Indonesia: KalTim Prima Coal. Available at: http://www.kpc.co.id/index.php?option=com_content&task=view&id=37&Itemid=51. Accessed May 13, 2012.

Kuehl, H.S., Nzeingui, C., Yeno, S.L.D., *et al.* (2009). Discriminating between village and commercial hunting of apes. *Biological Conservation*, 142, 1500–6.

Kühl, H., Maisels, F., Ancrenaz, M., and Williamson, E.A. (2008). *Best Practice Guidelines for Surveys and Monitoring of Great Ape Populations*. Gland, Switzerland: IUCN/SSC Primate Specialist Group. Available at: http://www.primate-sg.org/best_practice_surveys/.

La Republique Gabonaise (2007). *Journal Officiel De La Republique Gabonaise*. La Republique Gabonaise. Available at: http://medias.legabon.net/PROD/0000001278.pdf. Accessed July 19, 2013.

Lahm, S. (2001). Hunting and wildlife in northeastern Gabon. Why conservation should extend beyond protected areas. In *African Rain Forest Ecology and Conservation: An Interdisciplinary Perspective*, ed. W. Weber, L.J.T. White, A. Vedder, and L. Naughton-Treves. New Haven, CT: Yale University Press, pp. 344–54.

Lahm, S. (2002). *L'Orpaillage au Nord-est du Gabon. Historique et Analyse Socio-Ecologique*. (Gold panning in northeastern Gabon. History and socio-ecological analysis). Libreville, Gabon: Multipress Gabon.

Lambin, E.F. and Meyfroidt, P. (2011). Global land use change, economic globalization, and the looming land scarcity. *Proceedings of the National Academy of Sciences of the United States of America*, 108, 3465–72.

Laporte, N.T., Stabach, J.A., Grosch, R., Lin, T.S., and Goetz, S.J. (2007). Expansion of industrial logging in central Africa. *Science*, 316, 1451.

Lappan, S. (2008). Male care of infants in a siamang (*Symphalangus syndactylus*) population including socially monogamous and polyandrous groups. *Behavioral Ecology and Sociobiology*, 62, 1307–17.

Laurence, W. (2008). The real cost of gold. *New Scientist*, 2669, 16.

Laurance, W.F., Goosem, M., and Laurance, S.G.W. (2009). Impacts of roads and linear clearings on tropical forests. *Trends in Ecology and Evolution*, 24, 659–69.

Laurance, W., Useche, D.C., Rendeiro, J., *et al.* (2012). Averting biodiversity collapse in tropical forest protected areas. *Nature*, 489, 290–4.

Lawson, S. and MacFaul, L. (2010). *Illegal Logging and Related Trade: Indicators of the Global Response. Briefing Paper July 2010.* London: Chatham House (The Royal Institute of International Affairs). Available at: http://www.chathamhouse.org/sites/default/files/.../0710pr_illegallogging.pdf.

Layden, M. (2010). *The Status of Information on Corruption in the Forestry Sector: U4.* Bergen: Transparency International. Available at: http://www.u4.no/publications/the-status-of-information-on-corruption-in-the-forestry-sector/. Accessed March 3, 2013.

Lee, P.C. (1998). The meaning of weaning: growth, lactation, and life history. *Evolutionary Anthropology*, 5, 87–96.

Leendertz, F.H., Boesch, C., Ellerbrok, H., *et al.* (2004). Non-invasive testing reveals a high prevalence of simian T-lymphotropic virus type 1 antibodies in wild adult chimpanzees of the Tai National Park, Cote d'Ivoire. *Journal of General Virology*, 85, 3305–12.

Leendertz, F.H., Pauli, G., Maetz-Rensing, K., *et al.* (2006). Pathogens as drivers of population declines: the importance of systematic monitoring in great apes and other threatened mammals. *Biological Conservation*, 131, 325–37.

Leighton, D.S.R. (1987). Gibbons: territoriality and monogamy. In *Primate Societies*, ed. B.B. Smuts, D.L. Cheyney, R.M. Seyfarth, R.W. Wrangham, and T.T. Struhsaker. Chicago, IL: University of Chicago Press, pp. 135–45.

Leighton, M. (1993). Modeling dietary selectivity by Bornean orangutans: evidence for integration of multiple criteria in fruit selection. *International Journal of Primatology*, 14, 257–313.

LEITI Secretariat (2010). *Summary of LEITI Third Report: 1 July 2009–30 June 2010.* Monrovia, Liberia: LEITI Secretariat. Available at: http://www.leiti.org.lr/doc/leiti3rdSum.pdf. Accessed November 7, 2012.

Lewis, O.T. (2001). Effect of experimental selective logging on tropical butterflies. *Conservation Biology*, 15, 389–400.

Locatelli, S. and Peeters, M. (2012). Non-human primates, retroviruses, and zoonotic infection risks in the human population. *Nature Education Knowledge*, 3, 62.

Loken, B., Spehar, S. and Rayadin, Y. (2013). Terrestriality in the Bornean orangutan (*Pongo pygmaeus morio*) and implications for their ecology and conservation. *American Journal of Primatology* 75, 1129–1138.

Lomax, T., Kenrick, J., and Brownell, A. (forthcoming). *Case Study for FAO Implementation Guide on FPIC and Land Acquisition: Sime Darby Oil Palm and Rubber Plantation in Grand Cape Mount County, Liberia.* Moreton-in-Marsh, UK: Forest Peoples Programme.

Lopresti-Goodman, S., Kameka, M., and Dube, A. (2012). Stereotypical behaviors in chimpanzees rescued from the African bushmeat and pet trade. *Behavioral Sciences*, 3, 1–20.

MacKinnon, K., Hatta, G., Halim, H., and Mangalik, A. (1996). *The Ecology of Kalimantan.* Hong Kong: Periplus Editions.

MAF (2011). *Gibbon Conservation Action Plan for Lao PDR.* Vientiane, Lao PDR: Division of Forest Resource Conservation, Department of Forestry, Ministry of Agriculture and Forestry (MAF).

Maina (2009). *Tethered Sudan Chimpanzee Airlifted to Safety at Sweetwaters, Kenya.* Baraza: Wildlife Direct. Available at: http://baraza.wildlifedirect.org/2009/10/08/tethered-sudan-chimpanzee-airlifted-to-safety-at-sweetwaters-kenya/. Accessed March 11, 2013.

Maisels, F., Nishihara, T., Strindberg, S., *et al.* (2012). Great ape and human impact monitoring training, surveys, and protection in the Ndoki-Likouala Landscape, Republic of Congo. GACF Agreement 96200–9-G247. Wildlife Conservation Society (WCS). Unpublished report.

Maisels, F., Strindberg, S., Blake, S., *et al.* (2013). Devastating decline of forest elephants in Central Africa. *PLoS One*, 8, e59469.

Malla, Y.B., Neupane, H.R., and Branney, P.J. (2003). Why aren't poor people benefiting more from community forestry. *Journal of Forest and Livelihood*, 3, 78–90.

Manurung, E.G.T. (2002). Dampak Kebijakan Larangan Ekspor Kayu Bulat pada Periode 1985–1997 terhadap Sektor Kehutanan Indonesia. Unpublished analytical paper.

Marshall, A.J., Ancrenaz, M., Brearley, F.Q., *et al.* (2009a). The effects of forest phenology and floristics on populations of Bornean and Sumatran orangutans: are Sumatran forests more productive than Bornean forests? In

Orangutans: Geographic Variation in Behavioral Ecology and Conservation, ed. S.A. Wich, S. Utami Atmoko, T. Mitra Setia, and C.P. van Schaik. Oxford: Oxford University Press, pp. 97–117.

Marshall, A.J., Lacy, R., Ancrenaz, M., *et al.* (2009b). Orangutan population biology, life history, and conservation. In *Orangutans: Geographic Variation in Behavioral Ecology and Conservation,* ed. S.A. Wich. New York, NY: Oxford University Press, pp. 311–26.

Marshall, A.J., Nardiyono, Engstrom, L.M., *et al.* (2006). The blowgun is mightier than the chainsaw in determining population density of Bornean orangutans (*Pongo pygmaeus morio*) in the forests of East Kalimantan. *Biological Conservation*, 129, 566–78.

Marshall, A.J. and Wrangham, R.W. (2007). The ecological significance of fallback foods. *International Journal of Primatology*, 28, 1219–35.

Martell, L. (2007). The third wave in globalization theory. *International Studies Review*, 9, 173–96.

Masi, S., Chauffour, S., Bain, O., *et al.* (2012). Seasonal effects on great ape health: a case study of wild chimpanzees and western gorillas. *PLoS One*, 7, e49805.

Matsuzawa, T., Tomonaga, M., and Tanaka, M. (2006). *Cognitive Development in Chimpanzees.* Berlin: Springer.

Matthews, A. and Matthews, A. (2004). Survey of gorillas (*Gorilla gorilla gorilla*) and chimpanzees (*Pan troglodytes troglodytes*) in southwestern Cameroon. *Primates*, 45, 15–24.

Maze, K. (2003). Anglo-American and the Bushmanland Conservation Initiative. Vth World Parks Congress, Workshop II.5, on Building Support from New Constituencies, Durban, South Africa, September 11–13, 2003. PDAC. Avaiable at: www.pdac.ca/pdac/land-use/pa-manitoba.html Accessed December 13, 2012.

Mazina, N. and Masumbuko, M. (2004). The mercury situation in the Democratic Republic of Congo: another problem that needs to be addressed (La pollution par le mercure, une guerre que la République Démocratique du Congo doit mener). Presented at the Regional Awareness-Raising Workshop on Mercury Pollution: A Global Problem that Needs to be Addressed. Session 3. Current Knowledge with Regard to Global/Regional/National Releases of Mercury to the Environment, November 22–25, 2004, Dakar, Senegal. United National Environment Programme (UNEP) Chemicals.

Mbaza, G. (2011). *Rapport de Mission Étude Orpaillage Minkébé.* Libreville, Gabon: WWF-Gabon.

McConkey, K.R. (2000). Primary seed shadow generated by gibbons in the rain forests of Barito Ulu, central Borneo. *American Journal of Primatology*, 52, 13–29.

McConkey, K.R. (2005). The influence of gibbon primary seed shadows on post-dispersal seed fate in a lowland dipterocarp forest in central Borneo. *Journal of Tropical Ecology*, 21, 255–62.

McConkey, K.R. and Chivers, D.J. (2007). Influence of gibbon ranging patterns on seed dispersal distance and deposition site in a Bornean forest. *Journal of Tropical Ecology*, 23, 269–75.

McGrew, W.C. (2010). In search of the last common ancestor: new findings on wild chimpanzees. *Philosophical Transactions of the Royal Society London B: Biological Sciences*, 365, 3267–76.

McLennan, M.R. and Plumptre, A.J. (2012). Protected apes, unprotected forest: composition, structure and diversity of riverine forest fragments and their conservation value in Uganda. *Tropical Conservation Science*, 5, 79–103.

McMahon, G., Rasdiani Subdibjo, E., Aden, J., *et al.* (2000). *Mining and the Environment in Indonesia: Long-Term Trends and Repercussions of the Asian Economic Crisis.* Washington DC: East Asia Environment and Social Development (EASES) Group, World Bank.

McNeely, J.A. (2005). *Friends for Life: New Partners in Support of Protected Areas.* Gland, Switzerland and Cambridge, UK: IUCN.

McNeely, J.A. (2007). Addressing extreme conflicts through peace parks. In *Extreme Conflict and Tropical Forests*, ed. W. De Jong, D. Donovan, and A. Ken-Ichi. Dordrecht, the Netherlands: Springer, pp. 159–72.

McShane, T.O. and Newby, S.A. (2004). Expecting the unattainable: the assumptions behind ICDPs. In *Getting Biodiversity Projects to Work*, ed. T.O. McShane and M.P. Wells. New York, NY: Columbia University Press, pp. 49–74.

McShane, T.O. and Wells, M.P. (2004). Integrated conservation and development? . In *Getting Biodiversity Projects to Work*, ed. T.O. McShane and M.P. Wells. New York, NY: Columbia University Press, pp. 3–9.

Meijaard, E., Albar, G., Nardiyono, *et al.* (2010). Unexpected ecological resilience in Bornean orangutans and implications for pulp and paper plantation management. *PLoS One*, 5, e12813.

Meijaard, E., Buchori, D., Hadiprakoso, Y., *et al.* (2011). Quantifying killing of orangutans and human-orangutan conflict in Kalimantan, Indonesia *PLoS One*, 6, e27491.

Meijaard, E. and Sheil, D. (2007). A logged forest in Borneo is better than none at all. *Nature*, 446, 974.

Meijaard, E. and Sheil, D. (2008). The persistence and conservation of Borneo's mammals in lowland rain forests managed for timber: observations, overviews and opportunities. *Ecology Research*, 23, 21–34.

Meijaard, E., Sheil, D., Nasi, R., *et al.* (2005). *Life after Logging. Reconciling Wildlife Conservation and Production Forestry in Indonesian Borneo.* Jakarta, Indonesia: CIFOR and UNESCO.

Meijaard, E., Wich, S., Ancrenaz, M., and Marshall, A.J. (2012). Not by science alone: why orangutan conservationists must think outside the box. *Annals of the New York Academy of Sciences*, 1249, 29–44.

Melfi, V.A. (2012). Gibbons: probably the most endangered primates in the world. *International Zoo Yearbook*, 46, 239–40.

MIGA (2013a). *Environmental and Social Safeguards.* MIGA. Available at: http://www.miga.org/projects/index.cfm?stid=1822. Accessed October 2013.

MIGA (2013b). *Who We Are: Overview.* MIGA. Available at: http://www.miga.org/whoweare/index.cfm. Accessed October 2013.

MIKE (2005). *Monitoring the Illegal Killing of Elephants: Central African Forests. Final Report on Population Surveys (2003–2004).* Washington DC: MIKE-CITES-WCS.

Milner-Gulland, E.J. and Bennett, E.L. (2003). Wild meat: the bigger picture. *Trends in Ecology and Evolution*, 18, 351–7.

Ministry of Forestry (2006). *Forest Statistics of Indonesia 2005.* Indonesia: Ministry of Forestry. Available at: http://www.dephut.go.id/news.php?id=497. Accessed November 21, 2012.

Ministry of Forestry (2008). *Consolidation Report. Reducing Emissions from Deforestation and Forest Degradation in Indonesia.* Jakarta, Indonesia: Ministry of Forestry.

Ministry of Forestry (2009a). *Forest Designation Map.* Jakarta, Indonesia: Ministry of Forestry.

Ministry of Forestry (2009b). *Orangutan Indonesia Conservation Strategies and Action Plan 2007–2017.* Directorate General of Forest Protection and Nature Conservation, Ministry of Forestry of the Republic of Indonesia.

Ministry of Forestry (2013). Direktorat Jenderal Bina Produksi Kehutanan. Jakarta, Indonesia: Ministry of Forestry, Indonesia. Available at: http://www.dephut.go.id/index.php?q=id/node/898. Accessed September 2013.

Miranda, M., Burris, P., Bingcang Froy, J., *et al.* (2003). *Mining and Critical Ecosystems: Mapping the Risks.* Washington DC: World Resources Institute.

Mitani, J.C. (2009). Male chimpanzees form enduring and equitable social bonds. *Animal Behaviour*, 77, 633–40.

Mitani, J.C., Watts, D.P., and Amsler, S.J. (2010). Lethal intergroup aggression leads to territorial expansion in wild chimpanzees. *Current Biology*, 20, 507–8.

Mitra Setia, T., Delgado, R.A., Utami Atmoko, S., Singleton, I., and van Schaik, C.P. (2009). Social organization and male-female relationships. In *Orangutans: Geographic Variation in Behavioral Ecology and Conservation*, ed. S.A. Wich, S. Utami Atmoko, T. Mitra Setia, and C.P. van Schaik. Oxford: Oxford University Press, pp. 245–53.

Mittermeier, R.A. and Cheyney, D.L. (1987). Conservation of primates and their habitats. In *Primate Societies*, ed. B.B. Smuts, D.L. Cheyney, R.M. Seyfarth, R.W. Wrangham, and T.T. Struhsaker. Chicago, IL: University of Chicago Press, pp. 477–90.

MMG (2012). *Minmetals Resources Limited: Sepon.* MMG. Available at: http://www.mmg.com/en/Our-Operations/Mining-operations/Sepon.aspx. Accessed on July 17, 2012.

MMSD (2002). *Breaking New Ground.* London, UK, and Sterling, VA: Earthscan Publications Ltd.

Moilanen, A., Wilson, K.A., and Possingham, H. (2009). *Spatial Conservation Prioritization: Quantitative Methods and Computational Tools.* Oxford: Oxford University Press.

MONA Foundation (2013). *MONA Foundation: Who Are We?* MONA Foundation. Available at: http://www.fundacionmona.org/en/Fundacion/origenes.html. Accessed March 13, 2013.

Monkey World (2012). *Monkey World Rescue Centre: Meet our Primates.* Monkey World Ape Rescue Centre. Available at: http://www.monkeyworld.org/meet-our-primates. Accessed March 27, 2013.

Moore, N. (2012). *UK Timber Industry Certification* London: UK Timber Trade Federation. Available at: http://www.ttf.co.uk/. Accessed September 14, 2012.

Morgan, B.J., Adeleke, A., Bassey, T., *et al.* (2011). *Regional Action Plan for the Conservation of the Nigeria-Cameroon Chimpanzee (*Pan troglodytes ellioti*).* San Diego, CA: IUCN/SSC Primate Specialist Group and Zoological Society of San Diego.

Morgan, D., and Sanz, C. (2003). Naive encounters with chimpanzees in the Goualougo Triangle, Republic of Congo. *International Journal of Primatology*, 24, 369–81.

Morgan, D., and Sanz, C. (2006). Chimpanzee feeding ecology and comparisons with sympatric gorillas in the Goualougo Triangle, Republic of Congo. In *Primate Feeding Ecology in Apes and Other Primates: Ecological, Physiological, and Behavioural Aspects*, ed. G. Hohmann, M. Robbins, and C. Boesch. Cambridge, UK: Cambridge University Press, pp. 97–122.

Morgan, D., and Sanz, C. (2007). *Best Practice Guidelines for Reducing the Impact of Commercial Logging on Great Apes in Western Equatorial Africa.* Gland, Switzerland: IUCN/SSC Primate Specialist Group (PSG). Available at: http://www.primate-sg.org/best_practice_logging/.

Morgan, D., Sanz, C., Greer, D., *et al.* (2013). *Great Apes and FSC: Implementing 'Ape Friendly' Practices in Central Africa's Logging Concessions.* Gland, Switzerland: IUCN/SSC Primate Specialist Group. Available at: http://www.primate-sg.org/best_practice_logging/.

Morgan, D., Sanz, C., Onononga, J.R., and Strindberg, S. (2006). Ape abundance and habitat use in the Goualougo Triangle, Republic of Congo. *International Journal of Primatology*, 27, 147–79.

Morrogh-Bernard, H., Husson, S.J., Knott, C.D., *et al.* (2009). Orangutan activity budgets and diet. A comparison between species, populations and habitats. In *Orangutans. Geographic Variation in Behavioral Ecology and Conservation*, ed. S.A. Wich, S.U. Atmoko, T.M. Setia, and C.P. van Schaik. Oxford: Oxford University Press, pp. 119–33.

Morrogh-Bernard, H., Husson, S., Page, S.E., and Rieley, J.O. (2003). Population status of the Bornean orang-utan (*Pongo pygmaeus*) in the Sebangau peat swamp forest, Central Kalimantan, Indonesia. *Biological Conservation*, 110, 141–52.

Morvan, J.M., Deubel, V., Gounon, P., *et al.* (1999). Identification of *Ebola* virus sequences present as RNA or DNA in organs of terrestrial small mammals of the Central African Republic. *Microbes Infect*, 1, 1193–201.

Moser, J.H. (2011). *Global Infrastructure.* New York, NY: Bingham McCutchen LLP.

Muchaal, P.K., and Ngandjui, G. (1999). Impact of village hunting on wildlife populations in the Western Dja Reserve, Cameroon. *Conservation Biology*, 13, 385–96.

Muehlenbein, M.P., Ancrenaz, M., Sakong, R., Ambu, L., and Prall, S. (2012). Ape conservation physiology: fecal glucocorticoid responses in wild *Pongo pygmaeus morio* following human visitation. *PLoS One*, 7, e33357.

Muhtaman, D.R., and Prasetyo, F.A. (2004). *Forest Certification in Indonesia.* Bogor, Indonesia: Center for International Forestry Research.

Mulavwa, M., Furuichi, T., Yangozene, K., *et al.* (2008). Seasonal changes in fruit production and party size of bonobos at Wamba. In *The Bonobos: Behaviour, Ecology and Conservation*, ed. T. Furuichi, and J. Thompson. New York, NY: Springer, pp. 121–34.

Murdiyarso, D., Dewi, S., Lawrence, D., and Seymour, F. (2011). *Indonesia's Forest Moratorium. A Stepping Stone to Better Forest Governance? Working Paper 76.* Bogor, Indonesia: CIFOR.

Murphree, M.W. (1996). *Approaches to Community Participation. African Policy Wildlife Policy Consultation. Final Report of the Consultation.* London: Overseas Development Administration.

Murray, C.M., Heintz, M.R., Lonsdorf, E.V., Parr, L.A., and Santymire, R.M. (2013). Validation of a field technique and characterization of fecal glucocorticoid metabolite analysis in wild chimpanzees (*Pan troglodytes*). *American Journal of Primatology*, 75, 57–64.

Nakott, J. (2012). Grundrechte für Menschenaffen. *National Geographic Deutschland*, 38–71. Available at: http://www.nationalgeographic.de/reportagen/grundrechte-fuer-menschenaffen. Accessed March 12, 2013.

Nash, L.T., Fritz, J., Alford, P.A., and Brent, L. (1999). Variables influencing the origins of diverse abnormal behaviors in a large sample of captive chimpanzees (Pan troglodytes). *American Journal of Primatology*, 48, 15–29.

Nasi, R., Billand, A., and van Vliet, N. (2012). Managing for timber and biodiversity in the Congo Basin. *Forest Ecology and Management*, 268, 103–11.

Naughton, L. (1993). *Conservation versus Artisanal Gold Mining in Corcovado National Park, Costa Rica: Land Use Conflicts at Neotropical Wilderness Frontiers.* Available at: http://sites.maxwell.syr.edu/clag/yearbook1993/naughton.htm. Accessed January 10, 2013.

Nawir, A.A., Murniati, and Rumboko, L. (2007). *Forest Rehabilitation in Indonesia: Where to After More than Three Decades?* Bogor, Indonesia: CIFOR.

Ndumbe, L.N. (2010). Markets and market chain analysis for Eru (*Gnetum* spp.), a major non-timber forest product in central and west Africa. MSc thesis, University of Buea, Cameroon.

Neef, A. and Touch, S. (2012). Land-grabbing in Cambodia: narratives, mechanisms, resistance. Presented at Global Land Grabbing II, October 17–19, 2012, Department of Development Sociology at Cornell University, Ithaca, NY. Land Deals Politics Initiative (LDPI).

Nellemann, C., Miles, L., Kaltenborn, B.P., Viture, M., and Ahlenius, H., ed. (2007). *The Last Stand of the Orangutan – State of Emergency: Illegal Logging, Fire and Palm Oil in Indonesia's National Parks.* Norway: United Nations Environment Programme (UNEP), GRID-Arendal. Available at: www.grida.no.

Nelson, J. (2007). *Securing Indigenous Land Rights in the Cameroon Oil Pipeline Zone.* Moreton-in-Marsh, UK: Forest Peoples Programme.

Nelson, J. and Venant, M. (2008). Indigenous Peoples' Participation in Mapping of Traditional Forest Resources for Sustainable Livelihoods and Great Ape Conservation (November 2008). Report to the United Nations Environment Programme (UNEP). Moreton-in-Marsh, UK: Forest Peoples Programme.

Nguyen Vinh Thanh and Le Vu Khoi (2006). Results of study on Delacour's langur *Trachypithecus delacouri* (Osgood, 1932) in Van Long Nature Reserve, Ninh Binh Province. *Journal of Science*, 22, 73–8.

NIH Chimpanzee Working Group (2013). Section 3. Ethologically appropriate physical and social environments: a key concept in the IOM Principles. In *Council of Councils Working Group on the Use of Chimpanzees in NIH-Supported Research*, ed. US National Insititutes of Health. Washington DC: US National Insititutes of Health, pp. 19–27.

Nijman, V. (2005). Hanging in the balance: an assessment of trade in orangutans and gibbons on Kalimantan, Indonesia. Report for TRAFFIC Southeast Asia. Petaling Jaya, Selangor, Malaysia: TRAFFIC Southeast Asia.

Nilsson, S. (2011). The megatrends and the forest sector. Presented at the Royal Swedish Academy of Agriculture and Forestry, June 2011, Stockholm, Sweden.

Normand, E. and Boesch, C. (2009). Sophisticated Euclidean maps in forest chimpanzees. *Animal Behaviour*, 77, 1195–201.

Normand, E., Singo, B., and Boesch, C. (2010) *Rapport de suivi ecologique dans les forêts classées de Goin-Débé et de Cavally (2007-2010)*. Abidjan, Côte d'Ivoire: Wild Chimpanzee Foundation.

Norris, K., Asase, A., Collen, B., *et al.* (2010). Biodiversity in a forest-agriculture mosaic: the changing face of West African rainforests. *Biological Conservation*, 143, 2341–50.

Noss, A. (2000). Cable snares and nets in the Central African Republic. Evaluating the sustainability of hunting in tropical forests. In *Hunting for Sustainability in Tropical Forests*, ed. J.G. Robinson and E. Bennett. New York, NY: Columbia University Press, pp. 282–304.

Nussbaum, R. and Simula, M. (2005). *The Forest Certification Handbook.* London: Earthscan.

Nyame, F. and Grant, A. (2012). From carats to karats: explaining the shift from diamond mining to gold mining by artisanal miners in Ghana. *Journal of Cleaner Production*, 29–30, 163–72.

O'Brien, T.G., Kinnaird, M.F., Nurcahyo, A., Prasetyaningrum, M., and Iqbal, M. (2003). Fire, demography and the persistence of Siamang (*Symphalangus syndactylus*: Hylobatidae) in a Sumatran rainforest. *Animal Conservation*, 6, 115–21.

OCSP (2010). *Orangutan Conservation Services Program. Final Report.* Jakarta, Indonesia: DAI and USAID.

OECD (2012). *OECD Environmental Outlook to 2050. The Consequences of Inaction.* Paris: OECD.

OIE (2012). *Terrestrial Animal Health Code 2012*, 21st edn. Paris: World Organization for Animal Health.

Okimori, Y., and Matius, P. (2000). Impact of different intensities of selective logging on a low-hill dipterocarp forest in Pasir, East Kalimantan. In *Rainforest Ecosystems of East Kalimantan: El Nino, Drought, Fire and Human Impacts*, ed. E. Guhardja, M. Fatawi, M. Sutisana, T. Mori, and S. Ohta. Tokyo: Springer, pp. 209–17.

Olsen, C.S., and Helles, F. (2009). Market efficiency and benefit distribution in medicinal plant markets: empirical evidence from South Asia. *International Journal of Biodiversity Science and Management*, 5, 53–62.

Olson, D.M., and Dinerstein, E. (2002). The Global 200: priority ecoregions for global conservation. *Annals of the Missouri Botanical Garden*, 89, 125–6.

Onderdonk, D.A., and Chapman, C.A. (2000). Coping with forest fragmentation: the primates of Kibale National Park, Uganda. *International Journal of Primatology*, 21, 587–611.

Orellana, M.A. (2002). *Mining Certification: A Field of Growing Trade Interest.* Available at: http://www.ciel.org/Publications/BRIDGES_MiningCertif_NOVDEC02.pdf Accessed December 12, 2012.

Paciulli, L.M. (2004). The effects of logging, hunting, and vegetation on the densities of the Pagai, Mentawai Island primates. Anthropology, Stony Brook University. PhD.

Pact (2010). *PROMINES Study: Artisanal Mining in the Democratic Republic of Congo. DFID, World Bank, and PROMINES.* Washington DC: Pact Inc.

Pallisco and CIFM (2013). Plan Strategique de Protection de la Faune. Cameroon: Societés Pallisco and CIFM.

Palombit, R.A. (1992). Pair bonds and monogamy in wild siamang (*Hylobates syndactylus*) and white-handed gibbons (*Hylobates lar*) in Northern Sumatra. PhD thesis, University of California, California.

Palombit, R.A. (1994). Dynamic pair bonds in hylobatids: implications regarding monoganous social systems. *Behaviour*, 128, 65–101.

Palombit, R.A. (1995). Longitudinal patterns of reproduction in wild female siamang (*Hylobates syndactylus*) and white-handed gibbons (*Hylobates lar*). *International Journal of Primatology*, 16, 739–60.

Parnell, R.J. (2002). The social structure and behaviour of western lowland gorillas (*Gorilla gorilla gorilla*) at Mbeli Bai, Republic of Congo. PhD thesis, University of Stirling, UK.

PASA (2011). *PASA Moves Chimpanzees Amid Sudanese Unrest.* Pan African Sanctuary Alliance (PASA). Available at: http://pasaprimates.org/pasa-moves-chimpanzees-amid-sudanese-unrest/. Accessed March 3, 2013.

Pearce, F. (2012). *Land Grabbing: The New Tragedy of the Commons.* Available at: http://www.justconservation.org/land-grabbing-the-new-tragedy-of-the-commons. Accessed December 11, 2012.

Pedler, R., ed. (2010). *Best Management Practices for Orangutan Conservation: Natural Forest Concessions.* Jakarta, Indonesia: Orangutan Conservation Services Program (OCSP)/United States Agency for International Development (USAID).

Pérez, M.R., de Blas, D.E., Nasi, R., *et al.* (2005). Logging in the Congo Basin: a multi-country characterization of timber companies. *Forest Ecology and Management*, 214, 221–36.

Peters, S.L., Malcolm, J.R., and Zimmerman, B.L. (2006). Effects of selective logging on bat communities in the southeastern Amazon. *Conservation Biology*, 20, 1410–21.

Phoonjampa, R., Koenig, A., Brockelman, W.Y., *et al.* (2011). Pileated gibbon density in relation to habitat characteristics and post-logging forest recovery. *Biotropica*, 43, 619–27.

Plumptre, A., Amsini, F., Shamavu, P., and Kujirakwinj, D. (2009). Survey in Itombwe. *Gorilla Journal*, 39, 4–5.

Plumptre, A.J. and Grieser Johns, A. (2001). Changes in primate communities following logging disturbance. In *The Cutting Edge: Conserving Wildlife in Logged Tropical Forest*, ed. R.A. Fimbel, A. Grajal, and J.G. Robinson. New York, NY: Columbia University Press, pp. 71–92.

Plumptre, A.J. and Reynolds, V. (1994). The effect of selective logging on the primate populations in the Budongo Forest Reserve, Uganda. *Journal of Applied Ecology*, 31, 631–41.

Plumptre, A. and Reynolds, V. (1996). Censusing chimpanzees in the Budongo Forest, Uganda. *International Journal of Primatology*, 17, 85–99.

Plumptre, A.J., Rose, R., Nangendo, G., *et al.* (2010). *Eastern Chimpanzee (*Pan troglodytes schweinfurthii*): Status Survey and Conservation Action Plan 2010–2020.* Gland, Switzerland: IUCN.

Pollard, E.H.B., Clements, T., Hor, N.M., Ko, S., and Rawson, B.M. (2007). *Status and Conservation of Globally Threatened Primates in the Seima Biodiversity Conservation Area.* Phnom Penh, Cambodia: Forestry Administration and Wildlife Conservation Society.

Population Reference Bureau (2011). *2011 World Population Data Sheet.* Washington DC: Population Reference Bureau.

Porter-Bolland, L., Ellis, E.A., Guariguata, M.R., *et al.* (2011). Community managed forests and forest protected areas: an assessment of their conservation effectiveness across the tropics. *Forest Ecology and Management.* Available at: http://www.cifor.org/nc/online-library/browse/view publication/publication/3461.html. Accessed January 31, 2013.

Potts, K.B. (2011). The long-term impact of timber-harvesting on the resource base of chimpanzees in the Kibale National Park, Uganda. *Biotropica*, 43, 256–64.

Poulsen, J. and Clark, C.J. (2012). *Tropical Forest Conservation and Industry Partnership. An Experience from the Congo Basin.* New York, NY: The Wildlife Conservation Society and Wiley and Sons.

Poulsen, J.R., Clark, C.J., and Bolker, B.M. (2011). Decoupling the effects of logging and hunting on an Afrotropical animal community. *Ecological Applications*, 21, 1819–36.

Poulsen, J.R., Clark, C.J., Mavah, G., and Elkan, P.W. (2009). Bushmeat supply and consumption in a tropical logging concession in northern Congo. *Conservation Biology*, 23, 1597–608.

Powers, W. and Wong, A. (2011). *Fairly Trading the World's Timber: Lessons on Global Forest Governance and Trade from Europe and Liberia.* New York, NY: World Policy Institute and Demos.

Prasetyo, D., Ancrenaz, M., Morrogh-Bernard, H.C., *et al.* (2009). Nest building in orangutans. In *Orangutans: Geographic Variation in Behavioral Ecology and Conservation*, ed. S.A. Wich, S. Utami Atmoko, T. Mitra Setia, and C.P. van Schaik. Oxford: Oxford University Press, pp. 269–77.

President of the Republic of Indonesia (2012). Peraturan Presiden Republik Indonesia, Nomor 3 Tahun 2012, Tentang, Rencana Tata Ruang Pulau Kalimantan.

Presidential Regulation (September 20, 2011). Presidential Regulation of the Republic of Indonesia. No. 61/2011 on the National Action Plan for Greenhouse Gas (RAN-GRK).

Preuschoft, S., and Nente, C. (2012). *Last Step to Release: A Quarantined Forest High School.* Technical report. Wien: Veir Pfoten.

Prime Minister's Department of Malaysia (2010). *Economic Transformation Programme: A Roadmap for Malaysia.* Performance Management and Delivery Unit (PEMANDU). Available at: http://etp.pemandu.gov.my/download_centre.aspx. Accessed September 15, 2013.

Pruetz, J.D. and Bertolani, P. (2009). Chimpanzee (*Pan troglodytes verus*) behavioral responses to stresses associated with living in a savanna-mosaic environment: implications for hominin adaptations to open habitats. *Paleoanthropology*, 2009, 252–62.

PT Newmont Horas Nauli (2003). *Baseline Terrestrial Ecology Survey of the Martabe Project Area, North Sumatra Province, Indonesia.* Bogor, Indonesia: PT Newmont Horas Nauli, PT Hatfindo Prima, and LIPI.

Putz, F.E., Blate, G.E., Redford, K.H., Fimbel, R., and Robinson, J. (2001). Tropical forest management and conservation of biodiversity: an overview. *Conservation Biology*, 15, 7–20.

Putz, F.E., Dykstra, D.P., and Heinrich, R. (2000). Why poor logging practices persist in the tropics. *Conservation Biology*, 14, 951–6.

Putz, F.E., Zuidema, P.A., Pinard, M.A., *et al.* (2008). Improved tropical forest management for carbon retention. *PLoS Biol*, 6, e166.

Putz, F.E., Zuidema, P.A., Synnott, T., *et al.* (2012). Sustaining conservation values in selectively logged tropical forests: the attained and the attainable. *Conservation Letters*, 5, 296–303.

Quiatt, D., Reynolds, V., and Stokes, E.J. (2002). Snare injuries to chimpanzees (*Pan troglodytes*) at 10 study sites in east and west Africa. *African Journal of Ecology*, 40, 303–5.

Rabanal, L.I., Kuehl, H.S., Mundry, R., Robbins, M.M., and Boesch, C. (2010). Oil prospecting and its impact on large rainforest mammals in Loango National Park, Gabon. *Biological Conservation*, 143, 1017–24.

Raemaekers, J. (1978). Changes through the day in the food choices of wild gibbons. *Folia Primatologica*, 30, 194–205.

Raemaekers, J. (1980). Causes of variation between months in the distance traveled daily by gibbons. *Folia Primatologica*, 34, 46–60.

Rainforest Foundation (2012). *Seeds of Destruction, Expansion of Industrial Oil Palm in the Congo Basin: Potential Impacts on Forests And people.* London: The Rainforest Foundation.

Randeria, S. (2003). Cunning states and unaccountable international institutions: legal plurality, social movements and rights of local communities to common property resources. *European Journal of Sociology*, 44, 27–60.

Randers, J. (2012). *2052. A Global Forecast for the Next Forty Years.* London: Chelsea Green.

Rao, M. and van Schaik, C.P. (1997). The behavioral ecology of Sumatran orangutans in logged and unlogged forest. *Tropical Biodiversity*, 4, 173–85.

Ravat, A. and Ufer, A. (2010). *Toward Strengthened EITI Reporting: Summary Report and Recommendations. Extractive Industries and Development Series, No. 14.* Washington DC: The World Bank. Available at: http://documents.world bank.org/curated/en/2010/01/12166142/toward-strengthened-eiti-reporting-summary-report-recommendations.

Rawson, B.M. (2012). *Impact Assessment of Habitat Restoration Activities on The eastern Black Crested Gibbon* (Nomascus nasutus) *in the Cao Vit Gibbon Conservation Area and Best Practice Guidelines.* Hanoi, Viet Nam: People, Resources and Conservation Foundation.

Rawson, B.M., Insua-Cao, P., Nguyen Manh Ha, *et al.* (2011). *The Conservation Status of Gibbons in Vietnam.* Hanoi, Viet Nam: Fauna and Flora International and Conservation International.

REDD Desk (2011). *REDD Countries: A Database of REDD Activities on the Ground: Malaysia.* Available at: http://www.thereddesk.org/countries/malaysia/readiness_overview. Accessed September 2013.

Redford, K.H. (1992). The empty forest. *BioScience*, 42, 414–22.

Redmond, I. (2001). *Coltan Boom, Gorilla Bust: The Impact of Coltan Mining on Gorillas and other Wildlife in Eastern DR Congo.* Horsham, UK: Dian Fossey Gorilla Fund and Born Free Foundation.

Reichard, U. (1995). Extra-pair copulations in a monogamous gibbon (*Hylobates lar*). *Ethology*, 100, 99–112.

Reichard, U. and Barelli, C. (2008). Life history and reproductive strategies of Khao Yai *Hylobates lar*: implications for social evolution in apes. *International Journal of Primatology*, 29, 823–44.

Reimers, M., Schwarzenberger, F., and Preuschoft, S. (2007). Rehabilitation of research chimpanzees: stress and coping after long-term isolation. *Hormones and Behavior*, 51, 428–35.

Reinartz, G.E., Ingmanson, E.J., and Vervaecke, H. (2013). *Pan paniscus* gracile chimpanzee. In *Mammals of Africa. Volume II. Primates*, ed. T.M. Butynski, J. Kingdon, and J. Kalina. London: Bloomsbury Publishing, pp. 64–9.

Remis, M.J. (2000). Preliminary assessment of the impacts of human activities on gorillas *Gorilla gorilla gorilla* and other wildlife at Dzanga-Sangha Reserve, Central African Republic. *Oryx*, 34, 56–65.

Republic of Gabon (2013). *Emerging Policy, Le Gabon.org, Official Potal of the Gabonese Republic.* Republic of Gabon. Available at: http://www.en.legabon.org/emerging-gabon/emerging-policy. Accessed July 19, 2013.

République du Cameroun (1994). LOI No 94/01 du 20 janvier 1994 portant régime des forêts, de la fauna et de la pêche.

RESOLVE (2010). *Tracing a Path Forward: A Study of the Challenges of the Supply Chain for Target Metals used in Electronics.* Washington DC: RESOLVE Inc.

Rijksen, H.D. (1978). *A Field Study on Sumatran Orang Utans (Pongo pygmaeus abelii Lesson 1827): Ecology, Behaviour and Conservation.* Wageningen, the Netherlands: H. Veenman and Zonen B. V.

Rijksen, H.D. and Meijaard, E. (1999). *Our Vanishing Relative. The Status of Wild Orang-utans at the Close of the Twentieth Century.* Dordrecht, the Netherlands: Kluwer Academic Publishers.

Robbins, A.M., Stoinski, T., Fawcett, K., and Robbins, M.M. (2011a). Lifetime reproductive success of female mountain gorillas. *American Journal of Physical Anthropology*, 146, 582–93.

Robbins, M.M., Bermejo, M., Cipolletta, C., *et al.* (2004). Social structure and life-history patterns in western gorillas (*Gorilla gorilla gorilla*). *American Journal of Primatology*, 64, 145–59.

Robbins, M.M., Gray, M., Fawcett, K.A., *et al.* (2011b). Extreme conservation leads to recovery of the Virunga mountain gorillas. *PLoS One*, 6, e19788.

Robertson, J.M.Y., and van Schaik, C.P. (2001). Causal factors underlying the dramatic decline of the Sumatran orangutan. *Oryx*, 35, 26–38.

Robinson, J.G., and Bennett, E. (2000). Carrying capacity limits to sustainable hunting in tropical forests in evaluating the sustainability of hunting in tropical forests. In *Hunting for Sustainability in Tropical Forests*, ed. J.G. Robinson and E. Bennett. New York, NY: Columbia University Press, pp. 13–30.

Rogers, M.E., Abernethy, K., Bermejo, M., *et al.* (2004). Western gorilla diet: a synthesis from six sites. *American Journal of Primatology*, 64, 173–92.

Rogers, M.E., Tutin, C.E.G., Williamson, E.A., *et al.* (1994). Seasonal feeding on bark by gorillas: an unexpected keystone food? In *Current Primatology. Volume 1. Ecology and Evolution*, ed. B. Thierry, J.R. Anderson, J.J. Roeder, and N. Herrenschmidt. Strasbourg: Université Louis Pasteur, pp. 37–43.

Rogowitz, G.L. (1996). Trade-offs in energy allocation during lactation. *American Zoologist*, 36, 197–204.

Ros-Tonen, M.A.F. (1999). Introduction: NTFP research in the Tropenbos program. In *Seminar Proceedings. NTFP Research in the Tropenbos Program: Results and Perspectives*, ed. M.A.F. Ros-Tonen. Wageningen, the Netherlands: Tropenbos Foundation, pp. 15–32.

Rosati, A.G., Herrmann, E., Kaminski, J., *et al.* (2012). Assessing the psychological health of captive and wild apes: a response to Ferdowsian *et al.* (2011). *Journal of Comparative Psychology*, DOI: 10.1037/a0029144.

Ross, S.R., Lukas, K.E., Lonsdorf, E.V., *et al.* (2008). Inappropriate use and portrayal of chimpanzees. *Science*, 319, 1487.

Rouquet, P., Froment, J.-M., Bermejo, M., *et al.* (2005). Wild animal mortality monitoring and human *Ebola* outbreaks, Gabon and Republic of Congo. *Emerging Infectious Diseases*, 11, 283–90.

Rubin, J. (2012). *The End of Growth*. Toronto: Random House Canada.

Ruesto, L.A., Sheeran, L.K., Meatheson, M.D., Li, J.H., and Wagner, S. (2010). Tourist behavior and decibel levels correlate with threat frequency in Tibetan macaques (*Macaca thibetana*) at Mt Huangshan, China. *Primate Conservation*, 25, 99–104.

Ruggiero, R. (1998). The Nouabale-Ndoki Project: development of a practical conservation model in Central Africa. In *Resource Use in the Trinational Sangha River Region of Equatorial Africa: Histories, Knowledge Forms, and Institutions. Number 102*, ed. H. Eves, R. Hardin, and S. Rupp. New Haven, CT: Yale University Press, pp. 176–88.

Russon, A.E., Wich, S.A., Ancrenaz, M., *et al.* (2009). Geographic variation in orangutan diets. In *Orangutans: Geographic Variation in Behavioral Ecology and Conservation*, ed. S.A. Wich, S. Utami Atmoko, T. Mitra Setia, and C.P. van Schaik. Oxford: Oxford University Press, pp. 135–56.

Ryan, S.J. and Walsh, P.D. (2011). Consequences of non-intervention for infectious disease in African great apes. *PLoS One*, 6, e29030.

Sandker, M., Bokoto-de Semboli, B., Roth, P., *et al.* (2011). Logging or conservation concession: exploring conservation and development outcomes in Dzanga-Sangha, Central African Republic. *Conservation and Society*, 9, 299–310.

Sanz M.J., (2007). *Reducing Emissions from Deforestation in Developing Countries (REDD)*. Presentation at COM+ Media Training in Vienna, 29 August, 2007. UNFCCC Secretariat.

Savage-Rumbaugh, S., Wamba, K., Wamba, P., and Wamba, N. (2007). Welfare of apes in captive environments: comments on, and by, a specific group of apes. *Journal of Applied Animal Welfare Science: JAAWS*, 10, 7–19.

Schroepfer, K.K., Rosati, A.G., Chartrand, T., and Hare, B. (2011). Use of "entertainment" chimpanzees in commercials distorts public perception regarding their conservation status. *PLoS One*, 6, e26048.

Schultz, A.H. (1939). Notes on the diseases and healed fractures of wild apes. *Bulletin of the History of Medicine*, 7, 571–82.

Securities and Exchange Commission (2012). *Disclosure of Resource Extraction Issuers. Federal Register Release No. 34-67717*. Washington DC: Securities and Exchange Commission. Available at: http://www.sec.gov/rules/final/2012/34-67717.pdf. Accessed September 2013.

Seneca Creek Associates, L., and Wood Resources International, L. (2004). *"Illegal" Logging and the Global Wood Markets: The Competitive Impacts on the US Wood Products Industry. Paper prepared for American Forest and Paper Association, November 2004*. Poolesville, MD, and University Place, WA: Seneca Creek Associates, LLC, and Wood Resources International, LLC

Shearman, P., Bryan, J., and Laurance, W.F. (2012). Are we approaching "peak timber" in the tropics? *Biological Conservation*, 151, 17–21.

Sheeran, L.K. (1995). Behavior of wild black gibbons (*Hylobates concolor jingdongensis*). In *Chinese Primate Research and Conservation*, ed. W. Xia and Y. Zhang. Beijing, China: China Forestry Publishing House, pp. 221-225.

Sheil, D., Putz, F.E., and Zagt, R.J. (2010). *Biodiversity Conservation in Certified Forests*. Wageningen, the Netherlands: Tropenbos International.

Sicotte, P. (1993). Inter-group encounters and female transfer in mountain gorillas: influence of group composition on male behavior. *American Journal of Primatology*, 30, 21–36.

Simorangkir, D. and Sardjono, A.M. (2006). *Implication of Forest Utilization, Conversion Policy, and Tenure Dynamics on Resource Management and Poverty Reduction.* Rome: Food and Agriculture Organization (FAO).

Simorangkir, D. and Sumantri (2002). *A Review of Legal, Regulatory and Institutional Aspects of Forest and Land Fires in Indonesia.* Jakarta, Indonesia: IUCN/WWF International Project FireFight South East Asia.

Simula, M. (2006). *Public Procurement Policies for Forest Products and their Impacts.* Rome: FAO, Forest Products and Economics Division.

Singleton, I., Knott, C.D., Morrogh-Bernard, H.C., Wich, S.A., and van Schaik, C.P. (2009). Ranging behavior of orangutan females and social organization. In *Orangutans: Geographic Variation in Behavioral Ecology and Conservation*, ed. S.A. Wich, S. Utami Atmoko, T. Mitra Setia, and C.P. van Schaik. Oxford: Oxford University Press, pp. 205–13.

Singleton, I. and van Schaik, C.P. (2001). Orangutan home range size and its determinants in a Sumatran swamp forest. *International Journal of Primatology*, 22, 877–911.

Singleton, I., Wich, S., Husson, S., *et al.* (2004). *Orangutan Population and Habitat Viability Assessment: Final Report.* Apple Valley, MN: IUCN/SSC Conservation Breeding Specialist Group.

Skorupa, J.P. (1988). The effect of selective timber harvesting on rain-forest primates in Kibale Forest, Uganda. PhD thesis, University of California Davis, California.

Small, R. and Villegas, C.M. (2012). *Liberia Case Study Report.* Cambridge, UK: ASM-PACE Programme.

Smith, A.D. (1990). Towards a global culture? *Theory, Culture and Society*, 7, 171–91.

Smith, W. (2004). Undercutting sustainability: the global problem of illegal logging and trade. In *Illegal Logging in the Tropics: Strategies for Cutting Crime*, ed. R. Ravenel, I. Granoff, and C. Magee. New York, NY: Haworth Press, pp. 7–30.

SNL (2012). *SNL Metals Economics Group MineSearch Database.* SNL. Avaialble at: http://www.metalseconomics.com. Accessed December 2012.

SOS (2013). *Orangutan Rescue 1st April 2013.* Sumatran Orangutan Society (SOS). Available at: https://www.facebook.com/media/set/?set=a.10151512762289519.1073741825.352804059518&type=3. Accessed April 3, 2013.

Soulsbury, C.D., Iossa, G., Kennell, S., and Harris, S. (2009). The welfare and suitability of primates kept as pets. *Journal of Applied Animal Welfare Science (JAAWS)*, 12, 1–20.

Sousa, R., Veiga, M., van Zyl, D., *et al.* (2011). Policies and regulations for Brazil's artisanal gold mining sector: analysis and recommendations. *Journal of Cleaner Production*, 19, 742–50.

Southwick, C.H. and Cadigan, F.C. (1972). Population studies of Malaysian primates. *Primates*, 13, 1–18.

Spittaels, S. (2010). *The Complexity of Resource Governance in a Context of State Fragility: An Analysis of the Mining Sector in the Kivu Hinterlands.* London: International Alert.

Ssekika, E. (2012). FAO, partners move to curb deforestation. *The Observer*, February 29, 2012. Available at: http://www.observer.ug/index.php?option=com_contentandview=articleandid=17416:fao-partners-move-to-curb-deforestationandcatid=34:newsandItemid=114. Accessed January 31, 2013.

Stanford, C.B. (2006). The behavioral ecology of sympatric African apes: implications for understanding fossil hominoid ecology. *Primates*, 47, 91–101.

Steinhauer-Burkatt, B., Muhlenberg, M., and Stowik, J. (1995). *Kahuzi-Biega National Park. A Guide Book.* IZCN/GTZ-Project Integrated Nature Conservation in East-Zaire.

Stewart, F.A., and Pruetz, J.D. (2013). Do chimpanzee nests serve an anti-predatory function? *American Journal of Primatology*, 75, 593–604.

Stewart, K.J. (1988). Suckling and lactational anoestrus in wild gorillas (*Gorilla gorilla*). *Journal of Reproduction and Fertility*, 83, 627–34.

Stickler, C.M. (2004). The effects of logging on primate-habitat interactions: a case study of redtail monkeys (*Cercopithecus ascanius*) in Kibale National Park, Uganda. MSc thesis, University of Florida, Florida.

Stiles, D., Redmond, I., Cress, D., Nellemann, C., and Formo, R.K. (2013). *Stolen Apes: The Illicit Trade in Chimpanzees, Gorillas, Bonobos and Orangutans. A Rapid Response Assessment.* United Nations Environment Programme. Available at: http://www.un-grasp.org/news/121-download.

Stokes, E.J., Strindberg, S., Bakabana, P.C., *et al.* (2010). Monitoring great ape and elephant abundance at large spatial scales: measuring effectiveness of a conservation landscape. *PLoS One*, 5, e10294.

Strassburg, B.B.N., Rodrigues, A.S.L., Gusti, M., *et al.* (2012). Impacts of incentives to reduce emissions from deforestation on global species extinctions. *Nature Climate Change*, 2, 350–5.

Sugiyama, Y. and Fujita, S. (2011). The demography and reproductive parameters of Bossou chimpanzees. In *The Chimpanzees of Bossou and Nimba*, ed. T. Matsuzawa, T. Humle, and Y. Sugiyama. New York, NY: Springer, pp. 23–34.

Summerville, K.S., and Crist, T.O. (2001). The species richness of Lepidoptera in a fragmented landscape: a supplement to the checklist of moths of Butler Co., Ohio. *Great Lakes Entomology*, 34, 93–110.

Susila, W.R. (1998). *Development and Prospects of the Main Plantation Commodity.* Bogor, Indonesia: Center of Economic Study, Agriculture Research and Development.

Tanna, A. (2012). Chinese prosperity's hidden threat to African apes. *Channel 4 News*. Available at: http://www.channel4.com/news/chinese-prosperitys-hidden-threat-to-african-apes. Accessed January 12, 2013.

TBC (2012). *Indirect Impacts on Biodiversity from industry. Industry Briefing Note.* Cambridge, UK: The Biodiversity Consultancy.

Teleki, G. (2001). Sanctuaries for ape refugees. In *Great Apes and Humans, the Ethics of Coexistence*, ed. B. Beck, T. Stoinski, M. Hutchins, *et al.* Washington DC: Smithsonian Press, pp. 133–49.

Terborgh, J. (1999). *Requiem for Nature*. Washington DC: Island Press.

Thinh, V.N., Rawson, B., Hallam, C., *et al.* (2010). Phylogeny and distribution of crested gibbons (genus *Nomascus*) based on mitochondrial cytochrome b gene sequence data. *American Journal of Primatology*, 72, 1047–54.

Thorpe, S.K.S. and Crompton, R.H. (2009). Orangutan positional behavior: interspecific variation and ecological correlates. In *Orangutans: Geographic Variation in Behavioral Ecology and Conservation*, ed. S.A. Wich, S. Utami Atmoko, T. Mitra Setia, and C.P. van Schaik. Oxford: Oxford University Press, pp. 33–47.

Tieguhong, J.C., Ingram, V., and Schure, J. (2009). *Impacts of Artisanal Gold and Diamond Mining on Livelihoods and the Environment in the Sangha Tri-National Park Landscape.* Bogor, Indonesia: CIFOR.

Tomasello, M., Call, J., and Hare, B. (2003). Chimpanzees understand psychological states: the question is which ones and to what extent. *Trends in Cognitive Sciences*, 7, 153–6.

Townsend, W.R. (2000). The sustainability of subsistence hunting by the Siriono Indians of Bolivia. In *Hunting for Sustainability in Tropical Forests*, ed. J.G. Robinson, and E.L. Bennett. New York, NY: Columbia University Press, pp. 267–81.

TRAFFIC (2010). TRAFFIC Recommendations on Selected Agenda Items for the 15th Meeting of the Conference of the Parties to CITES. TRAFFIC. Available at: http://www.traffic.org/cites-cop-papers/TRAFFIC%20Recommendations%20on%20agenda%20documents.pdf. Accessed January 3, 2013.

Tranquilli, S., Abedi-Lartey, M., Amsini, F., *et al.* (2012). Lack of conservation effort rapidly increases African great ape extinction risk. *Conservation Letters*, 5, 48–55.

Tschakert, P. (2009). Recognizing and nurturing artisanal mining as a viable livelihood. *Resources Policy*, 34, 24–31.

Turner, S.D. (2012). *World Heritage Sites and the Extractive Industries. Consulting Report.* Gland, Switzerland: IUCN/World Heritage Center.

Tutin, C.E.G. (1999). Fragmented living: behavioural ecology of primates in a forest fragment in the Lopé Reserve, Gabon. *Primates*, 40, 249–65.

Tutin, C.E.G., and Fernandez, M. (1984). Nationwide census of gorilla and chimpanzee populations in Gabon. *American Journal of Primatology*, 6, 313–36.

Tutin, C.E.G., Parnell, R.J., White, L.J.T., and Fernandez, M. (1995). Nest building by lowland gorillas in the Lopé Reserve, Gabon: environmental influences and implications for censusing. *International Journal of Primatology*, 16, 53–76.

Tutin, C.E.G., Stokes, E., Boesch, C., *et al.* (2005). *Regional Action Plan for the Conservation of Chimpanzees and Gorillas in Western Equatorial Africa.* Washington DC: Conservation International.

Tutin, C.E.G., White, L.J.T., and Mackanga-Missandzou, A. (1997). The use by rain forest mammals of natural forest fragments in an equatorial African savanna. *Conservation Biology*, 11, 1190–203.

Tutin, C.E.G., Williamson, E.A., Rogers, M.E., and Fernandez, M. (1991). Gorilla dispersal of Cola lizae in the Lopé Reserve, Gabon. *Journal of Tropical Ecology*, 7, 181–99.

UN (2008). *Resolutions: 62nd Session of the UN General Assembly. Non-legally binding instrument on all types of forests: A/RES/62/98.* Blue Ridge Summit, PA: United Nations (UN).

UN (2011). *World Population Prospects: The 2011 Revision.* New York, NY: Population Division of the Department of Economic and Social Affairs of the United Nations (UN) Secerteriat.

UNDP (2011). *Human Development Report 2011.* New York, NY: United Nations Development Programme (UNDP).

UNDP (2012). *Human Development Indicators.* New York, NY: United Nations Development Programme (UNDP). Available at: http://hdrstats.undp.org/en/countries/profiles/CAF.html. Accessed October 2012.

UNDP (2013). *Human Development Indicators: Guinea.* New York, NY: United Nations Development Programme (UNDP). Available at: http://hdrstats.undp.org/en/countries/profiles/GIN.html. Accessed April 17, 2013.

UNEP (2011a). *Decoupling Natural Resource Use and Environmental Impacts From Economic Growth.* Nairobi: United Nations Environment Programme (UNEP), International Resource Panel.

UNEP (2011b). *The Democratic Republic of the Congo: Post-Conflict Environmental Assessment Synthesis for Policy Makers.* Nairobi: United Nations Environment Programme (UNEP).

UNEP and McGinley, M. (2009). *Kahuzi-Biéga National Park, Democratic Republic of Congo, October 15, 2009.* Available at: http://www.seoearth.org/article/Kahuzi-Bi%C3%A9ga_National_Park,_Democratic_Republic_of_Congo. Accessed September 27, 2012.

UNEP-WCMC (2011). Kahizu-Biega National Park Democratic Republic of the Congo. Report for UNEP, WCMC, IUCN and UNESCO. UNEP-WCMC. Available at: http://www.unep-wcmc.org/medialibrary/2011/06/24/39c633b6/Kahuzi%20Biega.pdf. Accessed October 15, 2011.

UNEP-WCMC (2012). Apes conservation and welfare status report: spatial overlap between mining operations and ape occurrence. United Nations Environment Programme World Conservation Monitoring Centre.

USAID (2010). *Best Management Practices for Orangutan Conservation in Mining Concessions.* Jakarta, Indonesia: USAID.

USDA (2012). *Animal Care Information System (ACIS) Search Tool.* Animal Plant Health Inspection Service, United States Department of Agriculture (USDA). Available at: http://acissearch.aphis.usda.gov/LPASearch/faces/CustomerSearch.jspx# Accessed March 15, 2013.

USFWS (2013). *US Fish and Wildlife Service Proposes Protection for all Chimpanzee – Captive and Wild – as Endangered.* Arlington, VA: US Fish and Wildlife Service (USFWS). Available at: http://www.fws.gov/home/newsroom/chimpanzeerecovery0610013.html. Accessed June 24, 2013.

van den Berg, S. (2006). Retirement home for ex-laboratory chimpanzees. *COSMOS Magazine.* Available at: http://www.cosmosmagazine.com/news/retirement-home-ex-laboratory-chimpanzees/. Accessed March 13, 2013.

van Kreveld, A. and Roerhorst, I. (2009). *Great Apes and Logging.* Zeist, the Netherlands: World Wide Fund for Nature.

van Kreveld, A., and Roerhorst, I. (2010). Impacts of certified logging on great apes. In *Biodiversity Conservation in Certified Forests,* ed. D. Sheil, F.E. Putz, and R.J. Zagt. Wageningen, the Netherlands: Tropenbos International, pp. 120–5.

van Noordwijk, M.A., Sauren, S.E.B., Nuzuar, *et al.* (2009). Development of independence: Sumatran and Bornean orangutans compared. In *Orangutans: Geographic Variation in Behavioral Ecology and Conservation,* ed. S.A. Wich, S. Utami Atmoko, T. Mitra Setia, and C.P. van Schaik. Oxford: Oxford University Press, pp. 189–203.

van Noordwijk, M.A., and van Schaik, C.P. (2005). Development of ecological competence in Sumatran orangutans. *American Journal of Physical Anthropology,* 127, 79–94.

van Paddenburg, A., Bassi, A., Buter, E., Cosslett, C., and Dean, A. (2012). *Heart of Borneo: Investing in Nature for a Green Economy.* Jakarta, Indonesia: WWF Heart of Borneo Global Initiative.

van Schaik, C.P. (2004). *Among Orangutans: Red Apes and the Rise of Human Culture.* Cambridge, MA: Harvard University Press.

van Vliet, N., Nasi, R., Abernethy, K., *et al.* (2012). The role of wildlife for food security in Central Africa: a threat to biodiversity? In *The Forests of the Congo Basin: State of the Forest 2010,* ed. C. de Wasseige, P. de Marcken, N. Bayol, *et al.* Luxembourg: Publications Office of the European Union.

van Vliet, N., Nasi, R., and Taber, A. (2011). From the forest to the stomach: bushmeat consumption from rural to urban settings in Central Africa. In *Non-Timber Forest Products in the Global Context. Tropical Foresty 7,* ed. S. Shackleton, *et al.* Berlin: Springer-Verlag, pp. 129–45.

Vidal, J. (2013a). Indonesia's forest fire smoke blows deeper into Malaysia. *The Guardian,* Monday June 24, 2013. Available at: http://www.guardian.co.uk/environment/2013/jun/24/indonesia-forest-fire-malaysia-singapore. Accessed July 2013.

Vidal, J. (2013b). The Sumatran rainforest will mostly disappear within 20 years. *The Guardian,* May 25, 2013. Available at: http://www.guardian.co.uk/world/2013/may/26/sumatra-borneo-deforestation-tigers-palm-oil. Accessed June 27 2013.

Villegas, C., Weinberg, R., Levin, E., and Hund, K. (2012). *Artisanal and Small-Scale Mining in Protected Areas and Critical Ecosystems: Global Scoping and Solutions.* Cambridge, UK: ASM-PACE Programme, Estelle Levin Ltd and World Wild Fund for Nature. Available at: http://www.asm-pace.org/projects/global-solutions-study.html.

Virah-Sawmy, M. and Ebeling, J. (2010). The difficult road toward real-world engagement: conservation science and mining in southern Madagascar. *Conservation Letters,* 3, 288–9.

Voorhar, R. and Myllyvirta, L. (2013). *Point of No Return: The Massive Climate Threats We Must Avoid.* Amsterdam: Greenpeace. Available at: http://www.greenpeace.org/international/Global/international/publications/climate/2013/PointOfNoReturn.pdf. Accessed January 2013.

Waldrop, C.S., Rawson, B.M., Henry, J., and Crowther, M. (2011). Using population viability analysis to assess threats and predict the potential for long-term survival of the northern white-cheeked crested gibbon (*Nomascus leucogenys*) in Vietnam. MSc thesis, University of Sydney, Australia.

Wales Ape and Monkey Sanctuary (n.d.). *Wales Ape and Monkey Sanctuary.* Available at: http://www.ape-monkey-rescue.org.uk/chimps.html. Accessed September 9, 2013.

Walker Painemilla, K., Rylands, A.B., Woofter, A., and Hughes, C. (2010). *Indigenous Peoples and Conservation: From Rights to Resource Management.* Arlington, VA: Conservation International.

Wall Street Journal (2011). UK miner challenges Indonesia. *Wall Street Journal*, December 2, 2011.

Waller, J.C. and Reynolds, V. (2001). Limb injuries resulting from snares and traps in chimpanzees (*Pan troglodytes scheinfurthi*i) at the Budongo Forest, Uganda. *Primates*, 42, 135–9.

Walsh, P.D. (2006). Ebola and commercial hunting: dim prospects for African apes. In *Emerging Threats to Tropical Forests*, ed. W.F. Laurance and C.A. Peres. Chicago, IL: University of Chicago Press, pp. 175–97.

Walsh, P.D., Abernethy, K.A., Bermejo, M., *et al.* (2003). Catastrophic ape decline in western equatorial Africa. *Nature*, 422, 611–4.

Walsh, S., Bramblett, C.A., and Alford, P.L. (1982). A vocabulary of abnormal behaviors in restrictively reared chimpanzees. *American Journal of Primatology*, 3, 315–9.

Ward, K. (2011). *The World in 2050. Quantifying the Shift in the Global Economy. HSBC Global Economics, January.* London: HSBC Global Research.

Ward, K. (2012). *The World in 2050. From the Top 30 to the Top 100. HSBC Global Economics, January.* London: HSBC Global Research.

Watts, D.P. (1984). Composition and variability of mountain gorilla diets in the central Virungas. *American Journal of Primatology*, 7, 325–56.

Watts, D.P. (1989). Infanticide in mountain gorillas: new cases and a reconsideration of the evidence. *Ethology*, 81, 1–18.

WAZA (n.d.). *Conservation Breeding Programmes. United for Conservation.* World Association of Zoos and Aquariums (WAZA). Available at: http://www.waza.org/en/site/conservation/conservation-breeding-programmes Accessed March 13, 2013.

WCD (2000). *Dams and Development: A New Framework for Decision-Making. The Report of the World Commission on Dams.* London and Sterling, VA: Earthscan Publications Ltd.

WCS (2012). *Congo: Where We Work.* Wildlife Conservation Society (WCS). Available at: http://www.wcs.org/where-we-work/africa/congo.aspx. Accessed December 12, 2012.

WCS/CIESIN (2005). Last of the wild data version 2: global human influence index (HII). Available at: http://sedac.ciesin.columbia.edu/data/set/wildareas-v2-human-influence-index-geographic.

Weinberg, R., Chishugi, A., Levin, E., and Beynon, G. (2012). *Artisanal and Small-scale Mining in the Protected Areas and Critical Ecosystems of the Democratic Republic of Congo.* Cambridge, UK: Artisanal and Small-Scale Mining in Protected Areas and Critical Ecosystems (ASM-PACE).

Weinberg, R., Chishugi, A., Levin, E., and Beynon, G. (2013). *Exploitation minière artisanale dans la Reserve Naturelle d'Itombwe, République Democratique du Congo: Rapport d'activité et recommandations mises à jour- Projet de rapport.* Geneva: ASM-PACE and WWF. Available at: www.asm-pace.org.

Weisenseel, K.A., Chapman, C.A., and Chapman, L.J. (1993). Nocturnal primates of Kibale forest: effects of selective logging on prosimian densities. *Primates*, 34, 445–50.

Weiss, A., Inoue-Murayama, M., King, J.E., Adams, M.J., and Matsuzawa, T. (2012). All too human? Chimpanzee and orang-utan personalities are not anthropomorphic projections. *Animal Behaviour*, 83, 1355–65.

Weiss, A., King, J.E., and Enns, R.M. (2002). Subjective well-being is heritable and genetically correlated with dominance in chimpanzees (*Pan troglodytes*). *Journal of Personality and Social Psychology*, 83, 1141.

Weiss, A., King, J.E., and Perkins, L. (2006). Personality and subjective well-being in orangutans (*Pongo pygmaeus* and *Pongo abelii*). *Journal of Personality and Social Psychology*, 90, 501.

Weitzner, V. (2011). *Tipping the Power Balance – Making Free, Prior and Informed Consent Work: Lessons and Policy Directions from 10 Years of Action Research on Extractives with Indigenous and Afro-Descendent Peoples in the Americas.* Ottawa: The North–South Institute.

Wells, P., Neil, F., and Paoli, G. (2011). *Preliminary Observations on the Indonesian Ministry of Forestry Decree SK.7416/Menhut-VII/IPSDH/2011: The First Revision of the Indicative Maps Concerning the Suspension of New Licenses for Forest and Peatland Utilisation. Daemeter Briefs on the Indonesian Moratorium No. 3.* Daemeter. Available at: http://www.daemeter.org.

Werdenich, D., Dupain, J., Arnheim, E., *et al.* (2003). Reactions of chimpanzees and gorillas to human observers in a non-protected area in south-eastern Cameroon. *Folia Primatologica*, 74, 97–100.

White, L.J.T. (1992). Vegetation history and logging disturbance: effects on rain forest in the Lopé Reserve, Gabon (with special emphasis on elephants and apes). PhD thesis, University of Edinburgh, UK.

White, L.J.T. and Tutin, C.E.G. (2001). Why chimpanzees and gorillas respond differently to logging: a cautionary tale from Gabon. In *African Rain Forest Ecology and Conservation: An Interdisciplinary Perspective*, ed. W. Weber, L.J.T. White, A. Vedder, and L. Naughton-Treves. New Haven, CT: Yale University Press, pp. 449–62.

Whitten, A.J. (1982). Diet and feeding behaviour of Kloss gibbons on Siberut Island, Indonesia. *Folia Primatologica*, 37, 177–208.

Wicander, S. and Coad, L. (2013). *Learning our Lessons: A Review of Alternative Livelihood Projects in Central Africa*. IUCN, CARPE, and Oxford University.

Wich, S.A., de Vries, H., Ancrenaz, M., *et al.* (2009a). Orangutan life history variation. In *Orangutans: Geographic Variation in Behavioral Ecology and Conservation*, ed. S.A. Wich, S. Utami Atmoko, T. Mitra Setia, and C.P. van Schaik. Oxford: Oxford University Press, pp. 65–75.

Wich, S.A., Fredriksson, G.M., Usher, G., *et al.* (2012a). Hunting of Sumatran orang-utans and its importance in determining distribution and density. *Biological Conservation*, 146, 163–9.

Wich, S.A., Gaveau, D., Abram, N., *et al.* (2012b). Understanding the impacts of land-use policies on a threatened species: is there a future for the Bornean orang-utan? *PLoS One*, 7, e49142.

Wich, S.A., Geurts, M.L., Mitra Setia, T., and Utami-Atmoko, S.S. (2006). Influence of fruit availability on Sumatran orangutan sociality and reproduction. In *Feeding Ecology in Apes and Other Primates: Ecological, Physical and Behavioral Aspects*, ed. G. Hohmann, M.M. Robbins, and C. Boesch. New York, NY: Cambridge University Press, pp. 337–58.

Wich, S., Koh, L.P., and Noordwijk, M.V. (2011a). The Indonesian deforestation moratorium: the devil is in the details. *Jakarta Post*, Monday February 21, 2011. Available at: http://www.thejakartapost.com/news/2011/02/21/the-indonesian-deforestation-moratorium-the-devil-details.html. Accessed July 2013

Wich, S.A., Meijaard, E., Marshall, A.J., *et al.* (2008). Distribution and conservation status of the orang-utan (*Pongo* spp.) on Borneo and Sumatra: how many remain? *Oryx*, 42, 329–39.

Wich, S.A., Riswan, J., Refish, J., and Nelleman, C. (2011b). *Orangutans and the Economics of Sustainable Forest Management in Sumatra*. Birkeland Trykkeri AS Norway: UNEP/GRASP/PanEco/YEL/ICRAF/GRID-Arendal. Available at: http://www.grida.no/graphicslib/collection/orangutans-and-the-economics-of-sustainable-forest-management-in-sumatra. Accessed October 11, 2012.

Wich, S.A., Usher, G., Peters, H.H., *et al.* (2013). Preliminary data on the highland Sumatran orangutans (*Pongo abelii*) of Batang Toru. In *High Altitude Primates*, ed. N.B. Grow, S. Gursky-Doyen, and A. Krzton. Berlin: Springer.

Wich, S.A., Utami-Atmoko, S.S., Mitra Setia, T., *et al.* (2004). Life history of wild Sumatran orangutans (*Pongo abelii*). *Journal of Human Evolution*, 47, 385–98.

Wich, S.A., Utami-Atmoko, S., Mitra Setia, T., van Schaik, C.P., eds (2009b). *Orangutans: Geographic Variation in Behavioral Ecology and Conservation*. Oxford: Oxford University Press.

Wich, S.A., Vogel, E.R., Larsen, M.D., *et al.* (2011c). Forest fruit production is higher on Sumatra than on Borneo. *PLoS One*, 6, e21278.

Wikelski, M. and Cooke, S.J. (2006). Conservation physiology. *Trends in Ecology and Evolution*, 21, 38–46.

Wikramanayake, E.D., Dinerstein, E., Loucks, C.J., *et al.* (2002). *Terrestrial Ecoregions of the Indo-Pacific: A Conservation Assessment*. Washington DC: Island Press.

Wilkie, D.S. (2001). Bushmeat trade in the Congo Basin. In *Great Apes and Humans: The Ethics of Coexistence*, ed. B.B. Beck, T.S. Stoinski, M. Hutchins, *et al.* Washington DC: Smithsonian Institution, pp. 86–109.

Wilkie, D.S., Sidle, J.G., Boundzanga, G.C., Auzel, P., and Blake, S. (2001). Defaunation, not deforestation: commercial logging and market hunting in northern Congo. In *The Cutting Edge: Conserving Wildlife in Logged Tropical Forests*, ed. R. Fimbel, A. Grajal, and J.G. Robinson. New York, NY: Columbia University Press, pp. 375–99.

Williams, J.M., Lonsdorf, E.V., Wilson, M.L., *et al.* (2008). Causes of death in the Kasekela chimpanzees of Gombe National Park, Tanzania. *American Journal of Primatology*, 70, 766–77.

Williams, M. (2002). *Deforesting the Earth: From Prehistory to Global Crisis*. Chicago, IL: University of Chicago Press.

Williamson, E.A. (in press). Mountain gorillas: a shifting demographic landscape. In *Primates and Cetaceans: Field Research and Conservation of Complex Mammalian Societies*, ed. J. Yamagiwa and L. Karczmarsk. Tokyo, Japan: Springer. DOI: 10.1007/978-4-431-54523-1_14.

Williamson, E.A., and Butynski, T.M. (2013a). *Gorilla beringei* eastern gorilla. In *Mammals of Africa. Volume II. Primates*, ed. T.M. Butynski, J. Kingdon, and J. Kalina. London: Bloomsbury Publishing, pp. 45–53.

Williamson, E.A., and Butynski, T.M. (2013b). *Gorilla gorilla* western gorilla. In *Mammals of Africa. Volume II. Primates*, ed. T.M. Butynski, J. Kingdon, and J. Kalina. London: Bloomsbury Publishing, pp. 39–45.

Williamson, E.A. and Feistner, A.T.C. (2011). Habituating primates: processes, techniques, variables and ethics. In *Field and Laboratory Methods in Primatology: A Practical Guide*, 2nd edn, ed. J.M. Setchell and D.J. Curtis. Cambridge, UK: Cambridge University Press, pp. 33–49.

Williamson, E.A., Maisels, F.G., and Groves, C.P. (2013). Hominidae. In *Handbook of the Mammals of the World. Volume 3. Primates*, ed. R.A. Mittermeier, A.B. Rylands, and D.E. Wilson. Barcelona: Lynx Edicions, pp. 792–843.

Williamson, E.A., Tutin, C.E.G., and Fernandez, M. (1988). Western lowland gorillas feeding in streams and on savannas. *Primate Report*, 19, 29–34.

Wilson, C.C., and Wilson, W.L. (1975). The influence of selective logging on primates and some other animals in East Kalimantan. *Folia Primatologica*, 23, 245–74.

Wilson, D. and Dragusanu, R. (2008). *The Expanding Middle: The Exploding Middle Class and Falling Global Inequality. Global Economics Paper 170*. New York, NY: Goldman Sachs.

Wilson, W.L. and Johns, A.D. (1982). Diversity and abundance of selected animal species in undisturbed forest, selectively logged forest and plantations East Kalimantan, Indonesia. *Biological Conservation*, 24, 205–18.

Wilson, M.L., Kahlenberg, S.M., Wells, M., and Wrangham, R.W. (2012). Ecological and social factors affect the occurrence and outcomes of intergroup encounters in chimpanzees. *Animal Behaviour*, 83, 277–91.

Wobber, V. and Hare, B. (2011). Psychological health of orphan bonobos and chimpanzees in African sanctuaries. *PLoS One*, 6, e17147.

Wolf, C. (2009). *Rescuing Apes from Conflict Requires more Flexibility in CITES* Bushmeat Crisis Task Force. Available at: http://www.bushmeat.org/node/86. Accessed January 9, 2013.

Woodcock, P., Edwards, D.P., Fayle, T.M., *et al.* (2011). The conservation value of South East Asia's highly degraded forests: evidence from leaf-litter ants. *Philosophical Transactions of the Royal Society Series B*, 366, 3256–64.

Woodford, M.H., Butynski, T.M., and Karesh, W.B. (2002). Habituating the great apes: the disease risks. *Oryx*, 36, 153–60.

World Bank (2008). *Assessment of the Central African Republic Mining Sector*. Newcastle-under-Lyme, UK: Wardell Armstrong LLP.

World Bank (2010). *Central African Republic Country Environmental Analysis: Environmental Management for Sustainable Growth. Volume I. Main Report*. Washington DC: World Bank.

World Bank (2011a). *OPCS Working Paper: Implementation of the World Bank's Indigenous Peoples' Policy: A Learning Review (FY2006–2009)*. Washington DC: World Bank.

World Bank (2011b). *World Development Report 2011: Conflict, Security and Development*. Washington DC: World Bank.

World Bank Group (2011). *The Inspection Panel: Panel Resolution and Mandate*. Available at: http://web.worldbank.org/WBSITE/EXTERNAL/EXTINSPECTIONPANEL/0,,contentMDK:20173262~menuPK:64129254~pagePK:64129751~piPK:64128378~theSitePK:380794,00.html. Accessed October 2013.

World Rainforest Movement (1998). *Underlying Causes of Deforestation and Forest Degradation. Summary of Indonesian Case Study*. Indonesian Working Group on Underlying Causes of Deforestation and Forest Degradation. Available at: http://www.wrm.org.uy/deforestation/Asia/Indonesia.html. Accessed September 20, 2013.

Wrangham, R.W. (1986). Ecology and social relationships in two species of chimpanzee. In *Ecological Aspects of Social Evolution: Birds and Mammals*, ed. D.I. Rubenstein and R.W. Wrangham. Princeton, NJ: Princeton University Press, pp. 352–78.

Wrege, P.H., Rowland, E.D., Thompson, B.G., and Batruch, N. (2010). Use of acoustic tools to reveal otherwise cryptic responses of forest elephants to oil exploration. *Conservation Biology*, 24, 1578–85.

WRI (2012). *Global Forest Watch/Forest Atlas of Cameroon*. Washington DC: World Resources Institute (WRI). Available at: http://www.globalforestwatch.org/english/interactive.maps/index.htm.

Wright J.S. (2010). The future of tropical forests. *Annals of the New York Academy of Sciences*, 1195, 1-27.

Wunder, S. (2003). *Oil Wealth and the Fate of the Forest. A Comparative Study of Eight Tropical Countries*. London: Routledge.

WWF (2011). *Living Forest Report*. Gland, Switzerland: World Wide Fund for Nature (WWF).

WWF (2013). *Bornean Orangutan* Pongo pygmaeus pygmaeus. Available at: http://www.wwf.or.id/en/about_wwf/whatwedo/forest_species/species/bornean_orangutan/. Accessed September 2013.

WWF International (2008). *Indigenous Peoples and Conservation: WWF Statement of Principles*. Gland, Switzerland: WWF International. Available at: http://www.worldwildlife.org/what/communityaction/people/partnering-with/guidelines.html.

Yamagiwa, J. (2003). Bushmeat poaching and the conservation crisis in Kahuzi Biega National Park, Democratic Republic of Congo. *Journal of Sustainable Forestry*, 16, 115–35.

Yanuar, A. and Chivers, D.J. (2010). Impact of forest fragmentation on ranging and home range of siamang (*Symphalangus syndactylus*) and agile gibbons (*Hylobates agilis*). In *Indonesian Primates. Developments in Primatology: Progress and Prospects*, ed. S. Gursky-Doyen and J. Supriatna. New York, Heidelberg and London: Springer Science, pp. 97–119.

Yerkes, R.M. (1943). *Chimpanzees; A Laboratory Colony.* New Haven, CT: Yale University Press.

Zhou, J., Wei, F., Li, M., *et al.* (2008). Reproductive characters and mating behaviour of wild *Nomascus hainanus. International Journal of Primatology*, 29, 1037–46.

Zimmerer, K.S. (2006). *Globalization and New Geographies of Conservation.* Chicago and London: University of Chicago Press.

Zimmerman, B.L. and Kormos, C.F. (2012). Prospects for sustainable logging in tropical forests. *BioScience*, 62, 479–87.

Index